American Democracy

Robert K. Carr and Marver H. Bernstein's
American Democracy

8th Edition

Walter F. Murphy
Princeton University

Michael N. Danielson
Princeton University

The Dryden Press
Hinsdale, Illinois

The author wishes to thank all sources for the
use of their material. The credit lines for
copyrighted materials appearing in this work
are placed in the Acknowledgments section at
the end of the book. These pages are to be
considered an extension of the copyright page.

For William O. Douglas
*Whose high ideals and dedicated energy
have made the United States a better place
for us and for our children.*

Preface

As this book makes its way through the dark passages of its publisher's labyrinth, the United States is once again beginning a peaceful change of governments. As has happened so many times since John Adams ruefully watched Thomas Jefferson take the oath of office in 1801, the party in the White House has fought and lost a bitter political campaign but has accepted its defeat and turned the machinery of government over to its foes. Such a peaceful transition is no small thing in this world of coups and counter coups, a tribute to this country's deeply rooted acceptance of constitutional democracy. The trauma of Vietnam, the crisis of Watergate, and the scandals of the Federal Bureau of Investigation, the Central Intelligence Agency, and the Internal Revenue Service have shaken but not broken popular faith in the capacity of the American political system to produce decent, efficient government. Whether the new regime will strengthen, weaken, or destroy that faith remains to be seen.

Like a new government taking office, authors revising a previous book do not start afresh. Continuity with the past, as Oliver Wendell Holmes said, is not a duty; it is only a necessity. But neither authors nor public officials need mindlessly repeat the past. Each has some measure of choice. In this edition, we have tried to retain the best of the old and add much that is new. We have kept a large amount of earlier editions' descriptive materials (albeit updated). We believe that without such basic knowledge beginning students are able neither to formulate nor to test empirical or normative theories about American politics. We have added, or at least sharpened, another dimension of political analysis by trying to stress how public policy gets made in the United States—to identify the points of access to power, to explain how citizens can and do utilize their opportunities for influence, and to demonstrate how formal and informal institutions interact to produce the decisions that shape our lives in so many vital ways.

We hope we have been able to analyze complexities of the American political system fairly, but our own values have undoubtedly influenced us. To allay doubts we set out a few of those biases at the outset: We believe that the fundamental value of the American system of constitutional democracy is the protection of human dignity. We believe that neither government nor a majority of the people has authority to degrade any citizen; more important, we also believe each person, and therefore government, has a duty to protect the dignity of every person—to help the poor, the old, the sick, and even "the different" to live lives that are touched with hope. But because we share the founding fathers' distrust of humans exercising political power, we do not expect that any government or any people can create heaven on earth. Yet we do believe that the United States has the wealth and the wisdom to make human life much more bearable than it now is.

As in previous editions our debts are both heavy and numerous. We mention only the most obvious: The late Dimmes McDowell for helping translate political science into English; Herbert Alexander of the Citizens Research Foundation for again placing at our disposal his encyclopedic knowledge of campaign financing; Mr. Harry Hirsch, Mrs. Lindi Sarno Kurtz, and Ms. Sharon Shervington of Princeton University and Mr. Bruce Snyder of Rutgers Law School for research assistance; Mrs. Zaida Dillon and Mrs. Rosemary Little of Princeton's Firestone Library for their patience and efficiency in responding to our frequent cries for help; Mrs. Barbara Keller, Mrs. Amy Kerlin, Mrs. June Traube, and Mrs. Helen Wright for cheerfully typing manuscripts that were indecipherable even to the authors; and last our families who once more stoically endured the agonies of our wrestling with American Democracy.

December, 1976

Marion, Massachusetts
Waltham, Massachusetts
Princeton, New Jersey

Robert K. Carr
Marver H. Bernstein
Walter F. Murphy
Michael N. Danielson

Contents

Part One
The Framework of American Politics

Contents

xi

Part Six
The Judiciary

Part Seven
Civil Liberties

Part 8
Conclusion

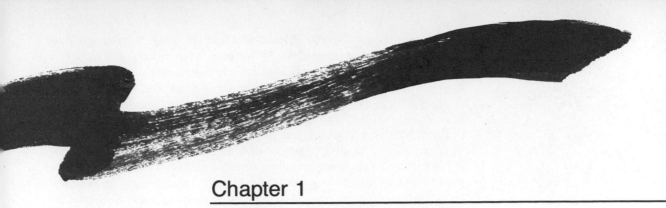

Chapter 1

Politics and Government

Democracy
The Inevitability of Conflict
Big Government
Public Policy
Summary

POLITICS DEALS WITH who governs and how. In pungent language, politics involves three questions: "Who gets what, when, and how?"* More elegantly, we can say that *politics is concerned with the authoritative processes that determine the goals of a society, mobilize its resources to achieve these goals, and distribute rights, duties, costs, benefits, rewards, and punishments among members of that society.*

Authoritative processes are those processes whose decisions the vast majority of the people accept as binding. People may accept them for a variety of reasons, including habit, tradition, respect for certain procedures, or loyalty to particular persons or institutions. In Western democracies, citizens tend to accept most governmental decisions as authoritative. In other systems, people may or may not see public officials as legitimate rulers, and in some circumstances large segments of a population may look on another organization or individual as the legitimate leader, at least for some purposes. A bishop or a guerrilla chief, for instance, may make decisions that a sizable minority or even a majority of citizens consider superior to those of presidents or parliaments. Considered this way, *politics encompasses all activities of individuals and groups, public and private, with respect to governing society.*

This definition is broader than that in everyday use, because people commonly limit the meaning of the term *politics* to political parties, campaigns and elections, and activities of elected officials. Of course, those are central aspects of politics, and much of the remainder of this volume examines them in detail. But politics also includes many other kinds of behavior that we cannot ignore. Equally important, politics is not a dirty word, nor are all politicians venal. That some are corrupt is as obviously true as that some bankers embezzle, some union leaders take bribes, some doctors pad their bills, and some lawyers pay for perjured testimony. In this world, politicians can claim a monopoly neither on sin nor on virtue. But the game they play — making decisions that can bring war or peace, prosperity or poverty, slavery or freedom — is vital to the survival of society.

Participants in politics usually seek the support of government for their goals. Thus, a group alarmed about the spread of pornography demands that the local police chief prevent showings of an X-rated film, while the theater operator goes to court to secure an injunction against picketing on his property by the antipornography group.† Advocates of women's freedom to control their bodies demand that state government enact legislation legalizing abortion on demand. Slum dwellers pay their rent to the city rather than to their landlords in the hope that their money will be used to make desperately needed building repairs. Federal officials are urged to lower waste discharge standards by meat packers, whose complaints about the high costs of

*This now-classic question is Harold D. Lasswell's and first appeared in his *Politics: Who Gets What, When, and How?* (New York: McGraw-Hill Book Company, 1936).
†An injunction is a court order which prohibits or requires a specified action.

Force can be used by government to ensure compliance with its policies on the part of those who feel no moral obligation to obey, as in the seizure by the U.S. Coast Guard of two smugglers and $5 million worth of marijuana off the Florida coast in 1973.

pollution control are echoed by local political leaders fearful of unemployment and loss of tax resources.

Government is the focus of political interaction because it makes and enforces many of the rules in modern society. Indeed, federal, state, and local governments regulate a wide range of individual, group, and corporate behavior; they levy taxes, set and enforce standards of behavior, confer licenses and franchises, and create rules regarding the distribution of all sorts of costs and benefits. As important as the scope of governmental rule making is the fact that governments usually can enforce their decisions more effectively than other social institutions. In a stable political system, citizens generally (although not always) feel a moral obligation to follow the law. It is this feeling of obligation that confers what is called *legitimacy* on governmental action. But should moral obligation fail, public officials have force—the police, the national guard, or even the army—to ensure by brute power that a policy will be carried out. Even though in the United States governmental use of force is subject to many important restraints, official use of raw power always remains a real possibility.

Furthermore, those with governmental authority usually command a preponderance of the instruments of coercion. This near-monopoly means that they can imprison people for real or alleged crimes, conscript young men and women for regular armies or guerrilla cadres, exterminate groups of people as Hitler did the Jews or Stalin his opponents, or allow the possession of slave laborers without rights or dignity as Americans did until the Civil War. Alternatively, political action can remove conditions of terror and slavery, end famine and pestilence, discourage drug abuse, wipe out gangland rule, and restore civil rights. At the international level, politics can trigger a war between individual countries and even incite a global conflict, but political action can also bring peace, orderly development, and a measure of prosperity.

Democracy

Americans commonly speak of the process by which their political decisions are made as *democratic.* Unfortunately, that word is among the most vague and value-laden terms in any Western language. Democracy can refer to a town-meeting style of government in which all citizens are present and have equal voting power; it can mean government by an Athenian assembly whose members are selected by lot or serve in rotation; it can refer to a representative form of government in which delegates are chosen by any of a variety of electoral processes. "Democracy" says nothing about the extent of governmental power. A democracy may, as in the United States, limit the authority of government, or it may exercise total authority. "Totalitarian democracy" is no contradiction in terms. "Democratic despotism" has a long history; the Greek city states were more totalitarian than many present-day "people's republics."

When we speak of *American democracy,* we are talking about a political hybrid, a government in which citizens can participate, operating in a particular cultural context, under certain legal rules, and through a certain set of institutions and informal processes. What is involved, as Chapter 4 explains in more detail, is a mix between popular government and limited government. In a pure democracy, the will of the people is supreme. In a limited government, the constitution imposes severe restraints on what the ruler—whether a single person, a small group, or a majority of the adult population—can do. Thus, to the extent that the people rule in the American political system, they do so subject to important legal restrictions, many but by no means all of which are spelled out in the Bill of Rights, the first ten amendments to the Constitution. As a result, we should speak of the United States as having a *republican form of government,* or a *free government*—a term the Founding Fathers liked—or a *constitutional democracy.*

The American version of constitutional democracy is also a *representative form of government.* To the degree that the people "rule," they do so by having a right to speak their minds on public issues, to organize other citizens, and, at stated intervals, to vote for or against candidates who wish to become their representatives. The people also "rule" in the sense that these representatives, who are subject to periodic re-election, are typically anxious to anticipate the moods and preferences of the voters—although how they anticipate or even discover those moods and preferences involves a process that is often more

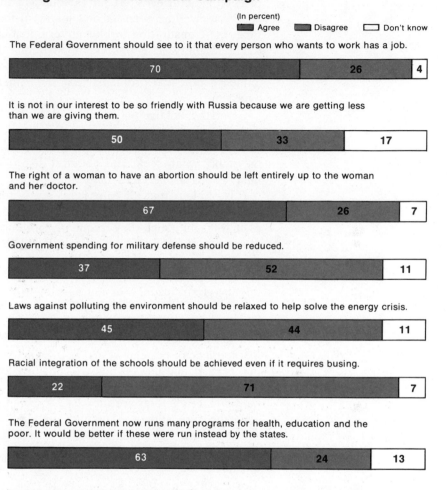

Figure 1.1
Public Attitudes on Major Issues during the 1976 Presidential Campaign

(In percent)
■ Agree ■ Disagree □ Don't know

The Federal Government should see to it that every person who wants to work has a job.

| 70 | 26 | 4 |

It is not in our interest to be so friendly with Russia because we are getting less than we are giving them.

| 50 | 33 | 17 |

The right of a woman to have an abortion should be left entirely up to the woman and her doctor.

| 67 | 26 | 7 |

Government spending for military defense should be reduced.

| 37 | 52 | 11 |

Laws against polluting the environment should be relaxed to help solve the energy crisis.

| 45 | 44 | 11 |

Racial integration of the schools should be achieved even if it requires busing.

| 22 | 71 | 7 |

The New York Times/CBS News poll surveyed by telephone 1,463 respondents in February 1976 as part of a continuous polling effort during the presidential year.

The Federal Government now runs many programs for health, education and the poor. It would be better if these were run instead by the states.

| 63 | 24 | 13 |

Source: *New York Times*, Feb. 13, 1976.

mystic than scientific. "To speak with precision about public opinion is a task not unlike coming to grips with the Holy Ghost," as V. O. Key* once remarked. Yet at election time public opinion can become as real to governmental officials as the Holy Ghost is to traditional Christian theologians.

Public Opinion and American Democracy (New York: Alfred A. Knopf, 1961), p. 8. Professor Key was one of the wisest analysts of American politics in the twentieth century. His work includes major contributions to the understanding of political parties, public opinion, voting behavior, and state and regional politics.

American government is also permeated with the concept of *equality,* a notion whose meaning is only slightly less varied than that of democracy itself.* At very least the Constitution's command of "equal protection of the laws," requires "one person, one vote" in the political sphere as well as even-handed justice from the courts. At the same time, the Constitution forbids governmentally imposed restrictions on social mobility or economic opportunity because of race, sex, religion, or ancestry. Living up even to these minimums has posed immense practical problems that the American system has not yet overcome.

Given the fact that people are not equal in talent and ambition and do not share the same interests and moral code, political equality is difficult for the government to maintain. If left alone, some individuals will inevitably want, seek, and obtain a disproportionately large share of many goods and services, including political power.

It is obvious that all Americans are not equal in terms of political influence. Candidates who compete for public office are rarely just plain folks, although they frequently pretend to be. They are members of an elite, typically better educated, wealthier, and far more astute in the arts of manipulation than the average citizen. They are often surrounded by other elites—bankers, financiers, union officials, lawyers, interest-group leaders, or journalists—whose political resources also set them apart from the average citizen. Even professional politicians are not equal in terms of political influence, and they must compete with each other for power. One of the arenas of competition is the marketplace of popular votes. It is principally because of competition in this particular market that we can speak of the United States as having a strong democratic element in its government. And because in that marketplace all votes are supposed to count the same, we can speak of some measure, at least, of political equality.

The problem of equality has other troublesome dimensions. In the United States, the notion of political equality has been coupled with an ideal of social equality, an ideal that goes far beyond equal treatment by governmental officials or "one person, one vote." It means an absence of informal, social barriers as well. But because social practice, like political practice, has not always lived up to its ideals, governmental action is necessary to strike down religious, economic, and, most important in the American context, racial barriers against social mobility. But actually the concepts of limited or constitutional government and representative democracy hamper this sort of governmental action. Ideals to the contrary, a majority of Americans have been quite willing to allow informal social barriers to exist. Indeed, they have spent a good deal of their ingenuity in constructing these barriers.

Equality is discussed in the context of political culture in the next chapter, in the context of voting rights in Chapter 10, and in the context of civil rights in Chapter 16.

The Inevitability of Conflict

The problem of equality, particularly racial equality, is at the heart of a persistent crisis in American domestic politics, and it is closely linked to problems of poverty and crime. Surrounding this trio is a band of other serious problems like inflation, unemployment, clogged transportation lines, urban growth, environmental pollution, and sickness, especially of the very young, the very old, and the very poor. International problems of foreign aid, war, peace, and survival create additional dimensions of concern. None of these problems has a simple solution. All are likely to generate conflict.

Conflict arises from disagreements about both ends and means. Individuals, groups, and governmental agencies differ over what should be done and how to tackle problems on the public agenda. One major source of political conflict is fundamental: should government intervene at all in a particular problem? Apartment dwellers battle with landlords over proposals for rent control. The American Medical Association and private insurance companies try to keep the federal government out of health insurance, while labor unions and other interests work for universal national coverage of medical expenses. Conflicts over governmental involvement are likely to be especially bitter when strongly held personal beliefs are challenged. Examples are conflicts over religious instruction in the public schools, use of public funds to provide abortions, and court orders requiring busing to desegregate schools.

Once government does become involved, the potential for conflict increases substantially. Some interests seek to enlarge government's role, others to restrict public activity. Conflict over the scope of governmental involvement is common. Welfare programs, for example, constantly generate conflict over who should receive public assistance as well as how much. Further conflict usually arises over the effectiveness of particular policies, programs, and agencies. Consumer groups, for instance, charge that the Federal Aviation Agency is not sufficiently independent of airplane manufacturers when it assesses the safety of commercial jets. Airlines, on the other hand, argue that FAA has inadequate funds and personnel to monitor the nation's airways safely and efficiently.

Allocating responsibilities among public agencies and levels of government also causes political conflict. City officials and their supporters in Washington quarreled for years with transportation interests about having federal transit programs in the Department of Housing and Urban Development or in the Department of Transportation. Similar disputes arise over whether food stamps for the poor should be administered by the Department of Agriculture or the Department of Health, Education and Welfare. Increasing the likelihood of conflict is the existence of 50 state governments and more than 78,000 local governments. State and local officials battle with the federal government, as well as with each other for control over various programs and tax resources. For their part, nongovernmental participants in politics favor assigning responsibilities to the agency or level of government most likely to advance their interests. Thus, residents of middle-class suburbs want to maintain local control over land use and housing programs, while civil rights and fair-housing groups want state or federal agencies to be responsible for locating subsidized housing.

Competition among existing programs and their supporters for scarce public resources is another important source of conflict. Building an antiballistic missile system may mean ending a school lunch program. Expanding foreign aid to Egypt and Israel is likely to reduce funds available for the poorest nations of Africa and Asia. Hiring more policemen can leave less money for public health. Paying teachers higher salaries often forces school officials to cut back on books and other supplies, reduce special forms of instruction, or delay the construction of needed facilities. Incessant pressures for more tax dollars for education also produce conflict, which is reflected in struggles over school budgets and bond issues and spirited campaigns between "spenders" and "economizers" for positions on local school boards. In recent years fiscal crises growing out of rejected budgets and vetoed tax increases have closed some schools for extended periods of time.

Conflict also results because public activities almost always involve costs and benefits that cannot be measured merely in dollars. A new network of highways may ease traffic congestion, but bring more air pollution. Heavy dependence on foreign sources of petroleum has led to strong demands for public policies that will foster use of domestic energy sources, such as soft coal, Alaskan oil, and offshore petroleum. At every turn, however, environmental interests have challenged proposals that threaten to increase sulphur and other pollutants from coal, or alter the ecology of northern Alaska, or imperil the fragile environment of coastal areas.

Political conflicts usually arise because of competing interests rather than lack of information or expertise. With the growth of government has come an enormous increase in availability of technical information to many participants in politics. Experts often disagree among themselves, however, and these developments probably have increased rather than decreased political conflict. Some top naval officers, for example, argue that giant aircraft carriers are essential to national defense. Other experts in the Navy and the Department of Defense contend that supercarriers are too vulnerable to attack to justify expenditure of $1 billion per ship. The point is that information and technical skills rarely are used neutrally in political conflicts. Instead, public agencies and other political participants tend to use expertise to advance their own interests and undermine the arguments of their opponents. Nuclear scientists within the atomic industry and the federal Nuclear Regulatory Agency produce analyses that conclude that atomic power plants are safe. Other scientists insist just as adamantly that

Almost everyone agrees that cleaner air is desirable. Conflicts arise, however, over specific *ends* — the question of how clean the air should be. Conflict also results from disputes over the *means* of reducing air pollution — what sorts of controls are needed at what cost. A major party to such conflicts has been the steel industry, which was forced to make significant reductions in emissions at plants such as this one in Gary, Indiana, following the enactment of the Clean Air Act of 1970.

nuclear generating facilities pose unacceptable risks of monumental disaster.

Despite the variety and intensity of political conflict in the United States, few of these disputes concern the fundamental arrangements of government. To be sure, large numbers of Americans are dissatisfied with the performance of public officials and agencies, with waste and corruption in government, and with rising tax burdens. But even so, most citizens do not seriously question the legitimacy of the basic features of the American political system. Groups seeking equal rights for women or higher social security benefits try to influence the government rather than overthrow it. Those not satisfied with Supreme Court rulings on school prayers are more likely to try to change the membership or jurisdiction of the Court than to have the Court abolished. Of course, these general rules have their exceptions, including such groups as the Symbionese Liberation Army and the Minutemen, radicals of the extreme left and right. And the Civil War stands as a bloody reminder of what happens when conflicts over difficult issues like slavery, tariffs, and territorial expansion come to involve basic governmental arrangements like the nature of the federal union.

Big Government

Government — the target of most political activity — has grown steadily in the United States. In 1975, the federal government, the states, and the more than 78,000 local governments spent $523 billion, which ac-

Figure 1.2
The Budget Dollar—1977

Where it comes from . . .

Individual Income Taxes	Excise Taxes	Social Insurance Receipts	Corporation Income Taxes	Borrowing	Other
39¢	4¢	29¢	13¢	11¢	4¢

Where it goes . . .

Direct Benefit Payments to Individuals	Grants to States and Localities	Other Federal Operations	Net Interest	Military
40¢	15¢	11¢	8¢	26¢

Source: *New York Times,* Jan. 22, 1976.

counted for 37 percent of the gross national product.* Almost $325 billion of this total was spent by the federal government, which was $44 billion more than it collected in taxes. To collect and spend these funds, government employed 14.6 million civilians in 1975, 11.7 million of whom worked for state and local governments.

Underlying the growth of government has been social, economic, technological, and political change. Urbanization and industrialization have made Americans less self-sufficient, and their increased interdependence has, in turn, generated demands for more public services and governmental regulation of private enterprise. In addition, these demands have brought about the organization of all sorts of interests, pressing for increased governmental activity of one kind or another — or for less of it. Political leaders have responded and have also generated new demands of their own, in the form of such programs as Woodrow Wilson's New Freedom, Franklin Roosevelt's New Deal, and Lyndon Johnson's Great Society. Paralleling urbanization and industrialization in the twentieth century has been the expanding role of the United States in world affairs, which has greatly increased the military, diplomatic, and other international activities of the national government and so its size and complexity.

Particularly striking in recent years has been the growth of government's social programs — such programs as medicare, food stamps, and antipoverty efforts. Between 1966 and 1976, federal spending for human resources increased almost fivefold, from $43 billion to over $202 billion. Underlying this rapid expansion of specific federal programs and assistance (and parallel developments at state and local levels) were many of the forces that account for the general growth of government.

Popular support for social security, for example, has produced a steady widening of eligibility for participation in the program. The lengthening of life spans also increased the number of recipients of benefits. As a result of these developments, one out of every seven Americans was collecting social security benefits in 1975. Equally important, benefits rose rapidly in recent years, because of both inflation and political pressures for more adequate levels of assistance for the elderly. Similar forces were at work in the medicare program, which provides health insurance for older Americans. During the program's first nine years, costs rose from $3 billion to $17 billion, while the number of recipients grew from 7 million to more than 13 million. In general, popular programs expand with population and political pressure, and government becomes bigger.

Even more spectacular was the growth of the food-stamp program. Food stamps were first distributed in the 1960s as a means of improving the diet of very poor families and individuals. Later, a series of leg-

*The gross national product (GNP) is all the goods and services produced within the United States.

One of the nation's 19 million food stamp recipients makes a purchase in Chicago.

islative changes and administrative actions broadened the program. The severe economic slump of 1974–75 further increased the ranks of those eligible. As a result, over 19 million people received food stamps in 1975, compared with less than a million a decade earlier. This enormous expansion combined with larger benefits to send federal outlays for food stamps from under $100 million in 1966 to over $6 billion in 1975 and the number of federal employees needed to administer the program from 240 to more than 2,000.

With all this growth has come specialization. Specialized agencies, personnel, and programs—in short, bureaucracies and bureaucrats—have developed at all levels of government. A single example of this process is the organization of the Department of Labor. At the top of this federal agency are the Secretary of Labor, the Under Secretary, Deputy Under Secretary for International Affairs, Assistant Secretary for Administration, Solicitor, and Director of the Office of Information, each with substantial staff. Most of Labor's work, however, goes on within its main divisions: the Manpower Administration, the Employment Standards Administration, the Occupational Safety and Health Administration, and the Bureau of Labor Statistics, each of which is headed by an Assistant Secretary, Administrator, or Commissioner. Within each of these major units are specialized offices that actually administer the department's many programs. For example, the Employment Standards Administration has units to insure that those who contract with the federal government comply with equal employment opportunity programs, equal pay and age programs, women's programs, fair labor standards, federal employees' compensation, wage determinations, evaluation and review, field operations management, and program regulations and procedures.

Governmental agencies like the Department of Labor produce rules, regulations, services, facilities, assistance, and information. Almost every kind of economic activity is affected by such rules and regulations. The federal government regulates transportation, communications, petroleum and natural gas, generation of electric power, atomic energy, food, drugs, consumer products, job safety, wages and hours, environmental protection, banks, securities dealers, and scores of other transactions and enterprises. State governments regulate insurance companies and public utilities and license lawyers, doctors, dentists, barbers, undertakers, engineers, and a host of other professionals. Local governments set taxi and transit fares, enforce building codes, regulate land use, and prescribe minimum health and sanitary standards for all sorts of enterprises.

Among the major services provided by governments are education, health, police, fire, public transportation, and mail delivery. Except for the postal service, the principal responsibility for actually providing these public services rests with local governments, although the state and federal roles in financing education, health, and transit have been steadily rising. Largely through federal funds, government provides assistance to millions of citizens in all income groups. Social security is available for the elderly, unemployment compensation for those out of work, welfare and social services for the poor, public housing for low-income families, aid to the blind and disabled, and medical assistance for the aged. Assistance also goes to veterans, farmers who have suffered crop damage, victims of floods and other natural disasters, and a wide variety of business enterprises. Many of these activities involve governments providing facilities—schools, police stations, firehouses, hospitals and clinics, community centers, welfare offices, housing units, and post offices. Other governmental responsibilities involve construction and operation of public facilities, such as highways, airports, transit systems, parks, military bases and equipment, research laboratories, and testing facilities.

In carrying out these responsibilities, and in collecting the taxes to finance them, governments consume an enormous amount of paper—statutes, regulations, reports, instructions, forms, press releases, and other documents. The federal government alone requires over 10,000 different forms and reports, which generate 556 million responses annually. A major corporation like Standard Oil of Indiana files 250 reports each year with more than forty governmental agencies. As programs evolve, new rules and regulations are constantly issued. Following enactment of the food-stamp legislation by Congress, rules for the program were developed in 1965, rewritten in each of the next three years, and again in 1972. After 1972 the rules were revised twenty-seven times before being rewritten once more in 1974. And in 1975 alone, almost 500 regulations affecting food stamps were issued.

"Go away . . . the post office is
already losing $250,000 an hour as it is."

Reprinted courtesy of the Chicago Tribune.

Big government, with its red tape, alphabet soup of agencies, and expanding programs, troubles most Americans. Rising taxes are universally disliked, as are mounting fees for all sorts of public services. When increasing costs are combined with declining levels of service, as in the case of the post office among others, concern is even greater. Widespread inefficiency, the ineffectiveness of many governmental programs, and the persistence of corruption further increase public dissatisfaction.

Big government also troubles some people because of the threat posed by its police and intelligence agencies to privacy, freedom of expression, and other basic rights. In recent years the Internal Revenue Service, the Federal Bureau of Investigation, and the Central Intelligence Agency have confessed to a series of felonies that would make a Mafia Don blush.

Others are deeply distressed by the prospect that social programs, high taxes, and economic regulation will undermine individualism, property rights, and free enterprise. "Any government big enough to give you anything you want," argued President Gerald Ford, "is big enough to take everything you have."*

While most people share these concerns about big government, they also tend to favor *more* public involvement in areas of particular concern to them. Almost everything that government does reflects long,

*Quoted in "Big Government," *Newsweek*, Jan. 15, 1975, p. 34.

hard work by some interest group pressing for governmental intervention. Elected political leaders typically are responsive to insistent demands that government do something about a problem. Thus, candidates who condemn big government, bureaucracy, and red tape rarely oppose all efforts to expand government after election to office. Once a program is begun, groups that benefit from that particular activity usually provide strong support for its continuation and enlargement. Few programs survive without strong backing from these "clientele" interests. And many of the most influential supporters of particular programs are outspoken critics of big government in general. Farmers, for example, tend to favor less government spending, but not in areas that benefit them directly—agricultural research, food programs, irrigation projects, and the like.

The fact that government with all its inadequacies plays an indispensable role in the everyday life of almost every American also partially offsets concerns about big government. Clean water to drink, disposal of sewage, schools, public safety, highways, public transportation, and scores of other essential services are provided by government. Because of federal environmental regulations, the air everyone breathes contained 25 percent less sulphur dioxide in 1975 than in 1970. Cars produced in 1976 under strict federal emission standards produced 83 percent less carbon monoxide than those manufactured in 1970. Mandatory federal requirements for seat belts and other safety devices on automobiles played a major role in reducing the highway death rate by one third between 1965 and 1975. During its first three years, the Consumer Safety Product Commission banned the sale of over 20 million unsafe items.

Also vital to life for millions of Americans are the social programs that are the cause of so much public concern and criticism. Over 11 million people receive sustenance through the federal government's program of Aid for Dependent Children. In addition, there are the 19 million individuals who have their diets and incomes supplemented through the food-stamp program. And 32 million people receive monthly social security benefits. Although benefits and costs keep rising and so increase political conflict, benefits under most social programs are grossly inadequate to provide a decent standard of living for recipients. Revised in 1972 to allow payments to rise with the cost of living, social security by itself still does not provide enough income for the aged to escape poverty. Payments under the Aid for Dependent Children program, which is administered by state and local governments, have been kept at miserably low levels in many states, and nowhere have they kept pace with inflation. Further reducing the help provided by most social programs is their incomplete coverage of those who need and are eligible for assistance. For example, because of ignorance, local administrative procedures, and plain red tape, less than half of the estimated 40 million Americans eligible for food stamps in 1975 actually participated in the program.

Public Policy

Public policy is what government does about a particular problem. Typically, public policies involve a series of decisions by public officials rather than a single decision. The nation's policy toward Panama, or its public-land policy, or its policy on tax credits results from a variety of public actions. First, certain officials make a decision to act, usually in response to particular problems and situations, pressures from various interests, and special concerns of key officials. Then they must select particular courses of action among alternatives. The importance of the problem, which will affect its claim to political, administrative, and budgetary resources, must be determined. Once an overall policy has been decided on, it needs to be implemented. Officials must assign responsibilities for carrying out the policy, settle administrative arrangements, and determine procedures. In the course of implementing the policy, all sorts of decisions have to be made about applying or not applying the general policy to specific instances.

Rarely, however, are public policies developed and implemented in a neat procession of decisions. Instead, new developments and considerations affect determinations at each stage. Experience with implementing a policy may lead to basic revisions or to changes in the administrative or intergovernmental arrangements. Group demands for certain policy goals that were not satisfied in the development of the general policy may be met in carrying out the policy. Benefits distributed by a policy may strengthen a particular interest group's ability to secure still more funds or more sympathetic treatment in the implementation of the policy. Moreover, other public policies constantly affect any one policy. Thus, policy toward Israel is influenced by foreign policies involving Egypt, the Soviet Union, and other nations, as well as by defense policies, foreign aid policies, and the government's need for support of other public policies by domestic interests favorable or hostile or indifferent toward Israel.

Public policy is expressed in a variety of ways, both formal and informal. Public policies dealing with the structure of the national government, the powers of its basic components, and the rights of the people and the states are set forth in the Constitution. State constitutions and municipal charters elaborate similar public policies. Many state constitutions also contain a variety of other policy statements—for example, descriptions of the highway system or allocation of aid for education, which in the case of the national government are the subject of legislation rather than constitutional provisions.

Law is an extremely important formal source of public policy. *Legislation* or *statutes* (also called *ordinances* in some local governments and collectively called *statutory law*) are those public policies formally enacted by legislative bodies. *Treaties* and *executive agreements* are policy statements that grow out of international relations. Treaties are agreements with foreign nations that are signed by the

A good example of the evolution of public policy is provided by the U.S. space program. Born in the late 1950s, the civilian space program grew rapidly under Presidents Kennedy and Johnson, reaching annual expenditures in excess of $5 billion in the mid-1960s and culminating in the landing of Apollo II on the moon in 1969. Growing political resistance to the costs of the space program, along with the press of other national needs, led to a tapering off of expenditures in the 1970s and a declining emphasis on manned space flights.

President and ratified by the U.S. Senate, whereas executive agreements are similar documents that do not require formal action by the Senate. *Executive orders* are policy determinations by the President, the governor of a state, or a mayor, and the authority to issue them is derived from constitutional or statutory law. *Administrative rules, regulations,* and *standards* are policy determinations by administrative agencies designed to implement constitutional provisions, laws, treaties, and executive orders. Another major source of formal policy statements are *court opinions* and the *rulings of quasi-judicial bodies* like the Federal Communications Commission or the Civil Aeronautics Board, whose decisions have much the same impact as court orders.

Despite the importance of such formal statements, many policies are expressed informally, particularly when they are being implemented. Every day, hundreds of thousands of governmental officials decide informally which laws to enforce and how strictly to apply administrative standards. The policeman who permits cars to exceed the speed limit by five miles an hour is revising the formal policy stated in statutes. So is the building inspector who does not enforce a section of the building code whose standards cannot be met by most older buildings. Laws, administrative regulations, and other formal policy statements may be informally altered for all sorts of reasons—convenience, practicality, constraint of time, bribery, fear, deference to the power of certain groups and individuals, racial or ethnic prejudice, or the desire for electoral support.

Informal determinations of public policy occur throughout the whole social system as well as in governmental processes. Policy can be vitally affected by the presidential aide who passes the word that only deserving Democrats (or Republicans) are to be considered for judgeships, by the civil service official who manages to find some serious flaw in the credentials of a homosexual, by the welfare investigator who turns his back on chiseling, by the executives of oil companies who secretly meet and agree to keep their tankers at sea to create an oil shortage to drive prices up, or by the union leaders who decide their men will not load ships bound for the Soviet Union.

Summary

We have said enough to make it clear that public policy results from an interplay among a complex mix of cultural, social, economic, constitutional, political, and institutional forces. The remainder of this volume examines many of those factors in detail. We shall concentrate on policy making at the national level, but the reader must keep in mind that formal and informal decentralization of power permeates the entire political system. Participants in state and local politics play a major role in making and implementing national policies.

Part I of this book describes the cultural, social, and economic setting in which political activity takes place. Part II looks at basic constitutional arrangements that affect policy making, the system that James Madison and other Founding Fathers designed to distribute and so restrict power within the national government and between the nation and the states. Part III then begins to analyze the processes of politics, examining such problems as the concept of power, the organization and functions of political parties, the electoral machinery for choosing public officials, and the diverse ways in which voters respond to appeals by parties and individual candidates. In Parts IV, V, and VI, the emphasis shifts to the political institutions that bear formal responsibility for making policy, the operations and mutual restraints among Congress, the Presidency, the bureaucracy, and the judiciary. Part VII takes up in detail certain problems of civil rights and criminal justice.

The final chapter tries to evaluate the performance of and the prospects for the American political system. A central concern in this concluding appraisal must be the capacity of the system as a whole to make and carry out public policies that can coherently and effectively attack problems that gnaw at the country. What we hope emerges from this discussion, as well as from the entire volume, is a more sophisticated appreciation of the difficulties of reconciling competing, even conflicting, demands. These conflicts and the power relationships that determine their outcome are the essence of politics.

Selected Bibliography

ANDERSON, JAMES E., *Public Policy-Making* (New York: Praeger Publishers, 1975). A succinct introduction to the policy-making process, which identifies the major aspects of policy formulation, implementation, impact, and change.

DAHL, ROBERT A. and CHARLES E. LINDBLOM, *Politics, Economics, and Welfare* (New York: Harper, 1953). A classic examination of planning and policy making within complex political systems.

DAVIES, J. CLARENCE III, *The Politics of Pollution* (New York: Pegasus, 1970). An analysis of the many participants in environmental politics, and the conflicts among them.

MOYNIHAN, DANIEL P., *The Politics of a Guaranteed Income* (New York: Random House, 1973). A detailed account of conflict over the Nixon Administration's family assistance plan by its principal architect.

REAGAN, MICHAEL D., *The Administration of Public Policy* (Glenview, Ill.: Scott, Foresman and Company, 1969). A description of the linkages between substance and process in the development and administration of public policy.

STEINER, GILBERT Y., *The State of Welfare* (Washington: The Brookings Institution, 1971). A thoughtful journey through the labyrinth of public programs aimed at lower-income Americans.

Part One

The Framework of American Politics

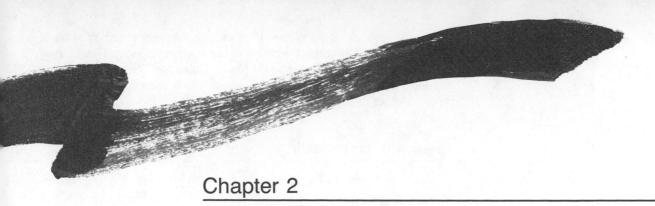

Chapter 2

American Political Cultures

The Continental Setting
Industrialization and Urbanization
American Society

The Concept of Political Culture

Systems of Beliefs

Cultural Diversity
The Silent Majority
The Professional Politician
The Poor
The Blacks
White Ethnics
Women

Violence as a Cultural Trait

Political Socialization

Patterns of Political Cultures

Summary

Selected Bibliography

POLITICAL BEHAVIOR AND governmental institutions are shaped by a nation's physical setting, patterns of development, social structure, belief systems, values, and goals. Most of these conditioning factors, in turn, are affected by the nature of a national political system and the public choices it makes and seeks to implement.

The Continental Setting

The political system of a nation is influenced by such physical factors as the country's location and natural resources. In these respects, the United States could hardly have been more blessed. When it was small, underpopulated, and weak, it was also remote, both in terms of interest to and distance from the great powers of the world. To the north Canada was a sparsely settled outpost of the British Empire; to the south Mexico, once it gained independence, wanted only peaceful coexistence. To the east was an ocean, and to the west an almost uninhabited subcontinent that invited exploitation.

Physical isolation was enhanced by natural wealth. On both sides of the Appalachian Mountains the climate was generally temperate and the soil fertile. A series of rivers provided a network of inland trade routes, and the seacoast was indented with sheltered harbors. Scattered about the country was an abundance of resources—wild animals for food, hides, and furs; grassy plains for cattle; timber for houses; gold and silver for adventure and quick wealth; and, for the industry that would later come, oil, coal, natural gas, iron, copper, lead, and bauxite.

In 1840 Alexis de Tocqueville, a Frenchman who traveled widely in the young nation, could speak of the "magnificent dwelling place" and the "immense booty" that fortune had left to Americans. That abundance has played a critical psychological as well as physical role in the American experience. Great prosperity, and an illusion of even greater prosperity, attracted wave after wave of immigrants and sent them as well as older inhabitants searching out and developing the natural wealth of the country. Often these people came as the downtrodden, but they came to better themselves, not to accept poverty. Until the early twentieth century, even their raw muscle power was much in demand. The myth of rags to riches may have seldom materialized, but social and economic advancement were possible and became the American dream, creating a surge of energy and hope.

Immigration and social mobility combined to help Americans maintain a myth of equality.[1] It was not that all people were equal—they certainly were not equal in wealth, education, talent, or political power. But the pull of an expanding economy and the push of the next sweep of immigrants, who represented both producers and consumers, did give most of the white-skinned poor more and more material benefits. It was not so much that their proportionate share of the good things of

Migrant children in the doorway of their home, Sequoia County, California, 1939. For more than two centuries, Americans have moved westward in search of opportunity and a better life. Joining this flow in the 1930s were tens of thousands of farmers from the plains states forced off the land by drought and the Great Depression.

life increased, but that the number of good things available at a low price multiplied.

Industrialization and Urbanization

Until 1900, the frontier played a major role in American development. So did industrialization, but before 1860 its impact had been gradual. Some small-scale manufacturing had appeared during the colonial period. After independence and shielded by a protective tariff, factories grew slowly but steadily. The Civil War, however, created massive demands and started American industry off on a spiraling curve that has continued, despite frequent recessions and occasional depressions, for more than a century. Technological advances in manufacturing occurred at the same time that technological advances in transportation opened vast markets and made raw materials easily accessible.

European demands during World War I further bolstered American industry, so that by 1918 the United States had become not only the creditor of much of the world but also the biggest of the industrial nations. After the disastrous years of the Great Depression, World War II catapulted the American economy off once more with a momentum that has sustained rapid economic growth for more than thirty years.

Industrialization changed the character of the American population. The new factories and their demands for labor stopped immigrants at the cities and also sparked a steady exodus from the farms to metropolitan areas. In 1800, only 6 percent of Americans were living in towns with populations over 2,500; by 1870 the proportion had risen to one

Figure 2.1
Immigration, 1820–1974

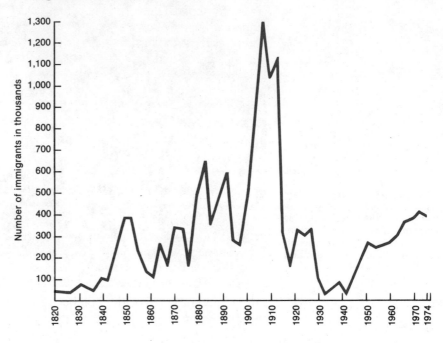

Source: U.S. Bureau of the Census.

quarter. By 1900 it was up to 40 percent, and by 1970 more than three out of four people in the United States were living in urban areas. Some 50 million of those people were in cities with populations of over 250,000. But even these figures understate urbanization. The arms of the megalopolis have been spreading out like the tentacles of a hungry octopus, scooping up surrounding land for industrial parks, research laboratories, shopping centers, and suburban housing developments. "Strip Cities," like the one reaching from north of Boston to south of Richmond, Virginia, the one bordering all the southern arc of Lake Michigan, and the one stretching from the Mexican border along the coast of California north above Santa Barbara, are turning huge stretches of country into urbanized belts that make old geographical and political boundaries impractical for control of many social problems.

American Society

This collage of wealth, work, isolation, immigration, industrialization, and urbanization has forged a complex society full of contradictions. The contrasts of American life abound: romantic love and high divorce rates, Hollywood sex symbols and Disneyland, urban blight alongside magnificent monuments, marvelous medical research and a mania for cigarette smoking, anger at the young for dulling their minds with marijuana but approval of cocktails before lunch and dinner, eminent symphony orchestras and blaring rock bands, resounding professions of human dignity and equality together with insidious racial and sexual discrimination.

The American people have succeeded in maintaining rates of production that enable them to have the shortest work week of any industrial nation, to provide most citizens with comfortable housing, good food, and excellent medical and dental care. They spend millions of dollars annually for recreation—color television sets, boats, second homes, golf, fishing, bowling, whiskey, and long vacations. Yet even play means hard work for Americans; they tend to consume leisure rather than enjoy it. At times it has seemed that the Protestant ethic of hard work has gone mad in America and has created a mass rat race of people working compulsively harder and harder to win higher salaries, more responsibility, and less enjoyment. In recent years, however, there has been a notable reaction against this kind of existence. Both in factories and among semiprofessionals and professionals, there has been a rejection, particularly by younger Americans, of the regimentation imposed by the discipline of large organizations. Many industries are now trying to develop ways of allowing employees more freedom, even at the expense of earlier standards of efficiency. At the same time, unions are pressing harder and harder for a four-day work week, a goal that a half-century ago appeared as foolishly utopian as the five-day work week did seventy-five years ago.

The frenzied labor of American adults has bought for future generations the advantage of the widest dispersion of educational opportunities in the world. The median number of years of schooling for adults in the United States is now twelve years. A college education for their children has become the normal expectation of almost all middle-class adults and probably a majority of working-class families as well. In 1975 about 9 million students were actually attending colleges and universities. The very high incomes earned by such professionals as doctors, lawyers, and engineers give evidence of the demands that a highly technological society makes on its members and the rewards it bestows for advanced training.

Despite the great emphasis on education and despite the great respect Americans accord academics, especially those in the physical sciences, there is a noticeable current of anti-intellectualism in American thought.[2] Perhaps the challenge of survival on the frontier and later of competition in the dog-eat-dog economy of the nineteenth century discouraged philosophical speculation and encouraged pragmatic approaches. Does it work? does it make a profit? and does it allow me to get ahead? were—and are—the typical questions Americans have asked, not: How does it fit into a broad interpretation of the cosmos?

"As I look back, I realize that everything I have I owe to the Protestant work ethic, and a few timely tips on the market."

New Yorker, June 7, 1969. Drawing by Donald Reilly; © 1969 The New Yorker Magazine, Inc.

Indeed, if Americans can be said to have developed any national philosophy, it is a philosophy of pragmatism, which pushes aside abstract speculation and favors more practical questions about actual results.

The permissive nature of society in the United States is notorious. With Dr. Benjamin Spock's books on child raising the bible of the last generation of parents, family life has become very democratic. In recent decades, many school teachers have urged children to express themselves, to give their own opinions rather than to regurgitate the rote recitations that used to characterize much of what we call education. The point is not that there is no discipline or authoritarianism in the family or school, but that there is considerably less than in the American past or in the present of most other nations.

The informality of American business life, where president or owner often insists on being addressed by first name or initials, may be partly a means of softening the savagery of competition. But the usual practice of the more successful corporations has been to encourage employees to exercise initiative, blue-collar workers as well as top officials. Even the military is becoming less authoritarian. The traditional model of the general as the "heroic soldier" who earned his reputation for blood and guts and demanded instant and unswerving obedience is being superseded by a managerial model, in which the general more often persuades and leads than commands.[3] Indeed, congressmen in 1973 put the blame for racial disorders aboard an aircraft carrier the previous year on the Navy's "permissiveness."

The Concept of Political Culture

Like a nation's physical setting and resources, its social customs and ideals can influence the character and operation of its governmental system. To take account of this shaping force, political scientists have developed the concept of political culture. In its most general—and useful—sense, *political culture refers to politically relevant ideas and social practices.* It is a concept that calls attention to the fact that habits of action, norms of conduct, symbols of good and evil, and even basic notions about the nature of God and man can influence the ways people behave in political contexts and the ways in which they evaluate the political behavior of others. To be sure, not all social arrangements and not all prevalent ideas are politically important, but many are. Even something as basic as language may play a significant role. One noted political philosopher[4] has speculated that the existence of the word "leader" has increased the chances for the success of democratic government in English-speaking nations over such countries as Germany and Italy, where the closest words are more equivalent to "commander" or "director."

One would expect a society in which fathers usually exercise authoritarian control over family life to foster very different sorts of political relationships than a society in which there is considerable give and take in family decision making. One would also expect people who grow up under a rigid class structure to have different patterns of political behavior than people reared in a classless society.

Although few societies provide neat contrasts, there is evidence to indicate that to a large extent the expected relations between society and politics do take place. People accustomed to participate in decision making in the family, at school, or at work tend to participate more in political life and to feel more competent to influence governmental decisions. The connections, however, between social background and political behavior are neither simple nor universal. Among other important factors is personality. For instance, people who feel least competent politically are usually not those who have been denied opportunities to participate in other social situations, but those who have had such opportunities but did not take advantage of them.[5]

Moreover, traffic between politics and other social relations is not along a limited-access throughway. New governmental policies frequently interact with old social customs to precipitate fundamental changes. And these changes occur not only in the way people behave politically but also in relationships within supposedly more basic groups like the family or the church.

"Our government," Supreme Court Justice Louis D. Brandeis once noted, "is the potent, the omnipresent teacher. For good or ill, it teaches the whole people by its example."[6] American concepts of equality owe much to Jefferson and Lincoln. George Washington and Chief Justice John Marshall helped shape our views on nationalism. Certainly Presidents Franklin D. Roosevelt, John F. Kennedy, and Lyndon B. Johnson were primarily responsible for converting minority views about the desirability of the welfare state into an accepted part of American life. Chief Justice Earl Warren's pronouncement for the Supreme Court in the School Segregation Cases of 1954 changed a great deal of thinking about human dignity in general and race relations in particular.[7]

More generally, it is a plausible hypothesis that much of the permissiveness of current American life is a by-product of political democracy. Extolling the virtues of debate and popular participation in governmental affairs has a perceptible spillover into the arena of the family, classroom, office, and church, even the once rigidly authoritarian Roman Catholic Church.

Systems of Beliefs

Basic ideas about human nature, authority, religion, and the purposes of life have broad political relevance. The framers of the American Constitution, for instance, were deeply aware of the frailty of virtue. Products of a Protestant religious culture, they were influenced by the doctrine of original sin—human nature is fundamentally weak; people want to do good but are inclined toward evil and selfishness. Thus the framers found attractive a governmental scheme for checking ambition against ambition. "But what is government itself," James Madison asked in *The Federalist*, "but the greatest of all reflections on human nature? If men were angels, no government would be necessary."[8]

Ideas about fundamental philosophic principles as well as beliefs directly linked to politics are more likely to be normative than descriptive. That is, they are more likely to consist of notions about what is right and proper than descriptions of what actually happens. These ideas thus form a kind of moral screen through which people filter information and perceive and pass judgments on political reality.

One can speak in two senses of a system of beliefs. First, there is evidence that an overwhelming proportion of Americans endorse democratic political principles. Most are convinced that democracy is the best form of government, that public officials should be elected by a majority vote, and that every citizen should have an equal opportunity to participate in politics. Americans also believe that members of the minority have a right to criticize the majority's choices and to try to win a majority over to their own views.[9] The concept of the basic equality of human dignity would probably receive an equally thumping endorsement.

Second, in many important respects, the political outlooks of Americans differ from those of citizens of other countries. In the late 1950s, for example, a study conducted by Almond and Verba showed that, compared to British, Germans, Italians, and Mexicans, Americans tended to be more trusting of their fellow man, to see more altruism in other people, to look more on political participation as a duty of the average citizen, to think of themselves as more influential in their national government, and, except for the British, more likely to expect fair and equal treatment from public officials.[10]

Almond and Verba also found that Americans were prouder of their governmental institutions, but more recent surveys show a marked drop in American trust in their political system. The Survey Research Center of the University of Michigan reported in 1964 that 62 percent of a national sample of adults had a high level of trust in the federal government. Over the next few years that figure fell steadily, and by 1974 had plummeted to 25 percent. These shifts in attitude are linked to reactions to governmental policies regarding Vietnam, race relations, urban problems, and, of course, the Watergate scandals.

Cultural Diversity

We must talk of *many political cultures* when we analyze most modern nations. Patterns of child raising, educational and religious training, and economic relations vary greatly from social group to social group in America. An immigrant child raised in a strict Irish-Catholic family and educated by authoritarian nuns is apt to have been exposed to a set of influences very different from that of a black child who came to maturity in an urban ghetto or on a Mississippi cotton farm, or of a white Protestant youngster who grew up in an affluent suburb where discipline was light.

In similar fashion, we should not expect anything approaching unanimity on most political issues. What we know about public opinion indicates that consensus on general principles rarely includes agreement on specific policies. To a middle-class white, for example, equality for blacks may refer to their right to live in decent housing in the central city, not next door in a suburb, or to compete for a blue-collar job, not a

Table 2–1.

Responses to Questions about Civil Rights

statement	percent agreeing
Antireligious speeches should be allowed	63
Socialist speeches should be allowed	79
Communist speeches should be allowed	44

statement	percent disagreeing
Only informed people should have the right to vote on a city referendum	49
Only taxpayers should have the right to vote on city tax measures	21
Negroes should not be allowed to hold public office	81
Communists should not be allowed to hold public office	46

Source: James W. Prothro and Charles M. Grigg, ''Fundamental Principles of Democracy: Bases of Agreement and Disagreement,'' *Journal of Politics*, XXII (1960), p. 285.

managerial position. To many blacks, equality means preferential treatment to compensate for centuries of injustice. To a conservative, the right of a minority to try to persuade the majority of the error of its ways may not include the right of a communist to speak in a public hall or at a street meeting. To radicals, free speech may mean the right to shout down those who advocate "immoral" or "fascist" positions.

Table 2–1 summarizes responses of a sample of adults in Ann Arbor, Michigan, and Tallahassee, Florida, who had averaged over 95 percent agreement on the democratic principles listed in the previous section and indicates just how quickly consensus disappears when it is confronted with practical problems of application. On only three of the seven statements listed—the rights of blacks to run for office and of socialists to speak and a desire to restrict voting on city tax measures to taxpayers—were about eight out of ten respondents in agreement. In no instance did the answers approach the consensus reached in reply to questions about general principles of democracy.

The Silent Majority

The dominant political culture in America has been shaped largely by the values of the white upper-middle class. Its general beliefs in popular participation and election, majority rule and minority rights, and equality before the law are widely shared. But these beliefs are usually abstract rather than particular. Often they have little to do with how people view concrete public issues. To many upper-middle class

Americans, political participation may mean only voting regularly and perhaps writing to a senator or calling a local official about a problem. To most other Americans, political participation means even less. On the whole, to the average citizen politics is neither a very important or interesting part of life's circus. In 1972, two out of every five American adults denied that they cared very much in a personal way about the outcome of the presidential election. During the same year, less than a third of the people indicated they were very much interested in the presidential campaign.

As such responses suggest, the political knowledge of most citizens is slight. Even during national campaigns, Americans are likely to have little detailed information about issues that candidates, journalists, and political scientists consider important. The citizen seldom engages in serious political discussion. When he or she does, it is likely to be with people who have the same opinions.

There is a cluster of private citizens, mostly but not exclusively from the upper and upper-middle class, who are highly informed and deeply concerned about politics. Among this group, an opinion about a specific problem tends to be a consistent piece of a more general and coherent political orientation. These people are typically well educated and sometimes have amateur experience in practical politics. But they form a small minority, accounting for less than 10 percent of the adult population.[11]

Apparently, despite lack of knowledge and lethargic participation, widely shared affection for the basic system continues even when levels of political trust are running low. A survey by Louis Harris and Associates in 1972 indicated that 90 percent of the respondents were convinced of the basic soundness of the American system of government despite the fact that fewer than 30 percent had a great deal of confidence in Congress or the federal executive. Throughout American history, foreign observers have been struck by the reverence with which Americans view their Constitution. Politicians and the institutions they man rise and fall in public esteem, but the Constitution seems to persist as a symbol of virtue as much as a charter for government.

Running alongside respect for the Constitution is usually suspicion of governmental power. "I am not," Thomas Jefferson wrote in 1787, "a friend to a very energetic government."[12] Something akin to that attitude can be seen today in the responses to questions put by the pollsters. Americans may say that they favor governmental action on problems that affect them directly—keeping railroads running or increasing social security benefits, for example. At the same time, those people are apt to respond negatively to broader questions about increasing governmental power. Although these reactions may seem logically contradictory, they reflect a recognition of the need for governmental action and at the same time a yearning for the independence and individualism that Jefferson treasured.

Even very interested and articulate private citizens often differ from professional politicians in the way they look at politics. The professional's world is shaped by the fact that he (or she) has far more political resources at his command. As a generalist—a nonspecialist—he may know less about some particular problems than do many highly educated private citizens, but he knows where to find expertise if he needs it. More important, he devotes his working time not just his leisure to politics. Acquiring and using political skills is his life's work; and success provides other resources. If an incumbent, he has the authority of his office and the prestige it provides. If not in office, the professional politician may still have considerable influence with those who head governmental agencies.

Private citizens seldom have a sophisticated understanding of how to translate general principles of democratic government into workable political rules. For the professional, on the other hand, "the rules of the game" are likely to be tangible guidelines.[13]

The most basic of these professional rules is acceptance of elections as the proper means of determining who should govern. To look at the frequency of coups d'etat around the world is to appreciate that respect for the ballot box is hardly an inborn trait. The political espionage and sabotage run by the White House in the infamous Watergate scandals of the 1972 presidential campaign indicates how brittle such respect can be even in the United States.

For legislators, other rules of the game include listening to all constituent complaints, permitting groups likely to be affected a chance to be heard before government takes action, allowing, even when in the majority, opposing legislators a reasonable opportunity to speak, keeping one's word to officials from the opposing party as well as one's own, not looking closely into the campaign financing or tactics of colleagues unless serious abuses come to light, and respecting the constitutional prerogatives of other governmental agencies even while sharply disagreeing with their decisions. Professional politicians generally observe these kinds of rules because they know that they have to work year after year with other professionals, that they will have to run for re-election at frequent intervals, and that in their careers they may hold a variety of offices in several branches of government.

Even the amateur activist who gets deeply involved in politics is apt to see a different world than does the professional. The amateur typically enters the political arena with a single, immediate policy goal in mind. The professional, on the other hand, is accustomed to dealing with many issues so steadily and constantly "that few of them have the ultimate soul-saving importance for him that they do for the amateurs. . . . Politics for them [amateurs] is a means to an end, and what counts is to gain that end. To the professional, in contrast, what counts is to endure."[14]

Figure 2.2
Percentage of Americans below the Poverty Line

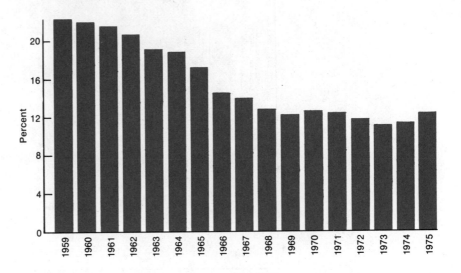

Source: U.S. Bureau of the Census

The Poor

Patterns of behavior, belief, and expectation are greatly influenced by an individual's economic circumstances. Most striking are the differences between those who are more or less affluent and those who live in dire poverty. In 1975, almost 26 million Americans lived below the poverty level.* Some of the poor are people who are too lazy, too undisciplined, or too oriented toward immediate gratification to cope with life in a technological society. Some, like the hobos of an older generation or the hippies of a more recent one, simply prefer a style of life that cannot be measured in economic terms. But the vast majority of the poor are poor neither by choice nor by sin. Instead they are "largely those unequipped by reason of some disability—age, sickness, or other physical incapacity, lack of education or training, discrimination because of race, or some other circumstance over which they have no control—to find gainful employment either in the private or public sectors of the economy."[15] Those who live in poverty are disproportionately black, members of other racial minorities, very old, or very young. Almost one out of every three blacks is poor. If old, the poor

*The poverty level line is defined by the U.S. Department of Commerce and the Bureau of the Census in terms of the amount of money it takes a family in a particular area to pay for minimally adequate food, shelter and medical care. In 1975, the poverty line for a nonfarm family of four was $5,469.

"Why can't <u>our</u> poor and needy be more picturesque?"

tend to be sick, unemployed, and unemployable. If young, they often come from broken homes and have received an education inadequate to equip them for competition in American society.

Michael Harrington, whose book *The Other America* played a major role in awakening national interest in the problems of the poor, sees poverty as "a culture, an institution, a way of life."[16] The poor have a family structure, sexual mores, and political outlooks different from those of middle-class citizens. "To be impoverished is to be an internal alien, to grow up in a culture that is radically different from the one that dominates society."[17] Those doomed to live in the empty shadows of poverty are vulnerable to hate—of themselves as well as of others—as they catch glimpses of the world of prosperity.

Poverty also has tremendous implications—although still largely potential implications—for the structure as well as the policies of the American political system. Until the late 1960s, the poor were politically mute and unimportant, despite their numbers. More recently, poor blacks, Chicanos, Puerto Ricans, Indians, and Appalachian whites have become "politically visible." Obviously, 26 million people represent an enormous political potential. The vast majority of the poor, however, remain ineffective in the political arena. Only about three out of five adults with an annual income of under $4,000 even claim to vote regularly, and the actual proportion is probably smaller. In comparison, about nine out of ten people with incomes over $15,000 go to the polls. Nor do the poor usually belong to unions, clubs, or other organizations that can dramatize their plight and represent their interests as poor people. In political life, the poor are fatally handicapped by their lack of resources. Most are too ignorant, too young and unsophisticated, too sick, too miserable, or too old to achieve anything like their political potential.

The Blacks

The National Advisory Commission on Civil Disorders stated in 1968 that the United States was "moving toward two societies, one black, one white — separate and unequal."[18] The striking eloquence of this sentence obscured the fact that it was fundamentally wrong. The United States has always comprised *many* societies, and race has drawn the most obvious and enduring line of division. Since the first slaves were taken ashore in Virginia in 1619, America has had a black society that has been distinctly separate from and decidedly unequal to the white societies. The black man, wrote W. E. B. DuBois at the beginning of this century, "ever feels his twoness — an American, a Negro; two souls, two thoughts, two unreconciled strivings; two warring ideals in one dark body."[19]

No more accurately, of course, than one can speak of *a* Caucasian can one speak of *a* black society. Many social, economic, educational, and political differences exist among blacks. There are some rich blacks, although not very many. More and more blacks have moved into the middle class and have incomes, education, attitudes, and values similar to those of white middle-class Americans. And there are the masses of the black poor, from the small rural farms to the large city ghettos. The poor of both races bear many of the same burdens, but the colors of their skin have usually generated enough prejudice and distrust to have kept them from acting as close allies. True assimilation of blacks into white American life at any social or economic level has been a rare phenomenon.

As a result of imposed separatism, a set of black subcultures has grown up, with some practices and speech patterns running back through the slave cabins to Africa. Not only do customs and habits of dress frequently differ, but rural and ghetto blacks often speak what is in many respects a different language from white-middle-class English.[20] The words are pronounced differently and have different meanings. The cadence is slower, more lilting, even the syntax is different. Gestures connote different kinds of emphases. Less formally, music plays a different role in the two subcultures. The Blues expresses much of the bitter lonesomeness of the black man's lot, and the concept "soul" signifies the greater seriousness and less inhibited pleasure that the black experiences.

Like whites, blacks have moved from lonely farms to even lonelier urban centers. In 1940, about two thirds of blacks lived in southern states; the proportion had fallen to 53 percent by 1970. But even more than from south to north, the pattern of black migration has been from farm to city. Wherever blacks live, most have grown up in an environment more hostile than that of the typical Caucasian. If they are poor or near-poor, blacks witness violence almost daily. The black trusts fellow humans less than does the white, and with good reason. A black male is four times more likely to be robbed than a white, and a black woman is three times more likely to be raped than a Caucasian woman. Blacks are also much more likely than whites to be stopped by police and subjected to humiliating searches or to be hauled off to a police station for questioning.

A black can expect to live, on the average, seven years fewer than a white person of the same sex, to enjoy a little more than half the income, and to suffer about twice the unemployment rate. Thus most blacks neither have nor can reasonably expect to gain in the near future the material goods that the average white earns. Discrimination is an integral part of a black's life.

In these circumstances, it is hardly surprising that blacks have created their own political subculture. They, too, may endorse the basic principles of democracy, but to them majority rule may mean white domination and minority rights a black dream. When they express their political views, blacks, compared to whites, assert greater general trust in the federal government and are much more strongly in favor of specific federal programs to carry out school desegregation, to enforce fair employment practices, and to provide jobs and a minimum standard of living for all citizens. On the other hand, blacks register far less satisfaction with local government. They are much more critical of such public services as garbage collection, recreational facilities, schools, and, most of all, police protection.[21]

James Baldwin has described the police as "an army of occupation" in the ghetto, imposing an alien law to keep black people in their place. Riots in Watts, Newark, and a half-dozen other communities in the

---

Table 2–2

White/Black Opinions about the Federal Government

statement	percent agreeing	
	Blacks	Whites
The federal government has gotten too powerful	15	59
The federal government should make sure everyone has a job and a good standard of living	81	30
The federal government should make sure Negroes get fair job treatment	89	38
The federal government should make sure Negro and white children can go to the same schools	89	37

Source: Center for Political Studies, University of Michigan, 1968 Election Survey.

Table 2–3
White/Black Opinions about the Police

statement	percent agreeing	
	Blacks	Whites
Police do not answer calls fast enough	51	27
Police show disrespect and use insulting language	38	16
Police search people without good reason	36	11
Police rough up people unnecessarily when arresting or questioning them	35	10

Source: Angus Campbell and Howard Schuman, "Racial Attitudes in Fifteen American Cities," in *Supplemental Studies for the National Advisory Commission on Civil Disorders* (Washington, D.C.: Government Printing Office, 1968), pp. 42–43.

1960s were sparked by minor incidents between blacks and police. To a middle-class white, a policeman may be an annoyance when it comes to a traffic ticket, but otherwise he is a welcome symbol of law and order. To the black, however, the policeman may be "the Man"—the Man who stops and searches people without, it often seems to the suspect and witnesses, good reason, the Man who chases kids off street corners, shuts off fire hydrants on hot summer afternoons, worries people with questions, and takes them off to jail, sometimes with what seems to be unnecessary force and verbal abuse. He is also the Man who is seldom around when a black is robbed. To the policeman, on the other hand, work in the ghetto is both hard and dangerous; the rate of crime is fantastically high and cooperation with and respect for legal processes very low. He believes that to enforce the law he must act quickly and decisively. He may be far less sympathetic to the plight of blacks than are social workers or educators, but there is evidence that he is more sympathetic than whites generally are.[22]

One of the more important political differences between blacks and whites is not merely the way in which they judge events but also the way each group tends to see—or not see—the same event. For instance, almost eight out of ten whites interviewed during the 1968 presidential campaign said they thought that most black protests had been violent, while fewer than three out of ten blacks so perceived the same demonstrations. The race riots of the 1960s underline these differences in perception. As Tables 2–4 and 2–5 show, blacks tended to find the causes of the riots primarily in social deprivation and saw them as the results of a discriminatory system. Whites, on the other hand, were far more likely to blame looters or "agitators." Moreover, blacks were more likely than whites to look for cures in social reforms, while close to a majority of whites saw a solution in stiffer police measures. Whites also claimed awareness of far less discrimination against blacks than did the blacks. Although Caucasians conceded that blacks were worse off than they themselves were, a majority felt the cause was in the

Table 2—4
White/Black Opinion about Causes of Urban Riots
"What do you think was the main cause of these disturbances?"

most frequent types of spontaneous response[a]	blacks (in percent)	whites (in percent)
Discrimination, unfair treatment	47	25
Unemployment	23	13
Inferior jobs	12	5
Poor education	10	7
Poverty	9	10
Police brutality	7	2
Black Power or other 'radicals'	5	24
Looters and other undesirables	11	34
Communists	0	7

[a]Since some people mentioned more than one cause, the percentages do not add up to a hundred.
Source: Angus Campbell and Howard Schuman, "Racial Attitudes in Fifteen American Cities," in *Supplemental Studies for the National Advisory Commission on Civil Disorders* (Washington, D.C.: Government Printing Office, 1968), p. 48.

Table 2—5
White/Black Opinion about Solutions to Urban Disorders
"What do you think is the most important thing the city government in _____ could do to keep a disturbance like the one in Detroit from breaking out here?"

first type of response mentioned	blacks (in percent)	whites (in percent)
Better employment	25	10
End discrimination	14	2
Better housing	8	4
Other social and economic improvements	6	4
Better police treatment	4	1
Improve communications between Negroes and whites; show Negroes whites care	12	11
More black control of institutions	0	0
More police control	9	46
Can't do anything; have already tried everything	4	8
Don't know	18	14
	100	100

Source: Angus Campbell and Howard Schuman, "Racial Attitudes in Fifteen American Cities," in *Supplemental Studies for the National Advisory Commission on Civil Disorders* (Washington, D.C.: Government Printing Office, 1968), p. 48.

blacks themselves rather than in social conditions brought about by discrimination.

Despite improving conditions for blacks and the easing of discrimination—even growing evidence of preferential treatment—race remains one of the fundamental sources of conflict in American society. Martin Luther King's dream of people of all races living together in harmony was still a distant goal in the late 1970s. King, and generations of blacks before him, had dreamed the American dream, the same dream that brought waves of immigrants from Europe, Asia, and the Caribbean to the United States. It was a dream of enjoying that equality of human dignity which the Declaration of Independence had proclaimed to be self-evident truth, that equality before the law which the Fourteenth Amendment had enshrined as a fundamental constitutional principle, and that material prosperity which had been achieved by millions of Americans.

For many blacks, the dream of equality in a racially integrated society is a dangerous fantasy rather than a guiding hope. A century of second-class citizenship, of living in sharecropper shacks or rat-infested urban ghettos, has cut an inevitable swath of bitter disillusionment. One response has been black separatism. In the 1920s, Marcus Garvey advocated a return to Africa. More recently, Black Muslims have

Table 2–6
Black Opinion on Racial Segregation

statement	percentage of blacks agreeing
Believe stores in "a Negro neighborhood should be owned and run by Negroes"	18
Believe school with mostly Negro children should have Negro principal	14
Prefer to live in all Negro or mostly Negro neighborhood	13
Believe school with mostly Negro children should have mostly Negro teachers	10
Agree that "Negroes should have nothing to do with whites if they can help it"	9
Believe that whites should be discouraged from taking part in civil rights organizations	8
Prefer own child to go to all or mostly Negro school	6
Believe close friendship between Negroes and whites is impossible	6
Agree that "there should be a separate black nation here"	6
Prefer child to have only Negro friends, not white friends too	5

Source: Angus Campbell and Howard Schuman, "Racial Attitudes in Fifteen American Cities," in *Supplemental Studies for the National Advisory Commission on Civil Disorders* (Washington, D.C.: Government Printing Office, 1968), p. 16.

preached the need for the creation of a black nation carved out of the southern states. Calls for "black power" and "black liberation" reflect the rejection of white society by many contemporary black leaders.

Few blacks, however, actively support racial separation. The results of the survey conducted for the Commission on Civil Disorders indicated that barely 6 percent wanted their children to go to a black school or believed there should be a separate black nation or that whites and blacks could not have close friendships. At the same time, running through these and other survey data was strong support for black cultural identity and economic independence. Almost all blacks believed that they should take more pride in their history and that there should be more businesses operated by blacks. A substantial majority agreed that, where possible, blacks should buy from stores run by blacks. A minority, but a large one, endorsed the idea of having black children learn an African language. What emerges is a portrait showing that "a substantial number of Negroes want *both* integration and black identity."[23]

White Ethnics

Rising self-consciousness among blacks has been accompanied by an intensification of ethnic consciousness among many working-class whites. The movement for black pride and power has not only generated fears among whites descended from immigrants from Ireland, Italy, and central and eastern Europe. It has also increased the sense of separation from the culture of white, Protestant, and affluent America that these people have long felt.

Disdained by WASPs (white Anglo-Saxon Protestants) and typically by the preceding waves of immigrants as well, the Irish, Italian, Poles, and other ethnic groups tended to settle initially in neighborhoods already populated by their own people. A common set of ties to family, friends, and customs in the old country, a common language, and a common religion (usually Catholic), plus a tightly knit family, held most of these people together against the strange and sometimes hostile behavior of the Anglos. "The point about the melting pot," Daniel P. Moynihan has written, "is that it did not happen."[24] Indeed, a smorgasbord would provide a more fitting analogy for American society: a rich variety of separate offerings, yet with a degree of similarity in flavor, much of it imparted in recent years by the leveling influence of television.

In some areas—big city banks, the large law firms or brokerage houses of Wall Street, or the managerial levels of giant corporations, for instance—the dominance of the WASPs has been so complete that the trickles of Irish and more recently Jews and blacks have had to conform to the style of the Protestant upper-middle class or be expelled. In fact, these newcomers have probably been allowed to enter because they had already conformed.

Ethnic differences also influence social behavior. One can see it most clearly in the working-class neighborhoods of large cities like New York or Chicago as one goes from an Irish to an Italian or Polish community. Similar distinctions appear more subtly in personal styles of life, most especially in family structure. The bonds of affection and, perhaps more significantly, of interdependence that still tie second-generation Italian or Polish families into a unit have weakened among the Irish and seldom exist at all among white middle-class Protestants.

To a large extent, the Germans, Scandinavians, and Jews have left the working classes and are diffused through the middle and upper classes of America and in the suburbs in which these classes largely live. Although the Irish have not yet reached the same degree of economic achievement, they have been more economically and politically successful—and more assimilated into middle-class mores—than the Italians, Poles and other Slavs, Greeks, Czechs. These groups, still disproportionately made up of manual and skilled laborers, remain aware of their differences from each other and from the rest of Americans.

The working-class ethnics are also acutely—and proudly—conscious of having earned the right to be Americans. They shed a disproportionate share of blood in the first three wars of this century. They also feel that they lifted themselves out of the stink of poverty, not the government. By their own hard labor, they sweated their way up from the slums. Thus white ethnics tend to be parochial in their outlook and wary of public welfare programs. Their own harsh struggle for survival has left scars of distrust of the world outside the family or neighborhood.

Historically, the ethnics have been loyal Democrats, although probably only the Jews have included a large share of ideological liberals. For most of the others, choice of party was usually determined less by political beliefs than by Republican indifference to economic insecurity and Democratic willingness to negotiate for votes in exchange for help in finding a job, a place to live, or a small loan. The Democratic party appeared to the immigrants and their offspring as the party of the little people, their people. When prosperity came, as it has for many Jews and Irish, ethnics have sometimes left the Democratic ranks. Defections have been more frequent among the Irish than the Jews, especially during the Eisenhower years. But as long as they felt threatened by economic insecurity, working-class ethnics have remained loyal to the Democrats.

In 1972, however, the presidential candidacy of George McGovern brought an abrupt change in these political loyalties. His condemnation of American policy in Vietnam offended the ethnics' deep sense of patriotism, and his proposal of a guaranteed annual income violated their belief in the necessity of hard work. Black power threatened their economic—and perhaps physical—security. Identification of the Democratic leadership with youthful protestors advocating sexual freedom and legalized marijuana affronted their moral codes. Despite their deep social conservatism and patriotism, however, a substantial number of white ethnics abandoned the Republican camp in 1976 and returned to their traditional political home.

Women

In many respects, the political behavior of women resembles that of men. More education and income increase the likelihood that women will vote and otherwise participate in politics. Class, racial, and ethnic affiliations have much the same effect on voting and political attitudes of women as of men.

Women, however, also face special obstacles that derive from their subordinate role in American society. Sexual stereotyping related to prospective social roles reduces educational and economic opportunities for many women. Automatic assignment to females of responsibility for child care and domestic life limits the horizons of large numbers of women. Male dominance of households, social groupings, and organizations restricts female participation and influence in all sorts of activities. Nor have women enjoyed the same legal rights as men, although recent changes have improved their legal position considerably. Women were not guaranteed the vote in federal elections until the enactment of the Nineteenth Amendment in 1920. As a consequence of these barriers, women fill a disproportionately small share of the positions of influence in American economic, political, and social life. They vote less often than men, tend to follow the lead of their husbands when they vote, and are less likely to run for public office than men.

During the past decade, growing numbers of women in the United States have rebelled against their subordinate status. In a variety of ways, Women's Liberation has raised the consciousness of females and males about the position of women. Given the enormous diversity of attitudes in the female population, however, the women's movement has been cross cut by other social, economic, and political forces. Catholic women are less likely to be mobilized in favor of liberalized abortion than other women. Black women are more concerned about sexual *and* racial discrimination than are their white sisters. Married women and single females have different interests on some issues, middle-class women differ from welfare mothers on others.

Despite this diversity, large numbers of women have mobilized politically to support efforts to eliminate sex discrimination in employment, to secure more effective and less humiliating laws dealing with rape, and to demand more positions of leadership in all aspects of American life. More and more women are running for—and winning—public office. Even more important, fewer women automatically accept the subordinate roles which the dominant male society traditionally assigned them.

Violence as a Cultural Trait

All social groups in the United States have been exposed to the glorification of *the rule of law* that runs through American culture.* Alongside the hallowed stream of traditional law and order, however, has run a clearly discernible trickle of thought justifying, and at times glorifying, violence. It may be a remnant from a frontier society that depended heavily on self-help for survival, for there is a strong theme of violence in the legends of Daniel Boone, Andrew Jackson, Davy Crockett, James Bowie, Wild Bill Hitchcock, and Buffalo Bill Cody. Moreover, much of what passes for literature today is often an assorted mixture of sex and sadism. In the popular novels about Lew Archer, Matt Helm, and Travis McGee and on the television screen or comic page are the stories of such upstanding peace officers as Starsky and Hutch or Dick Tracy, whose heroes automatically settle their disputes with guns, knives, lasers, knees, or, in moments of relative reason, fists. As one of Matt Dillon's victims observed from the perspective of a barroom floor, "That Marshal is awful sudden."

The Robin Hood theme of a generous criminal crusading against injustice has also been popular both in the movies and on television. The Hollywood productions of the lives of Frank and Jesse James made them out to be misunderstood lads whose murders and robberies were just boyish forms of social protest against overly acquisitive railroad officials. More recently, films like "Bonnie and Clyde" and "Butch Cassidy and the Sundance Kid" made light of the murder of dozens of human beings. The series of movies about "Shaft" added an element of black racism to bloody slaughter.

Even serious American writers like James Fenimore Cooper, Edgar Allan Poe, Stephen Crane, Jack London, Ernest Hemingway, John Dos Passos, and Norman Mailer have been fascinated by violence. At one level, they deplored its use, but again and again they returned to it, exploring in fine detail death struggles on the frontier, on the battlefield, or in the bullring.

Underlying this preoccupation have been frequent resorts to illegal or "extralegal" violence all through American history. Indeed, the country was conceived in a revolution against tax collectors and came to its maturity in a gruesome civil war. The gory chronicle of two centuries includes the Boston Tea Party; farmer rebellions; "Bloody Kansas"; riots against the draft in New York during the Civil War, against Catholics in Philadelphia, against blacks in the Midwest, and against Orientals in the Far West; bounty hunters; Indian fighters; feuds like

*The rule of law means that all governmental actions must be based on previously announced general rules, thus the idea of a "government by law" rather than a "government by men."

that of the Hatfields and the McCoys; the Molly Maguires of the mines; Pinkertons and union men beating and bombing each other; the gang warfare of Prohibition; wars among rival families of Mafiosi; the kidnappings and robberies by the Symbionese Liberation movement; the armed thugging of the Black Panthers or the White House plumbers; and assassinations of four Presidents.

Violence has been a recurring theme in the unhappy history of race relations in America. Before 1861, there were at least 250 abortive slave revolts, including Nat Turner's rebellion in 1831 and John Brown's raid in 1859. It took a civil war to end slavery, but even that bloody conflict did not eliminate violence from racial relations. The Ku Klux Klan and less-organized white mobs lynched more than 3,000 blacks from 1882 to 1959. The north experienced savage race riots, as in Springfield in 1908, East St. Louis in 1917, Chicago in 1919, and Detroit in 1943. Churches were bombed and civil rights workers in the south frequently beaten and sometimes murdered while white police actively or passively cooperated. In the 1960s, race riots in northern ghettos became such a common summer happening as to merit no headlines outside the affected city; and in the 1960s and 1970s, a few black gangs aped the Klan's racial terror by assassinating policemen and randomly robbing and sometimes murdering white private citizens. Police retaliated in some cities with brutal attacks on Black Panthers and other militant groups.

When H. Rap Brown, a black militant leader, said that violence was as American as apple pie, he was offering a reasonably accurate description of a part, although only one part, of American culture. The thread of legal, peaceful change may be the stronger one; but the recurrence of violence indicates a persistent failure of the political system to achieve its avowed goals of ensuring both justice and domestic tranquility. This failure is hardly unique to America. A generalization about European history that applies to Asia, Africa, and Latin America as well as to the United States holds that "collective violence has flowed regularly out of the central political processes. . . . The oppressed have struck in the name of justice, the privileged in the name of order, the in-between in the name of fear."[25]

In defense of the American system, one can note that a nation, carved out of a wilderness, has absorbed more than 44 million immigrants from almost every race, religion, and region of the world.[26] The significant points may be that there has been so little rather than so much violence and that such a small proportion of it has been directed against the system itself. Furthermore, there is a difficult moral dilemma here that has confounded political philosophers over the centuries: In many circumstances, violence may be the only alternative to submission to tyranny. On the other hand, resort to violence to correct major injustices when peaceful means are available can threaten the existence of society. No one has yet constructed a scale to weigh objectively and balance such matters.

Political Socialization

If a society is to survive for any substantial period of years, it has to pass on from generation to generation its morally approved beliefs and customs. Sociologists refer to this process as *socialization. Political socialization is the means by which a political system indoctrinates a new generation, as well as a means by which members of the new generation learn to become mature political participants following an old or a new set of values.*

Experiences in early childhood, even though not directly political, begin the educational process. In relations with parents, brothers, sisters, and other playmates, the child discovers something about authority, obedience, punishment, and the opportunities, benefits, and costs of freedom. Indoctrination with moral values by the family or church helps the child construct ideas about justice, fair play, and permissible limits of behavior.

Later, children transfer these more universal notions to the political world. In the United States, they begin to do so very early in life. Even before they go to school, American children are very much aware — and proud — of their national identity. By second grade, if not before, many of them think of themselves as Democrats or Republicans, although this partisan identification is almost totally emotional. Children usually have favorable attitudes toward those in positions of authority. Perhaps as a carry-over from a permissive family environment, most young American children look on the police, the mayor, and the President as "good men" who do "good things" for people. By their early teens, children are reasonably well informed — compared to their parents — about politics. By their mid-teens their views are usually sufficiently firm so that they can fit their specific policy preferences into a more general political orientation.

It is probable that this learning process continues through much of life. As a young person builds up experience with party workers and governmental officials, initially uncritical attitudes toward authority moderate and become more sophisticated. But psychologists still believe that early experiences make the most lasting impact on a person's outlook on life. It may well be that the strong emotional attachments of children to country and government are what keep people loyal in later years to their political systems, despite the frequent failures of all such systems to fulfill their promises.

Political socialization operates in a number of formal and informal ways. The patterns of trust, obedience, and freedom of preschool years have important political spill-overs. In addition, children may hear discussions of political affairs, and parents or other family members may "explain" some current event. These "explanations" are likely to be very simplistic and highly moralistic, couched in terms of the good guys (us) against the bad guys (them). In school, the authority of the teacher and the principal are added to those of the family. Children are taught, though they do not necessarily fully believe, such principles as "good boys and girls obey their teachers" or "good boys and girls settle their differences without hitting each other."

More formally, saluting the flag, reciting the pledge of allegiance, and singing the national anthem reinforce national identity. So does repeating legends of heroes like George Washington and Abraham Lincoln, whose truthfulness and honesty are often stressed more than their political accomplishments. Reading and teaching in history, geography, and civics provide a pool of specific, although simplistic, information about national ideals and traditions.

Even religious instruction may play a role. In inculcating ideas about the Deity, churchmen indirectly teach something about the nature of authority and the necessity of obedience. Furthermore, many religious groups, especially the Catholic Church, frequently go out of their way to praise the political system and to stress the smooth compatibility between fidelity to their theology and loyalty to America.

Not all groups in society go through the same processes of socialization, either formal or informal. Nor, of course, do all persons react to the same influences in the same way. Uniformity of socialization is impossible in a culturally diverse country, especially one where wealth is so unequally divided. Even among young children, differences in social class, religion, and race are accompanied by difference in political orientation. Black children, for instance, tend to display less feeling of political effectiveness than do whites. Blacks also develop earlier than whites a less idealized outlook on governmental officials.[27]

Adult immigrants go through a much different form of political learning. First of all, they have the difficult task of uprooting old national identifications and loyalties, building new ones, and perhaps accepting new standards of civic conduct. Many older blacks are experiencing similar problems of re-education. Some militant black leaders complain of being frustrated by the effectiveness with which the older generation was habituated to a subservient political role. One of the reasons for its low participation in politics has been its acceptance of the old idea that "politics is white folks' business," which has led to disinterest in governmental affairs and disbelief that public officials can or will do anything to better the lives of blacks.

Historically, socialization of waves of immigrants often reversed the usual generational process. It was the children who passed American culture on to their parents. They learned the new ways in the neighborhood and more importantly in school—more often than not for Catholic immigrants, a parochial rather than a public school—and brought the new customs and beliefs home to their parents both in words and in behavior that would not have been tolerated in the old country.

The foreign immigrant's socialization is usually more formal and direct than that of the natural-born citizen. Because he or she often goes through the process as an adult, the immigrant is likely to receive more political education from reading, from lectures, and from direct experiences with public officials than from the slow process of gradually being exposed to more and more complex relations. The federal government suggests that all aliens interested in becoming citizens read several volumes intended to provide quick socialization by providing lists of ideals of American government.[28]

Government plays a direct role in the process of all socialization, whether of the immigrant or of the native-born. As we have seen, the example of public officials can stir respect or contempt for prevailing customs, processes, and values. The speeches, opinions, and writings of Presidents, governors, legislators, and judges can help shape political beliefs. The way professional politicians campaign, run their offices, and train other professionals makes them carriers both of the general political culture and of the more particular rules that allow the system to operate.

Socialization, of course, does not mean merely preserving the cultural status quo, although it often has that effect. It can also be an instrument for change. The Russians, the Chinese, the Japanese after World War II, and the Germans both under Hitler and since World War II have deliberately tried to educate children away from old political standards and patterns of conduct. No educational system can ever be politically neutral. By its practices as much as by its teaching, it inevitably encourages some kinds of political conduct and discourages others, just as the political system inevitably influences the content of beliefs transmitted.

Moreover, socializing processes may be so effective that they promote unintended change. They may fill some people with such high political ideals that when they reach adulthood, they cannot accommodate those ideals to a world inhabited by fallible humans. In those circumstances people may react against the system and become either bitter revolutionaries or cynical apoliticals. In neither case are they likely to see much use in working within an existing political system.

Patterns of Political Cultures

One can speak of *an* American political culture only in the most general sense. It is much more accurate to talk of *political cultures*. Yet there are forces undermining diversity. Mass communications make up perhaps the most powerful of these. Movies, radio, and most of all television are providing common patterns of speech. More significantly, they generate, especially among young children, common standards for individual, social, and political behavior. These means of communication "set . . . the civic agenda."[29] This power to shape the collective psyche of the nation is awesome, apparently too awesome for most television producers to appreciate, or if they do, to bring them to agreement on what the content of this socialization should be.

Whatever the long-range effects of television and other means of communication in unifying American culture, at the moment the United States is still culturally pluralistic. These cultural divisions affect the way people look at and behave in politics. Among the more significant recent trends has been the erosion of some people's trust in the political system, an erosion that has expressed itself in violent outbursts and in quiet, reasoned replies to the questions of pollsters.

Without a deep and widespread belief that the governmental system, for all its faults, is basically fair and reasonably efficient, *political stability* cannot last, especially not in a nation whose people are so different from one another. Without a wariness of governmental power, *political freedom* may not last long. If stability and freedom are to have a substantial chance of coexisting, trust in and wariness of government have to coexist. Perhaps the greatest danger to freedom occurs when a low level of trust in a democratic regime is accompanied by a lack of fear of political power itself.

Summary

The American political system developed in a unique physical and social setting. A broad continent with abundant resources permitted the growth of a large, rich, and powerful nation. Within its boundaries, diverse peoples came together to produce a distinctive society. Despite the diversity of its citizens, agreement on basic democratic principles is substantial in the United States. On more specific issues, however, Americans tend to disagree, with political attitudes often reflecting class, racial, and ethnic cleavages. Political values are transmitted from generation to generation by the process of political socialization. This process in turn is influenced by the various political cultures that coexist in the United States. In some respects, these political cultures have been losing some of their distinctiveness because of the growth of national instruments of communication and other unifying influences on American life. In other ways, however, differences among political cultures continue to have a powerful influence on voting, attitudes toward authority, positions on many public issues, and feelings toward members of other races, classes, and groups.

Selected Bibliography

ALMOND, GABRIEL A., and SIDNEY VERBA, *The Civic Culture: Political Attitudes and Democracy in Five Nations* (Princeton, N.J.: Princeton University Press, 1963). A path-breaking study of political culture in five democracies.

BULLOCK, III, CHARLES S., and HARRELL R. RODGERS, JR., eds., *Black Political Attitudes: Implications for Political Support* (Chicago: Markham Publishing Company, 1972). A useful collection of articles dealing with the ways in which black children and adults perceive the world of American politics.

COMMAGER, HENRY STEELE, *The American Mind: An Interpretation of American Thought and Character Since the 1880's* (New Haven, Conn.: Yale University Press, 1950). An incisive and readable intellectual history of modern America.

DAHL, ROBERT A., *A Preface to Democratic Theory* (Chicago, Ill.: University of Chicago Press, 1956). An analysis of the underpinnings of American democracy that rejects much accepted lore.

DAWSON, RICHARD E., and KENNETH PREWITT, *Political Socialization* (Boston, Mass.: Little, Brown and Company, 1969). The best introduction to the study of political socialization.

FRAZIER, E. FRANKLIN, *Black Bourgeoisie* (New York: The Free Press of Glencoe, 1957). A jaundiced view of the black middle class, the group from which older black leadership was almost exclusively drawn until the mid-1950's.

GLAZER, NATHAN, and DANIEL P. MOYNIHAN, *Beyond the Melting Pot: The Negroes, Puerto Ricans, Jews, Italians, and Irish of New York City,* 2nd ed. (Cambridge, Mass.: The Massachusetts Institute of Technology Press, 1970). A study of the sociology and politics of ethnic groups that has far broader importance than for New York alone.

GREELEY, ANDREW M., *That Most Distressful Nation: The Taming of the American Irish* (Chicago: Quadrangle Books, 1972). A sometimes wistful, more often acerbic discussion of the absorption of the Irish into the mainstream of American culture.

HANDLIN, OSCAR, *The Uprooted* (New York: Grosset & Dunlap, 1951). A dramatic account of immigration to the United States and its impact on the immigrants.

HARRINGTON, MICHAEL, *The Other America: Poverty in the United States* (Baltimore, Md.: Penguin Books, 1962). A social reformer's angry account of the disgraceful number and condition of the American poor.

JENCKS, CHRISTOPHER, et al., *Inequality: A Reassessment of the Effect of Family and Schooling in America* (New York: Basic Books, Inc., 1972). An important—and much discussed—effort to gauge the effects of children's IQs, educations, and social backgrounds on their ultimate economic achievement.

LERNER, MAX, *America as a Civilization: Life and Thought in the United States Today* (New York: Simon and Schuster, 1957). A lengthy interpretation—always interesting and always controversial—of American political, social, and intellectual life by a thoughtful social scientist-turned-journalist.

LIPSET, SEYMOUR MARTIN, *Political Man* (New York: Doubleday & Company, Inc., 1960). A series of essays by a political sociologist evaluating the conditions that make for democratic stability.

LITT, EDGAR, *Beyond Pluralism: Ethnic Politics in America* (Glenview, Ill.: Scott, Foresman and Company, 1970). A concise introduction to the relevance of ethnicity to the functioning of the American political system.

LOWI, THEODORE J., *The End of Liberalism: Ideology, Policy, and the Cri-*

sis of Public Authority (New York: W. W. Norton & Company, 1969). An analysis of the problems of American politics that lays the blame squarely on acceptance of what the author calls "interest-group liberalism."

MASON, ALPHEUS T., ed., *Free Government in the Making,* 3rd ed. (New York: Oxford University Press, 1965). An extraordinarily useful collection of essays and documents illustrating the development of American thinking about politics.

MYRDAL, GUNNER, *An American Dilemma* (New York: Harper & Row, 1944). This book has become a classic in the study of race relations and has had a great impact on American political and social thought. It is also available in a second edition but that of 1944 is the one that has had great influence.

NOVAK, MICHAEL, *The Rise of the Unmeltable Ethnics: Politics and Culture in the Seventies* (New York: Collier-Macmillan, 1971). A well-written, hard-hitting yet sympathetic study of the working-class white ethnic, written by a man who is both a professional philosopher and a political activist.

POTTER, DAVID M., *People of Plenty: Economic Abundance and the American Character* (Chicago, Ill.: University of Chicago Press, 1954). A leading historian's view of the linkages between physical richness and the development of American life and "national character."

TOCQUEVILLE, ALEXIS DE, *Democracy in America,* Phillips Bradley, ed., (New York: Alfred A. Knopf, 1945). After more than 130 years still one of the most perceptive analyses of American democracy, a classic in the study of American politics.

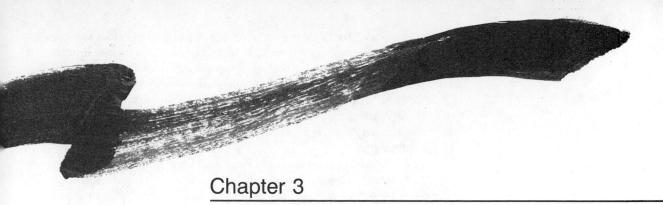

Chapter 3

An Urban Nation

CHALLENGED BY THE forces of change, the American political system reflects the dynamic, decentralized, and troubled urban society it serves. The continuous growth of government at all levels is primarily a response to urbanization, which draws some people to the cities and moves others out to the suburbs. In the transition from a rural to an urban society, government has taken over from the family, the church, and private charity such functions as the care of the old and the jobless. The interdependence of life in densely settled urban communities requires governmental involvement in health and housing, police and fire protection, water supply, and disposal of sewage and garbage. The complexity of urban life creates problems like traffic congestion, as well as a need for public services like rapid transit.

Urbanization also produces mobility and dislocation. One fifth of the population—or more than 40 million people—move to a new address each year. Residential patterns change as old neighborhoods decay and new ones spring up on the outskirts of the metropolis. Business firms leave the congested core of the city for a suburban industrial park. Urbanization also increases social interaction by bringing different ethnic, racial, and religious groups together in the metropolis.

In responding to the many needs and conflicts of an urban society, government has become increasingly complex. Existing governmental units have added a bewildering array of new agencies. Over the past century, cities have developed police, fire, water, sewage, health, planning, and traffic departments, housing, airport, and parking authorities, and urban renewal, antipoverty, and model-cities agencies. A similar process has occurred at the state and national levels. In most metropolitan areas, suburbanization has created a variety of new governments, many of which are special-purpose units needed to handle such problems as sewage, water supply, and flood control.

Emergence of the Metropolis

Only recently did the problems of an urban society move into the spotlight on the American political scene. Yet the history of the United States is one of continuous urban expansion. Since the first census was taken in 1790, urban population growth has in every decade outstripped the increase in rural areas except between 1810 and 1820. By 1920, more Americans were living in towns and cities than in the countryside. Thereafter, economic change, mechanization of farms, and prosperity speeded the flight of people from the countryside. By 1970, almost three quarters of the nation's population were living in areas classified by the Census Bureau as urban.

Even more important, over two thirds of the nation's citizens—or 151 million people—were residing in 1974 in metropolitan areas composed of cities and surrounding urban communities. The 264 *standard* *metropolitan statistical areas* covered almost 14 percent of the nation's land.*

Since the end of World War II, these areas have accounted for almost all population growth. Most of this expansion resulted from natural increase in metropolitan areas. The remainder was a product of development of smaller areas to metropolitan size, suburbanization of rural areas, and continuing migration to the cities and suburbs. As the Commission on Population Growth and the American Future emphasized in 1972:

Population growth *is* metropolitan growth in the contemporary United States. . . . The states with rapid population growth—for example, California, Florida, and Arizona—have been states with rapid growth of metropolitan population. The regional shifts in population, from north to west and south, from the midcontinent to the coasts, have been focused in rapidly growing metropolitan areas.[1]

Until recently, most urban growth has occurred in metropolitan regions having a million or more inhabitants. Such huge areas have been attractive because they promise their residents higher incomes, a wider range of economic opportunities, better schools and health services, and more cultural, entertainment, and recreational facilities. On the other hand, these big cities also are more congested, more polluted, have denser concentrations of poor people and greater distances separating lower-income groups in the old urban core from jobs and housing in the suburbs. At least in part because of these problems, the growth rate of large metropolitan areas tapered off in the 1970s, while metropolitan areas of less than one million inhabitants grew more rapidly in the 1970s than in the previous decade.

As they spread, metropolitan areas merge into vast urban regions, some hundreds of miles long. The largest of these stretches along the Atlantic seaboard from Boston to Richmond. An even bigger monster is incubating in California, threatening to sprawl from San Francisco Bay to San Diego. In 1970, two out of every three Americans lived within sixteen major urban regions. By the end of the century, five sixths of the population will live in two dozen urban regions, which will cover one sixth of the land in the continental United States.[2]

The Two Revolutions

The growth of cities, metropolitan areas, and urban regions is a consequence of what have been called "two revolutions," one piled on top of

---

*The Census Bureau defines a *standard metropolitan statistical area* as a county or two or more adjacent counties that contain at least one central city of 50,000 or a city of 25,000 which together with settled contiguous areas forms a community of 50,000. Other counties than the one or ones in which such a city is located are included in such a standard metropolitan area if they are essentially metropolitan in character and socially and economically integrated with the central city.

Figure 3.1 Standard Metropolitan Statistical Areas—1970

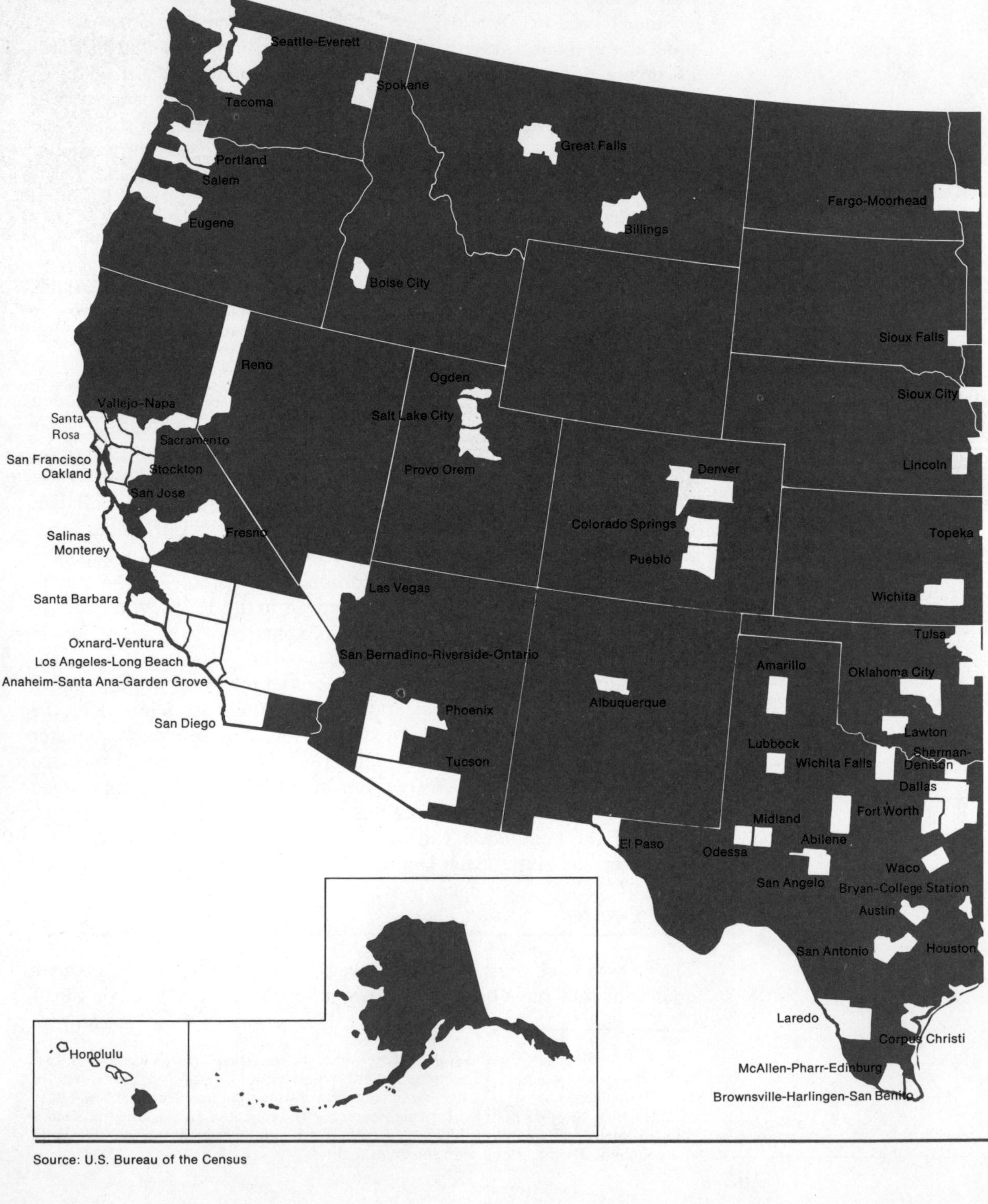

Seattle-Everett

Tacoma

Spokane

Great Falls

Billings

Fargo-Moorhead

Portland
Salem

Eugene

Boise City

Sioux Falls

Reno

Ogden

Sioux City

Vallejo–Napa

Salt Lake City

Santa
Rosa

Denver

Lincoln

San Francisco
Oakland

Sacramento

Provo Orem

Stockton

San Jose

Colorado Springs

Topeka

Salinas
Monterey

Fresno

Pueblo

Santa Barbara

Las Vegas

Wichita

Oxnard-Ventura

Tulsa

Los Angeles-Long Beach

San Bernadino-Riverside-Ontario

Amarillo

Oklahoma City

Anaheim-Santa Ana-Garden Grove

Albuquerque

Lawton

San Diego

Phoenix

Lubbock

Wichita Falls

Sherman-
Denison

Tucson

Dallas

Midland

Fort Worth

El Paso

Abilene

Odessa

Waco

San Angelo

Bryan-College Station

Austin

San Antonio

Houston

Honolulu

Laredo

Corpus Christi

McAllen-Pharr-Edinburg

Brownsville-Harlingen-San Benito

Source: U.S. Bureau of the Census

Figure 3.2
U.S. Central City
and Suburban Population, 1900–1974

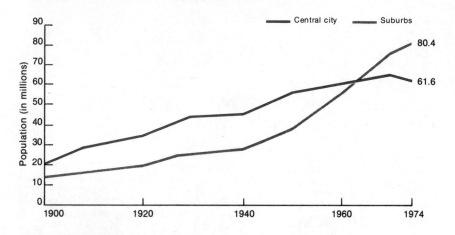

Source: U.S. Bureau of the Census

the other.[3] The first of these revolutions is the rise of an urban way of life. The second is its diffusion and dispersal over the countryside.

Underlying the "first revolution" has been migration to the city, a process that has had three major elements in the United States. The first has been the flow of white families from farm to small town, from farm and small town to the city, and, increasingly in recent years, from farm and small towns to suburbs. Second is the migration of immigrants, primarily from the rural areas of Europe, to American cities; at the height of European immigration in 1910, 72 percent of the foreign born lived in cities. The final element is the twentieth-century movement of blacks, Puerto Ricans, Chicanos, and whites from depressed areas such as Appalachia into the older cities.

The "second revolution," the rapid outward movement of urban populations, has resulted from acceleration of the natural tendency of cities to grow at their edges. Rapid outward expansion was made possible primarily by mass production of automobiles. Since 1920, suburban areas have been growing increasingly faster than central cities. By 1974, 80.4 million Americans lived in suburbs, 18.7 million more than resided in central cities, and 14.5 million more than lived outside metropolitan areas.*

The most dramatic source of new suburbanites is the central cities. Over 12 million Americans, most of them white, abandoned central cities for the suburbs between 1950 and 1974. Other new suburbanites

Central cities are cities which form the core of standard metropolitan statistical areas. These data do not include areas designated as standard metropolitan statistical areas after 1970.

Figure 3.3
Movement of Blacks, 1960-1970

Where they came from

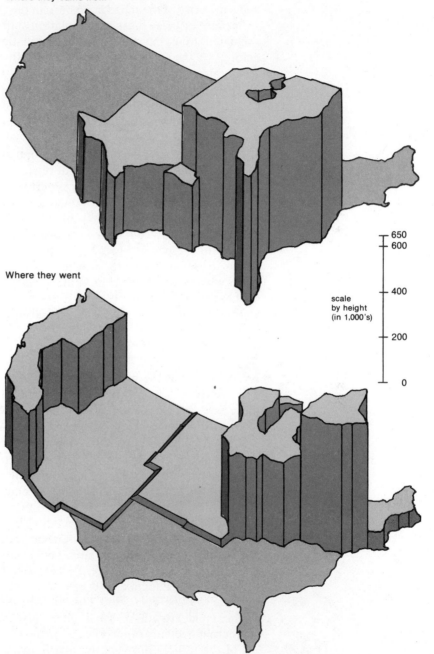

Where they went

scale
by height
(in 1,000's)

650
600

400

200

0

Source: *New York Times*, Jan. 26, 1975. Map prepared by Harvard University Mapping Service, Laboratory for Computer Graphics and Spatial Analysis.

are former rural dwellers who bypassed the city proper in the process of becoming urbanized. Most new suburbanites, however, are the off-spring of suburban parents. About 80 percent of all the people added to the population of the United States in the 1970s were suburbanites, and a majority of them had been born in the suburbs.

Because of these massive population shifts, most central cities have stagnated. Many have been losing population since the 1950s or even before. Of the twenty-one cities with 500,000 or more residents in 1960, fifteen lost population in the ensuing decade. Between 1950 and 1970, two of the ten largest cities—Detroit and Cleveland—lost 18 percent of their population. Even greater losses were experienced by such other old centers in the midwest and northeast as St. Louis, Boston, and Pittsburgh.

In all of these cases, losses in population would have been far greater had the outward movement of white families not been offset by the growing migration of blacks, Puerto Ricans, and Chicanos to the city—most of them poor and uneducated. Between 1950 and 1974, central cities added 7.3 million black residents through migration and natural increase, which raised the proportion of black central-city residents from 12 percent to 22 percent. At least three out of every ten blacks in the United States now lives in one of the twelve largest cities, six of which were 30 percent or more black in 1970. As a consequence of these trends, cities are separated from the surrounding suburbs by sharpening racial, income, housing, and educational differences.

Regional Variations

Exceptions to these patterns are found primarily among the younger cities of the south and west. Growing up in the era of the automobile, these cities developed at much lower densities than had the older cities of the northeast and midwest. As a result, many urban cores in Florida, Texas, Arizona, and California are more suburbs than cities in the traditional sense. As one would expect, central-city–suburban differences are less sharp in these metropolitan areas.

Unlike the typical older city, most of the newer cities have continued to experience rapid growth. Houston, the sixth largest city in the nation, more than doubled its population between 1950 and 1970 and continued to add 1,000 new residents a week during the 1970s. During the same two decades, even more spectacular growth rates were registered by Tampa (157 percent), Jacksonville (206 percent), El Paso (232 percent), Phoenix (440 percent), San Jose (585 percent), Albuquerque (597 percent), and Tucson (631 percent).

The rapid growth of these cities also reflects the westward and southern movement of the U.S. population, a migration toward the sun. All of the rapidly growing metropolitan areas are located in a broad band stretching from Florida to California and reaching north to include Atlanta, Charlotte, and Washington in the east and Portland,

Con Keyes/NYT Pictures.

Office buildings crowd out small houses in the expanding downtown area of rapidly growing Phoenix.

Seattle, and Denver in the west. Although the rapid growth areas of the Sunbelt encompassed only 14.5 percent of the metropolitan population in 1960, they accounted for 34 percent of metropolitan growth during the following decade.

As a consequence of rapid urban expansion in the Sunbelt, southern and western states accounted for 85 percent of all the nation's population increase during the 1970s. As people and jobs move southward and westward, entire metropolitan areas in the northeast and midwest have begun to lose population. During the 1960s, the Jersey City, Pittsburgh, and Wilkes-Barre areas experienced population losses. By

1980, more than one quarter of the nation's metropolitan areas, almost all of them older industrial areas in the northeast and midwest, will be losing residents.

Urban Change and the Central City

The explosive growth of the metropolis has exacted its heaviest toll from the older cities. Of the many factors that have contributed to the crisis of the American city, none is more basic than the failure of most central cities to extend their boundaries to encompass suburban growth. As a result, most older cities have received little benefit from newer residential, commercial, and industrial development. At the same time, central cities have had to bear most of the heavy social and financial burdens of urban change. Within their boundaries are most of the worn-out housing of the metropolis, a high proportion of its obsolescent factories and shopping districts, and most of its less fortunate citizens.

Decline of Annexation

Throughout the nineteenth century, urban growth was paralleled by the steady expansion of the cities' political boundaries. Annexation often was a marriage of convenience. Newly settled areas usually depended on the city for public services, while cities normally were eager to increase their tax base. Through annexation, Chicago grew from 10.5 to 222 square miles, Boston increased from 4.5 to 46 square miles, and Minneapolis from 8 to 55 square miles.

During the early years of the twentieth century, the pace of annexation slowed. In some cases, expansion was made difficult by physical barriers like rivers or by county or state boundaries. In others, city governments declined to finance unprofitable extensions of services to outlying areas. The principal barrier, however, was opposition from residents of newly settled areas. Then as now, most suburbanites preferred to live in small communities that promised neighborhood control over local taxes and services. They also wanted to be separated from the city's conflicts, immigrants, and corruption.

In response to the suburban desire for separation, many states prohibited their cities from annexing new territory without the approval of residents to be annexed. As a result, few older cities added significant new territory after 1920. Almost all large-scale annexations in recent years have been made by cities in the younger and rapidly growing metropolitan areas of the south and west where central-city – suburban differences are less pronounced than in the older areas of the northeast and midwest. Among the most successful of these cities during the past three decades were Houston, which grew from 160 to 447 square miles, and Oklahoma City, which became the second most extensive city in the nation by annexing 533 square miles of new territory.

The most important consequence of the failure of cities to add new territory is the politically fragmented metropolitan area. Before the decline of annexation, the city by and large *was* the metropolis. A single political jurisdiction encompassed the diversity of the urban community. Once the city stopped expanding geographically, its boundary became the line between city and suburb. On one side of the line, there is a single city government; on the other, usually a multitude of small suburban governments. People on the city's side of this political boundary are older, not as well educated, and less likely to own an automobile or home than those on the suburban side. City dwellers also are far more likely to be black, to live in substandard housing, to be on welfare, and to be victimized by crime.

The extent of these differences between city and suburb depends in part on when the city reached its territorial limits. Boston, for example, was encircled by independent suburbs as early as 1873. As a result, even the middle-class development that was spurred by the extension of street-car lines occurred largely outside the city limits. In contrast, the city of Los Angeles, by annexing over 200 square miles of undeveloped land in 1915, was able to encompass a sizable number of "suburban" neighborhoods, and as a result it now includes a much higher proportion of the middle-income population of its metropolitan area than does Boston.

Exodus of the Relatively Affluent

Emigration from the city is hardly new. City dwellers with the resources to buy or rent new residences have been moving out of the urban core for over a century. The oldest districts of New York and Philadelphia were losing population before the Civil War. But, as long as the city continued to annex newly settled neighborhoods, that outward migration of upper- and middle-income families did not have a great economic or political effect. Once the city ceased to expand its boundaries, however, the continued outflow removed most of its upper-income and middle-class residents. In the past quarter century, that exodus has been swelled by a growing number of blue-collar workers who want grass, fresh air, and safe streets for their families and can afford those items.

City finances have been particularly hard hit by the movement of the higher-salaried urban dwellers to the suburbs. Most of those who have left paid more local taxes and placed fewer demands on the city treasury than the lower-income newcomers who replaced them. In addition, many former city dwellers continue to work in the central business district where they and their families benefit from city services — parks, libraries and museums, as well as transportation facilities — to whose support they make relatively little direct contribution.

The exodus to suburbia also has deprived the city of the concerned involvement of those who once were its civic leaders and most active citizens. Many on whom the city's charitable, cultural, and civic organizations once depended for leadership and support have transferred to the suburbs their allegiances and energies along with their residences.

Influx of the Poor

One of the most important functions of the American city has been to take in impoverished newcomers and make them productive members of the urban community.

For the American city during the past hundred and fifty years, the raw material was the stream of immigrants pouring in from Britain, Ireland, Germany, Norway, Russia, Italy, and a dozen other lands. The city needed these immigrants to build its streets and offices, to man its factories, service its houses and hotels and restaurants, and do all the dirty and menial jobs that older residents disdained. But the city did more than use its newcomers: it equipped them to take their place as fully participating members of U.S. society. Doing this — bringing people from society's back waters into the mainstream of American life — has always been the principal business, and the principal glory, of the American city.[4]

Today, the city offers the newcomer considerably fewer opportunities than it did fifty or a hundred years ago. Part of this decline in opportunity results from the gap between the skills required by a more sophisticated economy and those possessed by the recent arrival or the graduate of an ineffective slum school. Lessened opportunity also reflects the movement of business and industry to the suburbs, which puts more and more jobs beyond the geographical reach of the city dweller. In addition, unions, civil service rules, and discriminatory practices have limited the access of blacks, Puerto Ricans, and Chicanos to the construction and public service jobs that provided employment to large numbers of earlier immigrants.

Intensifying all these problems is the fact that most recent newcomers to the older cities are black. Racial prejudice has narrowed the urban black's opportunities for employment, education, and housing. Instead of liberating the black man from a crippling heritage of slavery, repression, and segregation, the move to the city often has meant a lifetime spent

in the teeming racial ghettos [where] segregation and poverty have intersected to destroy opportunity and hope and to enforce failure. The ghettos too often mean men and women without jobs, families without men, and schools where children are processed instead of educated, until they return to the street — to crime, to narcotics, to dependency on welfare, and to bitterness and resentment against society in general and white society in particular.[5]

Such bitterness and resentment have produced demands for black power and race riots nearing rebellions in the ghettos. Violence and racial conflict have accelerated the flight of white families to the

Report of The National Advisory Commission on Civil Disorders

Summary

The summer of 1967 again brought racial disorders to American cities, and with them shock, fear, and bewilderment to the Nation.

The worst came during a 2-week period in July, first in Newark and then in Detroit. Each set off a chain reaction in neighboring communities.

On July 28, 1967, the President of the United States established this Commission and directed us to answer three basic questions:

What happened?
Why did it happen?
What can be done to prevent it from happening again?

To respond to these questions, we have undertaken a broad range of studies and investigations. We have visited the riot cities; we have heard many witnesses; we have sought the counsel of experts across the country.

This is our basic conclusion: Our Nation is moving toward two societies, one black, one white—separate and unequal.

Reaction to last summer's disorders has quickened the movement and deepened the division. Discrimination and segregation have long permeated much of American life; they now threaten the future of every American.

This deepening racial division is not inevitable. The movement apart can be reversed. Choice is still possible. Our principal task is to define that choice and to press for a national resolution.

To pursue our present course will involve the continuing polarization of the American community and, ultimately, the destruction of basic democratic values.

The alternative is not blind repression or capitulation to lawlessness. It is the realization of common opportunities for all within a single society.

This alternative will require a commitment to national action—compassionate, massive, and sustained, backed by the resources of the most powerful and the richest nation on this earth. From every American it will require new attitudes, new understanding, and, above all, new will.

The vital needs of the Nation must be met; hard choices must be made, and, if necessary, new taxes enacted.

Violence cannot build a better society. Disruption and disorder nourish repression, not justice. They strike at the freedom of every citizen. The community cannot—it will not—tolerate coercion and mob rule.

Violence and destruction must be ended—in the streets of the ghetto and in the lives of people.

Segregation and poverty have created in the racial ghetto a destructive environment totally unknown to most white Americans.

What white Americans have never fully understood—but what the Negro can never forget—is that white society is deeply implicated in the ghetto. White institutions created it, white institutions maintain it, and white society condones it.

It is time now to turn with all the purpose at our command to the major unfinished business of this Nation. It is time to adopt strategies for action that will produce quick and visible progress. It is time to make good the promises of American democracy to all citizens—urban and rural, white and black, Spanish-surname, American Indian, and every minority group.

Our recommendations embrace three basic principles:

- To mount programs on a scale equal to the dimension of the problems;
- To aim these programs for high impact in the immediate future in order to close the gap between promise and performance;
- To undertake new initiatives and experiments that can change the system of failure and frustration that now dominates the ghetto and weakens our society.

These programs will require unprecedented levels of funding and performance, but they neither probe deeper nor demand more than the problems which called them forth. There can be no higher priority for national action and no higher claim on the Nation's conscience.

The National Advisory Commission on Civil Disorders was appointed by President Lyndon Johnson in the wake of severe rioting that swept through the nation's black ghettos in the summer of 1967. Only a few of the commission's many recommendations had much impact on the development of urban policies by federal, state, and local government.

suburbs and have also intensified resistance of white neighborhoods to public housing and use of busing to integrate public schools.

Erosion of the Economic Base

Further complicating the difficulties of the older cities is the movement of jobs as well as people to the suburbs. Retail trade, service, and government jobs follow the people they serve out of the city. Cultural centers are being built in the suburbs; major-league ballparks are found in Bloomington, Minnesota, Foxboro, Massachusetts, and Anaheim, California; and organized crime finds lucrative new opportunities for profit in the spreading suburbs. Industrial jobs also have been

Chapter 3
An Urban Nation

moving outward at a rapid rate. In suburbia, industrial managers can find the space required by modern manufacturing processes much more easily than in the crowded urban core. In fact, over 75 percent of all the new industrial plants constructed in metropolitan areas in recent years were located in the suburbs. These locations bring industry closer to skilled workers, who increasingly live in the suburbs. Many of the firms that have suburbanized are in newer and rapidly growing industries like electronics and aerospace. Typical of this development are the factories and laboratories that line suburban Route 128 as it loops around Boston.

Even white-collar jobs, traditionally the most concentrated component of an urban economy, have been moving out of the city to escape high taxes, labor shortages, crime, and congestion in central business districts. Typical of the new suburban office centers are Towson, whose office buildings straddle the Baltimore Beltway, and Clayton, a self-styled "executive city" outside St. Louis, which has over 40,000 office jobs.

As a result of these trends, most of the older cities have declining or at best stable economies. Throughout the nation, downtown stores have lost customers to shopping centers, which are far more convenient for the auto-oriented suburbanite than the central business district with its inadequate parking. Similarly, central-city newspapers have lost both readers and advertisers to suburban dailies and weeklies.

Newer cities in the south and west have been less affected by these trends. Many encompass large tracts of undeveloped land suitable for commercial and industrial development. As a result, many shopping malls and industrial parks are located within rather than outside their city limits. Downtown office construction also has boomed in recent years in cities like Atlanta, Dallas, Denver, Los Angeles, and Phoenix. Substantial downtown development has continued in some older cities as well, such as Boston, Kansas City, Minneapolis, and New York. Most of the employment growth in the central business district, however, is in managerial and other skilled office jobs. These positions offer relatively few opportunities to the unskilled and poorly educated workers who form a growing proportion of the labor pool of older cities.

Intensified Pressures for City Services

Failure of older cities to grow has not been accompanied by leveling off of municipal services and costs. On the contrary, demands for expenditure are greater than ever. Higher salaries for teachers, policemen, garbage collectors, hospital workers, and other city employees produce sharp increases in municipal costs. Rising crime and juvenile delinquency lead to increased law enforcement costs. Welfare outlays soar as the proportion of poor residents increases. Efforts to woo back the middle class, to revive the city's flagging economy, and to im-

"Help!"

From *The Herblock Gallery* (Simon and Schuster, 1968).

prove housing and public services in slums add to financial problems.

In every older city, mounting governmental costs have placed tremendous pressures on local taxes. The tax resources available to cities have been declining with the departure of business firms and more affluent residents. The only way to stay solvent has been to raise taxes or reduce services, and some cities have had to do both. Each is counterproductive because each further reduces the attractiveness of older cities for both residents and businesses. In the face of these pressures, cities have borrowed more money and sought more state and federal assistance in an effort to minimize cutbacks in services. These rapidly rising costs for an exceptionally wide range of local services combined with unwise financing practices and inadequate state and federal aid to bring New York City to the brink of bankruptcy in the mid-1970s. Despite their scale and severity, New York's financial problems were not unique. As the mayor of Milwaukee, a city with more manageable problems, has emphasized:

We must remember that our better condition is only relative. We, along with other cities, are part of a deepening trend. That trend is toward an ever-growing concentration of the poor and the relatively poor in the central cities of America. New York just got hit first. It's time to factor out the real causes of the dilemma. All large cities are in the trend New York is in. It's a matter of time.[6]

Metropolitan Growth and the Suburbs

Suburbs come in a great variety of sizes and types. Most are small, but a few are larger than many central cities. Residential — or "bedroom" — suburbs are most common. Some, however, are primarily commercial or industrial, among them Cudahy, outside Milwaukee, and Teterboro, New Jersey, where 40,000 work and only 22,000 live. Among the residential communities, especially in the larger metropolitan areas, which can have dozens or even hundreds of suburbs, wide variations exist in income and status. At one extreme is the suburb with 3,000 low-priced homes squeezed onto one square mile, each built from one of four plans, and with little or no provision for schools, water, sewage treatment, and other public services. At the other is the enclave of the well to do, where fortunate suburbanites enjoy expensive homes on large lots, protected by strict zoning regulations and provided with a high level of community services.

Problems of Growth

Different kinds of suburbs face different problems. Many older suburbs have begun to experience difficulties familiar to central cities as neighborhoods decay, racial conflict grows, and commercial and industrial districts decline. The most common problems are those caused by growth. With growth come sprawl, congestion, and the ugliness of the city, creating a gaping hole between the suburban dream and its reality. Growth also brings demands for costly public facilities and services. New suburbanites want good schools, better roads, quick snow removal, an ample water supply, regular garbage and trash collection, efficient fire and police protection. The effect of rapidly expanding services on the local tax rate can be catastrophic. Some suburbs are fortunate in having within their boundaries business and industrial enterprises that pay a significant share of local taxes. Residential

The signs of urban growth look much the same from one end of the nation to the other. Gas stations, fast food outlets, discount stores, and motels crowd the highways as people and jobs move inexorably outward.

suburbs, however, are largely dependent on the taxation of homes for their local revenues.

Fragmentation of Suburban Government

In most metropolitan areas, providing public services in suburbia is complicated by the large number of separate local governments. Over 20,000 units of local government operate in American metropolitan areas. Half of all suburban municipalities have fewer than 5,000 residents and encompass less than one square mile. Some units are too small to afford anything but the most rudimentary public services. Often they lack adequate fire or police protection, and a public library is a vain hope. Moreover, the facilities and services that do exist are frequently duplicated at high cost in adjacent communities.

Fragmentation has its benefits as well as its costs, particularly from the perspective of the average suburbanite. Local autonomy permits community control over key elements of suburban life—real estate taxes, for example, land use (and therefore property values), and the local school system. Equally important, a fragmented governmental system provides the suburbanite with political independence from the central city; it separates him psychologically as well as physically from the city's people and their problems. As a leader in a working-class suburb in the Detroit metropolitan area emphasizes, "the most important thing to many people in Warren is just the simple fact that it isn't Detroit."[7]

"You should have been here in the old days,
before the budget cutbacks. . . . There were
cops and fire engines and planes buzzing around. . . ."

Mike Peters, Dayton Daily News.

The Divided Metropolis

Political fragmentation produces significant variations in the level and quality of public services in different sections of the metropolis. The political line between city and suburb concentrates the most serious urban problems in older cities. That separation also increases the political significance of social and economic differences in the metropolis. The nineteenth-century city fostered interdependence by including all elements of urban society within a single local government. The fragmented political system of the twentieth-century metropolis, on the other hand, reinforces social and economic differences between city and suburb as well as among suburbs.

Metropolitan Government

One answer to these problems is a single governmental unit for the entire metropolitan area. For more than fifty years, urban reformers have sought that goal. Despite their efforts, areawide government has won little popular acceptance in most of urban America. In the larger metropolises, size and complexity tend to rule out many of the advantages of areawide government, as New York City demonstrates. Another obstacle is the tendency of each of the major urban governmental activities to carve out its own ideal service area. The best geographic area in which to provide water and drainage, or secondary education, or police and fire protection rarely are the same.

The most important impediment to areawide government, however, is a lack of shared interests among residents of metropolitan areas. Suburbanites see a single metropolitan government as threatening the political independence of the local community. It implies "reunion . . . with the central city and its corrupt politics, its slums, immigrants, criminals, and the vicious elements from which they only recently escaped."[8] Areawide government brings threats of racial integration, public housing in the suburbs, and suburban children being bused to ghetto schools. Suburban interest in metropolitan government is further weakened by fewer suburban economic ties to the city; more and more suburbanites work outside the city, shop in suburban retail centers, and spend their leisure time beyond the city limits. Within the central city, blacks see metropolitan government as a menace to their political influence, diluting their power by adding white suburbanites to the local electorate.

Because of this formidable resistance, only a few of the many campaigns for metropolitan government have been successful. During the past thirty-five years metropolitan jurisdictions have been created in Baton Rouge, Indianapolis, Jacksonville, Miami, and Nashville. Most of these are newer areas that lack the sharp city-suburban differences of older metropolitan areas. For the future, the prospects for metropolitan government seem best among the rapidly growing centers of the south and west, which are less fragmented socially, economically, and politically.

The Adaptive Metropolis

Areawide government is not the only means of coping with problems that overrun local boundaries. Urban Americans have proved remarkably inventive in developing approaches that at the same time preserve the political independence of existing governmental units and provide necessary services.

One of the most popular approaches is the *special district* or *public authority*. These single- or limited-purpose units of government can have a jurisdiction as narrow as a residential subdivision within a city (as does a local water district) or as broad as an entire metropolitan area (as does the Metropolitan Water District of Southern California). Among the most common responsibilities of special districts and public authorities are water supply, sewage disposal, parks, airports, toll roads, bridges and tunnels, ports, and parking lots. Special districts are criticized because they add to the number of governments in the metropolis and in addition are rarely under the control of elected officials or citizens. Nonetheless, special districts and public authorities have the advantage of working reasonably well. They permit action toward meeting such community needs as a comprehensive water supply system, which simply exceeds the capacities of individual local governments in suburbia. Moreover, special districts do not appear to threaten local community control. They do not raise taxes directly but tend to be financed by fees imposed on users, such as bridge tolls or water charges. Special districts also are usually free from the tax and debt limits imposed by states on local governments. And they appeal to citizens who tend to distrust politicians and normal processes of local government.

Interlocal cooperation is another common means of dealing with urban growth and change. In many instances, central cities have rescued hard-pressed suburban towns by offering such services as water supply and public transportation on a pay-as-you-go basis. Similarly, police and fire departments of separate municipalities frequently have understandings, formal and informal, by which they come to each other's assistance in time of need and so increase the efficiency of both. County governments in many areas have assumed responsibility for a growing range of local services, including public health, administration of elections, library services, assessment and collection of taxes, fire and police protection, water supply, street maintenance, and recreation.

Suburbia is the prime beneficiary of these cooperative developments. By and large, they permit suburbanites to enjoy the benefits of smallness and autonomy without having to pay all the costs that would otherwise be imposed by fragmented government. Because all these approaches are voluntary, they rarely encompass controversial issues or deal with the central problems of the older cities. Public authorities are not created to build low-income housing throughout a metropolitan area. Interlocal cooperation seldom extends to large-scale transfer of students between suburban and city schools. Furthermore, most of these arrangements involve user charges and thus do not transfer resources from wealthier municipalities to poorer areas. As a result, these adaptive devices do little to ease the plight of the older cities or to reduce fiscal disparities among communities in the metropolis.

Urbanization and National Government

Throughout the twentieth century, urbanization has steadily and inevitably made urban voters and their problems more important in American politics. At the same time, federal involvement in the problems of the metropolis has increased rapidly (as has that of the state governments).

Federal involvement has reflected the complexity and diversity of urban America. Demands on the national government have been as varied as the competing needs of cities, suburbs, and metropolitan areas. Newer cities do not press the same claims in Washington as older cities. Within the same metropolitan area, cities and suburbs bring different concerns and priorities to the federal government.

Reinforcing Dominant Trends

In general, federal policies have encouraged the rapid spread of urban development. Massive federal highway programs greatly improved access to suburban areas. Federal mortgage policies helped to bring home ownership within reach of large numbers of Americans who then moved out of crowded cities.

Despite substantial federal investments within older cities, the overall effect has been to intensify rather than alleviate their problems. By accepting local boundaries, the federal involvement in public housing and urban renewal helped concentrate the poor and the black in cities. In addition, federal mortgage programs have fostered racial segregation in the metropolis.

The actions of the national government have also contributed to the fragmentation of the metropolitan political system. Most federal aid programs have accepted existing local boundaries, thus reinforcing the separation of city and suburb. By helping suburbs to overcome small size and limited resources, assistance from Washington has played an important role in permitting local governments to flourish within the metropolis.

Finally, federal investments in metropolitan areas have not been guided by over-all strategies. Instead, highways, post offices, military installations, and airports have been located haphazardly, usually in response to local needs or the criteria of a particular federal agency or the desires of a powerful member of Congress. As a result, important opportunities have been lost to guide urban development by planned and coordinated use of federal resources in public facilities.

Responding to Urban Change

Like other political participants in the dynamic metropolis, the national government is faced constantly with the need to adapt to social, economic, and political change. Most of the federal aid programs discussed in Chapter 5 resulted from the changing problems of cities and suburbs. At their inception, the war on poverty, model cities, urban-planning assistance, aid for local sewers, and scores of other programs were innovative federal responses to the forces of urban growth and change.

In some instances, Washington has encountered great difficulty in responding to changing urban problems. A case in point is the collapse of the welfare system in the face of drastic increases in the number of recipients, particularly in the older cities, and rapidly rising costs for the states and localities, which share the financing of the welfare system with the federal government. Efforts to develop a nationally financed minimum income, which would reduce the burden of poverty borne by local and state governments, failed repeatedly to attract adequate support from key interests in Washington during the 1970s. At other times, however, the federal government has moved swiftly to deal with changing urban circumstances, as in federal enactment in 1975 of a loan-guarantee plan designed to prevent the fiscal collapse of New York City.

Federal policies also have sought to stimulate governmental change in urban areas. One important effort was the Demonstration Cities and Metropolitan Development Act of 1966, which required that applications for a wide range of federal urban-development programs be reviewed by an areawide agency for consistency with metropolitan plans. As a result of this legislation, metropolitan areas across the nation created planning agencies and councils of local officials, some of which have had an important impact on local policies and programs.

The New Urban Majority

Changes in the urban population distribution also have had an important impact on the national government. Congressional representation is based on geographic districts. Population distribution also strongly influences the election of Presidents through allocation of delegates to the national conventions and votes in the electoral college. Inevitably, the steady movement of urban Americans to the suburbs and to the newer cities of the south and west has bolstered the influence of these areas in Washington.

Between 1966 and 1973, suburban districts in the House of Representatives increased 42 percent, from 92 to 131. During the 1970s, southern and western states will gain approximately fifteen seats in the House at the expense of northeastern and midwestern states. Both the winners and the losers in these shifts will be urban areas. Denver, Houston, Little Rock, Orlando, Phoenix, Tampa, and other newer areas will account for all of the gain. Chicago, Detroit, Newark, New

Table 3–1
Demographic Characteristics of House Districts 1966–1973

	1966	1973	Change 1966–1973
City	106	102	−4
Suburban	92	131	+39
Rural	181	130	−51
Mixed	56	72	+16

Source: *Congressional Quarterly Weekly Report*, XXXIX (Apr. 6, 1974), p. 878.

York, Philadelphia, Pittsburgh, St. Louis and other declining cities will lose seats.

Because of these population trends and shifts in representation, older cities find their influence in Washington declining as their need for federal assistance increases. The growing political power of the suburbs and suburb-like cities of the south and west reduces the prospect that federal programs will have a significant impact on the underlying racial, economic, and fiscal problems of the politically and socially divided metropolis. Increased representation from the suburbs and newer cities has diluted support for welfare reform, antipoverty programs, and federal housing subsidies for lower-income families.

School busing, among the most contentious domestic issues of the 1970s, offers a striking example of the new urban majority's increasingly decisive impact on American politics. Before federal district courts ordered the integration of schools on a metropolitan-wide basis in Richmond and Detroit, congressional support for restrictions on court-ordered school busing came primarily from southerners and conservatives. After federal judges directed exchanges of white suburban pupils and ghetto blacks outside the south, opposition to busing rose to a fever pitch in suburbs across the nation. Suburban voters put intense pressure on their congressmen, enough of whom joined the antibusing coalition to enable the House of Representatives to pass strong antibusing legislation (which died in the Senate) in the election year of 1972. Only after the Supreme Court overturned the lower court's ruling in Detroit, on the grounds that suburbs in the area bore no responsibility for the segregation of schools in the metropolis,[9] did the political furor subside in Detroit's suburbs.

To date, the institutions of an increasingly urban society have failed to distribute fairly either the benefits or the costs of urbanization. The central question for the future is whether the new urban majority will permit blacks and other disadvantaged groups to share in the prosperity that increasingly is focused in the spreading suburbs and the burgeoning metropolitan areas of the south and west. Based on present political trends, the outlook for change is bleak. The new urban majority does not appear willing to make the economic and political sacrifices necessary for the nation to deal effectively with the corrosive consequences of the poverty and racism that are rooted in its aging and declining urban centers.

Hopes that the federal courts would force basic changes in urban governmental arrangements were repeatedly dashed in the 1970s by a series of rulings by the Supreme Court. First, the Court ruled that local differences in tax resources to support public education did not violate the Constitution.[10] Next, the Court declined to merge city and suburban school districts in Detroit in order to foster racial integration.[11] Then, the Court restricted access to federal courts for poor city dwellers seeking to challenge exclusionary suburban housing and land-use policies.[12] Together, these decisions reinforced the significance of political boundaries in the metropolis, thus strengthening the barriers that separate older from newer areas, declining cities from growing suburbs and metropolitan areas, and the disadvantaged from the better off in urban America.

Summary

Urban growth has been a major feature of the development of American society for two centuries. Succeeding waves of rural Americans, immigrants from Europe and Asia, blacks from the south, and others have migrated to the cities. With the development of the automobile and the highway, rapid outward growth turned cities into metropolitan areas composed of a central city and surrounding suburbs. Most older cities stopped expanding their political boundaries decades ago; thus the suburban portions of their metropolitan areas tend to be large. Newer cities in the south and west, most of which have been growing rapidly, have been able to expand their territory by annexing developing areas. These newer areas, along with suburbs in general, account for almost all the urban growth in the contemporary United States. Older cities in the northeast and midwest, where most urban growth formerly occurred, now tend to have declining populations and large concentrations of lower-income and minority residents.

American politics is constantly affected by this pattern of urbanization. Federal programs have expanded in response to mounting urban needs and problems. Changes in urbanization also have a strong influence on national politics and policies. The growth of suburbia and the newer areas of the south and west has increased the political strength of these areas. Older cities bear the heaviest burdens of urbanization, but their political influence steadily declines with emergence of a new urban majority in the suburbs and rapidly growing metropolitan areas of the south and west.

Selected Bibliography

ADVISORY COMMISSION ON INTERGOVERNMENTAL RELATIONS, *Urban America and the Federal System* (Washington, D.C.: Government Printing Office, 1969). A comprehensive review of urban and metropolitan problems based on a decade of research and recommendations by the Commission.

BANFIELD, EDWARD C., *The Unheavenly City Revisited* (Boston: Little, Brown and Company, 1974). An iconoclastic examination of urban problems and the role of government in their resolution.

BOLLENS, JOHN C., and HENRY J. SCHMANDT, *The Metropolis: Its People, Politics, and Economic Life,* 3rd ed. (New York: Harper and Row, 1975). A detailed examination of the economic, social, and political systems of the metropolitan area.

BROWN, CLAUDE, *Manchild in the Promised Land* (New York: The New

American Library, Inc., 1965). A shocking but fascinating autobiographical account of life in the Harlem ghetto.

CANTY, DONALD, *A Single Society: Alternatives to Urban Apartheid* (New York: Praeger Publishers, 1969). A thoughtful essay that explores the prospects of creating an integrated urban community.

CLARK, KENNETH B., *Dark Ghetto: Dilemmas of Social Power* (New York: Harper and Row, 1965). A penetrating analysis by one of America's most distinguished social scientists.

COMMISSION ON POPULATION GROWTH AND THE AMERICAN FUTURE, *Population and the American Future* (Washington, D.C.: Government Printing Office, 1972). A thorough appraisal of demographic changes and their probable impact on American society in the decades ahead.

DANIELSON, MICHAEL N., ed., *Metropolitan Politics* (Boston: Little, Brown and Company, 1971). A collection of readings which explores urban politics from a variety of perspectives.

———. *The Politics of Exclusion* (New York: Columbia University Press, 1976). An analysis of the role of local governments, the states, federal agencies, and the courts in the development of exclusionary suburban housing and land-use policies.

LONG, NORTON, *The Unwalled City: Reconstituting the Urban Community* (New York: Basic Books, 1972). A provocative and optimistic analysis of the contemporary urban political scene.

NATIONAL ADVISORY COMMISSION ON CIVIL DISORDERS, *Report* (Washington, D.C.: Government Printing Office, 1968). The Kerner Commission report, which examines the urban riots of the 1960s and their causes.

STERNLIEB, GEORGE and JAMES W. HUGHES, eds., *Post-Industrial America: Metropolitan Decline & Inter-Regional Job Shifts* (New Brunswick, N.J.: Center for Urban Policy Research, Rutgers University, 1975). A series of essays that explores the implications of the southern and westward movement of jobs and people.

WILLBERN, YORK, *The Withering Away of the City* (University, Ala.: University of Alabama Press, 1964). An excellent introduction to the problems of governance of the American metropolis.

WOOD, ROBERT C., *The Necessary Majority: Middle America and the Urban Crisis* (New York: Columbia University Press, 1972). An optimistic appraisal of the prospects for dealing with urban problems in terms which are acceptable to most Americans.

Part Two

The Constitutional Framework

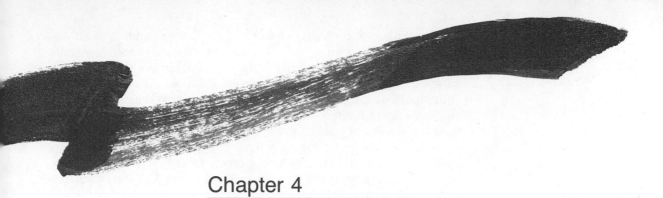

Chapter 4

The Constitutional System

The Nature of a Constitution
Constitution and Culture
A Constitution as an Instrument of Government
Constitutionalism and Democracy
Constitutional Permanence and Change

Framing the American Constitution
The Framers' Objectives
Government under the Articles of Confederation
The Framers
The Framers' Political Philosophy
Compromises

The Constitutional Structure
Limiting Power by Prohibitions and Elections
Limiting Power by Sharing Power
Networks of Jealousy
Restricting the Power of the People
The Bill of Rights

Watergate: A Case Study in Constitutional Checks

The Constitutional System and the Need for Energetic Government
Successes and Failures of the System

Summary

Selected Bibliography

THE PREVIOUS TWO chapters examined the cultural and physical setting of American politics. This chapter focuses on a related topic: the constitutional framework within which American politics functions. First we shall examine the nature of a constitution, the concept of constitutionalism, and its relation to democratic government. Then we shall look at the framers of the American Constitution, who they were, their basic political ideas, and the way they tried to blend elements of constitutionalism and democracy. Last, we shall take a brief overview of the way the political system they created has functioned at the national level, leaving to chapter 5 a similarly broad analysis of federal-state relations.

The Nature of a Constitution

Constitution and Culture

A nation's cultural and social systems, its physical setting, the state of its technology, and its relations with other nations all interact with that fundamental set of rules which we call a *constitution* and to which all governmental actions are expected to conform. Indeed, a constitution that did not fit a society's cultural patterns and physical needs would soon either change those patterns and needs or itself shrivel up and die. An effective constitution not only allows government to meet immediate problems but helps shape society's ideals and, although possibly less directly and immediately, its practices as well. The common expression "a living constitution" refers to a basic legal order that is truly part of a nation's life: it is capable of being adapted by public officials to fit changing problems; and in turn it frequently helps shape official and private judgments about what is proper and improper conduct in public affairs.

A Constitution as an Instrument of Government

Recognizing these reciprocal relations, some political theorists have viewed a constitution not as a document or even as a particular arrangement of political institutions, but as a way of life. Insofar as they are right, a nation's constitution is only one manifestation of its political culture, a statement of the objectives and ideals of that society and an explanation of the means that can be lawfully used to achieve those ends. Thus inherent in a constitution is a notion of change and development as society changes and develops.

Logically, then, we can restate what we have said and define *a constitution as an instrument of government expressing a set of general political principles about society's ideals, objectives, and legitimate processes*. To be effective, a constitution must not only fit existing cultural standards and be capable of meeting current problems but also of being "adapted," as Chief Justice John Marshall said in 1819, "to the various *crises* of human affairs," whether those crises be generated by economic, social, or technological changes or by shifts in power relations within a single country or between nations.[1]

As an instrument of government, a constitution distributes power among governmental institutions. It specifies—often in broad, sometimes in vague, and occasionally even in confusing terms—who can perform what kinds of publicly binding actions. As an instrument of government, however, a constitution usually does more than confer and distribute power. Even more important, it typically restricts governmental power in order to protect certain rights of the individual. This notion of individual rights against government or society is not one that citizens of ancient Greek city-states would have understood; nor is it intelligible in many modern "people's republics." Yet the purpose of protecting individualism is at the core of modern constitutionalism.

Although one can find scattered examples in antiquity, the idea of a constitution as a limitation on government is the product of long struggles in medieval and early-modern Europe against various forms of political tyranny. Intellectual justifications for those struggles have been rooted in such notions as *natural law* and *natural rights*—beliefs that human beings have certain obligations and rights that existed before organized society and that continue to exist within society, retaining superiority over any laws that society or its government may enact. Although the doctrine of natural rights flourished during a more religious age, today its groundings are likely to be purely secular. Occasionally, however, its theological foundation becomes clear. "Men," Supreme Court Justice William O. Douglas once wrote, "do not acquire rights from government; one man does not give another certain rights. Man gets his rights from the creator. They came to him because of the divine spark in every human being."[2]

As an instrument of government, a constitution may also serve as a symbol of the nation and its ideals. As such, it helps train new generations to accept both the political system itself and particular aspects of the nation's dominant political culture or cultures. In performing this kind of function, a constitution may allow government to cope with a variety of crises by applying old rules in new ways while at the same time retaining cherished links with traditional values and processes. Thus a constitution may help unify a people who are angrily divided over particular issues of public policy, reminding them that they are all citizens of the same country, believers in the same goals, and heirs to the same heritage.

Constitutionalism and Democracy

The heart of the notion of *constitutionalism* is that government and society are subject to a body of law that is superior to the immediate will of any governmental official, or to the majority of the community, or, as long as the constitution remains in force, even to the immediate will of the entire community. Most simply, the content of constitutionalism is often summed up in the phrase "the rule of law." Its heart is a moral principle that government, even government of, by, and for the people, can act legitimately *only* insofar as it follows certain procedures that the constitution specifies. For instance, if a constitution said that no one could be punished without a fair trial, a government would violate the essence of constitutionalism if it punished without a fair trial a single person for treason even if every private citizen (other than the accused) in the country and every public official were absolutely convinced that he was guilty.

Sometimes, the notion of constitutionalism includes a belief that some sorts of governmental action are prohibited, regardless of the procedures followed. In a country whose constitution forbade establishment of a religion, for example, it would not be legitimate for government to require, even by means of a properly adopted statute, all citizens to become Episcopalians, even if all but one person (or indeed if all persons) in the country were already Episcopalians.

Amending a constitution is almost always a possibility. (In the United States, each house of Congress must approve an amendment by a two-thirds vote, and then that proposal must be ratified by three-fourths of the states.) But in the absence of such an amendment, any official or private citizen who took his or her duty seriously (and in the United States every public official takes an oath to support the Constitution) would be obligated to vote against any policies that contradicted constitutional commands. If those policies won, even by an overwhelming vote, the conscientious individual would—in the absence of a constitutional amendment—still be obliged to refuse to carry them out. In short, one of a constitution's functions is to play a role similar to that performed by natural law in more religious times; that is, to serve as a body of principles that are superior to all other political obligations.

Constitutional Permanence and Change

If one could stop at this point, political science and the art of practical politics would be relatively simple. Unhappily, neither the world of action nor the world of ideas is quite so kind. Earlier we noted that an effective constitution had to be supple, to be capable of changing along with society's ideals and needs. Thus even constitutional clauses protecting individual rights do not necessarily retain quite the same meaning for every generation. It can happen, of course, that a constitution's commands or prohibitions will slow or even halt societal changes that involve certain values. But in a rapidly changing world even the wisest of constitutions could not lock a society into absolute stability of val-

Supporters of the Equal Rights Amendment campaign for ratification. The House of Representatives approved the proposed 27th Amendment in 1971, as did the Senate the following year; but the required three-fourths of the states had not ratified the Amendment as of the end of 1976.

ues and practices. One has only to look at the Roman Catholic Church before and after the Second Vatican Council (1962–1965) to see how much values can change even in an institution that prides itself on absolute fidelity to theological principles.

Some judges (and many theologians) justify such shifts by claiming that fundamental values do not vary, but their applications to shifting events may change. Dean Roscoe Pound summed up the dilemma: "The law must be stable, yet it cannot stand still." In this respect a constitution's symbolism may be vital for society, confirming the reality of great continuity with the past and imparting the appearance of greater continuity even as it permits some change. A constitution's fundamental purpose of protecting maximum feasible individual liberty may remain constant, but what is "maximum," or "feasible," or even "liberty" may change over time. Deciding when to oppose change, or when to go along and modify change, or when to accept it fully is, of course, one of the most difficult choices of statesmen, secular or religious.

Framing the American Constitution

The Framers' Objectives

The men who met in Philadelphia in 1787 to draft a new constitution for the United States were acquainted with the ideas and problems that we have been discussing. Nevertheless, they were confident that they could create political arrangements that would "bestow the blessings of liberty" on themselves and their "posterity" by combining both constitutionalism and popular participation. Indeed, had they not succeeded, they would have been hooted through history as arrogant fools who attempted the impossible.

An astute combination of *constitutional liberty* and *popular participation* were not the only objectives of the framers. They also tried to insure a high degree of *political stability*. And they also knew that, if their work were to endure beyond their own time, they would have to go beyond immediate problems and fashion a political structure that could cope with crises whose specific shapes they could not even dimly foresee. Thus they had to formulate general principles rather than a detailed code.

On the other hand, if their constitution were to have any future at all, it would first have to be suitable to solve existing difficulties, and those people at the Convention who wanted their ideas to develop into reality would have to persuade other delegates to join with them in proposing the plan as well as to convince political leaders in the states to agree to such a scheme. "We must," Gunning Bedford of Delaware urged the delegates, "like Solon make such a government as the people will approve."[3] His plea was echoed by colleagues who said they would accept the best constitution possible and not hold out for unrealizable ideals.

Government under the Articles of Confederation

At the time, the nation was seriously handicapped by shortcomings of government under the Articles of Confederation. That agreement had not created a national political system, but only "a firm league of friendship" among sovereign states. Under the Articles, each state retained "its sovereignty, freedom and independence, and every power, jurisdiction and right, which is not by this confederation expressly delegated to the United States, in Congress assembled." Congress itself consisted of a single house to which each state could send two to seven representatives who were more like ambassadors to the United Nations than like today's congressmen. Regardless of how many representatives a state sent or the size of its population, each state had only one vote. An affirmative vote of nine states was required to exercise any of the very few national legislative powers. Indeed, one could make a strong case for the proposition that Congress could not legislate at all in the modern sense. It could not, for instance, levy taxes on individuals or regulate commerce among the states. Its enactments were essentially proposals to state governments; and, lacking any effective executive department, Congress had no means of enforcing those suggestions. The central government under the Articles could "resolve and recommend but could not command and enforce."[4]

In foreign and military affairs, the Articles ostensibly gave Congress rather broad authority to speak for the United States. But, again, absence of an effective executive and inability to command individual citizens meant that Congress could only request the states to carry out whatever agreements its diplomats might be able to negotiate. In this context of political impotence, other nations tended to treat the Confederation with indifference or contempt.

Historians disagree about whether one should label as a crisis the events leading up to Congress' call to the states to send delegates to Philadelphia for the purpose of proposing amendments to the Articles. Certainly, however, inability to negotiate commercial treaties vital to the prosperity of a small agricultural nation contributed to dissatisfaction. And, in domestic affairs, widespread debt, a revolt of poor farmers in Massachusetts under the leadership of Captain Daniel Shays, and a threat of tariff wars among the states caused serious concern among governmental officials and politically aware private citizens. Thus one obvious and immediate objective of the framers had to be creation of a stronger national government that could further "prosperity" and "domestic tranquillity."

On the other hand, having just lived through a rebellion against an oppressive government, the framers were in no mood to obtain law and order by substituting American for British tyrants. The greatest need in constructing a government, James Madison wrote shortly before the Philadelphia Convention, is to "render it sufficiently neutral between the different interests and factions, to controul one part of the society from invading the rights of another, and at the same time sufficiently controuled itself, from setting up an interest adverse to that of the whole Society."[5]

The Framers

Like the old moral precept "Do good and avoid evil," Madison's constitutional prescription was not easy to fill. Fortunately, most of the fifty-five men who met at Philadelphia that summer were able and practical as well as ambitiously confident men. Although their average age was only forty-three, collectively they had already had considerable experience in the real world of politics. Forty-two had served in the Continental Congress; several were in fact officially serving while participating in the Convention. Seven had been governors and twenty

George Washington presides over the Constitutional Convention at Independence Hall, Philadelphia, in 1787.

had been members of state constitutional conventions. As a group, they were also extraordinarily well trained for the times. Twenty-six had a college education, more than thirty were lawyers, three were college professors, and two were college presidents.

In many ways these delegates were not especially representative of Americans. Most obviously, all the framers were males and all were white. Only the most extreme among radical democrats of the time considered women and blacks among "the people" entitled to political participation. Few delegates could speak for small yeomen farmers, and virtually no one had either himself been an urban worker or could claim to be a spokesman for these "mechanics and artisans." Rather, the framers were almost all men of some financial means, social stature, and professional reputation: creditors not debtors, gentlemen farmers, merchants, bankers, lawyers, and governmental officials. They had large, tangible, financial stakes in creating a political system that would provide both stability and freedom. Thus they were pushed by self-interest as well as by patriotism.

A few of the more famous leaders of the Revolution were at Philadelphia—George Washington, Benjamin Franklin, Alexander Hamilton, James Madison, James Wilson, George Mason, Oliver Ellsworth, and Edmund Randolph, for example. But other revolutionary leaders were absent. John Adams and Thomas Jefferson were serving abroad as diplomats; Tom Paine was living in Europe; Sam Adams was too old to come; John Hancock was governor of Massachusetts; and Patrick Henry, although chosen as a delegate, refused to attend, saying "I smelt a rat!" In all, only eight of the fifty-six who signed the Declaration of Independence were present.

Despite marked similarities in social class, the framers vehemently disagreed among themselves on many vital issues, such as how to divide power within the national government or between the national government and the states.* For John Dickinson of Delaware and Alexander Hamilton, monarchy had still not lost all appeal, whereas Ben Franklin, James Wilson, and sometimes even the wealthy New England merchant Nathaniel Gorham spoke for a more democratic form of government than finally emerged. Luther Martin of Maryland was among the principal advocates of retaining strong state governments, while Wilson and Madison were the leaders of the faction wanting a powerful national regime. Many delegates were also deeply troubled by slavery (Madison, for instance, argued that it was "wrong to admit in the Constitution the idea that there could be property in men"[6]), but no one could think of a way of abolishing the institution and keeping the south in the Union.

There were also broad areas of consensus among the framers. Moreover, what notes we have of their deliberations indicate that, like bright participants in a seminar, they learned from each other.[7] Most of them probably agreed with Madison's prescription for constitutional government—one strong enough to control any part of society but not so strong as to be able to set itself up against society. For these men, government was a dangerous but necessary institution; and, if they had been faced with a clear-cut choice between constitutionalism and democracy, they would have quickly opted for constitutionalism. Five years earlier, Jefferson had summed up their views: "an elective despotism was not the government we fought for."[8]

Given the heavy democratic element in most state governments, however, the framers never had any real option of excluding popular participation. Furthermore, most of the delegates actually wanted popular government both in the sense of widespread approval of the new constitutional system and also in the sense of the people's having a limited but real part in choosing public officials. Madison argued on sever-

---

*This disagreement focused on what we would today call *federalism,* a system of government in which authority is divided between local units (states in America) and the nation, with both sets of government having authority to act directly on individual citizens. A *confederation*—what the United States had in 1787—is an alternative system in which local units retain most of the important governmental powers. The central government in a confederation usually has only a limited set of powers, typically over matters such as international relations or perhaps trade among the system's local units. The central government may not directly command individual citizens, but must work through the local units. A *unitary* system forms a third alternative. Here, as in Great Britain, the central government possesses all political authority. Local governments exist only because the central government finds it convenient.

To settle on federalism, as the framers eventually did, by no means resolves all problems of distributing political power. In a federal system, a central government may be very powerful or very weak, depending on constitutional arrangements as well as a host of other factors in a nation's political life.

al occasions that popular election of at least one house of the legislature was "essential to every plan of free government."[9] Like many of his colleagues, he would have limited suffrage to those who owned property, but proponents of this restriction claimed that 90 percent of the population would still be able to vote.

Nevertheless, as a group, the men at Philadelphia feared tyranny by a majority as much as tyranny by a monarch. When they used the term *democratic,* it was typically a criticism. The label that they preferred for their bold plan to unite constitutionalism with democracy was *free government,* an imaginative but delicate marriage of liberty and restraint, of popular participation and constitutional limitations.

Much of the framers' notions about government derived from their view of human nature. On the one hand, they were aware of man's capacity for evil. They were influenced in part by the writings of the seventeenth-century English philosopher Thomas Hobbes, who claimed that "life is a restless seeking of power after power." Even more so, they were influenced by the Calvinist concept of original sin and the corruptibility if not the corruption of mankind. Having grown up in a relatively poor society but one rife with political struggles, they understood that power could be as luring a temptation as money. According to Bedford of Delaware, "Give the opportunity [to use power], and ambition will not fail to abuse it."[10] Then turning inward to the Convention itself, he reminded delegates:

Look at the votes which have been given on the floor of this house, and it will be found that their [delegates' states'] numbers, wealth, and local views, have actuated their determinations. . . . Pretences to support ambition are never wanting. . . . *I do not, gentlemen, trust you.* If you possess the power, the abuse of it could not be checked; and what then would prevent you from exercising it to our destruction?[11]

Madison spoke in more general terms: "In truth, all men with power ought to be distrusted to a certain degree."[12]

On the other hand, this bleak outlook was tempered by other ideas that were in the wind. As children of the European "Age of Reason," many of the framers also had some, although not unbounded, faith in the power of the human intellect; and many people of their generation, most notably Jefferson, hoped that by learning from experience and using his mind man could improve morally as well as intellectually. Writing in *Federalist* No. 55, Madison summed up the framers' mixed view of human nature: "As there is a degree of depravity in mankind which requires a certain degree of circumspection and distrust, so there are other qualities in human nature which justify a certain portion of esteem and confidence."

It was the framers' pessimism that made them see government as necessary to protect people against one another, and as dangerous because humans were no more apt to be moral in public than in private affairs. But it was their faith in reason that gave them the courage to believe that they could devise institutional arrangements that would channel behavior toward civilized conduct.

Besides a belief in the necessity of government and in constitutional limitations and a somewhat pessimistic view of human nature, the framers were empiricists, hard-headed men of practical experience. They had faith in reason, but wanted reason anchored to hard facts rather than wafting around abstract theories. "I believe," William Paterson of New Jersey told the delegates, "that a little practical virtue is to be preferred to the finest theoretical principles, which cannot be carried into effect."[13] As men of affairs, they knew politics first hand, but many of them had also read widely and knew a great deal about ancient Greek and Roman history as well as more recent political developments in England, on the continent, and in the American states.

Compromises

The framers' differences on many specific issues created a series of sharp disputes. But their agreement on certain fundamentals—coupled with their pragmatic outlook—allowed them to work out compromises on most of these. For the long run, the most important compromise involved slavery. On that question, John Rutledge of South Carolina told the Convention, hinged "whether the southern states shall or shall not be parties to the Union."[14] Faced with a choice between a single nation with slavery or two nations, one with and one without slavery, the framers largely gave in to southern demands, even though most if not all of the delegates, including the southerners, personally thought that slavery was morally wrong.

Probably to salve their consciences, the framers adroitly avoided ever using the term "slave" or "slavery" in the Constitution. Indeed, the document made few indirect references to this "peculiar institution," thus leaving it almost entirely to state control. Article I provided that, for purposes of apportioning representatives in Congress, a state's population would be computed "by adding to the whole number of free persons . . . excluding Indians not taxed, three fifths of all other persons." Furthermore, Article IV, section 2 placed on free states an obligation to return runaway slaves to their masters. The language of this section was a masterpiece of disingenuity:

No person held to service or labour in one State, under the laws thereof, escaping into another, shall, in consequence of any law of regulation therein, be discharged from such service or labour, but shall be delivered up on claim of the party to whom such service or labour may be due.

As a sop to strong moral sentiment against slavery, Article I empowered Congress after 1808 to forbid "the migration or importation of such persons as any of the states now existing think proper to admit"—a long-winded and indirect way of saying that Congress could prohibit importation of slaves. And in 1808 Congress promptly used this au-

Negroes for Sale.

A Cargo of very fine stout Men and Women, in good order and fit for immediate service, just imported from the Windward Coast of Africa, in the Ship Two Brothers.— Conditions are one half Cash or Produce, the other half payable the first of January next, giving Bond and Security if required.

The Sale to be opened at 10 o'Clock each Day, in Mr. Bourdeaux's Yard, at No. 48, on the Bay.

May 19, 1784.   JOHN MITCHELL.

Advertisement for a slave sale, 1784. Congress used its constitutional authority to prohibit the importation of slaves in 1808, but legal buying and selling of slaves within the United States continued until the Civil War.

thority, although that action did little to abate the slave trade *within* the United States.

At the time, the framers thought of the "great compromise" as that involving state representation in Congress. With larger states adamantly insisting on representation by population and smaller states just as firmly insisting on equality, the Convention almost blew apart. Oliver Ellsworth of Connecticut and John Rutledge finally worked out the obvious solution of equal representation of states in the Senate and representation by population in the House.

Another of several important compromises involved admission of new states into the Union. Some delegates feared the possible political orientation of western settlers and proposed a clause specifically providing for preferred status for the thirteen original states. Delegates who wanted free and rapid development of the west to enlarge and strengthen the Union urged a guarantee that new states would be admitted on the same basis as the original thirteen. The only compromise the framers could agree on was silence. Article IV, section 3 says only: "New states shall be admitted by the Congress into this Union. . . ." Later, Congress by law and the Supreme Court through constitutional interpretation opted for equality between old and new states.

The Constitutional Structure

"Happily for America," Madison modestly noted after the Convention adjourned, he and his colleagues at Philadelphia had pursued a "noble course." They had "paid a decent respect to the opinions of former times and other nations" without allowing "blind veneration for antiquity, custom, or for names to overrule the suggestions of their own good sense" and "the lessons of their own experience." Combining history and reason, Madison claimed, the men at Philadelphia had accomplished "a revolution which has no parallel in the annals of human society. They reared the fabrics of governments which have no model on the face of the globe."[15]

The new national government of which Madison spoke had far more power than the old. Congress could act directly on private citizens. It could tax and spend; "regulate commerce with foreign nations, and among the several states, and with the Indian tribes"; coin and borrow money; create a national system of courts; establish an army and a navy; and "make all laws which shall be necessary and proper" to carry out any of the powers granted to any branch of the national government. To enforce federal laws and treaties, the Constitution also established an executive department, chosen independently of Congress and headed by a President. By its own terms, the Constitution also provided that federal laws and treaties as well as the Constitution itself took precedence over state regulations.

The states, of course, retained much of their traditional political power, but were not the equal of the new federal government. At that, some delegates, including Madison, believed that the national government was not as powerful vis-à-vis the states as it should have been. But, as on most issues they were willing to compromise to obtain an agreement that could become operative.

Limiting Power by Prohibitions and Elections

As one would expect, the framers did more than grant and distribute power. In express terms they forbade Congress and/or the states to perform certain actions, for example, passing bills of attainder* or ex post facto laws.† But the framers were not naive, simple-minded men who thought that writing "thou shalt not" into a constitution would prevent abuse of power. They were, after all, familiar with the history of the Ten Commandments. As practical men they put their faith in a system in which institutions would share power and officeholders feud with one another rather than in "parchment barriers." Popular elections, Madison said, formed "the primary control on the government."[16] Officials who periodically were obliged to go, hat in hand, to the people to ask to be allowed to retain their jobs would find it difficult to behave arrogantly between elections.

*A legislative act that, without judicial trial, convicts a specific person of a crime and orders him punished.

Chapter 4
Constitutional System

†A law that makes an act, innocent when committed, a crime, or that retroactively lowers the amount of proof needed to convict for a particular crime, or that retroactively increases the punishment for a specific crime.

93

But this check by prohibition and election was not sufficient, Madison admitted; "experience has taught the necessity of auxilliary precautions." Responding to Bedford's argument about the abuse of power, Madison said that for those holding public office, "ambition must be made to counteract ambition. The interest of the man must be connected with the constitutional rights of the place."[17] To stir up a jealous clash among ambitions and to cement an identification of interest and rights, the framers divided—fractured is perhaps more accurate—governmental power. First, they made a virtue out of the necessity of the states' continuing to operate as important units of government. By increasing the power of the national government, leaving the states with a generous residue of power, and refusing to draw clear boundaries between the two, the Constitution made inevitable fears among state officials of federal encroachment and among federal officials fears of state trespasses.

At the national level, the framers further splintered power among three branches, the legislature, executive, and judiciary. They did not, as Madison conceded, provide for a "separation of powers" as is consistently and erroneously claimed. Rather they created a system in which separate institutions share power.[18] Congress—itself split into two houses that often compete with each other—must exercise its legislative power in conjunction with the President, who can call the two houses into special session, adjourn them if they cannot agree on a time for adjournment, recommend legislation to them, and veto bills that they pass. Moreover, in enforcing the law he, no less than judges, must interpret statutes. And, because the language of legislation is often vague and Congress has on occasion passed a new statute without fully explaining its effect on existing law, the President's discretion here can be quite broad. Moreover, a President's first obligation is to obey the Consitution, not Congress; and more than one Chief Executive has refused to carry out an act of Congress because he has believed it to be unconstitutional. Less dramatically, Presidents have typically not been zealous in executing laws they believe unwise. Much of the current controversy over executive "impoundment"* of money appropriated by Congress revolves around the unanswered, and perhaps unanswerable, question of the exact extent of presidential obligation to carry out the precise terms of every act of Congress.

The whole matter of responsibility for the legislative process is muddled for several reasons: executive agencies often draft the bills that congressmen debate, modify, and finally pass; the President or his staff often actively lobby in Congress and stir up public opinion for or against important proposals; and most important bills that become law

---

Impoundment refers to a blockage by executive officials, usually acting under direct orders from the President, of spending federal funds for certain specified purposes. The President simply orders that the money be retained in the U.S. Treasury.

confer a great deal of discretion on the President. In sum, as we shall see in Chapters 10–12, probably the most significant function of the President in domestic affairs is to act as Chief Legislator. With congressional power shared among 535 people, usually only the President can provide effective leadership.

Judges also share in legislative processes in that they must interpret the same statutes as does the President. Moreover, because the Constitution proclaims itself to be law, judges have asserted that they have authority to interpret that document. "It is, emphatically," Chief Justice John Marshall said in 1803, "the province and duty of the judicial department, to say what the law is."[19] As a result, judges can define the legitimate scope of Congress' power to enact laws, to conduct investigations, and even, in some circumstances, to seat its members.

In interpreting statutes and the Constitution, judges are often accused of "judicial legislation." Frequently if not always those charges are correct. By enacting vague statutes, Congress issues an open invitation for judges and administrators to indulge in creative interpretation. One cannot, for instance, mechanically apply a law that sets as a standard "the public interest." And the great clauses of the Constitution are often equally imprecise. For instance, Article I's listing of congressional power does not mention "interstate commerce." Rather, it confers on Congress authority to regulate "commerce among the several states," without defining "regulate," "commerce," or "among"—and the last omission may be the most serious of all, since the word "among" in the late eighteenth century was more likely to mean "within" than "between more than two." Similarly, the Fourth Amendment prohibits only "unreasonable searches and seizures," not all searches, not even all searches without a warrant. And the Fifth and Fourteenth Amendments do not flatly forbid federal and state governments to take life, liberty, or property, but only "without due process of law"; and no judge or lawyer or scholar has yet been able to offer a precise definition of *due process* that many other judges, lawyers, or scholars would accept. Faced with the task of interpreting such language, judges must act creatively, obtaining their values, as Justice Benjamin N. Cardozo said, not from law, but "from life itself."[20]

The President shares in judicial authority in that he directs, through the Attorney General, all civil and criminal suits begun in the name of the United States and may, except in cases of impeachment, pardon any person who may be convicted of, charged with, or suspected of violating federal law. The pardoning power even extends to those convicted of criminal contempt of court for disobeying or defying an order from a federal judge. In addition, the President nominates all federal judges and often selects people who he believes will decide cases in ways that he thinks correct. Furthermore, final responsibility for enforcement of judicial decisions falls on the executive, and Presidents have often treated this responsibility as requiring them to exercise careful discretion rather than automatic obedience.

Congress also shares in judicial power, the Senate in confirming or rejecting judicial nominees and both houses in regulating the size, organization, and jurisdiction* of the federal courts. Like the President, senators and representatives have often used their authority to try to shape the development of law, especially constitutional law.

Moreover, in their investigations of activities that might merit federal regulation, congressional committees frequently "punish" witnesses by forcing them to face television cameras while responding to questions about their pasts that can ruin reputations and wreck careers as well as merely embarrass. As an accusing body in impeachment cases, the House of Representatives exercises a quasi-judicial function; and if the House impeaches, the Senate sits as a trial court to determine the guilt or innocence of the accused federal official.

Nor is the executive branch immune from outside forces. Judges can interpret executive orders, just as they can statutes. And, in interpreting the Constitution, courts have on numerous occasions set limits to executive authority. Congress has even wider avenues of influence into administration. The Senate can confirm or reject the President's nominees for his own cabinet and several thousand other executive posts. Perhaps more important, Congress also determines the organization of all departments within the executive branch and by its control over appropriations can affect the minutest detail within federal agencies as well as the general direction of administrative policy. Indeed, many chiefs of federal offices are likely to pay more attention to the whims of senators and congressmen on the appropriations committees than to the President's policies.

Networks of Jealousy

The general picture that emerges from this description is that of several networks of overlapping grants of authority to separate institutions, each of which is staffed by people chosen in different ways and at different times, who have access to different sorts of information, are responsible to different constituencies, and are moved by different kinds of institutional loyalties as well as by competing personal and institutional ambitions. Each of the three branches has its own primary core of power, but each of the other branches to some extent shares in the exercise of that power. It is highly unlikely that either Congress, the President, or the Supreme Court can take any important action either without the cooperation of another branch or else without seeming to trespass on the domain of one or the other branch.

Thus wariness and jealousy form the normal state of affairs within the national government no less than between state and federal levels.

Jurisdiction refers to the basic authority of a court to hear and decide certain kinds of controversies. Article III of the Constitution allows Congress very broad authority to give jurisdiction to or take it away from federal courts.

Occasionally, as in the series of events called Watergate, which we shall discuss later in the chapter, jealousy flashes into open hostility. In fact, it is only a slight exaggeration to say that Madison and his colleagues tried to build a constitutional structure that would, on the one hand, stir up recurrent crises among envious governmental officials and, on the other hand, supply each of them with a sufficient number of checks on the others to keep those crises within tolerable limits.

Restricting the Power of the People

Because they distrusted all humanity and not merely governmental officials, Madison and the other framers also wanted to restrain the power of a majority of the people. "In all cases," Madison told the Convention, "where a majority are united by a common interest or passion, the rights of the minority are in danger."[21] The remedy, he said, was for government to encourage development of a whole range of interests within society. In short, he wanted "to enlarge the sphere, and thereby divide the community into so great a number of interests and parties, that in the first place a majority will not be likely at the same moment to have a common interest separate from that of the whole or the minority; and in the second place, that in case they should have such an interest, they may not be apt to unite in the pursuit of it."[22] One specific way to encourage growth of what we would call *pluralism** was to make sure, because it "was politic as well as just," that "the interests and rights of every class should be duly represented and understood in the public Councils."[23]

On the negative side, the framers were aware that federalism, vast distances, and poor means of communication would help keep a majority from identifying and uniting around a common interest separate from the rest of the community. If such a majority did develop, they also hoped that it would be hobbled by the system of restraints on public officials. The framers reinforced these barriers by staggering terms of office for national officials and by providing that they be responsible to different constituencies. Originally, only members of the House of Representatives were elected directly by the people. Having only one third of the senators chosen at the same time (and selected by state legislators who may have been elected a year or two earlier) would hamper any majority that managed to unite from gaining control of Congress at a single election. The Electoral College, as it initially functioned and still can function, put additional brakes on the ability of a

---

*In a general sense, *pluralism* refers to the existence within a particular community of people of different social classes, occupations, religions, ethnic backgrounds, educations, values, and races. That is the sense in which the word is used here. In a somewhat more specific sense, *pluralism* refers to particular arrangements for sharing political power among the different groups that make up a society. Pluralism is discussed in detail in Chapter 6.

"Under other forms of government,
the people don't have the right to elect
people to appoint people to run the government."

Grin and Bear It, by George Lichty and Fred Wagner, courtesy of Field Newspaper Syndicate.

national majority to choose a President. And, of course, federal judges, because they would be nominated by the President and confirmed by the Senate, would be even more insulated from pressures from any united majority.

The Bill of Rights

As drafted, proposed, and ratified, the Constitution had no separate bill of rights to protect individual liberties from governmental encroachment. The body of the document contained some prohibitions against state and federal action; but, as we have seen, the framers had little faith in "parchment barriers" preventing abuses of power. Moreover, as Madison put it:

Wherever the real power in a Government lies, there is the danger of oppression. In our Government, the real power lies in the majority of the Community, and the invasion of private rights is *chiefly* to be apprehended . . . from acts in which the Government is the mere instrument of the major number of Constituents.[24]

Thus the framers thought that they had already effectively protected individual rights by retaining the states, impeding the ability of a majority to control government at the expense of a minority, establishing a government under law, restricting the authority of the new government to powers expressly delegated or reasonably implied, and, most important, by creating a network of overlapping and interlocking grants of authority so that each branch of government would have a vested interest in preventing the others from abusing power.

Despite such weighty arguments, many delegates to the state ratifying conventions had opposed the new Constitution because it did not include a bill of rights; and two states, North Carolina and Rhode Island, had not yet ratified the document when the First Congress of the United States assembled in 1789. Although no explicit bargain had been struck to amend the Constitution in exchange for ratification, Congress was, nevertheless, under heavy pressure to add a listing of fundamental rights.

Earlier, Madison had not opposed a bill of rights, but he thought it unnecessary. He admitted to Jefferson, who was still in Paris, that such an enumeration of rights might become part of the political culture and so serve as an internalized check both on what private citizens demanded and on what officials tried to do. But, he concluded, given the sort of system that the framers had constructed and the inherent difficulties in formulating language that would protect rights and permit action needed in emergencies, omission was not a serious defect.

In reply, Jefferson took up point by point a whole series of objections to a bill of rights and attempted to rebut each of them. The major thrust of his reasoning, however, was brief:

In the arguments in favor of a declaration of rights, you omit one which has great weight with me, the legal check which it puts into the hands of the judiciary. This is a body, which if rendered independent, and kept strictly to their own department, merits great confidence for their learning and integrity.[25]

These men, Jefferson claimed, would be able to resist popular impulses and restrict governmental power.

Wanting to calm fears of the new government, desirous of persuading North Carolina and Rhode Island to join the Union, and intellectually convinced by Jefferson, Madison took the lead in guiding through Congress the Bill of Rights, the first ten amendments to the Constitution. In justifying such action, he adapted Jefferson's reasoning and incorporated it into his own general theory of checking power against power:

If they [the Bill of Rights] are incorporated into the constitution, independent tribunals of justice will consider themselves in a peculiar manner the guardians of those rights; they will be an impenetrable bulwark against every assumption of power in the legislative or executive; they will be naturally led to resist every encroachment upon rights expressly stipulated for in the constitution by the declaration of rights.[26]

Watergate: A Case Study in Constitutional Checks

We have spoken of the mutual checks that federal officials have on each other, and how those interlocking powers are increased by linking the ambitions of officials of one institution—whether the Presidency, the Congress, or the judiciary—to their institution's authority. Let us now look at the crisis called Watergate, a set of events that revealed serious threats to American civil liberties, and see how the system responded.

The power of the Presidency grew enormously in the twentieth century, and with that growth eventually came both arrogance and corruption. The crisis began in Washington on June 17, 1972, when a guard in Watergate—a posh complex of apartments, stores, and offices along the Potomac River—caught five armed men carrying eavesdropping equipment breaking into the Democratic National Committee's headquarters. At the same time that the Department of Justice reluctantly began a superficial investigation, two young reporters from the *Washington Post,* Carl Bernstein and Bob Woodward,[27] began to ferret out what was behind the burglary. The path quickly led back to Richard Nixon's White House and the Committee to Reelect the President, or CREEP, as friends and foes had appropriately dubbed it.

Bernstein and Woodward were soon joined by a host of other journalists. Together they rapidly uncovered layers of scandal. In contrast, the trial of the burglars was extraordinarily unrevealing. When it was completed, the presiding judge, John J. Sirica, commented that he had never seen a prosecutor so afraid to ask questions that might prove his case. Indeed, Sirica claimed that testimony at the trial had been a mishmash of half-truths and perjury; only the guilt of the accused was clear. He provisionally sentenced them to long prison terms ranging up to forty years, but promised to review that decision if they cooperated with an investigating committee that the Senate had established to look into the whole affair.

The story that came out of the committee hearings, testimony at later trials, and documented news stories was a jumbled saga of corruption, personal aggrandizement, betrayals of constitutional oaths, and a parade of assorted felonies. Specifically, the Watergate burglary had been directed from the White House. Then after the arrests, aides of Nixon, certainly with his knowledge and possibly under his orders, had tried to bribe the defendants with offers of money and eventual executive

The Senate's Select Committee on Presidential Campaign Activities opens its investigation of the Watergate scandal in May 1973.

clemency* to deny any connection with the President and his party.

More generally, the stench led to a trail of shakedowns of corporate executives for contributions to Nixon's campaign funds. One or both of two ploys were common: threat of governmental prosecution, or promise of governmental favors. The amounts pledged ranged from ten thousand to several million dollars, sometimes carefully "laundered" with the help of CIA so that they could not be traced. In addition, White House aides, again with Nixon's knowledge, organized a special unit called the "plumbers" to commit burglaries that might produce evidence that could be used to blackmail if not prosecute potential opponents. Another set of Nixon's men engaged in such "dirty tricks" as forging the signatures of Democratic candidates to politically damaging letters and stirring up disturbances to disrupt Democratic meetings.

In the whole process, the Internal Revenue Service played a major part. It gave White House officials the supposedly confidential tax returns of Nixon's political foes so that presidential aides might learn

---

*As part of the power to pardon, Presidents have claimed authority to free prisoners who serve less than their sentences or to return all or part of the fines that courts impose on convicted persons. Thus Presidents have looked on the power to pardon as including authority to wipe out all or merely part of a sentence.

about their activities. In addition, IRS agents swarmed over private citizens thought to be political opponents of Nixon, harassed them, and tried to embarrass them with false charges of income tax evasion. At the same time, the IRS closed its official eyes to Nixon's fraudulently underpaying his own taxes by $476,000. Further investigations brought out that Nixon had used hundreds of thousands of dollars of public funds to make improvements on his private home in California and had allowed his wife to keep gifts from foreign governments that, under law, were the property of the United States.

All these activities were carried out with little fear of discovery, for the Attorney General, John Mitchell, was directing and coordinating many of the crimes. And his successor, Richard Kleindienst, was not a lion of virtue. At the President's order Kleindienst not only dropped an investigation of a corporation that had given Nixon money but lied before a Senate committee by denying that he had ever received such an order. Furthermore, for at least part of the time, the Acting Director of the Federal Bureau of Investigation helped White House aides cover their tracks by turning over to them incriminating evidence his agents discovered and by burning other documents.

These revelations came in steady streams over a period of more than two years. During that time, Nixon tried to quiet public opinion by reassuring the people that he had no knowledge of his assistants' crimes. He also attempted to calm legislators. They had been generally concerned about the growth of presidential power since much of that accretion had come at their expense. More particularly, they had been angered by Nixon's efforts to deny Congress a voice in American foreign policy in Vietnam, his impoundment of money that Congress had appropriated for projects of which he disapproved, and his frequent rejection of requests by congressional committees for information that executive agencies possessed. To appease Congress, Nixon released some of the impounded funds, provided the Senate's special investigating committee with some of the tapes that he had made of conversations in the White House, and agreed to the appointment of a special prosecutor to handle criminal cases growing out of Watergate and related scandals.

The first compromise came too late; the second did not provide enough information to satisfy legislators (and some critical parts of the tapes were erased, while transcripts of other parts were altered). The third compromise backfired when the first special prosecutor followed the trail of corruption into the White House. Fearing exposure, Nixon fired him, but in the face of public and congressional outrage had to agree to the appointment of another independent attorney. The new prosecutor moved cautiously ahead along the same road and eventually obtained indictments against most of Nixon's chief assistants. One grand jury even named the President himself as an "unindicted co-conspirator."

As evidence of Nixon's personal involvement built up, the House of

Representatives began in early 1974 a formal inquiry into the question of impeachment. Nixon again refused to comply with subpoenas* to produce tape recordings and other documents. But the material by then made public by the Senate's special committee, testimony at various trials, and documents leaked to journalists were building a convincing case against the President. The crushing blow came in July 1974 when the Supreme Court ruled that the President was obliged to give the special prosecutor tapes of White House conversations that were needed in a criminal trial to determine the guilt or innocence of the accused.[28] Reluctantly Nixon produced the tapes. His case immediately collapsed because those recordings of his own conversations showed that he had persistently participated in a series of felonies and had consistently lied about that participation.

With impeachment by the House and conviction by the Senate a foregone conclusion, Nixon hastily resigned. Gerald Ford, whom Nixon had chosen to serve as Vice President after Spiro Agnew had resigned following his plea of guilty to not paying income tax on his bribes, immediately succeeded to the Presidency. Among Ford's first acts was to pardon Nixon of all federal crimes that he had committed while President.

The point of this account is not that Richard Nixon was venal and corrupt. Nor is the point that justice was done, for surely that was only partly true. The real point is to illustrate the way in which the Madisonian system of checks operates. Journalists wanted to report the news and, protected by the First Amendment, had an opportunity to do so and to stir up public opinion and to alert Congress and the judiciary. Legislators had a vested interest in controlling the presidency. John Kennedy's use of presidential power had worried them; Lyndon Johnson's had irritated them, Nixon's had infuriated them. In the arrogance of his power, Nixon thought he had nothing to fear, neither from Congress nor that mystic concept "the law." But neither Congress nor the courts are powerless, and when journalists began to produce weighty evidence of Nixon's criminal activity, legislators took advantage of the opportunity to strike back at the presidency and regain some of their lost power. Most senators and representatives did not act with great foresight, imagination, or even, at the beginning, courage. But during those two years, the interest of Congress in curbing the presidency gave legislators an institutional motive to pursue the truth. In the end,

---

*A *subpoena* (literally "under penalty") is an order, usually from a judicial official, directing a person to appear in court to offer testimony and/or to make certain documents available for inspection by parties to a lawsuit. Congress has given its committees authority to issue such orders. They are usually enforced through the judicial process. That is, the Department of Justice brings a normal criminal action against a person who defies a subpoena issued by a congressional committee. The charge is "contempt of Congress." Historically, however, Congress has claimed—but rarely used—authority to jail individuals it finds in contempt. If the offender is a federal officer, impeachment provides a third avenue of enforcement.

surprise at what they and the special prosecutor found gave them the courage to unlimber their ultimate weapon against a President—impeachment.

What one sees here is first of all that the affair was handled peacefully. There was no effort by any of the participants to use military force to achieve their goals. Although during the last few days before the resignation there was some fear among Nixon's closest advisers that he might try to use the army to set up a military government, he never attempted such a tactic.

Second, the slowness with which the system operates is evident. Nixon stayed in the White House for more than sixty-eight months, was re-elected four and a half months after the Watergate burglary, and served for more than two years after that event.

Third, one sees the importance of a free press. Jefferson, more sensitive to the significance of this than Madison, persuaded Madison at least enough to obtain the First Amendment. Newspapers provided not only the first real evidence of presidential criminality but also kept public attention focused on those crimes and continually gave legislators the courage to stand up and fight.

Fourth, one sees the results of pitting of ambition against ambition. A President guilty of many of Nixon's crimes but not so committed to dominating Congress might have eased his way out of the crisis. But in angering Congress before the Watergate burglary and in continuing afterward to treat Congress with contempt, Nixon gave legislators ample institutional reason to counterattack. In short, there was a group that had the power to check a President and the motive to do so as well.

The Constitutional System and the Need for Energetic Government

With its broad (critics said "sweeping") grants of power to the national government, the new Constitution inspired confidence both within the country and abroad that the United States could survive as a politically stable nation. Over the decades since 1787, the flexible and general (critics said "vague") nature of those broad constitutional clauses have allowed congressmen, Presidents, and judges to adapt grants of power in ways that enabled them to cope with most crises. During those years, the democratic element in the American system has grown in size and strength, as popular participation has expanded from white, male property owners, to white males, to whites, and finally to all citizens having a right not only to cast a vote for members of the House of Representatives but also for senators and, although still not directly, for the President as well.

If American government now includes more democracy than the framers would have included under "free government," the general wording of constitutional clauses has also allowed judges to protect, often in imaginative ways, constitutional rights against equally imaginative efforts at subversion. Perhaps most significantly, an executive order (the Emancipation Proclamation) and the Thirteenth Amendment extended the democratic notion of equality and the constitutional objective of individual liberty across racial lines.

Successes and Failures of the System

The framers did not believe they were constructing a utopia, nor did they succeed in doing so. As we have already indicated and will continue to point out, the warts on the American political system—for example, long tolerance of slavery—are large and sometimes ugly; moreover, as some old warts have fallen off new ones have grown. Yet, on the whole, the framers built well. The greatest success of the Madisonian system of federalism, popular elections, and interlocking power shared by separate institutions has been that the United States has generally had both *popular participation* and *limited government*. While many instances of serious oppression by federal officials have occurred, those instances, when compared with cases in similar spans of history in other nations, have been relatively few. To the extent that the framers tried to construct an enduring constitutional system that would increase the chances of prosperity, they also succeeded quite well. As Chapter 2 pointed out, Americans have historically been a "people of plenty," in large part because of natural resources, but also in part because of relative political stability.

On the other hand, the great weakness of the Madisonian system is that it makes *positive* action by the federal government always difficult and often impossible. And frequently positive federal action has been necessary to remove the tyranny of one citizen over others or of state officials over their own citizens. Freeing the slaves, protecting civil rights of minorities, guarding the public against the greed of giant monopolies in industry and labor, providing adequate medical care for the poor and aged, reversing the course of large-scale economic recessions or depressions—all these have required positive federal action. And that action has come slowly, even haltingly.

In short, the Madisonian system of sharing and checking power tends to foster the interests of people who are content with the status quo. And that system is hard on those who are political newcomers: in past generations, Indians, slaves and immigrants from Europe and Asia; more recently, blacks, Chicanos, and Puerto Ricans, the poor generally, and, somewhat out of the pattern, those who seek to conserve a portion of the country's resources for future generations.

Generally speaking, the Madisonian system can accommodate positive federal action in only three or four situations. First, where matters are not controversial, Congress, the President, and the Supreme

Court routinely agree. Little dispute, for instance, arises about paying salaries to civil servants or interest on the national debt, although there may be great controversy about the proper size of the national debt or the level of salaries. Second, in the opening stages of great national emergencies, especially those involving foreign affairs, Congress and the President, at least, tend to work closely together, with Congress usually deferring to presidential wisdom. As wars or other crises stretch out, however, presidential wisdom typically tarnishes, and legislators begin to reassert independent judgment.

Third, and more normal, are situations in which opposing leaders — and usually the President and his agents come off slightly the better in this game — can arrange a compromise that allows limited positive action in exchange for benefits to those who oppose such action. A fourth situation — perhaps really a variant of the second or third — may occur when an energetic and skillful President is able to mobilize patronage, patriotism, and public opinion to persuade congressmen to accept sweeping new policies. Perhaps the most striking example is Lyndon B. Johnson's astute manipulation of the public mood of sorrow and guilt after the assassination of John F. Kennedy to push Congress to adopt several meaningful civil rights statutes and to begin a bold "war on poverty."

Nevertheless, in its political orientation the Madisonian constitutional system is more negative than positive. "The purpose of the Constitution and the Bill of Rights," Justice William O. Douglas wrote for the Supreme Court, "unlike more recent models promoting a welfare state, was to take government off the backs of people."[29] The American Constitution, the first successful marriage of democracy and constitutionalism, has also been the most enduring union. But the fundamental difficulty is that this generation has entered an age in which positive federal action has become crucial. Whether the Madisonian Constitution can cope with current crises — or whether current political leaders possess sufficient skills to adapt that Constitution — remains an open question, one, however, that each generation of Americans has, from its own special perspective, asked.

Summary

This chapter has explored the concepts of constitutionalism and democracy and the way in which the framers of the American Constitution boldly tried to blend the two into a living political system. We have also taken a quick overview of how the national government functions under that system, leaving to the following chapter the task of examining federal-state relations, and to the rest of the book the work of filling in the skeleton of constitutional structure with the flesh and muscle of political processes.

Selected Bibliography

BAILYN, BERNARD, *Ideological Origins of the American Revolution* (Cambridge, Mass.: Harvard University Press, 1967). Analyzes the relationship between political thought in America during the Revolutionary period and European traditions, particularly libertarian ones.

BEARD, CHARLES A., *An Economic Interpretation of the Constitution* (New York: Crowell-Collier and Macmillan Company, Inc., 1913). Highly influential for more than half a century, this famous book argued the case that the Founding Fathers were strongly motivated by their own economic interests in drafting the Constitution.

BEITZINGER, A. J., *A History of American Political Thought* (New York: Dodd, Mead & Company, 1972). An excellent analysis of the origins and development of American political ideas.

BERNSTEIN, CARL, and BOB WOODWARD, *All the President's Men* (New York: Simon and Schuster, 1974). The account by two reporters of how they cracked the mystery of Watergate.

BOWEN, CATHERINE DRINKER, *Miracle at Philadelphia* (Boston: Little, Brown and Company, 1966). One of several accounts of the Philadelphia convention published in the last decade or two for the general reader.

BROWN, ROBERT E., *Charles Beard and the Constitution: A Critical Analysis of "An Economic Interpretation of the Constitution"* (Princeton, N.J.: Princeton University Press, 1956). With Forrest McDonald and Staughton Lynd, Brown has been one of the leading critics of Beard's views of the Philadelphia convention.

CORWIN, EDWARD S., *The Constitution and What It Means Today* (Harold W. Chase and Craig Ducat, eds.), 13th rev. ed. (Princeton, N.J.: Princeton University Press, 1973). A useful and authoritative analysis of the Constitution section by section and clause by clause, done briefly and concisely. (Paperback)

ELLIOT, JONATHAN, *The Debates in the Several State Conventions on the Adoption of the Federal Constitution* (Philadelphia: J. B. Lippincott Company, 1888). The standard source for the debates in the state conventions that ratified the federal Constitution.

FARRAND, MAX, *The Framing of the Constitution* (New Haven, Conn.: Yale University Press, 1913). One of the first popular accounts of the Philadelphia convention.

————, ed., *The Records of the Federal Convention of 1787* (4 vols.; New Haven, Conn.: Yale University Press, 1911, rev. ed., 1937). A compilation of documentary sources bearing on the work of the Philadelphia convention.

THE FEDERALIST, the title given to the collection of newspaper articles written by Alexander Hamilton, John Jay, and James Madison in support of the proposed constitution during the debates on ratification. Available in many editions; among the most useful is that by Benjamin F. Wright (Cambridge, Mass.: The Belknap Press of Harvard University Press, 1961).

FRIEDRICH, CARL J., *Constitutional Government and Democracy,* 4th ed. (Waltham, Mass.: Blaisdell Publishing Company, 1968). By now a classic examination of constitutionalism and constitutional systems by a leading scholar and teacher in this field.

GARVEY, GERALD, *Constitutional Bricolage* (Princeton, N.J.: Princeton University Press, 1971). An interesting reexamination of the process of American constitutional development.

JAWORSKI, LEON, *The Right and the Power: The Prosecution of Watergate* (New York: Thomas Y. Crowell, 1976). The second special prosecutor's inside story of his investigations and decisions to prosecute members of Nixon's staff.

JENSEN, MERRILL, *The Articles of Confederation* (Madison, Wis.: University of Wisconsin Press, 1940). An analysis of the drafting of the Articles and the system thereby established.

KELLEY, ALFRED H., AND WINFRED A. HARBISON, *The American Constitution: Its Origins and Development,* 5th ed. (New York: W. W. Norton Company, Inc., 1976). One of a number of excellent histories of constitutional development from colonial beginnings to the present.

LYND, STAUGHTON, *Class Conflict, Slavery, and the United States Constitution* (Indianapolis: Bobbs-Merrill Co., Inc., 1968). A provocative "radical" view of social and economic factors that shaped decisions during the revolutionary and constitutional periods.

MASON, ALPHEUS THOMAS, ed., *Free Government in the Making,* 3d ed. (New York: Oxford University Press, 1972). A superb collection of materials chronicling the development of American constitutional and political thought.

————, *The States Rights Debate: Antifederalism and the Constitution,* 2d ed. (Englewood Cliffs, N.J.: Prentice-Hall, Inc., 1976). A stimulating series of brief essays examining the "ambiguous interplay" of the polemics that influenced the formation of the Constitution.

———— and GERALD GARVEY, eds., *American Constitutional History: Essays by Edward S. Corwin* (New York: Harper & Row, Publishers, 1964). A collection of articles by the greatest of American constitutional historians.

MCCLOSKEY, ROBERT G., *The American Supreme Court* (Chicago: University of Chicago Press, 1960). A brief but insightful history of the Supreme Court as well as of American constitutional development.

MCDONALD, FORREST, *We the People: The Economic Origins of the Constitution* (Chicago: University of Chicago Press, 1958). One of the leading critiques of Beard's thesis concerning the economic motivations of the framers of the Constitution.

MCILWAIN, CHARLES H., *Constitutionalism, Ancient and Modern,* rev. ed. (Ithaca, N.Y.: Cornell University Press, 1947). A collection of essays by an American scholar whose studies of the history of political thought and of constitutional government are now read as "classics."

PRITCHETT, C. HERMAN, *The American Constitution,* 3d ed. (New York: McGraw-Hill Book Company, 1976). A distinguished analysis of current constitutional law.

ROSSITER, CLINTON L., *Seedtime of the Republic* (New York: Harcourt Brace Jovanovich, 1953). An excellent analysis of the intellectual ferment and political ideas current during the Colonial and Revolutionary periods.

WOOD, GORDON S., *The Creation of the American Republic, 1776–1787* (New York: W. W. Norton & Company, Inc., 1972). A thoughtful and perceptive study of the development of American political ideas from the Declaration of Independence to the framing of the Constitution.

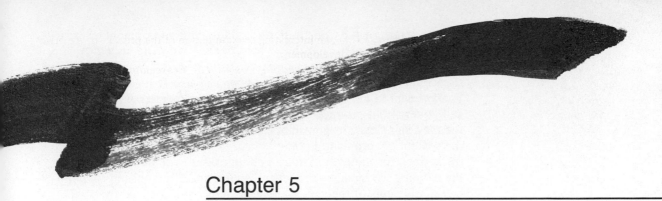

Chapter 5

The Nation and the States

THE FRAMERS OF the Constitution sought to limit government by creating a national government that would coexist with the states. At the same time that they wanted a set of strong national political institutions, they feared highly centralized power. These fears and the strong commitment of most Americans in the late eighteenth century to local self-government produced political arrangements in which the states retained significant responsibilities. By forging a partnership between the federal government and the states, the Constitution provided the framework for the evolution of a complex set of relationships among the national government, the several states, and the thousands of political subdivisions of the states—relationships characterized by conflict, cooperation, and, most important, constant change.

Federalism and the Constitution

Federalism refers to a political system that divides power on the basis of area—a national government and a series of local, state, or regional governments. Under a federal system, constituent units are guaranteed certain powers, and their consent is usually required for alterations in the basic arrangement. Federalism may be contrasted with a *unitary* or *centralized government,* such as that of Great Britain, in which local units are created by and subject to the control of the central government.

Every federal system reflects a compromise between concentration of power at the center and preservation of autonomy within the constituent units. To endure in the modern world, such a system must be able to adjust to change because no nation's social, economic, and political conditions—and thus problems—remain constant. In the United States, the bargain between nation and state was struck in an isolated, thinly populated, agrarian society. It has survived civil war, territorial expansion across a continent and beyond, a fifty-fold increase in population, development of an industrial economy and an urban society, global wars, and consequent multiplication of demands on all governmental institutions. In the process, American federalism has been transformed from a relatively simple set of constitutionally prescribed relationships between nation and state into a complex mosaic of interactions among public agencies and private associations at the national, state, regional, metropolitan, county, municipal, and neighborhood levels.

A Strong National Government

As we saw in Chapter 4, the Constitution created a central government that was much stronger than had existed under the Articles of Confederation. Since 1788 the national government has had authority to rule the people directly, not merely by recommendations to the states as was the case under the Articles. Moreover, the Preamble of the Constitution explicitly says that the national government draws its authority from "the people of the United States," not from the several states as separate political entities. The Constitution also denies the states a role in formulating foreign policy and forbids them to issue paper money, tax imported or exported goods except to the extent necessary to pay the cost of inspecting them, invalidate contracts, grant titles of nobility, enact bills of attainder, or pass ex post facto laws.

In addition, Article VI of the Constitution clearly announced a doctrine of national supremacy:

This Constitution, and the laws of the United States which shall be made in pursuance thereof; and all treaties made under the authority of the United States, shall be the supreme law of the land; and the judges in every State shall be bound thereby, any thing in the Constitution or laws of any State to the contrary notwithstanding.

Clearly, this clause renders invalid any effort by a state to infringe on the Constitution or any federal statute or treaty that lies within the authority of the national government to enact. Furthermore, it provides that in any area of public policy where both the national and state governments may legitimately be active — control of commerce, for example — the national law shall supersede inconsistent state law or even, the courts have ruled, a compatible state statute that may pose problems of different administrative interpretations.[1] In addition, state authority may have to give way completely before national authority in certain vital areas like national security, where Congress may claim a "dominant interest" and has woven a pervasive scheme of public policy for the nation.

To balance these provisions of the Constitution, the Tenth Amendment declared that all powers not delegated to the federal government were reserved to the states or the people. A hasty reading of this amendment might lead to the view that there are two watertight compartments of authority: the powers of the federal government as enumerated in the Constitution and a vast residue of state power. Unhappily for those who like simple political structures, no such clear-cut division of power exists.

While the Tenth Amendment serves as a constitutional reassurance of the viability of the states, it does not restrict national authority to those functions specifically listed in the Constitution. The amendment does not say that the powers not *expressly* delegated (that is, not specifically delegated in clear terms) are reserved to the states, only those "not delegated." Several times during the debate in Congress on this amendment, proponents of states' rights tried to insert the word "expressly," but each time they were voted down.

These matters are closely related to the provision of Article I, sec. 8, the "necessary and proper" clause, with its sweeping grant of implied power to the national government:

The Congress shall have power . . . to make all laws which shall be necessary and proper for carrying into execution the foregoing powers, and all other powers vested by this Constitution in the government of the United States, or in any department or officer thereof.

In 1819, in *McCulloch v. Maryland,* the Supreme Court spelled out the implications of the doctrine of implied powers.[2] In question was the constitutionality of Congress' establishment of the Bank of the United States. No clause of the Constitution mentioned congressional authority to charter banks or other corporations. But speaking for a unanimous Court, Chief Justice John Marshall held that, when coupled with the "necessary and proper" clause, the expressly delegated powers of Congress to borrow and coin money, to collect taxes, to regulate commerce, to raise armies, and to wage war implied that Congress also had authority to create institutions that would enable it to carry out its work. Marshall carefully rejected closely limiting the power of Congress to choose whatever means legislators thought most convenient:

we think the sound construction of the constitution must allow to the national legislature that discretion, with respect to the means by which the powers it confers are to be carried into execution, which will enable that body to perform the high duties assigned to it, in the manner most beneficial to the people. Let the end be legitimate, let it be within the scope of the constitution, and all means which are appropriate, which are plainly adapted to that end, which are not prohibited, but consist with the letter and spirit of the constitution, are constitutional.

The concept of *implied powers in the federal government* is not easy to reconcile with a doctrine of *reserved state powers.* Once it is conceded that the national government has implied as well as expressed powers, the exact limits of national authority become difficult to fix. As a result, the question of implied powers has been a constant source of controversy, conflict, and compromise among the parties to the American federal partnership.

Guarantees to the States

The Constitution protects the physical integrity of the states by forbidding the federal government to change a state's boundary without that state's consent. The Constitution also imposes some positive obligations on the federal government: it must guarantee the states "a republican form of government," guard them against invasion, and, at request of a state's legislature or governor, protect against domestic violence.

The guarantee of a republican form of government has had little impact on federal-state relations because the Supreme Court has said that enforcement of this clause belongs to Congress and the President, and

all three branches of the federal government have been extremely —
and understandably — reluctant to enter that briar patch.[3]

More controversial has been the obligation to protect a state against
domestic violence. In general, the President has waited for a request
from state authorities before acting. On occasion, however, he has
gone ahead without any such request and has defended his action by
asserting that enforcement of federal laws required intervention by
federal troops. For example, against the wishes of Governor John P.
Altgeld of Illinois, President Grover Cleveland sent an army regiment
to Chicago in 1894 during a railroad strike, claiming that this action
was necessary to protect interstate commerce and to keep the mails
moving.[4]

The practical effect of the federal guarantee of territorial integrity
has been to freeze state boundaries. Without the consent of state government, there is no way to satisfy those who would separate northern
and southern California or have New York City secede from New
York State. Not since 1820 when Maine was detached from Massachusetts as part of the Missouri Compromise has a state legislature
actually consented to a revision of its boundaries. At the opening of the
Civil War, when Virginia seceded from the Union, a group of western
counties refused to join the Confederacy and formed the state of West
Virginia. After the war, with Union troops in command, Virginia had
no alternative to "consenting."

Admitting New States

Awareness of the country's vast potential for further growth led the
framers of the Constitution to grant Congress virtually unrestricted
power to admit new states to the Union. Vermont and Kentucky came
in as the fourteenth and fifteenth states in 1791 and 1792. Alaska and
Hawaii became the forty-ninth and fiftieth states in 1958 and 1959.
There was early controversy over whether new states should have a
status secondary to the original thirteen, but a majority in Congress
opted for full equality.

Congress is under no legal obligation to admit a new state in any giv-
en situation. Generally, Congress has required local experience with
self-government (even if limited by federal control), support for statehood from a majority of the electorate of the proposed state, and sufficient population and resources to support state government and pay a
share of federal taxes.

Few territories, however, ever acquired statehood merely by meeting these conditions. Long after Alaska and Hawaii had met the traditional requirements, their admission was blocked in Congress. Because
both territories were noncontiguous to the existing states, many Congressmen felt a dangerous precedent would be established by breaking
the geographical solidarity of the country. Opposition also came from
southerners who believed that the congressmen from Alaska and

Hawaii would support civil rights legislation. Partisan considerations also played a role, since Republicans feared that Alaska would send Democratic members to Congress, and Democrats objected to Hawaii for the opposite reason. Not until 1958 did the supporters of Alaskan statehood prevail in Congress. With Alaska's admission, it proved easy a year later to admit Hawaii.

For three quarters of a century following adoption of the Constitution there was much argument as to whether states might withdraw from the Union. This issue was settled on the battlefields of the Civil War. In 1869 the Supreme Court gave legal approval to what had been already determined by force of arms when it declared that the "Constitution, in all of its provisions, looks to an indestructible union, composed of indestructible states."[5]

Interstate Obligations

In their relations with each other, the states are directed by the Constitution: (1) to give full faith and credit to each other's official acts; (2) to extend the same privileges and immunities to citizens from other states that they extend to their own citizens; and (3) to deliver up fugitives from justice at the demand of the executive authority of the states in which the crimes occurred.

The *full faith and credit* provision has been subjected to a great deal of intricate judicial interpretation. For example, the Supreme Court has held that the clause requires each state to recognize private contracts made under the laws of other states. Thus, a contract made in Ohio for the sale of land can be enforced in the courts of Texas. Similarly, marriages performed or granted under the laws of one state are valid in all other states. Divorce, however, raises more complicated problems, and judges have ruled that a state may refuse to recognize a divorce granted by another state.

The *privileges and immunities* guarantee means generally that a state must extend to citizens from other states the rights to acquire and hold property, make contracts, engage in business, and sue and be sued, on the same basis as its own citizens. But a state need not follow the literal meaning of the guarantee in all respects. It may, for example, deny to citizens of other states the "privilege" granted its own citizens to attend its university. On the other hand, a state cannot deny out-of-staters a privilege like use of its highways. Custom and common sense have had a good deal to do with drawing the line between privileges that must be granted and those that can be restricted. The same is true of the surrender of criminals. Although the obligation is prescribed in the Constitution in binding language, in practice state officials have occasionally refused to surrender fugitives at the request of other states. Federal judges have consistently refused to order state authorities to meet this obligation imposed by the Constitution.

Table 5–1
Local governments, 1972

Counties	3,044
Municipalities	18,517
Townships	16,991
Special districts	23,885
School districts	15,781
Total	78,218

The Place of Local Government

The Constitution deals only with relations between the national government and the states. It makes no specific reference to local units of government—counties, cities, school districts, townships, and the like. From the constitutional point of view, these 78,000 units are all state subdivisions, created by the states and responsible to them. As such, local governments are subject to all restrictions and prohibitions that the Constitution places on states. Their purposes, powers, and status, however, are determined by the states, except that a state cannot grant to a subdivision authority or functions that it does not itself possess.

National Power and States' Rights

Perhaps the most important feature of the Constitution with respect to federalism has been its flexibility concerning boundaries of power between the national government and state and local governments. This flexibility has permitted national power to expand to respond to social, economic, technological, territorial, and political changes. It also has facilitated innovation and adjustment in intergovernmental relations. Because of the fundamental issues involved, the evolution of the federal partnership has generated persistent conflict throughout American history between those favoring a stronger national government and those dedicated to preserving states' rights.

Growth of National Power

Underlying the national government's enormous expansion of activities has been the development of a modern industrial society with a national economy, nationwide networks of transportation and communications, and an increasingly interdependent and urbanized population. With these developments, more and more problems have become national in scope and impact and have generated demands for national action. State and local governments can deal with most national economic and social problems only in a piecemeal fashion. No state could control giant multinational corporations like Standard Oil or Du Pont or a national union like the AFL-CIO. The federal government, on the other hand, has the authority — though not always the capacity — to treat problems comprehensively. For example, in a period of widespread unemployment, the federal government can analyze the causes of unemployment without regard to states' political boundaries. It can attempt to eliminate gross differences among the states with regard to health, welfare, income levels, and economic development. Again, it can insist that there are certain essential standards of individual freedom, civil rights, and racial equality that must be accepted and maintained throughout the nation.

Development of national power has also produced national organizations — business, labor, farm, civil rights, and other groups — that naturally focus their political energies on the federal government. Concentrating on Washington means considerable economy of effort for organized interests, since there is only one Congress or Department of Labor compared with fifty state legislatures or state labor agencies. The fact that Congress and many federal agencies often have been more responsive to group demands than states and localities has reinforced the desire of many organized interests to achieve influence in Washington.

One major reason for the national government's greater responsiveness is the superiority of its financial resources. Throughout much of the nineteenth century, the expansion of federal activities was paid for by proceeds from tariffs and sales of the public lands, as well as through transfers of public lands to state and local units. During the past forty years, the growth of national government has rested on its formidable powers to raise money through income taxes and borrowing. Federal taxes also have the political advantage of nationwide application, which means they do not place the taxing unit at a competitive disadvantage as state and local taxes frequently do.

Federal involvement also has been spurred by the inability or unwillingness of states and localities to respond effectively to widespread demands for governmental action. Failure of most states to regulate effectively the industrial combines of the late nineteenth century led to the expansion of national controls over business during the progressive era (1885–1915). The devastating impact of the Great Depression of the 1930s on state and local fiscal capabilities created a governmental vacuum that was filled by the far-reaching innovations of the New Deal. Many of the newer federal programs have resulted from pressures from the cities, which, before the Supreme Court's reapportionment decisions of the 1960s, were systematically shortchanged by state legislatures dominated by rural interests.[6] A final stimulus to national action has been the ineffectiveness of many state and local governments. Given these financial, political, and administrative weaknesses, citizens and groups who want government to "do something" often turn to the national government for action.

States' Rights and Decentralization

"Government close to the people" has long been the rallying cry of those opposed to enlarging the role of the federal government. Defenders of states' rights see state and local officials as nearer and more responsive to the electorate than federal officials and thus better able to adapt governmental action to diverse local needs. From this perspective, diffusion of political power among state and local governments seems essential to democracy. A decentralized political system, its advocates argue, prevents national control by one party or group and affords minorities opportunities to control some of the system's many components. In addition, the political tasks of the national government in some respects are made more manageable by a decentralized system that provides many governmental units empowered to take official actions and resolve conflicts. Conflict may be moderated and experimentation encouraged because the existence of many relatively autonomous centers of power permits localities to adopt or avoid policies that do not command a national majority. Moreover, some measure of local self-government is a practical necessity in a country with the territorial expanse of the United States.

Although allocations of power and responsibility among the various units of the federal system have been in constant flux, it is difficult to conceive of any feasible arrangement under which the national government could assume direction of all the tasks now discharged independently by states, counties, and municipalities. Another benefit of the decentralization of American government is the wide variety of opportunities for active political participation offered by state and local governments. Almost half a million Americans fill state and local elective posts on school boards, city councils, and township committees and in state legislatures, while thousands more serve on planning boards, parking authorities, and advisory bodies of all sorts.

One may ask, however, whether state and local governments are really closer to the people than the federal government is. A larger proportion of voters participate in national than in state or local elections. News broadcasts, magazines, and newspapers devote more attention to national affairs than to state or local politics. Survey research indicates that the average citizen tends to be better informed on national issues than on issues contested at the state capitol or in city hall. Moreover, the decentralized administration of many national responsibilities means that citizens often have more frequent contact with federal officials in such agencies as the Post Office, Social Security Administration, Internal Revenue Service, or Department of Agriculture than with state and local officials.

Equally questionable is the assumption that small size automatically

Figure 5.1
Ages of Consent
in the United States, 1974

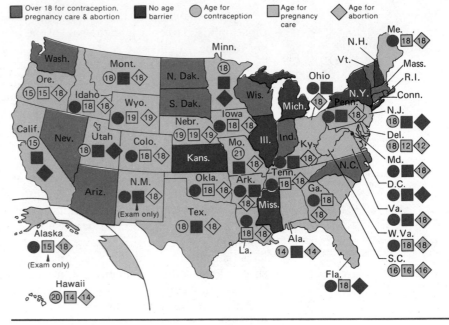

Variations in public policy among the states are an inevitable consequence of federalism. A good example is provided by the differences in the ages of consent required by states for individuals to obtain legally contraceptives, abortions, or publicly-supported pregnancy care. One of these variations, however, ended in 1976 when the U.S. Supreme Court held that parental consent was not needed to obtain an abortion *(Planned Parenthood v. Danforth).*

Source: *Time Magazine,* Nov. 25, 1974

promotes responsiveness, protection of minority rights, or democratic government. States and cities that are small have not been noticeably more responsive to citizens' demands than larger ones or than the federal government.

Moreover, minorities whose interests have been enhanced by decentralization frequently have used their influence to frustrate rather than to advance democracy and the general welfare. As one study of federalism emphasizes: "The main beneficiary [of federalism] throughout American history has been the Southern whites, who have been given the freedom to oppress Negroes, first as slaves and later as a depressed caste."[7] In general, the cause of states' rights has usually enlisted the staunchest defenders of the status quo. These interests have sought to minimize governmental activity by lodging responsibilities in state capitals where prospects of inaction were usually high, in part because their influence was greater than that of national majorities.

To be sure, the federal system does provide opportunities for those units which can muster the resources and the political support to innovate and expand. Wisconsin pioneered in developing unemployment compensation. California led the nation in evolving a superb and costly system of higher education in which some form of advanced training is available to every high-school graduate. New York City extended effective protection to a wide range of civil rights far in advance of most jurisdictions. But less enterprising or poorer states and localities have lagged far behind their more dynamic neighbors. Competition between states also limits experimentation. Policymakers in a state may hesitate to embark on costly social experiments that will raise taxes because they fear that businesses will move away to a state with lower taxes. Federal leadership, for example, was necessary to develop an adequate social security system. Furthermore, some experiments are beyond the fiscal resources of most state governments, or they involve problems too far-flung to be resolved by individual states or even adjoining, cooperating states.

Decentralization, then, involves costs as well as benefits. Government in the state capitals and at the grass roots abounds in anachronisms, ineffectiveness, and corruption. Perhaps the most serious weaknesses are the differences that result from the dependence of state and local services on taxable resources located within their boundaries. The cost and quality of education, availability of public health care, level of welfare and employment assistance, and burdens of taxes for every American are determined to a considerable degree by where he or she happens to live. These differences in services and taxes, particularly at the local level, are heightened by forces of urban growth and change that have widened disparities between metropolitan and rural areas, between city and suburb, and among suburbs.

The Zero-Sum Fallacy

A favorite image of the champions of states' rights pictures states and localities as shriveling appendages of an all-powerful national government manned by bureaucrats who seek to dominate every phase of public life. To support this contention, candidates on the stump and conservative political commentators point to the enormous growth in the activities and domestic expenditures of the federal government. Then they conclude that Washington's gains have been at the expense of the states and their subdivisions. This approach conceives of federalism as a "zero-sum" game, in which increased national power automatically means reduced state and local authority. The zero-sum approach, however, ignores the fact that governmental activity has been expanding at *all* levels.

Today, state and local governments are spending more money, employing more people, and engaging in more functions than ever before. In fact, state and local government is one of the fastest growing sectors of the American economy. Between 1950 and 1973, state and local expenditures increased 732 percent. During the same period, the gross national product rose only 455 percent. In 1973, states and localities spent $205 billion, compared with $168 billion spent by the national government for domestic purposes. Almost 12 million people worked

Figure 5.2
Government Employment, 1930–1975

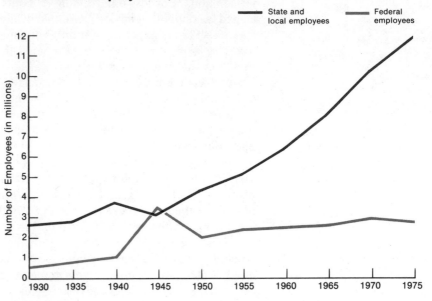

Source: U.S. Bureau of the Census

for state and local government in 1974, which was more than four times the number of federal civilian employees.

Equally important, state and local governments play a primary role in most of the areas of governmental activity that have the greatest bearing on the quality of individual and community life. Their activities have a direct, substantial, and often intimate impact on individuals. As parents, citizens are concerned about how the state and the community foster the health, welfare, and education of children; they are affected by municipal zoning and planning, by housing or slum-clearance programs, by fire and police protection, by collection of garbage, by recreational opportunities. If they live in a large city, they may ride to and from work on transportation owned and operated by the local government. If they live in the country, absence of a public water supply or a sewage-disposal system may make them drill wells or install septic tanks.

Federal Aid

Federal assistance provides an increasingly important source of funds for state and local government, making the superior resources of the national government available for financing locally administered services. A *grant-in-aid* is a sum of money derived from a tax levied and collected by a higher level of government for expenditure and administration by a lower level of government in accordance with certain standards or requirements.

Through grants, the federal government has often been able to advance national priorities without assuming full responsibility for functions within the traditional sphere of state and local jurisdictions. In the process, Washington has provided the states and their subdivisions with a substantial portion of the resources needed to tackle some of their most pressing problems. Federal aid has stimulated new state and local activity in a wide range of programs. Because recipients must meet federal standards, grant programs have raised the level of competence and professional skill of a substantial number of state and local employees. Federal grants have also redistributed wealth from prosperous to less prosperous areas, thus permitting higher standards of governmental service and performance to be set and implemented for the nation as a whole. Finally, development of the grant mechanism has moderated demands for more drastic forms of centralization that would clearly diminish the state and local role in the federal partnership.

Proliferation of Categorical Grants

Between 1955 and 1975, federal grants to state and local governments increased from $3 billion to over $47 billion. Equally dramatic was the increase in the number of federal programs. The Eighty-ninth Congress (1965–1966) alone enacted sixty-seven new programs, twenty-one dealing with health, seventeen with education, and others concerning development of resources, economic development, urban problems, and manpower. During the 1970s, federal assistance was available to states and localities from more than 500 programs, administered by over 150 bureaus and offices in a score of federal departments and agencies.

Paralleling the expansion of federal grant programs has been a vast increase in the number of state and local recipients of assistance. In response to federal requirements, states have created scores of regional comprehensive health planning agencies under the Partnership for Health Act and hundreds of regional law enforcement districts under the Safe Streets Act. Over 400 metropolitan and regional agencies have been established to comply with federal planning and coordinating requirements in programs affecting urban, community, and regional development. Federal aid has also been extended to nongovernmental groups, professional associations, and private businesses. In the War against Poverty, federal funds supported programs administered by community action agencies, often established outside regular governmental channels and administered by private boards of directors. Under Medicare, the federal government has in effect contracted with private insurance companies to handle claims of persons over six-

Figure 5.3
Federal Aid to State and Local Governments

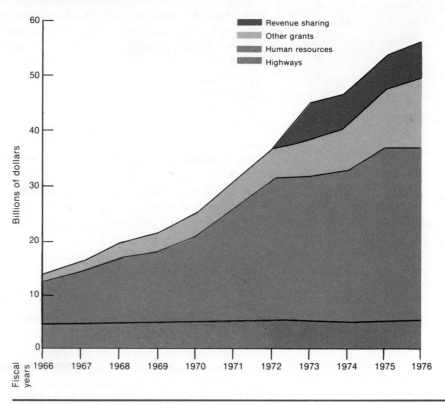

Source: *Office of Management and Budget*

ty-five and with professional associations to determine the eligibility of hospitals and nursing homes for participation in the program.

Until 1972, almost all federal assistance was provided in the form of *categorical grants,* that is, grants are made for specific purposes, such as constructing hospitals, providing school lunches, or financing public housing. Typically, categorical grants involve federal requirements or conditions. In addition to using the funds for the specific purposes of the particular program, the state or locality receiving federal aid must comply with a variety of program, performance, materials, administrative, and personnel standards. Most categorical grants also require that a proportion of the federal money be matched by the recipient, with the exact matching provisions varying from program to program. For interstate highways, the state share is 10 percent, for example, and for acquisition of open space, the matching requirement is 50 percent.

Development of federal assistance has brought mounting criticism of categorical grant programs. A major concern has been that conditions—or "strings"—attached to federal grants will undermine the independence of state and local governments. Federal grants, critics argue, inevitably shift control to Washington. At the same time, requirements for matching funds cause state and local budgets to reflect federal objectives rather than state or local priorities.

Complexity and proliferation of programs have also caused serious problems in administering categorical grants. At the state and local level, many agencies lack the political skills and organizational capabilities needed to master the esoteric art of "grantsmanship," which is loaded with complicated procedures and requirements. At the federal level, programs frequently overlap. Water and sewer grants, for example, are available from the Departments of Agriculture, Commerce, Interior, and Housing and Urban Development, as well as through the Appalachian Regional Commission. Coordination among agencies and programs is often weak, and interagency conflict common. Moreover, administration of many grant programs has been highly centralized in Washington. As a result, inflexibility, long delays in processing applications, and failure to adapt federal standards and guidelines to local conditions have been frequent.

State and local budget making has also been complicated by lack of any assurance that federal grants will be forthcoming. Every year, availability of federal aid depends on two uncertain processes—congressional appropriations and the approval of funding agencies like the Department of Health, Education and Welfare or the Department of Housing and Urban Development.

Another major concern has been the focus of most categorical grants on rather narrow objectives, such as a particular kind of housing or training program. Federal conditions and restrictions often prevent development of programs adapted to particular state or local circumstances. Even more important as pressures mount on state and local budgets, federal aid sometimes fails to provide funds for many public needs not covered by particular categorical programs. As more and more state and local officials came to share these concerns in the 1960s, support grew for a new approach, an unconditional sharing of federal revenue with state and local governments.

Revenue Sharing

Proposals for *sharing national revenues* are almost as old as the republic. In 1805, President Thomas Jefferson called for a "just repartition" among the states for "canals, roads, arts, manufactures, education and other great objects." Three decades later, President Andrew Jackson distributed a $30 million federal surplus to the state governments. A half century later, existence of federal surpluses generated pressures for revenue sharing, but Congress failed to act. Revenue sharing surfaced again in the 1960s in a plan that would have distributed, on the basis of population, 1 percent of federal income tax collections (about $2.5 billion in 1965) to the states for their unconditional use. President Lyndon Johnson dropped the plan when it stirred a hornet's nest of opposition from liberal, labor, and urban interests who argued that state governments would misuse unconditional grants. Similar protests came from federal agencies administering grants and from groups that were benefiting from specific federal programs. All these interests wanted federal funds to go to particular programs.

Despite these objections, support for revenue sharing mounted steadily, spurred by fiscal problems of state and local governments and criticisms of categorical programs. By 1967, one fifth of the members of Congress had sponsored revenue-sharing bills, and the Gallup Poll reported that 70 percent of the public favored the idea. During the 1968 presidential campaign, both candidates endorsed revenue sharing. Among the staunchest advocates were governors, who wanted shared revenues funneled through the state capitals. Mayors, on the other hand, demanded that a sizable portion of the funds be reserved for local governments. Local officials also wanted assurances that revenue sharing would supplement rather than supplant categorical assistance.

After extensive negotiations had produced consensus among state and local leaders, President Nixon, in his 1971 State of the Union Message, proposed to distribute $5 billion a year among the states and localities with no strings attached. Allocations among the states would be on the basis of population adjusted to reflect tax effort. Within the states, money would be earmarked for local governments, with all local units being eligible except such single-purpose units as school districts.

The debate that followed Nixon's proposal underscored the diversity of views and interests encompassed by the complex federal partnership. Pointing to mounting federal deficits, critics argued that there were no revenues to share. They also opposed distribution of national tax revenues without detailed federal controls, and the spending of federal funds by state and local officials who did not bear the political burden of imposing taxes. Questions of fairness were raised, both by those who felt that states and localities that taxed themselves lightly would be rewarded, and by those who wanted state and local needs, not population, to be the prime criteria for distribution of federal revenues. Many critics were not satisfied by the formula that assured a substantial share of funds for local governments. Some wanted the local portion enlarged; others wanted more federal money specifically earmarked for the cities.

Revenue sharing survived these attacks largely because the alliance of state and local officials remained cohesive and reached into every congressional district. The legislation that emerged from Congress in 1972 provided for distributing $5.3 billion in the first year, and a total of $30.1 billion over five years. Concern over the plight of the older cities led Congress to reserve two thirds of the revenue-sharing pool for localities, as well as to revise the formula for distributing funds to local governments so that it favored poorer jurisdictions. Congress also restricted use of revenue-sharing funds by local governments to public safety, environmental protection, public transportation, health, recreation, social services, financial administration, and libraries. These restrictions were dropped when Congress extended revenue sharing for four more years in 1976.

As expected, the money from revenue sharing has been used for a wide variety of purposes. A substantial portion has financed programs that were already in existence, like police and recreation. Also as anticipated, allocations for specific purposes have reflected state and local priorities, major public concerns, and the power of various interests. As a result, in the cities far more revenue-sharing funds have been expended for police and fire protection than for welfare programs and other activities that lack strong support from local voters.

Block Grants

The Revenue Sharing Act of 1972 added a new dimension to the complex arrangements of American federalism. Revenue sharing, however, supplemented rather than replaced categorical grant programs, and in 1975 revenue sharing accounted for only 13 percent of federal funds distributed to states and localities. Most of the remaining federal assistance continued to be allocated through categorical programs.

The same concerns that had stimulated development of revenue sharing led to efforts in the 1970s to reduce the number of categorical programs. To this end, President Nixon originally coupled revenue sharing with a proposal to consolidate 129 categorical programs into *block grants* for urban development, rural development, education, transportation, manpower training, and law enforcement.

As the name implies, block grants provide assistance for broad rather than narrow functions. A housing block grant, for example, can be used for any form of housing assistance. Categorical grants, on the other hand, are restricted to particular kinds of housing efforts, such as construction of low-rent public housing, or rent supplements, or urban renewal, or rehabilitation, or neighborhood preservation. Block grants typically involve fewer federal conditions, permitting the state or locality to determine how to spend the funds within the general program area. Block grants thus combine the program focus of categorical assistance with the fewer restrictions and greater flexibility of revenue sharing.

Among beneficiaries of federal aid, block grants raised many of the same concerns as did revenue sharing. Mayors resisted block-grant proposals that channeled federal funds to the states rather than to local governments. Large cities with the most serious crime problems, they claimed, had been shortchanged by the states in the distribution of block grants for law enforcement under the federal Safe Streets Act.

Governors from Appalachia opposed efforts to consolidate their special program out of existence. Civil rights groups argued that the interests of minorities would be more difficult to advance under block grants than in the more narrowly focused and more closely monitored categorical programs. Localities that had been particularly successful in securing categorical grants resisted changes that threatened to reduce their share of federal aid. In Congress, committee and subcommittee chairmen did not welcome dilution of their control over individual programs. Nor were congressmen eager to forego their personal identification with successful applications for specific grants and lose the gratitude of local officials who had been helped on their way through the federal-aid maze.

Because of this opposition, relatively few categorical programs have been replaced by block grants. One major exception occurred in 1974 when a number of housing, renewal, and urban facility grants were consolidated into block grants for community development. Enactment of this legislation, however, occurred only after a wide range of city, suburban, and congressional interests had agreed on the details of the plan that replaced individual grant applications with automatic allocations of federal funds.

The Decentralized Base of American Politics

Underlying evolution of federal assistance has been the decentralized nature of the American political system. Despite the development of a national economy and the growth of a strong central government, the political power of senators and representatives still derives from the voters in particular states and localities. As a result, Congress—and through Congress the federal executive—is highly responsive to the needs and demands of the states and localities.

This responsiveness assures state and local governments of a major role in federal programs. Despite conditions attached to categorical grants, primary responsibility for implementing federally aided activities belongs to state and local officials. In almost all grant programs, the federal role normally remains financial and supervisory. State highway engineers locate and build the roads, local school superintendents hire the teachers and establish the curriculum, state welfare officials set the levels of payment and criteria of eligibility for most forms of public assistance, and city aides negotiate complex arrangements for urban renewal. Other state and local officials make thousands of policy choices that largely determine who benefits from federal aid, under what conditions, and at what costs to the various components of a particular constituency. Revenue sharing and block grants further increase the scope of state and local influence over use of federal funds.

At the heart of this decentralized system are political parties that disperse rather than centralize power. It is difficult to find more decentralized national institutions in any modern society than the Democratic and Republican parties. The basic rules of the party system are largely determined by state law. Except for presidential elections, most party funds are collected and distributed by state and local party organizations. Both national party organizations are federations of fifty state parties. These committees exercise no significant control over party personnel in the states. Normally, the national party leadership plays no role in selecting candidates for Congress, governorships, state legislatures, or local offices.

Underlying the absence of centralized political parties is the decentralization of the rewards of political activity. For most participants in politics, the opportunities for elective office, government contracts, and other benefits are greater at the state and local than at the national level. Of more than 500,000 elected offices in the United States, only 537 are federal positions; and only the President and the Vice President among these 537 are elected nationally rather than from state or local districts. Opportunities for jobs and contracts are also more numerous at the state and local levels because three out of every four civilian government employees are hired by states or localities. Moreover, many patronage jobs in the federal government are distributed to the party faithful through state and local party leaders. Party decentralization is further enhanced by the broad scope of state and local activities. As a result, these governments control a significant proportion of the rewards essential to the sustenance of political parties. The fact that state and local officials play a major role in determining how more than $52 billion in federal aid will be spent also helps nourish the parties at the grass roots.

Of all the elements of the decentralized party system, none is more important than the fact that congressional constituencies are rooted in one state at most, and more commonly in one small area. Locally elected, congressmen usually make sure that officials from their constituency share in spending federal money. The sensitivity of the average congressman to the needs of his district also assures that state and local interests are protected in the federal administrative process: A state's objections to regulations proposed by the federal Welfare Administration, a city's failure to secure a manpower training grant, or a suburb's efforts to persuade the Bureau of Public Roads to reject a state highway department's proposed alignment for an interstate route all draw congressmen into the administrative aspects of intergovernmental relations.

A Government of Shared Power

The net effect of decentralized politics is to produce a widespread sharing of power within the American federal system. The money that comes from Washington is spent at the state and local level. Federal controls are tempered by political realities, as well as by bonds of professionalism, and sharing of goals among federal, state, and local officials who work together in a program area. As a result, there is no neat division of functions between the nation and the states and their subdivisions. Instead, the various components of the federal partnership cooperate in a multitude of ways to provide the ever-widening range of public services that are the shared responsibility of federal, state, and local government.

Federal-State-Local Cooperation

Intergovernmental cooperation extends far beyond activities financed by federal grants. Informal cooperation is the most pervasive form of sharing. Federal, state, and local agencies with common concerns find it mutually advantageous to keep each other informed about their activities and problems and to profit by one another's experience. All the levels of government cooperate in collecting and distributing information on everything from prices and incomes to births and deaths. Federal and state officials jointly inspect banks, utilities, and food processors; they investigate many crimes and accidents together; and they work side by side in preserving order and providing relief during disasters and riots. The federal partners share the services of many public servants such as health inspectors and agricultural specialists. They also lend personnel and equipment to one another, train personnel across intergovernmental lines, and provide each other with various goods and services.

Law enforcement, an area of paramount state and local responsibility, illustrates the variety and adaptability of the modes of federal-state-local cooperation. For years, the Federal Bureau of Investigation has helped train state and local police officers. Its fingerprint files were developed with the aid of local police officials, and those files as well as other information and technical resources are readily available to police departments throughout the nation. During the late 1960s, federal cooperation in law enforcement intelligence, planning, and training activities took on a new dimension in the wake of the racial violence that shattered Los Angeles, Detroit, Newark, and scores of other cities. Gathering information to prevent and control rioting was intensified and computerized so that it could be made available on short notice to state and local officials in a particular city. The Department of Justice organized conferences and seminars to exchange information and coordinate planning with police departments. A major aim of these efforts was to promote and provide instruction in techniques for riot control that minimized the use of force. In 1968 the federal government further expanded its activities by creating the Law Enforcement Assistance Administration, one of whose principal functions has been to funnel millions in national aid to state and local police.

Cooperation may ease problems of governmental officials, but occasionally the price is high. The U.S. Internal Revenue Service, for example, routinely makes files of citizens available to state tax officials, even though federal law forbids such action. Not only does this sort of cooperation violate a right to privacy that is protected both by the Constitution and by statute, but it encourages officials to believe that they are "above the law." Such an arrogant attitude made it easy for IRS officials to help Nixon and his henchmen use legally confidential tax returns to try to blackmail those people who dared oppose the President in a free election.

Given the scope of intergovernmental activities, conflicts inevitably arise among federal, state, and local officials. Among the causes of friction are differences in perspective, professional outlook, legal responsibilities, budgetary capabilities, constituency needs, and partisan affiliations of political superiors. Conflict also results from normal human desires to seek credit for things that go well and to avoid blame for those that go awry. Thus, the local police chief complains that the FBI receives all the praise when a joint federal-local operation foils an airline hijacking, while state and federal civil emergency officials blame each other for the inadequacies of relief measures in the wake of a disastrous flood. In a system as complex as the American federal partnership, the temptation to pass the buck is great, especially when pressures are intense, issues controversial, or partisan interests endangered. Yet, considering the volume and diversity of federal-state-local cooperation, the level of conflict in these relationships has been relatively low.

Decentralized Federal Activity

Both sharing of responsibilities and dispersion of power are promoted by the fact that most federal activities are administered in local communities by local people working for the national government. The great majority of employees of the largest federal agencies, including the Department of Defense, the Veterans Administration, and the Departments of Agriculture, the Treasury, and the Interior, are scattered throughout the country. By custom, U.S. Attorneys and marshals, federal district judges and, where possible, heads of FBI offices are residents of the areas in which they serve. Locally based federal employees staff veterans hospitals, maintain national dams and flood control projects, and keep the voluminous records of the old-age insurance program. By the nature of their work—and of congressional appropriations—most have to cooperate closely with their state and local counterparts. And almost all bring to their jobs the same range of values and attitudes that characterize Americans in each state and community throughout the country.

The Tennessee Valley Authority illustrates another way in which national government exercises broad authority and responsibility without necessarily concentrating additional power in Washington. In

Figure 5.4
The TVA'S Empire

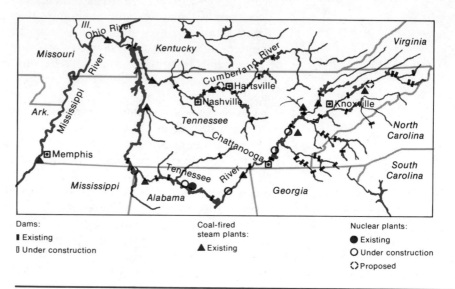

Dams:
▌ Existing
▯ Under construction

Coal-fired
steam plants:
▲ Existing

Nuclear plants:
● Existing
○ Under construction
◇ Proposed

Source: *Newsweek*, Nov. 3, 1975

TVA, Congress created an independent agency with broad power to encourage regional economic development and provide for comprehensive utilization of water resources for flood control, hydroelectric power, irrigation, and recreational purposes. Initiative and leadership was provided at the top without undermining the capacity of state and local units for self-government.

Interstate Cooperation

Sharing within the federal system does not always involve the national government. By their cooperative efforts, states have always met some of their needs for uniform or coordinated governmental activities without federal assistance. One example is the demand for *uniform state laws* that arises from the need for identical treatment of certain issues by individual states. Among the statutes recommended by the National Conference of Commissioners on Uniform State Laws, the most widely adopted are a criminal extradition* act, a gift-to-minors act, a partnership act, a narcotics act, and a simultaneous death act. But, because state courts are under no obligation to interpret identical laws in the same way, there is no guarantee that uniformity of administration will result from these enactments.

Extradition (technically the term should be "rendition" within the United States) is the process by which one government transfers a person within its jurisdiction to another government that wishes to try the person for a crime committed within its own jurisdiction.

Another means of securing cooperation among states is the *interstate compact,* an agreement between two or more states. Since 1921, over a hundred compacts have been concluded, many of which established continuing interstate agencies to operate bridges, ports, parks, and mass transportation, as well as to develop metropolitan and regional plans, coordinate state policies, and exchange information. The earliest and perhaps best know of such agencies is the Port of New York Authority, established in 1921 by joint action of New York and New Jersey to build and operate interstate transport and terminal facilities in the New York metropolitan area.

During the 1960s, a new form of interstate cooperation emerged with the creation of the Delaware River Basin Commission and the Appalachian Regional Commission. In contrast to interstate compact agencies, these commissions involve the national government as a full partner with the participating states. Federal officials share policy control with state governors in both agencies; and a part of each commission's operating funds is supplied directly by Congress (rather than indirectly through various federal grant programs, as is the case with interstate compact agencies that employ federal funds). Broad regulatory powers over water supply, water quality, watersheds, flood plains, recreation, and generation of electric power provide the Delaware River Basin Commission with an important planning and policy role in a valley that serves some of the most heavily urbanized areas in the nation. The Appalachian Regional Commission, primarily through investments in highways, seeks to stimulate economic development in a depressed area inhabited by 15 million people. Strong backing from most of the thirteen states in the region and their congressional delegations have maintained federal funding for the Commission.

Summary

Federalism involves a division of power between a central government and territorially based constituent units that have an independent base of authority. The Constitution established a strong national government with important specific powers and broad implied powers. The Constitution, as well as national laws and treaties, are the supreme law of the land and thus prevail in any conflict with actions taken by the states. Within this basic framework, national powers have steadily expanded in response to economic, social, and political changes. Dedication to local self-government and the pervasive decentralization of the American political system, however, have preserved major roles for states and localities. Much of the national government's growth in domestic affairs has come from the use of federal assistance to state and local governments in the form of categorical grants, block grants, and revenue sharing. As a result, state and local officials bear primary responsibility for implementing national programs. Despite constant conflict and controversy, the American federal system demonstrates remarkable durability because of its capacity for sharing of power and adjustment to change.

Selected Bibliography

ANDERSON, WILLIAM, *The Nation and the States: Rivals or Partners?* (Minneapolis, Minn.: University of Minnesota Press, 1955). One of the best general treatments of the American federal system.

ELAZAR, DANIEL J., *American Federalism: A View from the States* (New York: Thomas Y. Crowell Company, 1966). A useful analysis of federal-state-local relations from the perspective of the state capital.

GOLDWIN, ROBERT A., ed., *A Nation of States: Essays on the American Federal System* (Chicago, Ill.: Rand McNally and Company, 1963). A series of provocative essays on federalism by a group of leading scholars.

GRODZINS, MORTON, *The American System: A New View of Government in the United States.* Daniel J. Elazar, ed. (Chicago, Ill.: Rand McNally and Company, 1966). The major writings of one of the most influential students of American federalism.

MACMAHON, ARTHUR W., ed., *Federalism: Mature and Emergent* (New York: Doubleday & Company, Inc., 1955). A large collection of essays on various aspects of federalism in American politics.

MASON, ALPHEUS T., *The States Rights Debate: Antifederalism and the Constitution*, 2d ed. (Englewood Cliffs, N.J.: Prentice-Hall, Inc., 1972). An analysis of the historical origins of the current and recurrent debate about national power and states rights.

NATHAN, RICHARD P., et al., *Monitoring Revenue Sharing* (Washington, D.C.: The Brookings Institution, 1975). A report on the initial use of revenue sharing funds based on the experience of six states and sixty-one local governments.

REAGAN, MICHAEL D., *The New Federalism* (New York: Oxford University Press, 1972). A timely appraisal of revenue sharing and the implications of the Nixon administration's efforts to reshape the federal system.

RIKER, WILLIAM H., *Federalism: Origin, Operation, Significance* (Boston, Mass.: Little, Brown and Company, 1964). A systematic, original, and critical analysis of federalism.

SANFORD, TERRY, *Storm over the States* (New York: McGraw-Hill Book Company, 1967). An imaginative reappraisal of federal-state-metropolitan relations by a former governor of North Carolina.

Part Three
The Process of Politics

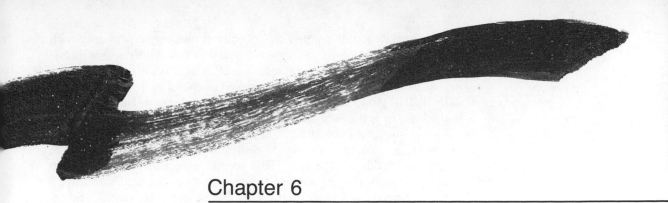

Chapter 6

Politics and Power

As THE FIRST chapter pointed out, politics is concerned primarily with power. *Political power involves having others feel, think, or act as one wants with respect to governmental and other authoritative decision making.* Political power can be exercised in one of two ways. First, an individual or group can shape decisions by government that affect other individuals or groups. Second, an individual or group can create an intellectual or emotional climate in which others are, for all practical purposes, unable to raise issues detrimental to the interests of the powerful individual or group.[1] This second aspect of power has been called the "mobilization of bias," since it involves the ability of powerful interests to shape values, attitudes, myths, and rules within a political system.[2] Thus, political power is exercised both in making governmental decisions and in excluding issues from the political arena.

Sources of Political Power

Political power comes from many sources. Among the more important are the right to vote, the right to speak out, wealth, official position, organization, popularity, knowledge, and force. Except for the right to vote, all these sources of influence are distributed unequally among citizens. And even the vote is used with varying skill and frequency by different individuals and groups. Moreover, the sources of political influence are not mutually exclusive. Knowledge, for example, can be purchased with wealth. Money certainly makes it easier to communicate with others or to organize for political action. Almost always, the legitimate use of force is reserved to those with official governmental positions.

Wealth

Money is one of the most significant sources of political power. As Jesse Unruh, a veteran of the political wars in California, once said, "Money is the mother's milk of politics." Wealth provides the resources for campaign contributions and other means of access to government officials. It can provide control over jobs and credit, which can easily be transformed into political influence. Corporate wealth creates sizable organizational resources—specialists, publicists, lobbyists, and lawyers ready and able to serve the political interests of the corporation's managers, directors, and larger stockholders. With wealth, particularly inherited wealth, come deference and social standing, both of which are important sources of political influence. Wealth can buy an excellent education, highly skilled assistance in dealings with government, and control over information through ownership of mass media of communications. Money can also supply the talents of pollsters, advertising experts, and campaign specialists—as well as

"To close on an upbeat note, I'm happy to report we received twenty-two per cent more in kickbacks than we paid out in bribes."

Drawing by Dana Fradon; © 1976 The New Yorker Magazine, Inc.

television time, billboards, and newspaper ads—to advance a cause or personal ambitions.

Durability is another important aspect of money as a source of political power. The wealthy tend to keep their economic resources over a long period of time, and usually pass their fortunes on to their heirs. As a result, wealth is "doubly powerful, not only for what it can purchase now but for what it can buy in the future. . . . Men of wealth can afford to wait, to bide their time while maintaining continual pressure on behalf of their interests."[3]

Money's usefulness and durability as a source of political influence have led many observers of the American scene to conclude that political power is concentrated largely in the hands of the wealthy. This *power elite,* as C. Wright Mills named it, is supposedly composed of top corporate, military, and governmental leaders, most of whose members come from wealthier families.[4] According to Mills, this tightly knit group rules in the interests of the rich and big business.

A similar picture of political power emerges from many studies of local influence. In them students of community power have found that political influence is derived almost exclusively from economic and social power. Control over the local political system, they believe, is exercised by a cohesive and stable business elite that rules in its own interests.[5] From the perspective of these studies of national and community power, the rich form a "governing class," which "owns a disproportionate amount of the country's wealth, receives a disproportionate share of the country's yearly income, contributes a disproportionate number of its members to governmental bodies and decision-making groups, and dominates the policy-forming process through a variety of means."[6]

There can be no doubt that the rich have more than their proportionate share of many of the resources on which political power is based. But is wealth the predominant source of political power? Does the political influence derived from economic resources overshadow other sources, permitting the wealthy to dominate politics? The supporters of the power-elite approach are right in saying that a cohesive economic elite dominates political life in some places and prevails more generally on some issues. But the power elitists have failed to demonstrate conclusively that the sources of political influence available to the economic elite enable them to prevail all the time.

The utility of political resources available to the economic elite depends on a number of other factors besides money: the sources of influence available to other participants in a particular political system, the nature of the issue at stake, and the characteristics of the political arena in which that issue is being contested. Also limiting the influence of the wealthy is a lack of agreement on all political issues among economic notables. The common fact of being multimillionaires produced little agreement on most political questions between liberal Democrat John F. Kennedy and conservative Texas oilman John Paul Getty.

Opposing the power elitists are scholars who have been labeled *pluralists*. They assign much less significance to wealth as a source of political power. Instead, they emphasize the variety of sources of influence and the dispersal of these sources across a wide range of individuals and groups. Pluralists do not believe that sources of power are evenly distributed among Americans, however; and they identify many kinds of elites, most of them not based on money alone. In their view, the wealthy share power with elected and appointed public officials, political parties, and all kinds of nongovernmental groups. Pluralists believe that:

businessmen, trade unions, politicians, consumers, farmers, voters, and many other aggregates all have an impact on policy outcomes; that none of the aggregates is homogeneous for all purposes; that each of them is highly influential over some scopes but weak over many others; and that the power to reject undesired alternatives is more common than the power to dominate over outcomes directly.[7]

Official Position

Formal roles within government — that is, being a congressman, agency head, school board member, or the like — provide a key source of political power. Unlike other participants in politics, who must persuade governmental officials to act, officials themselves have authority to act.

Legislators vote on bills, approve budgets, and confirm or reject executive nominations. They can also investigate other governmental officials as well as private citizens, including directors of huge corporations, presidents of labor unions, officials of presidential election campaigns, and kingpins of organized crime.

The President, governors, and mayors make thousands of decisions personally, and they delegate large amounts of their authority to political appointees and bureaucrats. Under the law, the President and other federal officials are empowered to enter into agreements with foreign nations, draft individuals into the armed services, and contract with private suppliers for everything from intercontinental ballistic missiles to toilet paper. Public officials determine eligibility for public assistance, inspect motor vehicles for compliance with safety regulations, and acquire private property for a wide variety of public purposes. Members of boards of education set local school policies and often school tax rates as well. Regulatory agencies determine airline fares, rates for gas and electricity, insurance premiums, and practices regarding sale of stocks and bonds. Judges have authority to levy fines, settle estates, and deprive individuals of their liberty. Judges can also set aside actions of other officials if judges conclude that those actions conflict with statutory authority or the Constitution.

By their nature, however, formal governmental roles are restricted sources of political power. In general, the influence derived from public office can be used only for specific functions within a particular governmental jurisdiction. A school superintendent may secure substantial political influence from his authority to manage a local school system. But his official position is not likely to provide him with much influence in such matters as the location of a new highway or the closing of a military base. Like most other officials, the school superintendent's official power is limited to a specific function and governmental jurisdiction.

Of course, holding an official position may provide an individual with other sources of influence. Knowledge and experience, popularity or deference, an important role in a political party, or a substantial increase in personal wealth can result from holding public office. By the same token, access to other sources of influence can bolster the utility of an official position. In addition to his formal powers, the President typically derives political influence from his popularity and his role as a national party leader. A wealthy governor or congressman may use personal funds in order to increase the expert assistance available in exercising official responsibilities. A federal administrator with a strong professional reputation may attract more support for his or her program than another official who is not well known.

The influence of most officials is also limited by their tenure in office. Official sources of power typically cannot be transferred from one office to another, or from public to private life. The city buildings commissioner who resigns to accept a judicial appointment has the same formal powers as other judges, who may or may not have held previous governmental positions. The state legislator who is elected governor derives formal authority solely from those provisions of the state's constitution and statutes dealing with the chief executive. In office, the President of the United States is one of the most powerful individuals in the world. But this source of influence terminates abruptly with the inauguration of his successor.

To be sure, popularity, experience, or wealth gained in one public position may increase influence in another governmental office or in private life. The former state legislator now serving as governor is likely to benefit from earlier experience in dealing with the legislature. A tax lawyer with previous service in the Internal Revenue Service and a retired Air Force general employed by a defense contractor will certainly draw on the knowledge and associations acquired in official roles to enhance their influence. An ex-President may derive influence from the prestige that follows him out of office and from his role as an elder statesman. These sources of influence, however, are a far cry from the enormous institutional power of the Presidency itself.

It is obvious that pluralists view official position as a critical source of power. In a classic pluralist study made in New Haven, Robert A. Dahl concluded that public officials play most of the central roles in political life. Officials were more likely than others to be full-time, knowledgeable, professional participants in politics. Dahl found the mayor to be the most influential individual in New Haven. His official sources of power enabled him to bridge a variety of issues and political arenas. As a result, the mayor's influence was broad in comparison with the more specialized political resources of nongovernmental participants, even wealthy citizens.[8]

Members of the power-elite school, on the other hand, downgrade the role of official position as a source of independent political influence. They see politicians and bureaucrats as dominated by the economic elite, whose members are statistically overrepresented in the highest positions of public leadership. Certainly public officials do not always exercise their authority without outside influences. Officials are often strongly influenced by wealthy individuals and corporations. But the notion that public officials are always subordinate to an economic elite is an oversimplification. Officials also are influenced by labor unions, organized crime, religious and racial groups, veteran's organizations, and many other interests. Equally important, public officials, because of the substantial sources of political power inherent in their official positions, frequently are *the* decisive participants in politics.

Organization

For large numbers of Americans *collective action* is a significant source of political influence. Business, labor, agriculture, professions, regional and neighborhood groups, religious faiths, racial and national groups, teachers, veterans, conservationists, consumers, pensioners, women, motorists, consumers, women's liberationists, sportsmen, homosexuals, public officials — most interests in the United States are organized to some extent.

All organizations facilitate collective activity by people who share common objectives and who try to influence government to promote their aims; but organizations differ widely in effectiveness as well as goals. Some have considerable financial resources, large staffs, and skilled leadership. Others are "letterhead" organizations with little behind them but a single individual's zeal. A few organizations have a broad range of political interests. Most, however, are specialized and become politically involved only when their particular interests are at stake. Some organizations are concerned primarily with politics, most notably political parties. A far larger number of groups that become involved in politics are organized primarily for other purposes like winning economic benefits from employers, facilitating exchanges of information within a profession, promoting a religious faith, or sharing a common recreational interest. The political effectiveness of an organization also depends on the unity of its members, their commitment to the organization's goals, and their willingness to support the organization.

Political parties are particularly important organizations. The Democratic and Republican parties are large organizations that seek to win the active support of millions of voters (and they will be discussed further in the next chapter). Consequently their appeals are broad and their programs deal with many problems. By contrast, because its appeal typically is narrow and its program limited, an interest group is usually supported by only a small minority of the population. In general, a party is primarily interested in winning control of the government, whereas an interest group is concerned mainly with influencing particular governmental decisions. But these distinctions are blurred in practice. Having won control of the government, a party cannot avoid responsibility for shaping many public policies. On the other hand, an interest group may find it necessary to elect its supporters to public office to secure its policy goals.

Historically, the most effective interest groups have been those based on economic interests. Business, labor, and agricultural groups have been the most successful in employing organizational resources to influence government. Nevertheless, these broad groupings are not very cohesive. Labor often is torn between rival aims of various unions and of skilled and unskilled workers. Dairy farmers of the middle west oppose cotton farmers of the south over such issues as taxation of oleomargarine. Manufacturers and independent retail merchants struggle with chainstore operators and discount houses over laws fixing minimum retail prices. Moreover, on some political issues, business and labor groups in the same industry may be more closely identified with each other than either is with other business and labor organizations.

Most professions also have strong organizations that from time to

In recent years, more and more minority groups have sought to enhance their political power through organizations such as La Raza Unida, a Chicano group organized by Jose Angel Gutierrez in southern Texas.

time become politically active. Through the American Medical Association, doctors have sought to block or curtail federal programs to finance medical care for the elderly and the poor. In 1965 the AMA admitted spending over $1.1 million in a vain effort to prevent the passage of Medicare, which it called "socialized medicine." The Association could claim some success, however, in restricting the coverage of the act and in having helped delay passage for seventeen years. The American Bar Association has a strong interest in the structure, procedure, and personnel of the courts, as well as in many specific issues of public policy that affect lawyers. In general, professional interest groups take very conservative positions. While claiming to be anxious about maintaining high professional standards or serving the public good, these groups often are mainly concerned with protecting the vested interests of their members, especially by limiting competition.

Organizations representing war veterans find a powerful incentive for political activity in such issues as pensions for former GIs and medical care for the disabled. But their political activity also has encompassed such issues as national defense and foreign policy. The largest veterans' organization is the American Legion, which is controlled and administered by a group of conservative leaders. This organization illustrates the enormous power wielded in all kinds of interest groups by their professional staffs. It is doubtful whether the average member of the American Legion shares—or even knows about—the views of the paid workers who run this organization. Similarly, the typical member of the Automobile Association of America probably does not fully agree with the strong prohighway views of AAA's Washington staff. One reason why public officials often ignore organizations is their awareness that the group's professional staff does not necessarily represent the views of rank-and-file members.

Pluralists point to the broad range of group and organizational activity as further evidence of the dispersal of sources of political power in the United States. "Few if any groups of citizens who are organized, active, and persistent," argues one pluralist, "lack the capacity and opportunity to influence some officials somewhere in the political system in order to obtain at least some of their goals."[9] But corporations, the wealthy, and middle-class citizens are far more organized, active, and persistent than the poor, the aged, members of minority groups, and others most in need of organizational resources. A recent study of political participation concluded that:

organizations increase the political gap [between more advantaged and less advantaged groups], for the simple reason that those who come from advantaged groups are more likely to be organizationally active. Upper-status groups are, to begin with, more politically active. They are also more active in organizations. And, because the latter type of activity has an independent effect in increasing political activity—over and above the effects of socio-economic status—their advantage in political activity over the lower groups is increased.[10]

Knowledge and Information

Knowledge may not be power, but it is a source of political influence whose importance steadily grows. In an increasingly complex society, knowledge and information are indispensable to all participants in politics. The substance of political life as well as its procedures require more and more technical competence. For example, intelligently settling disputes over hazards to health posed by nuclear generating plants necessitates obtaining and evaluating advice from nuclear physicists. Determining permissible contents of automobile emissions requires information and advice from chemical and mechanical engineers as well as specialists in respiratory diseases. The processes of electing public officials enlists the talents of campaign specialists, fund raisers, publicists, and pollsters. Operating the government requires personnel specialists, budget officers, efficiency experts, computer programmers, and hundreds of other kinds of technicians.

The wealthy, large corporations, governmental officials, and major organizations enjoy a tremendous advantage over others in the acquisition of knowledge and the use of experts. And the ability to control the contents and dissemination of information is as important as access to knowledge. Again this source of political influence in the United States is concentrated in the hands of a few hundred individuals and corporations. They control the broadcast networks, own radio and television stations, and operate wire services, newspapers, and magazines. In sum, they and their employees determine what the public sees, hears, and reads.

Control over information also provides the press with an important source of influence with other participants in politics. Most officials, groups, and individuals cannot communicate with the public unless the press and television pay attention to their activities and opinions. Moreover, public attitudes are shaped by the way in which reporters and editors present objectives and actions of various participants in politics.

Most political activists are quite aware of the importance of the media of communications. They hire press agents, hold news conferences, and prepare publicity releases. Government officials and other political participants leak stories to the press, withhold information, demand equal time, and curry favor with publishers, editors, columnists, commentators, and reporters. Organizations sometimes bring economic pressure to bear by contracting for or canceling advertising. Nor are public officials reluctant to criticize "biased" coverage of their activities or even, in the case of radio and television, to threaten greater federal regulation to insure "impartiality."

All participants in politics employ propaganda in order to influence public opinion. Propaganda may be true, false, partly both, biased, or distorted. It may be narrowly aimed, or it may seek the broadest national good. But its fundamental purpose is always to influence public opinion on a particular issue. To accomplish this objective, public relations experts generally rely on the same techniques used to advertise consumer products.

One of the more striking examples of political propaganda is afforded by the American Medical Association's long campaign against national health insurance.[11] Direct pressure on Congress by lobbying with individual legislators was only a small part of an enormous "educational" campaign conducted for the AMA by public relations experts. Thousands of billboards, newspaper advertisements, and radio commercials and millions of leaflets decried "socialized medicine." Almost 10,000 other organizations were persuaded to endorse the AMA's position. "Canned" editorials denouncing the evils of federal health assistance were distributed to newspapers. As a final touch, paintings of a physician at the bed of a sick child were sent to individual doctors to be displayed in their waiting rooms; the caption read:

KEEP POLITICS OUT OF THIS PICTURE

When the life — or health — of a loved one is at stake hope lies in the devoted service of your Doctor. Would you change this picture?

Compulsory health insurance is political medicine. . . .

Protest

Groups that lack other sources of political power are most likely to use protest as a means of bolstering their influence. The main purpose of protest is to dramatize grievances. By drawing attention to their problems, protesters hope to arouse the feelings of others, who will then put pressure on the target of the protest. When a group of black students in Greensboro, North Carolina, staged the first sit-in at a chain store in 1960, they did not impose a serious financial threat to the local store. But chain-store executives could not ignore sympathetic reactions from around the country. A demonstration in Greensboro was only a trivial incident, but pickets in major cities in the north and midwest, all presented on evening television programs, were a different matter.

Typically, the very condition that led them to protest in the first place — lack of other political resources — hampers effectiveness. Successful protests usually require excellent organization as well as leaders who can attract the attention of reporters. The activities themselves must be planned and led rather than just merely "happen." Funds have to be raised from sympathetic individuals and groups. Information needs to be distributed to protestors and the press. Technical skills often are required, such as those of lawyers if legal action is taken to halt the protest. Because those who are most likely to resort to protest usually lack these other sources of power, their demands often can be ignored or discredited.

Force

"Political power," in the words of Mao Tse-tung, "grows out of the barrel of a gun."[12] Because physical force is an extremely potent source of political influence, government in the United States exercises a virtual legal monopoly over its use. The military services and law enforcement agencies are authorized to employ deadly force in limited circumstances. Other officials, such as those who operate prisons and jails, may use physical force to detain individuals who have been convicted of violating the law or are suspected of crimes.

As demonstrated by the My Lai atrocities in Vietnam and the Chicago police "riot" during the 1968 Democratic National Convention, the use of "lawful" force by governmental officials can escalate into criminal acts. Moreover, governmental agencies often misuse their authority to employ force. One example is the brutal behavior of guards in many

Political protest takes many forms. In 1974, Minnesota farmers shot their cows and pigs rather than sell them at a loss. Their aim was to underscore for political leaders and the public their bitterness at the low prices they receive for the animals and the high costs of raising them.

prisons. Another is the forcible detention by the federal government of more than a hundred thousand Americans of Japanese descent during World War II. Local police power has often been employed to defend the status quo. Cities under the sway of political machines like that operated by Frank Hague in Jersey City used the police to intimidate voters, political opponents, and hostile newspapers. Not so long ago, city officials often repaid corporate executives for their campaign contributions by using police to break strikes and disrupt the organizing activities of labor unions. The power of the police has been used in recent years to put down demonstrations by blacks, striking farm workers, and opponents of the Vietnam War. On the national level, federal troops have been used to quell domestic disturbances ranging from the Whiskey Rebellion of 1794 to the ghetto riots of the 1960s. The Civil War represents the resort to force by government to settle a dispute that could not be resolved through more conventional sources of political influence.

Government's "legal" monopoly over force is not quite the same as a real monopoly. Other participants in politics have derived political influence from raw force. As Chapter 2 pointed out, there is a strong strain of violence in American culture. Political parties, organized crime, and agents of business and labor have threatened voters and political opponents and occasionally attempted to resolve political disputes through beatings or even shoot-outs. At times, law enforcement agencies have let groups violently settle disagreements among themselves or have—as the FBI did in the late 1960s and early 1970s with radical black organizations—even egged on groups to fight each other. And the assassinations of Presidents Lincoln, Garfield, McKinley, and

A stark reminder of the role of violence in American political life is provided by the funeral procession of President John F. Kennedy, who was killed by an assassin's bullets during a visit to Dallas, Texas, on November 22, 1963.

Kennedy, as well as the political murders of Martin Luther King and Robert F. Kennedy, and the attempted assassinations of Presidents Franklin Roosevelt, Harry Truman, and Gerald Ford and Governor George Wallace all illustrate that violence can be an extremely important, if very fleeting, source of power.

Using Political Resources

Political resources such as wealth, official position, organization, popularity, knowledge, and force are sources of power; they are not power itself. Availability of such means does not guarantee influence in a particular situation. Instead, the sources of power provide potential in political relationships. The usefulness of a particular source of power depends on the nature of an issue, participants' goals, and resources available to other parties. Moreover, some participants are more willing than others to use their resources for political purposes; and some are more expert in employing them. They may have more time available for political activity, as is the case with public officials in contrast with average businessmen. Or they may have acquired more skill in converting potential influence into actual power, as is often the case with elected officials and other political professionals.

A Multitude of Political Arenas

Relatively few participants in politics have political resources that are usable in a wide range of political arenas. Instead, the utility of sources of influence tends to be specialized. Like government itself, political activists specialize in functional responsibilities for defense, international trade, banking, taxation, education, housing, health, social security, welfare, public lands, or environmental protection. Equally important is the territorial distribution of responsibility within the federal system among national, state, and local governments.

Because of the specialization of influence, a lawyer experienced in immigration matters cannot use his resources as effectively in a dispute over the location of high-tension power lines in a residential area. An admiral responsible for procurement of antisubmarine weapons derives considerable influence over this activity from his official position, organizational resources, and expert knowledge. None of these specialized resources, however, is likely to make him a particularly active participant in political arenas dealing with baby-food additives or the design of public housing.

This multiplicity of political arenas contributes to dispersion of power in the United States. Power tends to be exercised in particular political arenas by different participants. A study of political influence in the nation's largest city concluded:

Decisions of the municipal government emanate from no single source, but from many centers; conflicts and clashes are referred to no single authority, but are settled at many levels and at many points in the system: no single group can guarantee the success of the proposal it supports, the defeat of every idea it objects to. . . . Each separate decision center consists of a cluster of interested contestants, with a "core group" in the middle, invested by the rules with formal authority to legitimize decisions . . . and a constellation of related "satellite groups" seeking to influence the authoritative issuances of the core group.[13]

As the chapters that follow indicate, similar statements can be made about political parties, Congress, the federal executive, and most of the other political arenas that comprise the American governmental system.

Participation

Participation in politics involves attempts to turn political resources into political influence. Most individuals and groups participate only in those political arenas in which they think they have an interest. Stakes are broader in some arenas than in others. Race relations and highway building, for example, attract more participants than does regulation of barbershops.

Those who participate most in politics tend to have roles that require substantial involvement, either as governmental officials or as holders of politically oriented positions in business, union, and other organizations. Most governmental and organizational roles, however, dictate a narrow range of political involvement. Bureaucrats typically participate only in those political arenas in which their authority is exercised. Private organizations usually do not become involved until they perceive a specialized interest of their own.

Only a small proportion of participants have sufficient resources or interests to participate in a wide range of political activities. Among the most active participants in politics are elected executives and their staffs, members of Congress and other legislative bodies, and judges. Private parties who participate in a broad scope of activities include the press, civic groups such as Common Cause and the League of Women Voters, and general-purpose business and labor groups like the Chamber of Commerce, the American Farm Bureau Federation, the Committee for Economic Development, and the AFL-CIO.

Aside from voting, most Americans participate in politics infrequently, and their scope of involvement typically is narrow. Less than 10 percent are members of groups that are primarily political in nature, and only one in five citizens has been in contact with a governmental official. Typically, involvement results from a local problem—a zoning change, a traffic accident, a proposal to integrate schools or housing, or the like—and that involvement usually ends when the issue is resolved or the conflict eases.

Participation is closely related to social and economic standing. Those who participate the most tend to have higher incomes, more education, and higher-status occupations. Conversely, those who are least involved tend to have low incomes, little education, and low-status jobs. For most Americans, "politics is a remote, alien, and unrewarding activity [that] lies . . . at the outer periphery of attention, interest, and activity."[14]

Some who fail to participate are totally inert politically. Others are satisfied with things as they are, or perhaps more frequently are not sufficiently dissatisfied to divert time and energy from other pursuits. Many do not participate because their resources are limited. Such people often see involvement as futile given the massive resources of public officials and established groups.

Voting, the only political resource employed by most people, has little direct effect on most political outcomes or the workings of governmental institutions. Elections rarely alter the behavior of bureaucracies with which citizens must deal. Moreover, connections between candidates and policies are often obscure. For example, the victors in the 1964 and 1968 presidential elections promised peace in Vietnam, but both President Johnson and President Nixon proceeded to wage war for the next four years.

A System of Many Elites

We have said enough to make it clear that, on the whole, we disagree with the belief of power elitists that political power in the United States is concentrated in the hands of a small group of wealthy people. The American political system, however, is hardly the participatory utopia pictured by some pluralists. Large numbers of Americans lack resources to participate effectively in any political arena. As a result, significant influence is distributed among a relatively small proportion of the population. People with power tend to be white males, among whom Protestants of native stock are overrepresented. The influential have college educations and incomes well above average. They usually hold positions of leadership in government, business and other organizations.

Those with substantial political resources secure many benefits from the political system. A supposedly progressive federal tax system places heavier relative burdens on lower- and middle-income families than on the very rich. Most federal housing subsidies—in the form of mortgage assistance and income tax deductions—benefit homeowners rather than the poor. Large farmers and agribusinesses have been the principal beneficiaries of massive agricultural programs. Public officials and businessmen defend huge subsidies for aircraft companies, the merchant marine, and the petroleum industry as essential to a healthy economy. Many of these same people, however, attack subsidies for unemployed mothers with dependent children as undermining self-reliance and thrift.

Alliances of public and private power tend to dominate many political arenas. Coal companies, the United Mine Workers, the Federal Bureau of Mines, and state regulatory agencies have been allies on such issues as mine safety and strip mining. Many government agencies with regulatory responsibilities—for example, the Federal Trade Commission, state utility commissions, and local zoning boards—are often dominated by the very groups they were created to control. Public power also is frequently delegated to influential private organizations. For example, county agents in the Department of Agriculture's extension program are appointed by a powerful private group, the American Farm Bureau Federation. Many state medical, bar, engineering, and other private associations exercise public power over licensing, certification, and other prerequisites to the practice of a profession. In the process, these private interests use their public authority to reduce competition.

Few such advantages are possible for those who lack political resources. The groups that are most dependent on government—the poor, blacks, the old, Chicanos, Puerto Ricans, Indians, migrant farm hands, and unskilled workers—have the least influence. On the whole, they vote less frequently and have fewer organizational resources than their fellow citizens. Because of their lack of power, governmental officials can afford to ignore or heavily discount the interests of these people.

Consequences of Powerlessness

The lives of the poor, the elderly, and racial minorities are in large part shaped by their lack of political power. The federal minimum wage system does not include many of the lowest paid jobs, such as farm labor. When workers in low-paying jobs reach retirement, they have to survive on inadequate social security benefits, supplemented by charity, private or institutional. At the same time that the Secretary of State negotiates grain sales to the Russians—who sometimes resell the food at a profit—hundreds of thousands of American poor go hungry and old people eat dog food. Under a national housing policy that proclaims the goal of decent shelter for all, urban renewal programs have replaced the slums of low-income families with lovely housing, but at rents that former residents can never even hope to afford.

Typically lacking education, legal assistance, and organizational resources, the poor are placed at a tremendous disadvantage by laws governing relations between landlord and tenant or between lender and borrower. Again because of their lack of politically useful skills and resources, powerless groups tend to receive the harshest treatment from police, judges, prison guards, and probation officers. Public health facilities for the poor are usually overloaded and understaffed, although poorer Americans have a much higher incidence of health problems than do middle-class people. Welfare recipients contend with a complex system that provides insufficient assistance at great cost in terms of human dignity. Moreover, because the children of the poor tend to attend the worst schools—when they attend at all—the outlook for the next generation remains bleak.

Political resources are difficult to create among impoverished groups. Few members of a powerless group have the time, energy, or personal resources to devote to political activity. Even protest, the most readily available means, is not a very effective substitute for more durable sources of political influence. Talented leaders like Cesar Chavez of the United Farm Workers Organizing Committee can help overcome some of these disadvantages. The efforts of skilled and dedicated professionals, such as those found in civil rights organizations, can provide the poor and minority groups with desperately needed political resources. So can the availability of organizational resources for the poor through such governmental programs as the ill-fated War on Poverty. Welfare clients, public-housing tenants, parents of black school children, and residents of poor neighborhoods also have orga-

A look at how millions of poor Americans are forced to live underscores the enormous difficulties the poor face in acquiring and using political resources effectively.

nized in recent years for political action. In so doing, some of these groups have gained influence in political arenas that most affect the poor.

Despite these successes, creating and maintaining political resources for the poor is an arduous task. Organizations serving the poor and minorities frequently depend heavily on governmental agencies, foundations, or other institutions controlled by outsiders. These groups must compete with other participants who hold official positions, have more reliable sources of political influence, and have more political experience. Without significant redistribution of wealth and access to other political resources, the poorer segment of the population is likely to remain relatively powerless. At the same time, poorer Americans' lack of political resources greatly reduces the likelihood of such a redistribution.

Black Power

Black Americans have faced particularly severe problems in acquiring political resources. First slavery, then segregation cut blacks off from most sources of political influence; thus they tended to receive few educational opportunities. And, even in an absence of prejudice, a poor education severely limits economic opportunities. Blacks—like Indians and Hispanic Americans—have lower average incomes than whites, are more likely to be poor, and have fewer organizational resources. Until recently, blacks were formally excluded from politics by the denial of the vote in many states. And when blacks have been able to participate in politics, their influence was often limited by the prevalence of racist attitudes among white Americans.

Inevitably, political involvement of blacks has been shaped by their unique position in American society. Because of segregation and discrimination, blacks have had to struggle for even the right to participate in politics. Almost all their meager political resources have been devoted to the fight for equality — for the right to be treated like other citizens in terms of jobs, housing, schooling, and other public services. Lacking access to most sources of political influence, blacks in the past relied heavily on legal action. Throughout the first half of the twentieth century, the courts were the key political arena for the National Association for the Advancement of Colored People and other groups representing black interests.

During the 1950s, frustration with the slow pace of change that courts could manage turned blacks to other means of registering dissatisfaction. Large-scale protests against racial separation began in Montgomery, Alabama, where a young minister named Martin Luther King, Jr., directed a successful boycott against the city's segregated bus lines. King and his organization, the Southern Christian Leadership Conference, stressed direct action in the form of demonstrations, protests, and boycotts, rather than lawsuits and lobbying, favored by traditional groups like the NAACP. The dramatic and direct aspects of protest appealed to frustrated blacks who lacked other sources of political influence. In the wake of the boycott in Montgomery, sit-ins, freedom marches, rent strikes, school boycotts, and other forms of mass protest were employed by increasingly militant blacks across the nation.

Out of these racial confrontations, and from the new leaders and organizations spawned by protest, came the demand for *black power*. In one sense, black power resembles the "Irish power" on which urban political machines were built during the nineteenth century. It involves using racial solidarity as a source of political influence by having black voters, black organizations, and black officials work for black interests. From this perspective, black power means capitalizing on the concentration of black voters in an area to elect black officials, or defeat hostile white candidates, or press for particular policies and programs.

For many blacks, however, black power involves more than following the traditional political strategy of ethnic solidarity. They see black power as essential to black self-determination. Their goal is freedom from the social, economic, and political domination of whites. Some black leaders stress use of black power to secure economic independence, urging blacks to build up and patronize their own business establishments. Even more important for many black spokesmen is freedom from white cultural dominance. For these people, black power must be expressed in terms of black pride. They urge blacks to develop values and institutions based on their own history, life styles, and aspirations.

Advocates of black power have differed widely on the best means to secure political power. Martin Luther King was a passionate advocate of nonviolence and peaceful protest. Demonstrations were also the principal weapon of the Congress of Racial Equality. The Student Non-violent Coordinating Committee emphasized working within the existing political system by concentrating on registering potential black voters in the south. More militant black groups, however, have embraced force, violent rebellion, and terrorism. Some leaders of the Black Panthers have said armed force is the only effective instrument of black power. "We must get it clear in our minds that we will shoot anyone who uses a gun, or causes others to use guns, to defend the system of oppression, racism, and exploitation," wrote one. "We must face the fact that we are at war in America."[15] More recently, however, the Panthers have de-emphasized violence in an effort to broaden their political base. Slogans like "All Power to the Sniper" frightened away much black support. Indicative of the changing perspective of the Panthers on political means was the candidacy in 1973 of one of the organization's leaders, Bobby Seale, for mayor of Oakland. Seale attracted sufficient support to force a run-off election with the victorious candidate.

Black leaders disagree about ends as well as means. Despite emphasizing mass action and radical rhetoric, Martin Luther King's dream of an integrated society linked him to the traditional objectives of the NAACP, middle-class blacks, and white liberals. Toward the other end of the spectrum have been outspoken separatists like the Black Muslims. For the Muslims—who have also begun to mellow—black power has been a means to create a separate black nation of Islam, which would be forged from a part of the United States. In between are those who see integration as unattainable and political separation as unrealistic. For them, black power is a means of providing blacks with the political resources to control those institutions that affect their lives—local schools, police departments, welfare bureaucracies, and public hospitals.

From these diverse views of black power, a few common themes emerged in the late 1970s. First was agreement on a need to bolster self-respect among blacks. Second were efforts to create greater unity among blacks. In the 1970s, black leaders spoke more and more of "nation time"—the time for black people to solidify as a single political force. In a massive effort to harness their potential, black community and political leaders from all over the country held a "Black Political Convention" in Gary, Indiana, in 1972. Unity was the overriding theme, although it was spoken in one tongue by politicians and in another by community activists. But despite pressing need and impressive eloquence, unity did not emerge from the convention. The platform that was adopted was too ambitious, and the general tone of black nationalism was too strident for many participants. The NAACP, for example, denounced it as racist.

Yet, the Gary convention did bring diverse black leaders together and allowed them to create a National Black Political Assembly to try to continue the work of building coordinated, if not unified, policies.

THE GARY MANIFESTO

We come to Gary in an hour of great crisis and tremendous promise for black America. While the white nation hovers on the brink of chaos, while its politicians offer no hope of real change, we stand on the edge of history and are faced with an amazing and frightening choice: We may choose in 1972 to slip back into the decadent white politics of American life, or we may press forward, moving relentlessly from Gary to the creation of our own black life. . . .

Our cities are crime-haunted, dying grounds. Huge sectors of our youth—and countless others—face permanent unemployment. Those of us who work find our paychecks able to purchase less and less. Neither the courts nor the prisons contribute to anything resembling justice or reformation. The schools are unable —or unwilling—to educate our children for the real world of our struggles. Meanwhile, the officially approved epidemic of drugs threatens to wipe out the minds and strength of our best young warriors.

Economic, cultural, and spiritual depression stalk black America, and the price for survival often appears to be more than we are able to pay. On every side, in every area of our lives, the American institutions in which we have placed our trust are unable to cope with the crises they have created by their single-minded dedication to profits for some and white supremacy above all.

And beyond these shores there is more of the same. For while we are pressed down under all the dying weight of a bloated, inwardly decaying white civilization, many of our brothers in Africa and the rest of the Third World have fallen prey to the same powers of exploitation and deceit. Wherever America faces the unorganized, politically powerless forces of the non-white world, its goal is domination by any means necessary—as if to hide from itself the crumbling of its own systems of life and work.

But Americans cannot hide. They can run to China and the moon and to the edges of consciousness, but they cannot hide. The crises we face as black people are the crises of the entire society. They go deep, to the very bones and marrow, to the essential nature of America's economic, political, and cultural systems. They are the natural end-product of a society built on the twin foundations of white racism and white capitalism. . . .

A black political convention, indeed all truly black politics must begin from this truth: The American system does not work for the masses of our people, and it cannot be made to work without radical fundamental change. (Indeed, this system does not really work in favor of the humanity of anyone in America.) . . .

Here at Gary, let us never forget that while the times and the names and the parties have continually changed, one truth has faced us insistently, never changing: Both parties have betrayed us whenever their interests conflicted with ours (which was most of the time), and whenever our forces were unorganized and dependent, quiescent and compliant. Nor should this be surprising, for by now we must know that the American political system, like all other white institutions in America, was designed to operate for the benefit of the white race: It was never meant to do anything else. . . .

If we have come to Gary on behalf of our people in America, in the rest of this hemisphere, and in the Homeland—if we have come for our own best ambitions—then a new black politics must come to birth. If we are serious, the black politics of Gary must accept major responsibility for creating both the atmosphere and the program for fundamental, far-ranging change in America. Such responsibility is ours because it is our people who are most deeply hurt and ravaged by the present systems of society. That responsibility for leading the change is ours because we live in a society where few other men really believe in the responsibility of a truly humane society for anyone anywhere.

The challenge is thrown to us here in Gary. It is the challenge to consolidate and organize our own black role as the vanguard in the struggle for a new society. To accept that challenge is to move to independent black politics. . . . White politics has not and cannot bring the changes we need.

A major part of the challenge we must accept is that of redefining the functions and operations of all levels of American government, for the existing governing structures—from Washington to the smallest county—are obsolescent. . . . For white politics seeks not to serve but to dominate and manipulate.

We will have joined the true movement of history if at Gary we grasp the opportunity to press man forward as the first consideration of politics. Here at Gary we are faithful to the best hopes of our fathers and our people if we move for nothing less than a politics which places community before individualism, love before sexual exploitation, a living environment before profits, peace before war, justice before unjust "order," and morality before expediency.

This is the society we need, but we delude ourselves here at Gary if we think that change can be achieved without organizing the power, the determined national black power, which is necessary to insist upon such change, to create such change, to seize change. . . .

We begin here and now in Gary. We begin with an independent Black political movement, an independent black political agenda, an independent black spirit. Nothing less will do. We must build for our people. We must build for our world. We stand on the edge of history. We cannot turn back.

Most of all, the convention underlined for blacks and for whites the national power that would accrue to the leader or leaders who might command the allegiance of 15 million blacks of voting age. Such recognition was hardly novel. Even groups like the Panthers had been getting involved in electoral campaigns. The fact that in 1976 there were more than 3500 black elected officials at the state and local level could hardly pass unnoticed.

At Gary and after, a number of observers pointed to the possibility of a black political party. As the next chapter points out, the attractions of organizing a new party are always tempting to leaders of a minority group. But blacks constitute only about 11 percent of the electorate, hardly enough to win control of any governmental structure above the county level. If, however, leaders can persuade more blacks to register and can offer a realistic threat of shifting their support to one party or the other or even of forming a third party at critical points, it is possible for blacks to exert far more political influence at the national level than they have in the past.

At the local level, results may be more immediate than in Washington. Although blacks could never control Congress or even a state legislature, simply by virtue of their numbers, they could, if they massed their power, dominate many older cities. Blacks already form a clear majority of the population in Atlanta, Gary, and Newark, and more than 40 percent in Baltimore, Birmingham, Detroit, New Orleans, Richmond, St. Louis, and Wilmington.

The fact that blacks are only now participating in politics as often as whites poses a serious obstacle to achieving black political aims. Compared to whites, blacks may now be voting in about the same proportions, but they engage less often and less actively in political campaigns and contact public officials less frequently about personal or community problems than do whites. But these differences are closely associated with differences in socioeconomic status.[16] Actually blacks with the highest socioeconomic status participate even more frequently and actively than do whites of similar backgrounds. The rub comes in the fact that a majority of blacks fall in the lowest one sixth of the country on the usual measure of socioeconomic status.

Thus, black leaders face the same circular problem as others who seek to bolster the political influence of disadvantaged groups. They need positive governmental action to improve the socioeconomic status of their people. Yet low socioeconomic status is typically accompanied by unawareness of political opportunities and an inability to exploit those that are perceived.

Neither calls to use the ballot more wisely and more often or to utilize other forms of participation offers an easy solution to the problem of political resources for blacks. The volatility of race in America imposes severe restrictions on both the speed and the quantity of gains that blacks can achieve by the political processes. Efforts to heighten the awareness of the black community may make whites more aware of their own identity and perhaps even frighten them into greater political activity. To avoid the dangers of a backlash while still mustering the black support needed to build political power requires skills of a rare sort.

An Inhospitable Tradition

One of the problems faced by those who lack political influence is the attitude of most Americans toward power and its role in public life. Demands for black power or brown power or student power disturb those who believe that conflict is undesirable. Most people apparently feel that issues ought to be settled on their merits rather than by exercise of political influence. The fact that most individuals or groups accept the resolution of an issue on its "merits" only when the merits or existing rules favor them does not diminish the widespread popular dislike for conflict, politics, and power.

Most Americans want statesmen rather than politicians or power brokers for leaders. Thus, those who exercise significant power usually mask its use. Typically, they claim that they are acting in the public interest, or following established procedures, or seeking economy, efficiency, justice, or some other admirable goal. Those who use power blatantly find themselves criticized for being selfish or undemocratic.

Public distrust of power has also contributed to the maintenance and elaboration of a complex governmental system that disperses authority widely. As Chapter 4 showed, desire to limit official power was a principal concern of the authors of the Constitution. The result was a sharing of powers, checks and balances, overlapping terms of office, and a federal system. State constitutions in the nineteenth century scattered governmental authority even further, providing for election of a host of executive officials, detailed restrictions on state officeholders and local governments, and creation of independent agencies to carry out governmental functions.

Pluralists see the fragmentation and dispersion of governmental authority in the United States as essential to prevent concentration of power, to protect minority rights, and to insure peaceful settlement of disputes. The importance of preventing tyranny, protecting minorities, and promoting peaceful resolution of conflicts should not be belittled. Equally important, however, is the fact that dispersal of governmental authority has not prevented concentration of great political power in the hands of certain public officials, most notably the President, governmental agencies like the Department of Defense, and large corporations, trade associations, major labor unions, and such organizations as the American Medical Association. Instead, fragmentation and decentralization of governmental responsibilities plays into the hands of influential and experienced participants who understand the complexities of the system.

The result is a political system which offers many advantages to the powerful in their quest to protect their interests. As one detailed study of political influence concludes: "Every proposal for change must run a gauntlet that is often fatal. The system is more favorable to defenders of the *status quo* than to innovators. It is inherently conservative.... If plans are radical, they seldom survive; if they survive, they seldom work major changes in the going system."[17]

Summary

Political power involves getting others to feel, think, or act as one wishes. It comes from a variety of sources — wealth, official position, organization, popularity, knowledge, force, and the right to vote. These resources are not evenly distributed in society, nor are skills in using such resources. Most sources of political power are specialized. Individuals and groups typically exert their influence in particular political arenas rather than in politics generally.

In the United States, power tends to be dispersed rather than highly concentrated in a power elite. Substantial influence, however, is distributed among a relatively small proportion of the population, composed primarily of white males with above-average incomes and educations who occupy positions of leadership in government, business, and other large organizations. The poor and members of disadvantaged minority groups have the least political influence, a circumstance that gravely handicaps efforts to improve their economic and social conditions. Because of the bitter heritages of segregation and discrimination, blacks, Indians, and Hispanic Americans have faced particularly severe problems in acquiring and using political resources.

For all individuals and groups, the exercise of political influence is conditioned by the hostility of most Americans to open use of power. Public distrust of power has shaped American politics from the colonial period to the present, in the process contributing significantly to the fragmentation and dispersion of authority at all levels of government.

Selected Bibliography

BACHRACH, PETER, *The Theory of Democratic Elitism* (Boston: Little Brown and Company, 1967). A succinct critical evaluation of the concept of the political elite.

BENTLEY, ARTHUR F., *The Process of Government* (Bloomington, Ind.: The Principia Press, 1949). A theory of the role of interest groups in politics.

BLAISDELL, DONALD C., *American Democracy under Pressure* (New York: The Ronald Press, 1957). A vigorous account of the operations of several interest groups, and a theoretical statement of their role and status.

CARMICHAEL, STOKELY, and CHARLES V. HAMILTON, *Black Power: The Politics of Liberation in America* (New York: Random House, Inc., 1967). An angry analysis of political power and the role of black Americans in the political process.

DAHL, ROBERT A., *Pluralist Democracy in the United States* (Chicago: Rand McNally, 1967). The pluralist perspective on the American political system.

————, *Who Governs?* (New Haven, Conn.: Yale University Press, 1961). A classic study of democracy and power in an American city.

DOMHOFF, G. WILLIAM, *The Higher Circles* (New York: Random House, 1970). An elitist analysis of the role of the "governing class" in American political life.

HUNTER, FLOYD, *Community Power Structure* (Chapel Hill, N.C.: University of North Carolina Press, 1953). A controversial analysis of the role of economic notables in a southern city.

KEY, V. O., JR., *Public Opinion and American Democracy* (New York: Alfred A. Knopf, 1961). A thoughtful attempt to place sociological knowledge about public opinion into a meaningful political context.

KING, MARTIN LUTHER, JR., *Stride Toward Freedom: The Montgomery Story* (New York: Harper & Row, 1958).

————, *Why We Can't Wait* (New York: The New American Library, Inc., 1963). Two introductions to King's philosophy of nonviolence and his tactics of mass action.

LOWI, THEODORE J., *The End of Liberalism* (New York: W. W. Norton and Co., 1969). An examination of the fusion of public and private power in American politics.

MCCONNELL, GRANT, *Private Power and American Democracy* (New York: Alfred A. Knopf, 1966). An analysis of the influential role of private groups in the making of public policy.

MILLS, C. WRIGHT, *The Power Elite* (New York: Oxford University Press, 1956). A classic and iconoclastic statement of the elitist perspective on American politics.

POLSBY, NELSON, *Community Power and Political Theory* (New Haven, Conn.: Yale University Press, 1963). A spirited critique of the political elitist approach to community power.

RICCI, DAVID, *Community Power and Democratic Theory* (New York: Random House, 1971). A critical review of elitist and pluralist approaches to power and democracy.

SALISBURY, ROBERT H., ed., *Interest Group Politics in America* (New York: Harper & Row, 1970). A useful collection of articles and selections from books dealing with pressure groups.

SKOLNICK, JEROME H., *The Politics of Protest* (New York: Simon and Schuster, Inc., 1969). Originally a task force report to the National Commission on the Causes and Prevention of Violence; a broad survey of protest movements with an excellent chapter on black politics.

TRUMAN, DAVID, *The Governmental Process* (New York: Alfred A. Knopf, 1951). A comprehensive analysis of the operation of the American political system as seen through interest group activities.

VOSE, CLEMENT E., *Caucasians Only: The Supreme Court, the NAACP, and the Restrictive Covenant Cases* (Berkeley, Calif.: University of California Press, 1959). A scholarly study of the NAACP as a pressure group.

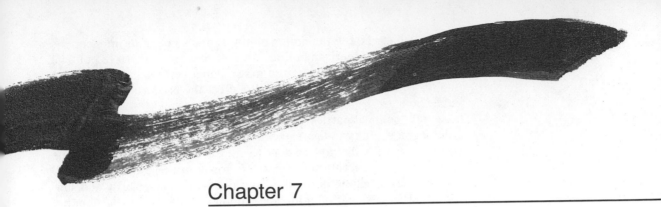

Chapter 7

The Party System

Parties and Interest Groups

The Two-Party System

Development of the Two-Party System
Why Two Parties?
Consequences of the Two-Party System
Exceptions to the Two-Party System

Parties and Ideology

Why Few Basic Differences?
Significance of Party Differences
Shifting Patterns of Difference

Decentralization of American Political Parties

Party Machinery for Winning Elections
Party Machinery for Running the Government
Federalism and Party Decentralization
Party Discipline: The Local Machine

Reform of the Party System

Critics of the Present System
Defenders of the Present System

The Pattern of the Party System

Summary

Selected Bibliography

CHAPTER 6 EXPLORED the notion of power and some of its implications for the study of American politics. In this chapter, we turn to political parties, the most obvious of the many nongovernmental institutions that try to organize and use power to affect the course and content of public policy.

Ideally, political parties perform a number of important functions in a democracy. For candidates seeking public office, a party mobilizes voters, organizes the government for those who are successful at the polls, and helps recruit new personnel for both these tasks. For citizens, parties supply information about political issues, clarify and simplify alternatives, and offer a choice among solutions. In addition, because political parties are continuing bodies, the citizenry can hold them responsible for achievements and failures, primarily by rewarding or punishing candidates at the next election.

Political parties in the United States do not always perform these functions effectively. Nevertheless, "the spirit and force of a party has in America been as essential to the action of the machinery of government as steam is to a locomotive engine," as Lord Bryce observed.[1]

Over the years, the American party system has developed three principal characteristics. First, at the national level, it is a two-party system. Since the 1790s, there have almost always been two, and only two, serious contestants for control of the national government. Second, the parties usually agree on many fundamentals of political philosophy and do not offer radically different programs to the voters. Third, each of the two national parties is decentralized. Party policy is more likely to be the result of bargaining among leaders at many levels of the party structure than of decisions made at the top.

Parties and Interest Groups

Before examining these characteristics of American political parties, we need to distinguish between political parties and interest groups. As we saw in the last chapter, an interest group is typically concerned with a single public policy or a set of related policies. In contrast, political parties involve themselves with a wide range of public policies. Specifically and more fundamentally, parties try to win control of the machinery of government in order to make those policies effective.

To attain its more limited goals, an interest group normally uses one or more of three basic techniques: electioneering, lobbying, and propagandizing. In electioneering, the group helps a party or individual candidates who appear favorably disposed to the group's objectives. Lobbying is an effort to persuade public officials, whatever their initial feelings about a group, to adopt and enforce its policies. Propagandizing is a longer-range version of the other two techniques. Essentially, it consists of "educating" the public to believe in the group's objectives and so to elect officials sympathetic to the group's goals.

Political parties also use these three techniques—including lobbying among their own members holding public office, because party leaders cannot always count on their support. For a party, however, the main techniques are, in the short run, electioneering and, over the longer haul, propagandizing. Interest groups may use these techniques to help a few candidates win office or to gain support on a small cluster of issues; party leaders are aiming for control of the government itself. The policy is *the* objective for interest group leaders. For most party leaders, on the other hand, policies are usually intermediate steps toward the primary goal of winning the next election.

Occasionally, an interest group that commands a large following is tempted to enter more directly into electoral affairs by becoming a political party. The Prohibition party, a one-issue organization that sought a ban on sale of alcoholic beverages in the years before adoption of the Eighteenth Amendment, provides a good example. For most groups, however, direct electoral involvement as a political party has few attractions. The variety of interests in the United States means that any group with too limited an aim will appeal to no more than a small segment of voters. Moreover, given the way in which the electoral system is organized, limited appeals are not likely to win any elections at the federal level and few at the state or even local level. On the other hand, if a well-organized interest group shrewdly bargains for the support of a party or candidate in exchange for help at the polls, the benefits can be both immediate and relatively inexpensive.

Unions, representing a large and frequently a well-organized minority, have been most often tempted to form parties. Labor parties have been organized in England, Ireland, Australia, and other countries, as well as in a few American states. Their efforts have met with some success, for labor in a highly industrialized area is a sufficiently numerous group to have a chance of winning an election. But labor's electoral prospects are not good unless a labor party is able to broaden its appeal to include farmers, professional men, trades people, or other groups. To become one of Britain's two major parties, the Labour party has had to pursue just such a course, and in so doing, it has ceased to be purely a workingman's party.

Interest groups can also function as political parties in countries that use an electoral system based on proportional representation. To win seats under proportional representation, parties need secure only a small proportion of the popular vote. Once in parliament, a narrowly based party may be able to negotiate its way into a governmental coalition and so exercise considerable direct influence on public policy. In the United States, however, a successful candidate usually must obtain a majority of the vote. Thus, most groups are discouraged from creating political parties to advance their particular interests.

The Two-Party System

The Constitution is silent about political parties and about such important party matters as presidential nominating conventions, direct primaries, and legislative caucuses. Because political parties were known in 1787 (though not in the fully modern sense) these omissions were probably deliberate. There is no record of any debate on political parties in the Constitutional Convention. At the end of his presidency, George Washington apparently expressed the attitude of many of the Founding Fathers when he warned against the "baneful effects of the spirit of party." It is also probable that some members of the Philadelphia convention realized the inevitability of political parties in American government. James Madison seemed to sense this in *The Federalist,* Number 10, originally published in November 1787:

A landed interest, a manufacturing interest, a mercantile interest, a monied interest, with many lesser interests, grow up of necessity in civilized nations, and divide them into different classes, actuated by different sentiments and views. The regulation of these various and interfering interests forms the principal task of modern legislation, and involves the spirit of party and faction in the necessary and ordinary operations of government.

Development of the Two-Party System

Whatever the thoughts and wishes of the men at the Philadelphia convention, by the beginning of Washington's second administration, two political parties were already operating. Washington had come under the influence of Alexander Hamilton and consistently sided with him against Thomas Jefferson in controversies over public policy. This factional dispute within Washington's cabinet became a party battle when Jefferson and James Madison created a coalition of small property owners and farmers to oppose Hamilton's policies. In 1793, Jefferson resigned from Washington's cabinet, and in a few years the *Republicans* (as they called themselves) were a full-fledged political party, challenging the administration's pro-British foreign policy and conservative economic policies.

During this period, the followers of Washington and Hamilton preempted for themselves the name of *Federalists*, although the Jeffersonian ranks included many of those who had led the original Federalist cause in the fight for adoption of the Constitution. The new Federalists, like the old, were predominantly an elite group composed of men of wealth and substance. In contrast to the imaginative and energetic Federalist campaign of 1787–1788 in support of the Constitution, the new Federalists were curiously negligent about forming local party organizations to compete with Jefferson's Republicans for support among the growing electorate. Out of touch with new voters and lacking the machinery to mobilize conservative voters, the Federalists were routed in the election of 1800. By 1816 they had ceased to exist as a party. The lesson of their disaster was not lost, however. Leaders of all succeeding parties have realized that to win office one must win votes; and to win votes one must have organizations working at every electoral level.

After the disappearance of the Federalists, the nation experienced a short period of one-party rule. Although the surviving party — the Jeffersonians — tried to encompass all points of political view, it could not satisfy every political, economic, and social interest. In the 1820s two warring factions developed within the party, the Democratic Republicans and the National Republicans. The split grew until by 1840 each of the two factions, now called *Democrats* and *Whigs,* had taken on the character of a national party.

Through the mid-1850s the two parties fought on almost even terms. But with the death of old Whig leaders like Henry Clay and Daniel Webster and the worsening of the crises over slavery, the Whig coalition between eastern capital and southern planters disintegrated. Of the various third parties competing for national status, Whigs as well as many northern Democrats found the new *Republican* party most attractive. In 1856, the Republicans rallied behind General John C. Fremont and made a respectable showing in the presidential campaign. In 1860, their candidate, Abraham Lincoln, carried only a minority of the popular vote but won a solid majority in the Electoral College. The Democrats and Republicans had become the main contestants in the American two-party system.

They were to remain so. No third party has come even close to capturing the White House in the years since 1860. Only in 1912, when the progressive wing of the Republican party broke from the regulars to nominate Theodore Roosevelt as the Bull Moose candidate, has a third party polled as many votes as the losing candidate of the major parties. Yet third parties have continued to have a voice in American politics. Henry Wallace and Strom Thurmond were heard in 1948 and George Wallace in 1968. In recent years some militant black leaders have advocated establishing a black party at the national level.

Why Two Parties?

One of the questions that has most puzzled foreign observers of American politics is why the United States has a two-party rather than a multiparty system. Most modern democracies have multiparty systems, and England and Canada have had a three-party system for much of the twentieth century. V. O. Key concluded that there is no satisfactory single answer. Instead, a number of forces have encouraged a two-party system.[2]

First, there are historical factors. The colonists brought with them a two-party tradition. It is easy to exaggerate its influence, however, because England in the eighteenth century did not have a party system in the modern sense. Yet the factional divisions between British Whigs and Tories had some effect on colonial ideas of politics. After independence, Federalists and Antifederalists divided over the adoption of the Constitution. A few years later came the split between the Federalists in power and the Jeffersonians out of power. The basic appeal to two social groups — by the Federalists to men of means and substance, and by the Jeffersonians first to small farmers and later also to the growing working classes in the cities — set the pattern that exists today.

Certain American institutions have also played a role in creating and preserving a two-party system. First the framers of the Constitution chose a presidential rather than a parliamentary form of government. Masses of voters owing allegiance to three or more parties will have more difficulty selecting a President than a majority of multiparty representatives in a legislature will have compromising their differences and picking a Prime Minister. Moreover, the constitutional requirement of majority agreement, whether the President is chosen by the Electoral College or by the House of Representatives, has further limited the number of presidential candidates and thus the number of political parties. The election of a single chief executive in each state and at local levels has also encouraged would-be factions to unite behind a single candidate and aim for that golden target, a majority vote.

Another institutional arrangement that has operated to foster a two-party system is the election of members of Congress from individual districts. In a single-member district only one party can win an election.* In such circumstances third parties are discouraged unless they can achieve voting strength sufficient to compete with the established major parties. The Constitution does not demand election of members of the House of Representatives from single-member districts, but Congress has by law required single-member districts throughout most of American history. Furthermore, the election of each of its two senators in different years makes each state a single-member district for senatorial elections. Many states, however, choose some members of their legislatures from multimember districts and there is no evidence that this procedure weakens the two-party system.[3]

Social factors have been more important than electoral arrangements in maintaining the American two-party system. Where a society is beset by political cleavages based on geographic, socioeconomic, ethnic, or religious lines, conditions are ripe for a multiparty system. Where there is relatively little class consciousness and where political divisions cut across religious, ethnic, geographic, and socioeconomic lines, a two-party system has a far better chance of taking firm root. In such a situation, "the stakes of politics are smaller, and the kinds of tolerance, compromise, and concession necessary for a two-party system's majoritarian parties can prevail."[4]

*A single-member district elects one representative to a legislative body. Districts that elect two or more legislative representatives are known as multimember districts.

"People are forgetting their old patriotisms . . . . like 'our party, right or wrong!'"

Grin and Bear It, by George Lichty and Fred Wagner, courtesy of Field Newspaper Syndicate.

There is class consciousness in the United States, as we saw in Chapter 2, as well as significant societal divisions along economic, ethnic, religious, geographic, and, most important, racial lines. Each of the two major parties does tend to direct its appeal to certain groups, and, as Chapter 9 will indicate, these groups often respond positively. Compared to countries such as France and Italy, however, class and other social divisions are relatively indistinct among whites in the United States. As long as blacks and other racial minorities were politically passive, racial differences imposed certain stresses on the governmental system, but stresses that the system could tolerate—although the pain to minorities was considerable. Now the situation has become more complex.

Appreciating the relative political, if not psychological, homogeneity of the white electorate, leaders of both parties have always tried to appeal to a wide spectrum of interests. Each party may gather its basic strength from particular ethnic, economic, or social groups, but each has usually tried to gain support from all segments of society. It has been a rare platform that has not offered something to all parts of white society, as well as to politically important parts of the black community. But the growing significance of racial cleavages has complicated the task of building biracial coalitions. In 1968 and 1972 the Republican party developed a "southern strategy," which gave up any hope of winning the black vote or any appreciable share of the liberal white vote of the northeast.[5] Instead, the Republicans successfully concentrated on capturing the white vote in the south and picking up enough support from traditional Republicans and worried white Democrats in the border states, the midwest, and California, as well as working-class whites in urban areas, to obtain a majority in the Electoral College. In 1976, the Republicans shifted their appeal more toward the rapidly growing states of the western as well as southern "rim" of the nation, but continued to ignore black voters.

Consequences of the Two-Party System

Because there are only two major parties, it is probable that in a presidential election year one or the other will win both the presidency and a majority of both houses of Congress. The peculiarities of the American electoral system make it possible, of course, for one party to gain the White House while the other wins a majority of seats in the House and the Senate. Such divided victories have happened only three times since 1848, however—in 1956, 1968, and again in 1972, and in each case, a Republican President faced a Democratic Congress. It is in off-year elections that the party not in control of the White House is more likely to obtain control of both houses of Congress. Such a division has occurred in eleven of twenty-three off-year elections since 1884.

By making it possible for one party to control the government, the two-party system puts great pressure on party leaders. To achieve the goal of party control they must win a majority, or close to a majority, of the popular vote. This requirement means that a party cannot concentrate on one interest (for example, organized labor) to the exclusion of all others. Nor can it depend solely on one segment of the country (for example, the south) for victory. Thus, the two-party system fosters the formation of electoral coalitions. Typically, the Republican party has brought together the financial interests of the northeast, the farmers and small-town residents of the midwest, and white-collar workers, professionals, and other suburbanites throughout the nation. More recently, Republicans have also focused attention on the prosperous states in the southwestern, Rocky Mountain, and Pacific Coast re-

gions. The Democrats, on the other hand, have historically united—at least for purposes of electing a President—the south, blue-collar workers in urban areas across the country, a portion of white-collar workers, small farmers, liberals, and blacks.

Exceptions to the Two-Party System

Although basically the United States has a two-party system, certain reservations must be made. First, for long intervals many states have had one-party systems. The south for almost a century after the Civil War offered the most obvious example of a regional one-party system. Furthermore, from 1914 to 1954, in only twenty-six of the then forty-eight states did the minority party win 25 percent or more of presidential, senatorial, and gubernatorial campaigns.[6] Examining elections from 1956 through 1973, Austin Ranney could classify only twenty-three of the fifty states as having truly competitive two-party systems.[7] Figure 7–1 shows how Ranney categorized individual states. In most election years, less than half the 435 congressional districts involve serious two-party contests, as we shall see in Chapter 10.

Now, however, these one-party monopolies seem to be giving way, both in national elections and, though less markedly, in state campaigns as well. In the 1960 presidential election, for example, the Republicans captured Florida, Tennessee, and Virginia; in 1964 they won Alabama, Georgia, Louisiana, Mississippi, and South Carolina; in 1968, Florida, North Carolina, Tennessee, South Carolina, and Virginia—all traditionally one-party states. And in 1972 Richard Nixon took every state in the old Confederacy from the Democrats. Although the Republicans were unable to consolidate their hold on the south in 1976, losing ten of the eleven states, President Ford ran almost as well in the south as he did elsewhere in the nation, winning 45 percent of the popular vote there compared to 49 percent nationally. The results of senatorial and congressional races have been less dramatic, but they tell a similar story of Republican gains. When the Ninety-fifth Congress convened in January 1977, 5 of the 22 senators from southern states were Republicans, as were 27 of the 108 southern members of the House.

The second reservation that must be made about the two-party system is that third parties have been a constant part of the American political scene. Freesoilers, Greenbackers, Populists, Farmer-Laborites, Prohibitionists, Bull Moosers, Socialists, Dixiecrats, Progressives, American Independents, and even Communists have been contestants for state and national office. No third party, however, with the possible exception of Theodore Roosevelt's Bull Moose group in 1912, has even come close to winning the presidency since the Republicans' success in 1860. On the other hand, third parties (for example, the Progressives in Wisconsin, the Non-Partisan League in the Dakotas, and the Liberals and the Conservatives in New York) have been influential

Figure 7.1
Party Competition in the United States

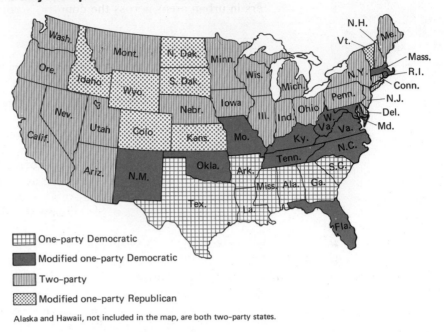

One-party Democratic

Modified one–party Democratic

Two-party

Modified one–party Republican

Alaska and Hawaii, not included in the map, are both two-party states.

Source: Austin Ranney, "Parties in State Politics," in Herbert Jacob and Kenneth N. Vines, eds., *Politics in the American States: A Comparative Analysis*, 3rd ed., p. 62. Copyright © 1976 by Little, Brown and Company. Reprinted by permission.

in state politics and occasionally have sent representatives and senators to Washington.

Despite short lifespans and influence restricted to single states or small geographic areas, third parties have often made important contributions to public policy. Many of them have won enough support among the voters to threaten the balance of power, and that threat has sometimes forced leaders of major parties to respond to pressures they would have preferred to ignore. Often the third party has taken a more decisive stand on issues than has either of the major parties. But whenever it has appeared that any large number of voters were being attracted to such a party, sooner or later one (or both) of the major parties has been sufficiently impressed to take over at least a part of the third party's program, thus cutting the ground from under it. For example, the small vote polled by Henry A. Wallace's Progressive party in 1948 resulted in part from the Democratic party's move to the left on civil rights and labor-management relations, caused by the Progressives' strength. So too in 1968 Richard Nixon undercut some of George Wallace's support by implying that a Republican administration would slow down the push for black civil rights. Furthermore, once in the White House President Nixon continued to erode Wallace's power by means of lax enforcement of civil right laws and by nominating for the Supreme Court a pair of southerners who had been staunch segregationists.

Parties and Ideology

A second key characteristic of the American party system is the lack of fundamental differences between the two major parties. Each presents to the voters an image that differs from the other's more in matters of style and policy detail than on fundamental issues of political philosophy. Both parties are likely to make appeals to citizens of all social classes and geographical areas. Both accept the basic, though vague, principles of democratic government as embodied in the American Constitution. Both reject socialism and endorse a free-enterprise system modified by a degree of governmental regulation.

Why Few Basic Differences?

Part of the explanation for the absence of fundamental differences can be traced to the lack of class consciousness of the bitter sort that has divided many nations. Most immigrants knew what a class-riven society was; they bore on their backs and in their souls many of its scars. As each new wave of immigrants came in, it was overwhelmed as much as absorbed by America, and the old hatreds softened into fears and suspicions. And the newcomers followed the twin American dreams of prosperity and equality. Without a high degree of class antagonism, development of parties with strong commitments to particular programs or ideas becomes very difficult. In this country an appeal pitched only to blue-collar workers may well fall on uncomprehending, if not deaf, ears, as members of the Students for a Democratic Society discovered in the late 1960s when they moved off the campuses and tried to "radicalize" factory workers. America's relative lack of class struggle can be traced to the absence of a feudal tradition, the comparative prosperity of the economy, the existence of a frontier to absorb dissident elements, the ideals of egalitarianism, and the political castration of blacks. As a result, the dominant political standards of American society have been those of the white middle class. No nationally oriented party can yet wander very far from its standards without risking disastrous defeat.

Furthermore, the two-party system encourages formation of coalitions. As we have seen, to control the national government party leaders must make a broad appeal. Given the diversity of American backgrounds, outlooks, aspirations, and loyalties, it has been difficult, even in times of severe crisis, to organize a majority coalition behind a specific and all-encompassing party program. An easier alternative for national party leaders is the vaguely worded statement of ultimate goals—glowing allusions to "The Great Society," for example, or to "binding up the nation's wounds"—with little systematic development of general ideas and few specific proposals for achieving these noble purposes. Even the New Deal, which was the closest thing to a comprehensive governmental program the United States has ever had, was a combination of uncoordinated and at times conflicting individual policies, geared as much to satisfying each of the diverse groups in Roosevelt's grand coalition as to overcoming the Great Depression through a coherent, coordinated governmental system.

An additional factor militating against clearly defined party positions is the indifference of many Americans to politics. In 1953, for example, at the height of debate in Congress and in the press over Senator John Bricker's proposed constitutional amendment to limit the President's treaty-making power, the Gallup poll reported that 81 percent of the persons interviewed disclaimed knowing anything about the proposal.

Even when people are not indifferent, public opinion is not likely to be neatly divided into two camps. Just before the 1968 election, after several years of intense public debate on American policy in Vietnam, the Survey Research Center of the University of Michigan found the following distribution of opinion about what the United States should do:

Pull out of Vietnam entirely	19.5%
Keep our soldiers in Vietnam but try to end the fighting	36.7
Take a stronger stand even if it means invading North Vietnam	33.5
Other	3.3
Don't know, no answer	7.0
Total number = 1557	100.0%

Public opinion may also be internally contradictory. The same people who disapprove of big government in Washington and want to cut federal spending may favor building new atomic-powered aircraft carriers, increasing aid to veterans, or expanding highway networks.

Significance of Party Differences

Despite the absence of a deep ideological gap between the major parties, Democrats and Republicans do differ in their general orientations toward public policies. The popular impression of the Democrats as the more liberal and the Republicans as the more conservative party is essentially accurate, although there are liberals and conservatives in each party. Delegates to the two national conventions—a group that includes senators, congressmen, governors, state and county chairmen, and other party officials, as well as private citizens—in their attitudes

Figure 7.2
Opinions of Administrative Assistants

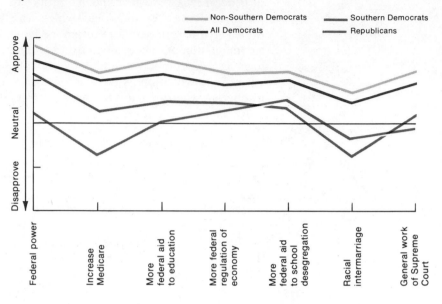

(Mean scores: The higher the score the more the group approves) Differences between "All Democrats" and "Republicans" are significant at the .005 level

Source: Walter F. Murphy and Joseph Tanenhaus, *Public Opinion and the American Supreme Court* (forthcoming).

toward a whole series of political issues have differed markedly along party lines. The Democrats have favored more governmental activity to protect the civil rights of minority groups, more governmental regulation of business, less regulation of labor, more public ownership of natural resources, higher taxes on business and upper income groups, and more of an internationalist orientation toward foreign policy than have Republican leaders.[8]

Administrative assistants of senators and congressmen have similar disagreements. As Figure 7–2 shows, Democratic staff members were much more favorably disposed toward use of federal power in general and more specifically to increase medical care for the aged, improve education, control the economy, and desegregate public schools. In addition, Democrats were far more likely to find nothing wrong with racial intermarriage and to approve both the liberal decisions of the Warren Court and the over-all way the justices had been performing their governmental functions. As a whole, even southern Democrats tended to be more liberal than Republicans on most of these issues.

The different approaches of the two parties can also be seen in a comparison of the concepts of the presidency held by Democratic Presidents Wilson, Franklin Roosevelt, Truman, Kennedy, and John-

Table 7-1
Party Unity[a] Scoreboard

	total roll calls	party unity roll calls	percent of total
1976			
Both Chambers	1349	493	37
Senate	688	256	37
House	661	237	36
1974			
Both Chambers	1081	399	37
Senate	544	241	44
House	537	158	29
1972			
Both Chambers	861	283	33
Senate	532	194	36
House	329	89	27
1970			
Both Chambers	684	219	32
Senate	418	147	35
House	266	72	27
1968			
Both Chambers	514	172	33
Senate	281	90	32
House	233	82	35
1966			
Both Chambers	428	198	46
Senate	235	118	50
House	193	80	41
1964			
Both Chambers	418	171	41
Senate	305	109	36
House	113	62	55

[a]"Party Unity" roll calls are those on which a majority of voting Democrats oppose a majority of voting Republicans. This is only one possible index of party cohesiveness in Congress. Source: Congressional Quarterly Weekly Report, April 3, 1964, p. 650; October 25, 1968, p. 2934; January 16, 1970, p. 172; November 18, 1972, p. 3018; January 25, 1975, p. 199; and November 13, 1976, pp. 3173-3174.

son with those of nearly all the Republican incumbents of this century. The most notable Republican exception, Theodore Roosevelt, took a grand view of his office, as did each of the Democrats. For these men, the presidency was a position of dynamic power, a post from which to control the executive bureaucracy, to push social and economic legislation through Congress, and to shape public opinion in favor of strong governmental action. For Taft, Harding, Coolidge, Hoover, and Eisenhower, the presidency was more a place for repose than for energetic action. Nixon and Ford differed in some respects from this Republican pattern: In foreign affairs, both were active and energetic. In domestic policy, however, Nixon and Ford essentially tried to stop Congress from acting, to reduce spending, and to cut back on programs aimed at social welfare.

The voting records of Congress provide another indication that there is a meaningful difference between the two parties. Party affiliation is the most significant factor associated with voting behavior of congressmen. While party unanimity is rare in Congress, party cohesion is not. Althouth in recent years there has been a decline in party unity on Capitol Hill, especially in the House, nonetheless, as Table 7–1 shows, party still exerts a strong pull on most representatives and senators. (Chapter 11 will further examine congressional voting behavior.)

Shifting Patterns of Difference

While party activists continue to show identifiable characteristics, there are within the electorate seethings that cannot easily be described in terms of traditional distinctions between liberals and conservatives. Agitation over the war in Vietnam, student radicalism, the fight first for civil rights and then for black power, the reaction against black demands by white ethnics, the political appeal of Governor George Wallace to millions of Americans, and the struggle for women's liberation, all reflect fundamental changes in the patterns of political attitudes and orientations. The customary image has been an American electorate clustered about the center, much as in Figure 7–3. These recent changes suggest that the old image mistakes the developing popular mood. That new state may be more accurately represented by the distribution presented in Figure 7–4. Even more precise may be a circular model (Figure 7–5) that shows how close in many respects—attitudes toward violence, for example—the radical right and the radical left have become and how the middle position is likely to be squeezed.

There are few hard data for any of the three figures. The 1972 election, like that of 1964, makes a strong case against any sizable popular abandonment of middle-of-the-road politics. But a large number of people (still a minority) are deeply worried about the course of American politics, and some proportion of those citizens is clearly alienated from the system. The Watergate scandals and the crass efforts of the White House to use bribery and perjury to hide earlier crimes scarcely

Figure 7.3

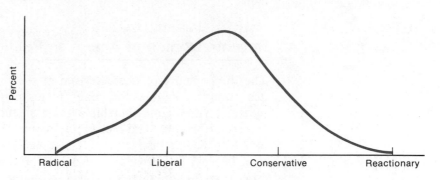

Figure 7.4

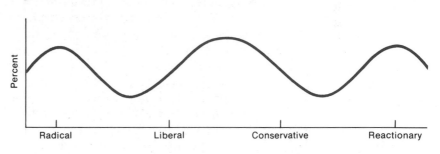

Figure 7.5

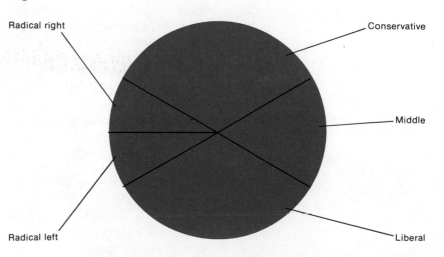

increase confidence in either the competence or the integrity of government.

Decentralization of American Political Parties

The third important characteristic of the American party system is decentralized organization. Each major party is often pictured as a pyramid, with the membership at the base, the President (or opposition leader) at the apex, and a chain of command running from top to bottom. This analogy is picturesque but misleading. Instead, power within each party is diffused. Rather than a chain of command running down from the top of the party hierarchy, there are only many avenues of persuasion, requests, demands, threats, and bargaining. Each of these is a two-way street, and sometimes the traffic in demands and threats is heavier going up than down.

Neither party enlists or organizes members on a national or centralized basis. In fact, membership in either party is difficult if not impossible to define. It does not involve paying dues or subscribing to any particular set of doctrines. Frequently, party membership is nothing more than a state of mind because many people who call themselves Democrats or Republicans never bother to vote. Among those who participate in elections, a vote cast in the party primary is the usual indication of party membership. In most states, a citizen who votes in the primary of one party is barred from voting in the primary of another for a period of several months or years. In a few states, however, primaries are "open," and voters are legally free to change party allegiance and vote in either primary, or, in the state of Washington, both. Nothing, of course, prevents any individual from voting for the other party's candidates at the general election.

Decentralization also is apparent in the complexity and disorder of party organizations. Overlap and conflict in organizational structure are common. In addition, formal organization is frequently supplemented by informal organizations that wield actual power. For example, presidential candidates typically put together personal staffs that usurp many of the campaigning functions of their respective national committees, Nixon's Committee to Re-elect the President (CREEP) being a striking example. As we have already seen in Chapter 5, federalism also plays an important role in decentralizing American parties because it provides independent bases of political power.

Party Machinery for Winning Elections

Generally speaking, party machinery, whether formal or informal, has one of two functions: winning elections or running the government. Of these two types of party organization, the first is more decentralized.

The basic unit of the party machinery for winning elections corresponds to the basic unit of electoral administration, the *precinct*. Here the party organization may consist of only one person, the precinct captain or executive. Particularly in large cities, he or she may have a small staff of assistants, usually part-time volunteers. Historically, it was at the precinct level that most of the personal contact between party officials and party constituencies occurred, although this is far less true today. Above the precinct in urban areas is the *ward organization,* again perhaps consisting of only a few people. In small towns and rural areas the unit above the precinct is the *county committee*. Its members are usually the precinct captains, and its chairman is often "a local political potentate of considerable significance."[9] As a result, the 3,000-odd county chairmen wield real power within each party organization.

One step above the county committee, at least on paper, is the *state committee*. Depending on local laws and customs, its members may be elected or may hold their offices by virtue of their position in county organizations. The functions that state committees are supposed to perform vary widely from state to state, but they frequently include coordinating the campaign work of county committees, calling state party conventions to nominate candidates for office, and arranging the administrative details for primaries.

Although much of the organization and operation of party machinery at the local and state level is prescribed by state law, at the national level party machinery is strictly a matter of custom. The two parties, however, have established very similar patterns of organization. There are four main agencies, or agents, heading the national parties: the *national convention,* the *national committee,* the *national chairman,* and the *national committee secretariat.*

The *national convention* is the formal assembly of some 1,200 to 3,200 delegates* from the fifty states and the federal territories who meet every four years† amid television cameras, bunting, bands, and extravagant oratory. The national convention's task is to select the party's candidates for President and Vice President and to determine party policy by writing and approving a document called the *party platform,* in which a stand, forthright or evasive, is taken on the issues of the day. Apart from these functions, the national convention has little authority. It has nothing to do with the nomination of the party's candidates for Congress, nor can it compel congressional candidates to pledge support to the party's platform. Between conventions it has no authority at all.

During the four-year period between conventions a party is supposedly run by the *national committee* and the national chairman. The national committees are composed of members from each state, territory, and the District of Columbia. Ordinarily, a national committee meets

---

*There is a difference between *delegates* and *votes* in a national convention. Some delegates may have only a half-vote.
†In 1974, the Democrats held a mid-term convention, which provided a national forum for various factions and leaders.

only on call by the chairman, and such calls are infrequent. Its main task is to determine the date and place of the national convention. The committee never actually runs the party, nor does it determine party policy, although it may ratify proposals laid before it by the chairman or party members holding public office. Individual national committee members, however, frequently wield considerable power in their own states and within the federal government.

The *national chairman* is chosen by the national committee every four years after the nomination of the presidential and vice-presidential candidates. In practice the chairman is the personal choice of the presidential nominee, and the committee merely ratifies the name suggested. The first and most important task confronting the new chairman is the party's campaign for the presidency. The national chairman is also active in congressional campaigns, but here power and responsibility are shared with the Senate and House campaign committees organized by the party groups in Congress. Between elections, the national chairman's day-to-day duties are varied. He keeps in close touch with state and local party organizations, makes many speeches, and works constantly to raise party funds. Never has a national chairman become a "boss" in the sense that state and local chairmen sometimes have. Rarely does the national chairman have anything to do with the actual operation of the government itself unless he also holds a governmental post.

The party *secretariat* attracts little attention, but this salaried staff attached to the national committee and its chairman is extremely important to the vitality and the effectiveness of the party. Its organization varies from time to time and from party to party. Its functions are to write speeches for important party members, supply research assistance, help raise money, keep track of political trends, prepare publicity releases, handle correspondence with state and local party agencies, and engage in a great many housekeeping tasks whose successful performance, although not publicized, does much to build party unity and strength for the next campaign.

Party Machinery for Running the Government

Party machinery for winning elections has relatively little to do with running the national government. Indeed, any attempt by the national chairman or national committee to exert pressure on congressmen is apt to be vigorously resisted. To be sure, county chairmen and other party officials offer advice on the distribution of patronage and convey to officeholders requests for favors that may affect the formation or administration of important public policies. More important in Washington, however, are the party organizations that parallel governmental machinery. Each party has units inside Congress, including a caucus, a steering or policy committee, and a floor leader to try to shape policy making. (These we shall examine in Chapter 11.) National party officials are supposed to be in close touch with the executive branch if the party controls the presidency. In reality, the White House staff, other presidential advisers, and the Cabinet are more often the instruments through which party control of the administrative aspects of government is exercised.

The President, of course, is the chief of his party. In staffing an administration, Presidents seek not only to run the government efficiently but also to keep the party organization together by rewarding friends and punishing enemies. Although the President's control over party machinery is far from absolute, his immediate access to the press and the television networks, the enormous prestige of his office, and his power over patronage provide him with party leadership if he cares to use it. Like it or not, other party leaders have to live with the fact that the public at large usually identifies the President with his party, and the fate of most of the party's candidates at the next election is strongly influenced by the public image of the President.

The opposition party on the other hand has no powerful, national leader around whom to rally. Supposedly, the leader of the minority party is the defeated presidential nominee, but his actual position is ambiguous. His rejection by the voters to some extent counterbalances his nomination by the party for the country's highest office, and commonly he is leader in name only. As Adlai Stevenson, twice titular head of the Democratic Party, commented:

The titular leader has no clear and defined authority within his party. He has no party office, no staff, no funds, nor is there any system of consultation whereby he may be advised of party policy and through which he may help to shape that policy. There are no devices such as the British have developed through which he can communicate directly and responsibly with the leaders of the party in power.[10]

Adding to the difficulties of the titular leader are rivals within the party. Leaders who opposed his nomination are rarely persuaded of the error of their ways by having the electorate confirm their views. Other presidential hopefuls, looking to the next nomination, are rarely eager to increase the prestige and power of a prominent rival.

If there were no more to the story, then the titular leader's position would be unambiguously impotent. But, as Stevenson himself admitted, the press and public often look on the titular leader as the spokesman of his party. Whether or not he deserves that role, there is rarely any other person who has a legitimate claim to speak for the party. Senators, congressmen, and governors represent interests that are too parochial, and aspiring presidential candidates have not yet won the approval of the national convention. "Despite its ambiguity, perhaps even because of it," three close students of the American party system conclude, "the titular leadership has become a post that offers many opportunities for initiative, at least for a first time incumbent."[11]

As Chapter 4 pointed out, federalism in the formal governmental structure increases the decentralization of power within the party system. There are more than 78,000 units of government in the United States that are empowered to levy taxes and more than a half million elective political offices. An independent source of revenue or an elective office means a potentially independent base of power for state and local party leaders and elected officials. A mayor who refuses to support an urban renewal program on which the President's prestige depends cannot be fired by the President, even though they are of the same party. Nor can the President dismiss a senator or representative who consistently attacks the administration's foreign policy or votes against administration bills. Each of these officials is elected by a local constituency and is legally responsible only to that constituency. If the locally based official is sure of electoral support, he can thumb his nose at the President, at party colleagues, or at any other official.

Congress has been wary of centralizing power in Washington and usually stipulates that state and local officials share in administering national programs. State and local officials actually spend federal grants, as we saw in Chapter 5, and so power moves away from national party leaders. In addition, almost every congressman takes up a considerable part of his time—and his staff spends even more—talking to administrators about problems his constitutents at home are experiencing, once again diffusing national party influence. A congressman can apply more formal pressure in questioning agency heads or bureau chiefs during annual appropriations hearings or at special investigations. A President's ability to control his bureaucracy is typically proportional to his ability to control Congress; and seldom can even the most astute President exercise real control (as opposed to influence) over senators and congressmen from his own party.

Party Discipline: The Local Machine

Decentralization does not always affect parties at the state or local level, and in some areas, discipline is strict and real power centered in the hands of one man or a small group of men. The literature and folklore on colorful, and not always honest, city and county bosses is as enormous as it is fascinating. The fragmented power structure of the national parties helps bosses run their machines. Decentralization of government and party power means local control and "plays into the hands of the boss . . . he has contact with all the elements of the party system, but he usually is beyond the authority of any higher echelon of the party. He has and uses the weapons of discipline to keep control over his organization, but he is usually free of effective control or discipline from above."[12]

Harper's Weekly, December 18, 1886.

The Spirit of Tweed Is Mighty Still.
"And even yet you don't know what you are going to do about it!"

Increased prosperity, the spread of civil service, and wider assumption by governmental agencies of social welfare functions once exercised by party officials to keep poor immigrants loyal have cut into the number and efficiency of bosses. Even fabled bosses like Mayor Richard J. Daley of Chicago have encountered problems keeping their machines running smoothly. Yet many of these disciplined local political organizations survive, particularly in the older cities of the northeast and midwest.

Although these organizations have less power than in the past, they continue to play an important party role, largely because of their ability to control disciplined blocs of voters in primary elections. Political bosses also survive because citizens need, or believe they need, a political broker who listens sympathetically to problems and has enough organizational strength to intervene with a particular agency of government. A father, for example, who has denounced politicians and bossism all his life may turn to a state or local political leader when his son has trouble getting into the medical school of the state university. A contractor who wants a bigger share of paving jobs complains not to a purchasing agent of the county but to its political taskmaster. Citizens like these represent sources of power as much as did the impoverished and disoriented immigrants of the gaslight era. The individual who can help them soon becomes a repository of good will—the substance of which bosses are made.

If Americans widely believe that politicians are engaged in a dirty business, it is partly because many private citizens persist in using party organizations for personal gain, from fixing a traffic ticket to legitimizing by ordinance and statute otherwise illegal business practices worth thousands or even millions of dollars. In boss-ridden cities, the party boss and his aides are accessible to citizens who want some governmental act of commission or omission for which they are willing to make some suitable payment. In other areas, a party functionary may merely be an intermediary who "introduces" a citizen to appropriate governmental officials and tries to get him a sympathetic hearing. Often, particular party leaders are known for their close relationship with governmental officials, one with the police department, another with the prosecutor's office, another with the tax assessor, and so on.

Even when an activity is legal—for example, the operation of a race track under license granted by the state or a city—relations between operators and government or party officials may be intimate and questionable. The list of stockholders in such enterprises often includes a large number of party leaders, perhaps to ensure adequate police assistance in handling traffic and large crowds. These enterprises are by no means exceptional. For decades, the liquor business has put large sums of money into politics in order to maintain valuable operating privileges.

Reform of the Party System

At the turn of the century the American party system was the principal target of political reformers. Their goal was to curb the power of the party politician. To this end they fought for nonpartisan elections in which candidates' party affiliations would not appear on the ballot. In other areas, they fought for primary elections, which would take the power to nominate candidates away from party leaders.

The party system is still the target of political reformers, but ironically the goal of many is now to strengthen party leadership, to centralize power within the parties, to shore up party discipline, and to broaden the representation of women, blacks, younger people, and others within the party structure. The over-all objective of the newer critics is to make the parties more responsive to the popular will and more responsible for the behavior of their elected candidates.

Critics of the Present System

The decentralized, compromising character of the national parties has been severely criticized on the ground that such parties fail to fulfill two essential functions. First, they do not present the voters with a clear choice on the really important public issues. Indeed, they frequently fail even to discuss the really important issues. There is, critics charge, "a vast boredom" in America with party politics. "Because it has failed to engage itself with the problems that dog us during our working days and haunt our dreams at night, politics has not engaged the best in us."[13]

The second criticism of the American party system is that its diffusion of power causes a diffusion of responsibility. Because no one individual or one committee or one convention can set party policy, no individual or committee or convention can be held responsible. Some critics argue that the United States now has a four-party rather than a two-party system, with the Democrats and Republicans each having a congressional party and a presidential party. The parties are not able to effect consistent governmental policies and the voters are unable to hold either party, as a party, responsible for the action or inaction of its members while in office.

Defenders of the Present System

Some political scientists defend as well as criticize the existing party system. Pendleton Herring, for example, claimed that a democratic society can survive only where there is a constant reconciliation of conflicting economic and social interests. Herring argued that a party politician performs an essential social role by acting as mediator. He also defended the political party because of the way in which it appeals to a wide variety of groups and wins their support by offering something to each. "The accomplishment of party government," Herring wrote, "lies in its demonstrated ability for reducing warring interests and conflicting classes to cooperative terms."[14] Herring and others have asserted that the vague ideologies of the two parties make it possible for people who have clashing interests to live together in peace. If the lines of conflict were ever drawn too clearly and the stakes in politics set too high, the danger of the defeated faction's refusing to accept the result of an election would increase. Its members might conclude that, having lost so much, it would be better off opposing the result with violence than permitting the government to pursue unacceptable policies.

The Pattern of the Party System

We deliberately chose the term *party system* for this chapter, because "to speak of a party *system* is to imply a patterned relationship among elements of a larger whole."[15] What we have described and analyzed is a pattern of relationships. The three main characteristics of the American party system—two parties, with few fundamental differences, and with decentralized organizations—are so interrelated that it is difficult to say which are causes and which are effects of the others, or how the consequences of each shape the consequences of the others.

Because a two-party system encourages efforts to form majorities, it encourages the formation of broad-based electional coalitions. The relative absence of deep and antagonistic class cleavages also discourages ideological stands, as does a respected written Constitution. These factors also encourage electoral coalitions, which in turn facilitate a two-party rather than a multiparty system. A presidential form of government and a winner-take-all electoral arrangement for congressional seats also encourage two parties and move parties to stress social unity rather than divisiveness. At the same time, such political arrangements are feasible only where class consciousness is low. A pluralistic society spread over half a continent makes federalism an attractive political arrangement. Federalism, in turn, creates independent bases of power for local politicians and works against disciplined national parties. Undisciplined national parties are not likely to be able to unite on ideology and comprehensive programs. The dangling bait of a majority vote and the apparent middle-of-the-road and rather indifferent political attitude of large portions of the electorate move the parties to make similar appeals to similar groups of voters. At the same time, the similarity of these appeals may tend to make large blocs of voters somewhat lukewarm in their attention to politics and, after being educated in an environment of political moderation, to adhere to the middle of the political road.

This reasoning does not lead to a conclusion that the party system has never changed or can never change. Surely in many respects it has changed over the years, and inevitably it will change in the future. The attempt in 1964 by elements within the Republican party to swing that party from the center would have, if continued for any length of time, brought about sweeping changes in the nature of the party system. The stinging defeat of Senator Barry Goldwater in the presidential election of that year convinced Republican leaders to halt the voters' abandonment of their party by uniting behind Richard Nixon, a more moderate conservative. In 1972, many of Senator George McGovern's supporters and at times the Senator himself saw his campaign as an effort to restructure the party system by ousting conservatives from the Democratic party and moving the organization decisively to the left. The disastrous results of that election convinced most Democratic leaders that a feasible reshaping of the party system cannot stray too far from the middle of the political road.

Nor does the description of the patterns of party behavior as a system imply that positive steps should not be taken to reform that system. What the concept of a party system does indicate is that reform is a much more difficult process than merely tinkering with the mechanics of party organization. The concept of a party system suggests that successful reform of the party system is likely to have widespread effects throughout the entire governmental and social system in the United States. If power within the parties were to be effectively centralized and if they were thus converted into disciplined, programmatic bodies, headed by leaders who had real power, changes in the basic structure of American politics would follow. Not only would relations between the President and Congress be affected. Relations between the nation and the fifty states would also change. Furthermore, fusion of the scattered fragments of power into the hands of leaders of disciplined parties might very well materially affect the relationship of the individual to government.

The existing splintering of power makes governmental action difficult and thus often frustrates demands for new and needed policies. But by making governmental action difficult that splintering also sometimes helps protect individuals and minorities against oppressive governmental action.

Summary

Political parties perform extremely important functions in a modern democracy. They mobilize electoral support at the polls, simplify alternatives for voters, dramatize issues and candidates, and provide a means of organizing government after elections. Unlike interest groups, which usually concentrate on a particular policy goal, political parties seek to win control of the machinery of government. In the United States, a party system has evolved characterized by the existence of two major parties that are highly decentralized and not separated by fundamental social, economic, or ideological differences. The result is a party system that encourages the formation of governing majorities, but does not provide sufficient party cohesion or discipline to permit parties to dominate the government.

Selected Bibliography

AGAR, HERBERT, *The Price of Union* (Boston, Mass.: Houghton Mifflin Company, 1945). Stresses the role that political parties have played in American history in furthering compromise and building consensus.

BASS, JACK and WALTER DEVRIES, *The Transformation of Southern Politics*

(New York: Basic Books, 1976). An informed effort to update the analysis in Key's *Southern Politics* listed below.

BINKLEY, WILFRED E., *American Political Parties,* 4th ed. (New York: Alfred A. Knopf, 1963). Provides historical background for the present-day party system.

BURNHAM, WALTER DEAN, *Critical Elections and the Mainsprings of American Politics* (New York: W. W. Norton, Inc., 1970). A "revisionist" interpretation of American politics that argues that the party system is on the verge of a drastic realignment.

COTTER, CORNELIUS P. and BERNARD C. HENNESEY, *Politics without Power* (New York: Atherton Press, 1964). An analysis of the national committees of the two major parties.

DUVERGER, MAURICE, *Political Parties: Their Organization and Activity in the Modern State* (New York: John Wiley and Sons, Inc., 1954). Still a leading comparative study of party systems in several countries.

GREENSTEIN, FRED I., *The American Party System and the American People,* 2d ed. (Englewood Cliffs, N.J.: Prentice-Hall, Inc., 1970). A short but insightful introduction to American parties.

HOFSTADTER, RICHARD, *The Idea of a Party System: The Rise of Legitimate Opposition in the United States, 1780–1840* (Berkeley, Calif.: University of California Press, 1969). An analysis by a distinguished historian of the gradual establishment of what we have come to call political parties.

KEY, V. O., JR., *Politics, Parties, and Pressure Groups,* 5th ed. (New York: Thomas Y. Crowell Company, 1964). The most recent (and the last) edition of the standard—and, in many ways, the classic—textbook on American political parties.

———, *Southern Politics in State and Nation* (New York: Alfred A. Knopf, 1949). A brilliant analysis of the politics of one section of the United States.

MCKEAN, DAYTON, *The Boss* (Boston, Mass.: Houghton Mifflin Company, 1940). A detailed study of the late Mayor Hague of Jersey City and his political machine.

MICHELS, ROBERT, *Political Parties* (New York: Dover Publications, Inc., 1959). A sociological study of the emergence of leadership, the psychology of power, and the oligarchic tendencies of organization, first published in English in 1915.

ROYKO, MIKE, *Boss: Richard J. Daley of Chicago* (New York: The New American Library, 1971). A fascinating journalistic account of the most prominent of extant American political bosses.

SARTORI, GIOVANNI, *Parties and Party Systems: A Framework for Analysis* (New York: Cambridge University Press, 1976). The first volume in a sweepingly ambitious multi-volume effort to construct a general theory of political parties.

SCHATTSCHNEIDER, E. E., *The Struggle for Party Government* (College Park, Md.: University of Maryland Press, 1948). In contrast to volumes by Agar, Herring, and others, this pamphlet presents a plea for stronger and more highly disciplined parties.

SUNDQUIST, JAMES L., *Dynamics of the Party System* (Washington, D.C.: The Brookings Institution, 1973). An analysis of party realignments, which seeks to explain changes in the American party system.

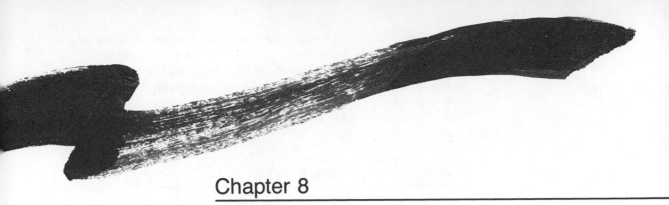

Chapter 8

Elections and Campaigns

IN DISCUSSING THE American party system, Chapter 7 spoke of winning public office — gaining control of government — as the primary goal of political parties and the chief characteristic setting them apart from interest groups. This chapter looks at the electoral processes, the means by which the federal political system as a functioning constitutional democracy chooses all of its legislators and two of its executive officials.

Suffrage and Democracy

A minimum requirement of democratic government is that *principal officers who make public policy should be elected by the people for limited terms.* Although hardly controversial, this prescription leaves open such vital questions as who are the "principal officers"? from what constituencies shall different sets of officers be chosen? what constitutes a "limited term"? and, of course, just who are "the people"?

"Principal Officers"

There is no objective test to distinguish "principal officers" from minor political officials. Certainly heads of executive offices such as the Attorney General and the Secretary of Defense make important policy decisions, but to some extent so do almost all governmental officials. Even a policeman modifies a legislative policy when he decides not to give speeding tickets unless offenders exceed posted limits by more than five miles an hour. So too a judge in interpreting general phrases of the Constitution or ambiguous wording in a statute inevitably makes both law and policy.

Yet at the national level a citizen can only vote for a senator twice every six years, a congressman every two years, and, by a single X on the ballot, a President and a Vice President every four years. At the state and local level, far more offices are elective. Indeed, some states sin by overwhelming voters with a "jungle ballot," a long list of candidates for offices ranging from governor, lieutenant governor, cabinet officials, three levels of judges, state, county, and municipal legislators and perhaps a mayor, coroner, and dog catcher. There are, in fact, more than a half million elected officials serving in state and local governments. Voters seldom even know the names of most of the candidates for minor offices, and where candidates' party identification is unclear, choice has a large element of randomness. There is, apparently, something to the old myth that being listed first on the ballot confers an advantage.

Perhaps related to the tangles of the jungle ballot are rather startling findings from a study of eighty-seven cities in the San Francisco Bay area.[1] There, about a quarter of municipal councilmen were not in the first instance elected to office but were appointed to serve out the terms of people who had died or resigned. Furthermore, candidates running as incumbents won in 80 percent of the elections, indicating the tremendous advantage conferred by the familiarity of their names.

Constituencies

American colonial history made it inevitable that national legislators would be chosen from within the states. Once the Constitutional Convention had decided that there was to be a single executive who would not be selected by or from Congress, a national constituency also became inevitable for the election of the President.

"Limited Terms"

"Limited terms" posed additional problems for the framers; and in their typical fashion, they adopted a pragmatic compromise: two years for members of the House of Representatives, six for senators, and four for the President, all being eligible for re-election. Like many compromises, this solution has not ended debate. Proposals have frequently been made to lengthen representatives' terms to four years and to restrict the number of terms a national legislator may serve. In the latter vein, the Twenty-second Amendment limits a President to two four-year terms or, if he initially succeeds to the presidency on the death or disability of the incumbent, to a maximum of ten years.

"The People"

The framers spoke eloquently of "We, the people," but they skillfully avoided offering any definition of who those people were. Alexander Hamilton's alleged reference to the people as a "great beast" probably did not accurately reflect the delegates' sentiments. Nevertheless, many of them deeply feared democracy. As we saw in Chapter 4, the framers wanted popular *approval* of the political system but not necessarily much active popular *participation*. As part of their artful dodging, they left the question of suffrage* pretty much to the states. Senators were to be elected by state legislatures, congressmen by voters who possessed "the qualifications requisite for electors of the most numerous branch of the state legislature," and members of the Electoral College, who formally choose the President, were to be selected in each state "in such manner as the legislature thereof may direct." Again, this compromise marked the beginning not the end of debate and development.

*Suffrage refers to the right to vote.

The March toward "One Person, One Vote"

Despite the framers' serious reservations, their republic evolved into democracy. As the idea of equality gained strength and its logic extended to politics, the concept of "one person, one vote" gradually became an ideal of American political culture.

Constitutional Changes

Formal constitutional amendments have played a part in broadening the suffrage and in shifting control over decisions about who can vote from the states to the federal government. In forbidding states to deny persons equal protection of the laws, the Fourteenth Amendment, adopted in 1868, generally prohibits discriminatory regulations of the right to vote. The Fifteenth Amendment, approved in 1870, specifically bars state or federal abridgment of the right to vote "on account of race, color, or previous condition of servitude." The Nineteenth Amendment, which became part of the Constitution in 1920, forbids discrimination because of sex. The Seventeenth Amendment, adopted in 1913, provides for direct, popular election of U.S. senators by those persons qualified to vote for members of Congress. The Twenty-third Amendment, which went into force in 1961, gives the District of Columbia three votes in the Electoral College, but that amendment makes no provision for representation in Congress. The Twenty-fourth Amendment, operable since 1964, forbids denials of a right to vote because of failure to pay poll taxes* or other levies, and the Twenty-sixth Amendment, adopted in 1971, lowers the minimum voting age to eighteen.

Formal constitutional amendments do not in actuality tell all of the story. White, male suffrage had become almost universal before the Civil War, and these advances had come through political processes at the state level. Furthermore, when constitutional amendments have been quickly successful, they have reflected earlier deep-rooted changes in political attitudes. For example, before the Seventeenth Amendment was proposed, most states already had informally provided for popular choice of senators. Similarly, adoption of the Twenty-fourth Amendment occurred while the poll tax was dying a painful but natural death. The story was much the same with the Nineteenth Amendment's extension of suffrage to women. Adoption in 1920 cli-

---

*A *poll tax* (or *head tax* or *capitation tax*) is a general tax of a fixed amount levied on all persons regardless of income or property. When used in the south, it was typically collected either some months before an election in order to establish a citizen's eligibility to vote or at the election itself. In either case payment was a prerequisite to receiving a ballot. Those who did not wish to vote were usually not asked to pay the tax. To increase its effect on the poor, it was usually cumulative. For example, failure to pay the tax in 1944 and 1945 meant that before a citizen could vote in 1946 he or she would have to pay the tax for all three years.

maxed nearly a century of agitation, marked toward the close by mass demonstrations, violence, and jailings. But the amendment came after fifteen states had granted full female suffrage and many others had conferred limited voting rights. The Twenty-sixth Amendment also came after years of debate over the unfairness of drafting eighteen-year-olds into the armed forces while refusing to allow them to participate in choosing officials who decided on war and peace.

The history of the Fourteenth and Fifteenth Amendments was radically different. They were not anchored in established customs, nor were they products of long debates on black suffrage; even many abolitionists had before and during the Civil War argued against allowing freed slaves to vote. Moreover, in southern states, where almost all blacks then lived, the amendments lacked legitimacy among the white majority. Not only did they violate the wishes of most whites, but the Radical Republicans—those in control in Washington—had also made ratification of these two amendments a prerequisite for southern states to regain their prewar status. Worsening the situation was a general lack of even elementary political knowledge among newly freed slaves and consequent scarcity of black leadership. These amendments thus represented the hopes of a group of northern whites and blacks only temporarily dominant in the federal government. But without a strong base of power in either the north or the south, the amendments signaled merely a small beginning to full political participation by blacks.

Black Ballots

After 1877 and the end of Reconstruction, which had involved federal military rule of the former Confederate states, there was some acceptance among whites of black voting, even in the south. The movement to disfranchise blacks did not gain real momentum until the 1890s. Then, after the failure of the Populist Revolt of small farmers and poor city dwellers to capture political power in the south, many Populists turned on the black man as a scapegoat, blaming their defeat on the conservatives' ability to buy black votes.[2] (One must keep in mind that the secret ballot that we know did not come into wide use in the south until a decade later. During the 1890s voting was open, not secret, and often oral rather than written, making purchasing votes and other sorts of fraud quite easy.)

Historically, whites used three different means of keeping blacks from the polls. The first, simple physical violence or threats of violence, was patently illegal, although no less effective for this fact. The second means, economic reprisal—for example, firing a black man who tried to vote or denying him credit at local stores—was also sometimes illegal but more subtly so. Third, there was a continuous search for a "legal" means of keeping blacks from voting: "literacy" tests administered in such a way as to allow discrimination against both blacks and poor whites; "understanding clauses" that required a voter to explain to a state official's satisfaction that he "understood" the state or federal Constitution; "grandfather clauses" that permitted a citizen to vote without taking a literacy test if his grandfather had voted; "white primaries" that barred blacks from participation in primary elections, which, until recently, were the real elections in the one-party south; and poll taxes that again discriminated against poor whites as well as blacks.

The Supreme Court declared many of these legal charades unconstitutional, but southern officials could pass new laws as fast as judges could invalidate them. Not until after the School Segregation Cases[3] of 1954 did public and official moods become receptive to national legislative and administrative action to end discriminatory voting practices. After passing a pair of ineffective statutes in 1957 and 1960, Congress, prodded anew by federal judges, by the U.S. Commission on Civil Rights, and by the growing political power of northern blacks, zeroed in on the principal evils of literacy tests and other procedures for registering voters.

In much of the south, however, resistance to black voting continued. White Citizens' Council leaders and state officials—in many instances state officials *were* White Citizens' Council leaders—cooperated to purge already registered blacks from voting lists. Blacks trying to register for the first time were often confronted with a battery of evasive maneuvers. Some registrars held office hours at irregular times and were simply not available when blacks showed up. Other registrars arbitrarily refused to accept such standard identification as a driver's license, declared blacks to be illiterate, or required that a prospective black voter bring in two already registered voters (that is, whites) to identify him. There were also cases in which registrars rejected black applicants for such minor errors as underlining rather than circling "Mr." on an application form.

To counter these tactics, the Civil Rights Act of 1964 made a sixth-grade education a presumption of literacy and required that all literacy tests be administered in writing, unless the Attorney General of the United States gave special permission. The statute also forbade unequal administration of registration requirements and made it illegal for state officials to refuse to allow a prospective voter the franchise because of immaterial errors on registration forms. In addition, the 1964 act strengthened earlier statutes permitting the Attorney General to intervene in voting cases and directed the Bureau of the Census to gather registration and voting statistics based on race and national origin.

Although more effective than its predecessors, this statute proved to be defective in many respects, leading Congress to pass a new law in 1965, the Voting Rights Act. The heart of the 1965 statute—which applies to all elections, state or national, primary or general—is a series of specific, practical remedies. The act allowed the U.S. Attorney General to suspend operation of any state, county, or parish voting test

Blacks flock to the polls in rural Peachtree, Alabama, in 1966, part of the dramatic increase in voting by southern blacks which resulted from enactment of the Voting Rights Act of 1965.

of literacy, education, or character that he believed had been used to discriminate. It also provided that any new local or state regulations affecting voting rights had to be approved by the U.S. Attorney General. Then, in 1975 Congress simplified the statute by outlawing all literacy tests. The Voting Rights Act also allows the U.S. Attorney General to declare that federal supervision in some specified place is necessary to ensure fair voting procedures there. The U.S. Civil Service Commission must then assign federal examiners to determine who are qualified voters, and state officials must register anyone so certified. If requested by the Attorney General, the Commission must also assign federal officers as poll watchers to ensure that qualified voters are allowed to cast their ballots.

Although early enforcement of the Voting Rights Act was hampered by a lack of trained personnel who could investigate complaints or serve as examiners, this federal show of force nevertheless encouraged black organizations to intensify their registration drives in the south and in the north as well. Black registration figures climbed dramatically. Now, even in the deep south, black voters are an important political force. By 1976 more than 3,500 elected black officials were serving in Congress and in state and local governments—a figure that represents a remarkable change over the previous decades but appears less impressive when one realizes that it represents less than one percent of all elected officials currently serving.

Today voters are required to meet four general conditions. These pertain to citizenship, age, residence, and registration.

There is nothing in the Constitution that limits voting to citizens, and in the past many states allowed aliens to vote. Now, however, citizenship is an absolute requirement in every state. Historically, states have also required citizens to be residents for rather lengthy periods before they could vote, often twelve months or occasionally even several years. In an amendment to the Voting Rights Act Congress in 1970 effectively eliminated residence requirements for voting in presidential elections. Two years later, the Supreme Court declared a Tennessee law requiring a year's residence to vote in a state election to be a violation of equal protection of the law.[4] Thirty days, the Justices said, provided ample time for the state to prevent fraud.

Each state administers these requirements by means of a system of registration. Typically, a prospective voter must go to a local governmental office during specified times of the year, offer proof of age, residence, and citizenship, and have his or her name entered on the electoral rolls. Most states now provide for permanent registration; that is, once a voter is enrolled he or she may continue to vote at each election. To prevent fraudulent "voting" using names of those who have died or moved away, some states still require reregistration every few years.

While useful in keeping elections honest, registration acts as a real deterrent to voting, particularly when offices are not open year-round or periodic reregistration is necessary. In 1974, less than 65 percent of people otherwise eligible to vote had actually registered. Those who do not register come disproportionately from blacks, Hispanic Americans, the poor, and those under thirty and are also more likely to be Democrats than Republicans.

Dilution by Legislative Apportionment

Unfair apportionment* of legislative seats may dilute the value of a vote. That dilution can be accomplished by *gerrymandering*—drawing lines of electoral districts to give one party, area, or set of interest groups advantages over others either by making districts unequal in population or by placing the boundaries in such a fashion that certain interests are likely always to lose. Malapportionment may also result from inaction in the face of major shifts of population. Inaction has been widely "used" and, with the mass exodus from farms to cities, was effective for many years in overweighing rural representation. As late as 1964 it was not unusual to find urban and suburban congres-

---

*Apportionment refers to the distribution of legislators among electoral districts within a state. Normally legislators are not chosen by an entire state (U.S. senators form an obvious exception) but from geographical regions within a state.

sional districts with populations three to four times those of rural districts in the same state, and imbalances were even more dramatic in most state legislatures.

In 1962, the Supreme Court made a landmark decision, ruling in *Baker v. Carr* that it was a violation of the Constitution that courts could remedy for a state to allow, by official inaction, the lower house of its legislature to become malapportioned.[5] Two years later, the Court extended *Baker* and held that states had a constitutional obligation to insure that the districts from which members of the U.S. House of Representatives are chosen are approximately equal in population.[6]

Then, in 1964, *Reynolds v. Sims* held that both houses of a state legislature had to be apportioned on the basis of population.[7] The Court said that the democratic ideal of "one person, one vote" was a constitutional command subject only to the specific exceptions of the U.S. Senate and the Electoral College. "Legislators," Chief Justice Earl Warren wrote for the Court, "represent people, not trees or acres. Legislators are elected by voters, not farms or cities or economic interests."

These decisions and their extension to local elections created a potential for vast change in American politics by strengthening the electoral power of metropolitan — and more specifically, suburban — areas. Since 1962, every state has reapportioned at least once (and many have done so several times) both its own legislative and congressional districts. During the 1970s, the Supreme Court moved away from the near-mathematical uniformity among districts that had been demanded by the Warren Court. While retaining the general principle of "one person, one vote," the Court under Chief Justice Warren Burger has permitted states rather wide leeway in applying that maxim, allowing, for instance, Virginia's electoral districts to vary in population by as much as 16.4 percent.[8]

Advocates of reapportionment had hoped that reform would produce better-qualified legislators, more effective lawmaking institutions, and far greater concern for urban problems. Redistricting, however, has not achieved anything like its potential for change. One set of reasons lies in the way in which power is diffused in both state and federal legislative systems. Typically two sets of rules are in force in any legislative body, one open and published, the other informal, cliquish, and more important. These rules function within several complex structures of power. To bring a bill to a vote it is often less useful to have the support of a majority of legislators than the approval of the committee chairman or two or three party leaders. Something approaching total replacement of old personnel might clean out these nests of power and allow immediate, sweeping changes. But the piecemeal replacement that has occurred in Congress and state legislatures has caused newcomers to get lost in a maze for a few years, with the most astute of them obliged to cooperate with the old guard in order to accomplish many of their aims.

Table 8-1
Relationships between Seats and Votes in U.S. House of Representatives

| | Percent Democratic | |
Year	Votes	Seats
1964	57.5	67.8
1966	51.3	56.9
1968	50.9	55.4
1970	53.4	58.6
1972	51.7	55.9
1974	57.6	66.9

Source: Adapted from Edward R. Tufte, "The Relationship between Seats and Votes in Two Party Systems," *American Political Science Review,* LXVII (1973), p. 540.

Related to the peculiar functioning of legislatures is the fact that new district lines have often been drawn to protect incumbents. This kind of bipartisan log-rolling reflects interests that professional politicians share with each other, regardless of party. "It is hardly surprising," one scholar has commented, "that legislators, like businessmen, have collaborated with their nominal adversaries to eliminate dangerous competition."[9]

An additional factor restricting effects of reapportionment has been simpler. It is not possible to draw electoral lines without conferring some partisan advantages; and where one party has been able to do so, it has usually taken full advantage of every opportunity to cling to power. Judges are well aware of the possibility of gerrymandering districts of equal population, and on one occasion the Supreme Court struck down a crude effort to district blacks out of a city government.[10] But it remains to be seen whether judges can—or will try to—cope with more subtle efforts where there are no racial overtones.

Even if most House districts were approximately equal in population, there would still be wide variations in representation in Congress. First, the Constitution's guarantee to each state of two senators—a provision that requires unanimous consent of the states to change—means that in 1977 California had one senator per 10.5 million people and Alaska one senator for every 180,000. The House also poses problems. Each state must have at least one congressman, and in 1977 three states had total populations below that of the average district (about 500,000 people).

There is another way in which the democratic nature of the House is skewed, the so-called "swing ratio"; that is, electoral results do not always correspond completely to patterns of voting. In a perfectly representative system, a party receiving 51 percent of the votes would obtain 51 percent of the seats, but no country can be divided into electoral districts that always produce such mathematically pure results. Assuming equality in districts' sizes, a party that won 100 percent of the votes in fifty districts would gain a larger number of votes but a smaller number of seats than a party that won 50.1 percent in fifty-one districts. Sometimes this swing ratio between votes and seats in the House has helped Republicans, but more recently it has benefited the Democrats, as Table 8-1 shows.

Electing Congressmen

Provisions of the Constitution

Every other November, voters choose the entire membership of the House of Representatives and one third of the Senate. The Constitution allows Congress to determine the number of seats in the House, and currently that number is 435. Every ten years, following the census, Congress redistributes those seats among the states according to population—with the proviso, of course, that each state has at least one representative. The Constitution itself fixes terms and minimum qualifications for Congress. Senators must be thirty years old, or even more ancient, and have been citizens for nine years. Representatives must be at least twenty-five and have been citizens for seven years. All are required to be residents of their states at the time of election, but "resident" has sometimes been liberally construed. Representatives are not legally obliged to be inhabitants of the districts they serve, but almost invariably they are.

Article I of the Constitution and the various voting amendments discussed earlier in this chapter give Congress broad authority to regulate elections, both primary elections and general elections, at which national officials are nominated and chosen. But although Congress has passed important legislation protecting voters against racial discrimination and various forms of fraud, it has by and large left other kinds of regulation to the states.

Nomination of Congressmen

Elections in the United States are typically a two-step process. First comes formal nomination, then a general election.

As with most public officials other than President and Vice President, the *party primary* is the normal, almost exclusive means of nominating both senators and representatives; but the form of these elections differs widely from state to state. Most use *closed primaries,* in which participation is limited to voters who have declared their party allegiance either at registration or at the primary itself. There are, of course, provisions for changing loyalty, but having voted in the primary of one party usually bars a citizen from voting in the primary of

Table 8–2
Party Changes in the U. S. House of Representatives

Year	Number of seats		Seats changed	
	Dems. won from Reps.	Reps. won from Dems.	Total number	Percent
1960	8	28	36	8.2
1964	48	10	58	13.3
1968	9	5	14	3.2
1972[a]	14[a]	8[a]	22[a]	5.1[a]
1974	49	6	55	12.6
1976	12	10	22	5.1

[a]Creation of new districts because of reapportionment after census of 1970 makes it difficult to compare figures before and after 1972.

another for a period of a year or longer. A few states use a system of "open" primaries, allowing voters at each primary to decide in whose election they will participate. In practice, the distinction between the two types is not always sharp; a closed primary can be so loosely administered as to be almost indistinguishable from an open system.

Timing provides another variation in primaries. There is no national primary day; dates for House and senatorial contests range from March through October. This staggering makes it virtually impossible to focus the attention of voters in different states on the same issues of public policy, and it reinforces the power of local politicos at the expense of national party leaders.

In many states, especially in the south, the primary often serves as the real election. Between 1896 and 1946 more than 53 percent of congressional candidates won the general election by at least a margin of 60–40, indicating that the outcome was never seriously in doubt. Data from 1956 through 1976 demonstrate an even clearer pattern. On the average, about 261 seats, 60 percent of the total, were won by margins of 60–40 or higher.

Although "safe" districts in one election can become bitterly contested battlefields a few years later, the fact remains that only a rather small number of seats change party hands at any one election. Table 8–2 presents some figures from recent years to demonstrate this point. Even in recent landslides turnover in seats has not exceeded 13 percent of the House.

Off-Year Campaigning

In presidential election years, candidates for the House and Senate, and more especially for the House, usually try to ride the coattails of presidential nominees. They tend to leave what discussion of vital national issues there is to presidential aspirants and to concentrate on

Figure 8.1
Losses in House Seats by Party in
White House, Off-Year Elections, 1936-1974

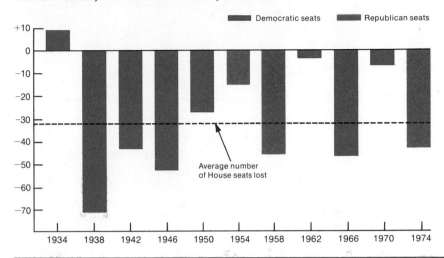

Sources: *The New York Times*, November 6, 1966; *Congressional Quarterly Weekly Report*, November 6, 1970, and November 9, 1974.

local affairs. In *midterm* or *off-year elections* for Congress, the national parties are relatively inactive. There is no party platform and, more important, no presidential contest to focus attention. As a result, the process seems more like several hundred individual campaigns than a single election.

But, as in other phases of real life, appearances are sometimes deceiving in politics. Off-year congressional campaigning is most certainly a highly decentralized process, with each candidate having great leeway in choosing his or her own strategies. Still, there is strong but indirect evidence that national affairs do exert a powerful influence that brings more coherence to the result than individual candidates may intend or prefer. Practicing politicians and students of politics have long been aware that, as Figure 8–1 sketches, the President's party almost invariably loses congressional seats in off-year elections.

Explaining this phenomenon and predicting its magnitude in any election are obviously politically important. And it was an effort to wrestle with these problems that led Edward R. Tufte to a relatively simple formula that accurately predicts the national distribution of votes in off-year congressional elections.[11] Two elements are involved: the President's popularity just before the midterm election as measured by the Gallup Poll, and general economic conditions as measured by the real, disposable income per person.* Statistical techniques aside,

*The actual distribution of seats, as we saw earlier, is affected by the so-called swing ratio, for which Tufte has also devised a formula.

the significant point here is that, in the aggregate, midterm elections function as a sort of national referendum on the President's general performance and more particularly on his management of economic affairs.

Electing the President

The Original Method

After much debate, the framers compromised on an Electoral College to select a President and Vice President. (Actually "colleges" would have been more accurate since these groups never sit as a national body.) Each state legislature can choose its members of the College — equal to the number of the state's representatives and senators — as it sees fit, although all now use popular elections. Technically, it is for a slate of such electors and not for a President or Vice President that voters cast their ballots. The winning electors meet in their respective states at a time designated by Congress and vote for a presidential and vice-presidential candidate. The ballots are forwarded to Congress and counted in the presence of both Houses. Originally, the electors voted for two persons without designating either office. The person receiving the largest number of votes, providing it was a majority, would be President, and the person with the second-highest number Vice President. If no person had a majority, the House of Representatives was to select one of the five highest on the list to serve as President; each state was to have one vote in this process, and a majority of all the states was required for election.

The election of 1800, when party lines were drawn tight, revealed a serious flaw in this plan. All the electors from the Jeffersonian party cast their two votes for Thomas Jefferson and Aaron Burr, intending the first to be President and the latter Vice President. But, since both men had the same number of electoral votes, the only way of breaking the tie was for the House of Representatives to choose. Because it was clear that the same result would prevail in subsequent elections if political parties continued to be active, the Twelfth Amendment was added to the Constitution, directing electors to cast one vote specifically for President and one for Vice President. If no person obtains a majority, the House chooses the President from the three candidates with the largest number of electoral votes, and the Senate chooses the Vice President from the two leading candidates.

Nominating Presidential Candidates: Primaries

For almost a century and a half, the major parties as well as many minor organizations have nominated presidential candidates by national conventions. Historically, state party organizations used their own conventions or caucuses to choose delegates to the national convention, and many still do. In this century, however, most states have at one time or another provided that delegates be chosen by primary elections.

The importance of these primaries varies from year to year and state to state. A strong incumbent President eligible for re-election can usually ignore them all—a rule that underscored Gerald Ford's weakness in 1976. At the other extreme, such contests may be decisive for the party out of power when the competition is among several candidates whose ability to attract votes outside of their own state or region is untested. How "important" primaries are likely to be in any year largely depends on: (1) the number of primaries (the greater the number, the greater the opportunity for candidates who lose in some contests to recoup in others and so neutralize primaries' impact); (2) the number of delegates chosen in primaries (importance increases with numbers); (3) the number of active candidates (the larger the number, the more likely primaries are to sift out at least a few who cannot generate public support); (4) timing; and (5) technical rules under which primaries are conducted.

The last two points require elaboration. Because these contests are scattered from February until June, timing of victories and defeats can be crucial in creating the illusion of momentum. An early victory may thrust a candidate into prominence and attract further support and money. In 1976, for instance, Jimmy Carter's early victories persuaded *Time* and *Newsweek* to put his picture on their covers and to structure feature stories around him, transforming him from a little known former governor of Georgia into a household word across the country. Similarly a victory in one of the last major primaries—California or Ohio, for example—may propel a candidate into the convention with a considerable psychological advantage.

Conversely, an early defeat may crush a candidate before he gets started, and a late defeat may give the impression of ebbing strength and frighten supporters away. It is always desirable, of course, for an aspirant to do well in any primary he enters (and thus it is prudent for him to stay out of any contest in which he is doomed to be drubbed). But, if his time and other resources are scarce, he is generally wiser to concentrate his efforts on winning early and late. One important and obvious qualification is that the candidate must also gain a share of large delegations (like those from California and New York) regardless of when the primaries occur.

The technical rules under which primaries are run also affect both strategy and results. Occasionally, what are called primaries are really little more than public opinion polls, and the results do not bind delegates. Winning these contests is less useful than winning in states that require delegates to support candidates on one or more ballots at the convention.

A second critical issue of technical rules pertains to who gains what from a primary. One rule may give the state's entire delegation to the candidate who wins the most votes; a different rule may provide that each candidate will receive a share of delegates proportional to his share of the popular vote, providing he obtain a certain minimum level of support, perhaps 15 percent. A third rule may divide delegates by electoral districts and provide either that the winner in each district will take all the votes or that the front runners will share those votes proportionately. These rules can make a decisive difference. In 1972, for example, "proportionate shares" would have sent George Wallace into the Democratic convention with by far the largest number of committed delegates. Under a winner-take-all system, Hubert Humphrey would have had the most delegates, although not a majority. Only under the districting rule, which the Democrats used most frequently in 1972, could George McGovern have been the front runner.

For 1976, the Democrats adopted a rule forbidding winner-take-all primaries and encouraging proportionate shares. In the context of thirty-two primaries and at least a dozen candidates for the nomination, one result was the elimination by mid-spring of most candidates. A second outcome was that more than eighty percent of the delegates to the convention arrived with at least their first round votes already pledged; and of course Carter had a clear majority. Thus the change in the Democrats' rules obviously did not accomplish its principal purpose of re-establishing the convention as the arena in which the real as well as the formal choice would be made. Party leaders were thereby denied their cherished role as brokers, pasting together a winning coalition from among various factions.

An unresolved problem, one that is certainly unresolvable as long as primaries are scattered across such a wide period of time, is that these contests usually draw only a small portion of eligible voters to the polls. In fact, as little as 2 percent of a party's registered voters may actually participate; seldom does the figure exceed one third, and rarely one half. On the average from 1932 until the present, about 15 percent of those who vote in a state's general election turn out for the primary. The matter is complicated because, while it is true that most of those who vote in primaries are party loyalists, it often happens that participants include a substantial share of dissidents who are voting *against* a set of policies or people rather than *for* the candidate they are seemingly supporting. Thus a candidate's ability to win a primary is frequently a very poor measure of real popular support.

Nominating Presidential Candidates: Conventions

Democratic and Republican national conventions may have from 1,200 to 3,200 delegates, many with only a half vote. The size of a state's delegation is determined by complex formulas that weigh both the state's population and its support for the party. Nevertheless, the more populous states tend to be underrepresented as do states where the party is stronger and the turnout higher. In the past especially, delegates have underrepresented females, blacks, and young people, but since 1968 both parties have been trying to correct such imbalances.

The first item of business is to seat delegates. Normally, a credentials committee routinely certifies those who have been chosen by their states. Occasionally, however, a rival faction challenges a delegate or even an entire state delegation. The decision, ultimately made by those members of the convention who are already seated, may materially affect aspirants' chances.

Adoption of a platform is the second important item of business. A special committee that has long been in session presents its report, sometimes with strong dissenting views. Normally, convention leaders are able to march the document through without serious debate; but when challenges occur, they are apt to be bitter and to reveal cleavages within the party that can have a vast impact on the campaign strategies open to the eventual nominee. It is easy enough to ridicule the average platform, for, as V. O. Key said, it "speaks with boldness and forthrightness on issues that are already well settled; it is likely to be ambiguous on contentious questions."[12] But evasive platforms often make it possible for parties to hold together long enough to elect a President who has the backing of 40 or 50 million voters—an achievement that should not be minimized. At the same time, the price is sometimes heavy in terms of muddling issues vital to the nation.

The convention's next step is to nominate a presidential candidate. A simple majority of votes is needed. If the party controls the White House and the President is eligible for re-election, the outcome is usually clear from the moment the President decides to run again. For the Republicans, two exceptions stand out: 1912, when Teddy Roosevelt tried to deny William Howard Taft renomination, and 1976, when Ronald Reagan attacked Gerald Ford's claim to be the leader of the party. In both cases, however, the challenge to the President failed. A convention without a serious contest for the nomination also may occur if a candidate had won enough delegates in primaries to have or be close to a majority, as Carter had done in 1976. In most other situations, bargaining, maneuvering, and negotiation among candidates and delegates—often conducted before the convention meets—will be decisive. Only twice from 1932 until 1976 did the Democratic or Republican nominee not win on the first ballot.

The dynamics of the nominating process are much more complex. They probably began at the previous convention when far-sighted would-be candidates befriended delegates and sized up potential rivals. In the intervening years, aspirants traveled around the country, meeting and negotiating with local leaders, carefully grooming themselves to appear reluctantly but dutifully ready to accept responsibility for the good of the country. Later, of course, came grueling primary campaigns and more jockeying for support. Holding public office is useful so that the candidate's name can stay in the news — which helps explain why governors and senators are so often among the presidential contenders taken most seriously.

The candidate's religion and region can also help. With few exceptions, leading candidates for major party nomination have been Protestants (and all have been white males). Historically, candidates from large states have had an advantage, but the visibility provided by national television has dulled that edge considerably.

Selection of a vice-presidential nominee provides the convention's final work. Usually the presidential candidate announces his preference, and the convention quickly ratifies it. A, if not *the,* central concern of the presidential nominee has typically been the ability of a running mate to "balance the ticket," to appeal to important segments of voters whom the presidential candidate cannot easily reach. The capacity of the vice-presidential candidate to succeed to the presidency in an emergency often is a marginal consideration, as Richard Nixon's cynical choice of Spiro Agnew attested.

Political Campaigning

A campaign and election perform a number of functions. From the citizen's point of view, they provide an opportunity to obtain at low cost a great deal of information about politics and politicians, as well as an opportunity to participate in determining who will govern. In so doing, campaigns and elections also permit him or her to have a voice, although only a very small voice, in affecting the policies that will shape much of public and private life over the next few years.

From the point of view of the parties and their candidates, a campaign and election provide means of obtaining control of the government that are nonviolent and legitimate in the eyes of the governed. Further, by winning office, candidates and their colleagues can dispense patronage to keep their party together and can create new public policies that they hope will both increase votes at the next election and even do some good for the country.

From the point of view of the political system, a campaign and election allow peaceful means of change, permitting shifts in personnel and policies while maintaining a high degree of stability. By involving masses of the people, a campaign and election also reconfirm the basic legitimacy of the system itself and foster support for future governmental decisions, thus lowering the amount of force needed to preserve public order. The fact that Presidents, senators, and representatives all have apparently been chosen by the people provides a frequently powerful emotional argument for almost automatic compliance with their decisions — although the intellectual problems raised by such terms as "chosen" and "people" are formidable.

The difficulties of campaigning vary from office to office. We shall

Jimmy Carter begins the long campaign for the presidency in a beauty parlor, seeking Democratic votes in the New Hampshire presidential primary.

concentrate on the most dramatic, that for the presidency. Candidates for congressional, state, and local posts face some of the same problems, although the scale may be far smaller and the electorate far more homogenous in economic, social, and ethnic terms.

Campaigns and Debates

An American presidential campaign involves expenditure of hundreds of millions of hours and only slightly fewer dollars. Candidates preempt prime television time to deliver speeches, splatter radio and TV with spot announcements, and crisscross the country in jets specially equipped as flying dormitories for politicians and journalists. At the same time, thousands of volunteers ring doorbells, distribute literature, chauffeur hundreds of thousands of people to registration offices and later to voting booths. But when ears stop ringing from torrents of booming oratory and superficial analyses by television commentators, one cannot escape doubts that the campaign provided citizens with the quality of information needed to make intelligent appraisals of issues or competitors.

Candidates tend to talk past each other, not to the issues. More often, both come out strongly for virtue and against sin. Each campaign seems to emphasize the candidate's charm rather than sharply outlining the nation's problems, exploring alternatives, and justifying solutions in an intellectually respectable way. Differences in policy can

Gerald Ford campaigns with his wife on the "Presidential Express" in Michigan. Once the main means of reaching voters, campaign trains today are one of the many devices used by candidates to attract the attention of television and newspaper reporters.

sometimes be divined both from speeches and previous public records. But a campaign seldom forms a stage on which presidential aspirants perform according to the script of democratic government, giving voters a choice between legible scenarios of and reasoned justifications for proposed policies. Even the televised debates of 1960 and 1976, as interesting as they sometimes were, found the candidates often talking around rather than at the questions.

The causes of these performances are not hard to find. Two factors are basic. First, in peacetime, politics is usually not a fundamental concern of most Americans, and there is constant competition for attention. To compete successfully for voters' ears and eyes, most politicians believe, one cannot offer complicated discussions of political issues. To rally supporters a candidate must first attract attention; and a pretty wife and children, an emotional charge of corruption in the opposition's ranks, and Madison Avenue gimmickry can be more effective than discussing specific policies that would reduce unemployment without aggravating inflation.

A second factor relates to the very broad spectrum of support that a successful candidate needs. To win, he must stitch together a large and diverse coalition that transcends regional, religious, class, and ethnic lines. Because of the fragility of that coalition, he may find it expedient to speak in vague terms that will offend no one of his targeted groups or to make promises that, if not actually incompatible, can be reconciled only with extreme difficulty.

Table 8–3
Time of voting decision in presidential elections (voters only)

QUESTION: *"How long before the election did you decide that you were going to
vote the way you did?"*

	Percentage						
	1948	*1952*	*1956*	*1960*	*1964*	*1968*	*1972*
Before the conventions	41	36	60	31	41	36	47
At the time of the conventions	31	32	19	31	25	24	18
After the conventions, during campaign	15	21	12	26	21	19	22
Last two weeks of campaign	10	9	7	9	9	14	8
On Election Day	3	2	2	3	4	7	5
	100	100	100	100	100	100	100

Source: Center for Political Studies, University of Michigan.

Do Campaigns Make a Difference?

There is no simple answer to the reasonable question of how much difference all this frenzied activity makes on election day. Public opinion polls,[13] summarized in Table 8–3, indicate that in presidential elections about one half to three quarters of those who actually vote make up their minds by the time the national conventions have nominated candidates. Thus, presidential campaigns have, at most, a real chance of shaping choices of only half of the voters.

These figures also suggest what further research substantiates: a large share of the uncommitted are independents, who are generally less informed about and interested in politics than those who profess loyalty to a party. This fact, of course. reinforces campaign strategists' temptations to substitute drama for debate.

On the other hand, the figures in Table 8–3 conceal one of the purposes of a campaign: to bring the committed to the polls. Without a campaign, many who actually did vote might not have done so. A preference expressed at a cocktail party is welcome, but only when that preference is registered at the ballot box does it do a candidate much good. Gross statistics also obscure the fact that in many presidential elections — 1948, 1960, and 1968, for example — a small switch in votes can be decisive. Harry Truman's hard-hitting, whistle-stop tour in 1948 eroded just enough of Dewey's support to put Truman back in the White House. John F. Kennedy's effectiveness in the television debates of 1960 has been widely credited with providing his margin of victory. When a shift of only one or two percentage points means the difference between winning and losing, campaigns become vitally important. They are waged "to make marginal changes in political alignments."[14]

Campaign Strategy

The object is to win, but that is hardly a simple job in most precincts, much less in a country of more than 215 million people. The first problem a candidate faces is that of choosing a campaign manager and building a staff of close advisers on various issues of campaigning as well as public policy; while the candidate himself may have to make many decisions, he can know about only a small fraction of the hundreds of problems that arise daily.

In turn, lest the campaign manager be quickly swamped, he has to select a large staff of trusted assistants. These people will include a press secretary to oversee arrangements for newsmen, a finance director to coordinate myriad fund-raising activities, and often a vice president of a Madison Avenue public relations firm that will "package" the candidate's message. Both parties now routinely employ these people to merchandize candidates with all the skill and good taste that they use to huckster laxatives and lingerie.[15]

The manager and his chief advisers have the additional—perhaps primary—duty of helping to map the candidate's strategy. The first problem is that of raising money, for American campaigns are wonderfully expensive enterprises. The matter of money in politics is sufficiently important that we make it the subject of a full section of this chapter. Here we stress only that a presidential candidate must spend many millions of dollars to get—and keep—his name before the public. In the face of such costs, the question of how much money can be raised necessarily precedes that of how to reach voters most effectively. The question of raising money also affects other strategic choices, because a candidate cannot safely offend those whom he asks to pay his bills.

The next major decision involves how to form a coalition that offers maximal opportunities for winning and does so at minimal costs—in terms of budget as well as in terms of programs that the candidate wants to carry out. A labor leader, for instance, may promise a large bloc of union votes, but only in exchange for a higher minimum-wage law; a governor from the southwest may claim to be able to deliver several states if the candidate agrees not to prosecute oil companies for violating the antitrust laws. Moreover, an appeal to one group may bring votes at the expense of lost votes in another sector. A strong civil rights speech may garner black support in northern cities, but reduce support from white ethnics in those same cities.

The candidate's most rational approach is to set out clearly, at least in his own mind, his objectives and what he is being asked to trade and then begin to do his arithmetic. To bring his total up to 50.1 percent of the electoral vote, he has to be willing to pay a high price. After he

Table 8–4
Party identification

	1940	1950	1960	1964	1968	1972	1976
Democratic	42%	45%	47%	53%	46%	43%	46%
Independent	20	22	23	22	27	29	32
Republican	38	33	30	25	27	28	22
	100%	100%	100%	100%	100%	100%	100%

Source: Press releases, The Gallup Poll, April 5, 1973, and May 27, 1976.

passes that magic mark, additional increases in support become less and less valuable. Nevertheless, although a particular price—some particular trade-off—may be too high, the worth is never zero, for a candidate can never be sure that his computations have been correct. Besides, "winning big" brings immense psychological advantages. In addition to demoralizing the opposition and attracting donors for the next campaign, a President who runs ahead of his ticket will have a much easier time leading Congress. If he can attract votes, senators and representatives who are concerned about re-election will want his help; and nothing in politics is ever free, not even a campaign endorsement.

All these calculations have to be made with a precision that disguises the fuzziness of the data on which they are based. Past records do not necessarily predict the future accurately, and even evidence from current surveys of public opinion is often elusive. Both parties have certain historic strengths, however, on which they can build their coalitions—Democrats with blacks, Jews, Catholics, blue-collar workers, small farmers, and intellectuals; Republicans with white-collar workers, middle-class Protestants, large farmers, and more affluent businessmen. But none of these allegiances is permanent. In 1964, the Democrats wooed away many businessmen and white-collar workers from Barry Goldwater's ultraconservatism; and in 1972 the Republicans pried away a large portion of white ethnics (who were typically Catholic) by painting George McGovern as a man who would "run up the white flag" in international relations and at home take away the workers' hard earned money to lavish it on blacks.

Strategists must also consider party allegiance in mapping their plans because these loyalties often exert strong emotional pulls. As Table 8–4 shows, to win, the Democrats in recent decades have usually needed only to keep their adherents together and pick up a small portion of independents. This task is often neither easy nor simple, since the Democratic party draws its strength from such different social groups as conservative southerners, militant blacks, liberal white intellectuals, and white working-class ethnics. Moreover, party *identification* is not the same as party *loyalty*. The Electoral College adds another complicating dimension. The candidate must win not a majority of the popular votes but a majority of electoral votes.

The Republicans have an even more difficult task. They must keep their own followers in line, pick up a large share of independents, and also lure away a sizable number of Democrats. And, of course, Republicans have to be as concerned as Democrats about distribution of support in the Electoral College. These sorts of considerations led Republicans in 1968 and 1972 to follow a "southern strategy" and in 1976 to adopt a modification called the "rim strategy," that is, appealing to white voters in the states that sweep around the southern rim of the United States from Florida to California. While still courting working-class voters in the northeast, Nixon and later Ford gave up hope of cutting deeply into the Jewish, black, or Hispanic vote. In sum, they concentrated on holding on to traditional Republican support in rural areas and small towns of the midwest and adding to those supporters:

(1) whites from the deep south, who tend to be more conservative than northern whites;

(2) southwesterners and westerners—who also tend to be politically conservative—clustered in the Sun Belt states such as Florida, Texas, New Mexico, Arizona, and California;

(3) urban, working-class whites, the so-called white ethnics, people normally Democratic and liberal on such economic issues as minimum wage laws but fearful of a breakdown of law and order often attributed to black migration to their neighborhoods and resentful of "welfare giveaways."

A third set of problems involves interlocking questions of focus, timing, and style. Most candidates focus their energy and resources in states with large electoral votes and where the outcome is in doubt. It takes considerable political intelligence—usually gathered by analyses of past elections and of current public opinion polls—to select these states; and if a choice has been unwise, the candidate may not only lose a state in which he has been working but also others that his efforts might have brought into the fold.

Timing is critical both in scheduling visits to specific areas and in setting the over-all tempo of the campaign. Activity must start neither too early nor too late and must come to a crescendo at just the right moment—clearly identifiable only in retrospect—to sway the greatest number of voters. Candidates who start out far behind their opponents, as John F. Kennedy did in 1960, usually find it necessary to race at maximum speed every day, a tactic that risks killing the candidate and supersaturating the electorate.

Questions of style inevitably relate to substance. Whether a candidate shall attack relentlessly as Harry Truman did in 1948 and Kennedy in 1960, or speak glowingly (although with appropriate humility) of his record as Lyndon Johnson did in 1964 and Nixon in 1972, or present a new and complicated program to revitalize society as McGovern did in 1972 affects the kinds of issues to be discussed and the format that can be best used to bring them to voters' attention. A forty- or sixty-second spot message on radio or television is ideal to blast the opposition or call attention to simple accomplishments. It is totally inadequate to explain a new program.

When all these kinds of decisions have been made, attacks slashingly delivered, defenses righteously proclaimed, money collected and spent, votes counted, and results announced, both candidates are probably acutely aware of the huge role that sheer chance played in the outcome. The "ifs" are numerous. If Richard Nixon's makeup man had been more skilled before the first television debate in 1960, if someone had probed more deeply into Watergate in 1972, if Gerald Ford had known in 1976 that Poland was not a "free" Country — if, on and on. Yet despite the capricious play of luck, a candidate who does not meticulously plan and carefully execute an intelligent strategy has no hope of being more than the leader of the loyal opposition for four years.

The Final Election of a President

By midnight of election day, it is usually obvious who will be the next President. But the outcome is not official until the new Congress assembles in January, counts the ballots of the members of the Electoral College, and proclaims the result. It is at this point that the House of Representatives would proceed to elect a President if no candidate had a clear majority of electoral votes.

Defects of the Electoral College

Although the Electoral College has functioned reasonably well through the years, the system has three serious weaknesses. First, there is no provision in the Constitution or in federal law requiring an elector to vote for his party's candidates, and in 1948, 1960, 1968, and 1972 at least one elector voted for an "outside" candidate. Only a few states expressly compel electors to fulfill their pledges to vote for particular candidates, although several others have laws that hint at it.

The second weakness is that the victor in the electoral vote might actually receive fewer popular votes than his opponent. This possibility results primarily from the fact that in each state the winning candidate receives the state's entire electoral vote, equivalent to the total of the state's two senators plus its representatives in Congress. Such an imbalance has occurred in two elections since the Civil War, 1876 and 1888. Moreover, the same result could have occurred in many other elections had very small blocs of popular votes been cast the other way in certain states.

A third weakness is that the Electoral College could fail to give a majority to any candidate and throw the election into the House of Representatives. The House has had to make such a choice only once (1824) since the adoption of the Twelfth Amendment. But there have been other elections in which strong third-party candidates almost succeeded in deadlocking the Electoral College. In 1968 George Wallace won in five states and received forty-six electoral votes. Had Humphrey rather than Nixon carried Alaska, Delaware, Missouri, Nevada, and Tennessee (Nixon's combined margin of victory in these states was less than 91,000), Nixon's electoral vote would have been 269 and Humphrey's 223. Both would have been short of a majority—270.

It takes only a moment's reflection to understand the problems caused by having the House choose a President. Most obviously, voting in the House for President is by states and not by members, with states as different in population as Alaska and California each having one vote. It is also entirely possible for the minority party in the House to control a majority of state delegations and thereby to elect its candidate to the presidency even though he stood second in both popular and electoral votes. The constitutional requirement that the winning candidate receive the votes of a majority of states poses yet another problem. It is possible for party control of state delegations to be so scrambled that the House would have great difficulty in selecting a President, if it could do so at all.

If the House were unable to choose a President by Inauguration Day, the Vice President, elected by the Senate from the two candidates with the highest electoral votes for that office, would serve until the House could reach a majority decision or, if that did not happen, until the end of a regular four-year term. If the Senate were unable to elect a Vice President—fifty-one votes are needed and enough senators might abstain to keep either candidate from winning—the Speaker of the House of Representatives would serve as President, again until the House reached a decision or until the end of a four-year term. These defects have been obvious for many years, but conservative congressmen and those from the smaller states have been reluctant to upset the status quo lest they increase the political power of states with huge metropolitan areas.

Campaign Financing[16]

Chapter 6 pointed out that money is an important element in political power; nowhere is it more important than in financing the extravaganzas called political campaigns. The costs of winning election to public office in the United States are tremendous. Together all the candidates for the presidency in 1972 spent $138 million in the campaigns for nomination and election. Nixon and his supporters spent $68 million, almost all of it after he was renominated. Securing the Democratic nomination that year cost George McGovern $12 million, and his campaign in the general election consumed another $34 million.

How Money Is Spent

It is not possible to compile an exhaustive list of the ways in which campaign money is used, but we can suggest six legitimate purposes that are illustrative:

(1) *general overhead*—for headquarters at national, state, and local levels, including salaries, office rent, postage, and telephones;

(2) *field activities*—candidates' speaking trips, often by leased jet aircraft (in 1972 airlines charged candidates from $5,000 to $8,000 a day

Table 8–5
1971–72 Republican presidential expenditures of CREEP and related organizations: Pre- and postnomination

Expense Category	$ Millions
Advertising (broadcast, including production costs and fees)	$ 7.0
Direct mail to voters (not including fund raising)	5.8
Mass telephoning to voters	1.3
State organizations (primary elections, personnel, storefronts, locations, travel, voter contact, etc.)	15.9
Campaign materials	2.7
Press relations, publications, and literature	2.6
Headquarters (campaign, personnel, rent, telephone, travel, legal, etc.)	4.7
Travel and other expenses of President, Vice-President, surrogates, and advance men	3.9
Citizen group activities	1.9
Youth activities	1.0
Polling (including White House-directed surveys)	1.6
Convention expenses	.6
Election night	.2
Fund raising (direct mail, $4 million; and major events, $1 million)	5.0
Fund raising (national administration and gifts for contributors)	1.9
Legal fees	2.0
Democratic settlement	.8
Democrats for Nixon	2.4
Total[a]	$61.4

[a]Does not include $1.4 million in miscellaneous cash, some used for dirty tricks or hush money in 1972–73, and some used for political or other purposes in 1969–70–71, not directly related to the 1972 presidential election.
Source: Herbert E. Alexander, *Financing the 1972 Election* (Lexington, Mass.: D. C. Heath and Company, 1976), p. 272.

Table 8–6
1972 presidential expenditures by five central McGovern committees, general election

Expense Category	Amount
Media—broadcasting	
TV and radio time	$ 5,035,000
TV and radio production	793,000
Media—nonbroadcasting	
Newspapers and magazines	962,273
Telephone canvassing	96,160
Direct Mail	3,135,334
Campaign materials	176,049
Crowd events	25,200
Personal services	
Staff payroll	914,401
Outside professional services and consultant fees	269,763
Office Expenses	822,339
Air charter	
Net cost	755,473
(Gross cost, $1,898,795; press and secret service reimbursement, $1,143,322)	
Field campaign	
Transportation	286,485
Other expenses	431,378
Transfers	
To state McGovern committees	3,074,541
To other organizations (e.g., for voter registration)	1,498,610
Payment of preconvention debts	267,410
Total expenditures	18,543,416
Loan repayments	2,634,969
Total disbursements	$21,178,385

Note: These figures cover the expenditures from national campaign headquarters in Washington, D.C. Additional expenditures were made by numerous state and local committees not closely controlled by McGovern headquarters during 1972.
Source: Herbert E. Alexander, Financing the 1972 Election (Lexington, Mass.: D. C. Heath and Company, 1976), p. 290.

to lease each plane), renting of halls, stadiums, and auditoriums, and other expenses involved in organizing mass meetings;

(3) *publicity*—telecasts and radio broadcasts, spot commercials, newspaper advertisements, campaign literature, special buttons and souvenirs; and the fees charged by the public relations firms that handle the campaign;

(4) *grants to subsidiary committees*—transfers of funds from national organizations to state and local organizations and to special committees and groups;

(5) *election day expenses*—transportation of voters to the polls and payments to watchers at the polls and to party workers who try to bring out the vote;

(6) *public opinion polling* to gauge the effects of various campaign strategies (in 1972 the two parties spent almost $2 million for such surveys during the presidential primaries and the general election).

Tables 8–5 and 8–6 offer some examples of general expenses from 1972, but one should note that they include only payments by national committees. The totals spent for each candidate were actually much higher because a number of local groups both collected and disbursed funds to help their candidates.

In state as well as presidential campaigns, television eats up a large share of campaign funds. Tables 8–5 and 8–6 show that Nixon and McGovern spent a total of almost $14 million for broadcasting in 1972, actually a surprisingly low figure because Nixon alone had spent $12.6 million in 1968. In 1976 Carter budgeted $13 million for television. That medium gives splendid coverage, but at a very high price. Each sixty-second "spot" political advertisement costs about $30,000 if aired with full network coverage during prime time.

Where the Money Comes From

Apart from the huge amounts of money needed for campaigning, the most striking feature about party finances, at least before 1976, has been how much of the cash comes from so few donors. In 1972, for example, the five largest contributors to Nixon gave him a total of $4,328,000, and five other persons gave him more than a quarter of a million dollars apiece. Historically, however, most Americans, so generous in other respects, have been unwilling to make political contributions. The Gallup Poll reported in 1954 that only one family in eighteen had given in that year's campaign, and in 1968 the Survey Research Center of the University of Michigan found that the proportion had increased only to one family in thirteen. To spur small giving and thus protect parties and candidates from domination by a few rich donors— "fat cats," politicians call them—Congress now allows each taxpayer to allocate one dollar of his or her income tax to a political party or to a fund to be divided among the parties. The 1974 Election Campaign Act, which we shall discuss shortly, makes further efforts to encourage small gifts and outlaws most large donations.

In addition to fat cats, most of whom give in expectation of future favors or in payment for past help, politicians who are not themselves wealthy have had to rely heavily on three other sources of funds: labor unions, governmental employees, and the underworld. Since 1943 federal law has forbidden direct gifts by unions to candidates for national office, but unions have avidly spent money in conducting their own campaigns for friends of labor. Although it is always illegal to ask a federal civil service employee for money and usually illegal to ask a state civil service worker, many civil servants and appointive officials contribute as a form of job insurance. In 1972, for example, the American ambassador to France gave Nixon $1 million, and many states have unofficial (and illegal) sliding scales of contributions that party leaders expect from employees.

The underworld, from petty hoodlums to Mafiosi Dons, constitutes another source of funds. No matter how astute, no criminal can long conduct large-scale operations in loan sharking, narcotics, prostitution, gambling, milking labor unions, and shaking down legitimate businessmen without heavy governmental insulation. To survive, lucrative criminal enterprises need police officials who look the other way or who warn about impending crackdowns, district attorneys who do not prosecute, judges who set minimum bail, dismiss charges, or give light or suspended sentences, state and federal legislators who, along with executive officials from the mayor's staff on up, will pressure police, prosecutors, and judges to go easy. Returns from rackets are immense, totalling untold — and untaxed — billions each year; and campaign contributions to cooperative politicians or, perhaps without his knowing it, to an opponent of an uncooperative official, are cheap forms of insurance.

Election Reform Act of 1974

Political parties or public officials who are beholden to a few large donors are a danger to honest government, but so are debt-ridden parties. The Democrats, for instance, entered the 1972 campaign with a debt of $9.3 million, a financial burden that imposed severe restrictions on their candidates' ability to campaign, to charge expenses rather than pay cash, and to borrow more money. Over the years, Congress has occasionally passed legislation to protect the integrity of the electoral process by regulating campaign contributions and expenditures. Although exceedingly complex, this legislation has been largely ineffective. Finally the scandals of Watergate and revelations that Nixon's aides had in 1972 routinely used promises of governmental aid or threats of governmental prosecution to collect millions of dollars led Congress to adopt the first regulatory scheme that has had any real chance of success, the Election Reform Act of 1974.

The nucleus of the statute is a system of heavy federal subsidies for presidential campaigns and restrictions on raising and spending money from other sources. (We shall limit analysis to provisions relating to presidential campaigns.) The act sets up three special funds, one for national nominating conventions, a second for presidential primaries, and a third for the general election.

Subsidies for national conventions. The national committee of each major party (one whose candidate for President received at least 25 percent of the votes at the last election) is eligible for $2.2 million to finance the national convention on the conditions that the national committee not spend any more money for the convention and that none of the funds be used to help any particular candidate or candidates. (Incidentally, the amounts of money specified in the statute are tied to an "escalator clause," that is, the sum automatically increases with inflation as calculated by governmental economists.) National committees of minor parties (those whose presidential candidates polled from 5 to 25 percent of the vote at the last election) can receive a smaller amount based on a formula that takes into account the number of votes received by any minor party and the number received by the major parties at the last election. New parties and those whose candidates received less than 5 percent of the votes at the last election are not eligible for federal assistance in holding a national convention.

Presidential primaries. In general the act provides for matching federal funds to defray costs of campaigning. To be eligible a candidate must generate contributions of at least $5,000 (only the first $250 of any contribution counts) in each of twenty states. The candidate must also agree that his total expenditures will not exceed a specified maximum (in 1976 it was a little over $13 million). The federal subsidy matches dollar for dollar approximately the first $5.5 million a candidate raises (again through contributions that do not exceed $250 per donor); but, of course, the candidate may not receive federal funds that exceed half of what he actually spends. In 1976, none of the three leading candidates, Jimmy Carter, Gerald Ford, and Ronald Reagan, received the maximum subsidy, but the federal government in all disbursed about $24 million for the presidential primaries that year.

Presidential elections. During the campaign, each candidate of a major party is entitled to another federal subsidy—in 1976 it was $21.8 million—on the condition that the candidate not accept any donations (including advertising material as well as money) in excess of the maximum federal grant. (National, state, local, and district committees, however, can spend additional money to help their candidates. In 1976, national committees were allowed to spend $3.2 million and the smaller committees a total of $4.5 million for each candidate.) Minor party candidates receive lesser federal aid based on the same sort of formula for subsidies to their national conventions. Independent candidates and candidates of new parties or parties that received less than 5 percent of the vote at the last presidential election may also be eligible for federal aid. But because the formula used takes into account how many votes they received in proportion to other candidates, these independents and candidates of new parties receive federal support only after the campaign is over and the votes counted. On the other hand, candidates from established parties receive their subsidies, in the form of a "draw-

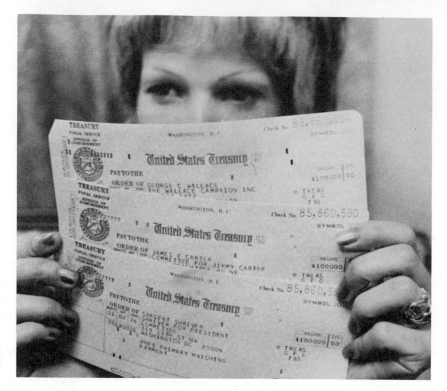

Three of the checks, each for $100,000, distributed by the federal government to candidates in the presidential primaries are shown by an official of the Treasury Department at the beginning of the 1976 campaign.

ing account" at a central bank of the federal reserve system, immediately after formal nomination by their parties.

The Election Reform Act also established an Election Commission to enforce the statute, requires detailed reporting by candidates and parties of fund raising and spending, and specified heavy penalties for violations. In addition, the act set limits on how much money an individual may contribute to political campaigns in any year: $1,000 to any one candidate; $5,000 to any political committee (except a national party committee, the limit there is $20,000); and $25,000 to all candidates and committees.

As one can imagine, this statute was highly controversial both as a matter of wise public policy and as conforming to constitutional provisions regarding equal treatment and freedom of political expression. Its constitutionality was immediately challenged in the courts by people as politically diverse as James Buckley, conservative senator from New York, and the liberal American Civil Liberties Union.

The Supreme Court[17] sustained most of the provisions of the act, but it did strike down, as violations of freedom of communication and association protected by the First Amendment, sections that set limits on the amount that a candidate could spend from his own private resources and on the sums that private citizens, acting without the consent of a candidate, could spend for that candidate. Somewhat surprisingly the Court upheld the constitutionality of different subsidies to major, minor, and new parties and their candidates.*

Summary

Elections and campaigns are among the most visible (and expensive) aspects of American politics. They also provide the most obvious expression of the democratic nature of the political system. But, as this chapter has tried to point out, the march to "one person, one vote" has been long and slow. We have also tried to emphasize that certain institutional arrangements, such as the electoral college and gerrymandering, the costs of running for public office, the character of campaign rhetoric, and widespread inattention to politics, leave the United States far short of achieving the democratic ideal. Even if, as is now unclear, the Election Reform Act of 1974 radically improves financial problems, all the other difficulties will remain.

Selected Bibliography

ALEXANDER, HERBERT E., *Financing Politics: Money, Elections, and Political Reform* (Washington, D.C.: Congressional Quarterly, 1976). An introduction to the problems of money and political campaigns, written by the foremost American expert on the topic.

———, *Financing the 1972 Election* (Lexington, Mass.: D. C. Heath and Company, 1976). An intensive, detailed analysis of fund raising and spending during the 1972 campaigns.

DAVID, PAUL T., RALPH M. GOLDMAN, and RICHARD C. BAIN, *The Politics of National Party Conventions,* paperback edition, K. Sproul, ed. (Washington, D.C.: The Brookings Institution, 1960). Brings together a wealth of information on and interpretations of the operations of national party nominating conventions.

DIXON, ROBERT G., JR., *Democratic Representation: Reapportionment in Law and Politics* (New York: Oxford University Press, 1968). An examination by a lawyer-political scientist of the problems, past and future, of legislative reapportionment.

DOWNS, ANTHONY, *An Economic Theory of Democracy* (New York: Harper & Row, Publishers, 1957). A challenging investigation of the rational bases of political behavior.

DUNN, DELMER D., *Financing Presidential Campaigns* (Washington, D.C.: The Brookings Institution, 1972). An effort to sketch reforms that would

---

*The justices also invalidated the way in which members of the Election Commission were appointed—only two were chosen by the President. As administrators, the Court ruled, all the commissioners would have to be nominated by the President, subject, if Congress wished, to confirmation by the Senate. Congress amended the law in 1976 to conform to the Court's ruling and also made several other changes in the act that are incorporated in the analysis in the text.

both minimize the role of wealthy donors and enable less affluent candidates to compete for office.

HEARD, ALEXANDER, *The Costs of Democracy* (Chapel Hill, N.C.: University of North Carolina Press, 1960). A study of money in politics; its data are dated, but the broad analyses are still useful.

JENNINGS, M. KENT AND L. HARMON ZEIGLER, eds., *The Electoral Process* (Englewood Cliffs, N.J.: Prentice-Hall, Inc., 1966). A collection of original and sometimes insightful essays on campaign strategy and finance.

KEECH, WILLIAM R., and DONALD R. MATTHEWS, *The Party's Choice* (Washington, D.C.: The Brookings Institution, 1976). A thorough re-examination of the whole process of nominating presidential candidates.

KELLEY, STANLEY, JR., *Political Campaigning: Problems in Creating an Informed Electorate* (Washington, D.C.: The Brookings Institution, 1960). The central concern here is how the discussion of policies and candidates in campaigns might make a greater contribution to electoral rationality.

———, *Professional Public Relations and Political Power* (Baltimore, Md.: The Johns Hopkins Press, 1956). An interesting account of the use of high-pressure public relations techniques on behalf of issues and candidates for office.

KESSEL, JOHN H., *The Goldwater Coalition: Republican Strategies in 1964* (Indianapolis, Ind.: The Bobbs-Merrill Company, Inc., 1968). A scholarly but readable analysis of how the Republicans tried to capture the White House in 1964.

LANE, ROBERT E., *Political Life* (New York: The Free Press, 1959). A study of "why people get involved in politics."

PHILLIPS, KEVIN P., *The Emerging Republican Majority* (New Rochelle, N.Y.: Arlington House, 1969). A description of the so-called southern strategy that Richard Nixon followed in 1968 and to a lesser extent in 1972.

POLSBY, NELSON W., and AARON B. WILDAVSKY, *Presidential Elections: Strategies of American Electoral Politics,* 4th ed. (New York: Charles Scribner's Sons, 1976). An excellent introduction to the American electoral process and the implications of some proposals for reform.

SALE, KIRKPATRICK, *Power Shift: The Rise of the Southern Rim and Its Challenge to the Eastern Establishment* (New York: Random House, 1975). An examination of the political effects of the major shifts in population toward states of the "sun belt" or southern and southwestern "rim" of the United States.

U.S. CONGRESS, HOUSE COMMITTEE ON THE JUDICIARY, *Report: Direct Popular Election of the President,* Ninety-first Congress, first session (1969). A detailed examination of the Electoral College and a reasoned justification for changing to a system of direct elections.

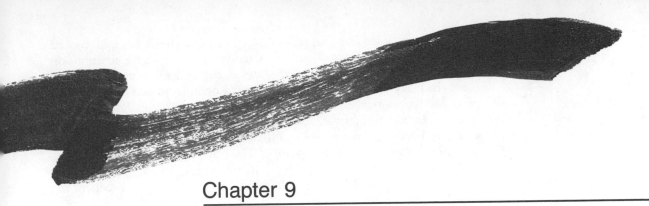

Chapter 9

Political Participation and Voting Behavior

THE THREE EARLIER chapters in this part of the book have discussed some of the processes of politics. Chapter 6 looked at the distribution of political power in the United States; Chapter 7 examined the nature of the party system, one of the principal organizers and mobilizers of collective political power; and Chapter 8 analyzed campaigns and elections. In this chapter we shall look at the ways individual citizens participate in political processes and then narrow our focus onto patterns of voting behavior. From one point of view, this chapter forms an evaluation of the successes of parties in their appeals to particular groups. From a second point of view, these pages reanalyze some facets of the distribution of power: who participates and how in politics? who votes for whom? From yet another perspective, this chapter examines the problem of rationality in political behavior. Given their varied objectives, to what extent do private citizens maximize their opportunities to influence public policy?

Political Participation: The Decision to Vote

A citizen's act of voting represents perhaps the simplest form of political participation. It costs no money, takes only a small amount of time (although registering to vote can be more burdensome), and, according to democratic folklore, is a precious right. Yet in the United States seldom do as many as two thirds of potential electors go to the polls, even for presidential elections; and local contests often bring out only a small fraction of citizens. Indeed, about 10 percent of those who vote in presidential elections do not even bother to mark their ballots to choose among candidates for Congress. The turnout for off-year congressional elections (those when a President is not chosen) is anywhere from 20 to 50 percent less than for presidential elections. In short, the right to vote may be sacred, but a substantial percentage of Americans seldom if ever avail themselves of its potential saving grace.

Who Is More or Less Likely to Vote?

More men than women vote, although the gap has narrowed since 1920 as women, having gained the vote, acquire more political experience. Education directly affects the proportion of people casting ballots, the better educated being more likely to vote. Similarly, people in upper-income brackets are more likely to vote than those in lower-income groups. Persons between thirty-five and fifty-five show greater interest in voting than do people either younger or older. A larger portion of urban dwellers turn out than do rural residents. Persons with strong attachments to a political party vote in relatively larger numbers than do political independents or those with weak party affiliations. Westerners have the highest rate of voting, and southerners the lowest. Protestants are less likely to vote than Catholics and Jews.

Although the legal and extralegal devices of southern communities have historically discouraged blacks from voting, so have, as the Civil Rights Commission has said, lethargy, lack of education, and simple despair.[1] Even in the north, blacks have in the past been less likely to vote than whites, but this statement is somewhat misleading. Blacks have been as likely to vote as whites of the same socioeconomic status, but blacks have tended to come from the lower-income and lower-educated strata of society, in which nonvoting almost always runs high. In 1972, however, blacks as a group did vote as frequently as whites.

Why People Stay at Home

Some people do not vote because they have only recently moved into a state or are ill, disabled, or away on vacation or business. Local party organizations try to minimize such problems by helping arrange for transportation and absentee ballots. Thus the number of people unable to vote for purely physical reasons is normally quite small, probably less than 6 percent of nonvoters.[2]

Some people, again a relatively small number, do not bother to vote because of their faith that whatever the rest of the people want will be right. Others—relatively fewer than we might expect—may feel that one side is so certain to win by a large majority that to cast their votes is to waste their time. Perhaps more important in keeping people at home are cross-pressures; for example, a person's general sympathy with the Republican party but deep concern about disagreement with a spouse who is a Democrat, or approval of Republican foreign policy but preference for Democratic approaches to welfare.

In addition, the issues and personalities featured in a campaign confuse some potential voters and bore others. Or they see no viable choice: they may be bored by Ford but suspicious of Carter. More generally, nonvoting may indicate a lack of faith in the political system and its processes, a belief that the system itself is too corrupt and inefficient to cope with important problems.

Nonvoting thus may result from from a rational decision. Registration and voting consume time and energy; small amounts of each are involved but still they bring what economists call "opportunity costs." Similar and higher costs attend the process of obtaining information needed to choose intelligently between available alternatives. These costs also explain in part why many people find party labels handy guides to decision making. And, democratic ideals to the contrary notwithstanding, the effect of any one vote must be discounted by the total number of other voters. That a single vote could ever swing an election above the ward or precinct level is an infinitesimally small probability. What we know of typical nonvoters, however, does not fit the model of shrewdly calculating people meticulously employing their resources. On the contrary, nonvoters are usually relatively uneducated people, indisposed to tolerate coldly rational analysis.

A traditional lion dance is used in New York City to attract attention to a voter registration drive for the 1976 election. Bilingual registration forms and information were available to Chinatown residents at tables like the one in the center of the photo.

Paul Hosefros/NYT Pictures.

Several factors stand out in scholarly diagnoses of possible causes of nonvoting. First is the difficulty of registration. States that allow prospective voters only brief periods during the year to enroll have a much higher percentage of nonvoters than do states in which registration is relatively easy. And of those people who register, about three quarters actually vote in presidential elections.[3] Of course, no one who is unregistered can legally vote in any election. Parenthetically, we might note in anticipation of later sections of this chapter that because less well-educated and less affluent groups are the least likely to register and are also among the most likely to vote Democratic if they do register and go to the polls, registration campaigns should logically be the first order of business of Democratic candidates.

A second critical factor relates to civic mindedness and perhaps to civic education. What we have said about the very tiny effect of any single vote is absolutely true, but apparently not especially important for most people. (Less than one half of one percent of nonvoters in a national sample interviewed in 1974 gave such an explanation for not going to the polls.) The point is that many people feel an obligation to vote and in addition actually enjoy the sense of power that voting gives them. Indeed, almost three quarters of respondents in one study reported that voting gave them emotional satisfaction.[4] People who lack civic training or who have not on their own developed this peculiar democratic belief that one should enjoy voting as well as profit from it in some material fashion are not likely to go to the polls.

Electoral competitiveness may be a third factor in voting or nonvoting. The evidence is not clear-cut: some studies have found that when

Table 9–1

Percentage of people engaging in certain kinds of political activity

Type of political participation	Percentage
1. Vote regularly in presidential election	72
2. Always vote in local elections	47
3. Active in at least one organization involved in community problems	32
4. Have worked with others to try to solve some community problems	30
5. Have attempted to persuade others how to vote	28
6. Have ever actively worked for a party or candidates during a campaign	26
7. Have ever contacted a local government official about some issue	20
8. Attended at least one political meeting or rally within last 3 years	19
9. Have ever contacted a state or national governmental official about some issue	18
10. Have ever formed a group or organization to attempt to solve some local community problem	14
11. Have ever given money to a party or a candidate during a campaign	13
12. Presently a member of a political club or organization	8
Number of people interviewed: 2,549	

Source: Sidney Verba and Norman Nie, *Participation in America* (New York: Harper & Row, Publishers, 1972), p. 31.

political contests may be close, more people take the time to register and vote. Other investigations have found at most a weak relationship between voting and anticipated closeness.[5] At least, however, the probability of a close election can move political organizations to mobilize likely supporters and so increase registration and voting.

Other Forms of Political Participation

Voting, we said, is among the simplest, cheapest, and most obvious ways of participating in politics. But there are dozens of other ways by which a private citizen can influence the choice of public officials or public policies. (Some are listed in items 3 to 13 in Table 9–1.) Because more than one third of people fail to vote even in presidential elections, it is reasonable to expect that far fewer attempt more expensive and difficult forms of participation. The data in Table 9–1 confirm that expectation. In fact, these figures are somewhat higher than those found by other respected researchers.

The most thorough study of political participation in American politics is that of Sidney Verba and Norman H. Nie.[6] Under their direction, the National Opinion Research Center interviewed a national sample* of 2,600 adults as well as officials in sixty-four of the communities from which the sample was drawn. The findings (partially reported in Table 9–1) enabled Verba and Nie to distinguish six categories of citizens, one group that was politically inert, one that was fully active, and four that more or less specialized in certain kinds of participation:

(1) *The Inactives.* These people seldom vote and rarely take part in other aspects of political life; indeed, they usually demonstrate neither knowledge of nor interest in matters political. This group constitutes a little more than one fifth of the adult population, and it heavily overrepresents blacks and those from lower socioeconomic levels, as well as young adults, very old people, and women.

(2) *The Voting Specialists.* These citizens typically vote but only occasionally perform other politically relevant activities, even though they often express strong identifications with a political party. These people are about as numerous as the Inactives, and they overrepresent older persons, those from lower socioeconomic strata, and inhabitants of big cities.

(3) *Parochials.* This group is quite small, forming less than 5 percent of the sample. Its members vote less frequently than anyone except the Inactives. The Parochials' principal form of political participation comes through personal contacts—which they themselves initiate—with public officials, asking for assistance with problems peculiar to them or to a small segment of the population to which they belong. The Parochials overrepresent people of lower socioeconomic status, but not blacks. They are quite likely to be Catholics and to live in large urban centers.

(4) *Communalists.* These people usually vote regularly, but seldom engage in other electoral activities such as campaigning. On the other hand, they, like the Parochials, make direct contact with public officials but do so about problems of wide significance within the community. The Communalists are also likely to form associations or join existing organizations to cope on a bipartisan or nonpartisan basis with social and political problems. They form about a fifth of the sample, underrepresenting blacks and Catholics and overrepresenting upper socio-

---

*Pollsters cannot, of course, interview every person, even in a small town. Instead they interview only a portion (or sample) of the people in the particular town, city, county, state, or nation being studied. A *national sample* refers to a sample of people selected from every geographical region of the country. Although not free of problems, sampling has reached the status of a rather fine art. Most pollsters now use *random samples* of adults for voting studies, that is, samples in which every adult in the region being studied has an equal chance of being interviewed.

economic strata, Protestants, and people living in smaller towns and rural areas.

(5) *Campaigners*. These are the citizens who are heavily involved in partisan political activities. They almost always vote, and they spend time urging others to do so—but in support of their own candidates. They often work energetically for candidates or parties, ring doorbells, distribute literature, attend rallies, and solicit and contribute money. The Campaigners have a number of political skills and are deeply partisan; but they tend to lack the sense of contribution to a community that the Communalists talk about. The Campaigners constitute about 15 percent of the population, overrepresenting persons of higher status, blacks, Catholics, and those who live in big cities.

(6) *The Complete Activists*. These are the few (a little more than 10 percent of the sample) who fit the classic democratic model of the active, informed citizen. They immerse themselves deeply in political life, voting, campaigning, contacting officials about personal and communal problems, and joining with others in both partisan and nonpartisan efforts to solve political and social problems. They heavily overrepresent the better educated, the more affluent, and people of middle age. And, despite expectations, blacks make up a fully proportional share of this group.

Why People Participate in Politics[7]

If a sense of civic obligation and simple enjoyment of power are among the causes of political participation, very closely allied is the need that many people feel to understand the world around them and to exercise some control over what happens to their lives. Other motives vary from narrow self-interest—for instance, the Parochials—to selfless concern for the good of the whole community.

Desire for social activity—meeting with, talking to, and helping others—moves some people to political participation. Others, sometimes unconsciously, find in politics an outlet for emotional tensions, caused perhaps by personal problems, perhaps by broader concerns. Some white men who actively advocate busing to achieve integration may be assuaging the guilt they feel about past injustices done to blacks. Some wives who are dissatisfied with housework may find the politics of women's liberation an emotional godsend. Some public issues, especially those involving race or sex, can attract people with deep-seated neuroses. For some of them, participation acts as therapy. For others, it may be a frenzied symptom of mental disturbance. There is no evidence, however, that those who participate in politics are more likely to be neurotic than less active citizens. In fact, nonparticipation can be linked to emotional disorders that cause sufferers to withdraw from problems of the real world.

Actually, participation is intuitively easier to understand than is nonparticipation. After all, politics makes a constant impact on the lives of most citizens. Yet the simple fact remains that relatively few people make the effort to become politically well informed or to take advantage of the range of opportunities open to them.

Results of Political Participation

The way an individual citizen votes is not likely to have much political impact—unless he or she acts in concert with others. And, of course, organizing individuals and massing their power is precisely what interest groups and, with a broader base, political parties try to do. It is necessary to read only an occasional newspaper to be aware of the effect that organized interest groups can have when they mobilize—or even seem to be able to mobilize—voters who share common concerns. If such organizations have money and some social prestige, their power further escalates.

The National Rifle Association, for example, has for decades been able to block effective federal gun-control laws despite the far more widely shared but unorganized concern about reducing the availability of weapons that contribute so hugely to violent crime and to thousands of accidental deaths. Despite such daily demonstrations of the power of political organizations, only 8 percent of Americans were members of such groups, as Table 9–1 shows. That figure would rise considerably, however, if it included such organizations as the American Legion, labor unions, chambers of commerce, or medical and bar associations, which, although ostensibly functioning for social, economic, or professional purposes, often work hard to block or secure passage of legislation to their own selfish advantage.

Even a private citizen initiating contact with a public official can sometimes, on his own, exercise real influence. Most elected officials pride themselves on their efficiency (usually their staff's efficiency) in hearing constituents' views and at least considering them in making decisions. In senators' and representatives' offices, much of the time is consumed in processing constituents' requests for help in dealing with various governmental agencies. And an elected official who has no strong personal views on some issues may find contacts initiated by individual citizens an excellent means of divining public opinion when he wants to build up a record that will please voters.

In general, public officials do listen to and try to heed the suggestions, advice, requests, and even demands of politically active citizens, Verba and Nie concluded from their interviews with officers in sixty-four of the communities from which their national sample was drawn. "If we accept," they explained, "as a measure of responsiveness the extent to which community leaders adopt the same agenda for community action as that of the citizenry, then our data support the conclusion that where those citizens are participant, leaders are responsive."[8]

Studying Electoral Behavior

So far we have been discussing individual citizens' decisions to participate in political affairs and the general patterns of their participation. Now, before moving to other aspects of political behavior, we shall explain how researchers have obtained data about voting (and, incidentally, about most other forms of political participation).

Data for Study

The raw materials most readily available for the study of electoral behavior are the official voting returns, that is, the actual records of the division of votes. These *aggregate data,* to use the technical term, are normally available down to the precinct level. They are useful for many purposes in analyzing either the results of a single election or changes over time in patterns of support. On the other hand, aggregate data have limited utility in explaining how different groups—Catholics or Jews, men or women, whites or blacks—voted. The means most frequently used to explore these differences is *survey research,* almost synonymous in the popular mind with the Gallup Poll.

To obtain information about how and why citizens vote (or participate in other ways), pollsters interview a sample of people—a small number randomly drawn so that all persons in the population have an equal chance of being selected—from an electoral district. For a presidential election, that "district" may be the entire nation; and in comparison with the entire population, "small" is indeed small. As few as 1,300 people, if truly randomly selected, meet statistical standards for a representative national sample. The questions pollsters ask vary in sophistication, but if sensibly constructed they can tell a great deal about electoral decisions.

A variant of interviews with respondents at a single point in time is the so-called *panel.* Here pollsters interview each respondent on at least two occasions, perhaps once before and once after an election, or perhaps even a third and fourth time, before and after the next election. The advantages of a panel in discovering and accounting for changes over time are obvious. But the cost of any kind of survey research is high. And, because of the mobility of Americans, those costs spiral when a pollster tries to reinterview the same people after a lapse of several years.

Incidentally, there is no reason why students of voting behavior cannot combine analysis of aggregate voting data with survey research. And, in fact, most of the more sophisticated analysts do use both sorts of information.

Limitations on Research and Analysis

Several cautions are in order before we look at the substantive findings about electoral behavior, cautions that also apply to what we said earlier about electoral behavior, and about other kinds of political participation. First, none of the voting studies claims to explain the choices of all the voters. Each explanation is hedged by such words as "usually" and "typically." Second, most intensive studies of electoral behavior concern presidential or off-year congressional campaigns. We can generalize from national elections to all state and local contests, but only as hypotheses worth testing. Third, even at the national level, we have close investigations of only a handful of elections over a span of forty years. We should be careful not to assume that we are dealing with a static phenomenon. We may have discovered permanent patterns of behavior, but we should not reach such a conclusion without research extending over a much longer period.

This third qualification requires elaboration. Historically, presidential elections can be classified[9] as (1) *maintaining,* in which prevailing patterns of party loyalties persist; (2) *deviating,* in which basic partisan loyalties remain intact, but for some reason enough voters support the minority party candidate to swing this particular election to him; (3) *reinstating,* in which the majority party regains control following a deviating election; (4) *realigning,* in which old loyalties are disrupted to such an extent as to reshuffle majority and minority party statuses. The elections of 1940 (Roosevelt v. Wilkie), 1944 (Roosevelt v. Dewey), and 1948 (Truman v. Dewey) were all *maintaining* elections. Thus similarities in findings during those years may mean only that in the same kind of electoral situation most people reacted in the same fashion.

The contests of 1952 and 1956 produced *deviating* elections. Dwight D. Eisenhower won handily in both, but a large number of those who voted for him continued to think of themselves as Democrats, and in 1954, 1956, and 1958 they elected a Democratic majority to both houses of Congress. The election of 1960 (Kennedy v. Nixon) was a *reinstating* election, and 1964 (Johnson v. Goldwater) provided another *maintaining* election. 1968 (Humphrey v. Nixon) again produced a *deviating* election. Richard M. Nixon captured the White House but with only 43 percent of the popular vote, and, at the same time, the Democrats retained control of both houses of Congress. In 1972 (McGovern v. Nixon), the Democrats were still bitterly divided among themselves, and their nominee clumsily pushed party loyalists into Nixon's camp. The result was a peculiarity, a *deviating* election in which the Republicans won the presidency by a huge landslide but lost both houses of Congress. In 1976, most of the Democratic loyalists came home and reinstated their party in power.

There having been no *realigning* election in these years of political research, we lack a study in depth, a lack that makes a full comparison impossible. Such contests, however, are relatively rare, those of 1896 and 1932 being the two that experts usually identify. The panic of 1893 apparently served as a catalyst to raise Republicans to the status of majority party. They retained this dominance, despite deviating elections in 1912 and 1916, until the Great Depression of 1929 started another cycle that brought the Democrats into power. Some explanations of political behavior may change considerably when data of the same kind are available on each type of presidential election. Even without such data, there have already been some modifications of early theories. The first studies, which involved only *maintaining* elections, agreed that a person's party preference was the best single determinant of his or her final vote. In the *deviating* elections of 1952 and 1956, however, large numbers of voters who continued to call themselves Democrats voted Republican, clearly attracted to General Eisenhower. Even in the *reinstating* election of 1960, a considerable number of Democrats again voted Republican. In 1964, vast numbers of Republicans supported the Democratic candidate; and in 1972, an equally vast number of Democrats voted for Nixon.

We cannot, therefore, think of parties as holding together "like a sticky ball of popcorn." Rather, as V. O. Key put it, "no sooner has a popular majority been constructed than it begins to crumble."[10] Even a finding that the proportion of votes going to each party remains constant does not necessarily mean that the same people are always voting the same way. New voters come of age or participate in politics; old ones die or lose interest. Other voters become disenchanted with the administration and support the opposition; still others may be won over to administration policies and, for this election at least, vote for the incumbents.

Patterns of Partisanship

Political Knowledge

Despite different techniques of research and analysis, their limitations, and different interpretations of results, students of electoral behavior have produced a set of findings that are quite consistent with each other. Those who, despite what passes for political campaigning in the United States, hope to find an intelligent, informed electorate carefully weighing policy alternatives and candidates' records before voting can expect small comfort from available data. One nearly universal finding has been that a large majority of adults have little knowledge of politics, even during a national campaign when the media are saturated with political information. In the fall of 1966, for example, only one out of five respondents in a national sample could recall the name of any congressional candidate for whom he or she could have voted a few weeks earlier.

Furthermore, people's opinions and preferences about policies are highly unstable over time. For example, questioned three times over a four year period by the University of Michigan's Survey Research Center, a large segment of individuals in one panel gave answers to identical questions that varied from strongly opposed to strongly in favor of certain policies. And these questions concerned such apparently basic issues as the proper roles of the federal government and private enterprise in the fields of housing and public utilities.[11]

Socialization

Even when a voter believes that he or she has made a clear-cut choice based solely on considerations of public policy, a number of factors in that person's background may have helped form attitudes affecting and even distorting the images that the candidates have tried to project. Psychologists have often demonstrated the phenomenon of *selective perception* — what people see in a particular situation is greatly influenced by their own values. And early political education may affect both perceptions and preferences.

Cohesiveness of voting within families was a striking finding of an intensive study of Erie County, New York, in 1940,[12] a finding that has cropped up again and again in subsequent surveys. Because husbands and wives have tended to vote the same way, children have usually been reared in a one-sided political atmosphere. It is hardly surprising to find, then, that when they come of age children are inclined to vote in the same way as their parents. This pattern, however, forms only a general rule. Changes in social status or disagreements on important policy questions may weaken the "inherited" party allegiance. Lowering the voting age to eighteen, an age at which the young often take great pride in seeming to differ with their parents even when they really agree, may also widen cleavages between generations. Moreover, families' political coherence in the past normally resulted from wives following their husbands. What effect Women's Liberation will have on this coherence — and on children's inherited loyalties — remains to be seen.

Social Class

If we use occupation, income, and education as indexes of class (or what is called *socioeconomic status*), then we can say that, generally, the higher their education and income and the more professional the nature of their work, the more likely voters are to be Republican. Conversely, the lower their income and education and the more closely their occupations are related to manual, unskilled labor, the more likely they are to be Democrats. There is, therefore, some evidence behind the old cliché that the rich are Republicans and the poor Democrats, but the full truth is far more complex. Republican strength is largely based on middle-class white-collar workers and semiprofessionals, and the Democrats often draw their leaders from the wealthy. There is also a striking exception to the rule of the better educated being Republican. Intellectuals, particularly social scientists, are overwhelmingly Democratic. Moreover, many blue-collar workers supported Nixon in 1972 and Ford in 1976, although without transferring any permanent allegiance to the Republican party.

Despite unions' claims to the contrary, there is probably more political cohesiveness among businessmen than among workers. If there were not and if general socioeconomic divisions were followed in every election, the Republicans would be hard put to win office above the ward level, or they would be forced into becoming a more liberal party. Perhaps one of the basic reasons for absence of political solidarity among working-class people is that American culture has been predominantly white middle class. Geographical influences also cut across class lines. For example, in those small cities that are normally Republican communities, factory workers are less inclined to vote Democratic than are people who do the same sort of work in large urban centers.

Furthermore, the general relationship between class and party loyalty has declined since World War II. The Democratic party has made deep inroads into the middle class, especially its younger people, in part because of the upward mobility of traditionally Democratic families, and in part because of changing attitudes about the proper role of the federal government in social and economic affairs.[13]

Religion

Religion, too, is associated with partisan political loyalty, as Table 9–2 shows. White Protestants in northern states tend to vote Republican. Since the 1920s, the Jewish vote has been heavily Democratic by about a four to one margin. Historically, Catholics, even those in upper-income brackets, have been much more likely to vote Democratic, although this tendency has been more pronounced among Irish- and Polish-Americans than among Italian-Americans. Despite this traditional orientation, Catholic voters in 1952 and 1956 shifted their votes to Dwight Eisenhower and the Republican column. With John Kennedy the candidate in 1960, however, four out of five Catholics voted Democratic. 1972 brought another reversal. Large numbers of working-class white ethnics—who are predominantly Catholics—voted for Nixon, as did a substantial number of middle-class Catholics. But in 1976 most of these people again voted Democratic.

Religion can be an explosive issue when it comes out openly in a campaign, and most politicians are careful to avoid the subject. In 1928, Al Smith's Catholicism was a major factor in his defeat. Again in 1960, it played a significant role, although its actual effect is more difficult to assess because the number of Catholic voters had greatly increased in the intervening thirty-two years. On balance, however, it seems that John Kennedy's religion cost him more votes than it gained him. "Probably the best guess," V. O. Key wrote, "is that

Table 9–2
**Voting trends among social categories since 1952
(presidential vote, 1952–1972)**

Percent Democratic of two-party vote for President (three-party in 1968)

	1952	1956	1960	1964	1968	1972
National	45	42	50	61	43	38
Men	47	45	52	60	41	37
Women	42	39	49	62	45	38
White	43	41	49	59	38	32
Nonwhite	79	61	68	94	85	87
College	34	31	39	52	37	37
High school	45	42	52	62	42	34
Grade school	52	50	55	66	52	49
Prof. and Business	36	32	42	54	34	31
White collar	40	37	48	57	41	36
Manual	55	50	60	71	50	43
Under 30 years	51	43	54	64	47	48
30–49 years	47	45	54	63	44	33
50 years and older	39	39	46	59	41	36
Protestants	37	37	38	55	35	30
Catholics	56	51	78	76	59	48
Republicans	8	4	5	20	9	5
Democrats	77	85	84	87	74	67
Independents	35	30	43	56	31	31
Members of labor union families	61	57	65	73	56	46

Source: The Gallup Poll, press release, December 14, 1972.

Kennedy won in spite of rather than because of the fact that he was a Catholic."[14] Anti-Catholicism may still be alive, but Catholics have become the largest religious sect in the United States. Because they are heavily concentrated in large metropolitan areas, no sane national candidate can afford to antagonize such a large group. Ironically, in 1976, Carter's fundamentalist Baptist religion caused deep concern among many liberal Catholics and Jews.

Race

Minority racial status, like religion, indicates probable party choice. From Emancipation to the New Deal, blacks, at least those who voted, were strongly Republican; then Franklin D. Roosevelt won them away from the party of Lincoln. Although the Republicans have made a number of attempts to woo black support and black leaders frequently urge their followers to vote more selectively, blacks have remained since 1932 solidly Democratic. It was in part Republican despair at cracking the black vote in northern metropolitan areas that made the southern strategy in 1968 and 1972 and the modified "rim" strategy in 1976 attractive.

Age

From 1948 to 1960, more than half of voters claimed never to have crossed party lines in a presidential election, but 1964 and 1972 sent that statistic sprawling. Despite those two landslide years, there is a general pattern: age tends to stabilize party preferences. Typically, younger voters' party loyalties are not firm. In fact, young citizens who vote for the same party as their parents often initially call themselves independents. If a switch in party allegiance does occur, it is likely to come during early adulthood, along with changes in income and social status. As voters grow older their attachment to a party very often hardens to the point where it becomes psychologically quite difficult to vote for the opposition.

Older voters are more apt to vote Republican than are younger voters, as Table 9–2 shows, the usual explanation being that age brings greater conservatism and, at least until retirement nears, larger income. But that table also shows considerable variations within each age group at any given election and indicates that voting behavior of any particular group varies from election to election. More specifically, Table 9–2 demonstrates that it is wrong to think that most younger voters always vote Democratic, much less side with the radical left that was once so vocal on campuses. In 1968, at the peak of student unrest, George Wallace drew heavy support from the young. Indeed, outside the south, he received stronger support from voters under thirty than from any other age group. Activists among college students may have visualized themselves as battling a corrupt older generation, but:

A more head on confrontation at the polls . . . was with their own age mates who had gone from high school off to the factory instead of college. . . . Outside of the election period, when verbal articulateness and leisure for political activism count most heavily, it was the college share of the younger generation—or at least its politicized vanguard—that was most prominent as a political force. At the polls, however, the game shifts to "one man, one vote," and this vanguard is numerically swamped even within its own generation.[15]

Again in 1972, young adults were somewhat more likely to have voted for Nixon than McGovern, and even college students were about equally divided between the two candidates. In 1976, however, about 56 percent of voters under thirty chose Carter.

Geography

Immigration from urban centers to the suburbs might benefit Republicans because this change normally involves moving from a lower to a higher income bracket and to an environment generally less hospitable to the Democratic party, or so some writers have speculated. While Republicans are somewhat more likely than Democrats to move out of the cities, there is little evidence of conversion among former city dwellers to Republicanism.

Farmers and city people react to politics in very different ways. But it is possible to speak of a rural or an urban vote only in gross terms. Any remarks about voting behavior must be made with qualifications about income, race, religion, and a host of other factors. Northern farmers, for example, generally have a Republican tradition; southern farmers, at least until recently, a Democratic one. Outside the south, however, a considerable number of small farmers are quite likely to be Democrats; and even in the deep south, there have been rural Republican enclaves that trace their loyalty back to the Civil War.

Historically, farmers have been a prolific source of radical third parties that have received impressive rural support at one election only to vanish within a few years. This tendency to support third parties may be dying out; but the two-party division among farmers outside the south still shows sharp fluctuations. Moreover, not only are farmers disinclined to be loyal to a party over time, but they are also less likely than city dwellers to vote a straight party ticket in any one election. And farmers' voting participation is erratic: they may turn out in mass for one election only to stay quietly at home for the next.

Many explanations have been offered for the lack of a coherent pattern in rural political behavior. Economic vulnerability is undoubtedly partially responsible. Another important aspect is the farmer's isolation—not only physical but also cultural. He tends to have less formal education. He is less exposed to the mass media. One could make similar observations about semiskilled factory workers, but there are differences. The farmer usually works pretty much alone. He is less likely to be approached by a party worker or to be reminded of his duty to vote "correctly" by a group official. (Despite lobbyists' claims, few farmers are active in farm organizations.) In other words, many factors that operate in an urban environment to stir up and maintain political interest and partisan loyalty function far less efficiently in rural areas. Unencumbered by party loyalty, farmers are free of one of the principal emotional attachments that steady the vote of urban workers. Without compunction farmers can "vote the rascals out," whether they be Republicans, Democrats, or members of some agrarian party. This political style, of course, is not altogether different from that of independent voters in the city, but urban independents are greatly outnumbered by their committed neighbors. Independent farmers, on the other hand, are often a majority within their occupational grouping.

The Independents

Because membership in American political parties is loose and informal, it is not easy to determine what proportion of the electorate can

Figure 9.1
**Percent of people claiming political identification
as Republicans, Democrats, or Independents**

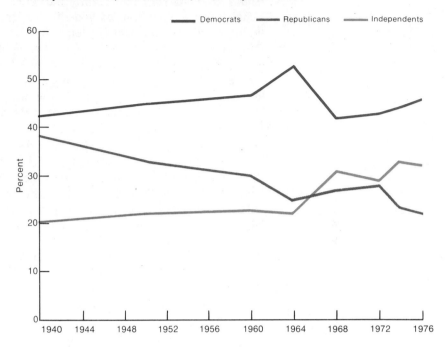

accurately be labeled "independent." Many people who claim to be
independents actually support one party with considerable regularity.
The best guesses place the proportion of real independents at somewhere between one quarter and one third of the electorate.

There is a venerable body of opinion that asserts the moral and intellectual superiority of independent voters. It is true that national
surveys have found that a majority of the most knowledgeable respondents call themselves independents, but this group is small. Furthermore, the typical independent tends to have less political interest,
awareness, concern, and information than the voter who asserts party
allegiance.

Reactions against the war in Vietnam and the scandals of Watergate
have reduced citizens' trust in government and these, along with the
adoption of the Twenty-sixth Amendment in 1971 that lowered the
voting age to eighteen, have also reduced willingness to identify with a
political party. As Figure 9–1 shows, for decades about 75 to 80 percent of adults claimed to be Democrats or Republicans; but since 1967
the proportion of potential voters denying affiliation with either party
has risen to almost one third.

Rationality and Political Choice

The classical democratic model of a politically interested, informed, and active citizenry intelligently participating in the choice of public officials and public policies finds little support in available data about political information and participation—at least on first examination. Nor do these data seem to fit a model of highly informed "opinion leaders" guiding the political choices of the less sophisticated. The critical causes for the actual state of things, we have said, appear to lie in citizens' failing to appreciate the importance of politics, not understanding ways to influence public officials, and not enjoying participation, or at least lacking a feeling of civic duty to take part in politics. These shortcomings, as we shall discuss in a moment, are related to socioeconomic status. More immediately, we concentrate on the question of how rationally the mass of citizens behave. *Rationality* in this discussion is not a synonym for intelligence. Rather it concerns efficient allocation of available means (resources such as time, energy, and money) to achieve desired goals.

Rationality, Candidates, and Politicians

First of all, whatever one can say about private citizens, it seems clear that, as a group, candidates for office behave rationally. The campaigning techniques described in Chapter 8 appear quite suited to the behavior of the American public, to whom "politics is a sideshow in the great circus of life."[16] Moreover, such traditional party appeals as those of the Democrats to the working class, blacks, Jews, and Catholics and those of the Republicans to whites, Protestants, professionals, semiprofessionals, and other members of the middle class seem to hit a large share of their targets. More specifically, the fact that elected officials try to respond to the requests and suggestions of citizen-activists also indicates rational behavior by people who wish to be re-elected.

Rationality and Private Citizens

A closer look at private citizens shows, as we would expect, both far less political sophistication and much less rational behavior, in an objective sense, than among professionals. For, whether they believe it or not, politics vitally affects the lives of all citizens. Thus—and leaving aside voting for the moment—insofar as people do not take full advantage of their constitutionally guaranteed rights to contact government officials and join with others to engage in a whole range of activities that are politically relevant, those people seem to be making very inefficient use of their resources.

That evaluation is correct, however, only to the extent that these people cannot act as "free riders" or actually do not want to destroy the system. It could make very good sense, of course, for a person opposing the system to refuse to use the means it offers to satisfy citizens' needs, thus increasing their dissatisfaction. The problem of the free rider is much more complex. In brief, insofar as a group or another individual (such as Ralph Nader) will effectively further the interests of the inactive as well as the active, it is perfectly rational for a person to sit back and let others do the work. For example, a conservative lawyer who knows that the powerful and highly politicized American Bar Association will fight vigorously to protect both his professional interests as a lawyer and his conservative ideology can quite rationally devote his time to making money.

Doing nothing, however, is not rational when such organizations or individuals either do not exist or lack money, skills, and other instruments of political power. And it is likely to be the poorer, less well educated, aged, or sick—the very people who need governmental action most—who lack powerful organizations to fight for them. Thus it is objectively irrational for such people not to participate actively in politics. But these are also likely to be the people who lack the knowledge and verbal skills to participate effectively, and, in the case of the aged and the sick, the physical capacity to do so. As Chapter 6 pointed out, it is people of higher socioeconomic status who are best equipped to wield political instruments effectively.

Americans like to think that because the opportunity to participate politically is, as a matter of constitutional law, open to all, it is therefore *equally* open to all. As a matter of logic, the second proposition simply does not follow from the first. Nor is it empirically true. Of the ten countries that Verba and Nie have studied (Austria, Germany, Great Britain, Holland, India, Italy, Japan, Mexico, Nigeria, and the United States), only in India is political participation tied as closely to socioeconomic status as it is in the United States. The tight linkage in this country, they believe, is a paradoxical result of a relative absence of class consciousness and class-oriented political institutions. If most Americans were aware of the differences in political rewards received by different classes, and if there existed parties or interest groups that could awaken and exploit such an awareness, then, Verba and Nie believe, people of lower socioeconomic status would take fuller advantage of the political opportunities that are open to them. And there is some evidence to support this proposition. For instance, blacks who are able to articulate concern about racial problems tend to be more politically active than whites who have similar incomes, education, and social position.

Rationality and Voting Behavior

Assuming that it is rational to vote, the actual electoral behavior of almost two thirds of American citizens demonstrates considerably more rationality than their generally low level of information might indicate. The small core of *Complete Activists,* of course, neatly fits the classic democratic model. But before dismissing as irrational the way the relatively inactive and uninformed general public votes, we must carefully re-examine much of what was said earlier in this chapter.

First, there is a problem with our information, a methodological problem inherent in most of survey research. Having a stranger come into one's home and ask questions about politics for as long as two hours creates emotional stress; and the questions require a degree of verbal articulation that the respondent may simply not possess under the best of circumstances. The point is not that most voters are well informed, but rather that the way in which pollsters test their information tends to exaggerate their ignorance. Less structured and more informal interviews, involving talks with an interviewer who over a period of weeks becomes a friend, have produced a different picture.[17] It shows somewhat more coherence—though not necessarily more sophistication—among opinions that at first glance seem confused and even contradictory. This type of interview, however, may itself help produce coherence and consistency by forcing respondents to think hard about political problems, something they might never do unless prodded by a persistent interrogator.

Second, there is a distinction between acting on little information and acting irrationally. One cannot say that a gut reaction is irrational or even unintelligent. Rationality depends on the person's gut and the nature of the reaction. For example, it makes excellent sense in terms of economic self-interest for blacks and poor whites to vote for Democratic presidential candidates, just as it makes economic sense for middle- and upper-class white Protestants to vote Republican. By and large, Democratic Presidents of this century have tried to use federal power to help the economically less fortunate. Republican Presidents have been more concerned to protect middle- and upper-class whites.

Furthermore, those voters who want social change may reasonably prefer the more liberal party, just as those who look to the past for guidance may prefer the more conservative. Catholics and Jews, underdogs in a predominantly Protestant society and strongly motivated by religious teachings about government's positive obligations, act rationally in picking the candidate who preaches social justice through governmental action. Candidates and parties may give the public weak or even confusing clues to their stands on *specific* problems, but since 1932 the *general* policy orientations of presidential candidates has been clear. And the data in Table 9–2 are consistent with a rational response by most voters to those orientations.

Relationships between responses to policy questions and actual votes are weak, but, as we have said, this weakness may be due in part to difficulties in responding to interviewers' formal questions. This weakness may also be partly due to the fact that parties take stands on a great many issues, and the relative importance of these issues may vary widely among voters. It would hardly be surprising to see a white laborer, worried about his job and afraid of having blacks live next door, vote for a Democratic presidential candidate who was pressing for civil rights, *if* the white worker also associated the Democrats with prosperity and better jobs. Economic advancement might be more important to him than dislike of blacks. Besides, with more money he might be able to move to an all-white suburb. If this man used such social science jargon as "rank ordering of values" and "efficient allocation of resources," political scientists would be quick to proclaim the rationality of his decision, although they might deplore his goals. In short, we should be slow to equate lack of sophistication and academic knowledge with irrational behavior.

There is a third, straightforward reason why one should hesitate to dismiss as irrational voters' reactions in presidential elections. There is a close relationship between how voters perceive parties and candidates and how voters cast their ballots. To explain this linkage, Stanley Kelley and Thad Mirer stated what they called the Voter's Decision Rule:

> The voter canvasses his likes and dislikes of the leading candidates and major parties involved in an election. Weighing each like and dislike equally, he votes for the candidate toward whom he has the greatest net number of favorable attitudes, if there is such a candidate. If no candidate has such an advantage, the voter votes consistently with his party affiliation, if he has such. If he does not identify with one of the major parties and if his attitudes do not incline him toward one candidate more than toward another, he will not vote.[18]

To test the validity of this rule, Kelley and Mirer analyzed the results of surveys of panels conducted just before five presidential elections. For each respondent they constructed a scale of attitudes toward parties and candidates based on his or her replies to questions asking what the person liked about the leading presidential candidates and major parties.* The farther the person was located on the negative (Republican) side of the scale, the more likely he or she was to vote Republican; the farther on the positive (Democratic) side of the scale, the more likely he or she was to vote Democratic. In fact, the scale accurately predicted the way an overwhelming percentage of voters would decide, as Table 9–3 shows. The scale's poorest performance came in 1968, when there were three major candidates and many Democrats, especially in the south, viewed George Wallace as the party's real candidate.[19] In addition, the Voter's Decision Rule accurately predicted a larger percentage of votes than did any other explanation,

---

*For each respondent, Kelley and Mirer counted the number of favorable comments about Democrats and subtracted from that number all unfavorable comments the respondent made about Democrats. They performed the same simple arithmetic with each respondent's comments about Republicans. Then Kelley and Mirer subtracted each respondent's pro-Republican score from his or her pro-Democratic score. (The formula is more easily seen than said: [D+− D−] − [R+−R−]=scale score.) The resulting scale gave pro-Democratic respondents positive scores and pro-Republicans negative scores. "The Simple Act of Voting," *American Political Science Review*, LXVIII (1974), p. 572.

Table 9–3
Percentage of voters whose presidential vote the rule accurately predicted

Year	Percentage	Number of respondents
1952	87	1184
1956	85	1270
1960	88	1413
1964	90	1113
1968	81	1027

Source: Stanley Kelley, Jr., and Thad W. Mirer, "The Simple Act of Voting." *American Political Science Review*, LXVIII (1974), p. 572.

including party identification and even respondents' own statements given in interviews shortly before the actual election about how they planned to vote.

The results produced by the Voter's Decision Rule accord with Edward Tufte's analysis of off-year congressional elections (which was reported in Chapter 8).[20] Tufte, it will be recalled, found that combining an index of economic well-being with presidential popularity accurately predicted the percentage of the national vote that the President's party would win. Thus it is reasonable to see off-year congressional elections as referendums on the President's performance in office.

There is additional evidence that many voters exercise rational choice. One piece of that evidence is indirect, but in the long run likely to be of great importance. The level of education in the United States has risen dramatically during the last generation. In 1948, almost half the electorate had not gone beyond grammar school. In 1972, adults who had some college education outnumbered by 5 to 3 those who had not gone beyond grammar school. Given the correlations among education, political interest, and political knowledge, we would expect that more voters are now giving thoughtful attention to politics than was the case thirty years ago, when pollsters were first putting together an accurate picture of the American voter.[21]

The data that we have from surveys do not allow a definitive test of an increase in political sophistication (and thus, we would infer, rationality). But we can note three sorts of changes in answers to the questions that the Survey Research Center asks people regarding their likes and dislikes about presidential candidates.[22] First, the number of replies referring to candidates' personal characteristics remains steady over the years. Second, the number of answers regarding candidates' party affiliation plummets. In 1952 almost half the people interviewed mentioned candidates' parties; but 1972 only one in five did so. Third, there has been a marked increase in responses referring to candidates' stands on particular issues of public policy. Before 1964 only about half the people interviewed mentioned issues; after 1964 about three out of every four respondents do so. Moreover, correlations between voting choice and each of these sorts of responses show a parallel course, steady for personal characteristics, a sharp decrease for party affiliation, and a noticeable rise for stands on issues.

Neither individually nor collectively do these data *prove* that most people vote rationally. What the data do show, however, is that *in the aggregate* American electoral behavior meets at least minimal standards of rational choice—which is not to say, we repeat, that that choice is necessarily wise.

What complicates discussion—as well as practical politics—is that a sizable minority of voters, typically the least informed, least interested, and least committed to a political party, often supply the decisive margin of victory. And, as we saw in Chapter 8, campaign managers aim much of their propaganda at such people. With the uninformed, uninterested, and uncommitted a principal target, campaign strategists understandably prefer to rely on gimmickry rather than on hard evidence and cold logic.

Summary

This chapter has described varying patterns of participation and nonparticipation in American politics and has offered a set of explanations about why some people do but most do not take anything like full advantage of available opportunities to influence politics. We also noted that the better educated and more affluent citizens were more apt to participate than other people. More specifically, this chapter described the voting behavior of various groups and concluded that, despite low levels of information and the inability of a large portion of citizens to respond in a sophisticated fashion to pollsters' questions, the bulk of American voters make electoral choices that appear to be quite rational.

Selected Bibliography

BURNHAM, WALTER DEAN, *Critical Elections and the Mainsprings of American Politics* (New York: W. W. Norton & Company, Inc., 1970). A study of American voting behavior that challenges many of the basic interpretations of the "Michigan School," exemplified by the work of Campbell, Converse, Miller, and Stokes listed below.

BURNHAM, WALTER DEAN, PHILIP E. CONVERSE, JERROLD G. RUSK, and JESSE F. MARQUETTE, "Political Change in America," *American Political Science Review*, LXVIII (1974), p. 1002. A debate among experts on electoral behavior.

CAMPBELL, ANGUS, PHILIP E. CONVERSE, WARREN E. MILLER, and DONALD E. STOKES, *The American Voter* (New York: John Wiley and Sons, Inc., 1960).

———, *Elections and the Political Order* (New York: John Wiley and Sons, Inc., 1966). Two thorough and insightful analyses of voting behavior in national elections, based on polls conducted by the University of Michigan's Survey Research Center.

FUCHS, LAWRENCE P., ed., *American Ethnic Politics* (New York: Harper & Row, 1968). A collection of essays dealing, as the title implies, with the political participation of white ethnic groups.

KEY, V. O., JR., *The Responsible Electorate: Rationality in Presidential Voting, 1936–1960* (Cambridge, Mass.: The Belknap Press of Harvard University Press, 1966). "The perverse and unorthodox argument of this little book," Key said shortly before his death, "is that voters are not fools."

LANE, ROBERT E., *Political Ideology: Why the American Common Man Believes What He Does* (New York: The Free Press, 1962). An effort to describe the sources and consequences of the ideology latent in the mind of "the urban common man," based on long and intensive interviews with fifteen lower-middle-class workers.

———, *Political Thinking and Consciousness: The Private Life of the Political Mind* (Chicago, Ill.: Markham Publishing Company, 1969). A study, based on indepth interviews with twenty-four young men, of how motivation shapes thinking about politics.

LAZARSFELD, PAUL F., BERNARD BERELSON, and HAZEL GAUDET, *The People's Choice: How the Voter Makes Up His Mind in a Presidential Campaign* (New York: Duell, Sloan and Pearce—Meredith Press, 1944). The first of the modern voting studies, interesting for its status as a piece of intellectual history.

MILBRATH, LESTER, *Political Participation* (Chicago: Rand McNally, Inc., 1965). An insightful analysis of the modes of private citizens' involvements in politics.

NIE, NORMAN H., SIDNEY VERBA, and JOHN R. PETROCIK, *The Changing American Voter* (Cambridge, Mass.: Harvard University Press, 1976). A systematic effort to review, re-analyze, and rethink available evidence about voting behavior to discern patterns of change over the years.

POMPER, GERALD, *Voters' Choice: Varieties of American Electoral Behavior* (New York: Dodd, Mead & Company, 1975). Stresses changes in the way American voters in the 1970s are behaving compared to older generations in the 1950s and 1960s.

ROGERS, LINDSAY, *The Pollsters* (New York: Alfred A. Knopf, 1949). An examination of the failure of the pollsters to predict the 1948 election that questions many of the fundamental assumptions and techniques of mass opinion surveys.

SCAMMON, RICHARD M., and BEN J. WATTENBERG, *The Real Majority* (New York: Coward-McCann, Inc., 1970). An interesting and controversial analysis of the political attitudes and voting behavior of the "middle American."

THOMPSON, DENNIS F., *The Democratic Citizen: Social Science and Democratic Theory in the Twentieth Century* (Cambridge: Cambridge University Press, 1970). An interesting effort to reconcile the empirical findings of voting studies with attempts of normative political philosophers to construct a democratic political theory.

TUFTE, EDWARD R., ed., *The Quantitative Analysis of Social Problems* (Reading, Mass.: Addison-Wesley Publishing Company, Inc., 1970). A good collection of quantitative studies, many of which deal with voting behavior.

VERBA, SIDNEY, and NORMAN H. NIE, *Participation in America: Political Democracy and Social Equality* (New York: Harper & Row, 1972). The most thorough and painstaking analysis of the varied patterns of political participation and what those patterns imply for the functioning of the political system.

Part Four

The Congress

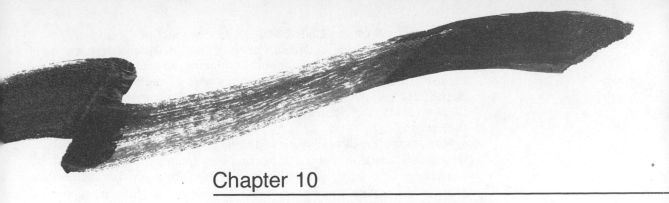

Chapter 10

Congress and Congressmen

THE CONGRESS OF the United States was a product of the golden age of legislatures. In the eighteenth century the doctrine of legislative supremacy strongly influenced political thinking. Reflecting their commitment to representative democracy, as well as the young nation's distrust of executive power, the founders created a strong national legislature to determine public policy, spend public funds, and command the executive.

Now, however, development of the modern state and its large bureaucracies, expansion of the stakes and instruments of diplomacy and warfare, and the ability of mass communications to dramatize and personalize presidents and prime ministers have all contributed to the eclipse of the legislature by the executive. Congress has not been immune to these worldwide trends. Its relative importance has inevitably declined; but unlike most other national legislatures in the contemporary world, Congress has survived the growth of executive and bureaucratic power without losing its central role in the American system.

In recent years, however, the House of Representatives and the Senate have been severely tested. Presidential warmaking has largely bypassed the legislative process. Various Presidents, particularly Richard Nixon, have asserted sweeping executive powers. In the wake of the Watergate scandals and Nixon's forced resignation, Congress sought with some success to regain its power over the purse and its checks on the executive branch. These efforts seem unlikely to restore Congress to its constitutional role as the first branch of government. But they demonstrate the underlying political strength of a national legislature unwilling to become a rubber stamp for the chief executive and his agents.

Congress' Policy-making Functions

According to the traditional theory of representative democracy, the legislature has primary responsibility to determine public policy through its power to make laws. Article I of the Constitution provides that: "All legislative power herein granted shall be vested in a Congress. . . ." Laws such as the Social Security Act, the Wages and Hours Act, the Elementary and Secondary Education Act, and various civil rights, housing, and highway statutes passed by Congress over the past half century are among the most important public policies currently being pursued in the United States.

As Chapter 1 pointed out, a statute is only one of many forms of policy statements. Policy also emerges from customs, court decisions, executive orders, and administrative rulings. Often a rule of society begins as a custom that men observe more or less voluntarily. Later this custom may find expression in judicial decisions or administrative orders. Thus, when the time arrives for the legislature to enact a statute in a particular field, a good deal of relevant policy may already exist.

Indeed, in most law-making situations the legislature does not initiate completely new policy. Instead, Congress selects from or ratifies certain rules that have already taken shape.

Nor does the process of policy formation come to an end when Congress has acted. No matter what the character of a law, refinement and extension of policy is inevitable as it is enforced. The complex problems of modern society encourage legislatures to enact laws in more and more general terms, indicating broad lines of policy and leaving details to other governmental agencies.

Constitutionally, Congress always retains power to erase or alter the actions of those agencies by passing new laws. But the national legislative process is exceedingly difficult and complex, and Congress does not legislate easily. Once a statute is passed, its moment is usually gone. Public attention is diverted elsewhere, legislative coalitions dissolve, and new ones take their place. As a result, Congress has been unable to follow up initial policy decisions with periodic revisions. Nor can individual Congressmen be familiar with the work of the hundreds of courts, regulating bodies, and administrative agencies that interpret and enforce the law.

Policy Making without Statutes

Congress is not, of course, the only initiator of governmental policy. Policies can evolve without law making, particularly in the area of foreign affairs. The Constitution gives so much power to the President in this field that he is capable of acting independently of Congress in many ways. The Monroe Doctrine is a famous example. So are the Korean and Vietnam wars, both of which began and ended without the formal involvement of Congress. Usually, the President takes influential members of Congress into his confidence in an effort to make the legislative branch a cooperative partner in his foreign policy. Occasionally, as in the case of the Gulf of Tonkin Resolution which Congress passed in 1964 during the initial stages of American involvement in the Vietnamese conflict, the President seeks direct congressional approval of actions he has already taken in the international sphere.

To be sure, Congress has an important general check on presidential policy making because it controls the purse strings. But this power is of limited usefulness in checking the executive in most important areas of foreign affairs—especially once the President commits the armed forces. As congressional behavior during the Vietnam war illustrates, few congressmen are willing to leave themselves open to the charge that they failed to support "our boys" who are risking their lives abroad. Only in 1973 after the withdrawal of American troops from Vietnam did both houses of Congress reject a presidential request for funds to pursue military operations in Southeast Asia.

The President also can make domestic policy without benefit of action by Congress. A good example is provided by the loyalty program for federal employees originally announced by President Truman in 1947 by means of an executive order. This controversial program subjected federal employees, actual and prospective, to intensive loyalty and security checks. Congress might well have made the first move by enacting a statute to provide for such a program. But it chose to permit the President, as Chief Executive, to decide how the loyalty of federal employees should be judged.

Sharing the Legislative Function

The role of Congress, then, is limited by the fact that policy making in a complex government inevitably involves more than passing laws. It is further circumscribed because Congress must share legislative functions with the President. From the Constitution the chief executive derives power to veto legislation, call Congress into special session, report to the House and Senate on the State of the Union, and "recommend to their consideration such measures as he shall judge necessary and expedient."

Only in the twentieth century, however, have Presidents regularly employed their constitutional powers so as to occupy an increasingly important role in the legislative process. Today, the President is the chief source of legislative initiative and leadership in the Congress. The executive branch drafts most of the major bills considered by Congress. Because it prepares the budget, the White House proposes national priorities and, as a consequence, sets the legislative agenda. The President and his staff also organize support for his program in Congress, using their own lobbyists and those of various departments and agencies. In addition, the President has means to reward and punish congressmen through federal programs that could distribute benefits in every congressional constituency. Because of his instant access to television and the press, the President can influence public opinion far more effectively than any congressional leader can, particularly on matters involving foreign policy or affecting national security.

Despite constant grumbling, frequent frustration, and an occasional revolt, Congress by and large accepts the President's legislative initiative, although not necessarily his specific policies. Given the size and complexity of its legislative task, Congress has no alternative. Congressional leaders rarely have the power to establish priorities or a legislative agenda. The President fills this gap with his legislative program and the leadership he provides for its enactment. In the process,

Congress gains . . . a prestigeful "laundry-list," a starting order-of-priority to guide the work of each committee in both houses in every session. Since it comes from downtown [the White House], committee and house leaders—and all members—can respond to or react against it at their option. But coming from downtown it does for them what they, in their disunity, cannot do for themselves: it gives them an agenda to get on with, or depart from.[1]

Congress usually "gets on" with a fair amount of the President's program, but never with all of it. Congress inevitably views the President's program from a perspective different from that of the White House. No congressman shares the President's national constituency. Few congressmen, including party stalwarts, see their political careers as closely tied to the fate of the President's program. Moreover, influential members of Congress enjoy far longer tenure than the President. As President Kennedy pointed out in speaking of a powerful committee chairman: "Wilbur Mills knows that he was chairman of Ways and Means before I got here and that he'll still be chairman after I've gone—and he knows I know it. I don't have any hold on him."[2] Indeed, Mills lasted as chairman until 1975, a dozen years after Kennedy's death.

Between 1964 and 1966, Lyndon Johnson dominated Congress as no President has since the early years of the New Deal. Yet the Eighty-ninth Congress rejected Johnson's proposal for home rule for the District of Columbia, blocked the administration's plan for merging the National Guard and the Reserves, refused to appropriate funds for the newly enacted rent-supplement program, forced the White House to accept limitations on the Secretary of Defense's power to close military bases, and killed the attempt of the President and organized labor to repeal the provision of the Taft-Hartley Act that permits states to enact "right to work" laws.

In recent years, most tax legislation has been written by the House Ways and Means Committee rather than the White House or the Treasury Department. This committee's leadership also played a central role in determining the fate of revenue-sharing and welfare reform during the early 1970s, helping to enact the first and to kill the second. Congressional influence has been substantial in legislation affecting agriculture, atomic energy, education, housing, labor-management relations, and social security.[3] In addition, much of the legislative initiative in air and water pollution, mass transportation, consumer protection, reform of the Electoral College, and women's rights has come from congressmen. Often, the congressman responsible for legislative innovation is chairman of a key committee or subcommittee, as in the case of Representative John Blatnik of Minnesota, who became Washington's prime mover on water-pollution control after assuming the chairmanship of the Subcommittee on Rivers and Harbors of the House Committee on Public Works. In other instances, local concerns produce congressional innovation. The problems of rail commuters in the New York and Philadelphia metropolitan areas led Senator Harrison Williams of New Jersey to develop legislation to provide federal aid for mass transportation. Foresight in selecting an issue can catapult an obscure congressman into the national limelight, as occurred with Senator Edmund Muskie of Maine, the prime architect of the Clean Air Act of 1963.

Other Functions of Congress

Lawmaking usually is considered to be the paramount function of the legislature. But the work of Congress is not limited to enacting statutes. Congress also controls—formally, if not always actually—the budget, supervises administrative agencies, represents interests of constituents, and influences public opinion. In performing these functions, Congress often has more influence on policy making than it does through its power to legislate.

The Power of the Purse

Controlling the purse strings is one of the oldest and most important functions of any legislative body; for example, it had much to do with the emergence of Parliament as an important part of the British government by the eighteenth century. The rallying cry of the American revolution was "no taxation without representation," indicating how the idea of legislative control of tax policy had grown. The related notion that funds could be appropriated from the public treasury only by legislative action was a firmly established concept of Anglo-American political practice by 1787. Without hesitation the framers of the Constitution prescribed that "no money shall be drawn from the treasury, but in consequence of appropriations made by law." Writing in the *Federalist Papers,* James Madison argued that congressional control of the purse strings was the chief safeguard against abuse of executive power:

This power over the purse may, in fact, be regarded as the most complete and effectual weapon with which any constitution can arm the immediate representatives of the people obtaining a redress of every grievance and for carrying into effect every just and salutary measure.[4]

Over the years, Congress has delegated much of its power over the purse to appropriations committees, the House committee being more important than that of the Senate. Acting through subcommittees, the House Appropriations Committee each year reviews the President's budgetary requests. Hearings are held to permit agency officials to explain and justify proposed expenditures; there, legislators' questioning of administrators may be penetrating and even hostile. After holding hearings, the subcommittees make their recommendations to the full committee for action, which then submits its proposed appropriations bills to the House. The House measure is then transmitted to the Senate, which follows a similar procedure. When congressional action is completed, an appropriations bill goes to the President, who can veto it as a whole, but not specific items in it.

The President, however, can impound (that is, refuse to spend) the funds appropriated by Congress. Before 1972, the White House tended to impound funds on a highly selective and usually temporary basis. After his landslide re-election in 1972, President Nixon claimed con-

Figure 10.1
The Congressional Budgetary Process

Stage 1.
Nov. 10 –
Apr. 15

Information gathering, analysis, preparation and submission of congressional budget by congressional budget office and budget committees.

Stage 2.
Apr. 15 –
May 15

Debate and adoption of congressional budget by both houses; establishment of national spending priorities.

Stage 3.
May 15 –
Early Sep.

Enactment of spending bills.

Stage 4.
Sep. 15 –
Sep. 25

Reassessment of spending, revenue, and debt requirements in second budget resolution; enactment of reconciliation bill.

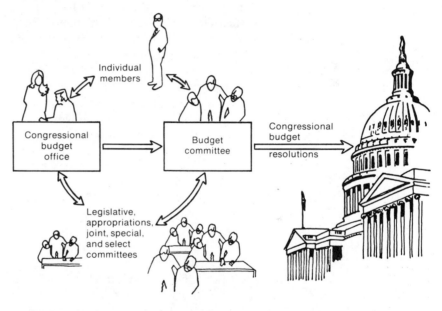

Source: U.S. Congress, Senate, Committee on Government Operations, *Congressional Budget Reform* (Washington: U.S. Government Printing Office, 1974), pp. 15-16.

stitutional authority to refuse to spend $12 billion, asserting that as President, he was the sole representative of the national interest.

Part of Congress' problem in controlling the purse arises from the fact that its powers are exercised "pluralistically, parochially, and episodically."[5] In 1971, for example, authority over appropriations was splintered among thirteen subcommittees in each house. These subcommittees were subject to only general oversight by the full appropriations committee and to even less control by the entire House or Senate. Many subcommittees were dominated by powerful chairmen with great personal influence over broad areas of federal activity. As a result, Congress gave piecemeal rather than comprehensive consideration to the budget as a whole. Until recently, the many segments of the appropriations process pursued their particular tasks in splendid isolation from each other. Moreover, the House and the Senate consider each appropriations bill separately, with no formal reference to its impact on the budget as a whole.

Growing concern over the weaknesses of the decentralized appropriations process led Congress to enact sweeping reforms of its budgetary procedures in 1974. Under the new arrangements, Congress annually adopts an over-all spending ceiling that must be honored in the appropriations process. If appropriations exceed the ceiling, both houses are obligated to impose new taxes or a higher national debt limit. To perform these functions, budget committees were created in the House and Senate. Staff assistance to the new committees is provided by the Congressional Budget Office, the legislative counterpart to the President's Office of Management and Budget.

The budgetary reforms of 1974 gave more cohesion to Congress' efforts to control the purse. They also restricted the President's ability to impound funds appropriated by Congress. The reforms, however, did not alter significantly the power of appropriations committees and subcommittees, or of the influential congressmen who control these committees. Nor did the new budgetary procedures have much impact on the pre-eminent role of the President in establishing the basic outlines of federal spending policy.

Administrative Oversight

Supervising administrative agencies is another major function of legislatures. The American Constitution does not spell out this legislative function in so many words. But, the framers made congressional oversight inevitable when they assigned Congress control over appropriations, provided for senatorial confirmation of appointed executive officials, and permitted Congress to create and reorganize the administrative machinery of the national government. With the tremendous growth in the activities and personnel of the federal government in the twentieth century, administrative oversight has become an increasingly important congressional task, even overshadowing law making.

The Legislative Reorganization Act of 1946 charged congressional committees with maintaining "continuous watchfulness" over administration of the laws, a function most committees were already performing and since have continued with considerable zeal. The appropriations committees and their subcommittees monitor programs and personnel through their control of the annual appropriations process. Other committees exercise influence because of requirements for annual review of such programs as foreign aid and space exploration by Congress. A number of committees and subcommittees also have involved themselves directly in the administrative process. Appropriations subcommittees use detailed provisions in the appropriations statutes, subcommittee reports, and communications to executive agencies to instruct administrators on how to spend funds in order to avoid punitive action in the next round of the appropriations process. Some committees insist on a veto over such executive actions as closing military bases or require agencies to submit administrative determinations for committee clearance. More generally, committees use hearings and investigations to expose mismanagement and corruption, to advocate projects and priorities they favor, and to compel policy changes in the administration of federal programs.

Congress also influences the operations of the federal executive through the power of the Senate to confirm or reject the President's nominations. For example, senatorial criticism of the conservation and natural-resources policies of Governor Walter J. Hickel of Alaska, President Nixon's nominee as Secretary of the Interior, stimulated a great deal of concern on the part of Hickel with ecological issues after his confirmation.

Another major source of congressional involvement in administrative matters results from Congress' responsibilities for structuring and staffing the executive branch. Acts of Congress are necessary to create departments or agencies. Congress also can reject administrative reorganizations proposed by the White House. It has vetoed one third of the reorganization plans submitted by Presidents over the past quarter of a century. In 1971, it rejected President Nixon's proposal to consolidate the Departments of Agriculture, Commerce, Health Education and Welfare, Housing and Urban Development, Interior, Labor, and Transportation—with their hundreds of programs and thousands of special relationships with committees, subcommittees, and individual congressmen—into four new departments responsible for community development, human resources, economic development, and natural resources.

Congress also provides the legislation that establishes, regulates, and nourishes the Civil Service and the armed forces, as well as such special groups of personnel as the Foreign Service, the Secret Service, and the Federal Bureau of Investigation. In the process, Congress influences the managerial practices of federal executives and the pay, working conditions, and morale of millions of federal workers. Through committees such as Armed Services, congressmen become intimately involved with personnel issues and enormously influential with administrative officials and groups which promote the interests of federal employees.

A final, if rarely used, source of congressional control over the executive branch is the removal power. Responsibility for impeaching, or indicting, the President, Vice President, and other civil officers for "treason, bribery, or other high crimes and misdemeanors" rests with the House of Representatives. The Senate is responsible for trying those impeached by the House, and conviction by the Senate results in removal from office. (We discuss the process in Chapter 12.)

CONGRESSIONAL OVERSIGHT

©1976 HERBLOCK

Copyright 1976 by Herblock in The Washington Post.

Despite the scope of these various powers, congressional oversight resembles Congress' attempts to control the nation's purse strings. Oversight rarely is systematic or comprehensive. Instead, various committees and subcommittees "look at programs . . . in a hop, skip and jump fashion."[6] Many programs and agencies have been largely immune from congressional oversight because of their political popularity, the influence of their administrators, the sensitivity of their tasks, or the sheer size and complexity of the federal establishment. For more than a quarter century, no arm of Congress scrutinized closely the Social Security program, which distributed $58 billion in benefits to 31 million retired and disabled Americans in 1974. Before 1975, the Federal Bureau of Investigation and the Central Intelligence Agency were free from any effective congressional oversight, despite growing evidence of policies of questionable legality, constitutionality, and morality.

Representing Constituents

Representation of the people is supposedly the principal reason for Congress' existence. More than any other political institution in Washington, it reflects the diversity of the American people and their interests. In practice, representing the people of a particular district or state usually means advancing and defending local interests in the nation's capital.

Most congressmen spend a good deal of their own time—and most of their staffs'—servicing needs of constituents who want help on everything from information about voting to intercession in a federal criminal case. During a typical day, a congressman or staff member may check with the Department of Agriculture on availability of agricultural agents to help suburban homeowners fight crabgrass, call the Defense Department to arrange an interview for a local businessman seeking a federal contract, and contact the Civil Service Commission to inquire about how a constituent performed on a recent examination.

Representation of constituency interests also involves congressmen in a wide range of federal programs (as Chapter 5 pointed out). The growing impact of federal spending on state and local economies has made congressmen increasingly active in the promotion of their localities as sites for federal facilities and in seeking federal contracts for industries within their district. Of particular importance are federal outlays for defense, aerospace, and science, which can make the difference between prosperity and depression in a congressional district. Most congressmen understand that federal expenditures for research and development "have an extraordinarily powerful impact on the educational, industrial, and employment sectors of every region's vitality."[7]

The larger the prize, the greater the legislative involvement, as indicated by the major roles of congressmen from Texas and Washington in the celebrated battle between General Dynamics (Fort Worth) and Boeing Aircraft (Seattle) for the $6.5 billion TFX fighter plane contract in the 1960s. Prospects of congressmen delivering on such campaign promises as Senator Edward M. Kennedy's 1962 pledge to "do more for Massachusetts" depend largely on increasing their constituency's share of defense and space contracts. Several state delegations in Congress have organized committees to work closely with state and local officials and lobbyists of local industry in the quest for contracts and installations. One of the most active congressional delegations in this respect is California's, whose goal is to maintain and expand the state's dominant role in military and space spending. Midwestern congressmen, on the other hand, have sought to increase that region's small share of federal military and science dollars.

Shaping Opinion

A democratic government has a particular obligation to acquaint the people with the nature of social problems and with possible courses of action. Moreover, it is to the legislature — the chief agency representing the people and their interests — that a considerable part of this educational responsibility falls.

A speech on the floor of the House or the Senate by a well-known member of Congress may influence both public opinion and administrative action. In January 1945, Senator Arthur Vandenberg of Michigan publicly repudiated his earlier isolationist leanings and announced that he would henceforth support an American foreign policy looking toward closer international cooperation. That address influenced many Americans who had previously hoped that their country might "go it alone" but who trusted Senator Vandenberg's integrity and judgment. It also encouraged the Roosevelt administration to adopt a bolder course of action. Similarly, Senator William Fulbright's attacks on President Johnson's policies in Vietnam established an important rallying point for all groups who had doubts about the wisdom of American military participation in the Vietnamese war.

Such influential speeches are not made in Congress every day or even in every session. But from time to time the stage is set for an address that will profoundly affect the thinking of important segments of the American public. Such remarks need not even be spoken on the floors of Congress. So great is the attention paid by the press, radio, and television to certain congressmen that a few words uttered at a press conference or over the air may drastically alter the course of public thinking or administrative policy. For instance, Senator Joseph McCarthy's speech in 1950 in which he announced that he held in his hands the names of 205 persons "that were made known to the Secretary of State as being members of the Communist party and who nonetheless are still working and shaping policy in the State Department" marked the beginning of McCarthy's strong influence on American public opinion. That he never succeeded in documenting his charge — and kept changing the number of alleged communists in the State Department — did not alter the effect of his speech. When a United States senator makes sensational charges, many people listen and are impressed.

In performing its many functions, Congress often employs investigating committees. A congressional investigation differs from routine consideration of bills by standing committees. An investigation involves an inquiry into a subject or a problem—like domestic spying by the CIA and the FBI, cost overruns in the Department of Defense, windfall profits for grain exporters, or the safety of food additives—rather than scrutiny of a particular legislative proposal. The most formal investigation occurs when Congress specifically authorizes an inquiry into a particular subject, designates a committee to make this study, votes an appropriation to cover costs of the inquiry, and grants the committee power to subpoena witnesses.

The motives that lead congressmen to authorize an investigation are varied. First is the obvious need to obtain detailed and accurate information if Congress is to take intelligent action. A second purpose is to supervise or check administrative agencies. Each house has a committee on government operations, which frequently conducts such inquiries. A third purpose of investigations is to influence public opinion by giving wide circulation to certain facts or ideas, as Senator William Fulbright tried to do in his committee's 1966 hearings on the Vietnamese war.

These three purposes are often supplemented by others of a more personal and partisan character. More than one member of Congress has advanced his career because of a reputation as a hard-headed investigator. Accordingly, it is not surprising that hope of political profit should strongly motivate congressmen to new investigations. Similarly, a political party often undertakes investigations to further its own interests or to embarrass its adversary. When the Republicans won control of Congress in 1946, they facetiously announced that each day's session of the Eightieth Congress would "open with a prayer and close with a probe" of the Truman administration.

Congressional investigating committees sometimes encounter witnesses who refuse to appear before a committee or to answer its questions. Out of such episodes have come congressional statutes and Supreme Court decisions concerning the relative status and rights of investigating committees and witnesses. The Supreme Court has held:

It is unquestionably the duty of all citizens to cooperate with the Congress in its efforts to obtain the facts needed for intelligent legislative action. It is their unremitting obligation to respond to subpoenas, to respect the dignity of the Congress and its committees and to testify fully with respect to matters within the province of proper investigation.[8]

As early as 1857, Congress enacted a statute directing private persons to appear before investigating committees when subpoenaed and answer pertinent questions or to risk a criminal prosecution in the

An official of the Committee for Re-election of the President explains the organization of President Nixon's re-election organization to the Senate committee that initially investigated the Watergate scandals in 1973.

courts and imprisonment up to one year for failure to do so. The constitutionality of this statute has repeatedly been upheld by the Supreme Court. But the Court has also ruled that a witness may properly refuse to cooperate with an investigating committee of Congress if the subject under examination lies outside the authority of the investigating committee, if a committee asks a witness questions that are not pertinent to the subject under investigation, or if a witness's answers would provide evidence that might be used against him or her in a criminal proceeding.[9]

The Members of Congress

Whatever else it is, Congress is not an accurate cross section of the American people. In 1977, the "average" member of Congress was a forty-nine-year-old white male. Only seventeen women and sixteen blacks (including three women) were serving in Congress that year, and all the women and blacks, except for Senator Edward W. Brooke of Massachusetts, were in the House. While younger Americans, women, and blacks continue to be significantly underrepresented in Congress, their ranks have been increasing steadily in recent years. Only ten women were elected to the House of Representatives in 1964, compared with seventeen in 1976. During the same period, black representation in Congress increased from six to sixteen. Between the Ninety-third and Ninety-fourth Congresses alone, the number of representatives under forty rose more than 50 percent, to a total of eighty-seven.

Most members of Congress are professionals or businessmen with college educations who have been active in politics before coming to

**Figure 10.2
Use of Free Mailing Privileges
by House Members, 1971–1974.**

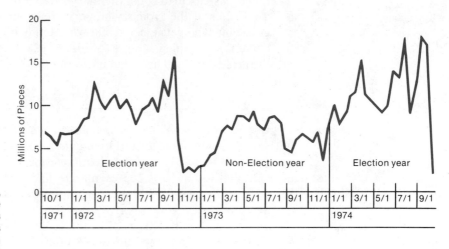

"As the figure indicates, House members increase their free mailings dramatically in the months immediately preceding an election."

Washington. In 1976, 54 percent were lawyers, and 30 percent had been (or still were) active in business or banking. In addition, seventy-one members of the Ninety-fourth Congress were teachers, forty-one farmers, twenty-nine journalists, six doctors, and four clergymen. Over 80 percent of the membership of the two houses had previously been elected to public office or had otherwise been involved in governmental service before their arrival in Congress. Members of Congress are much wealthier than most Americans. In 1976, a majority of the hundred Senators admitted to assets of $250,000 or more, and twenty-two were millionaires.

Election to Congress provided a job in 1976 that paid $44,600 a year and provided, in addition, $227,000 a year for representatives and between $413,000 and $818,000 for senators to employ an office staff (the exact amount of senator's allowance depending on the population of his state). A member also receives a travel allowance for twenty-six trips a year between Washington and home, free office space in Washington and in his state, generous postal allowances, access to television and radio studios in the Capitol, and substantial allowances for stationery, long-distance calls and telegraph messages, newsletters, and such special office equipment as automatic typewriters and signature machines.

Staff assistance, mailing and telecommunications privileges, radio and television studios, and travel allowances offer substantial political advantages to the congressman seeking re-election. At government expense, the incumbent can stay in constant touch with residents of his district, as well as travel home for campaigning. He also benefits from his status as senator or representative, from the news his congressional seat allows him to generate, and from the favors incumbency permits him to distribute to constituents. The advantages are so great, contends a member of the House who served seventeen terms, that "no Congressman who gets elected and who minds his business should ever be beaten. Everything is there for him to use if he'll only keep his nose to the grindstone and use what is offered."[10]

Increasing Tenure and Professionalization

In part because of the advantages provided by incumbency, congressional careers have tended to lengthen. During the nineteenth century, turnover in the House after elections ranged from 30 percent to 60 percent and the average representative had less than two terms of prior service. Not until 1900 was a Congress elected in which less than 30 percent of House members were newcomers and the average prior service more than two terms.[11] In the Ninety-fourth Congress, which experienced the largest turnover in a quarter of a century, only 21 percent of the representatives were first termers, 48 percent had won five terms or more, and the average member had served almost nine years. Lengthening tenure reflects proliferation of safe seats throughout the nation. During the past fifteen years, approximately three fourths of the seats in the House have been safe. With the exception of the presidential landslide of 1964 and the post-Watergate election of 1974, very few incumbents have been defeated in any recent election.

With increased tenure have come profound changes in the nature of congressional service. Lengthening service has shifted "the balance in the careers and life styles of legislators from amateur to professional, from the status of temporary ambassador from home to that of member of the legislative group."[12] It also has bolstered the importance of seniority and made very long tenure a requirement for leadership, especially in the House of Representatives. These developments, in turn, have increased the power of committees and subcommittees, encouraged specialization, and contributed to the general dispersion of power in Congress, all of which are discussed in Chapter 11.

Rewards and Frustrations

The fact that most congressmen seek re-election suggests a relatively high level of satisfaction with their jobs or at least a preference for staying in Congress rather than practicing law in Pocatello, Pascagoula, or Portland. Almost all congressmen enjoy the prestige conferred by their office and derive satisfaction from being in Washington at the center of national affairs. All acquire some influence, and a few are rewarded for their service and skill with great power. For most, being in Congress is itself a reward, either as the culmination of a political career begun in

Figure 10.3
**Seniority and turnover
in the House of Representatives**

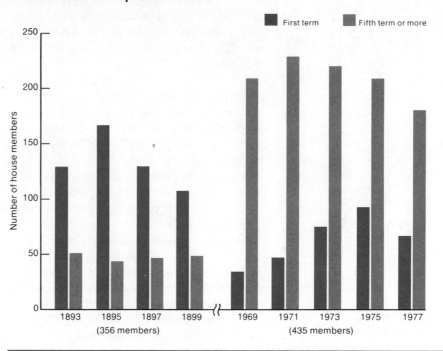

Source: Adopted from H. Douglas Price, "The Congressional Career Then and Now," in Nelson W. Polsby, ed., *Congressional Behavior* (New York: Random House, 1971), p. 17. Data from various sources.

local government or as a way station on the road to higher office. For some, election to Congress is an opportunity for public service, a once-in-a-lifetime chance to advance a cause or change the nation's course. For others, a seat in the House or Senate becomes an easy job with a good salary, influential colleagues, and plentiful opportunities for personal gain and travel to the far corners of the earth at taxpayers' expense.

The average congressman works hard, spreading himself too thin across the many tasks that compete for his time and attention. For a member of the House, a typical day might begin with breakfast with a lobbyist, followed by two hours at his desk sampling the mail, consulting with staff on his weekly newsletter, meeting visitors, editing a speech to be given to a veterans' group, and helping constituents by making telephone calls to various administrative agencies. Next comes an hour at the executive session of a subcommittee, lunch with a group of colleagues to discuss tactics on a forthcoming bill, and an afternoon divided among the House floor, where amendments to a water-pollution control measure are being considered, the corridors, where he talks briefly with colleagues and lobbyists, and a meeting with Labor

Department officials to discuss a manpower-training grant to the largest city in his district. Before leaving for home the congressman may spend another hour dictating and signing letters. After dinner, he works his way through a bulky briefcase containing the *Congressional Record* for the previous day's session, the morning newspapers, the rough draft of a committee report, and a thick file of housing data on his district supplied by the Department of Housing and Urban Development.

As Congress spends more and more of the year in session, such schedules become increasingly common. Because longer sessions shorten the time available to renew constituency ties and to campaign, weekends and recesses must be spent in the district. The pressures are particularly severe for House members, who must run for re-election every two years.

The growing volume of legislation, the mushrooming of federal programs and spending, and the steady rise in communications from constituents also increase demands on congressmen. Because of these pressures, most have less time to master any subject. Even the more conscientious members find it necessary to vote on numerous issues that they only vaguely understand and on a vast amount of legislation that they have not read. The sheer volume of business increases reliance on their staffs, party leaders, committee associates, other congressmen, and lobbyists.

The hectic pace of life in Congress also strains family life and the personal resources of many members. Increasing the sense of frustration for many, particularly among the more junior and activist members, is the slow pace of Congress, the long apprenticeship required by the seniority system, the concentration of power in the hands of committee and subcommittee chairmen, and the fact that "it takes so long to get anything done here."[13] For a growing number of congressmen in recent years, these frustrations lead to early retirement. Representative William L. Hungate, a fifty-two-year-old five-term Democrat from Missouri, retired in 1976, explaining:

My enthusiasm for public service has been waning under the weight of my frustrated hopes, others' unreasonable pressures and the job's persistent demands. Since I entered office, the duties have increased dramatically, exceeded only by public dissatisfaction with the Congress.[14]

Congressional Ethics

Public attention tends to focus on congressional ethics only when attracted by spectacular scandals involving personal appropriation of campaign money, diversions of public funds for private pleasures, or use of a congressman's name, office, and influence to further personal financial interests. More serious than an occasional scandal, however, is the widespread practice of senators and representatives engaging in

Copyright 1976 by Herblock in The Washington Post.

private business while in public office. Congressmen frequently sit on committees considering new laws and overseeing administration of existing statutes that regulate the very businesses in which themselves are involved. A member of the House Banking or Senate Finance Committee who maintains his position as a bank executive, a member of the Commerce Committee who owns an interest in a radio or television station, or the owner of a large farm who sits on the Agriculture Committee, each has an impossible job of serving the twin masters of the public good and personal financial interest. Even if he miraculously succeeds, it is not likely that he can appear to succeed. At the very least, he leaves not only himself but Congress open to a charge of corruption.

Despite the serious implications of widespread mixing of public and private responsibilities, Congress has been remarkably insensitive to conflicts of interest involving its own members. On the other hand, congressmen have been quick to attack administrators and judges for possible violation of ethical standards. Except in the most flagrant cases, Congress has been unwilling to take action to clarify the ethical standards expected of senators and representatives. In 1962, Congress passed a far-reaching conflict-of-interest statute governing the behavior of almost all employees of the federal government. Neither in 1962 nor in the intervening years, however, have congressmen seen fit to include themselves under the terms of such laws. Resolutions passed in the House and Senate in 1968 provided for a code of conduct for members and staff, as well as requiring congressmen to file financial statements with committees on standards and conduct in both houses. But disclosure rules are riddled with loopholes and the detailed financial statements are not available to the public.

Staffing Congress

Over the years, the rising volume of government business has led Congress to build up a bureaucracy that employs more personnel than many federal agencies. These professional staff members, who often have more technical experience and greater expertise than the representatives and senators for whom they work, have come to play an increasingly important part in the legislative process.

Each member of Congress is given an allowance for the maintenance of a personal office staff. In the case of representatives, these funds provide for eighteen people, including an administrative assistant, a legislative assistant, a professional secretary, two or three other aides, and several clerk-stenographers. A senator's allowance is more generous, and a senator from a populous state may have fifty or more persons working in his office. Administrative assistants and other aides answer a congressman's mail, deal with visitors, keep in touch with the executive agencies of the government, run errands to these agencies for constituents, and offer the congressman advice and assistance in studying bills, researching, writing speeches, and running for re-election.

Each of the standing committees also employs a sizable corps of professional and secretarial staff members, although compared with the executive departments, congressional committees employ few economists, statisticians, demographers, operation analysts, and other specialists. Committee chiefs of staff are frequently extremely knowledge-

An aide to a House member assists a constituent with an immigration problem at the Congressman's district office in New York City.

able and influential and often have years of experience. They organize committee hearings and investigations, draft legislation, and direct as many as seventy-five assistants. While many appointments to committee staffs are made on the basis of merit, party affiliation remains an important factor in filling these positions.

General staff services also are available to Congress. Chief among these are the Congressional Research Service, the Office of Legislative Counsel, the Congressional Budget Office, and the Office of Technology Assessment. The Congressional Research Service is a general research agency in the Library of Congress. It supplies various services and materials—pamphlets, digests of bills, data for use in speeches, abstracts of current literature, and studies of special legislative problems—requested by individual congressmen or by committees. The Office of Legislative Counsel's chief function is to draft bills at the request of congressmen or committees, making certain that their legal language accomplishes the purposes that their sponsors have in mind.

Less closely tied to Congress is the General Accounting Office, the independent auditors of the federal government for Congress. GAO, with a budget of $140 million and 3600 employees in 1977, investigates all sorts of governmental activities to insure that congressional appropriations are spent in the manner intended by law. Over the years, GAO's function has broadened to include a consideration of "whether the programs are really accomplishing their objectives or not."[15] As a result, GAO's investigators increasingly include engineers, statisticians, and medical experts as well as accountants.

Despite a budget that exceeded $950 million in 1977, Congress has made relatively little use of modern methods available to assist organizations in coping with the vast flow of information characteristic of complex societies. A growing chorus of reformers, both inside and outside Congress, argue that the House and Senate with their nineteenth-century procedures and techniques cannot deal effectively with the executive branch and its banks of computers, program budget specialists, and the like. Reformers advocate widespread congressional use of computers and other electronic information storage and retrieval devices, as well as the employment by Congress of technicians trained in systems analysis, operations research, and related skills.

Summary

Congress is the most representative of our national political institutions. Its 535 members reflect the diverse interests of a complex society. Congressmen, however, are less diverse than the people they represent. Most are middle-aged college-educated white males with professional or business backgrounds. Congressmen and their growing staffs perform many functions: they make laws, control the purse, oversee the federal executive, and inform the public. Over the nation's history, Congress' *relative* influence in the American system of government has declined, largely as a result of the enormous increase in the power of the presidency. Among legislative bodies, however, Congress is perhaps the most influential representative assembly in the world. It initiates a good deal of important legislation, modifies much of what the executive branch proposes, and influences a wide range of other governmental activities.

Selected Bibliography

BOLLING, RICHARD W., *House Out of Order* (New York: Dutton, 1965). A critical analysis of the House of Representatives by an experienced congressman who favors far-reaching reforms.

CARR, ROBERT K., *The House Un-American Activities Committee* (Ithaca, N.Y.: Cornell University Press, 1952). A thorough account of the role and activities of one of the most publicized congressional committees in decades.

CLAPP, CHARLES L., *The Congressman: His Work As He Sees It* (Washington, D.C.: The Brookings Institution, 1963). The House of Representatives from the perspective of the individual congressman.

Congress and the Public Trust (New York: Atheneum, 1970). Report on the Association of the Bar of the City of New York Special Committee on Congressional Ethics, James C. Kirby, Executive Director. A study of conflicting interests and ethical standards in Congress with recommendations designed to increase public confidence in the legislative process.

DeGrazia, Alfred, ed., *Congress, The First Branch of Government* (Garden City, N.Y.: Anchor Books, 1967). Twelve studies of congressional organization based on the premise that Congress itself must be strengthened, not made more dependent on party or the presidency.

Kofmehl, Kenneth, *Professional Staffs of Congress* (West Lafayette, Ind.: Purdue University Studies, 1962). A useful analysis of the development since 1946 of professional staffs for congressional committees.

Miller, Clem, *Member of the House* (New York: Charles Scribner's Sons, 1962), ed. by John Baker. A view of life in the House of Representatives as seen by a brilliant young congressman.

Tacheron, Donald G., and Morris K. Udall, *The Job of the Congressman* (Indianapolis and New York: The Bobbs-Merrill Company, 1966). A handbook for members of the House, full of useful insights into the congressional setting.

Taylor, Telford, *Grand Inquest* (New York: Simon and Schuster, Inc., 1955). Probably the best general account of congressional investigating committees, treated historically and critically.

Wilson, Woodrow, *Congressional Government: A Study in American Politics* (Boston: Houghton Mifflin Company, 1885). A classic study analyzing the way in which nineteenth-century Congresses predominated over the presidency.

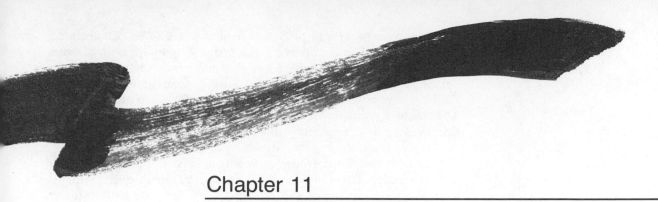

Chapter 11

The Legislative System and Lawmaking

The Congressional Setting

The Role of Political Parties in Congress
The Party and Congressional Voting Behavior
Role of the Party Caucus

Congressmen and Their Constituencies
Constituency Interests and Voring in Congress
The Shifting Constituency Base

The Structure of Congress
Two Houses
A New Congress Every Two Years

The Leadership
Presiding Officers
Floor Leaders and Whips

The Committee System
Committees and Subcommittees
Membership on Committees
Role of Committee Chairmen

Lobbying
Techniques of Lobbying
Interdependence of Legislator and Lobbyist
Federal Regulation of Lobbying

The Making of a Federal Statute
Drafting and Introduction of Bills
Committee Action on Bills
Floor Action on Bills
Limitation of Congressional Debate
Methods of Voting
Conference Committee Action on Bills
Final Hurdles

Summary

Selected Bibliography

VISITORS TO THE House or Senate galleries are often disillusioned. Having imagined an impressive parliamentary panorama with ceremonial pageantry, dignified debate, and dramatic clashes between famous personalities, they find instead that the usual scene is dull and inactive. Of the 435 representatives, perhaps thirty or forty are present, of the 100 senators, perhaps a dozen. A lone figure has the floor, and while he drones along in an unexciting monologue a few inattentive colleagues read newspapers, work at their desks, or sit talking in back rows.

Such a glimpse of the House or Senate in session is hardly a reliable guide to the legislative process. "Like a vast picture thronged with figures of equal prominence and crowded with elaborate and obtrusive details," Woodrow Wilson once wrote, "Congress is hard to see satisfactorily and appreciatively at a single view and from a single standpoint."[1] Congress goes about its work by means of a complex institutional system that has evolved slowly over the years, only a small part of which can be understood by observing the House and Senate in formal session.

The Congressional Setting

Congressional behavior is influenced by many factors, not the least of which is the fact that no two of the 100 senators and 435 representatives have identical personal philosophies, perceptions of their roles, or habits of work. Some are conservatives, other liberals. Most, but not all, work hard, seek the respect of their colleagues, and conform to the customs of the House or Senate. Concerns about their constituencies preoccupy numerous congressmen. But many of the more senior and influential representatives and senators have relatively safe seats and are less restricted by the periodic necessity of facing the voters. A majority are ready to follow the party line—if there is one—when they or their constituents have little concern with a measure. On the other hand, a sufficient minority are mavericks who pursue an independent course much of the time.

Despite these individual differences, every congressman is influenced by certain common factors. Almost all are Democrats or Republicans and have certain obligations to party. But, as Chapter 7 showed, national party organizations are typically weak. Also important in terms of pressure are each member's constituents, state or district. Because at the next election these people can end or continue a legislator's career, their wants—or the legislator's perception of their wants—typically form the single most powerful influence on his behavior. Complicating matters, all states and a large number of districts contain a wide variety of economic, social, ethnic, and other groups whose interests compete if not conflict. Moreover, all congressmen work in an institutional arena with specific structural characteristics such as two houses and a committee system, formal rules and procedures such as

A typical scene on the floor of the House of Representatives as the Seventy-ninth Congress reconvened after a three-week recess.

those that govern the role of presiding officers and consideration of legislation, and informal practices such as seniority and specialization.

The dominant characteristic of Congress in the twentieth century has been an increasing dispersion of power. More safe seats have lengthened tenure, increased the importance of seniority, lessened party leaders' influence, and bolstered the independence of individual members. In the House, party leadership is much weaker than it was during the half century following the Civil War. And in neither house do leaders have many resources to reward the faithful or punish the wayward.

Committees and especially subcommittees have steadily increased their power, contributing further to decentralization. More recently, reforms that reduced the importance of seniority in selections of committee chairmen dispersed power more widely in both houses. So did changes that permitted new members to secure seats on major committees. Other reforms have improved access of the press, lobbyists, and the public to formerly closed committee sessions and party caucuses, thus increasing the number of knowledgeable participants and further reducing the influence of committee and party leaders. Underlying these changes was the arrival in Congress during the 1970s of large numbers of aggressive younger members who insisted that authority be broadly distributed rather than concentrated.

As a result of these decentralizing forces, coalitions must be constructed on each major legislative issue; "inevitably the politics of

Chapter 11
The Legislative System
and Law Making

279

such an institution is compounded of persuasion, bargaining and log-rolling."[2]

The Role of Political Parties in Congress

Behavior in every legislative assembly is conditioned in part by the way its members are nominated and elected to office. In the case of Congress, these procedures are highly decentralized, reflecting the geographic fragmentation of influence in the American party system. For nomination, campaign assistance, and re-election, congressmen rely on party leaders and supporters within their constituency rather than on national parties. The two parties' weak national organizations cannot even control the use of their party's label: whoever wins the primary in a particular state or district can claim the tag. Except in rare landslides like those in 1936 and 1964, holding a safe seat insulates most congressmen from the ebb and flow of national party fortunes. And party mavericks are protected from purges by either the President or the party's leadership in Congress by the decentralized base of constituency support.

Despite these weaknesses, the two political parties are the most comprehensive groupings in Congress. All but one member of the Ninety-fifth Congress elected in 1976 was a Democrat or a Republican.* A congressman's party is his primary identification both in Congress and on the ballot. Party affiliation determines which legislative leaders he will consult and follow. And on election day his party's label will provide him with a large share of the support he receives, because "the candidate's party is the one piece of information every voter is guaranteed. For many, it is the only information they ever get."[3]

Party also symbolizes the traditions and convictions a congressman shares with most of his fellow party members in Congress. Shared identities, hazards, and rewards provided by party shape the general orientation of most senators and representatives toward policy and also provide the basis for most associations with congressional colleagues. Party also offers a source of support for efforts to enact a bill, investigate the bureaucracy, or secure a prize for a constituent. For the typical congressman,

The life of an habitual maverick would be intolerable. Acting against the party involves a substantial amount of personal discomfort, which can even be expressed physically. The only Republican to vote against his party's recommital motion on a major administration bill in 1963 answered the roll call while

---

*Originally elected to the Senate as a Democrat, Harry F. Byrd, Jr., of Virginia was re-elected in 1970 and 1976 as an Independent. Despite changing his party affiliation in 1970, Byrd retained his Democratic seniority and two choice committee assignments — Armed Services and Finance.

crouching behind the rail on the Democratic side of the House chamber. He explained: "It's 190 degrees over there [pointing to the Republican side]."[4]

In short, party is something to be loyal to and to expect loyalty from, albeit not all of the time, and certainly not when important constituency interests point the other way.

Party and Congressional Voting Behavior

Party, constituency, group pressures, and personal beliefs all affect the way a representative or senator votes in Congress. Of all these factors, however, party has the most frequent influence on congressional voting behavior.

During the past half century, between two thirds and three quarters of the Democrats and Republicans in Congress have voted with a majority of their party colleagues on contested votes. Voting in the House and Senate is more closely related to party affiliation than to constituency factors like urban-rural or sectional differences. Most Republicans tend to think and vote more like other Republicans than like Democrats—which is why they are Republicans. The parties tend to be most cohesive on votes involving partisan and ideological considerations, organization of the House and Senate, for example, and patronage, the size of the federal government, economic issues, taxation and fiscal policies, housing, and welfare. Party is less important on foreign policy and on questions dealing with ethics, morals, and prejudice.

Nevertheless, except in periods like 1935–1938 and 1965–1966 when congressional majorities are exceptionally large, party cohesiveness is not sufficient in either house to guarantee victory to the majority party on most major issues. With the lengthening of congressional careers, the decentralization of power to committees and subcommittees, and the weakening of party discipline, parties have become less cohesive than they were earlier in the century. Among the Democrats, the majority party in Congress for all but four years since 1933, party cohesiveness has been further weakened by the insurgency of many southern Democrats on a substantial range of issues, including civil rights, labor, tariffs, foreign aid, and social welfare. For example, in the Ninety-second Congress (1971–72), a majority of southern Democrats opposed a majority of northern Democrats on more than one third of the recorded votes in the House.

Reflecting these differences among congressmen of the same party are informal and formal groupings, or factions, which strongly influence party voting patterns. These groups have been particularly important among Democrats in the House. Ties among southern Democrats have been informal, with leadership provided by southern committee and subcommittee chairmen. Liberal Democrats, mostly from the north and west, are formally organized into the Democratic Study Group, which enlisted almost 60 percent of the 243 Democrats in the

Ninety-third Congress (1973–74). In addition to marshaling voting strength on the House floor, the Democratic Study Group provides research and campaign assistance to its members. Recently, middle-of-the road Democrats in the House organized the Democratic Moderates of Congress as a counterweight to the liberal Democratic Study Group.

Role of the Party Caucus

A *caucus* is a meeting of all members of a party in a legislative chamber. At the beginning of the twentieth century, caucuses determined party positions on controversial issues in Congress, particularly in the House of Representatives, and members were expected to cast their votes in accordance with the decision made in caucus.

Over the past half century the role of the caucus in binding congressional votes has declined, primarily as a result of the weakening of party discipline and the decentralization of power in Congress. During the 1970s, younger liberal Democrats in the House tried to reinstate the caucus as an instrument for setting party policy on key legislative issues. They were able to adopt caucus positions on a few issues, including halting bombing in Cambodia and eliminating the oil-depletion allowance, but the caucus proved too large and unwieldy and party differences too great for agreement on most questions.

Although party members often break ranks over legislation, both parties' caucuses stand firm in organizing the House and Senate. Caucuses select the party's candidates for Speaker of the House and President pro tempore of the Senate, as well as party floor leaders, whips, and policy committees. In addition, caucuses have ultimate authority to determine committee assignments and chairmanships. Committee reforms of the 1970s greatly enhanced this authority, particularly among Democrats in the House. Now chairmen unable to retain the support of a majority of the caucus face a very real threat of losing their positions, as did three chairmen of House committees when the Ninety-fourth Congress organized in January 1975.

Congressmen and Their Constituencies

Seats in the Senate and House depend on state and local constituencies, and national party leaders and organizations play a minor role in congressional campaigns. As a result, constituency influence is pervasive in Congress:

An understanding of the risks of the electoral arena is important for an understanding of Congress, not because local pressures are always decisive on particular votes but because the local basis of election tends to promote a local orientation toward issues in general. Specific local pressures may only infre-

Congress of the United States
House of Representatives
Washington, D.C. 20515
OFFICIAL BUSINESS

Charles E. Bennett
M. C.

A Report

from

CONGRESSMAN CHARLES E. BENNETT

April 3, 1976

Dear Friends:

Last week, I testified before the House Appropriations Committee in support of Florida's public works appropriations requests and especially those in our Third Congressional District. My requests for this area included: $7.8 million to complete the deepening of Jacksonville Harbor from 34 to 38 feet and $580,000 for operation and maintenance of the harbor; $500,000 to study the need to deepen Jacksonville Harbor to 45 feet; $3.9 million to initiate construction on the Duval County Beach Erosion Project; $102,000 to continue a study to eliminate sedimentation and provide water circulation in the Mill Cove area; $500,000 to continue the study of Metro Jacksonville water resources; $265,000 for operation and maintenance of Fernandina Harbor; $2 million for operation and maintenance of the Jacksonville-Miami Intracoastal Waterway section; $24.4 million as requested by the Jacksonville City Council for resumption of construction on the Cross-Florida Barge Canal on a contingency basis, depending on the outcome of the Corps of Engineers' Environmental Impact Statement; and $957,000 for maintenance of the completed section of the canal.

The Committee to Investigate a Balanced Federal Budget held hearings last month on my bill to require a balanced budget each year except in time of war or national economic emergency. As a member of the committee, I attended the hearings and listened to the testimony of several expert witnesses who called for an end to Federal deficit spending. The witness list included such notable figures as Federal Reserve Board Chairman Arthur Burns and New York Stock Exchange President James Needham. All of the witnesses stressed the need for a balanced Federal budget and I am hopeful that Congress will heed their advice. The hearings will continue later this month with Treasury Secretary William Simon heading the witness list.

Concern with constituency interests is evident in a typical congressional newsletter. Note that the first item in Representative Bennett's "report" deals with his efforts to "bring home the bacon" in the form of federal projects for his district.

quently be decisive, but they constitute the pervasive milieu within which congressmen and senators operate.[5]

Congressional opposition in the late 1960s to the deployment of an antiballistic missile weapons system provides a good example of this local orientation toward issues. Relatively few congressmen initially opposed the $58-billion Sentinel ABM system proposed by the Johnson administration as a means of protecting American cities from nuclear missile attack. Once Congress approved the program, the Army began to acquire sites in a number of metropolitan areas. What happened next was graphically described by John W. Finney in the *New York Times:*

In Boston, Chicago, Detroit, Seattle, San Francisco, Los Angeles and Honolulu, objections [were] raised by city councils, church groups, conservationists, union leaders, real estate developers, peace groups and scientists to the emplacement of nuclear-tipped missiles in their cities or suburbs. . . . What had been an abstract, highly technical issue suddenly acquired a direct political interest for many Senators and Representatives. When opposition began mounting in Hawaii, for example, Senator Daniel K. Inouye, a Democratic member of the Senate Armed Services Committee, came out firmly against Sentinel deployment on the ground that it would be "a dangerous step backward" into a nuclear arms race. Senator Harry M. Jackson of Washington, who had championed the system on the Senate floor, found himself running into a political flak back home when the Army proposed to put a Sentinel site at Fort Lawton in the heart of Seattle. At Senator Jackson's suggestion, the Army agreed to move the site to Bainbridge Island, across Puget Sound, but that only served to arouse Representative Thomas M. Pelly, who has a home on the island. . . . The Army [also proposed] to establish a Sentinel base at Cheli Air Force Base in the southeastern section of Los Angeles, only half a mile from [Representative Chet] Holifield's home in Montebello. This . . . brought protests from the Los Angeles County Board of Supervisors, which [wanted] to use the World War II base for industrial and housing development, and suggestions from Mr. Holifield that the Army should not build its Sentinel bases in populated areas.[6]

Constituency Interests and Voting in Congress

The importance of constituency concerns does not, however, make congressmen robots who automatically serve the interests of their districts. Indeed, such interests are not clear-cut on most issues. Districts typically encompass a variety of interests, which often cancel out one another, giving congressmen considerable freedom of choice. On many questions, constituents express little or no concern, and most Americans never communicate with their senator or representative. In the average House district, a majority does not even know the name of its congressman.

Despite the general public's lack of information and interest, most congressmen believe their voting records are of concern to their constituents. Usually, they vote in accord with their perception of their district's interest. But this perception is significantly shaped by the kind of contacts a congressman has with his constituents:

The communications most Congressmen have with their districts inevitably puts them in touch with organized groups and with individuals who are relatively well-informed about politics. The Representative knows his constituents mostly from dealing with people who do write letters, who will attend meetings, who *have* an interest in his legislative stands. As a result, his sample of contacts with a constituency . . . is heavily biased.[7]

The average congressman's contacts among politically active constituents tend to be with members of his own party who already share his general outlook on national issues and district interests. As a result, "the Representative's perceptions and attitudes are more strongly associated with the attitude of his electoral *majority* than they are with the attitudes of his constituency as a whole."[8]

Because congressmen are responsive to the views of their partisan electoral supporters, they tend to see party and constituency interests as similar on many issues. Contributing to this coincidence of interests is the fact that Democrats and Republicans typically represent states

and districts that reflect the differing socioeconomic bases of the two parties. Thus, congressmen often are able at the same time to vote for the interests of their party and of the dominant majority in their districts.

Party and constituency are most likely to conflict for congressmen who represent districts that differ greatly from the party norm—urban Republicans and rural Democrats. Over the past three decades, Democrats in the House have divided along urban-rural lines nearly half of the time, while urban and rural Republicans have parted company on more than a fifth of all important votes in Congress.[9]

As in the case of party, constituency interests stimulate formation of groupings within Congress. Representatives and senators from a state organize, regardless of party, to advance common interests, some being far more effective than others in coalescing voting strength, securing federal aid, and influencing the location of federal installations and contracts. Larger constituency-based groupings include the rural caucus, composed of congressmen from farm districts, and the New England caucus. Black members of Congress, almost all of whom represent inner-city districts, created the Congressional Black Caucus in 1970. Initially, the Black Caucus focused on broad national issues affecting blacks in general rather than on specific legislation. Recently, however, the caucus has concentrated more on advancing the interests of black city dwellers.

The Shifting Constituency Base

Congressional constituencies change over time. National demographic shifts have affected the composition of the electorate in every state and district—increasing the number of voters in the rapidly growing states of the south and west, reducing the number of farmers and younger people in midwestern states, replacing white voters with blacks in inner-city districts, and adding new residents to voting rolls in suburban districts. These population movements require substantial reallocation

Chapter 11
The Legislative System
and Law Making

of seats among the states each decade. Between 1948 and 1972, California gained twenty seats in the House and Florida nine, while Pennsylvania was losing eight and New York six. During the 1970s, another fifteen House seats shifted from the northeast and midwest to the south and west. Within states, metropolitan growth necessitates redistricting to provide more representation for spreading suburbs.

Legal changes also alter constituencies and their electorates. In *Wesberry* v. *Sanders*,[10] the Supreme Court ruled that congressional districts within a state must have equal populations, thus ordering an end to the widespread malapportionment of House districts that had benefited rural areas and disadvantaged growing cities and suburbs. The Civil Rights Act of 1965 enfranchised hundreds of thousands of southern blacks, while the Twenty-sixth Amendment gave an opportunity to 11.2 million young people between eighteen and twenty-one to join the electorate.

Inevitably these changes affect congressmen's electoral chances. Redistricting following the 1970 census was a major factor in the defeat of nine of the thirteen incumbent House members who lost their seats in November 1972.

In addition to increasing incumbents' electoral hazards, changes in constituencies have steadily augmented the number of congressmen oriented to the interests of suburbs and newer cities, lowered the average age of congressmen, and reduced the number of southern districts in which candidates can ignore black voters. Constituency changes have also affected the internal workings of Congress. Younger and newly elected congressmen played key roles in democratizing the selection of committee chairmen and in securing seats for less senior members on important committees.

Change has broadened the perspectives of newer members of Congress. Many are less localistic in their outlook than senior congressmen. They are less likely than older members to have spent their entire lives in their district, and more likely to have worked for the federal government or some nationally based organization before coming to Congress. "We represent the mobile generation of postwar America," noted one of the ninety-two freshmen representatives elected in 1975. "We don't have the local roots that some others have. Our group would style ourselves as national Congressmen. . . . We're concerned about our districts, but we're even more concerned about national problems."[11]

No matter how concerned about national problems, however, members of Congress cannot afford to ignore their constituencies. In fact, constant changes within constituencies reinforce continual efforts of congressmen to build a solid political base in their district and state. Job security is the object of much legislative activity. The necessity for such activity is reinforced by the fact that control over House districting is largely decentralized in the American federal system. State legislatures, not Congress, determine boundaries of congressional districts,

Figure 11.1
Projected House Apportionment
After the 1980 Census

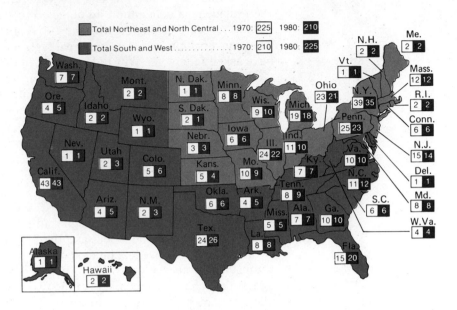

Source: *The New York Times*, Jan. 23, 1976

a task they often perform with considerable imagination. Careers in the House have been abruptly terminated by redistricting following a shift in party power in the state legislature. For example, after capturing control of the California legislature in 1960, the Democrats ensured the defeat two years later of Republican John Rousselot, a member of the John Birch Society, by moving heavily Republican sections of Rousselot's district to an adjoining district.* Other House members have been shielded from electoral risk by friendly state legislators. For years, House Speaker Sam Rayburn and Rules Committee Chairman Howard Smith represented undersized rural districts that the Texas and Virginia legislatures protected from urban voters.

The Structure of Congress

Two Houses

The most obvious structural fact about the American Congress is its bicameral organization. At the constitutional convention, bicameralism

Chapter 11
The Legislative System
and Law Making

---

*Rousselot returned to the House of Representatives in 1970, winning election from a district that contained many of his old constituents.

was required to accommodate the interests of the larger and smaller states. It also was consistent with the principle of checks and balances, one of the strongest forces that motivated the work of the framers. The story is told that when Thomas Jefferson returned from France after the Philadelphia convention he objected to the bicameral feature and asked George Washington why the convention had taken such a step. The conversation occurred at breakfast, and Washington is said to have asked Jefferson, "Why did you pour that coffee into your saucer?" "To cool it," was Jefferson's reply. "Even so," answered Washington, "we pour legislation into the senatorial saucer to cool it."[12]

This original expectation has long since ceased to be realized. The Senate does not function primarily as a "check" on the House. Legislation, with very few exceptions, originates as readily in one house as in the other. Under the Constitution, the Senate has exclusive jurisdiction over the ratification of treaties, trials of impeachments, and the confirmation of presidential appointments. The House initiates impeachment proceedings, revenue bills, and, by custom, appropriations. Otherwise, the two houses are equal in power, and *all* legislation requires action by both the House and the Senate.

Bicameralism, however, influences the nature of the congressional setting in a number of ways. The difference in their constituency bases affects the behavior of members of the two houses. Representatives are chosen from districts with an average population of approximately 500,000, whereas senators represent states that range in population from about 300,000 (Alaska) to well over 20 million (California). Regardless of their size, statewide constituencies tend to be more diverse than most House districts, and senators are subject to a greater variety of pressures than the typical House member. As a result, there are fewer safe seats and less immunity to national political trends in the Senate than in the House of Representatives.

Because the Senate is much smaller than the House, senators function in a less formal environment than do the 435 representatives. The pace in the Senate is more leisurely, the rules more flexible, and real debate and deliberation more frequent. The House is an impersonal institution, with rigid rules that limit consideration of legislation on the floor. Because senators normally serve on twice as many committees as representatives, specialization is less intensive and opportunities for leadership come more quickly in the smaller Senate. In the Ninety-fourth Congress, 90 percent of the Democrats in the Senate were committee or subcommittee chairmen, compared with 47 percent in the House. All these differences provide individual senators with greater independence and visibility than their counterparts in the House.

Senators also enjoy a six-year term, while representatives must face the ordeal of re-election every two years, which in a competitive district means almost perpetual campaigning. Because of the advantages of the Senate's size and term of office, as well as the greater prestige associated with being a Senator, many representatives aspire to and eventually win a seat in the Senate.

A New Congress Every Two Years

Congress operates on a two-year cycle. The Congress that convened early in January 1977 was the Ninety-fifth Congress, there having been ninety-four previous Congresses in one hundred and eighty-eight years. While not prescribed in the Constitution, this biennial cycle was the logical result of an electoral system whereby all the seats in the House of Representatives and one third of the seats in the Senate become vacant every two years. Accordingly, the Congress that meets in January of an odd-numbered year is a new body, many of its members having just been elected two months before. The meeting in the odd-numbered year is called the *first session*. Assuming that no special session is called, the meeting in the following, even-numbered year is the *second* and final *session* of a Congress. Very early in the first session the two houses proceed to organize, and the resulting arrangements continue for the two-year period. Any bill introduced in the first session of a Congress may be taken up during the second session. But when the final session in the two-year cycle comes to an end, all unfinished business automatically dies.

The opening days of a new Congress, when the business of organizing is done, are marked by activity and excitement. The presiding officers and other officials must be elected, members assigned to standing committees, a chairman selected for each committee, and in the House parliamentary rules of procedure agreed upon. These organizational tasks give the House a good deal more concern than they do the Senate, because only one third of the senators have been involved in the recent election. Unless party control of the Senate is changing in a new Congress, organizing is a relatively simple process. Moreover, the Senate has always regarded itself as a continuing body and therefore does not reconsider its rules every two years.

The Leadership

The primary centralizing force within Congress is the leadership, composed of the presiding officers and party leaders who manage the flow of business through the House and the Senate. The leaders organize the parties in Congress, prepare the legislative schedule, promote attendance of party members for votes on important bills, collect and distribute information, try to persuade members to follow their lead, and maintain liaison with the White House.

As one would expect, the leaders are among the most influential and respected members of Congress. Because the average length of service has grown, most leaders are career congressmen with long tenure. The leaders, however, have modest formal powers with which to influence individual members. As we have seen, the White House rather than the leaders in the House and Senate really sets the legislative agenda. Congressional leaders are further hampered by their lack of rewards and punishments. "How do you discipline a man? What goodies are there?" asks the majority leader of the House. "If a fellow says 'No' to us what can the Speaker and I do about it? What can we give them? There are no little goodies, no patronage."[13] A legislator with a strong constituency base usually can get re-elected, even if he has thumbed his nose at his party's leaders in Congress. Also limited is the authority of leaders over chairmen of committees and subcommittees. Thus, leaders with small powers attempt to steer a diverse legislative party whose members are largely independent of direct control.

Presiding Officers

The most important formal officers of Congress are those who preside over the two houses: in the House, the *Speaker,* chosen by the majority party caucus; in the Senate, the *Vice President,* who under the Constitution holds the post of presiding officer. In the Senate, the *President pro tempore* is chosen on a party basis to preside in the absence of the Vice President. (In fact the Vice President or the President pro tempore rarely presides; this dull duty is usually passed around among junior senators.)

The presiding officers' authority and influence depend only in part upon their formal powers. To a large extent, the leaders' importance is controlled by such intangible factors as their personalities, the respect they command from their colleagues, their skills in human relations, their party standing, the over-all strength and cohesion of their party, and the state of relations between Congress and the President. The Speaker of the House is almost always one of the most respected and influential members of the majority party. Unlike the Vice President, the Speaker is a party leader, chosen by his colleagues. He is a regular member of the House who retains his right to vote and speak on any proposal. When the Speaker does leave the chair to enter the debate, he is likely to exert great influence. The Vice President, on the other hand, has no regular right to participate in debate and may vote only to break a tie.

No member of the House or Senate may speak on the floor or offer any motion without first being recognized by the presiding officer. Occasionally, the course of the legislative process may be significantly affected by the recognition of a certain member at a particular moment, and the Speaker and the Vice President sometimes deliberately weigh such considerations when they give the floor to members. But the power of recognition usually is exercised on an impartial basis.

The presiding officer also has authority to interpret and apply the rules when a procedural question arises. Usually, reference to prece-

Representative Sam Rayburn of Texas moves to the podium after re-election by the Democratic majority as Speaker of the House at the opening of the Eighty-seventh Congress in 1961. "Mr. Sam," as he was known to his colleagues, served eighteen years as Speaker, a period which spanned the administrations of four Presidents.

dent is enough to indicate the proper interpretation, but occasionally the presiding officer makes a creative and important decision. In 1890, for instance, Speaker Thomas B. Reed changed the interpretation of the quorum rule so as to include in the count members present but not voting on a bill. In so doing, Reed frustrated the attempts of the Democratic minority to prevent the transaction of business by not voting either way. Generally, however, opportunities to make new and significant interpretations of the rules are rare. Besides, any ruling of the presiding officer may be appealed to the floor and reversed by a majority of the members present.

In both houses, the presiding officers refer bills introduced by the members to standing committees for consideration and action. Various legislative reform acts delineate the jurisdiction of committees in detail, but when a bill can be assigned to one of two or more committees, the presiding officer may have the option of chosing a friendly or unfriendly committee.

In addition, the presiding officers of the House and Senate name members of special committees, among them conference committees (those organized to compromise the differences in the bills passed by the two houses) and special investigating committees. This function is usually so controlled by tradition, however, that it leaves very little freedom of choice. For example, members of conference committees normally are named in order of seniority from the standing committees that originally considered a bill.

Chapter 11
The Legislative System
and Law Making

291

Before 1910, the powers of the Speaker of the House were far greater. As chairman of the Rules Committee, which determines what proposals reach the floor, the Speaker controlled the flow of legislation in the House. He also appointed committee members and chairmen and had absolute discretion in recognizing members on the floor. All these powers were lost as a result of the revolt of 1910–11 against the strong leadership of Speaker Joe Cannon. Since then, "the Speaker's formal authority has been modest, and his centralizing influence has been more informal and interstitial than formal and comprehensive."[14]

Most of the Speaker's informal influence is derived from his role as the central party leader in the House. His views usually are influential in selecting the rest of the majority party leadership and in assigning members of his party to committees. He is at the center of a communications network that links committee chairmen, other powerful members of his party, and the minority leadership. He is also his party's chief persuader. As former Speaker Joseph Martin explained:

The Speaker himself is the grand strategist and guiding spirit. Each Speaker, of course, exercises his leadership according to his own character and the prevailing political situation. For my own part I was never dictatorial. I worked by persuasion and drew heavily on long-established personal friendships. I found that I could best keep my members with me by tact and discretion. Unless it was absolutely necessary I never asked a man to side with me if his vote would hurt him in his district. Whenever I could spare a man this kind of embarrassment I did so and saved him for another time when I might need him more urgently.[15]

Floor Leaders and Whips

Next to the Speaker, the most important officers in Congress are the *majority* and *minority floor leaders* in each house. These leaders are chosen by the party caucuses. As their titles indicate, their main duty is to watch over and try to control business on the floor of the Senate and House in the interests of their parties. A floor leader keeps in touch with ordinary party members and key committee members, as well as leaders of state delegations and other groupings like the Democratic Study Group and the Black Caucus. He tries to persuade them to act in committee and vote on the floor in accordance with party policies and the wishes of party leaders. In addition, floor leaders supervise debate, direct the activity of party whips, and serve as their party's legislative strategists. In consultation with the presiding officer and the minority leader, the majority leader in each house also plans the order of business, a function shared in the House with the Rules Committee.

Each party in each house employs a *whip,* who is appointed by the floor leader. Aiding the whip are a number of assistant whips, all of whom are members of Congress. The basic function of the whips is to secure the support of party members when major issues reach the floor. In the process, whips find out how party members intend to vote, convey the wishes of the leadership to members, inform the party leaders of the views of the rank and file on pending bills, notify members when key votes are scheduled, and ensure that supporters are present to vote. In the House, particularly, the activities of whips often affect the outcome of votes on important legislation.[16]

Both parties also have created *policy committees* in each house of Congress. These committees are supposed to develop general legislative programs for their respective parties. None, however, has been able to formulate broad policies, largely because of the diversity of viewpoints within each of the parties and the decentralization of power within Congress.

The Committee System

Power is dispersed in Congress primarily because most of the work of the House and Senate is done in *standing committees* and their *subcommittees*. Furthermore these committees exercise their considerable power independently of one another. In large measure, they also operate independently of the presiding officers, floor leaders, and other centralizing forces in Congress.

The committee system permits a division of labor in dealing with the numerous and complex proposals that come before Congress. It also encourages specialization by congressmen, most of whom develop detailed knowledge only in those areas of governmental activity that fall within the range of their committees. Respect and influence among colleagues, particularly in the House of Representatives, are won primarily by working hard in committee and developing expertise. In the words of one representative:

The members who are most successful are those who pick a specialty or an area and become real experts in it. As a consequence, when they speak they are looked upon as authorities and are highly respected. Even though they may be an authority in only one field, their influence tends to spread into other areas.[17]

The congressman who relies on a colleague's judgment on some issue within his special sphere of competence expects that colleague's support on matters that come before his own committee. The relationship is reciprocal and so committee influence increases.

Committees and Subcommittees

While the number of standing committees in the two houses differs slightly (twenty-two in the House, eighteen in the Senate), the division of responsibility among committees is similar. Both have committees on agriculture, appropriations, armed services, banking and housing, budget, commerce, the District of Columbia, foreign affairs, govern-

"You'll find 80% of the work is done in the committees, my boy . . . and 90% of the goofing off."

Grin and Bear It, by George Lichty and Fred Wagner, courtesy of Field Newspaper Syndicate.

ment operations, interior, the judiciary, labor, post office and civil service, public works, rules, science, taxation, and veterans.

Over the years, responsibilities of various committees have expanded as new problems and issues have come before Congress. Movement of the banking committees into housing and urban policy provides a good example. Housing issues initially arose in the context of mortgage policies, which the banking committees handled. Once involved in housing politics, these committees began handling other urban issues such as planning, mass transportation, and open space. Eventually, the committee names were changed to reflect their responsibilities in housing and urban affairs—to the Banking, Currency and Housing Committee in the House and the Banking, Housing and Urban Affairs Committee in the Senate.

Table 11–1
Committees and subcommittees in the Ninety-fourth Congress

(Number of subcommittees shown in parentheses)

House of Representatives	Senate
Agriculture (10)	Agriculture and Forestry (6)
Appropriations (13)	Appropriations (13)
Armed Services (7)	Armed Services (9)
Banking, Currency and Housing (9)	Banking, Housing and Urban Affairs (8)
Budget (0)	Budget (0)
District of Columbia (6)	District of Columbia (0)
Education and Labor (9)	Labor and Public Welfare (11)
Government Operations (7)	Government Operations (5)
House Administration (9)	
Interior and Insular Affairs (7)	Interior and Insular Affairs (6)
International Relations (10)	Foreign Relations (9)
Interstate and Foreign Commerce (6)	Commerce (13)
Judiciary (7)	Judiciary (15)
Merchant Marine and Fisheries (5)	
Post Office and Civil Service (6)	Post Office and Civil Service (3)
Public Works and Transportation (6)	Public Works (6)
Rules (0)	Rules and Administration (7)
Science and Technology (7)	Aeronautical and Space Sciences (0)
Small Business (6)	
Standards of Official Conduct (0)	
Veterans' Affairs (5)	Veterans' Affairs (4)
Ways and Means (6)	Finance (11)
Totals: 22 committees	*Totals:* 18 committees
141 subcommittees	127 subcommittees

Periodically, Congress has tried to rearrange its committee structure to reduce overlapping responsibilities, organize functions more logically, and provide better balance in the workload of committees. One such effort produced the Legislative Reorganization Act of 1946, which eliminated almost fifty standing committees. In 1974, another reform eliminated the Internal Security Committee, as well as altering the responsibilities of a number of committees in the House. Most transportation programs were gathered into the Public Works Committee, renamed the Public Works and Transportation Committee. A number of medical programs were moved to the Interstate and Foreign Commerce Committee, responsibilities for scientific research were focused in the Science and Technology Committee (formerly the Science and Astronautics Committee), and a variety of international food and trade programs transferred to the International Relations Committee (formerly the Foreign Affairs Committee). In addition, jurisdiction over revenue sharing was shifted from Ways and Means to the Government Operations Committee, and legal services from Education and Labor to the Judiciary Committee.

Overhauling committee responsibilities intimately affects the fortunes of large numbers of legislators. Eliminating committees and subcommittees directly threatens the chairmen of the targeted bodies. Shifting a function such as mass transportation or health care from one committee to another means an irretrievable loss of influence for congressmen who have specialized in that activity because members of Congress cannot move with their area of specialization to a new committee. Thus, carefully nurtured relations with federal officials, state and local agencies, interest groups, and others with a concern in a particular policy area are bound to suffer. Because of the high stakes congressmen have in existing allocations of responsibilities, committee reform has been an extremely controversial issue, and opposition from potential losers within the House prevented many proposed committee reforms from being enacted in 1974.

Each standing committee in Congress is organized on a bipartisan basis. Ratios of Democrats and Republicans on committees reflect the over-all division between the two parties in the House and the Senate. Each representative is assigned to one or two committees, and the typical senator to three. Committees in the House tend to be twice as large as those in the Senate, averaging thirty-five members in the Ninety-fifth Congress compared with fifteen in the upper house.

Subcommittees have proliferated since the streamlining of the committee system in 1946. House and Senate standing committees now have more than 260 subcommittees, a growth that also reflects the increasing volume and complexity of legislation. Obviously, subcommittees permit greater specialization; and, even more important, subcommittees mean that more members of Congress occupy positions of leadership, a condition that further disperses power in Congress.[18]

Membership on Committees

Committee assignments largely determine the areas of public policy in which a congressman will specialize, the administrative agencies on which he will have the greatest influence, and the subjects on which he will generate the most publicity. Both houses limit the number of committee assignments available to individual legislators. In the House, membership on the extremely important Appropriations, Rules, or Ways and Means Committees usually precludes service on other standing committees.* All other House members are permitted to

---

*The Appropriations Committee handles all spending bills, that is, those that *appropriate* public funds. The Rules Committee is the "traffic cop" of the House, because it determines what proposals reach the floor for debate and a vote. The Ways and Means Committee considers tax legislation and related matters, such as revenue sharing and social security.

serve on two committees, but only one of these assignments can be on a major committee. The Senate restricts members to two major committees.

The party caucuses assign congressmen to standing committees. In both the House and the Senate, the party caucuses have delegated this task to party committees. Because standing committees are reasonably continuous bodies (most members carrying over from the previous Congress), the prime task of each party committee is to fill vacancies. Usually, there are more applications than openings on the important committees as some senior congressmen try to obtain assignments that provide more influence and visibility. Pressures from younger members, however, have diluted the significance of seniority in committee assignments. The Democrats in the Senate try to give each newly elected Democratic senator an appointment to a major committee. In the House, the party committees consider a number of factors in addition to seniority, including the member's record as a legislator, his or her state or region, the nature of his or her district, the contribution of a particular committee assignment to chances for re-election, and the legislator's background before entering the House. Constituency considerations are especially important in assignments to such committees as Agriculture, Armed Services, Banking, Currency and Housing, Education and Labor, Interior and Insular Affairs, Merchant Marine and Fisheries, and Science and Technology.

Policy can also play an important role in some assignments. Over the years, various factions have tried to bolster their influence by placing particular individuals on a committee. For example, in 1975 southern Democrats pressed for the assignment of Senator James B. Allen, a conservative from Alabama, to the Judiciary Committee. Allen was blocked in the Democratic Steering Committee by liberals strongly opposed to having another conservative on the committee that handles civil rights, criminal justice, and judicial nominations.

Particularly in the House of Representatives, personal factors have strongly affected assignment of members. For many years, the prime criterion for securing a place on powerful committees such as Appropriations, Rules, and Ways and Means was whether the congressman had been judged as "responsible" by his elders. A "responsible" representative was a good team player who would not prove troublesome to his colleagues. Such congressmen typically were moderates or conservatives whose views on key issues differed little from the leaders of these committees. Resentment by liberal Democrats in the House against this tight control led to the expansion of the Ways and Means Committee from twenty-five to thirty-seven members after the 1974 election, with most of the new seats filled by younger, less conservative Democrats.

Normally, ratification by the party caucus of recommended committee assignments is a mere formality. Congressmen disgruntled with a committee assignment have no choice but to wait two years for another chance. Some freshmen, however, have successfully challenged their committee assignments in the Democratic caucus. In 1969, Shirley Chisholm — the first black woman elected to Congress — objected to her assignment to the Agriculture Committee as inappropriate to her inner-city district. Her appeal was accepted by the caucus, and she was assigned to the urban-oriented Education and Labor Committee. Two years later, another New York City Democrat — Herman Badillo, the first congressman of Puerto Rican descent — also successfully challenged his assignment to the Agriculture Committee and won appointment to the Education and Labor Committee.

Role of Committee Chairmen

Because so much of Congress' work is done in committees and sub-committees, chairmen play a critical role in the legislative process. To a chairman belongs most of the power to arrange committee meetings and select staff to work with committee members. Chairmen establish most subcommittees, appoint their members and chairmen, determine how specialized and independent they will be, decide what matters will be referred to them, and assign them staff and funds. The chairman also determines the order in which a committee considers bills, decides whether public hearings shall be held, arranges to have bills that the committee has approved brought to the floor, and manages floor debate on the committee's bills. If a conference committee is required to resolve differences with the other house, the chairman serves on it and usually plays a central role in selecting the other conferees from his house.

In both houses of Congress, committee chairmen are selected primarily on the basis of seniority on the committee. Rank within committees also is similarly determined; and subcommittee chairmen normally are selected from among the most senior committee members. The Senate has used seniority since early in the nineteenth century, and the House since the revolt in 1910–11 against Speaker Cannon. For much of the twentieth century the only exception to the seniority rule has been the prohibition in both houses against a member's serving as the chairman of more than one standing committee.

Probably no aspect of the congressional system has been more controversial than reliance on this criterion to select committee chairmen. Critics argue that seniority rewards continuous service rather than hard work, skill, or even party loyalty. Seniority also sentences junior congressmen to a long period of apprenticeship that frustrates newcomers and deters àble and mature individuals from seeking election to Congress. New members, as one House freshman pointed out in 1974, do not want to "wait around five years to have a voice in making this a viable institution."[19] It is further argued that the seniority rule is undemocratic in that it tends to place in office as committee chairmen men from safe congressional districts that are little affected by —

Figure 11.2
Seniority and committee chairmanships in the House of Representatives, 1881–1975.

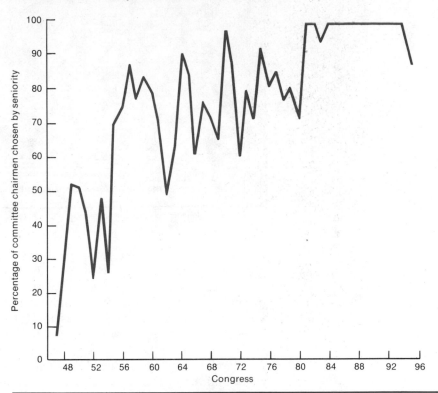

Source: Adapted from Nelson W. Polsby, Miriam Gallaher, and Barry Spencer Rundquist, "The growth of the Seniority System in the U.S. House of Representatives, *American Political Science Review*, LXIII (1969).

and often insensitive or even opposed to—national political tides.

The seniority rule also comes under fire from those who want to strengthen the role of the parties in Congress. Under the seniority system, a committee chairman can usually ignore the party leadership. As long as he has the support of a majority of voters in his state or district, his seat in Congress is safe. So too is his chairmanship of a committee, provided his party retains its majority. Critics of the seniority rule argue that one of the most effective ways of increasing party discipline in Congress would be to assign committee chairmanships on the basis of service and loyalty to the party and to insist on continued loyalty as the price of retention of a chairmanship.

Seniority is defended on a number of grounds. It has brought or promises rewards to many congressmen. Conservatives favor a system that has strengthened their hand in both parties and reduces the influence of liberals. Supporters also contend that seniority contributes to the stability of committee membership by rewarding experience, thus

THE HOUSE EXAMINES THE COMMITTEE CHAIRMEN

promoting specialization and expertise. Defenders further argue that no workable alternative exists. Abandoning seniority, they insist, would lead to endless factional and personal conflicts over distribution of chairmanships. The result would weaken Congress in its dealings with the President, federal agencies, and lobbyists.

None of the arguments in favor of seniority has proved very persuasive to congressmen elected in recent years. In the House, pressures from junior members produced significant modifications in the selection of committee chairmen. Since 1971, nominations for chairmen and ranking minority members of committees have been submitted to party caucuses for approval. In 1975, the Democrats in the House dramatically broke with the seniority tradition. With the reformers' ranks bolstered by the addition of seventy-five freshmen, the Democratic caucus voted to deny reappointment to three venerable chairmen who had served a total of 118 years in the House.*

Despite these reforms, seniority continues to play an extremely important role in selecting committee chairmen. Nineteen of the twenty-two House chairmen chosen during the "revolt" of 1975 were the most senior members of their committee. In two of the three cases where chairmen were removed in 1975, the position went to the next senior Democrat on the committee. And all thirteen of the chairmen of Appropriations subcommittees, who also are subject to caucus approval in the House, held their posts on the basis of seniority.

Thus most chairmen still are older members with long tenure who

---

*Ousted were Wright Patman of Texas, the eighty-one-year-old chairman of the Banking and Currency Committee, W. R. Poage of Texas, seventy-five, who had headed the Agriculture Committee, and F. Edward Hebert of Louisiana, seventy-four, chairman of the House Administration Committee.

tend to represent districts or states in which competition between parties is relatively low. In the Ninety-fourth Congress, the average chairman was 63, and had served more than twenty years in Congress. Half of the chairmen in the two houses were from southern and border states.

Although modification of seniority has had relatively little impact on the *selection* of chairmen, the necessity to win caucus approval has significantly affected the *behavior* of chairmen. In the past, they could reward and punish individuals with little fear of retaliation. Now, in the words of one representative, chairmen "recognize they are not serving by divine right, but as elected representatives of the caucus."[20] Accountability to the party caucus had made them more responsive to committee members, junior congressmen, and party leaders. Because chairmen exercise less control than in the past, there is more debate, conflict, and compromise.

These developments have further dispersed power within Congress. Both floor leaders and committee chairmen must largely deal with subcommittee chairmen as equals and, increasingly, even with individual legislators. Paradoxically, greater democratization within Congress had made it more difficult to carry out any policy, even one that is popularly approved.

Lobbying

Congress is a constant target of vigorous activity by groups that try to shape policy decisions. Lobbyists are involved in every stage of the legislative process, directly pressuring senators and representatives. They draft legislation, support or oppose proposals at hearings, urge committees to advance or block issues, and try to influence votes on bills that reach the floor of the House or Senate. Many groups also actively promote or oppose changes in the legislative process. For example, Common Cause, a national citizens group, energetically supported the revolt of younger House members against the seniority system in 1975. Labor unions, on the other hand, successfully fought the proposed division of the House Education and Labor Committee into two committees.

An extraordinary range of groups seeks to influence Congress. Lobbyists for corporations and trade associations as well as a host of Washington law firms advance business interests. The AFL-CIO, individual unions, state labor federations, and large union locals all have agents in Washington to "inform" legislators. The diverse concerns of farmers are pressed by such national organizations as the American Farm Bureau Federation and the Farmers Union, as well as by commodity and cooperative groups. Veterans' groups, doctors, lawyers, conservationists, owners of firearms, religious organizations, welfare recipients, proponents of birth control, public-housing tenants, and

Ralph Nader, perhaps the nation's best-known lobbyist in the 1970s, urges a congressional committee to reject energy policies which impose heavy burdens on consumers.

hundreds of other organized interests also lobby in Congress. Expansion of federal aid to states and localities has led to more and more lobbying by governors, state highway officials, public universities, county officials, mayors, school boards, local health officers, housing authorities, metropolitan planning agencies, and a multitude of other public bodies. Even representatives of foreign governments contact congressmen, seeking economic aid, military assistance, trade advantages, and similar benefits.

The largest employer of lobbyists is the federal executive, whose corps of legislative representatives constantly try to advance agency interests in Congress. In the 1970s the Defense Department alone budgeted more than $3 million annually for legislative relations. Even the Supreme Court lobbies in Congress. The Chief Justice and one or two Associate Justices often are invited—or get themselves invited—to testify on budgetary matters that concern the judicial system. Sometimes individual Justices have pressed hard—albeit informally—for and against bills. Indeed, an occasional statute has been drafted by members of the Supreme Court.

Senators and congressmen are more susceptible to pressures from lobbyists than would be the case if the political parties were highly disciplined. The dispersion of influence among committees and subcommittees also provides lobbyists with a multitude of access points to decision-making processes. Perhaps the most successful groups are those that exploit the opportunities offered by the decentralization of power to forge an alliance of lobbyists, committees (or subcommittees), and a federal bureau, which together control a particular area of policy. These "sub-governments," as they have been called, function in a variety of fields, including defense, oil, sugar, housing, and public works.[21] In the case of public works, the main allies are the National Rivers and Harbors Congress, the Public Works Committees, and the Army Corps of Engineers.

Techniques of Lobbying

Lobbying methods vary greatly. An approach that is effective with one congressman may put off another. The techniques that attract the most public attention—wining and dining, free plane trips and hotel rooms, gifts, sex, and money—are not necessarily the most profitable.

Lobbyists typically concentrate on those legislators who are either already disposed to vote their way—the object is to re-enforce loyalty and to secure active support—or on those who are uncommitted and thus open to persuasion. Seldom do lobbyists spend time, energy, and other scarce resources on those who are committed to the other side. Threats are only rarely used. Senators and representatives, as a general rule, are simply too powerful and independent to look kindly on those who threaten them. And legislators have nasty weapons that can be turned against annoying lobbyists.

A lobbyist has four principal instruments of persuasion. First are *campaign contributions* from his clients and their friends. As we said in Chapter 8, the costs of winning a contested election for a major office are always high. Because the Election Reform Act of 1974 only limits spending in congressional campaigns and fails to provide money as it does for presidential races, even the most honest legislator is tempted to be more sympathetic to the pleas of special interests that make heavy contributions to his or her campaign. These contributions need not be monetary. They might include helping with registration drives, actually engaging in campaign debates, or getting out the vote on election day.

The second instrument is *friendship*. Many organizations hire former congressmen or staff members to represent them, because these people usually can gain access to their former colleagues. Obtaining access is critical, but using it fruitfully is even more so. Operating in a selfish world of demands and counter demands, a legislator usually finds that he can trust only a small portion of those who come to him for help. As as result, he tends to listen more to those whose reliability and personal loyalty have been tested over time. The mark of a successful lobbyist is that officials on Capitol Hill look on him as a trusted friend and ally, not as an agent of a particular group.

Information is the lobbyist's third instrument. Congressmen need accurate information about the nature and extent of a problem, the feasibility of proposed solutions, and, not least, how constituents feel about the matter. Because of the thousands of demands on their time, legislators can be personally familiar with only a narrow range of problems. Even with the help of a large staff, many important matters cannot be given anything like the attention they deserve. One particularly persuasive kind of information concerns what a proposal will do for—or to—a legislator's constituents. Lobbyists often try to generate a grassroots movement by having members of their group send letters and telegrams to their congressmen. As a variant, some lobbyists prefer to have a few friends of the legislator speak privately with him or her about what a bill is likely to do and how the people at home are viewing it.

Fourth is the ability of the lobbyist and his group to *deliver votes* in the constituencies of individual congressmen. For example, "a congressman from a district with a high proportion of union members will not often risk alienating the labor lobby through his votes on the floor."[22] Of course, most lobbyists represent groups with far more limited clienteles than organized labor. Such groups either do not try to mobilize their supporters at the grassroots, or they focus their resources on a smaller number of congressmen. The latter strategy was followed in 1972 by environmental groups who sought to demonstrate their electoral strength to Congress by concentrating their grassroots' efforts on the defeat of the "dirty dozen," twelve congressmen who had opposed environmental measures.

Interdependence of Legislator and Lobbyist

Lobbying is not a one-way street. Congressmen frequently use lobbyists for their own purposes. A bargaining process is at work. The legislator can do things for the lobbyist—give his cause publicity, leak some inside information to him, talk to an uncommitteed colleague for him, introduce him to a member of an important committee, invite him to social functions so he can enlarge his contacts, and, of course, speak and vote for his proposals. Negatively, the legislator can refuse to cooperate with the lobbyist or can even publicly attack him for trying to pressure votes.

The lobbyist can help the legislator by doing research, writing speeches, running errands, lining up friendly witnesses for committee hearings, soliciting campaign contributions, supplying information, and using influence with other lobbyists and legislators to support proposals that the legislator wants enacted. In short, lobbyists and legislators need each other and use each other.

In addition, lobbyists' efforts to build up friendships are often based on mutual, if selfish, interests. Lobbyists and legislators frequently have the same aims. Planning and carrying out a coordinated campaign to secure or block passage of legislation comes easily to them in such circumstances. A senator from Kansas has little difficulty cooperating with lobbyists from farm organizations, a senator from Texas readily accepts the help of the petroleum industry in working out details of an oil bill, and a representative from Akron or Pittsburgh is likely to be predisposed to support organized labor's position on a full-employment bill.

Federal Regulation of Lobbying

In 1946, Congress for the first time undertook to control interest groups by the Regulation of Lobbying Act. Actually, the law is poorly named, because it provides for little actual *regulation*. Any person or organization soliciting or receiving money to be used "principally to aid," or any person or organization whose "principal purpose" is to aid, passage or defeat of legislation before Congress is required to register with the clerk of the House of Representatives. Each lobbyist is required to disclose the name and address of the person by whom he is employed and in whose interest he works, the duration of such employment, how much he is paid and is to receive, by whom he is paid or is to be paid, how much he is to be paid for expenses, and what expenses are to be included.

Lack of clarity in the law, as in the use of vague phrases like "principal purpose," allow some active organizations to refuse to register on grounds that lobbying is only incidental to their objectives. Compounding difficulties, Congress did not establish any special agency to enforce the statute. Nor does publication of required data in the *Congressional Record* do much to improve the situation. The *Congressional Record* is hardly regular reading fare even for well-informed voters, and newspaper and television analysts have generally shown scant interest in the information available, perhaps because it is incomplete and at times misleading.

.Federal regulation of lobbying also suffers from the difficulty of having to operate under tight constitutional restrictions. The First Amendment, which forbids Congress to make any law abridging the right of the people to assemble and to petition the government for a redress of grievances, protects the basic right of lobbying against any outright federal prohibition. In upholding the Regulation of Lobbying Act, the Supreme Court in 1954 gave the statute the narrowest possible interpretation. According to the majority opinion, the act applies only to lobbyists who enter into direct communication with members of Congress with respect to pending or proposed federal legislation and does not cover lobbyists who try to influence the legislative process indirectly by working through public opinion.

The Making of a Federal Statute

The cards are stacked against action by Congress. Bills can be pigeonholed as a result of committee or subcommittee inaction in either

92D CONGRESS
1ST SESSION

H. R. 9058

IN THE HOUSE OF REPRESENTATIVES

JUNE 10, 1971

Mr. MOORHEAD (for himself, Mr. ADDABBO, Mr. BINGHAM, Mr. BROWN of Michigan, Mr. CONYERS, Mr. DENT, Mr. DIGGS, Mr. FRASER, Mr. KOCH, Mr. HECHLER of West Virginia, Mr. LEGGETT, Mr. MATSUNAGA, Mr. MIKVA, Mr. PEPPER, Mr. PODELL, Mr. QUIE, Mr. REES, Mr. RODINO, Mr. ROSENTHAL, Mr. RYAN, and Mrs. SULLIVAN) introduced the following bill; which was referred to the Committee on Banking and Currency

A BILL

To amend the Housing and Urban Development Act of 1970 to provide a more effective approach to the problem of developing and maintaining a rational relationship between building codes and related regulatory requirements and building technology in the United States, and to facilitate urgently needed cost-saving innovations in the building industry, through the establishment of an appropriate nongovernmental instrument which can make definitive technical findings, ensure that the findings are made available to all sectors of the economy, public and private, and provide an effective method for encouraging and facilitating Federal, State, and local acceptance and use of such findings.

1   *Be it enacted by the Senate and House of Representa-*

2   *tives of the United States of America in Congress assembled,*

One of the thousands of bills introduced in each Congress. This particular bill was the 9,058th introduced in the House of Representatives during the Ninety-second Congress. It was introduced by Representative William Moorhead of Pennsylvania and cosponsored by twenty other House members. The bill was referred to the Committee on Banking and Currency, which in turn sent it to the Housing Subcommittee for consideration.

house, blocked by a negative vote in committee or subcommittee, or beaten by failure of the Rules Committee in the House to act. A negative vote by the Rules Committee or defeat of a proposed rule for the bill on the House floor, a successful motion in either house to send the bill back to committee, a negative vote on final passage by the House or Senate, failure of a conference committee to resolve differences between the houses, or rejection of the conference compromise on the floor of either house can each effectively kill a bill.[23] Those who want action must win at every stage of the process in both houses. Opponents, on the other hand, can lose at five stages, win at the sixth, and carry the day.

Drafting and Introduction of Bills

With very few exceptions any member of either house may introduce a *bill* dealing with any subject over which Congress has authority. A bill carries the prefix "HR" in the House, "S" in the Senate, and a number that indicates the order of its introduction. Bills enacted into law are also numbered in sequence. The Voting Rights Act of 1965, for example, is Public Law (or P.L.) 89–110, the 110th public law adopted by the Eighty-ninth Congress. The title *public law* is used to differentiate statutes of general application from *private laws,* such as an act to admit a particular person to the United States as an exception to current immigration rules.

The wording of a major statute is usually determined by many persons. Few congressional committees report bills in exactly the original language, which may have been suggested by an executive agency or interest group. On the other hand, almost no major legislation, even on taxes, is written in Congress without outside help or advice.

Committee Action on Bills

Almost all bills are referred to standing committees for consideration. The committee stage is the most crucial in the life of a bill since most proposals die there. Each bill is carefully scrutinized in committee, and often its final language is determined at this stage, either by the committee or subcommittee.

Committees usually hold public hearings on important bills, and these hearings may be impressive sessions at which members seek the advice and assistance of informed persons interested in the proposed legislation. On the other hand, they may be carefully staged productions in which a committee chairman seeks to confirm and give publicity to his own prejudices. Because the two houses accept so many committee recommendations without change, interest groups and lobbyists are very active at committee hearings.

After these public hearings, the committee or subcommittee meets to determine a bill's fate. Before passage of the Legislative Reorganiza-

tion Act of 1970, most of these sessions were closed to the public. Today, both houses impose strict limits on secret or "executive" sessions. If a committee views a legislative proposal favorably, it usually proceeds to "mark up" (revise) the bill and to prepare a formal report on it. Often the committee is split and submits both majority and minority reports to the floor.

Floor Action on Bills

A bill that has been reported by a committee is listed on a calendar, although its position there has little to do with the order in which it is actually considered. Instead, both houses have developed varying procedures for determining the order of business.

Under Senate rules, any senator is entitled to move that the Senate take up any bill that has been reported by committee. If the motion is adopted by a majority vote, the Senate turns to the bill in question. In practice such motions are usually offered by the majority leader, who acts after consultation with committee chairmen who have bills awaiting consideration.

Because of the size of its membership, the House uses a more complex system to determine the order of business. Very few bills can be called up by a simple motion from the floor. A few committees, such as Ways and Means, Appropriations, and Rules, may do so and are said to be "privileged" in this respect.

Important public bills are normally brought to the floor of the House by means of a *special rule* or order prepared by the Rules Committee and adopted by a majority vote of the House. It is standard procedure for the chairman of the committee reporting a bill to go to the Rules Committee to ask for such a rule. (Often the Rules Committee has refused a special rule to bills supported by committees and by the majority leadership.) If granted, the special rule usually fixes the time that consideration by the House shall begin, limits the period of debate, and guarantees that the bill will be brought to a final vote. Most special rules are "open," but a few are "closed" or "gag" rules, which limit or forbid offering amendments to that particular bill from the floor.

A bill may also be brought to the floor of the House by *discharging a committee* from further consideration of it. Discharging a committee requires that a majority of all House members sign a petition and that the House then approve the motion to discharge by a majority vote of those present. If the Rules Committee refuses to report a special order for a bill, the same discharge petition method can be used to force a House vote on the special order. This procedure is rarely successful, in part because of the influence of senior members of committees, who are able to take revenge by pigeonholing bills supported by those who sign a discharge petition.

Limitation of Congressional Debate

Under House rules, each member is entitled to speak for one hour on the subject under consideration, but this right means little in practice. First, it is usually in order for the member who has the floor to move to close debate. This motion must be voted on immediately. If it is supported by a majority, debate ends at once, and the bill or proposal is brought to a final vote. Furthermore, the House debates virtually all important measures while sitting as the *Committee of the Whole.** Here, debate is divided into two sections: a period of general debate on a bill and a period when the bill is read section by section for amendment. The length of the period of general debate is fixed in advance by the Rules Committee. In the second period, debate occurs under the so-called five-minute rule, by which five-minute speeches are in order for or against proposed amendments. Debate in the House is thus apt to be brief and lively. General debate on important bills may consume two or three days. Further debate under the five-minute rule may on occasion lengthen House consideration of a bill to a period of a week or more.

Under Senate rules, senators may speak as long as they please on any matter under consideration. It is this privilege plus that of a senator who has the floor to yield it temporarily to a colleague whom he chooses that allow a *filibuster*—a prolonged discussion by one or a few senators to prevent the majority from passing a bill.

*All 435 members serve on the Committee of the Whole. By sitting as the Committee of the Whole, the House is able to operate under rules that are designed to expedite business.

Opponents of unlimited debate argue that the filibuster enables a minority to frustrate the will of the majority. Defenders contend that unlimited debate protects a minority's right to present its views and so prevent hasty action. In fact, filibusters have defeated relatively few bills that would have been passed. Most casualties have been civil-rights bills; and the most ardent defenders of the filibuster traditionally have been southern conservatives, with northern liberals the most outspoken critics. But liberal senators who had repeatedly gone on record as favoring a change in Senate rules to curb unlimited debate filibustered unsuccessfully against the Communications Satellite bill in 1962. In the early 1970s, liberal filibusters killed federal aid for the development of a supersonic transport and legislation opposing school busing.

As the pressure of legislative business has mounted over the years, the Senate has been forced to use certain means of limiting debate:

Two-Speech Rule: No member may speak more than twice on a single subject on the same legislative day. By recessing, rather than adjourning, at the end of a day's session, the Senate can prolong a "legislative day" indefinitely, and thereby limit the amount of speaking that can be done on a single item of business.

Cloture Rule: In 1917, prior to American entry into World War I, the Senate adopted a specific rule to close debate as the result of a particularly unpopular filibuster against a proposal by President Wilson for arming American merchant ships. Under the present version of the rule, a vote of sixty senators closes debate on a pending measure. After cloture has been voted, no senator can speak for more than one hour on the measure and its pending amendments. In practice, cloture has been extremely difficult to invoke. Senators attempt to invoke it only in the face of an extensive filibuster against a highly controversial bill. Of 104 cloture votes between 1917 and 1975, the necessary vote was attained only twenty-four times.

Curtailment of Debate by Unanimous Consent Agreements: Debate on major bills is usually brought to a close in the Senate by unanimous consent that a final vote will be taken at a set hour. Debate is closed by unanimous consent as a matter of convenience where there is no real opposition to letting a bill come to a vote, particularly if the majority has allowed a reasonable time for debate.

Methods of Voting

Both House and Senate employ several methods of voting. The simplest and most common is a *voice vote,* in which the members in turn call out the yeas and nays and the presiding officer judges which side has prevailed. Any member who doubts the results can ask for a *rising,* or *division, vote* in which the two groups rise alternately and are counted. In the House only, one fifth of a quorum may request a *teller vote,* by which the two groups leave their seats, pass between tellers, and are counted. Finally, in both houses, one fifth of the members present may demand a *record vote,* in which the clerk calls the roll and members vote yea or nay. The House now has an electronic system that allow such roll calls in a matter of seconds.

Prior to passage of the Legislative Reorganization Act of 1970, teller votes in the House (and in the Committee of the Whole) were not recorded. As a result, the voting records of individual congressmen on amendments were not available. Often, congressmen used nonrecorded teller votes to conceal their position on an issue. As a House member explained:

A member can vote for any number of amendments which may cripple a water pollution bill or render ineffective a civil rights bill or fail to provide adequate funding for hospital construction or programs for the elderly, and then he can turn around on final passage and vote for the bill he has just voted to emasculate by amendment. While on record he can pose as a champion of environmental protection, of the elderly and of the sick, he has in fact voted against their very interests.[24]

In 1971, the first year under the new requirement that individual votes be recorded, participation in teller votes increased 90 percent. One of the most significant teller votes in 1971 was a 204–217 defeat for the Administration's request for funds for development of a supersonic transport. It was the first recorded vote on the SST in the House, which had approved a similar request the previous year in an unrecorded teller vote in which only 188 members participated.

Conference Committee Action on Bills

Most important public bills pass each house in a different version. These differences must be compromised if the bill is to become law. Where differences are slight, time short, or the bill unimportant, one house often accepts the version approved by the other. But if each house stands fast on its own version, it is necessary to use a *conference committee* to effect a compromise. The members of conference committees are usually drawn in a bipartisan fashion from among the more senior members of the standing committee in each house that originally considered the bill.

A conference committee is supposed to produce a bill that falls somewhere between the House and Senate versions. Sometimes, however, conference committees find it expedient to introduce new provisions into bills, even though that practice is a violation of congressional rules. Members of conference committees are also expected to defend their house's version in the negotiations. But this does not always occur, especially when the conferees do not sympathize with the legislation passed by their house.

To become law, a conference committee's proposal must be accepted as it stands by both houses, and no amendments may be proposed on the floor of either house. Either house, however, may reject a conference report and send a bill back to conference a second time, making clear that a particular change is required before it will accept the bill.

Final Hurdles

Following final affirmative action by both House and Senate, a bill is signed by the Speaker of the House and the President of the Senate, and then transmitted to the White House for the President's signature. The President may sign the bill, whereupon it becomes law. Or he may let it become law without his signature by doing nothing for ten days following congressional approval. But if Congress adjourns during that ten-day period (as often occurs because of the rush of legislation in the last days of a session), the bill is dead. Or, finally, the President may veto the bill. Congress in turn can override the President's veto by a two-thirds majority in each house. (The President's role is examined in greater detail in Chapter 12.)

Summary

Power is decentralized in Congress. Most of the work of the House and Senate is done in committees and subcommittees. Legislative leaders cannot enforce party discipline on most issues, although party affiliation has a strong influence on the behavior of most congressmen. Decentralized constituencies reinforce the independence of most congressmen. Because representatives and senators enjoy considerable freedom of action, they are more receptive to pressures of lobbyists than would be the case if the parties would effectively discipline their members. Recent reforms have further dispersed power by making committee chairmen accountable to party majorities for their posts. This decentralized environment makes positive action difficult. The existence of two houses, complex rules, highly independent committees, and crowded legislative agendas provide opponents with many opportunities to defeat proposals. Most bills—wise and foolish—never survive the run through the congressional gauntlet.

Selected Bibliography

THE AMERICAN ASSEMBLY, *The Congress and America's Future,* ed. David B. Truman (Englewood Cliffs, N.J.: Prentice-Hall, 1965). Perceptive essays by eight leading students of congressional behavior and national politics.

BAILEY, STEPHEN K., *Congress Makes a Law* (New York: Columbia University Press, 1950). A lively study of the enactment of the Employment Act of 1946.

——, *Congress in the Seventies* (New York: St. Martin's Press, 1970). An interpretative analysis which stresses the growing strength of centralizing forces in Congress in recent years.

BERMAN, DANIEL M., *In Congress Assembled* (New York: Crowell-Collier & Macmillan, Inc., 1964). A fine introduction to the national legislative process.

FENNO, RICHARD F., JR., *The Power of the Purse* (Boston: Little, Brown and Company, 1966). An exhaustive account of the political processes involved in congressional appropriations.

FROMAN, LEWIS A., JR., *The Congressional Process: Strategies, Rules, and Procedures* (Boston: Little, Brown and Company, 1967). An analysis of the effects of congressional organization and rules of procedure on public policy formulation.

GRIFFITH, ERNEST S., *Congress: Its Contemporary Role* (New York: New York University Press, 1951). A defense of congressional pluralism and an argument against the need for more party discipline in Congress by a former director of legislative reference in the Library of Congress.

GROSS, BERTRAM, *The Legislative Struggle: A Study in Social Combat* (New York: McGraw-Hill, Inc., 1953). A portrayal of the legislative process in terms of inter-group conflict.

JEWELL, MALCOLM E. and SAMUEL C. PATTERSON, *The Legislative Process in the United States* (New York: Random House, 1966). An extremely thorough comparative analysis of Congress and the state legislatures which synthesizes a great deal of contemporary research on legislative behavior.

MATTHEWS, DONALD R., *U.S. Senators and Their World* (Chapel Hill, N.C.: University of North Carolina Press, 1960). A detailed and well-written analysis of the formal and informal ways of the Senate.

MAYHEW, DAVID R., *Congress: The Electoral Connection* (New Haven, Conn.: Yale University Press, 1974). An incisive essay which argues that congressional behavior is best understood in terms of the congressman's constant quest for re-election.

MILBRATH, LESTER W., *The Washington Lobbyists* (Chicago, Ill.: Rand McNally and Company, 1963). An interesting analysis of the strategy and tactics of lobbyists, based on a series of interviews with both lobbyists and legislators.

ODEGARD, PETER H., *Pressure Politics: The Story of the Anti-Saloon League* (New York: Columbia University Press, 1928). A classic account of the efforts of one group to control the legislative process.

POLSBY, NELSON, ed., *Congressional Behavior* (New York: Random House, 1971). A stimulating selection of readings on behavior in the Congress, past and present.

REDMAN, ERIC, *The Dance of Legislation* (New York: Simon and Schuster, 1974). A fascinating account of Congress at work as seen by a bright young man just out of college serving on a senator's staff.

RIESELBACH, LEROY J., ed., *The Congressional System* (Belmont, Calif.: Wadsworth Publishing Co., 1970). A useful collection of readings organized around the theme of Congress as a social system.

STEINER, GILBERT Y., *The Congressional Conference Committee* (Urbana, Ill.: University of Illinois Press, 1951). A case study of this committee's operations from the Seventieth to the Eightieth Congress.

TRUMAN, DAVID, *The Congressional Party* (New York: John Wiley & Sons,

Inc., 1959). A case study of party leadership and cohesiveness in the Eighty-first Congress.

TURNER, JULIUS, *Party and Constituency: Pressures on Congress.* Revised edition by Edward V. Schneier, Jr. (Baltimore, Md.: The Johns Hopkins Press, 1970). A thorough revision of a pioneering work which sought to measure the influence of party and constituency factors on the voting behavior of members of the House of Representatives.

Part Five

The Presidency

Chapter 12

Presidential Leadership

BEFORE RICHARD NIXON, the presidency had become an almost sacred institution. Crisis after crisis in international and domestic affairs, the President's capacity and willingness to dramatize *his* solutions to those crises, and the development of swift and awesome weapons demanding equally swift and awesome decisions helped the power of the presidency expand to become at least as powerful as any political office on this planet. Presidential authority symbolized the strength of American character and of American arms. Regardless of party, the President had come to personify American government. He stamped his image on the country, whether that of the patrician dynamism of Franklin Roosevelt or John Kennedy, the patient integrity of Dwight Eisenhower, the homespun shrewdness of Harry Truman, or the sly manipulation of Lyndon Johnson.

In much the same way, Richard Nixon represented much that was wrong with America—and with human nature. Slick, glib, and unctuous, he was a man with no apparent moral standards beyond his own self-interest. His ambitions were grand, however, and his zeal tenacious. He disciplined himself to work doggedly for more than twenty years to achieve the presidency. But his ambitions were also shallow. He was willing to trade his own and his nation's honor for personal gain. Nixon, to be sure, had not been the first sinner in the White House. James Buchanan was a weakling, Ulysses Grant a drunk, Woodrow Wilson a racial bigot, Warren Harding a philandering fool, and Lyndon Johnson a harsh master who delighted in verbally lashing the hide of human dignity off his aides. But, whatever their personal failings, none of these earlier Presidents had cynically, systematically, and deliberately betrayed the integrity of his office.

Coming so soon after bitter public reactions against Johnson's tragic escalation of the war in Vietnam and his crude efforts at deception, revelation of Nixon's misdeeds left the prestige of the presidency in shambles. Even intellectuals, who since the New Deal had been chanting hymns of praise to the presidency as the hope of the American people, attacked the "imperial" power and corruption of that office.

When Gerald Ford came to the White House after Nixon's hasty resignation in August 1974, he faced an aroused Congress that was controlled by a Democratic majority determined to regain political dominance. A few months later, the midterm elections increased the Democrats' majority above the two-thirds mark in both houses. Notwithstanding these signs of great decline in presidential power, it quickly became obvious once again that effective American government must be presidential government. Congress can certainly frustrate a Chief Executive. It can formulate ideas for alternative policies that a President or his successors might adopt. It can even play creatively around the edges of policy. But, for all the reasons detailed in Chapter 10 and 11, Congress simply cannot lead the nation in a sustained fashion.

Like the United States, the presidency has survived the scandal of

Richard Nixon. This chapter concentrates on the powers of the presidency and the opportunities for leadership that those powers provide. We shall look first at the way in which the office is shaped and reshaped by the personal style of each "man in the White House" and then systematically examine presidential power.

Presidential Styles

Strong versus Weak Presidents

In the abstract, if one were interested in presidential power it might seem that one should talk first about sources of, limitations on, and instruments of the President's authority and only afterward discuss ways in which various Presidents have tried to maximize their advantages and minimize their disadvantages. But the presidency is such a personal office that one cannot speak intelligently about it without first fully understanding that the character, ambition, skill, and, not least, the vision of the incumbent are critical elements.

We might range all American Presidents along a spectrum of attitudes toward their office. At one extreme would be the "literalists."[1] Men like William Howard Taft, Warren Harding, and Calvin Coolidge viewed the presidency as a place of rest and repose. They saw carrying out congressional policies as the President's main function. Any positive presidential action had to be justified by a clear constitutional command. As Taft wrote:

The true view of the Executive functions is . . . that the President can exercise no power which cannot be fairly and reasonable traced to some specific grant of power or justly implied and included within such express grant as proper and necessary to its exercise. Such specific grant must be either in the Federal Constitution or in an act of Congress passed in pursuance thereof. There is no undefined residuum of power which he can exercise because it seems to him to be in the public interest.[2]

At the other end of the spectrum have been "strong" Presidents like Jackson, Lincoln, both Roosevelts, and Woodrow Wilson. They have thought of the presidency as the center of a tornado of activity, an ideal vantage point from which to lead the nation. Theodore Roosevelt summed up the outlook of these men:

My view was that . . . every executive officer in high position was a steward of the people bound actively and affirmatively to do all he could for the people. . . . I declined to adopt the view that what was imperatively necessary for the Nation could not be done by the President unless he could find some specific authorization to do it. My belief was that it was not only his right but his duty to do anything that the needs of the Nation demanded unless such action was forbidden by the Constitution or by the laws.[3]

Most Presidents do not fall so neatly at one extreme or the other. Many sometimes behave more like literalists, sometimes more like strong Presidents. But it is becoming less and less probable that the kind of role outlined by Taft remains a viable option. The problems of modern society and the demands as well as opportunities for leadership are likely to be too pressing for anyone who enters the White House with a modest conception of his functions to follow Taft's model. One might even argue that the driving ambitions that propel most of those who seek the presidency are not apt to be satisfied with such a humble role, except perhaps as a tactical — and temporary — maneuver.

Recent Presidents

Among recent Presidents, only General Dwight D. Eisenhower might be described as an antipolitician. He achieved national support as a great war hero and grandfather figure. In his attempt to place the presidency "above partisan politics," Eisenhower emphasized tidy administrative arrangements, careful staff work, and reliance on assistants for information, ideas, analyses, and insights. His staff made the President's tasks, as he perceived them, more manageable. But, in the process "he became typically the last man in his office to know tangible details and the last to come to grips with acts of choice."[4]

Given the irrelevancy of much of Eisenhower's military experience to running the country, his insensitivity to political factors is understandable. He sought national unity, not personal power; disliking partisan politics, he saw his main task as reconciling differences among Americans and among nations. He preferred to moderate change rather than initiate it.[5]

John F. Kennedy, from the moment he assumed office, gave every indication of relishing his job. Reporters repeatedly described him as a bubbling source of fresh ideas and energy, the focus of action in American politics. Kennedy maintained an enormous command of information on a wide range of issues. Impatient with staff meetings and Cabinet sessions, he preferred to expose himself directly to free-flowing arguments. He rejected summaries of reports and avidly sought details. Eisenhower functioned like a chairman of the board, waiting for his staff to resolve controversies, but Kennedy tackled problems personally, seeking out information. Although individual assistants tended to concentrate more on some subjects than on others, they had few carefully staked-out areas of sole responsibility. They worked *with* the President, never *instead of* him.

As a result, Kennedy's presidency was not very neat, and failures of coordination were sometimes embarrassing. But, like Franklin Roosevelt, Kennedy believed that it was *his* job to make decisions; and to do so intelligently he needed to know as many of the facts as he could absorb. To obtain the information he needed, again like Franklin Roosevelt, he cut across normal administrative channels.

President Kennedy's style mixed energy, confidence, and good humor, all of which are evident as he recognizes a reporter at a 1963 news conference.

In style and temperament, Lyndon Johnson differed dramatically from both Kennedy and Eisenhower. But, like Kennedy, Johnson was a restless political leader. He had worked closely with Presidents and members of Congress for almost thirty years before coming to the White House and had acquired a reputation for political genius in his astute management of the Senate. As a country school teacher in the hills of Texas, as majority leader of the Senate, and then as President, he displayed cyclonic energy, great persuasiveness, and iron will. Whereas Kennedy had been dashing, even electric, in style, Johnson was flamboyant, emotional, and something of a ham. Yet with all his affectation of "cornpone," he was acutely sensitive to "the art of the possible" in domestic affairs. But in foreign policy in general and Vietnam in particular he showed none of his usual cunning and political skill. There he demonstrated much iron but little wisdom.

Johnson lacked the warmth of Eisenhower and the wit and grace of Kennedy. Rather, he was hard-driving, purposeful, willful, and often spiteful, able to beg a man one day to join his staff, the next day to dominate him, and the third day to humiliate him with vulgar sarcasm. Yet for all his meanness as a person, Johnson kept his attention on using power — and people — to achieve public policies. The many facets of the War against Poverty and the Civil Rights Acts of 1964, 1965, and 1968 were all *his* measures, parts of *his* grand design for a "Great Society." And he enjoyed the whole business. As he summed up his years in the White House: "If the Presidency can be said to have been employed and to have been enjoyed, I have employed it to the utmost, and I had enjoyed it to the limit."[6]

Nixon's presidency mirrored his own character, tight, somewhat paranoid, and erratic. He mixed considerable managerial talent, political shrewdness, and great energy with rigid control — that sometimes slipped embarrassingly — over his emotions. In foreign policy his record was more positive than in domestic affairs. He did, however slowly and bloodily, end American participation in Vietnam, establish relations with Mainland China, and lessen tensions with the Soviet Union. In domestic affairs his presidency was much less successful. Despite new directions in revenue sharing and environmental protection, his primary concern was keeping himself in power at any price. His style was heavily sanctimonious, interspersed with occasional slashing attacks on the intelligence, integrity, and patriotism of those who refused to accept his hyperbolic rhetoric as eternal truth. Nixon tended to make policy in secret and to reveal decisions in surprise announcements that stressed their "historic" importance and originality.

Part of the explanation for Nixon's erratic style lay in his need for power (a need he shared with most modern Presidents), but part can also be found in other facets of his personality.[7] Essentially an introvert, he preferred quiet meditation to free-wheeling debates about policy. To keep himself insulated — many who supposedly worked for him thought "isolated" a more accurate description — he gave his top aides licenses to act more as Assistant Presidents than as presidential assistants. Not only did they apparently make many decisions themselves, but much to the annoyance of legislators as well as executive officials, they also determined who could see or speak to the President. In effect, Nixon's lieutenants exercised precisely the kind of control over his sources of information — and so his choices — that the Roosevelts, Truman, Kennedy, and Johnson had so carefully avoided.

Gerald Ford's simplicity etched a striking contrast to Johnson's guile and Nixon's duplicity. Personally honest and outgoing, Ford made no pretense of being an intellectual like Kennedy, a dynamic leader like Johnson or either of the Roosevelts, or a self-styled world leader like Nixon. Ideologically a conservative, he wanted to cool both anger against the presidency and demands for governmental action to solve domestic problems. Somewhat accident prone, his habit of stumbling over obstacles or bumping into doors made him the butt of many jokes, but the humor was more sympathetic than cruel.

Ford's apparent directness and simplicity concealed the fact that he was an able manipulator of men. He was ill at ease with ideas, but his long tenure in the House of Representatives had taught him how to deal effectively with people. That legislative background brought him to the White House with a determination to heal the wounds that Nixon had inflicted on Congress. But within a few months Ford had his own disagreements: his frequent use of the veto relit the inevitable coals of presidential-congressional tensions, although with nothing like the intensity that had burned during the Nixon administration.

Personal Style and Presidential Power

In a formal, constitutional sense, the authority of the presidency has remained pretty much constant from Washington to Carter, but in another sense the office has changed markedly from one man to another. The presidency of Andrew Jackson was simply not the office he had taken over from John Quincy Adams any more than that of Lincoln was the same as Buchanan's, or Franklin Roosevelt's that of Herbert Hoover.

Thus the first source of presidential power is the President himself: his peculiar skills and the ideas that he has about his own roles and those of his staff, of Congress, of the courts, and his notion of what is good for the country and his own position in history. The presidency at any given moment is in large part the creature of the political vision of its temporary possessor. The other sources of his power come either from grants in the Constitution or from less formal practices that have built up around the institution of the presidency. It is to these that we now turn.

Sources of Presidential Power

Most of the President's work, Harry Truman liked to say, consists of "trying to persuade people to do the things that they ought to have sense to do without my persuading them."[8] A President's judgment about what others should do may not always be correct, but Truman was certainly right in stressing that the power of the President, in national as well as international politics, is based on persuasion rather than command. In domestic affairs, both state and national legislators, as well as governors, mayors, and a host of other officials, have independent electoral bases, and federal judges have virtual life tenure. Thus, there are few people outside the executive branch whom the President may command, and even there he may have problems. In dealing with foreign nations, the need to rely on persuasion is obvious. Threats of force, like Kennedy's in dealing with Soviet missiles in Cuba, or uses of force, like bombing North Vietnam, are typically designed to compel an opponent to negotiate rather than to obliterate him.

The unique constitutional and political position of the President allows him to play many different roles, and in each role he may exercise different kinds of persuasion. But two facts must be kept in mind when looking at these roles as sources of power and opportunities for leadership. First, the President "plays every 'role,' wears every 'hat' at once. Whatever he may do in one role is by definition done in all. . . . He is one man, not many."[9] Second, in no one role or combinations of roles is the President sure of exercising effective persuasion. Even as canny a man as Lyndon Johnson may end in tragedy. Each facet of the presidency presents the incumbent with an opportunity — and in another sense, a menace — but never a guarantee.

Party Leader

When a candidate for the presidential office receives the nomination, he becomes head of his party. Whether he becomes the party's leader as well as its head depends on his ability. But without his party's support he cannot be elected or, after election, effectively perform his duties. Because American parties are loose coalitions of state and local factions, they cannot be easily directed by the President or anyone else. If he is a strong vote-getter, state and local leaders may feel indebted to him for helping them stay in power. As often as not, however, these leaders boast of *their* achievement in electing the President. If he is to be at all successful, a President as party leader must use charm, patience, patronage, and federal funds to weld these factions into some reasonable facsimile of a political organization.

Chief of State

The President is the representative of the entire nation as well as party. He symbolizes the government of the United States. Like the British monarch, he reigns; like the British prime minister and cabinet, he governs. Thus, when he thinks it necessary, the President can try to rise above partisan politics and claim authority to lead in the name of America, gathering to himself all the emotions aroused by appeals to patriotism. It is very difficult for any American to ignore a President who says that the national interest requires a certain policy. A member of Congress or a private citizen may not necessarily be convinced by the President's logic, but very probably he or she will listen attentively and respectfully.

Chief Legislator

The Constitution makes the President part of the legislative process. Article II instructs him to "give the Congress information of the state of the Union" and to "recommend to their consideration such measures as he shall judge necessary and expedient." In addition, he can

The ritual of inauguration symbolizes the President's role as chief of state and representative of the entire nation. Except in the case of re-elected Presidents, inauguration also marks the peaceful transfer of power from one administration to another, as when Franklin Roosevelt succeeded Herbert Hoover (at the far right in the first row), Roosevelt's bitter foe in the critical 1932 election.

call Congress into special session to act on his recommendations and adjourn a session if the two houses cannot agree on a date. Furthermore, he may veto bills that he does not like. These formal grants of authority and the diffusion of power within Congress reinforce the President's influence over legislation.

At least as important as these factors is the President's access to mass media of communications. The presidency is, in Teddy Roosevelt's words, a "bully pulpit" from which a man may preach to the nation and the world. The President, as Chapters 10 and 11 said, has the legislative initiative. He can set the agenda of Congress because he can set the political agenda for the nation. If he has the skill and courage, he can, as Lyndon Johnson phrased it, put "Congress' feet to the fire" by stirring up public opinion.[10] Presidents of this century, especially Franklin Roosevelt and Lyndon Johnson, have dramatized their role as legislative leader, and Thomas Jefferson still stands out as one of the most effective Presidents in this respect.

Chief Administrator

Article II of the Constitution charges the President "to take care that the laws be faithfully executed." The vague language of many statutes increases that burden, but it also increases the President's discretion and so his power. As a means of compromise or as the only feasible way of coping with a complex problem, legislators often choose general rather than specific phrasing, leaving final resolution of difficulties to administrators, judges, or future legislators. And a President can read much policy — *his* policy — into broad statutory language.

Translating law — vague or specific — from statute books into rules of real life requires sets of enormous administrative apparatuses. Later in this chapter and in the next, we discuss some of the President's difficulties in dealing with the vast federal bureaucracy. Here we note only that, despite existence of a merit system in the career civil service, the President can appoint — usually subject to the approval of the Senate — several thousand people at the top ranks of executive agencies. Skillful use of this authority in selecting people who will serve him loyally and ably can materially enhance his power to lead, just as can deft use of the discretion allowed by vague or general statutory language.

Chief Diplomat

The Constitution makes the President the principal officer in foreign affairs, although in some respects he shares authority with Congress. The President alone receives ambassadors and thus "recognizes" foreign governments. With "the advice and consent of the Senate" he appoints American ambassadors and top-level State Department officials. Only the President or his agents can communicate with other governments in the name of the United States. Only the President or his agents can negotiate treaties or other international agreements, although to become binding a treaty must be approved by a two-thirds vote of the Senate. In addition, to become fully effective some treaties need to be supplemented by legislation, such as an appropriation, that must be passed by both houses of Congress.

Presidential authority has been enhanced by judicial interpretations of the Constitution that have decreed that the conduct of foreign affairs is a virtual federal monopoly. The authority of the federal government in international politics, the Supreme Court has ruled, is complete, limited neither to those powers specifically listed or implied in the Constitution nor by authority reserved to the states.[11] As Edward S. Corwin once remarked, power over foreign affairs is inherent in the federal government in the sense that it "owes its existence to the fact that the American people are a sovereign entity at international law."[12]

On occasion, the Justices have also spoken glowingly about the President's authority in foreign policy. In 1936, for instance, a unanimous Court waxed lyrical about "the very delicate, plenary and exclusive power of the President as the sole organ of the Federal government in the field of international relations — a power which does not require for its exercise an act of Congress."[13] On other occasions, the Court has held that the President's conduct of foreign policy is subject to congressional restraints.[14] But the President's ability to act swiftly and his access to secret information give him enormous advantages over Congress in this area of policy making.

Personal diplomacy has become an increasingly important source of presidential power and visibility in the twentieth century. In February 1972, President Richard Nixon met with Premier Chou En-lai in Peking during a presidential visit which marked the end of a quarter century of hostility in the relations between the United States and the People's Republic of China.

Commander in Chief

Closely related to the President's diplomatic power is his designation by the Constitution as "commander in chief" of the armed forces of the United States. As part of their fracturing of power among the various branches of government, the framers gave to Congress authority to declare war and to the President responsibility for the way a war is fought. Indeed, Presidents from Washington to Ford interpreted their authority as permitting them to commit American forces to combat without any congressional declaration of war. (We discuss later in this chapter some of the problems such a claim raises.)

The way a President plays his role as commander in chief can have a significant impact on domestic politics. Increased military spending can generate inflation. New defense priorities can force cutbacks in peaceful programs, even much needed programs. A decision to fight an undeclared war as in Korea or Vietnam can also drastically change a President's popularity at home and affect his ability to push measures through Congress or to carry out existing programs. The saddest case in point is the way the war in Vietnam blasted Lyndon Johnson's plans to build a Great Society that would conquer poverty and racial discrimination. Lesser decisions, such as hiring and firing professional soldiers, can change a President's standing with Congress or the electorate, as Lincoln found out when he shuffled generals during the Civil War and Truman when he dismissed the legendary General Douglas MacArthur during the Korean conflict.

As commander in chief, the President may make another, very different kind of impact on domestic affairs. Section 4 of Article IV of the

Constitution directs the national government to protect each state "on application of the legislature, or the executive (when the legislature cannot be convened), against domestic violence." Congress has authorized the President to use federal forces, including the National Guard, in discharging this obligation. It was on this authority that Lyndon Johnson in 1967, at the request of the governor, sent troops into Detroit to help put down race riots. Congress also has provided for use of troops when enforcement of federal laws by ordinary judicial proceedings is, in the President's judgment, impracticable. President Eisenhower used this latter authorization in 1957 to dispatch troops to Little Rock, Arkansas, and President Kennedy in 1962 to send troops into Mississippi to enforce federal court decisions ordering school desegregation.

The President's responsibility to "take care that the laws be faithfully executed" also carries with it authority to use federal troops when federal property or activities are endangered. In its most drastic form, use of military power within the United States means establishment of martial law — replacement of civil law and civilian courts by military law enforced by military tribunals. Such a suspension of civil government must be authorized by Congress and is valid only, the Constitution stipulates, when the United States is invaded or a rebellion is in progress.

Limitations on Presidential Power

The President and Public Opinion

When a President wants to have his policies accepted and put into operation, he must persuade large segments of the voting public, a working majority of Congress, executive officials, and, often, many state officers. All can limit his effectiveness. He must also consider judicial opinions, for in very different ways federal judges may also block attainment of presidential goals.

In dealing with other public officials, a President's professional reputation for having both the ability and the desire to make the most of his position is crucial. So too is the President's prestige — what other political leaders believe the general public thinks about the President. Although voters can defeat the President or his party only at election time, their opinions, at least what politicians perceive to be their opinions, can ignite or extinguish enthusiasm in Washington or in state capitals, for a President's plans. Many legislators are as reluctant to support an unpopular President's programs as they are to oppose the proposals of a popular Chief Executive. Administrative officers are also often sensitive to fluctuations in both congressional and popular opinion. Thus public opinion, which can be a whip the President can

Instantaneous access to the press is one of the President's many advantages in seeking to mold public opinion. In the photo, President Lyndon Johnson has called reporters into the Oval Office to relate his version of the Gulf of Tonkin incident, a naval action in 1964 which contributed heavily to the massive American intervention in Vietnam.

crack against Congress, can snap back and coil around an unskilled user.

The President and Congress: Checks and Needs

Congress, like public opinion, poses major checks on presidential power. A President needs Congress to pass new legislation, to modify existing statutes, and, most of all, to appropriate money to carry out his policies. To the extent that Congress refuses to perform such acts, it restricts presidential power. More positively, Congress can harass the President by adopting, perhaps over his veto, policies that he opposes. The reasons for presidential-congressional friction are varied.

First, conflict is built into a system of shared powers. The purpose of this constitutional arrangement, as Chapter 4 pointed out, is to check the power and ambition of one group of officials by the power and ambition of another group so that no one person, faction, or institution can obtain a monopoly of political authority. The system works well in that its overlapping grants of authority do generate suspicion and antagonism among the three branches. Whether the President is a Democrat or a Republican, to all senators and representatives he is to some extent a dangerous rival.

Second, the President and members of Congress are elected by very different constituencies. Chosen in a national election with the support of 40 million or more voters, a President naturally tends to think in terms of a grand strategy of national policy. A senator or representative, on the other hand, is chosen by a single state or district and must necessarily be sensitive to more parochial demands. Indeed, a legislator is likely to be turned out of office if he or she persistently supports national interests to the neglect of widespread local concerns.

Third, not only do constituencies differ, but so do responsibilities and perspectives. While a flood in central Pennsylvania may seem catastrophic to a congressman from that district, it may seem rather minor to a President trying to negotiate an agreement with the Soviet Union to limit nuclear weapons. Similarly, a President's requests for new federal programs for big cities may look to a senator from Wyoming or Idaho like just another give-away of taxpayers' dollars.

Complicating all presidential-congressional relations is the fact that often Congress is not a single entity. As a former presidential adviser put it:

A President does not face anything so simple as *the* Congress: such a cohesive assembly does not exist. Instead, he must confront a confounding array of Senate and House committees and subcommittees—each clutching its proud prerogatives and special responsibilities, all responding to chairmen as personally varied as the nation's Congressional districts in their presumptions and procedures.[15]

The growth of over-all executive power in this century has displeased many legislators, and one might suspect that as a result Congress would easily and frequently stymie the President completely. Certainly it does frustrate the President, yet less often than one might predict simply by looking at formal relations. In fact, the needs are mutual. Legislators often need what the President can give: his influence on other congressmen to vote for their bills; his signature on legislation that helps their constituents; his power to make useful appointments; or his support in campaigns for re-election. Thus the relationship between congressmen and the President is hardly simple. Despite deep differences, they need each other, especially if they are members of the same party. If either is to accomplish any policy goal other than stagnation, there must be some cooperation.

In such situations, the most likely outcome is negotiation and compromise. At times, especially if the White House and Congress are controlled by different parties, relations may verge on all-out war, as happened in 1973–74 when a Democratic majority in Congress, with the help of a sizable number of Republicans, revolted against Nixon's leadership. At other times, a weak President like Warren Harding, untroubled by personal ambition or ideas about policy, may enjoy quite chummy relations with Congress. At still other times, a strong President may dominate Congress, the extreme cases being Franklin Roosevelt in 1933–34 and Lyndon Johnson in 1964–66. Periods of total war, honeymoon, and domination have, however, usually been short. More often there is the give and take of bargaining, sometimes expressed, sometimes tacit. And as Lyndon Johnson once remarked: "I've never seen a Congress that didn't eventually take the measure of the President it was dealing with."[16] "Eventually," however, can be a long time; and Johnson's own legislative record in domestic affairs demonstrates that a President can accomplish a great deal before being stalemated.

The President and Congress: Impeachment

The Constitution creates an additional check on the President — and on federal judges as well — by allowing Congress to impeach and remove officials from office. This weapon is powerful but seldom used. Indeed, after the Senate in 1805 failed to convict Justice Samuel Chase, Thomas Jefferson called impeachment "a scarecrow." As a general description, that was only a slight exaggeration. Specifically, it would be difficult to imagine a person more clearly guilty than Chase. He had used his power as a judge — in those days Supreme Court Justices spent much of their time riding around the country sitting as trial judges — to treat with scandalous unfairness any lawyer or other person who appeared before him in court and disagreed with his conservative politics. Over all, from 1789 to the present, only twelve federal officials have been impeached (nine of them judges) and only four (all judges) convicted.*

If one speaks about the Presidency itself, for much of American history Jefferson appeared to be guilty of understatement. Growth of political parties and the normal state of affairs in which the same party controlled both Congress and the White House made impeachment an extraordinarily unlikely event. In fact, until Richard Nixon's troubles in 1974, Andrew Johnson had been the only President to be impeached, and he had been acquitted. Nixon was to learn to his sorrow, however, that, like ghosts, scarecrows sometimes walk and even slay.

The Constitution speaks with deceptive simplicity about impeachment. Article II states that:

The President, Vice-President and all civil officers of the United States, shall be removed from office on impeachment for, and conviction of, treason, bribery, or other high crimes and misdemeanors.

But nowhere does the Constitution define "high crimes and misdemeanors." From the time of Jefferson through Gerald Ford's attack on Justice William O. Douglas in 1970, some legislators have argued that impeachment need imply no more than that the group in control of Congress wants to take a public office from one person and give it to

*These figures somewhat underestimate the effectiveness of impeachment. At least seventeen judges resigned during impeachment proceedings and a large number of officials have left office at the first serious threat of such action. See Raoul Berger, *Impeachment: The Constitutional Problems* (Cambridge, Mass.: Harvard University Press, 1973), p. 166, and literature cited.

another. The House of Representatives, however, has taken the narrower view that an impeachable offense includes only crimes serious under ordinary law.

Article I of the Constitution gives the House sole power to impeach. Individual representatives introduce resolutions for impeachment as they do other proposals, and these resolutions go to the Committee on the Judiciary. Most of them, like that to impeach Chief Justice Earl Warren for writing the Court's opinion in the School Segregation Cases, are silly and die in the committee's files. If, however, the committee takes the charges seriously, it holds hearings much as it would for any complex bill, except that the procedures are likely to be much more formal and the "accused" given many of the rights he or she would receive in a court. At the conclusion of hearings and deliberations, the committee reports its recommendations (with minority views, if any) to the House. If the committee's recommendation is to impeach, the House debates and votes on the question. A simple majority is sufficient to impeach—to accuse formally.

If the resolution passes, the Senate then sits as a court and proceeds much as any criminal court would. The impeached official is represented by counsel (as he or she was in the proceedings in the House), and one or more members of the House act as prosecutors (officially called *managers*). Both sides may make opening and closing statements, call, examine, and cross examine witnesses, and present documentary evidence. The Senate's rules provide that to pose a question an individual senator must submit it in writing to the presiding officer, who shall ask it. When the President or Vice President is on trial, the Chief Justice of the United States presides, otherwise the Vice President or the president pro tempore if there is no Vice President. A two-thirds vote is required to convict.

Punishment can extend no further than removal from office and a ban against ever again holding federal office. But the Constitution specifically states that conviction and punishment upon impeachment does not bar trial and additional punishment in regular criminal courts. The President's power to pardon—which reaches all other federal offenses, past, present, and possibly even future—does not extend to conviction upon impeachment, lest he pardon himself or his cronies. Whether there can be any judicial review of impeachment proceedings remains an unsettled and fascinating question.

The President and Congress: Foreign and Military Affairs

Congress has a number of means of checking the President's power in foreign affairs. By refusing to consent to treaties and appointments of ambassadors and other officials, the Senate can frustrate the President's policies, as can both houses when determining appropriations and setting the size and composition of the armed forces. Historically, however, Congress has not restricted presidential power in foreign pol-

"Why do I still think Presidents
are above the law? Because one told me so . . ."

icy nearly as much or as consistently as in domestic affairs. The needs
for secrecy and speed in international relations, although often exag-
gerated, are real; and Congress finds it difficult to act with dispatch and
impossible to keep secrets. Moreover, constituents are apt to put far
less pressure on legislators to intervene in foreign than in domestic
affairs.

As did George Washington, some Presidents have taken seriously
the implicit constitutional command to share with Congress responsibility for foreign policy. Most recent Presidents, however, have taken a
sweeping view of their powers and have controlled not merely the day-
to-day conduct of foreign relations but also dealt summarily with crises
that threatened violence. In fact, in well over a hundred instances,
Presidents have ordered American forces into combat without an explicit congressional authorization, much less a declaration of war.

Almost always, a few senators or representatives have vigorously
protested these "usurpations" of legislative authority, but the typical
response of Congress as a whole has been sluggish inaction. Indeed, on
occasion, as when it adopted the Gulf of Tonkin Resolution in 1964,
approving "the determination of the President, as Commander in
Chief, to take all necessary measures to repel any armed attack against
the forces of the United States and to prevent further aggression,"
Congress has given the executive what amounts to a blank check.

On some occasions, however, one or both houses of Congress have
attempted to reassert authority over foreign policy. In 1848, for instance, the House of Representatives adopted a resolution branding

President Polk's military operations against Mexico as "unnecessarily and unconstitutionally begun." Several times during the 1950s both houses came close to proposing the so-called Bricker Amendment to the Constitution, a measure that would have restricted the scope of the treaty-making power and would also have subjected executive agreements* to senatorial approval. And during the late stages of the war in Vietnam, Congress rescinded the Gulf of Tonkin Resolution and prohibited use of American ground forces in Laos or Cambodia.

More generally, in the War Powers Act of 1973 Congress claimed that the Constitution gives the President authority to commit armed forces to combat only after "(1) a declaration of war, (2) a specific statutory authorization, or (3) a national emergency created by attack upon the United States, its territories or possessions, or its armed forces."

In that act Congress ordered the President to consult with Congress "in every possible instance" before sending troops into combat in an undeclared war. If the President does commit troops to combat without a declaration of war, the act requires him to submit a report to Congress within forty-eight hours. He must withdraw those forces, the statute says, when Congress so directs or within sixty days unless during that period Congress (1) declares war; (2) extends the time limit; or (3) is unable to meet because of a physical attack upon the United States.

The extent to which such legislation is constitutional is an open question. Certainly a test in court would be difficult to arrange. Perhaps more critical is how Congress could enforce such a policy once the President actually sent troops into combat. As the most ardent doves discovered during the Vietnamese war, it is very difficult for congressmen to vote to cut off supplies for the "brave young American men" who are being shot at, even if congressmen disapprove of the war.

The President and the Bureaucracy

Officials of administrative agencies may present a third set of limitations on presidential power. One might think that, as Chief Executive, the President would be able to command his subordinates in much the same way a general commands an army. In practice, however, bureaucracy "more nearly resembles the arena of international politics

---

*An executive agreement is a covenant between heads of government. In international law, it is binding on the President who signs it but not on his successors. As domestic law, however, it has much the same effect as a treaty. See *United States v. Belmont,* 301 U.S. 324 (1937); and *United States v. Pink,* 315 U.S. 203 (1942). According to one count, between 1945 and 1970 the United States publicly signed 368 treaties and 5,590 executive agreements. In addition, the United States was a party during that period to about 400 secret executive agreements. Emmet John Hughes, *The Living Presidency* (Baltimore: Penguin Books, 1974), p. 230.

than a group of disciplined subordinates responsible to the control of common superiors."[17] The next chapter talks in detail about the President's problems in leading *his* bureaucracy. Here we note only that the sheer magnitude of the President's work forces him to rely heavily on subordinates to carry out his policies. In turn, these officials must rely on their own subordinates to complete the tasks.

In effect, then, the same people who can contribute to the President's power by providing the means to execute his policies may also be able to frustrate policies with which they disagree. The President may have been unwise in his appointments, choosing some people who were not especially competent or not staunchly loyal to him and his goals. The possibility of doubtful loyalty is increased by the frequent necessity for a presidential candidate, or even a President, to trade appointments for votes or support on some specific issue before Congress. Moreover, the tradition of senatorial courtesy gives senators from the President's party a large—sometimes decisive—share in choosing federal officials who will serve in their states. Local U.S. Attorneys, for example, are the federal equivalent of district attorneys. They are in charge of most prosecutions in federal courts; and because they are apt to owe their position to a senator or a local politico, they may be quite unsympathetic to the President's goals.

In a related fashion, the merit system of appointment and promotion within the civil service may mean that at any particular time many of the men and women who run day-to-day governmental operations want policies that differ widely from those of the President and his immediate subordinates. Having considerable technical expertise and having seen Presidents and their assistants come and go do little to make career officials ready to surrender their professional judgment, much less their agency's interests. Even when they do not openly or consciously oppose the President, their lack of enthusiasm may hamper execution of a program.

Judges and State Officials

Once nominated and confirmed, federal judges are virtually immune to presidential control. And many executive policies face major tests before the courts. Judges may pass on the constitutionality of legislation or executive orders or interpret a statute to determine whether Congress in fact has authorized a particular course of action.

State officials may also check presidential policies. Given the federal nature of American political parties, state and local officials can help shape the reactions of senators, legislators, and even administrators to proposals from the Chief Executive. Moreover, again in part because of the federal nature of the party structure, the success of many supposedly national presidential programs depends on cooperation by state and local officials.

Most Presidents have been restrained by a sense of what is morally right and wrong in politics. As professional politicians, they have in most instances worked in public affairs for decades before coming to the White House, and to move ahead they have had to follow if not absorb at least a fair share of widely accepted norms about right and wrong, the so-called rules of the political game. Even when they do not personally believe in the prevailing standards of public morality, most Presidents, ambitious (even vain) men, have been deeply concerned about their place in history. The judgment of future generations thus usually acts as a powerful reinforcement to private conscience in restricting a President's choices. In an ironic way, it was a concern for history that hastened Nixon's downfall. His complicity in assorted felonies was proved beyond doubt by the record that he kept in the form of tapes of conversations in the White House.

Instruments of Persuasion

Despite these interlocking checks, a President is in a position of immense influence — provided he has the desire, energy, and ability to exploit his opportunities for persuasion. He has at his command a number of instruments, not the least of which are availability of evidence to support his arguments and use of reason to convince other people. In addition, he has the prestige of his office, the hopes of his party, easy access to mass media of communications, and certain specific constitutional grants such as the nominating power. He may also have personal charm and skill in human relations. None of these instruments is likely to be effective alone; but, if several of them are expertly combined, they may yield some measure of success.

To a certain extent, a President may be hampered by the Twenty-second Amendment, which stipulates that a President may not be elected for more than two terms.* In his second term, and especially in his last year, rival candidates for the nomination may attract considerable political support to themselves and away from the incumbent. But, if a President uses his instruments of persuasion to control his party's choice of a candidate, he may still retain much of his power during this bowing-out period. Furthermore, he may, if he is extraordinarily gifted, even increase his power during this time by persuading others that, with his own career done, he is acting only for the good of the nation. Whether or not members of his own party are convinced, they may be

---

*The amendment allows a person who succeeds to the presidency and serves for not more than two years to run twice for election on his own. If such a person serves an unexpired term of more than two years, he can run only once. Thus a person may serve not more than ten years as President.

willing to compromise with a President in such circumstances, because they, and not he, have to face the voters on *his* record.

Molding Public Opinion

With mass media at his disposal, the President has an unequaled opportunity to convince the public to approve his policies, to elect other officials who approve, or to pressure incumbents to cooperate with him. For important speeches he may preempt prime television and radio time, newspapers carry his remarks on their front pages, and magazines publish feature articles on him and his family. By displaying confidence, knowledge, and intellectual agility, an adroit President can do much to build up a favorable image not only with the general public but also with legislators and administrators.

Press conferences, allowing exchanges with reporters, can be especially valuable not only in nabbing the next day's headlines but in persuading journalists that the President knows what he is doing. Franklin Roosevelt was the first real master of this sort of exchange. John Kennedy took advantage of his quick wit by allowing television coverage of some of his conferences, a practice that later Presidents have continued with less but still some success. Any such triumphs, of course, are not merely the product of a President's intellect. Each conference is preceded by days of research by the White House staff to cope with, if not answer, questions that advisers think are most likely to be asked. Then come hard hours of briefing the President so that he may appear to be a spontaneous font of wisdom.

Influencing Congress: Formal Powers

Recommending legislation. To induce members of Congress to cooperate or at least compromise, a President has a number of instruments. First is his ability to recommend legislation and, in effect, to set the agenda of Congress. Article II of the Constitution instructs the President to "give the Congress information of the state of the Union" and to "recommend to their consideration such measures as he shall judge necessary and expedient." This power is most important because it gives the President the initiative in the legislative process. In addition, the President can call Congress into special session to act on his recommendations.

The veto. The President has another powerful weapon, the veto, that he can use both as a roadblock against unwanted legislation and as a prod to move congressmen to pass bills that he wants in the form that he wants. The Constitution is specific in its provisions: Every bill, order, resolution, or vote to which the concurrence of the Senate and the House of Representatives may be necessary (except a question of adjournment) shall be presented to the President of the United States for his approval or disapproval.*

The President has four choices when he receives a bill. The first and most obvious is to sign it, in which case the bill becomes law. He may also veto the bill and return it without his signature to the house where it originated. If each house repasses the bill by a two-thirds majority, it becomes law without the President's approval; otherwise the bill dies. Or he may let a bill remain on his desk for ten days without either signing it or returning it to Congress; in this case it becomes law without his signature. The fourth possibility is the so-called *pocket veto*. If during the ten-day period during which a bill may sit on the President's desk Congress ends its session and adjourns, the bill automatically dies if the President does not sign it. Because Congress tends to pass a great many bills during the closing days of a session, a President has extensive opportunity to employ this weapon.

Early Presidents used the veto very seldom. Until the time of the Civil War, they justified most vetoes on grounds of a bill's doubtful constitutionality. Some people even contended that this was the only valid reason for a veto. Since the Civil War, however, Presidents have far more often based their objections to a bill on its lack of wisdom.

Relatively few measures are ever repassed over a presidential veto.[18] Congress made no serious efforts to override any of Kennedy's or Johnson's vetoes, and even heavily Democratic Congresses overrode only 11 of Ford's 59 regular vetoes. The Constitution makes reconsideration mandatory, but this requirement is fulfilled by referring the bill to the standing committee that reported it to the house in which it originated.

Impoundment. The President cannot veto specific items in a bill (as can governors of some states). He must accept or reject a measure in its entirety. But some Presidents have claimed authority not to spend — to impound — funds appropriated by Congress, thus giving themselves an *item veto* as far as appropriations are concerned. And programs without money are unlikely to survive.

The constitutional authority of the President to impound funds is unclear. Taft's conception of the presidency would sternly deny such authority. On the other hand, Teddy Roosevelt's stewardship theory would just as firmly justify presidential refusal to spend money if he thought such action was in the public interest. The only time that the Supreme Court decided a case arising out of impoundment, the Justices restricted themselves to the narrow question whether in the Clean Waters Act of 1972 Congress had delegated to the President power to withhold funds. The Court unanimously agreed that Congress had

President Lyndon Johnson signs the Civil Rights Act of 1964 into law. The other signatures are those of the Speaker of the House of Representatives and the President Pro Tempore of the Senate.

made no such delegation,[19] but the Justices offered no views on the larger constitutional question, whether the President could act on his own authority.

Practical problems complicate the issue of impoundment. Most legislators would not want the President to spend money unnecessarily. Suppose, for example, Congress appropriated $10 billion for communications equipment for the armed services, and the Pentagon found that improved technology could provide even better equipment for $5 billion. A President who tried to force the manufacturer to accept $10 billion would surely incite screeches of congressional wrath. Because one can easily multiply such examples, congressmen are loath to require the President to spend all funds they appropriate. The real dispute comes over priorities. A President may believe that government must reduce spending or bring on disastrous inflation. And he may impose cuts on programs of which he disapproves (such as welfare) but not on others (such as purchases of military hardware), which he likes. Faced with that same choice, a majority of Congress may well have set precisely the opposite priorities.

An astute President may use a threat of impoundment just as he would a threat of veto. That is, he might allow it to be "understood" that if Congress passed a certain program, he would not carry it out. How effectively a President can use such tactics depends not only on his prestige, personal skills, control over his party, and his party's strength in Congress, but also on what more he wants from Congress.

The fundamental point is that, if important programs are involved, impoundment is certain to anger many if not most legislators. If the President has already achieved all or most of his principal legislative goals, he can shrug off such resentment. If, however, he is in the process of bargaining with congressional leaders and needs — or fears — congressional action, he must be very flexible.

Presidential spending power. Money is the lifeblood of governmental programs no less than of political campaigns, and according to Article II of the Constitution, "no money shall be drawn from the Treasury, but in consequence of appropriations made by law. . . ." On its face, this clause gives Congress complete control over what can be spent from the public purse, subject only, of course, to the President's veto. Chief Executives, however, have found some loopholes here.[20]

First of all, because of the complexities of governmental operations, Congress usually appropriates money in large lump sums to agencies or programs rather than specifying precise amounts to be spent for every purpose. The "understanding" among executive officials and appropriations subcommittees is that the money will in fact be spent for specific items spelled out in the President's budget and explained in testimony before Congress. Nevertheless, administrators sometimes take advantage of these broad grants to initiate programs that were never mentioned to Congress and occasionally programs that Congress specifically rejected.

Second, because of a need for secrecy in some phases of foreign and military policy, Congress normally gives the President certain blocks of money to be used at his discretion. And if he is imaginative, he can spend these funds in ways that help his programs. Because of the clandestine nature of the payments, monitoring either by Congress or its financial watchdog, the General Accounting Office, is very difficult.

Third, Congress also typically appropriates "contingency funds," especially for defense agencies, to meet emergencies or unforeseen major problems. The amounts involved can run into the hundreds of millions of dollars. Since there can be no exact definition of a "major" unforeseen problem or even of an emergency, the President and his subordinates have wide discretion. In 1973, for example, Nixon used $10 million of a contingency fund for disaster relief and national security to aid research on raising livestock in the Bahamas and less than $5 million to help victims of a catastrophic drought in Africa.

Additionally, a President may sometimes authorize an official to transfer funds given for one purpose to another. For example, to finance operations by American troops in Cambodia in 1970, Nixon used money that had been appropriated for economic and military aid to foreign nations. There is still on the statute books an old "feed and forage" law that allows the armed services to purchase needed supplies in the absence of an appropriation; in effect, Congress promises to appropriate the money once obligations are incurred. Presidents have also allowed agencies to use secret or contingency funds or unspent money from other accounts to begin projects and then explained to Congress the following year that unless the money to complete the project is forthcoming, the millions of dollars already spent will have been wasted.

Several of these techniques raise serious questions of breaches of faith with Congress, and a few raise questions of legality. But some executive discretion in using money is obviously necessary, especially in an era of rapidly changing technology. Thus the problems of presidential spending parallel those of impoundment. Congressmen simply cannot lay down fifteen to eighteen months in advance absolutely rigid rules specifying exactly how each dollar is to be spent. Historically, however, even when abuses have been flagrant, senators and congressmen have done little more than whine. On the whole, they have tended to be too lazy or too timid to challenge the President. In the aftermath of the war in Southeast Asia and the scandals of Watergate, Congress passed the Budget and Impoundment Control Act of 1974. It is an effort to tighten formal, legal controls over spending in the executive branch. But whether its actual effect will be to stop shrewd Presidents from continuing their art of picking Congress' purse remains to be seen.

Executive privilege. Congress needs information if it is to function intelligently, and often that information can be secured only from an executive agency. Thus, a President can sometimes stymie Congress by claiming "executive privilege," that is, authority to refuse to supply, or allow other executive officials to supply, information.

Presidents have sometimes justified such refusals on claims of "national security," or protecting the good names of innocent people, or safeguarding informants or spies whose safety would otherwise be endangered, or preserving the Chief Executive's ability to obtain candid advice — advice that would not be forthcoming were assistants not guaranteed confidentiality. More broadly, some Presidents have made a constitutional argument: In separating institutions, the Constitution makes the President independent of the legislature. Congress has no more "right" to learn about the President's information and his sources than he has a "right" to know what goes on in closed sessions of Congress or its committees or in conversations among individual legislators or between a legislator and his staff.

These arguments have convinced many Presidents since George Washington, and even senators and congressmen have often accepted them. On the other hand, early Presidents admitted, even while invoking the privilege, that Congress could override the claim. The Constitution itself makes no mention of executive privilege, and the scope of its legitimacy remains obscure. In ordering Richard Nixon to deliver to a special prosecutor tapes of certain conversations in the White House — and one should note that the conflict there was not specifically between Congress and the President — the Supreme Court implied the legitimacy of at least a limited privilege:

The President's need for complete candor and objectivity from advisers calls for great deference from the courts. However, when the privilege depends solely on the broad, undifferentiated claim of public interest in the confidentiality of such conversations, a confrontation with other values arises. Absent a claim to protect military, diplomatic, or sensitive national security secrets, we find it difficult to accept the argument that even the very important interest in confidentiality of Presidential communications is significantly diminished by production of such material for in camera* inspection with all the protection that a district court will be obliged to provide.[21]

Like impoundment, presidential invocation of executive privilege is almost wholly negative in effect. That is, its use is not likely to persuade Congress to act in the way the President wishes. On occasion a President may give up a claim of executive privilege or "un-impound" funds in exchange for congressional action. But usually the most he can hope for is to make it impossible for Congress to act at all. Because of the fuzzy nature of the constitutional question and the vital legislative need for information, use of executive privilege, like impoundment, may anger or even outrage many congressmen. Thus a President can use it freely only when he wants nothing and fears nothing from Congress.

Influencing Congress: Informal Means

To lead Congress a President has to use informal as well as formal means of persuasion. Most obviously, he may invoke party loyalty. While that loyalty may be a sometime thing for most senior legislators, it can tug at their self-interest more insistently than at their emotions. Even if their own re-election is certain, congressmen's abilities to influence appointments may vanish if their party does not win the presidency again. If their party does not retain control of Congress, their positions of leadership and committee chairmanships will go to other people.

Still, a President cannot depend on the weak, decentralized party structure to bridge the gap between the executive and legislative branches. Far more often than not, only by means of bipartisan majorities is the President able to get measures through Congress. Piecing these majorities together is delicate work. Thus, in dealing with members of the opposition as well as of his own party, a President must learn to be a consummate manipulator of his fellow politicos, alternately friendly and stern, now shrewd and calculating, now seemingly open and frank, by turns acting as suppliant and commander, flatterer and

*The term *in camera* means in closed session. Thus the judge would examine the papers in the privacy of his office and there decide which could be used in the courtroom and seen by both sides, the jurors, and eventually the public.

President Gerald Ford addresses a joint session of Congress in April 1975 in a futile effort to secure nearly $1 billion to prop up the collapsing government of South Vietnam.

sharp critic. As Lyndon Johnson recalled about his own presidency, "I pleaded. I reasoned. I argued. I urged. I warned."[22] And he also threatened and badgered.

To translate his legislative proposals into actual policy, a President has to weld congressmen into an effective team if he wants action — or play them off against each other if he wants inaction. His immediate goal is to persuade a working majority of senators and representatives that his program is good for the country, good for their constituents, and therefore good for themselves. For, as a former director of the Bureau of the Budget remarked, "Virtue is so much easier when duty and self-interest coincide."[23]

To ease the inevitable friction with senators and representatives, Presidents try to find ways of making friendly overtures. Harry Truman now and then appeared suddenly at the Capitol and modestly asked to eat lunch with some of his old colleagues; Dwight Eisenhower offered lunch at the White House to Republicans and Democrats alike. John F. Kennedy often extended the hospitality of a formal White House dinner with vintage wine, French cuisine, and music from the Marine band. Lyndon Johnson used the telephone to keep in touch with members of Congress at all hours of the day — and night — and his entertaining was more folksy than that of his recent predecessors.

It is doubtful that these efforts have often paid off directly in bills passed or not passed by Congress. But no President can afford to ignore friendly gestures. There are so many occasions when he must play the tough taskmaster that he must seize every opportunity to persuade legislators that he is a decent human being.

As we have seen, the President can sometimes swap with legislators. A promise of support for a congressman's pet bill, or a threat of presidential opposition to it, may produce support for the President's program. Frequently the President must bargain with congressmen about details, and one of the chief purposes of regular consultations between the President and congressional leaders is to determine whether the lines can be held fast for a presidential proposal or whether compromise is in order and if so how much.

Perhaps the most famous of the President's informal powers to influence Congress is patronage. Use of the appointing power to win over senators and representatives dates back to George Washington. Usually Presidents do not crudely offer to make a particular nomination if the congressman votes as the President wants. He is likely to use patronage more subtly as a means of cultivating friendly relations with legislators, thereby encouraging sympathetic consideration of his proposals. This kind of approach was illustrated in the special session of Congress in 1933 at which many of Roosevelt's New Deal measures were passed. The administration let it be understood that patronage would not be distributed until after the session. In this way, congressmen eager to control certain appointments were compelled to give favorable consideration to the President's legislative requests.

Patronage, however, is a two-edged sword. For one thing, an appointment that pleases one congressman may irritate other legislators as well as disappointed job seekers. Second, by trading patronage for congressional votes a President may be weakening his control over administration, because the appointees may feel a stronger loyalty to members of Congress than to the Chief Executive.

A promise of presidential support at the next election can be an effective instrument of persuasion. In extreme circumstances, the President may hint at political reprisals against uncooperative congressmen. But he must be wary of actually carrying out this threat. He cannot dissolve Congress and call a new election as can a prime minister. Even though a regular election may be near, if his quarrel is with members of his own party the President cannot very well ask for election of members of the opposition. To purge his party of dissidents he must go into state primaries and try to persuade party voters to replace them with new legislators who will be more loyal to him. Historically, this practice has not had great success.

Persuading the Bureaucracy

The following chapter examines in detail the President's relations with the federal bureaucracy. We note here only that the President can increase his influence, first, by exercising great care in his appointments. Neither personal loyalty, professional ability, nor political skill is sufficient in itself to make an administrator an especially useful subordinate. The President needs assistants who have a combination of these virtues. Second, the President can enhance his capacity to lead career officials by showing them that he understands the problems that his policies create and appreciates the difficulties of carrying them out. Third, congressmen, like the President, try to shape decisions of administrators, and the President's ability to protect the bureaucracy from congressional retaliation is critical to the way administrators will respond to competing demands from the White House and Capitol Hill.

Persuading Judges and State Officials

In dealing with state officials a President can use almost the same instruments and tactics that he employs with Congress—reason, prestige, publicity, personal charm, promises of campaign support, patronage, and old-fashioned bargaining. In contrast, a President has as little chance of charming judges into agreement as he does of overawing them with his prestige or with promises of patronage. Of course, since federal judges are not elected, campaign support is of no value to them, although a chance of promotion might be enticing to those on lower courts. Reasoned argument, usually presented by local U.S. Attorneys or the staff of the Department of Justice, is the instrument most often used in dealing with judges. But a President's nominating power can also be important, both in selecting people to run the solicitor general's office* and in choosing and promoting judges whose basic views tend to coincide with his own.

In addition, if courts hand down a decision or series of decisions that threaten his policy objectives, the President may deploy his instruments of persuasion on Congress to obtain some counteraction—perhaps a constitutional amendment, a more clearly worded statute, a change in the kind of cases federal courts can hear, or an increase in the number of judges. As a last resort, a President may refuse to enforce a court decision, as Lincoln declined to do during the Civil War when Chief Justice Roger B. Taney ordered a southern sympathizer released from a military prison.[24]

In influencing public opinion in general, a President may also influence judges because he creates a climate of opinion in which all citizens must live. "The great tides and currents which engulf the rest of men," Justice Benjamin Cardozo once wrote, "do not turn aside in their course and pass the judges by."[25]

Summary

This chapter has stressed the political nature of the presidency. Emphasis on the necessity of manipulation and maneuvering does not in

---

*The solicitor general works directly under the Attorney General and functions as the head of a team of lawyers who handle almost all federal cases before the U.S. Supreme Court. In addition to other duties that the President or the Attorney General may give him, the solicitor general and his staff usually decide which cases that the U.S. government has lost in lower courts should be appealed.

any way question the necessity of the President's having, or being receptive to, creative policy ideas that have great substantive merit. Rather, the point is that many other governmental officials, officials who have power to check the President, also have firm policy views of whose worth they are sincerely convinced. Faced with these conditions and armed with only a limited authority to command, the President must persuade, negotiate, bargain, and compromise if he wants to achieve a positive program. As James David Barber remarks, the presidency represents a contradiction in power, for the President, "like most actors in the political system, is dependent on his dependents, subject to his subjects, forever in the position of supplicant for renewal of his license to rule."[26]

Knowing what policies to pursue requires the vision of a statesman; putting those policies into actual operation requires the talents of a masterful politician. A successful President needs not only strength of character and a thorough understanding of the long-run needs of the nation but also professional skills, personal charm, a feel for shifting winds of public opinion, a delicate sense of timing, and that quality which in enemies we call ruthlessness and in friends total dedication. For a President must be able to use, drain, and discard other people to achieve national goals. He must be able to distinguish among what is worth fighting for to the bitter end, what is worth compromising on, and what is worth only capitulation. He must know when to move and when to wait, when to argue and when to agree, when to stand firm and when to compromise, when to reason and when to bargain, when to cajole and when to command. Without doubt, such paragons of virtue and intelligence are rare. The amazing thing is that some have made their way through the labyrinthine paths of American politics to the White House.

Selected Bibliography

BARBER, JAMES DAVID, *The Presidential Character: Predicting Performance in the White House* (Englewood Cliffs, N.J.: Prentice-Hall, Inc., 1972). An ambitious effort to develop tools of psychological analysis to explain, predict, and evaluate presidential performance.

BERGER, RAOUL, *Impeachment: The Constitutional Problems* (Cambridge, Mass.: Harvard University Press, 1973). A scholarly and detached study of an explosive political problem.

BLUM, JOHN M., *The Republican Roosevelt* (Cambridge, Mass.: Harvard University Press, 1954). A sparkling study of Theodore Roosevelt as President.

CORNWELL, ELMER E., JR., *Presidential Leadership of Public Opinion* (Bloomington, Ind.: Indiana University Press, 1965). The best study of the President as leader of public opinion.

CORWIN, EDWARD S., *The President: Office and Powers,* 4th ed. (New York:

New York University Press, 1957). The authoritative study of the presidency from a constitutional and legal perspective.

CRONIN, THOMAS E., *The State of the Presidency* (Boston: Little, Brown and Company, 1975). An effort to answer two questions: how can the presidency become a more efficient executive institution and how can it be made more accountable to the people? (Paperback.)

EVANS, ROWLAND, JR., and ROBERT D. NOVAK, *Lyndon B. Johnson: The Exercise of Power* (New York: The New American Library, 1966). A critical—and readable—analysis of Johnson by two veteran reporters.

FISHER, LOUIS, *Presidential Spending Power* (Princeton, N.J.: Princeton University Press, 1975). A careful examination of the ways in which Presidents have methodically picked Congress' purse. (Paperback.)

HUGHES, EMMET JOHN, *The Living Presidency: The Resources and Dilemmas of the American Presidential Office* (Baltimore, Md.: Penguin Books, 1974). A beautifully written, sweeping examination of the character of the Presidency from Washington to Nixon. (Paperback.)

JOHNSON, LYNDON BAINES, *The Vantage Point: Perspectives of the Presidency, 1963–1969* (New York: Holt, Rinehart, and Winston, Inc., 1971). Vintage LBJ. A gold mine of vinegary, delightfully opinionated, and egoistic reminiscenses of five years in the presidency.

KEARNS, DORIS, *Lyndon Johnson and the American Dream* (New York: Harper & Row, Publishers, 1976). A fascinating and controversial interpretation of Johnson the man and Johnson the President.

MALONE, DUMAS, *Jefferson the President: First Term, 1801–1805* (Boston: Little, Brown and Company, 1970); and *Jefferson the President: Second Term, 1805–1809* (Boston: Little, Brown and Company, 1974). The fourth and fifth volumes of the authoritative biography of Jefferson, focusing, as the titles indicate, on his years in the White House.

NEUSTADT, RICHARD E., *Presidential Power: The Politics of Leadership* (New York: John Wiley and Sons, Inc., 1960). A perceptive study that deals not with the presidency as an institution, not with its legal and constitutional position, nor with the politics of winning nomination and election, but rather with the President's problem of obtaining power for himself while holding office. (Paperback.)

SAFIRE, WILLIAM J., *Before the Fall: An Inside View of the Pre-Watergate White House* (Garden City, N.Y.: Doubleday & Company, 1975). A detailed and sympathetic account by one of Nixon's speechwriters.

SCHLESINGER, ARTHUR M., JR., *The Age of Roosevelt,* a three-volume history of the years preceding and during F.D.R.'s administrations: Vol. 1: *The Crisis of the Old Order;* Vol. 2: *The Coming of the New Deal;* Vol. 3: *The Politics of Upheaval* (Boston: Houghton Mifflin Company, 1957, 1959, 1960). A distinguished history, colorful and brilliant, illuminating an exciting era of ideas, events, and personalities.

———, *A Thousand Days* (Boston: Houghton Mifflin Company, 1965). A controversial but lively insider's analysis of Kennedy's presidency.

———, *The Imperial Presidency* (New York: Popular Library, 1973). A scathing indictment of presidential power by a man who helped it grow.

SHERWOOD, ROBERT, *Roosevelt and Hopkins* (New York: Harper & Row, 1948). An extraordinarily rich biographical study of the Roosevelt administration.

SORENSEN, THEODORE C., *Kennedy* (New York: Harper & Row, 1965). A well-written and thoroughly detailed account of Kennedy as a senator and President, written by his former Special Counsel.

WILDAVSKY, AARON, ed., *The Presidency* (Chicago: Rand McNally, Inc., 1969). A useful collection of articles on many aspects of the office.

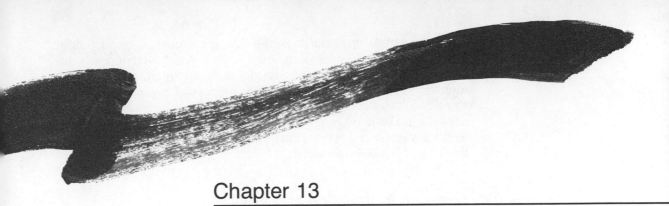

Chapter 13

The President and the Executive Branch

Securing Information and Advice

Executing Public Policy

Summary

Selected Bibliography

THE PRECEDING CHAPTER looked at the presidency as an institution that offers a bundle of opportunities for political leadership and discussed ways in which various Presidents have exploited these opportunities. This chapter focuses on two aspects of presidential leadership: how the President obtains the information and advice that he needs to make intelligent decisions and how he can exercise control over the vast federal bureaucracy that is supposed to carry out policies that he and Congress formulate.

Securing Information and Advice

Before being able to recommend policies to Congress or to carry out policies under his own authority, a President needs a great deal of information as well as advice about what that information means in practical terms. No matter how intelligent and widely read he is, a President cannot be an expert, nor does he have time to become an expert, on all the problems that confront the nation. Neither could any small group of people provide the knowledge to deal with such a variety of problems as how to gather and evaluate military intelligence about Soviet strategic planning, the implications of changes in personnel within the Chinese government, the causes of tensions in the Middle East, how most effectively to equip and deploy American armed forces, or ways of helping friendly countries like Britain weather their financial straits. Similarly in domestic affairs, a President needs a comparable range of expert advice in deciding how to dispose safely of nuclear wastes, coordinate medical research, maintain prosperity while curbing inflation, manage a huge and decentralized political party, carry on congenial relations with congressional leaders while pushing them to adopt his legislative program, find able executives for government, unearth bright and honest lawyers for federal judgeships, settle feuds between officials in different bureaucracies, and conduct press conferences so as to convey an image of informed, forceful leadership.

Obviously a President has to surround himself not just with a few but with a whole array of advisers. We shall divide these people—and the institutions they head—into two categories, *formal* and *informal advisers*. Formal advisers are those whom a statute or executive order designates as presidential advisers; informal advisers are those whom the President chooses without regard to such legalistic criteria.

Formal Advisers: The Cabinet and Its Meetings[1]

In most constitutional democracies the prime minister and his cabinet are chosen by and are immediately responsible to parliament. In those countries, there is, as in the United States, a great deal of informal discussion among top officials; but the cabinet meeting is the formal institutional setting where the prime minster calls for discussion of almost all important questions of policy. At the end a vote is taken. By definition, an effective prime minister leads rather than follows his ministers, and he may on occasion go against the collective advice of his cabinet. But to do so is to run a grave risk of a rash of resignations by those ministers, collapse of his support in parliament, and the fall of his government.

In the United States, the situation is very different. The President is not responsible to Congress, nor, at least in a constitutional sense, are cabinet members, called *Secretaries* (except for the Attorney General, who heads the Department of Justice). Instead, they are supposed to be the President's men (or women). To appoint them, he needs the consent of the Senate, but it is normal for nominees to the cabinet to win easy approval. As a matter of constitutional law, the President can dismiss any Secretary when he wishes. But, we have hinted earlier and shall explain later, a President does not, as a practical matter, always have complete freedom to hire and fire cabinet officials. Thus the pressures on him to consult with his cabinet are exerted by prudence, not the Constitution.

How individual cabinet members run their particular departments is of vital concern to the President, for ultimately he bears responsibility for whatever goes on in the executive branch. Thus a President may keep in very close touch with each Secretary. But Presidents seldom seek the *collective* advice of the cabinet and are not apt to follow it if given. It is true that any major policy decision inevitably has an impact on all other governmental action; at minimum it affects the amount of money available. But there is no reason to expect the Attorney General, for example, to have an expert opinion about how to negotiate with the Chinese. Nor should anyone expect the Secretary of State to be able to offer informed advice on how to cope with crime in the cities.

Perhaps even more important than lack of expertise is a presidential fear that the advice of a Secretary may be biased toward the parochial concerns of his or her own department or the particular interests that department protects. That sort of special advocacy is easier to discern when the department's involvement in a problem is clear and direct. It is far more difficult to detect when a recommendation is supposedly objective. To be sure, a President may often ask an individual cabinet member for advice about problems that technically do not fall within his or her jurisdiction. But, when that happens, the President is far more likely to consult in private with that Secretary rather than defer to him or her in a cabinet meeting.

Having all the members of the cabinet periodically sit down with the President around a table undoubtedly performs many useful functions. It allows the President to emphasize his priorities and to explain how each department will be affected; it gives the President an opportunity to convey his mood in a direct and personal manner and to stress the force with which he intends to carry out his job. A cabinet meeting also allows Secretaries an additional few moments to chat with each other

and with the President—not easy tasks for busy people in the hectic
rush of their usual routines. But as a means of offering a President advice on general problems, the cabinet meeting has been a failure.

Formal Advisers: White House Staff

By far the most important set of formal advisers are the men and wom-
en whom the President appoints to his personal staff in the White
House. At barest minimum, he needs a press secretary, a liaison officer
to be in charge of dealing with Congress, a speechwriter, and a personal secretary. Just how many more assistants a President has, how
they are organized, and how much power they have depends almost
totally on the President's personal wishes. In 1976, for instance, the
White House staff under Gerald Ford included two presidential "coun-
sellors," three "counsels to the President," two general assistants, five
assistants to the President for specific matters of management and
budget, economic affairs, domestic affairs, public liaison, and legislative affairs, nine special assistants, a staff secretary, a personal secretary, and sixty-six others whose offices were of sufficient importance
to rate a special title listed in the *United States Government Manual.*
Each of these people, in turn, had his or her own staff of assistants.

UNEMPLOYMENT

TOTAL | FULL-TIME | MARRIED MEN

A key member of the White House staff is the press secretary, who has the difficult job of representing the President's interests with the White House press corps. In the photo, Press Secretary Ronald Ziegler explains the Nixon administration's position on unemployment to reporters.

As we saw in Chapter 12, Presidents have followed many models of organizing their staff. Dwight Eisenhower and Franklin D. Roosevelt fall at the polar extremes. Eisenhower, relying on his experience as a general, preferred to arrange his staff in a structure much like that of a military command, with a chief of staff channeling an orderly stream of information and recommendations to the President and directing neat rivers of decisions from the White House to various departments and agencies. Roosevelt, on the other hand, demanded a free-flowing system—or nonsystem—in which aides had vague and overlapping missions and information and recommendations tumbled around the President like clothes spinning in a gigantic dryer. FDR would not have tolerated a "chief of staff" to run *his* White House. Rather he "intended his administrative assistants to be eyes and ears and manpower for *him*, with no fixed contacts, clients, or involvement of their own to interfere when he needed to redeploy them."[2] Presidents Truman, Kennedy, and Johnson were more like FDR, although none had his tolerance for turmoil and disorder. Nixon was quite close to Eisenhower; and Ford, while tending toward Eisenhower, did not rely on his assistants as much as Nixon had.

However a President wishes to use his staff, one thing is evident: the enormous growth in the size of that group. Abraham Lincoln handled the business of the White House with the aid of two or three clerks and even allotted time almost weekly for appointments with private citizens. Even in the early twentieth century, President Taft thought it strange that he needed twenty-five clerks and stenographers. In recent decades, the President's personal staff and the Executive Office of the President—which supplies much specialized help—has numbered from 2,500 to 4,000 people. Most of these, to be sure, are members of the staffs of the President's staff. They rarely, if ever, consult directly with the President; but they gather, process, and evaluate much of the information that comes to the White House and make recommendations to the few people at the top who deal directly with the President.

Formal Advisers: Office of Management and Budget (OMB)

Next to the White House staff, the Office of Management and Budget is the most important of the agencies whose primary mission is to help the President control and direct the executive branch. It acquired its present significance in 1939 when its predecessor, the Bureau of the Budget, was transferred from the Treasury Department to the Executive Office of the President. President Nixon converted the Bureau of the Budget into the Office of Management and Budget in 1970. It is headed by a Director, who is appointed by the President without Senate confirmation. Its primary activities are formulation and execution of the federal budget that the President sends to Congress each year.

By law, all executive agencies must submit their budgetary estimates to the President. He, however, rarely gets involved in the details of budgetary decision making. Rather, he makes the grand decisions that express his priorities and general policies and leaves main responsibility for making detailed judgments to the OMB Director and his aides, with help perhaps from the White House staff. Because the budget is of necessity one of the most important instruments of executive direction and influence, it is difficult to overestimate the impact of these judgments. As President Johnson's Budget Director wrote:

Whereas the budget may have looked from the perspective of the Senate like an intricate collection of compromises among the interests of separate and often conflicting constituencies, it is suddenly seen from the White House as the central focus of efforts to achieve the Presidential vision of national purpose. What appears from lower vantage points to be a catalogue of discrete decisions is viewed from the highest perspective as a series of *choices* among alternatives, many of them perplexing and some of them agonizing.[3]

Another major task of OMB is to help improve management of the executive branch, a function it performs in two ways. It provides technical assistance in preparing plans for reorganizing executive agencies. The Office also offers advice to executive departments and agencies about how to improve their internal organization and operating procedures.

A third activity involves acting as a clearing house for legislative matters. OMB participates in developing legislative programs by clearing and coordinating departmental advice on proposed legislation and by recommending presidential action on legislative enactments. It also reviews legislative proposals submitted by various agencies, examines them for conformity with the President's general program, and seeks views of other agencies that have an interest in the legislation. The

OMB's staff is thus often able to discover conflicts in proposals from different agencies and perhaps prevent incompatible plans from being submitted to Congress as administration bills. Armed with information from OMB, the President is able to tell legislative leaders whether a particular bill has his support, whether he is indifferent, or whether it is contrary to his program.

In addition, OMB surveys interested departments and agencies to find out how they would be affected by any bills that have been passed and on which the President must act. If the consensus is against a bill, OMB drafts a veto message for the President. The President, of course, consults legislative leaders as well as executive officials; but he finds it easier to make up his own mind because of the information assembled by the Office of Management and Budget.

Formal Advisers: The National Security Council (NSC)

The National Security Act of 1947 placed the three military departments—army, navy, and air force—under one cabinet-level office, the Department of Defense, and established a National Security Council to help advise the President on international relations and military affairs. The Council's functions are to "assess and appraise the objectives, commitments, and risks of the United States in relation to our actual and potential military power" and to coordinate the various political, technological, and military factors necessary to plan for national security.

By statute, the NSC's members are now only the Secretaries of State and Defense, the President, and the Vice President; but the President normally invites a scattering of other people to participate. Frequently these include—but are by no means limited to—the Chairman of the Joint Chiefs of Staff, the Director of the Central Intelligence Agency, and the Secretary of the Treasury. To assist deliberations, the NSC has its own professional staff, mostly experts on loan from the Department of Defense, the military, and various intelligence agencies.

While more effective than cabinet meetings in formulating policy, the National Security Council has been less than an ideal institution. Each President has used it in his own fashion, and in varying degrees each has felt that it does not include precisely the people whose advice he needs—which explains why "outsiders" so often participate in its deliberations.[4]

Formal Advisers: The Council of Economic Advisers

The Employment Act of 1946 requires the President to send an annual economic report to Congress. It also created the Council of Economic Advisers to help the President prepare that report, which usually describes trends in employment and production and appraises federal programs that are affecting the economy. The Council has three members, usually highly respected academic economists who are sympathetic to the President's general political goals. He appoints all three with the advice of the Senate. Their function, in addition to preparing the annual economic report, is to recommend actions to maximize employment, production, and purchasing power.

Educating the President and other public officials is an inescapable part of advising in any technical field. As Walter Heller, a former chairman of the Council, put it, "The explanatory and analytical models of the economist must be implanted—at least intuitively—in the minds of Presidents, congressmen, and public leaders if economic advice is to be accepted and translated into action."[5]

Because the President knows that the Council's advice is not diluted by interests of particular governmental agencies or pressure groups, its members tend to have relatively easy access to the White House. But influence on presidential decisions is by no means automatic. According to Heller:

Unless the White House took a hand in directing economic traffic through the Council, the policy train often flashed past before we could get out the flag to stop it. One of our major tasks was to establish constructive relationships with the men around the President to help insure that the Council's voice would be heard before final decisions were made, even if it had not been drawn into the early stages of the policy-making process.[6]

In an environment often characterized by bureaucratic aggrandizement, the Council has remained compact and flexible. Its professional staff is limited to about fifteen, many of whom are on leave from universities in order to serve full-time for a year or two and perhaps part-time thereafter.

Formal Advisers: Special Boards, Task Forces, and Commissions

Depending on his personal style or the image that he wishes to transmit, a President may also appoint a bevy of special boards, commissions, and task forces to gather data and offer recommendations. In 1976, for instance, Gerald Ford had operating within the White House special groups charged with advising him on conservation of energy, environmental protection, telecommunications, drug abuse, international trade, international economic policy, executive clemency, wage and price stabilization, and uses of federal property. In addition, a President may utilize special task forces composed of officials from a variety of agencies to study and advise on certain problems that cut across normal lines of responsibility within the executive branch.

Since Herbert Hoover, Presidents have frequently used a variant of the last group, a presidential commission.[7] Typically made up of prominent private citizens and perhaps a few senior public officials, these commissions are asked to investigate and report on problems ranging from reorganization of the executive branch to civil rights to criminal justice. The period of time such an outside commission—aided by a professional staff of its own choosing—needs to study a problem and prepare a report generally prevents hasty action and allows the President an opportunity to plan his own approach. Perhaps even more important, precisely because most of these people are outsiders, they can approach a problem free from commitment to any particular policy or to the interests of any bureau and its clientele. They can take a fresh look and, if they think it feasible, offer a solution that cuts across established jurisdictional lines of existing agencies. Furthermore, since commission members are distinguished citizens, their report can win congressional and administrative attention and also generate reactions from reporters and analysts from the news media.

The principal disadvantage of advisory commissions is inherent in their chief advantage. Because the members tend to be outsiders without roots in the federal bureaucracy, they will not remain in office to carry through on the long, hard process of translating ideas into viable, operational policy decisions. A second disadvantage lies in their vulnerability to abuse. It is not uncommon for Presidents (or governors or mayors or university officials) to establish commissions as means of burying rather than confronting problems. Indeed, a commission report that does not accord with the policy that a President may have already chosen is typically shelved in a very dark corner.

Informal Advisers: Friends, Relatives, and Public Officials

Whatever the differences of presidential style and the effectiveness of formal sources of advice, most Presidents have drawn heavily on advice from people outside the official chain of command or even outside of government. Indeed, during the last fifty years, informal advisers have often exerted decisive influence on critical presidential choices. Nor is that practice new. Andrew Jackson had his "kitchen cabinet" of old friends—the two most prominent were journalists—and Woodrow Wilson's relationship with Colonel Edward M. House is legendary.[8] Wilson's reliance on Louis D. Brandeis, while less famous, was also significant. Brandeis was, according to Wilson's biographer, "the chief architect" of the President's economic program of "the New Freedom."[9]

As one would suspect, it was Franklin Roosevelt who most thoroughly exploited unofficial advisers. His friendship with Harry Hopkins was, if anything, more productive of policy recommendations than Wilson's with Colonel House.[10] And in the early days of the New Deal, Brandeis, though a Supreme Court Justice, was in spirit if not in body at the center of debates in the White House. In those days, FDR referred to him as "Old Isaiah" and continually sought his opinions on economic policy. But Roosevelt also gathered opinions from dozens of other people, prominent government officials, young men fresh out of

Harvard Law School, journalists, professors, and even, his opponents claimed, his dog Fala. He sent his wife around the country as an ambassador to discover what formal advisers could have never learned or would have feared to report. Visitors who came to talk about one problem might find their whole appointment consumed by the President's inquiries about totally unrelated matters. Newsmen who tried to question Roosevelt often found themselves being used as sources of information.

One could recite whole litanies of presidential reliance on unofficial sources of information and advice. Truman, Eisenhower, Kennedy, Johnson, Nixon, and Ford all kept old friends busy pondering the President's problems. Many of these people were private citizens; some of them, like Clark Clifford and Abe Fortas under Lyndon Johnson, were later given official positions; others, like James Reston, were journalists. Some held governmental offices but not positions that would normally include offering advice to the President. Truman's reliance on Fred Vinson and Johnson's on Abe Fortas, for example, continued after the two had gone to the Supreme Court.

The essential elements in these informal relationships have been intellectual respect, loyalty, and friendship, usually old friendship. Needing advice he can rely on and suspicious of most of those who offer suggestions, Presidents understandably tend to turn to those whose personal loyalty has been proved by time.

Information, Advice, and Decision Making

All these advisers, councils, staff members, and friends are critical in formulating policy. A decision maker—whether a President, a governor, a business executive, or a dean—can act only on the information that he or she has. Thus by screening information, by keeping out some kinds of data and stressing other kinds, officials in supposedly subordinate positions can severely narrow the choices that a decision maker sees as open. Furthermore, to the extent that the information contains technical material outside the decision maker's expertise, the people who evaluate the data can further restrict his opinions.

It is important to keep in mind that no effort at sabotage or selfish thinking need be involved. All of us see the world only through our own eyes. And even the most conscientious assistant can overlook or under- or overestimate a fact. Problems here are magnified by the possibility of less innocent distortions. Insofar as each governmental agency has its own character and peculiar goals, its officials are likely to have their own institutional, clientele, and perhaps even personal objectives to pursue. Indeed, to promote their particular goals is the reason why special-interest groups such as farmers or businessmen or union leaders have fought to have cabinet-level departments. Frequently if not invariably, bureaucrats have come to associate the interests of their "clients" with those of their department or agency. Even

A major source of information for presidential decision making during an international crisis is the National Military Command Center in the Pentagon.

those departments supposedly without clients, such as State and Defense, have their own institutional commitments, whether to certain policies, such as containment of communism, or to particular weapons, such as manned bombers, or to allocations of authority to certain kinds of personnel, such as professional Foreign Service Officers.

Thus, the President who relies solely on a single source for information or advice becomes to some extent a captive of that source. As FDR explained to Wendell Willkie in 1941:

Someday you may well be sitting here where I am now as President of the United States. And when you are, you'll be looking at that door over there and knowing that practically everybody who walks through it wants something out of you. You'll learn what a lonely job this is, and you'll discover the need for somebody like Harry Hopkins, who asks for nothing except to serve you.[11]

But if even the most loyal person can have blind spots and pet theories that color his or her outlook, so too friends can build up certain interests apart from those of the President, if only to be known as a person with influence. The President's need, therefore, is for advice that is unpolluted by institutional or personal biases, something that mere humans are not likely to be able to give on a regular basis. The improbability of achieving semidivine assistance leaves the President with three basic alternatives: (1) to consult with several agencies and individuals who have different—and if possible competing—perspectives; (2) to rely principally on his own staff and friends, for at least he is apt to know their biases and to be able to discount them with greater accuracy; or (3) to combine the first two and at the same time read as widely as possible while cultivating or maintaining friendships with academics and journalist. The more successful Presidents have tended to follow the third alternative. When Presidents have narrowed their circle of communication to keep out dissenting views, as Johnson did regarding Vietnam and Nixon after Watergate, they have courted—and sometimes won—disaster. The basic point is that if a President is to choose intelligently, he must have alternatives from which to select and know more about each alternative than any single person can tell him.

Executing Public Policy

On occasion, every President must have looked out the window of the Oval Office and imagined that he saw not a garden but a creeping jungle that was about to engulf him. The Constitution says that he is the head of the executive branch of government. But a weary President must sometimes have grave doubts.

Some agencies are legally outside his control. The Federal Power Commission, the Federal Reserve Board, and the Interstate Commerce Commission are examples of so-called independent regulatory commissions. They are partly legislative, partly judicial, and partly administrative bodies that are supposed to formulate, within broad statutory guidelines, specific rules to control aspects of economic and social life—how much, for example, producers can charge for natural gas, how much the "prime rate of interest" will be, or how much truckers or railroads can charge for their services. These commissions also apply those rules to particular situations and, subject to appeal to federal courts, can impose monetary penalties.

With the advice and consent of the Senate, the President appoints the commissioners to each board. In that respect, he has some control. But Congress has stipulated that there must be representation from both political parties and that commissioners serve for set terms. A President may not fire them except for neglect of duty or criminal actions. The Supreme Court has ruled that disagreement with the President, no matter how deep, on matters of policy is not grounds for removal.[12] Since these commissions can have immense impacts on national policy—affecting, for instance, the amount of energy available, or the volume of money in circulation, or priorities in transportation among truckers, airlines, and railroads—their actions can either reinforce or sap the strength of presidential decisions.

Unlike the independent regulatory commissions, most federal agencies are legally under the President's authority. But many enjoy considerable informal autonomy. Just as gathering and evaluating masses of information about any serious problem of policy are impossible tasks for a single person, so too is controlling millions of civilian employees and members of the armed forces.

To make decisions that are both intelligent and his own, we just said,

Secretary of State Henry Kissinger briefs President Gerald Ford on foreign policy problems. To assist the Secretary in developing and implementing the nation's foreign policies, the Department of State employed over 40,000 individuals in 1977.

a President needs information and advice. To control "his" bureaucracy to make sure that it is "his" policy that is being carried out, a President also needs advice and information. Compounding the difficulties is the fact that to some extent one of his major sources of information about the people he is trying to control is those people themselves. At least some of them may see little advantage in telling him all they know.

The Chain of Command?

The Constitution and various statutes establish a chain of command from the President's desk to the janitor in a social security office in Topeka. Each member of the cabinet is directly responsible to the President for the operations of his department.* So are the heads of other major agencies headed by officials who are not members of the cabinet, such as the Veterans Administration, the Environmental Pro-

---

*In 1976 there were eleven cabinet-level departments: Agriculture; Commerce; Defense; Health, Education, and Welfare; Housing and Urban Development; Interior; Justice; Labor; State; Transportation; and Treasury.

tection Agency, and the Central Intelligence Agency. In turn, each Secretary has various deputy secretaries, undersecretaries, assistant secretaries, and directors of programs who are responsible for specific functions and suboffices. Each of these officials has his or her line of subordinates. On paper, the system is clear, if complicated by great masses of people. One can see the chain of command run through organizational charts like a bright—and thick—red line. But yanking on that chain often gives a Secretary, or even a President, only a strained back.

One of the basic facts of life with which a President or any other executive official must come to terms is that the federal bureaucracy is not a monolithic unit. And it certainly is not neat. It operates much more like the two decentralized political parties than like a disciplined semimilitary organization. The analogy to the two political parties is no accident. As Chapters 5 and 7 indicated, there is a causal relationship here. Legislators, drawing the vital juices of re-election from state and local constituencies, work hard to ensure that the bureaucracy will be less the creature of the President's will and more the benefactor of their constituents. The armed forces may be an exception to this rule in actual combat, but not the way in which the various services purchase supplies or build bases.

Pluralism and Perspective

Factors other than congressional ambitions and jealousies are at work, of course. The bureaucracy's diversity of interests reflects and contributes to American pluralism. As we have several times noted, many governmental agencies exist to help rather than regulate special interests; and some created to regulate certain industries, like the Interstate Commerce Commission, soon become their captives rather than their controllers.

Also involved are the interests and perspectives of the agencies themselves, something we alluded to earlier in this chapter. All but the very top few layers of federal officials are likely to be careerists. Middle- and upper-level civil service employees are apt to be the officials who make specific decisions about whether a university is complying with guidelines relating to equal employment opportunities or what new tax statutes actually mean for taxpayers. These people were initially appointed on merit after taking examinations or possessing certain professional qualifications, and since then they have risen through the ranks. Bureau or agency chiefs have probably worked for the government for at least a decade, many for several decades. They have seen Presidents, Secretaries, undersecretaries, and lesser political appointees come and go. As professionals, these career employees have built up a sense of personal identification with and pride in their work. They think they know their jobs, and they are usually right.

Most of these men and, more frequently now, women live in a world that includes not only a specific bureau but the organized interests and individuals who are affected by that bureau's activities, the congressional subcommittees that help shape the bureau's missions, and the specialized press that covers its actions. Compared to the immediate reality of this world, the rest of the federal government tends to appear remote and the President a shadowy and transitory figure.

Most bureau chiefs and program managers in the federal government may be loyal to the President in the sense that they try to accept his decisions and support them. Some bureaucrats, however, may have goals of their own, which they try to advance by mobilizing support among their clientele and concerned congressional subcommittees. Some may be weak or inept in managing their activities and thus unable to follow the President's lead. Some may be so zealous in behalf of their programs that they lose their sense of proportion and fail to relate effectively to their department or to the rest of the executive branch. As a close observer and former member of the bureaucracy has noted:

It would be unreasonable to expect this official to see his program in the Presidential perspective. The President wants him to be a zealot about his mission, to pursue the goals of his program with skill, enthusiasm, and dedication. To ask him at the same time to be Olympian about his role and his claim on resources — to see in a detached way that he is part of a hive in which many other bees have missions of equal or greater urgency — is to ask him to embrace a combination of incompatible attitudes.[13]

Sabotage

When an agency chief simply cannot believe that the President's policies are correct, the situation is worsened. In those circumstances, a harassed President may be among the last to realize what has happened. William O. Douglas recalled that, when he was Chairman of the Securities and Exchange Commission and Jesse Jones Secretary of Commerce, Franklin Roosevelt summoned them to the Oval Office and ordered them to coordinate their activities to develop regional electric systems. "Now, Jesse," FDR ended, "you get together with Bill and work this out." As they left the White House, Douglas asked: "Jesse, when shall we get together? How about now?" "Not now, not tomorrow, never," Jones replied. Then taking off his hat and pointing to his gray thatch, he added:

When your hair gets the color of mine, you'll be wise. You will know by then that the President is a very busy man. He's so busy that he'll never remember this talk we've had.[14]

Nor are examples confined to domestic affairs. When Richard Nixon ordered destruction of American stores of deadly nerve gas, some CIA officials, believing the President was wrong, simply neglected to carry out the order. A decade earlier, during negotiations over the Cuban missile crisis, President Kennedy was surprised to hear the Russians ask the United States to withdraw its medium-range missiles from Turkey. In fact, Kennedy had issued that order some months earlier, but the Air Force had failed to obey. In each of these instances, the President simply did not know that his policy had been ignored.

Temptations to sabotage a President's program may afflict even members of the cabinet. Those officials, Vice President Charles Dawes used to assert, "are the President's natural enemies."[15] Dawes was exaggerating, but there is a hard kernel of truth in his claim. Some Secretaries may covet the presidency for themselves and recall that in the founding period Jefferson, Madison, Monroe, and John Quincy Adams were cabinet members, and in this century so were William Howard Taft and Herbert Hoover. More often—and more realistically— some Secretaries may earnestly wish to pursue policies that differ markedly from those of the President.

The bases of conflicts over policy are not hard to find. Hardly ever has every member of the cabinet represented the President's own choice of people to head executive departments. American presidential hopefuls typically "run scared," and to gain votes in nominating conventions and to accrue electoral support during campaigns, they often bargain away some cabinet positions. Perhaps they will give a large union the prerogative of naming a new Secretary of Labor or a group of corporate executives a similar privilege regarding the Secretary of Commerce. Later, to obtain leverage to move his legislative program through Congress a President may have to bargain away other posts, or at least agree not to dismiss officials who are siding less often with him and more often with chairmen of important congressional committees or subcommittees. To win or keep the support of local politicos he may also have to place their people in important positions below that of Secretary. As a result of these maneuverings, even high-level political appointees may feel no gratitude and little loyalty, personal or programmatic, toward the President.

Federalism

Federalism, in the subtle ways it permeates the entire political system, further complicates the President's problems. Congressmen, to strengthen their own bases in state and local politics, have not only tried to influence federal bureaucrats directly, they have also, as Chapter 5 explained, provided that state rather than federal officials actually spend much of the money to carry out federal domestic policies. Congress sets some minimal and typically flexible standards, but within those limits state bureaucrats have broad legal leeway. And, of course, a President can usually exercise very little control over state governmental processes.

When a President wants or fears little from Congress, his control over the executive branch increases because he can crack down on administrators without fear of having angry legislators tie up his programs in committees. Because Richard Nixon, for example, wanted to cut back federal involvement in domestic affairs rather than maintain or increase it, he could preside over the bureaucracy with a ruthlessness that more activist Presidents would have envied. But even Nixon did not have a free hand. When, for example, he dismissed the first special prosecutor appointed to investigate the Watergate scandals, he stirred up such virulent threats from Congress that he was obliged to agree to extraordinary means to protect the tenure of the succeeding special prosecutor. And, as the final days drew on, firing this second man as he neared the truth would have meant automatic impeachment and removal from office.

No President, of course, is helpless in exercising considerable control over the bureaucracy. Even a President who wants a great deal from Congress has important instruments of persuasion and command. Our references to the *possibility* of bureaucratic resistance should not be read to mean that all or most federal officials amuse themselves by attempting to wreck presidential programs. On the contrary, most try to be loyal, and presidential appeals to that faithfulness, especially if phrased in terms that indicate understanding and appreciation of the problems of administrators, can be quite effective.

A President can further reduce—although he can never erase—his difficulties by negotiating shrewdly, even tightfistedly, for support both before and after election. At very least, he can insist on retaining a veto over who will receive the posts that are bargained away. He can insist on a high degree of professional skill and some amount of personal loyalty. When he makes the choices himself, he can insure even higher standards on both scales of values.

Close control over the budget provides another instrument of command. A President can insist that agencies give to the Office of Management and Budget detailed explanations of how they intend to use requested funds and, later, progress reports on how they are spending that money.

The sort of crosschecking of sources of information that we have been discussing can also be important. Obviously, to control his subordinates a President must first know what they are doing. If he depends solely on the bureaucrats themselves for information, he again becomes their prisoner. That is why Franklin Roosevelt instructed an old friend: "Go and see what's happening. See the end product of what we're doing. Talk to people. Get the wind in your nose."[16]

In monitoring what his agencies are doing, a President has the same sorts of alternatives available as in gathering information and advice about formulating policy. Some, like talking to journalists and reading newspapers, may be especially valuable in tipping off a Chief Executive about his subordinates' actions. But no single means is likely to be sufficient, and successful Presidents are likely to use combinations of techniques, as they do in gathering advice. FDR added a twist of his own: He would sometimes deliberately assign two departments or agencies the same or overlapping missions in the hope that competition would spur each to do a better job or at the very least give each an incentive to tattle on any sins by the other.[17]

The Vice President

In overseeing the variegated operations of the executive branch, one might think that the Vice President would make an ideal chief of staff. After all, he has precious little else to do. To date, however, no Vice President has ever played that role. In part, the explanation may lie in the sort of people who have been Vice President. Even a man as dour as Richard Nixon would have laughed at the suggestion that a petty criminal like Spiro Agnew could have helped run the federal government. And Dwight Eisenhower retained deep suspicions about Nixon's character. But that can only be part of an explanation, because many able and honest men have filled the office.

For some Presidents much of the rest of the explanation may lie in a subconscious reaction against close relations with the man who will gain the White House if the President dies in office. Furthermore, many Presidents have refused to include the Vice President on their "team" because of a deliberate choice regarding power. To the extent that a President delegates power, we have seen, he loses a measure of control. Much delegation is necessary, of course; but the Vice President is the only member of the executive branch whom the President cannot legally dismiss.

Bureaucratic Independence and Limited Government

The independence of bureaucratic structures can impose high costs on the coherence of presidential programs. As conceived in the White House, an attack on a particular problem may involve closely coordinated sets of action by several federal agencies. If one agency drags its heels, another proceeds in a ploddingly begrudging fashion, while a third and fourth leap enthusiastically into the battle, the final program is not likely to be particularly successful. Nor is the President likely to appear to be a careful planner.

Such a price in programmatic coherence may be steep, but as long as bureaucrats maintain their independence, some such costs are inevitable. It is easy to bemoan these costs and to think of ways to "reform" the system. But reformers have to ask themselves precisely how far they wish to go in making bureaucracy responsive to the White House. An answer to that question must consider several points.

Reprinted courtesy of the Chicago Tribune.

Although the Vice President is not dependent on the President for his current term of office, his political future usually is heavily conditioned on continued support by the President. For a variety of reasons, Vice President Rockefeller was unable to sustain the support of President Gerald Ford, who replaced Rockefeller on the 1976 Republican ticket with Senator Robert Dole.

First of all, because of the complexity of serious political problems, Congress tends to legislate in general terms, setting broad objectives rather than specifying details. For all the reasons already discussed, no President or small group of advisers can possibly know enough to fill in every major gap in legislation, much less complete every detail. And, even if they had the technical knowledge, they would lack the time.

As a result, if most policies are to be effective, administrators, from cabinet Secretaries to bureau chiefs to heads of field offices around the country, have to make intelligent, imaginative decisions. The kinds of people who can make such choices are not apt to come to or remain in jobs that limit them to shuffling papers and filling out forms. If the federal government is to recruit and retain effective executives, it must provide reasonably regular opportunities for creative leadership. Choices made by such executives will not always coincide with those the President would have made. But until some scientist devises a machine that can rearrange the President's molecules so that he can be a hundred places at once and instantly acquire years of professional training and skill required by each of those hundred places, he has to rely on others.

Here is a dilemma that is common to popes and prime ministers, to dictators and corporate executives, as well as to Presidents. To cope with complex problems, a leader needs subordinates who are loyal, diligent, and creative. Otherwise the leader will be overwhelmed with decisions. On the other hand, to the extent that creative people, even though loyal and diligent, exercise *their* judgment, they will shape policy in ways that are likely to diverge from what the leader had in mind. In so doing, those subordinates subtract from their leader's power. The chiefs of most governments of constitutional democracies are sufficiently realistic—and tolerant of disagreement—to be satisfied with keeping bureaucratic independence within bounds rather than trying to stomp it out.

There are other potential benefits to bureaucratic independence in a *constitutional* democracy founded on the desirability of *limited* government. A President who cannot command absolute, unquestioning obedience is restricted from doing evil as well as good. In this regard, it should be remembered that many of the sordid details of Watergate became known in 1973–74 partly because of officials and former officials of the White House who became disgusted with the immorality of Nixon and his henchmen. The famous "Deep Throat," who fed or confirmed reports to the two newsmen who did the most to break the full story of Watergate, may have been a mythical composite of several informants, but his—or their—resistance to the President was an important factor in Nixon's fall. Less publicly noticed but equally significant, during the late summer of 1974 when impeachment seemed close, the Secretary of Defense, with the help of several White House aides, took special precautions to short-circuit any effort by Nixon to use the armed forces to defy Congress or the Supreme Court.

American government has been and remains presidential government, but presidential government is not the same as presidential dictatorship. Checking the President is not a trivial matter in a constitutional system. Indeed, what is at work here is another manifestation of the now familiar Madisonian strategy of preserving liberty by fracturing and fragmenting power.

Summary

This chapter has had two major objectives. First, it has tried to explain the President's need for information and advice in order to make decisions, and to describe the formal and informal systems of advice that are available to him. Second, and closely related, this chapter has attempted to show how a President's reliance on others to carry out his decisions inevitably reduces his power—but need not, if the President is astute, drain his ability to see that his program is carried out. Nor do these checks on presidential power constitute mere flaws in the political structure. They can serve positive functions in preserving limited, constitutional government.

Selected Bibliography

ALTSHULER, A. A., ed., *The Politics of the Federal Bureaucracy* (New York: Dodd, Mead, 1968). A useful collection of readings.

APPLEBY, PAUL, *Big Democracy* (New York: Alfred A. Knopf, 1945). Stimulating lectures on administrative problems of the federal government; just as fresh today as they were when originally published, by a distinguished public executive and academic administrator.

BERNSTEIN, MARVER H., *The Job of the Federal Executive* (Washington, D.C.: The Brookings Institution, 1958). Contains reflections of thoughtful federal executives, both career and political, about their experience in the complex setting of the federal government.

CRONIN, THOMAS E. and SANFORD D. GREENBERG, eds., *The Presidential Advisory System* (New York: Harper & Row, 1969). An excellent collection of articles with comments by the editors.

FENNO, RICHARD F., JR., *The President's Cabinet* (Cambridge, Mass.: Harvard University Press, 1959). The best account of the cabinet as a political institution, pointing up its weaknesses as a policy-making body.

FLASH, EDWARD S., JR., *Economic Advice and Presidential Leadership* (New York: Columbia University Press, 1965). A thorough analysis of the machinery of economic advice in three presidential administrations.

FRANKEL, CHARLES, *High on Foggy Bottom* (New York: Harper & Row, 1970). A former Assistant Secretary's tale of his tribulations as a federal political executive.

HALPERIN, MORTON H., with the assistance of PRISCILLA CLAPP and ARNOLD KANTER, *Bureaucratic Politics and Foreign Policy* (Washington, D.C.: The Brookings Institution, 1974). An effort by a former national security adviser to explain the process by which decisions are made regarding international relations and military affairs.

JOHNSON, RICHARD TANNER, *Managing the White House: An Intimate Study of the Presidency* (New York: Harper & Row, 1974). A former White House fellow's analysis of the President's problems in organizing and running his own office.

KOENIG, LOUIS W., *The Invisible Presidency* (New York: Holt, Rinehart and Winston, Inc., 1960). Interesting portraits of persons who have wielded power "behind-the-scenes" in the White House, including Hamilton, Van Buren, Loeb, House, Corcoran, Hopkins, and Adams.

PRESSMAN, JEFFREY L., and AARON WILDAVSKY, *Implementation: How Great Expectations in Washington Are Dashed in Oakland: Or, Why It's Amazing That Federal Programs Work at All, This Being a Saga of the*

Economic Development Administration as Told by Two Sympathetic Observers Who Seek to Build Morals on a Foundation of Ruined Hopes (Berkeley, Cal.: University of California Press, 1973). As the lengthy subtitles indicate, this book attempts to show (and prescribe remedies for) the many slips between the cup of policy as formulated in Congress and the White House and the lip of the ultimate consumer of what is left of that policy.

PRICE, DON K., *The Scientific Estate* (Cambridge, Mass.: Harvard University Press, 1965). An urbane discussion of key issues of public policy in science and the proper role of science advisers.

ROURKE, FRANCIS E., *Bureaucracy, Politics, and Public Policy* (Boston: Little, Brown and Company, 1969). A thoughtful treatment of the design and operation of the bureaucracy and its contribution to the formulation of public policy. Contains selected bibliography of relevant books and articles.

SEIDMAN, HAROLD, *Politics, Position, and Power: The Dynamics of Federal Organization,* 2d ed. (New York: Oxford University Press, 1975). A penetrating analysis of the ways in which the federal bureaucracy operates — both its internal politicking and its ultimate external effects on national policies.

SELZNICK, PHILIP, *Leadership in Administration: A Sociological Interpretation* (New York: Harper & Row, Publishers, 1957). A general discussion of the problems of leadership in large organizations.

STANLEY, DAVID T., DEAN E. MANN, and JAMESON W. DOIG, *Men Who Govern* (Washington, D.C.: The Brookings Institution, 1967). An analysis of those who served in political executive positions in the departments, agencies, and regulatory commissions of the federal government.

STEIN, HAROLD, ed., *Public Administration and Policy Development* (New York: Harcourt Brace Jovanovich, 1952). A pioneering collection of case studies in administrative action, with a seminal essay on public administration by the editor.

SUNDQUIST, JAMES, *Politics and Policy: The Eisenhower, Kennedy, and Johnson Years* (Washington, D.C.: The Brookings Institution, 1968). Six case studies of the contributions of key participants in the federal executive and legislative branches to the passage of major domestic policy measures.

THOMAS, NORMAN C., and HANS W. BAADE, eds., "The Institutionalized Presidency," *Law and Contemporary Problems,* XXXV (1970). A valuable set of analyses of problems relating to presidential advisory groups, White House-departmental relations, budgeting, management, and reorganization.

TREWHITT, HENRY L., *McNamara: His Ordeal in the Pentagon* (New York: Harper & Row, 1971). Lucid, perceptive account of McNamara as Secretary of Defense under Kennedy and Johnson.

VAN RIPER, PAUL, *History of the United States Civil Service* (New York: Row, Peterson, 1958). The standard history of the federal civil service system.

WILDAVSKY, AARON, *The Politics of the Budgetary Process,* 2d ed. (Boston, Mass.: Little, Brown and Company, 1974). A thorough study of the role of the OMB and other participants in the formulation of the President's budget.

Part Six
The Judiciary

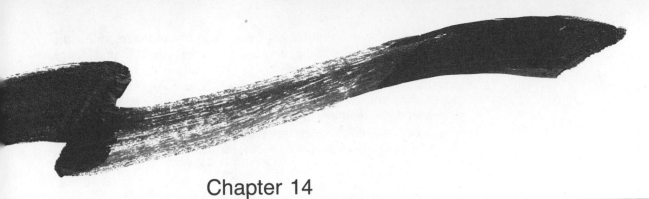

Chapter 14

The Judicial Process

Judges and the Development of Anglo-American Law
The Common Law
Equity
Toward an Independent Judiciary

Political Effects of Judicial Decisions

Judicial Discretion

The Federal Court System
Jurisdiction: The Authority to Decide Cases
State Courts
Federal Judicial Organization: District Courts
Federal Judicial Organization: Courts of Appeals
Federal Judicial Organization: The Supreme Court
Special Federal Courts

Judicial Recruitment
Federal Recruitment
Nomination
Confirmation
Federal Judges
Retirement of Federal Judges

Summary

Selected Bibliography

PARTS FOUR AND FIVE of this book examined two of the major institutions of American national government, Congress and the presidency. This chapter and the one that follows look closely at the third branch of government, the judiciary. Here we shall try to vivisect the roles that judges, "the oracles of the law," play in the political system. First, in this chapter we shall examine in general terms the origins, discretion, jurisdiction, organization, and personnel of the entire system of federal courts. The next chapter will focus on the Supreme Court of the United States.

Judges and the Development of Anglo-American Law

The history of the development of political institutions has been in large part an attempt to establish impartial umpires who could settle disputes between individuals and between individuals and public authority. In Western democracies this search has led to familiar divisions among legislators, executives, and judges. But, as we have seen, these divisions are clear neither in the abstract nor in the tangled webs of real government. In countries that trace their legal institutions to England, as the United States does, judges often have themselves created the rules that they are supposed to interpret. Indeed, in England and the United States, until well into the second half of the nineteenth century, judges made far more law than did legislators. And, of course, we have just seen that congressmen become involved both in administration and in adjudication and that it is frequently difficult to tell whether an executive official is creating, interpreting, or applying rules.

The Common Law

There are solid historical reasons for the fusion of these functions of making, interpreting, and applying law in American politics. The roots of American law run far back into medieval Britain, where judges—if one can even use the word—were executive officials and Parliament was a court whose basic legislative function was to levy taxes. Early English "judges" some of the time conferred with the king at Westminster, and at other times traveled around the country to settle disputes on the basis of "common" custom, rather than the particular usages of any single region. Undoubtedly, judges' own biases were important elements in deciding what was "common" and what was local practice. Rather early in this process, judges adopted a rule called *stare decisis;* that is, they tried to follow their own earlier decisions when they encountered similar cases. It was not until centuries later, when reports of important courts were published, that stare decisis could actually become a firm and general rule. But even its loose application soon began to make the *common law* that emerged from application of common custom a system of judge-made rules.

During the nation's early years, justice was brought to remote settlements by judges who rode the "circuit," moving from town to town to hear cases that fell within their jurisdiction.

Equity

As the English common law developed, it slowly hardened into rigid forms that covered only certain standard situations. The English social system, on the other hand, was still evolving, and old rules could not solve all the new problems. Therefore, as aggrieved persons came to the king for justice, his staff referred them to the royal chancellor. Gradually the chancellor's office, the chancery, also developed into a court, separate from the courts of the common law, and it applied a different set of rules, which came to be known as *equity*.

Equity acted as a force for reform in English society. It operated by relatively informal procedures, and at first judges of chancery claimed to apply "natural justice" rather than fixed legal rules. But soon precedents, what had been decided before, came to have much the same force as in the common law. Procedures, too, soon became fairly well set, although they remained less formal than in courts of law.

The most important difference between equity and common law lies in their objectives. Common law mainly provides *compensatory* justice; its chief remedy is money to pay for damages. Equity, on the other hand, offers *preventive* justice. It can order a defendant not to act, to stop acting, or to undo the effects of a former action.

Federal seizure of the steel mills in 1952 supplies a good illustration of these differences. When President Truman ordered the Secretary of Commerce to take over the mills to prevent a national strike, the owners of the mills could, under the common law, have sued the United States, the Secretary, or both for damages. Putting a price on the loss that the owners might suffer would have been difficult, however; and it is doubtful whether the United States or the Secretary could have been forced to pay any money at all. Equity offered a different remedy, an *injunction* (a court order) directing the Secretary to return control of the mills to their managers. Naturally, management sought an injunction.[1] In other situations, one might seek an injunction to forbid an official or a private citizen to take a particular action; for example, a black might ask for an injunction prohibiting a registrar from enforcing a literacy test for voting.

Although in England courts of law and courts of equity were historically separate institutions, the American Congress in 1789 authorized federal judges to hear cases arising under either common law or equity, a practice accepted today in most of the states (and even in Britain).

Toward an Independent Judiciary

Over time, the personnel who staffed the British tribunals of common law and equity began to split off from the rest of the king's court and gradually began to develop a new professional identity as judges. By the early seventeenth century, they could claim a monopoly in interpreting the law. True independence from the king, however, came even more slowly. It was not until 1701 that judges served for good behavior during the reign of the king who appointed them, with removal during the king's life subject to Parliamentary approval. And it was not until 1760 that judges did not have to surrender their offices when the king died.

Eventually, the notion of a judiciary independent of executive and legislative took firm hold in British and American culture. Royal abuse of this principle was one of the grievances against George III listed in the Declaration of Independence. Today, even though about two thirds of American states provide for popular election of judges, the American political system still gives them a great degree of independence.

Political Effects of Judicial Decisions

The rules that judges apply can have an important impact on the political system. In deciding cases that appear to concern only two private citizens, a court may be doing one of three things: mechanically applying an old rule, modifying that old rule, or creating a new one. That rule, old, new, or modified, if followed by other judges, can affect the rights of many other citizens, either because of lawsuits or because of out-of-court advice given by lawyers. More broadly, the interests involved in a case may be widely shared by individuals in society and perhaps even represented by organized groups. For instance, a case may revolve around the reciprocal rights and duties of manufacturers and their customers. Here a decision holding a car manufacturer liable to a customer for injuries suffered because of inadequate safety features can immediately affect the lives and property of millions of people.

At another level, a lawsuit, or perhaps a criminal prosecution, may raise issues fundamental to relationships between citizens and government. For example, how free is free speech? Another kind of case may concern relations among governmental officials. In what circumstances, for instance, can the President invoke executive privilege to withhold documents from Congress or the courts?

Like governmental officials, leaders of interest groups have been aware of the potential effects of judicial decisions. The National Association for the Advancement of Colored People, for instance, is no less interested in securing a favorable interpretation of civil rights laws than in having such statutes enacted in the first place. Thus interest groups frequently try to shape the content of judicial rulings. Lobbying, in the sense that the term is used in the legislative process, has little or no legitimate place in the judicial process. Private contacts with judges or jurors about a matter before a court are always unethical and usually illegal.

Yet, in a broader sense, interest groups can legitimately lobby in the judicial process in several ways. First, leaders of a group can use their influence to help select judges whose general political philosophy is favorable to the group's objectives. For instance, the American Bar Association, a conservative group that does not represent all or even a majority of lawyers and that for much of its life barred Jews and blacks from membership, has managed to finesse for itself an institutional voice in the selection of federal judges and so can exercise its influence to limit the number of liberal judges.

Second, interest groups can often file law suits or help others do so. This sort of aid can be critical. The legal process is typically slow and costly. Lawyers are expensive, and there are usually certain court fees and perhaps large bills for research. Facilitating group access to courts is a technical procedure known as a *class action*. Here, a single person or a few people sue not only for themselves but for all other members of a clearly defined group who share a common legal right, and the resulting decision affects the entire "class." For example, a black man might file a class action for an order forbidding voting registrars to discriminate not only against him personally but also against all qualified black voters.

A group can legitimately lobby in a third way. If it can meet certain technical requirements, an association can enter a legal dispute already in progress as an *amicus curiae*, a friend of the court, and offer its views about the proper way to resolve the dispute.

These kinds of activities surprise many people because they conflict with a naive view that judges are remote from struggles over public policy. But judges are intimately involved in these conflicts, and the U.S. Supreme Court has held that the First Amendment's protection of freedom of speech, association, and petition gives organizations as well as individuals a constitutional right to use the courts to further their goals.[2]

Because of the significance of judicial rulings, a decision, even by the Supreme Court, does not necessarily end conflict over policy. Because the political process provides avenues of attack on judicial decisions just as it provides ways to contest legislative or administrative action, a decision by the Supreme Court that is unfavorable to the objectives of a particular interest group may signal the start of a fresh campaign in the legislative or administrative process. Groups hurt by a decision seek a remedy in the form of new legislation, constitutional amendments, or new judges; groups who benefit from the ruling talk about the sanctity of law and fight to prevent counteraction.

Judicial Discretion

The effects of their decisions on public policy make judges major political actors; they do not function as dispassionate computers, searching a memory bank of prefabricated rules and then applying relevant rules to a factual matrix. Judges frequently exercise choice among competing values and competing policies, and they are forced to do so by the nature of their office.

If the streams of the law — customs, previous judicial decisions, statutes, and constitutional clauses — were crystal clear and all ran in the same direction and if the needs of society were static, judges might be able to exercise only technical skills. But none of these conditions obtains. Most basically the problems and the needs of society are constantly changing. "The law," Dean Roscoe Pound once observed, "must be stable, yet it cannot stand still." This dilemma of providing a known set of rules while adapting the principles embodied in those rules to cope with changing conditions makes judging an inherently creative process. Furthermore, the sources of the law rarely settle difficult cases. Custom is usually of only marginal help when a new problem arises; indeed custom — the custom of dumping industrial wastes in the nearest stream, for instance — may be the cause of the problem. Previous judicial decisions may not cover the situation or, what is more likely, may offer conflicting guidelines. American courts have been functioning for such a long time that it takes an incompetent attorney not to be able to unearth a half dozen precedents to support either side of almost any kind of claim.

Statutory and constitutional clauses may be of more help, but they do not necessarily settle the problem. The Constitution contains a wide variety of vague prohibitions and commands. The Fourth Amendment does not forbid *all* searches and seizures but only those that are "unreasonable." The Fifth and Fourteenth Amendments forbid not the taking of "life, liberty, and property," but only their taking "without due process of law," and that phrase defies precise definition.

Like constitutional clauses, important statutes tend to be general—in part because vagueness of language is one way of maximizing agreement, in part because there are inherent problems in using words, and in part because congressmen have at times wanted to encourage, or even force, judges to become creative partners in the legislative process. The Sherman Antitrust Act, for example, declares that it is illegal to "monopolize, or attempt to monopolize" trade in interstate commerce. But the statute offers no definition of *monopoly* or *monopolization*. As Senator Sherman candidly conceded:

I admit that it is difficult to define in legal language the precise line between lawful and unlawful combinations. This must be left for the courts to determine in each particular case. All that we, as lawmakers, can do is to declare general principles, and we can be assured that the courts will apply them so as to carry out the meaning of the law.[3]

Even when Congress appears to speak precisely, it may not be consistent. At different times, Congress may enact statutes with mutually incompatible provisions and, because of oversight or inability to reach agreement, may not specify which provisions take precedence. The antitrust field again provides an example. In one series of statutes, Congress has instructed federal agencies to attack restraints on trade and to foster free competition. In another series of laws (and in niggardly appropriations to run enforcement agencies), Congress has opposed too much competition and too vigorous federal attacks on monopolistic practices.

When judges can exercise discretion, when they have some freedom in choosing among policy alternatives, they, like other human beings, are apt to be influenced by their own values when they choose. Judges are also influenced by their perceptions of the nature of a problem. To a judge like William O. Douglas, who as a poor young man trying to ride a freight train from Yakima, Washington, to get to law school in New York was almost killed by a railroad detective, police brutality seemed a more real danger than it did to a judge who was reared in a socially prominent family.

Perception and values reinforce each other to the point that judges, like the rest of men, may well see much that they want to see in particular controversies. A number of empirical analyses of the voting behavior of Justices of the Supreme Court have found a strong relationship between those votes and the values the Justices endorse.[4] When he was still a judge on the Court of Appeals of New York, Benjamin Cardozo summed up the matter:

My analysis of the judicial process comes then to this, and little more: logic, and history, and custom, and utility, and the accepted standards of right conduct, are the forces which singly or in combination shape the progress of the law. Which of these forces shall dominate in any case must depend largely upon the comparative importance or value of the social interest that will thereby be promoted or impaired. . . .

If you ask how [the judge] is to know when one interest outweighs another, I can only answer that he must get his knowledge just as the legislator gets it; from experience and study and reflection; in brief from life itself.[5]

One must be very careful, however, in discussing judicial discretion. It is not the same as judicial license. Judges do not fit the model of completely impartial arbiters; they have prejudices and predilections. But these are usually not biases for or against particular persons but for or against certain principles and policies. If the ideal judge is one who is impartial between litigants—that is, those persons who sue or are sued or prosecuted in the courts—then most federal judges come reasonably close to this model. But judges are not intellectual eunuchs; they are not impartial between competing ideas. Before lamenting this fact, one should consider whether a judge who had no respect for the dignity of man would be a proper official in a civilized society. The troublesome aspects about judicial discretion are how much of it a judge exercises and for what purposes he or she uses it.

The Federal Court System

Jurisdiction: The Authority to Decide Cases

One of the chief features of American law is a dual court structure, one for the federal government and a different set of tribunals run by each state government. Federalism itself does not require this double system. In Australia, Canada, and India, state courts handle most judicial business and a national supreme court at the top of the hierarchy furthers uniformity. Although the U.S. Constitution permits a similar arrangement, the First Congress opted in 1789 for a complete set of federal courts. Nevertheless, to the despair of litigants and the profit of lawyers, Congress has given federal courts exclusive *jurisdiction** only in certain kinds of controversies—bankruptcy and patents, for instance—listed in Article III of the Constitution as being under national control. The official rationalization is that the workload of federal judges must be kept within manageable limits, and allowing state courts to exercise some federal jurisdiction eases some of the burden that might otherwise fall on federal judges. Far more important, however, has been the pressure of local officials to enhance their own power and that of state judges.

Because of overlapping patterns of jurisdiction, a potential litigant often has a choice of using state *or* federal courts. Moreover, in matters of criminal law, a defendant may be prosecuted in *both* state and fed-

*The authority of a court to hear and decide a case.

UNITED STATES DISTRICT COURT

FOR THE DISTRICT OF COLUMBIA

```
RICHARD NIXON, individually        )
    and as the former President    )
    of the United States,          )
                                   )
            Plaintiff              )
                                   )   Civil Action No.  74-1852
            v.                     )
                                   )
ADMINISTRATOR OF GENERAL SERVICES) 
                                   )
            and                    )
                                   )
THE UNITED STATES OF AMERICA,      )
                                   )
            Defendants             )
_____)
```

AFFIDAVIT OF RICHARD NIXON

County of San Diego
State of California   ss:

Richard Nixon, being duly sworn under oath, deposes and says as

follows:

1. I am a citizen of the United States and a resident of the

State of California, my residence being at San Clemente, California.

2. From January 3, 1947 to November 30, 1950 I served as a Member

of the House of Representatives. From December 1, 1950 to January 1,

1953 I served as a United States Senator from the State of California.

Thereafter, from January 20, 1953 until January 19, 1961 I served as

Vice President of the United States. I was elected President of the

United States and served in that office from January 20, 1969 until my

resignation on August 9, 1974.

3. During the time I served in each of these four Constitutional

offices it was my practice to retain and preserve nearly all of the

materials produced or received by myself or my staff. Following the

practice of all other Congressmen, Senators and Vice Presidents, when I

Contests in the courts involve a variety of legal documents, such as the affidavit or sworn statement. After Richard Nixon's resignation from the presidency in 1974, Congress passed a law ordering that the papers and tapes amassed during his years in the White House remain under governmental control. Nixon then sued to have them returned to his custody, alleging that the statute was unconstitutional. This is the first page of the affidavit justifying his claims.

eral courts, since by one act — robbing a national bank, for example — he may violate the law of both governments. The Supreme Court has ruled that such a possibility constitutes "double amenability" not double jeopardy; the resulting confusion, the Court has comfortingly said, is a price of federalism.[6]

Article III limits the jurisdiction of federal courts to *cases* and *controversies*. These are technical terms and refer to situations in which opposing litigants have real interests that are in conflict and that conflict either has injured or threatens imminent injury to a right that the law protects, such as the right to travel between states or to petition Congress. The gist of this restriction is that federal courts are not supposed to give advisory opinions* or settle academic arguments, however interesting or even important. To these "case" requirements, judges have added rules regarding "standing to sue." Basically these rules require that a person who invokes federal jurisdiction show that: (1) the question raised is one that courts can answer and not one whose solution the Constitution leaves to Congress or the President; and (2) this particular clash of interests involves one of the litigant's legally protected rights, not a right of the public in general or of some other person. The Supreme Court has sometimes relaxed the latter requirement when it would be difficult for the individual whose rights were threatened or denied to bring suit.[7] A class action does not violate the standing rules, because the one who brings suit must demonstrate that a real personal interest of his or her own is involved, an interest that is shared by members of a definable group of other people.

Further, Article III restricts the kinds of cases federal courts may decide. Federal jurisdiction depends either on the nature of the controversy itself or the status of one of the parties to the suit.

A. Nature of the Controversy
   If the case involves:
   1. a question of the interpretation of the federal Constitution or any federal statute or treaty;
   2. a question of admiralty or maritime law.
B. Status of the Parties
   Where one of the parties is:
   3. the United States government or one of its officers or agencies;
   4. an ambassador, consul, or other representative of a foreign government;
   5. a state government suing:
      a. another state;
      b. a citizen of another state;
      c. a foreign government or its subjects;
   6. a citizen of one state suing a citizen of another state;
   7. an American citizen suing a foreign government or citizens of a foreign nation;
   8. a citizen of one state suing a citizen of his own state where both claim land under grants of different states.

State Courts

Because of the limited scope of federal jurisdiction, most lawsuits begin and end in state tribunals. Indeed, the courts of a large state like California or New York may handle more cases in any year than does

---

*An *advisory opinion,* as its name implies, is a statement of a court's opinion about a legal question where no real case, in the technical sense of the word, exists. A few American state courts and many courts in other countries are required, when requested, to offer such advice to the executive or legislative branch of government.

the entire system of national courts. The organization of state courts varies widely, but normally, in addition to such specialized tribunals as juvenile courts, there are two sets of trial courts, one for minor criminal and civil matters, the other for more serious litigation. There is also always at least one appellate court to oversee the administration of justice in trial courts, and in some states there are two such layers, headed, as in the federal system, by a supreme court.

Federal Judicial Organization: District Courts

For the federal system, Congress has created three tiers of courts plus several special tribunals. At the first, or trial, level are the district courts. In 1976 there were ninety of these, at least one in every state. At the next level are eleven U.S. courts of appeals, which review decisions of district courts, and at the top is the U.S. Supreme Court, which reviews decisions of federal courts of appeals and also decisions of state supreme courts on federal questions.

The bulk of federal judicial work is done at the trial level, that is, in the *district courts*. Except for some local matters in the District of Columbia and the territories, all federal criminal cases and most civil cases start here, as do all federal suits in equity. Almost 160,000 cases a year are filed in district courts, but a large share of them are informally settled by the parties themselves without any action by the court. Except for relatively infrequent civil litigation requiring a special panel of three judges, a single judge presides over a trial, although the court itself may have as many as twenty-seven judges attached to it.

District judges are important public officials. In pretrial conferences they act as mediators and try to persuade litigants to settle their differences without further judicial proceedings. These solutions are seldom appealed because the parties themselves have agreed to them. Even when a formal trial is held, only a bit more than half of the decisions in civil cases will be appealed and less than a quarter of the decisions in criminal cases (although the latter figure represents about two thirds of the convictions obtained after full trial). Thus the district court's decision is not only the first, but more often than not the final, judicial ruling in a case. This fact alone gives district judges considerable practical leeway.

Other factors widen that leeway. First, legal rules are no more clear when a district judge has to interpret them than when the Supreme Court does. Indeed, they may be far less so, because, if the case presents a new problem, the Supreme Court has the advantage of the district judge's insights. In addition, even where the Supreme Court has apparently spoken, the Justices may not have spoken clearly. In addition to having normal problems of communication, judges, like framers of constitutions and statutes, often have difficulty coming to full agreement. One way of compromising differences is to use vague phraseology and leave some issues for future resolution. Supreme Court Justices may also take this course when they are simply unsure of what is the best solution, hoping to gain wisdom from the experience of lower court judges as they transform broad pronouncements into specific rules. The generality of the Supreme Court's directives in the School Segregation Cases[8] and early Reapportionment Cases[9] was in part an attempt to learn by experience.

When a district judge faces a muddy pronouncement by the Supreme Court or if he senses that the Justices are about to change an old rule, he must exercise choice, not completely unfettered choice, but still choice. And his selection can shape public policy as well as public law. Even if his decision is appealed, argument at the next level will be shaped by his work.

Fact Finding. The process of determining the facts of a case also widens a trial judge's discretion. Cases seldom present only questions about what rule to apply to a problem that is neatly outlined. Probably most lawsuits center on disputes of fact. Witnesses to the same act vividly recall quite different actions; experts often offer conflicting diagnoses of a defendant's mental health or financial condition. Allegations of police brutality are among the most difficult. Police swear great oaths they never touched the accused, while he vows that he confessed to escape being beaten to death. Even when witnesses have nothing at stake, there is real difficulty in accurately recalling what happened months or even years earlier.

An appellate judge is reluctant to disturb a trial judge's or a jury's weighing of conflicting testimony. A witness's nervousness, confidence, or dress may strengthen or weaken his or her credibility, and appellate judges never see or hear witnesses. They must depend on a record of the trial.

Trial courts perform an ancillary emotional function by providing a forum in which disputants may angrily, but peacefully, attack each other. In the courtroom, friendly witnesses are gently examined and hostile witnesses mercilessly cross-examined, and it is here that opposing counsel make eloquent pleas to the judge, to the jury, and to the Deity for justice, mercy, or revenge. This function is so important that "a day in court" is synonymous with a fair chance. Disruptive tactics of some defendants—Black Panthers and alleged leaders of riots, for instance—who during trials shout obscenities at the judge threaten not only to disrupt formal processes but to destroy the role of the trial as a substitute for brute force.

Trial by Jury. The judge's tasks narrow when a jury is used. In federal courts, a litigant may ask for a jury trial in any law suit (but not in a suit in equity) where the amount in dispute exceeds $20. In a federal criminal prosecution, a defendant must be tried by jury unless both he and the prosecution waive that right. The jury takes over the task of fact finding, and the judge is supposed only to ensure that the trial follows regular procedures and to instruct the jury on the rules to be applied to the facts. Yet, a clear distinction between facts and law is frequently impossible. In deciding what evidence the jury can hear, a judge participates in fact finding; moreover, a judge can often comment to the jury on the weight that should be given to certain kinds of evidence. In turn, the jury in its deliberations probably often interprets or creates new legal rules to decide a case.

Although still numerous, jury trials are becoming less common in the United States. There is considerable debate whether that decrease bodes good or ill for the legal system. Only two facts are clear: (1) jury trials typically take much longer and so contribute to growing burdens of administering justice; (2) juries are much freer than judges in arriving at a judgment because they do not have to explain or justify their decisions.[10] A court hearing a case on appeal can never be sure what mixture of law and fact a jury used to decide a case. And a trial judge or an appellate court can overturn a jury's decision only on a finding that its judgment could not have been based on the evidence presented—a most difficult conclusion to justify, though sometimes easy to suspect.

Federal Judicial Organization: Courts of Appeals

Trial judges may make mistakes. More often, litigants who have lost think that trial judges have erred. Even when judges have made no mistakes in a technical sense, other trial judges may have offered different solutions to the same kind of problem. Thus, for greater certainty, faith in the courts, and uniformity, most judicial systems have established a way to review trial judgments.

Generally speaking, an American *court of appeals,* or *appellate court,* does not retry the facts of a case, but the distinction between facts and law is as blurred at the appellate as at the trial level. Appellate judges frequently must decide for themselves whether congressional districts are as equal in population as they can be, or whether a business is mostly in local or interstate commerce. The Supreme Court's duty to review, it has said, is "not limited to the elaboration of constitutional principles; we must also in proper cases review the evidence to make certain that those principles have been constitutionally applied."[11]

The federal judicial system has two appellate layers, courts of appeals and the Supreme Court. Congress has divided the country into eleven circuits, each presided over by a court of appeals. In 1976, ninety-seven judges staffed these tribunals, ranging from three in the first circuit (encompassing Maine, New Hampshire, Massachusetts, Rhode Island, and Puerto Rico), to fifteen in the fifth circuit (Georgia, Florida, Alabama, Mississippi, Louisiana, Texas, and the Canal Zone). Circuit judges normally sit in panels of three, but in rare and important instances all those in a circuit may sit together—*en banc*—to decide a controversy.

As its name implies, a court of appeals hears only cases initially decided elsewhere. A few decisions can be taken directly from a district court to the Supreme Court, but most litigation begun in district courts must go to a court of appeals for review. In addition, a court of appeals may review orders of certain federal administrative agencies, such as the Interstate Commerce Commission and the Federal Trade Commission.

Federal Judicial Organization: The Supreme Court

The Constitution refers to a Supreme Court but leaves it to Congress to determine the Court's size and organization and to establish its appellate jurisdiction. From time to time, Congress has set the number of Justices at from five to ten. Changes in the Court's size, or attempts to change its size as in 1937, have usually been at least partially the result of partisan efforts to shift the direction of the Court's decisions. Nine has no inherent magic, but because this has been the number of Justices since 1869, it has taken on sanctity over the years. The Court's appellate jurisdiction has also been a frequent target of congressional attacks but has survived most of these assaults intact. The most significant exception occurred after the Civil War, when in 1868 the Radical Republicans (northern extremists), fearing with good reason that the Justices would declare much of military Reconstruction unconstitutional, removed the Court's jurisdiction to hear an appeal. The Justices then dutifully declared they were without authority to decide the controversy.[12]

The Supreme Court is almost exclusively an appellate tribunal. Article III does provide that the Court shall have original, that is, trial, jurisdiction in a few instances, but as a practical matter, the Supreme Court exercises that jurisdiction almost solely in suits between states and, less frequently, between a state and the federal government.

The procedure by which cases reach the Supreme Court under its appellate jurisdiction is complex. Generally speaking, cases come up in one of three ways: *certification, appeal,* or *certiorari.* Judges of a U.S. court of appeals may "certify" to the Supreme Court a question of federal law in a case before them, a question that the judges feel is of such importance or difficulty that it should be resolved immediately by the highest tribunal in the country. This procedure is uncommon.

Appeal is more often used. Under existing statutes a losing party may appeal his case to the Supreme Court when: (1) a federal court has declared a state or federal law unconstitutional; (2) the highest court of a state has declared a federal statute, executive order, or treaty unconstitutional; or (3) the highest court of a state has sustained the validity of a state law that has been challenged as violating the U.S. Constitution. Cases under the last heading are numerous, and, while jurisdictional statutes appear to oblige the Supreme Court to hear nearly all of them, the Justices dismiss the overwhelming majority on grounds that the constitutional challenges are insubstantial.

At the apex of the federal court system is the U.S. Supreme Court, whose majestic building proclaims the lofty goal of "equal justice under law."

The bulk of cases are brought to the Supreme Court by a *writ of certiorari* (from the Latin, "to be made more certain"). The losing party in a U.S. court of appeals or in the highest court of a state, if the claim involves a question of federal law, may petition the Supreme Court for review. Granting certiorari, that is, agreeing to hear the case, is strictly a matter of discretion. The Justices vote on whether or not to take each of these cases, four votes, one less than a majority, being necessary to accept the dispute.

Special Federal Courts

There are also several federal courts of special jurisdiction, among them the Customs Court, the Court of Customs and Patent Appeals, the Court of Claims, and the Court of Military Appeals. Decisions of these tribunals are reviewable by the Supreme Court under much the same procedures as cases from courts of appeals.

Judicial Recruitment

Judicial office in a constitutional democracy is not a simple concept. On the one hand, judges are supposed to be "animate justice." On the other hand, they are governmental officials who possess considerable political power. Periodically, cries are raised to take judicial appointments "out of politics" and leave recruitment of judges to bar associations. In practice, this suggestion means taking selection out of one kind of politics, where voters indirectly exercise some measure of control, and putting it into another, the politics of bar associations, where voters have no control at all.[13]

Historically, the British king appointed judges and still officially does, although the prime minister and his cabinet, especially the minister of justice and the lord chancellor, make the actual choice. Older practice in the United States tended toward election by state legislatures or nomination by the governor subject to legislative consent. At the end of the Revolutionary War, only Vermont provided for popular election of judges; but in the nineteenth century the tides of Jacksonian democracy swept over the courts. Every state admitted to the union since 1846 provides for popular election of all or most judges, as do many older states. Federal judgeships, however, have remained appointive offices.

The status of judges in common law countries differs from that in European nations whose legal systems draw on the Roman law tradition. On the continent, judges form a distinct profession separate from the practicing bar. One usually enters the judiciary immediately after graduating from law training and having passed a special set of examinations and undergone apprenticeship. Promotion is regulated much as for career civil servants. In contrast, American judges come from the ranks of practicing lawyers, public officials who went to law school, and from law professors. These judges seldom have any special training other than having once studied law; indeed, many minor state judges may have had no legal education at all.

Federal Recruitment

The formal steps in appointing federal judges are deceptively simple. The President nominates a candidate whom the Senate confirms or rejects. If confirmed, the judge takes an oath of office and serves during good behavior at a salary that cannot be lowered.

The informal processes are far more complex. A campaign for appointment usually begins long before any particular vacancy occurs. Judgeships are marvelously rich pieces of patronage, "grand political plums," Senator Everett Dirksen once called them. It is not salary; federal judges are not especially well compensated* when compared to successful practicing attorneys. The critical factors are the power and prestige a judge commands. Many, perhaps most, ambitious lawyers covet these rewards and begin early in their careers to try

---

*Federal judges' salaries are now adjusted annually to include a cost of living increase computed according to governmental economists' estimates of inflation. In 1976, district judges were receiving $42,000, circuit judges $44,625, Associate Justices of the Supreme Court $63,000, and the Chief Justice $65,625.

to achieve them by working hard and faithfully for political organizations or by running for office themselves.

Before disparaging this ambition, one must look carefully at its effects. It may make judges appear less like high priests and more like public officials, but such an image is not necessarily bad for democratic government. Second, this ambition helps keep able, highly trained people in politics. A third effect is to provide a large pool of professionally qualified and practically experienced candidates from which both parties can draw.

Ambition also provides appointing officials with a basis for predicting performance. If a judge turns out to be incompetent or corrupt, the country will suffer and the President and his party may be punished at the polls. Thus, it is prudent for appointing officials to prefer harder evidence of a person's strength under fire than his or her friends' assertions of steadfastness.

There is also the matter of a judge's basic political philosophy. A President would be a fool willingly to put on the bench a judge who would declare the administration's most cherished policies unconstitutional or interpret statutes so as to block the administration's goals. In his angry denunciation of senators who rejected the nomination of G. Harrold Carswell because they said he was a mediocrity with a racist background, President Nixon candidly stated the primary criterion that most Presidents have applied in selecting judges: "First and foremost, they had to be men who shared my legal philosophy. . . ." It may turn out, of course, that the President misjudges a person or has to choose the lesser evil; but when he has free choice, a President opts for a judge whose constitutional philosophy accords with his own. It is no accident that more than nine out of ten federal judges have come from the same political party as the President who nominated them and that Presidents tend to pick people whose views have been tested. As Lincoln said:

We cannot ask a man what he will do [if appointed], and if we should, and he should answer us, we should despise him for it. Therefore we must take a man whose opinions are known.[14]

Given the wide spectrum of views encompassed by both political parties, a President is not limited to his own party for "right thinking" people. A President can put members of the other party on the bench to enhance an image of nonpartisanship while hoping to secure a judge favorably disposed toward his general politics. A President may also reward senators or congressmen from the other party by naming some of their candidates to the bench. Although a President or his staff rarely bargains openly along straight lines of "You support my bill and I'll nominate your man," Presidents cannot consistently ignore the wishes of those legislators on whom they depend. And the President often has to rely on members of the opposing party to supply critical votes for his programs.

Once a vacancy occurs, a dramatic game begins. Unlike most American contests, the object is to get off the field and onto the bench. Candidates quickly mass the support they have been building up over the years and prod bar associations, friendly interest groups, local politicos, senators, and even congressmen. Interest groups concerned about the courts rally around their own candidates or endorse or oppose candidates already active. Public officials join in, sometimes to make sure one of their people is selected, sometimes to win the post for themselves.

Most recent Presidents have delegated their authority in the nominating process to the Attorney General, who passes this authority down to the Deputy Attorney General, who, in turn, usually works through a small staff. The amount of leeway the President's agents have in selection depends on the level of the judgeship. Since George Washington's time, senators have played a crucial—at times a dominant—part in naming district judges. If one of the senators from the state in which the vacancy occurs is from the President's party, senatorial courtesy gives that legislator a great advantage. A senator cannot capriciously invoke this tradition to blackball any nominee, but he or she can come close to doing so. If both senators are from the President's party, his agents may gain leverage by playing one senator off against the other. But even where the two senators are both in the opposition party, the Deputy Attorney General's staff is well advised to listen to their views, although probably—and usually quite acceptably—local leaders in the President's party will carry more weight.

When a vacancy occurs on a court of appeals, the President has much more freedom. Every circuit includes at least three states—except the District of Columbia circuit but the District has no senators—and while considerations of geographical representation do come into play, a senator cannot assert the same proprietary interest as when a judgeship falls totally within his or her own state.

When filling vacancies on the Supreme Court, the President is least restricted. But, as the nomination of Abe Fortas to be Chief Justice and Homer Thornberry, Clement Haynsworth, and G. Harrold Carswell to be Associate Justices in 1968, 1969, and 1970 showed, the President is not completely free.

Before a vacancy occurs, the Deputy Attorney General's staff also usually begin to make a list of candidates. Senators, congressmen, local leaders, interest-group representatives, officials of other executive departments, and perhaps members of other presidential staffs will be in constant touch, suggesting, supporting, or criticizing candidates. Incumbent judges may also be drawn into this process; indeed, they may inject themselves with gusto. During William Howard Taft's Chief Justiceship (1921–1930), the scent of a vacancy on the federal bench triggered a series of letters, telephone calls, and visits from "Big Chief" to the Department of Justice and the White House.

When the Deputy Attorney General's staff has completed its list — and in the case of district judges that list invariably overlaps with those of the state's senators — they ask the Federal Bureau of Investigation to investigate the moral characters and professional reputations of at least the front runners. At the same time, the staff usually asks the American Bar Association's Standing Committee on Federal Judiciary to report on candidates' professional qualifications. Their report rates candidates on a three-point scale: "Meets the highest standards," "Not opposed," and "Not qualified."

These investigations may screen out some candidates, but they rarely determine the winner. For district judgeships and to a lesser extent circuit judgeships, the remaining names on the list are subjects of continuing negotiation among the staff and the senator or senators. Even for a district judgeship, a senator cannot dictate final choice, unless the President has given that prerogative in exchange for other considerations. What a senator can do is to block almost any nominee from being confirmed. Faced with a potential stalemate, both sides typically negotiate a compromise.

Confirmation

The President announces the nomination by sending the candidate's name to the Senate, where the matter is referred to the Committee on the Judiciary. The committee chairman and his staff have usually long been in contact with the Deputy Attorney General and his staff and have completed some preliminary investigations of their own. A member of the Justice Department goes over the FBI report with the chairman, but no other senator is supposed to see it. The American Bar Association's committee formally submits its evaluation to the committee. Meanwhile, the committee's staff solicits views of senators from the nominee's state so there will be a clear record of the senators' views, then sets a mutually convenient time for hearings. Because of the work that has preceded nomination, hearings on district or circuit judgeships are generally dull recitations of virtue more appropriate to funeral eulogies.

In contrast, hearings on Supreme Court nominees are frequently dramatic performances. A few crackpots may provide comic relief by explaining how the nominee's refusal to march against the United Nations spells corruption of American youth. More seriously, some legal experts may offer searing critiques of his judicial philosophy while others present stirring panegyrics; and the debate may expand to such broad topics as the nature of the Union or the relationships between Congress and the courts. Committee members and other senators may join in discussion and praise or damn the nominee's political opinions, questioning him with the zeal of an ambitious district attorney cross-examining a notorious kidnapper.

The 1968 hearings on Abe Fortas provide a vivid illustration of what can happen, as Senator J. Strom Thurmond of South Carolina thundered at the nominee:

Mallory — I want that word to ring in your ears — Mallory. . . . Mallory, a man who raped a woman, admitted his guilt, and the Supreme Court turned him loose on a technicality. . . . Can you as a Justice of the Supreme Court condone such a decision as that? I ask you to answer that question.[15]

His ears, and those of most people within a hundred yards, ringing from the senator's shouting, Fortas did refuse to comment and exposed himself to hours of additional berating.

After the hearings, the committee deliberates and recommends that the Senate confirm or reject the nominee. Both majority and minority members may file reports. The question is then discussed on the Senate floor. Again the matter has usually been long settled for district and circuit judgeships. It is not unusual, however, for debates over confirmation of Supreme Court nominees to be both angry and informed. Nominations of Louis D. Brandeis, Charles Evans Hughes, and John J. Parker caused fights comparable to those over Fortas, Haynsworth, and Carswell.

At this stage, lobbying is normally at a minimum; by this time opponents know they are beaten and content themselves with formal speeches. When the opposition has a chance, however, lobbying may become intense, with agents of the AFL-CIO, the National Association of Manufacturers, the NAACP, the American Bar Association, Justice Department officials, members of the President's personal staff, and senators crossing each others' trails with promises, blandishments, and fresh evidence about the nominee.

Federal Judges

The products of this nominating process have generally been honest, competent, and politically knowledgeable public officials. Again, the sanction of punishment at the polls reinforces the moral imperatives that a President, his assistants, and senators bring to bear on such problems. To speak of judgeships as one form of patronage by no means implies that they are auctioned off to loyal party workers or parceled out to the opposition like green stamps. As one official said, "We feel that we owe certain people jobs but we do not feel that we owe them *specific* jobs."[16] Judgeships are very special kinds of jobs requiring very special qualifications.

In addition to being competent and honest, the typical federal judge has been a white, male, upper-middle-class, highly educated Protestant, who is in middle to later life. Ethnic pressures affect this area of politics, too, and there are many members of white ethnic groups on

The nine justices of the U.S. Supreme Court in 1977. Sitting, left to right: Byron R. White, William J. Brennan, Jr., Warren Earl Burger (Chief Justice), Potter Stewart, and Thurgood Marshall. Standing, left to right: William H. Rehnquist, Harry A. Blackmun, Lewis F. Powell, Jr., and John P. Stevens.

the bench, although blacks and women are grossly underrepresented. Of the more than five hundred judges on lower federal courts, in 1976 only five were women and nineteen were blacks.

Perhaps more important than ethnic or socioeconomic backgrounds of judges is that they are almost all successful lawyers whose commitment to the existing system has been tested in the crucible of practical politics. Most of them are "establishment men" in the broadest sense of that term. Some may be mavericks who relish tweaking the system, as Justice William O. Douglas did, and many other jurists may be equally devoted to political, legal, and social reform. But they come almost exclusively from people clustered just to the right and to the left of the political center. This collective biographical fact may help account for what many observers have noted: the inherent conservatism of the bench. Judges may work actively for social change, but for change that preserves and perhaps perfects the existing system rather than creates a new system.

Retirement of Federal Judges

Judges on many state courts serve for specified terms, and many countries have set ages for compulsory retirement from the bench. Article III of the Constitution, however, specifies that federal judges shall serve "during good behavior." Unhappily, judges are subject to the same problems of ill health and old age as the rest of humanity, and they may stay on the bench after they can no longer function effectively. Justice Stephen Field, for example, cast the decisive vote in 1895 to invalidate the income tax after his mental faculties had failed. He, like

Robert Grier before him and Joseph McKenna and Oliver Wendell Holmes after him, was asked by his colleagues to resign.

Since impeachment is an inappropriate remedy for bad health or old age, policy makers have sought other solutions. Many people have suggested a constitutional amendment setting a compulsory retirement age. More positively, Congress has enacted generous retirement provisions. A judge who reaches seventy and has had ten years of service — or sixty-five after fifteen years' service — may retire at full salary. If he or she is in ill health, both the stipulations about age and length of service may be waived. Nevertheless, most judges do not retire at seventy. "It is extraordinary," Charles Evans Hughes once remarked, "how reluctant aged judges are to retire. . . . They seem to be tenacious of the appearance of adequacy."[17] Hughes himself stayed on the Supreme Court until he was seventy-nine.

Congress may have unwittingly established a procedure to remove from service those district and circuit judges who are no longer able to perform their duties. A federal statute provides that each judicial circuit should have a council composed of judges and members of the bar. The law authorizes this council to "make all necessary orders for the effective and expeditious administration of the business of the courts within its circuit." And in 1965 the judicial council of the tenth circuit ordered that a district judge accused of inefficiency should not hear any additional cases or decide cases already on his docket. The Supreme Court refused to review this order, in effect allowing the judge to retain his office and salary but without authority.[18] Whatever solution this sort of procedure offers for lower court judges, there is still no way short of impeachment to force an infirm Supreme Court Justice to retire. The only remedy remains persuasion by the ailing Justice's colleagues.

Summary

This chapter has tried to offer some insights into the development of judicial institutions, to begin a discussion of the capacity of federal judges to shape public policy, to explain the jurisdiction and organization of federal courts, to outline the procedures by which those judges are chosen as well as some of the problems raised by tenure "during good behavior," and to sketch a composite silhouette of the jurists who staff the federal bench.

Selected Bibliography

ABRAHAM, HENRY J., *The Judicial Process: An Introductory Analysis of the Courts of the United States, England, and France,* 3d ed. (New York: Oxford University Press, 1975). A first-rate introduction to the business of judges and their inevitable involvement in making public policy.

AUERBACH, JEROLD S., *Unequal Justice: Lawyers and Social Change in Modern America* (New York: Oxford University Press, 1976). A blasting criticism of the American legal profession for its failure to achieve justice.

BERMAN, HAROLD J., ed., *Talks on American Law,* rev. ed. (New York: Vintage Books, 1971). A useful although very elementary series of lectures on American law broadcast by members of the faculty of the Harvard Law School to foreign audiences.

CARDOZO, BENJAMIN N., *The Nature of the Judicial Process* (New Haven, Conn.: Yale University Press, 1921). An eloquent and insightful description of the problems of judicial decision making.

CHASE, HAROLD W., *Federal Judges: The Appointing Process* (Minneapolis, Minn.: University of Minnesota Press, 1972). The most thorough study yet produced of the appointing process.

DANELSKI, DAVID J., *A Supreme Court Justice Is Appointed* (New York: Random House, 1964). A fascinating analysis of the events that led to the appointment of Pierce Butler to the Supreme Court.

FRANK, JEROME, *Law and the Modern Mind* (New York: Brentano's, Inc., 1930). A brilliant and provocative analysis of the role of law in modern society.

FRIEDMAN, LAWRENCE M., *A History of American Law* (New York: Simon and Schuster, 1973). A one-volume history of the development of American legal institutions and doctrines.

GROSSMAN, JOEL B., *Lawyers and Judges: The ABA and the Politics of Judicial Selection* (New York: John Wiley and Sons, Inc., 1965). A case study of the efforts of a pressure group to influence federal judicial appointments.

JACOB, HERBERT, *Debtors in Court: The Consumption of Government Services* (Chicago: Rand McNally and Company, 1969). An investigation of the consequences flowing from efforts of debtors and creditors to use the courts—a broader and more useful book than the title implies.

————, *Justice in America: Courts, Lawyers, and the Judicial Process,* 3d ed. (Boston: Little, Brown and Company, 1977). A brief but useful "political analysis of how justice is administered in American courts."

KALVEN, HARRY, and HANS ZEISEL, *The American Jury* (Boston: Little, Brown and Company, 1966). A fascinating empirical study of the work of juries and how their decisions differ from those of judges.

McWHINNEY, EDWARD, *Judicial Review,* 4th ed. (Toronto: University of Toronto Press, 1969). An excellent introduction to judicial review as it operates in seven countries.

MURPHY, WALTER F., and C. HERMAN PRITCHETT, *Courts, Judges, and Politics,* 2d ed. (New York: Random House, Inc., 1974). An introduction to the judicial process in the United States.

MURPHY, WALTER F., and JOSEPH TANENHAUS, *The Study of Public Law* (New York: Random House, 1972). An explanation of why and how political scientists study courts and judges.

————, *Comparative Constitutional Law* (New York: St. Martin's Press, Inc., 1977). An effort to view the political functioning of American courts from a comparative perspective.

PELTASON, JACK W., *Federal Courts in the Political Process* (New York:

Random House, Inc., 1955). A stimulating analysis of judges' involvement in American government.

PLUCKNETT, T.F.T., *A Concise History of the Common Law,* 5th ed. (Boston: Little, Brown and Co., 1956). A scholarly but readable account of the development of English legal rules and institutions.

WATSON, RICHARD A., and RONDAL G. DOWNING, *The Politics of Bench and Bar* (New York: John Wiley and Sons, Inc., 1969). A close examination of the political maneuverings of lawyers and judges to influence judicial selection under a supposedly nonpartisan method of choice.

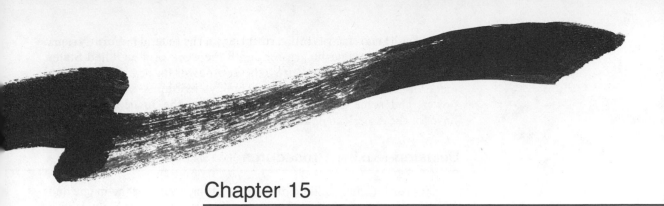

Chapter 15

The Supreme Court at Work

CHAPTER 14 PROVIDED a broad overview of the federal judicial system. This chapter examines in greater depth the work of the United States Supreme Court—its procedures, the sources of its power, the instruments it may use to affect public policy, restraints on the Court's power, and some general consequences that the Justices' decisions have for the American political system.

Decision-Making Procedures

The Supreme Court building provides a fitting home for the magic and majesty that surround law. On the outside, the huge marble palace—modeled on a Greek temple—reflects the solidity and integrity of established legal rules. Inside, the long, cool corridors radiate the serenity of a temple of justice. From the first Monday in October until sometime in July, the Justices meet here to hear the mass of cases that roll in. The issues directly involved are always legal, but the ramifications of those issues affect political rights or powers.

The long summer vacation and the Court's practice of recessing every several weeks during the term to read, write, and reflect make the Justices' pace seem far more leisurely than it really is. In fact, their workload is staggering, and as much in self-pity as in jest the Justices, as they confront each year's docket of more than 5,000 cases, have referred to themselves as "a chaingang."

Just before ten o'clock Mondays through Wednesdays when the Court is in session, the Justices meet in the robing room behind the red veloured courtroom, shake hands, and put on their black robes. Precisely at ten, the curtains part and the Justices take their places behind the great mahogany bench that dominates the small room. As they enter, the crier slams down his gavel and chants:

The Honorable, the Chief Justice and Associate Justices of the Supreme Court of the United States!

Oyez, oyez, oyez! All persons having business before the Honorable, the Supreme Court of the United States are admonished to draw near and give their attention, for the Court is now sitting. God save the United States and this Honorable Court.

Administrative matters may consume a few minutes; then the Chief Justice calls the first case. Probably months before, the Court had agreed to hear the controversy, and each side's contentions have already been explained at length in carefully documented written arguments called briefs and reply briefs. Now counsel have a chance at oral argument. Usually, the Justices allot only thirty minutes to each side, although in extraordinarily important disputes, such as the School Segregation Cases, they may allow more time. In front of the Justices in their high-backed leather chairs, counsel stands at a lectern and begins, "Mr. Chief Justice, may it please the Court. . . ." A white light on the lectern flashes when five minutes are left; when a red light goes on, the

Figure 15.1
Supreme Court Workload
Number of Cases on Docket, 1941–1975.

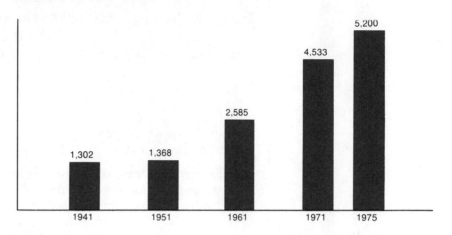

Source: Based on data in *Congressional Quarterly Weekly Report*, September 23, 1972, p. 2371, and

lawyer stops instantly. Chief Justice Charles Evans Hughes supposedly once called time on an attorney in the middle of the word "if."

Oral argument can be a traumatic experience for a lawyer. The Justices prefer a Socratic dialogue to a lecture, and lucid explanation to rhetoric. Questions, sometimes three and four at once, fly at counsel, as the Justices probe for clearer exposition of the facts in the dispute and for informed speculation on probable consequences of alternative solutions. The Justices can be ruthless in their pursuit of the truth — or of the lawyer, if he annoys them.

If the Justices find a presentation tedious, they do not hesitate to show their feelings. They may stare glumly at the ceiling, whisper and send notes to each other, or dispatch messengers to bring them law books. When he was solicitor general, William Howard Taft complained that the Justices chose his turn to speak as the best time to write letters; few who were familiar with Taft's oratorical style questioned the Justices' taste. Oliver Wendell Holmes used to sketch an outline of an attorney's probable argument and, if counsel followed a predictable course, catch a short nap.

At noon, the Court recesses for an hour's lunch, then goes back into session until three. On Fridays (and often on Thursdays as well), the Justices meet in their conference room to discuss and vote on the cases they have just heard argued, and to decide what other cases to accept. These conferences are secret. Only the Justices may enter the room, but some, Frank Murphy and Harold Burton, for example, have scribbled notes to guide themselves in writing opinions and perhaps to en-

Decisions are the final product of those cases heard by the Supreme Court. This is the opening page of the ruling in 1976 validating the death penalty. The case is referred to as *Gregg* v. *Georgia*.

lighten history. The Burton and Murphy papers show that discussions are usually informed, lively, and often long and heated. As at oral argument, the Justices are concerned about more than technical legal rules; they explore—and debate—with each other possible impacts of decisions on public policy. The Chief Justice speaks first, then the others in order of seniority. Each is supposed to be allowed to talk without interruption, but ideas—and sometimes tempers—flash. When the Chief feels that further discussion would serve no useful purpose, he calls for a vote. Until recently, voting was in reverse order of seniority, with the Chief last. In the 1960s, however, Earl Warren changed this historic procedure and surrendered his prerogative of casting the final vote. The Justices now vote in the same order in which they spoke.

If the Chief Justice is with the majority—and before Warren some Chiefs followed John Marshall's tactic of using the advantage of voting last to join the majority—he assigns responsibility for writing the opinion of the Court either to himself or to one of the other majority Justices. If the Chief Justice is in the minority, the senior Associate Justice in the majority appoints the opinion writer. That Justice circulates drafts to all his colleagues, so that those in the majority can make suggestions for changes and the minority may have an opportunity to answer his arguments. The Justices usually do suggest changes—Oliver Wendell Holmes complained that "the boys generally cut one of the genitals" from his opinions. In an important case, an opinion is likely to go through at least a half-dozen versions. Each Justice may write his own opinion, dissenting or concurring, although custom requires that he circulate it to all the Court. Occasionally a concurring or dissenting opinion persuades other Justices to change their minds and so becomes the opinion of the Court. A Justice is free to switch his vote up to the moment the decision is announced, and even after that if the loser petitions for a rehearing.

Judicial Power

In opposing ratification of the Constitution, one delegate to the Virginia convention complained of "the stupendous magnitude" of power conferred on the Supreme Court.[1] American constitutional history makes the gentleman appear guilty of understatement. The Justices function as members of a coordinate branch of government, and they have sometimes fully exploited their potential to influence not only immediate public policy, but also long-range development of the political and social systems. John Marshall's nationalism, Stephen Field's classic economic liberalism, and Earl Warren's civil libertarianism have been dynamic forces shaping American society. Yet the Justices are not all-powerful. They operate from a strong political base and can wield sharp weapons, but they are also subject to many restrictions. Without understanding the sources and instruments of judicial power and the limitations on that power, one cannot begin to grasp the kinds of roles that the Supreme Court—indeed all courts—play in American government.

Sources of Judicial Power

Legal Sources

As are all American judges, the Justices are legitimate heirs of the English jurists who staffed the courts of common law and of equity, and so have authority, recognized by custom, statute, and the Constitution, to adjudicate certain kinds of disputes. Like their British ancestors, American judges can also interpret acts of the legislature. As Chapter 14 showed, the multiplicity of legal rules and the generality of language of many important statutes force judges to act as policy makers, and the Constitution reinforces this push. By its own terms, the Constitution is law—"the supreme law of the land"—and, so the Justices have successfully claimed, as subject to judicial interpretation as other kinds of law.

In practice, *constitutional interpretation means judicial review, the authority to declare invalid actions of other public officials.* Yet the Constitution makes no mention of any such authority. In several early cases, however, the Justices assumed they could declare statutes unconstitutional.[2] The first clear use of judicial review came in *Marbury v. Madison* (1803).[3] The specific point involved was a narrow, technical one of jurisdiction; but, as frequently happens, there were important political issues below the surface.

Before going out of office, President John Adams had persuaded the lame-duck Federalist Congress to create a number of new judgeships, which Adams filled up with deserving Federalists. Some of these appointments were made so late that John Marshall, who saw no ethical problem in serving as Adams' Secretary of State while he was also Chief Justice, did not have time to deliver them before Jefferson took office. President Jefferson refused to send out the remaining commissions, and William Marbury, a disappointed justice of the peace in the District of Columbia, went to law to gain his judgeship.

Marbury filed suit in the Supreme Court for an order directing James Madison, the new Secretary of State, to deliver the commission. Marbury claimed that the Judiciary Act of 1789 gave the Court original jurisdiction to issue a mandamus—an order to a public official to do his duty—in such a case. As Chief Justice, Marshall, who like many conservatives was fearful of the havoc a radical like Jefferson might wreak on the country, was determined to establish once and for all the character of judicial power. He put aside the easy course, which was to declare that the Act of 1789 did not give the Court original jurisdiction in this kind of case—a fair reading of the statute.

First, Marshall wrote a biting 9,000-word indictment of Jefferson's refusal to deliver the commission, concluding that Marbury indeed had been wronged. The next question, Marshall said, was whether Marbury had sought the correct remedy. At that point the Chief Justice took up the constitutional issue and found a conflict between Article III's description of the Court's original jurisdiction and what was supposedly added by the Act of 1789. He then deduced the principle of judicial review by means of a syllogism. Major premise: The Constitution is the supreme law. Minor premise: It is the function of judges to interpret the law, and they take an oath to support the Constitution. Conclusion: Courts must declare invalid any inferior law—for example, an

Act of Congress—in conflict with the higher law, that is, the Constitution.

Marshall's tactics were clever: he had declared a statute unconstitutional in a case whose political context made it impossible for the President to defy the decision. Jefferson, after all, did not want to give Marbury his commission, and Marshall ruled that the Court could not order him to do so because Marbury had sued under an unconstitutional statute. On the other hand, the Chief's logic was not invulnerable. Jefferson and his supporters attacked it as an assertion of judicial supremacy and as an effort to retain Federalist control of government. The Constitution, critics noted, was different from ordinary law; it was a political document. As for the judicial oath, every office holder took a similar pledge to support the Constitution. Perhaps the most telling point was made by Senator Breckinridge of Virginia: "Is it not extraordinary," he asked, "that if this high power was intended, it should nowhere appear [in the Constitution]?"[4]

Marshall's decision enraged the Jeffersonians, though more because of his blasting attack on the administration than for his assertion of judicial review. In retaliation, they impeached Justice Samuel Chase and came within a few votes of convicting him (as we described in Chapter 12). Had they succeeded, Marshall might have been next; but they failed, and the principle of judicial review—next used by Marshall to declare invalid an executive order issued by President Adams,[5] a decision with which the Jeffersonians found it difficult to quarrel—soon became part of the American political tradition.

Although few people today seriously question the legitimacy of judicial review itself, just how far a Supreme Court decision obligates coordinate branches of the federal government is still unsettled. Probably most responsible critics would not deny judges' supremacy over the kinds of courtroom procedures covered by Article III of the Constitution. For instance, were Congress to provide for a conviction for treason on testimony of one witness rather than two as Article III commands, few would claim that the Court should enforce the statute. Probably also a broader policy that uniformly denied other officials use of judicial machinery to enforce laws that the Justices thought unconstitutional would find little opposition.

Some writers, however, have implied a much wider claim: A Supreme Court decision binds not only the parties to a case; it also binds the President and Congress in their own policy-making roles. Without a doubt, the possibility of an adverse Supreme Court decision has inhibited administrative and legislative behavior, but the extent of legal and moral obligations involved poses a different sort of question. Strong Presidents like Thomas Jefferson, Andrew Jackson, Abraham Lincoln, and Franklin Roosevelt have asserted that in performing their duties they must follow their own interpretations of the Constitution. Jackson vetoed the bank bill of 1832 because he thought a national bank unconstitutional,[6] even though the Supreme Court had held in

McCulloch v. *Maryland* (1819)[7] that Congress could establish such an institution. In his veto message the President said:

If the opinion of the Supreme Court covered the whole ground of this act, it ought not to control the coordinate authorities of this Government. The Congress, the Executive, and the Court must each for itself be guided by its own opinion of the Constitution. Each public officer who takes an oath to support the Constitution swears that he will support it as he understands it, and not as it is understood by others.

Lincoln put it more generally. He first conceded that a Supreme Court decision was binding on the parties to a case and that public officials must treat with great respect the principles announced by the Court. He then added:

At the same time the candid citizen must confess that if the policy of the government, upon vital questions, affecting the whole people, is to be irrevocably fixed by decisions of the Supreme Court, the instant they are made, in ordinary litigation between parties, in personal actions, the people will have ceased to be their own rulers, having to that extent, practically resigned their government, into the hands of that eminent tribunal.[8]

Jackson's and Lincoln's arguments, incidentally, would not support *state* officials who claimed authority to nullify a Supreme Court decision, because they are not officers of a *coordinate* branch of government.

It is worth noting that judicial review is not a power unique to the U.S. Supreme Court. It is shared by every federal court and by all state courts of general jurisdiction, although usually the Supreme Court can, if asked, review decisions of these other courts. Other countries—including Australia, Canada, West Germany, India, Ireland, Italy, Japan, and the Philippines—have also adopted judicial review, more or less modeling their processes on those of the United States.

Prestige

In democratic politics prestige can be a vital source of power, and judges may have a firm hold on public esteem. Because judges lack physical force, they ultimately have to depend on the feeling that one *ought* to obey a court decision and that if one of the parties does not, then other public officials *ought* to use their power to compel obedience.

From time to time, scholars, newspapermen, lawyers, elected politicians, and judges themselves point to the high or low prestige in which the Supreme Court is currently held. Unfortunately, we have little hard data to gauge the relative popularity of the Court in different periods. Decisions constantly irritate some groups, ethnic, regional, or ideological, while other decisions please other groups. But the correlation between general public opinion and noisy praise or condemnation by a few groups is doubtful. It is even hazardous to generalize from editorial opinions to those of newspaper readers. What does seem clear, however, is that if one looks at what critics have said over the years, the Justices began with no prestige whatever and have since fallen steadily in public esteem. "The Supreme Court is not what it used to be, and what's more it never was."[9]

Mass polling promises some clarifications, but its use on a scientific basis goes no further back than the 1930s: and even since then there has been relatively little sampling of public attitudes on judicial issues. One systematic study reveals some awareness of specific Court decisions.[10] About 45 percent of national samples of voting-age adults in 1964, 1966, and 1975 could recall a recent Supreme Court action — names of cases were not, of course, asked. When a respondent could recollect a decision, it was likely that he or she disapproved of what the Court had done. Yet more than two out of three of the people who had an opinion — including 40 percent of those who had expressed only critical views of particular decisions — thought that the Court was doing its basic job very well. This difference between criticism of individual decisions and approval of the Court as an institution indicates that the Justices have a reservoir of public support on which they can draw in emergencies. Additional surveys of practicing attorneys and administrative assistants of senators and congressmen, as well as analyses of views expressed by better-educated people in the national samples, indicate that this institutional support is deeply and widely shared among those who could be termed political activists and opinion leaders.

Yet three pieces of evidence imply that the Justices' reservoir of public support is not unlimited. First, and perhaps most critical, replies to open-ended questions — that is, questions to which respondents frame their own answers rather than choose among those suggested by the interviewer — showed a wide range of emotions: from respect, admiration, pleasure, and approval on the one hand, to disapproval, anger, and contempt on the other. But there was little evidence of anything like awe or adulation that would remotely imply automatic acceptance of Court decisions.

Second, variation in evaluations of the Court was closely associated with respondents' over-all political views, usually lumped under liberalism and conservatism. This connection indicates a complex relationship. In part, public approval of certain policies may be due to Supreme Court decisions; one simply cannot say to what extent this is true. On the other hand, this connection may mean that certain kinds of decisions can severely drain the Court's reservoir of support and also that as general political attitudes change so must those of the Justices if they are to retain support.

Third, a large portion of the public either is not aware of the Court's work or so slightly aware as to be unable to answer simple questions.

Thus we do not know how deeply, if at all, the support of this silent mass runs. We said earlier that more than two out of the three persons who answered the question thought the Court was doing its job very well, but only a little more than half of those asked could make any response at all. Moreover, ignorance or apathy may occur among those most helped by judicial decisions and whose political support the Court would most need in time of crisis. In the mid-1960s, for example, one would have expected blacks to be among the most ardent defenders of the Court, and so knowledgeable blacks were. But far fewer blacks than whites, proportionately, had much knowledge of the Court in particular or politics in general.

The Need for an Umpire

A third source of judicial power is a practical one; a federal system that divides power among state and national units of government, denies some power to each level, and then further fragments power among units of the national government needs some kind of umpire. The framers planned this division to cause friction, and in that sense it works very well indeed. But if anything is to get done, there must be ways of overcoming, at least temporarily, that friction. Just as individuals living together in society need some sort of arbiter to settle disputes, so do governmental officials who share power.

In a related fashion, other governmental officials may need the Court to help legitimize controversial decisions.[11] In a pluralistic society, any important public policy is likely to hurt the interests of many individuals and groups. Opposition will be based in part on the *wisdom* of a policy; but, especially when a vaguely worded constitutional clause is involved, doubts about the policy's *validity* will occur.

To survive, every governmental structure must provide some means of quieting basic constitutional doubts of this kind. In American politics the campaign speech, the ballot box, and the constitutional amendment can perform this legitimizing function, but so may a Supreme Court decision. Indeed, the Justices are far more likely to declare a contested congressional statute constitutional than unconstitutional. From 1789 to 1976 the Supreme Court invalidated national laws in less than 100 instances.

Instruments of Judicial Power

The most basic instrument of judicial power is *jurisdiction,* the authority to hear and decide certain kinds of cases as well as to issue orders to the parties involved. The potential political effectiveness of this instrument increases if, as American judges can, courts can issue orders to governmental officials. Reinforcing this authority is the practice of writing opinions. These may be merely turgid explications of technical rules. In the hands of a master, however, they can become means of influencing not only immediate but also future public opinion. The eloquent rhetoric of John Marshall, Louis Brandeis, Oliver Wendell Holmes, and Harlan Fiske Stone all took on lives of their own in helping to mold the thinking of later generations.

Just as *prestige* is an important source of judicial power, so it can also become a weapon of judicial power—precisely what an opinion writer wants it to be. Prestige can be strongly reinforced by *professional reputation,* the respect that other governmental officials have for the skill and determination with which the Justices use their power. When the Justices can combine a popular feeling that their decisions ought to be obeyed with a belief that the Justices can create a political backfire to burn those officials who do not aid compliance, they have forged an instrument to bludgeon the very people who have at their command the physical force to defy them.

The Justices also have available certain passive instruments. Almost completely they can determine what cases they accept—which is not to say they can control what cases are brought before them; that is another problem. But without giving any reason whatever, they can refuse to hear almost any case. Moreover, even when they take a case, they can if they wish use a variety of technical devices to delay a decision on the merits until a time they consider more favorable for the objectives they wish to achieve.

Limitations on Judicial Power

Technical Checks

A series of interlocking restrictions limit judicial power. As judges, the Justices must follow certain formal procedures. These are generally flexible, but not infinitely so. Unlike administrators, judges cannot initiate action. Someone must bring a case to them, and in a form that meets jurisdictional and standing requirements. The Justices can, for instance, sustain the conviction of a brutal sheriff under a civil rights law, but they cannot start such a prosecution themselves. Even when a case has been brought and formal criteria met, the Justices are restricted, usually, to giving no more than what the parties ask for. For example, if a group of dissidents appeals a city's injunction forbidding a protest march, the Justices cannot put the mayor out of office.

A second restriction limits the effect of a decision. A court order legally obligates only the parties to that particular case, those who cooperate with them, and those who succeed to their office or status. A decision that the legislature of Tennessee is gerrymandered does not, of itself, *legally* oblige the government of another state using exactly the same representational formula. A separate suit must be brought, although, of course, existence of the first judgment might well move officials of the second state to act on their own. Earlier, we mentioned the class action, a procedure that allows one litigant or a small group of litigants to sue for themselves and all others similarly situated. These kinds of options widen access to the courts, but the resulting order still binds only the specific persons named in the court's final order.

The kinds of orders that a court can issue also limit judicial power. In general, judges can far more easily forbid action than they can command positive action, especially where public officials are involved. The Justices can hold a civil rights statute or social security law constitutional, but they cannot compel Congress to pass such a statute. They can, of course, liberally interpret existing statutes and surprise congressmen with more policy than they realize they had set. In 1956, for example, Rep. Howard Smith, author of the Smith Act which punishes advocacy of violent overthrow of the U.S. government, expressed stunned disbelief at the Court's decision[12] that this statute forbids the states to adopt similar laws to protect the United States. Despite occasional opportunities to reap a bigger harvest than Congress has thought it has sown, the basic limitation on the kinds of orders a court can issue are very real.

Public Opinion

If the Court draws much of its power from public esteem, popular attitudes can also check judicial power—unless, of course, the Court is considered incapable of error and, as we have seen, there is no evidence of such adulation. Like the Lord, the public taketh away as well as giveth, and it may act considerably more capriciously than the Deity.

Internal Restrictions

The Justices are also limited by their own ideas of how they, as judges, ought to act. Because they come to the bench after a long period of legal training and usually a far longer period of apprenticeship in public service, they probably have absorbed many prevailing norms about judicial action. These norms may be vague, yet in broad terms they do distinguish between behavior perfectly proper for legislators and administrators but improper for judges. For instance, a legislator who seeks a solution to a problem by supplementing official information with informal consultations with friends and experts and a great deal of personal research might be looked on as energetic. On the other hand, a judge who discusses a pending case with a person not a member of the court when attorneys for both sides are not present is skirting the very edge of unethical conduct.

In addition, the Justices cannot help but be aware to some extent that they are appointed officials serving what amounts to life terms in a supposedly democratic government. The apparent oddity of this situa-

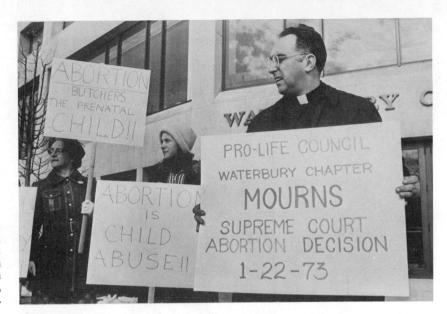

Opponents of the Supreme Court's favorable ruling on abortion seek to mobilize public opinion by a demonstration outside a courthouse in Waterbury, Connecticut.

tion has caused many, but by no means all, Justices to hesitate to substitute their own judgment for that of popularly elected officials. (Candid judicial acknowledgement that the United States is a *constitutional* democracy, as explained in Chapter 4, would ease but not remove the difficulty.)

Institutional Limitations

The simple fact that the Supreme Court is staffed by nine Justices constitutes another check. To hear a case requires a vote of four members and to decide it requires five votes. Since nine is an uneven number, one might expect clear-cut decisions in all cases where every Justice sat; but in complex litigation there are usually more than two options open. Furthermore, an opinion, to be labeled the opinion of the Court, must win the assent of at least a majority of the Justices. It is no easy matter to persuade five or more individualistic, strong-willed lawyers to agree on a complicated legal document that is based on certain fundamental and perhaps controversial assumptions of political philosophy that may have immediate as well as long-run effects on public policy.

A Justice who is determined to write exactly as he himself wishes is apt to write for himself alone. Not since the days of John Marshall has a single Justice been able to dominate the Court. Decisions and opinions are products of what Justice Felix Frankfurter once described as an orchestral rather than a solo performance.[13] When the Justice assigned the task of writing for the Court circulates each draft, suggestions for change may pertain to literary style or to the heart of the

"My dissenting opinion will be brief: 'You're all full of crap!'"

substance of a case. Securing agreement, if the case is at all important, typically involves negotiation, compromise, and even bargaining. This sort of operation is complex, for a change demanded by one member of the majority may anger another. The opinion writer thus sometimes finds himself deliberately writing vaguely so as to alienate as few of his colleagues as possible. The final product, as Justice Holmes once observed, may be a mass of dough. But if no single judge or small coterie can dominate the Court, the alternatives to bargaining are each judge writing for himself, as is done in England and Australia, or no opinion at all.

The Justices have incentives and sanctions for their bargaining. The main incentive, of course, is to enshrine as that of the Court the principles that each Justice thinks most fitting to cover this and similar situations. The major sanction available to the opinion writer is to ignore a colleague's wishes—if he can somehow still muster five votes. His colleague's sanctions are to write a separate opinion and to persuade other

Justices to join him. Clearly, the effectiveness of either sanction depends in part on the closeness of the vote and in part on the intellectual powers of individual Justices. A 5–4 division puts the opinion writer at a considerable disadvantage, just as an 8–1 judgment gives him great leeway. So too a threat to circulate a separate opinion means much more from a Holmes, a Brandeis, or a Black than from a less skillful writer. Helping to keep negotiations within bounds is the knowledge among the Justices that they will work together for many years, and during that time each is likely to have to write a hundred or more opinions of the Court.

A second set of institutional checks arises from the fact that the Supreme Court rarely makes either the first or the final decision in a case. As the preceding chapter showed, the Court's jurisdiction is almost totally appellate. It reviews a lower court decision, reverses or affirms it, writes an opinion explaining the principles behind choices, and usually sends (remands) the case back to the court where the litigation began for final disposition. Thus, like the President, the Justices must often operate through a bureaucracy; but they have far less control over their bureaucracy than does the President over his. The Justices can exercise little if any formal or informal control over appointment, retention, or promotion of lower federal judges and probably no control whatever in state judicial affairs. The sheer volume of business in state and federal courts, the frequency with which new issues arise, the vagueness of many legal rules and of some Supreme Court interpretations of those rules mean that the Justices are at most leaders of their branch of government, not its masters. The analogy of bureaucracy—judicial or administrative—to international politics, where independent and semi-independent leaders negotiate, is apt.[14] The military model of disciplined subordinates saluting and unquestioningly carrying out orders is one that Presidents and Supreme Court Justices may sorely envy but never see.

Political Restraints

The Supreme Court can say what statutes and executive orders really mean; it can even declare them unconstitutional. These are great powers, but both Congress and President have a series of weapons they can turn against the Justices. Congress can impeach and remove any judge, increase the number of Justices, withdraw most of the Court's appellate jurisdiction, cut off money for the Court's administrative staff or deny funds to execute specific decisions, enact new statutes to "correct" judicial interpretations of old law, and propose constitutional amendments to counter the effects of a judicial decision, as the Fourteenth and Sixteenth Amendments did, or even to strike at judicial power itself, as the Eleventh Amendment did. During Jefferson's administration Congress, although its action was unconstitutional, abolished a whole tier of federal courts and turned the judges out without salaries; and after the Civil War, several Radical Republican legislators threatened to abolish the Supreme Court itself.

The President, as Chief Executive, may forbid any administrative officials to enforce Supreme Court decisions, and he can pardon anyone convicted of criminal contempt of court for disobeying judicial orders. In choosing judicial nominees, the President can try to influence future decisions, as can senators in approving or disapproving a nominee. The President can also try to persuade Congress to use any of its powers against the Court; and, as can senators or congressmen, he can draw on his own prestige to attack the Justices.

Although the wording of the national supremacy clause of Article VI of the Constitution puts state officials on a lower level than federal officers, state officials can still challenge the Court. They too can pass new statutes or issue fresh orders and so force apparent winners back to court for additional battles. Like national officials, state officers may try to undermine the Justices' prestige. And because the feudal structure of both political parties makes senators, representatives, and even federal administrators dependent on local politicos, state officials may be in a strong position to pressure federal officials into opposing Supreme Court decisions. Efforts to impede implementation of the Court's rulings regarding segregation in education, prayers in public schools, and reapportionment of state legislatures demonstrate how effectively states may retard judicial action.

Power and Prudence

So many restraints coming from so many sources raise the question of why the Supreme Court has not been curbed severely and frequently. In part, the answer lies in the fact that these checks are limitations, not barriers. Having usually had practical political experience, judges are typically aware of these restrictions and know how to work within them and how to reduce their strictures. Moreover, judicial decisions that offend one group usually delight (and help) another. And defenders of the Court as well as its attackers can use channels of political influence; it is always easier to prevent Congress from acting than to persuade it to act.

A President, too, is likely to be subjected to cross-pressures. Much of the real power he can wield against the Court requires congressional cooperation. Furthermore, refusal to enforce decisions can expose him to political dangers, not only from public opinion, but from the fact that recalcitrants are usually state officials whose challenge to the Court can become a threat to national supremacy. And on that supremacy much of the President's own power rests.

Another part of the answer lies in the internal restraints to which all governmental officials are subject. Presidents, members of Congress, and most state officials take their oaths of office as seriously as do judges and are usually as devoted to preserving the political system. And an independent judiciary exercising judicial review is an integral part of that system. Closely related is the fact that public officials often feel they *ought to* obey Supreme Court decisions even when they disagree with them. There are, of course, limits on how far officials will go in following a judicial decision—limits determined partly by the official's guess about how far those people who form his particular public will push him or let him go.

In short, Supreme Court Justices and other public officials are commonly products of the same general political culture—the white middle class—and of the same political subculture—professional politicians. They share beliefs in the "rules of the game" and existing governmental processes. Presidents, senators, congressmen, and Justices are held together by the additional bond of all being officers of the *federal* government.

Furthermore, because of the frequency with which vacancies occur on the Court (about once every twenty-seven months), it is usual for at least a sizable minority, if not a majority, of the Justices to be quite sympathetic with the general and even the specific goals of an administration. Bitter disagreements may arise, as in the early 1800s or the mid-1930s, when a majority of the Justices are from a political generation other than the President's and a majority of the Congress. More likely to occur are difficulties with state officials whose local orientation may put them out of the mainstream of national politics.

Prudence may for other reasons deter Congress and the President from using their weapons against the Court. The President and Congress are inevitably rivals for power, and each may need the Court to check the other. Because of the President's easy access to mass media, legislators may believe that by crushing judicial power they would give the Chief Executive the upper hand in that rivalry. Even when for the most part they agree with him on substantive issues, they may feel that their status as members of the legislative branch is protected by a strong judicial check on the White House. In 1937, for instance, many liberal Democrats who had been foes of the Supreme Court attacked Roosevelt's plan to add six new Justices. These people sensed what one of FDR's advisers put into words: "If the President wins the court fight, everything will fall into his basket."[15]

Moreover, either branch may need the Justices, as John F. Kennedy and Lyndon Johnson did in the civil rights field, to help push the other into taking certain courses of action. The President and Congress may also need the Court to legitimize certain controversial policy decisions or to take the blame for failures to act.

As a result of all these factors, there has been intermittent guerrilla warfare between Congress and the Court and between the Court and the President, but not since Jefferson was in the White House have Congress and the President joined to launch a major attack against the Justices, and even that alliance was short-lived. The three branches of government coexist, occasionally in harmony, more often in armed truce, even more frequently in competition, and sometimes in open conflict; but the conflict has typically been for limited objectives.

Summary

In this and the previous chapter, we have been describing a whole set of roles that Supreme Court Justices and to some extent all federal judges play in the American political system. The Supreme Court is a legal tribunal operating within a flexible but still recognizable set of procedural rules; it is also a dispenser of justice as well as an interpreter of legal rules; at the same time the Court is a coordinate branch of government responsible in an important way for helping to formulate public policy while deciding individual cases.

Like the President, Supreme Court Justices simultaneously play many roles. First, they are arbitrators of disputes between individual citizens and thus often between conflicting social interests. Second, where public officials are involved in a case, the Supreme Court often has the task of defining boundaries of authority between various governmental agencies and between government and individual citizens. Third, in defining boundaries of public authority, the Supreme Court may not only check governmental power but also help legitimize controversial policies. Fourth, as appellate judges, the Justices supervise the federal judicial system, and even the fifty state judicial systems insofar as federal law is concerned. Fifth, in deciding cases, the Court often modifies existing rules or fashions new rules for new problems. Thus, Justices play a legislative role, much to the anger of losing litigants and of public officials who fear judicial encroachments on their power, disagree with the substantive policy involved, or are vulnerable to pressure from those who lost in the judicial process.

Sixth, like bureaucrats, Supreme Court Justices may play a representational role in the sense of being "chosen from" rather than "acting for." Customs surrounding Supreme Court appointments require that the Justices come from all sections of the country and that there usually be at least one Catholic and one Jew on the Court. The appointment of Thurgood Marshall has probably begun a tradition of having at least one black Justice. Searches for a woman to fill recent vacancies indicate that women may soon secure at least token representation. The Court may perform an additional representational function by providing a forum for those who have too little political power to secure a real voice in other governmental processes. Last, the Justices may also play an ancillary representational role by protecting the integrity of the electoral processes, by trying to safeguard, as in the white primary cases,[16] the rights of racial minorities to vote, or, as in the reapportionment decisions,[17] the right of every person to have his or her vote counted equally with those of every other citizen.

Seventh, by the opinions they write, the Justices may help educate the public at large and governmental officials in particular. It is true that few of these opinions are read by other than a cluster of lawyers, public officials, newsmen, scholars, and students experiencing the joys of political science courses. Yet, because these people also write and talk, a general idea of what courts do percolates through some of the community. And knowledge that the Justices have declared that the Constitution permits or forbids certain kinds of policies may well affect public attitudes. Like the Presidency, the Supreme Court can be a "Great Pulpit" in American politics. Here, incidentally, may be the most important legacy of the Court under Chief Justice Earl Warren (1954–1969): it frequently reminded Americans of the basic concepts like democracy, constitutionalism, legal equality, and the presumption of innocence that underlie their political system.

The Justices may play any or all of these roles well or badly. The *Dred Scott* decision,[18] for instance, held in 1857 that Congress had no authority to regulate or prohibit slavery in the territories, and what the Justices thought would stabilize the Union by ending debate on slavery helped bring on the Civil War. The School Segregation Cases,[19] on the other hand, supplied a much-needed sermon that democratic government cannot rest on a caste society.

Three points are fundamental: First, the Justices play these roles whether they want to or not. As Justice Robert H. Jackson once said, "We act in these matters not by authority of our competence but by force of our commissions."[20] A decision that school segregation was constitutional would have had different but no less important political and educational effects from those of the actual decision.

Second, the direction that Supreme Court decisions take and the persuasiveness and persistence with which the Court pushes its jurisprudence are all highly dependent on the values, talents, and courage of the Justices themselves. Neither precedents nor procedural rules predetermine the course the Court will follow and rarely do statutes or the Constitution. All of these permit choice.

A third point we have alluded to several times. A judicial decision, even when it interprets the Constitution, is not necessarily final. New statutes, new constitutional amendments, even new judges are practical possibilities. The American political system forces judges to participate in policy making and requires them to share power not only with each other but also with a large number of other public officials.

Selected Bibliography

BEVERIDGE, ALBERT J., *The Life of John Marshall* (Boston: Houghton Mifflin Company, 1916), 4 vols. The first major biography of a Supreme Court Justice: a classic of its kind.

BICKEL, ALEXANDER M., *The Supreme Court and the Idea of Progress* (New York: Harper & Row, 1970). A well-written evaluation of the work of the Warren Court by a former law clerk of Justice Felix Frankfurter.

CARR, ROBERT K., *The Supreme Court and Judicial Review* (New York: Holt, Rinehart and Winston, Inc., 1942). A brief analysis of the Court's use of judicial review.

FRIEDMAN, LEON, and FRED L. ISRAEL, eds., *The Justices of the United States Supreme Court 1789–1969: Their Lives and Major Opinions* (New York: Chelsea House Publishers, 1969). A 4-volume work containing a lengthy biographical article on each Justice who sat from 1789 until 1969, with a reprinting of one or two of his most important opinions.

FREUND, PAUL A., ed., *History of the Supreme Court of the United States* (New York: Macmillan Company, 1971–). A projected 11-volume history of the Court, financed through a bequest of Justice Oliver Wendell Holmes. As of 1976, 3 volumes had been published, written by Charles Fairman, Julius Goebel, Jr., and Carl B. Swisher.

JACKSON, ROBERT H., *The Supreme Court in the American System of Government* (Cambridge, Mass.: Harvard University Press, 1955). A Justice's short, trenchant essays on his Court.

KLUGER, RICHARD, *Simple Justice: The History of Brown v. Board of Education and Black America's Struggle for Equality* (New York: Alfred A. Knopf, 1976). By focusing on the School Segregation Cases shows the way the Court functions in the political system.

MASON, ALPHEUS T., *Harlan Fiske Stone: Pillar of the Law* (New York: Viking Press, 1956).

———, *William Howard Taft: Chief Justice* (New York: Simon and Schuster, Inc., 1965). Two richly detailed political biographies of Chief Justices of the United States.

McCLOSKEY, ROBERT G., *The American Supreme Court* (Chicago, Ill.: University of Chicago Press, 1960). A superb historical introduction to the work of the Court.

MILLER, CHARLES A., *The Supreme Court and the Uses of History* (Cambridge, Mass.: The Belknap Press of Harvard University Press, 1969). A delightfully written analysis of the gropings of Supreme Court Justices to find historical footings for their decisions.

MURPHY, WALTER F., *Congress and the Court* (Chicago, Ill.: University of Chicago Press, 1962). A case study of the efforts in the 1950s to curb the Supreme Court.

———, *Elements of Judicial Strategy* (Chicago, Ill.: University of Chicago Press, 1964). An analysis of the political power of the Supreme Court, based on the private papers of several Justices.

PRITCHETT, C. HERMAN, *The Roosevelt Court: A Study in Judicial Politics and Values, 1937–1947* (New York: Crowell-Collier and Macmillan, 1948.) A path-breaking study of decision making in the Supreme Court.

SCHMIDHAUSER, JOHN R., *The Supreme Court* (New York: Holt, Rinehart and Winston, Inc., 1960). A useful analysis of the social backgrounds of Supreme Court Justices.

TWISS, BENJAMIN R., *Lawyers and the Constitution: How Laissez-Faire Came to the Supreme Court* (Princeton, N.J.: Princeton University Press, 1942). An important case study of the influence on the Supreme Court by lawyers who argued before it.

Vose, Clement E., *Caucasians Only: The Supreme Court, the NAACP, and the Restrictive Covenant Cases* (Berkeley, Calif.: University of California Press, 1959). An interesting account of how a pressure group utilized judicial power to achieve one of its goals.

Part Seven
Civil Liberties

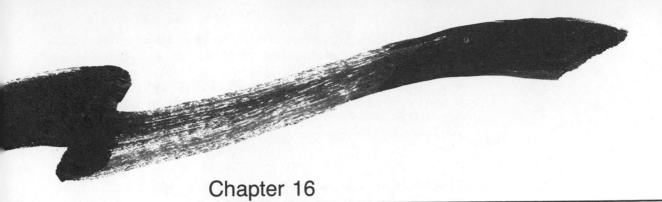

Chapter 16

Civil Liberties in a Free Society

The Historic American Concept of Rights

The Bill of Rights
States and the Bill of Rights

Fundamental Substantive Rights

Right to Be Free
Citizenship
Right to Travel
Equal Justice
Freedom of Religion
Privacy
Bodily Integrity

Basic Rights: Communication and Association

Preferred Position
Balancing
Reasonableness
Literalness
Public versus Private Issues
Judicial Practice

The Darker Side of Civil Liberties

Summary

Selected Bibliography

THE CHAPTERS IN Parts Three through Six centered on various political processes or on particular governmental institutions. In discussing topics like campaigning, electoral behavior, and lobbying, we occasionally alluded to such issues of civil liberties as the right to vote and to petition government. This chapter focuses directly on some other fundamental rights, while Chapter 17 moves on to analyze more specifically the American system of criminal justice.

The Historic American Concept of Rights

Every American schoolchild can repeat from memory the second paragraph of the Declaration of Independence:

We hold these truths to be self-evident, that all men are created equal, that they are endowed by their Creator with certain unalienable rights, that among these are life, liberty, and the pursuit of happiness. That to secure these rights, governments were instituted among men, deriving their just powers from that consent of the governed, that whenever any form of government becomes destructive of those ends, it is the right of the people to alter or abolish it. . . .

Embodied here is more than stirring rhetoric. Jefferson was summarizing a political philosophy that was shared by the leaders of the Revolution and probably by most educated colonists. In a later fit of jealous pique against Jefferson's fame in writing the Declaration, John Adams, who had also been a member of the drafting committee, complained that, "There is not an idea in it that had not been hackneyed in Congress for two years before." Jefferson himself freely conceded that he had meant only to paraphrase the "sentiments of the day." His task, he told a friend, had not been to discover new principles of government or to advocate new political arrangements, but "to place before mankind the common sense of the subject, in terms so plain and firm as to command their assent."[1]

The fact that the Declaration's ideas were commonplace made them all the more useful for the immediate purpose of uniting the colonies. Jefferson had succinctly outlined the essential elements of a political philosophy around which the new nation should be organized: (1) by their human nature, not by the gift of society, or government, or particular officials, *all* men have certain fundamental rights, their *"natural" rights;* (2) men created government not for its own sake but to protect their natural rights and thus governmental action that violates those rights is a violation of the purpose of government's existence; (3) thus natural rights form a standard, a higher law, by which to judge the legitimacy of governmental action, and habitual governmental abuse of those rights gives citizens the right, if not the duty, to overthrow that government.

The roots of the idea of natural rights run back through medieval theologians, Roman lawyers, and ancient Greek philosophers. But for the colonists there were more recent sources. First were Sir Edward Coke (1552–1634) and Sir William Blackstone (1723–1780). These men were the authors of treatises on English law that were required readings—often the *only* required readings—for fledgling lawyers in colonial America. In explaining the law of England, Coke and Blackstone argued that no act of government could validly abridge natural law or natural rights. Thus one could expect that every colonial lawyer was familiar with this doctrine and, judging from writings and legal arguments of attorneys, most of them accepted it.

The writings of the English philosopher John Locke (1632–1704)—the "divine Locke," as some colonists called him—formed a second source. Among English writers he set forth most systematically the concepts of natural rights and limited, representative government that were so congenial to the revolutionaries. Because of the influence of his ideas in America, Locke was the spiritual grandfather of the Declaration of Independence.

For the generation that fought the Revolution and later accepted the Constitution no less than for people of the twentieth century, civil liberties were goods to be enjoyed for their own sake or means to achieve other ends, such as individual self-development. Without the rights to enjoy privacy, to express oneself in words and symbols, to talk and associate with others in order to discover and pursue common goals, to worship or not worship, to own and use property, and to be secure from arbitrary arrest and imprisonment, the good life, however defined, would be impossible, at least in western culture.

The doctrine of natural rights also formed an important theoretical cornerstone to the concept of limited government that we discussed in Chapter 4. All constitutionally protected rights limit government. This is especially true of those concerning protection against arbitrary arrest and, in any system that allows elections, freedom to communicate, associate, and vote. Freedom of speech and press, for instance, not only permit self-expression, but, along with freedom of assembly, they provide a legitimate means of organizing opposition that can protest governmental policies and at the next election challenge and perhaps unseat incumbents. In this sense, freedom of communication and association form the basis of constitutional and democratic government. If opposition is illegal, if alternative policies cannot be formulated, defended, and put to a test in the market of the ballot box, then constitutional democracy cannot exist. The right to discuss public affairs, Justice Oliver Wendell Holmes once said, "is more than self-expression; it is the essence of self-government."[2] In a similar fashion, other protections, such as a fair, public trial by jury in a criminal case, function not merely to defend the rights of a particular person but also to protect society as a whole from overzealous, overambitious, or corrupt guardians.

But civil liberty also depends on governmental power. Without strong government to keep the peace and protect people from fellow citizens who feel little moral restraint in taking what they want or in venting their aggressions, real freedom in modern society would be impossible. On the other hand, possession of a near monopoly of physical force can tempt governmental officials to use their power for personal benefit. The history of Nazis and Fascists in Germany, Italy, and Spain provides a set of horror stories about the dangers from unchecked "defenders of the people" that are as vivid as the records of Stalinism in the Soviet Union.

Civil liberties, whether expressed in terms of natural rights or merely those rights specifically guaranteed by a country's constitution, thus pose a delicate problem of blending freedom with governmental power. "It is a melancholy reflection," James Madison wrote to Jefferson in 1788, "that liberty should be equally exposed to danger whether the Government have too much or too little power, and that the line which divides these extremes should be so inaccurately defined by experience."[3]

The Bill of Rights

The original Constitution did not contain a bill of rights, although it did provide some protections. Article I forbade states to pass bills of attainder, ex post facto laws (both are defined in Chapter 4), or "law impairing the obligation of contracts." Article IV provided that citizens of each state would be entitled to "all privileges and immunities of citizens in the several states"—a vague clause that makes sense only as a shorthand for the contemporary doctrine of natural rights outlined in the Declaration of Independence. Article I also forbade Congress to enact bills of attainder or ex post facto laws, or to suspend the writ of habeas corpus*—the common law's basic protection against arbitrary arrest and imprisonment—"unless, when in cases of rebellion or invasion the public safety may require it." Article III guaranteed trial by jury in federal criminal cases, established a narrow definition of treason, and outlawed the historic British practice of punishing a traitor's children.

These protections were hardly trivial, but they certainly did not guard the whole sweep of what contemporaries thought were the natural rights of men or the historic legal rights of Englishmen. The framers' basic justification for the omissions was that the Constitution gave the federal government no authority to violate any of these rights. They also argued that to try to list such rights would be dangerous, because if one were accidentally omitted governmental officials could later deny its existence. Moreover, most of the framers apparently thought that

---

*A *writ of habeas corpus* (literally, "if you have the body") is an order from a court, usually issued at the request of a friend or attorney of the prisoner rather than the prisoner himself (being in jail, he finds it difficult to go to court), directing a jailer or other official who is holding the prisoner to bring that person before the court and justify his detention or to release him immediately.

the Constitution's complex system of pitting power against power and ambition against ambition better protected civil liberties than would the "parchment barriers" of a bill of rights.

But, bowing to pressure from those who deeply regretted the absence of a bill of rights and to induce Rhode Island and North Carolina to join the Union, the First Congress proposed twelve amendments to the Constitution. The states ratified ten of these, and collectively they have been called the Bill of Rights. (Inclusion of the Ninth Amendment—"enumeration . . . of certain rights, shall not be construed to deny or disparage others retained by the people"—met the problems of possible omissions.)

Despite sponsoring these amendments in the House of Representatives, Madison had greater faith in the checks built into the body of the Constitution as armor for civil liberties. But, he argued, inclusion of a bill of rights might serve as an educating (modern social scientists would say "socializing") instrument to remind citizens of the sacredness of their fundamental rights. In addition, like Jefferson, Madison stressed that a written bill of rights would encourage judges to protect civil liberties by providing them with an explicit list of constitutional guarantees.

As Madison predicted, American judges have come to "consider themselves in a peculiar manner the guardians of those rights," though by no means have they always functioned as an "impenetrable bulwark" against popular frenzy or governmental arrogance. Despite frequent judicial failings, it remains true that to understand civil liberties in the United States, one must begin by learning what judges—especially Justices of the U. S. Supreme Court—have said about them. As we have already seen, decisions and opinions of the Supreme Court can act as powerful influences on the policies governmental officials pursue and, by helping to shape the general political culture, can affect the ways in which members of the general public think and behave. But a Supreme Court ruling seldom immediately settles a policy problem. Before a problem is solved—or outlived—Congress, executive officials, state and local officers, and many private citizens usually become involved.

States and the Bill of Rights

Much of the wording of the Bill of Rights is general enough to prohibit state as well as federal action. But the records that remain of discussion of the amendments indicate that there was a widespread assumption that they would restrict only the *federal* government. In 1833, speaking for a unanimous Court in *Barron* v. *Baltimore,* Chief Justice John Marshall wrote that assumption into constitutional law.[4]

It did not follow, however, that individuals—at least white individuals—were at the mercy of state officials. First of all, most states had their own bills of rights. Second, the doctrine of natural rights retained its grip on the judicial mind. Indeed, until well after the Civil War, that doctrine flourished among American judges, although in keeping with the Constitution's compromise they exempted slavery from the doctrine's reach. But when other issues, most especially property, were concerned, judges frequently announced that they would invalidate state or federal legislation that offended natural rights.

By the time the doctrine of natural rights had begun to wane, the Fourteenth Amendment—ratified in 1868—had become part of the Constitution, and it specifically restricted state power. Its second sentence reads:

No State shall make or enforce any law which shall abridge the privileges and immunities of citizens of the United States; nor shall any State deprive any person of life, liberty, or property, without due process of law; nor deny to any person within its jurisdiction the equal protection of the laws.

Gradually that sentence, especially its second clause, became a protection against state and local efforts to regulate business and property. (It should be kept in mind in this discussion that, in terms of constitutional law, there are only two levels of government, state and federal. All city, county, or other local officials are *state* officers.)

Nevertheless, for many decades the Supreme Court refused to protect against state action rights other than those relating to property. Then in 1925, without warning, the Court held that the "liberty" guaranteed by the "due process" clause of the Fourteenth Amendment included freedom of speech.[5] In the 1930s, the Court included freedom of religion and, although only under limited conditions, a right to free legal counsel. In 1937, speaking through Justice Benjamin Cardozo, the Court offered a justification for its process of "selective incorporation." Some rights are

of the very essence of a scheme of ordered liberty. . . . If the Fourteenth Amendment has absorbed them, the process of absorption has had its source in the belief that neither liberty nor justice would exist if they were sacrificed. . . . This is true, for illustration, of freedom of thought and speech. Of that freedom one may say that it is the matrix, the indispensable condition of nearly every other form of freedom.[6]

Within a few years, Justice Hugo Black was claiming that the Fourteenth Amendment incorporated all of the Bill of Rights. Much of his argument was based on the intent of the framers of the Fourteenth Amendment, but he also objected to the broad scope that "selective incorporation" gave to judges in asserting authority to distinguish between rights essential "to ordered liberty" and those that were unessential. The Supreme Court has never accepted Black's reasoning, but has pretty much accepted the same results. The slow process of inclusion has now encompassed all of the first nine amendments except the requirements of indictment by grand jury and trial by jury in civil cases where the amount in controversy exceeds $20.

Still, a majority of the Justices continue to follow Cardozo's distinction to the extent that most of them see a hierarchy of values in the Bill of Rights, indeed, in the entire Constitution and all its amendments. Needless to say, the Justices also continue to disagree among themselves about the nature of that hierarchy. Insofar as there is consensus, it is that among the most important rights — and therefore among those most deserving of judicial protection — are those to freedom and citizenship, to travel, to equal justice under law, to liberty of conscience and protection against state-imposed religion, to privacy, to bodily integrity, to freedom to speak, to publish, to associate with others, to petition government, and to vote.

Fundamental Substantive Rights

Earlier we noted that from one point of view all civil liberties are values in themselves or stepping stones to achieve other substantive values, while from another point of view those same civil liberties function as limitations on government. Some rights obviously partake more of one character than the other. In this section we shall look at several fundamental rights that are more values in themselves. In the next section we shall analyze those that function more as means to restrict government.

Right to be Free

Slavery blatantly contradicted the whole notion of natural rights and, so some Tories claimed, made a mockery of the Declaration of Independence. The existence of slavery as a legal institution caused much soul searching in the early days of the Republic. In fact, Jefferson's early drafts of the Declaration had contained a searing indictment of the slave trade as "execrable commerce" that "waged cruel war against human nature itself, violating it's [sic] most sacred rights of life and liberty." But fear of alienating southern colonies caused removal of those sentences from the final draft.

As Chapter 4 pointed out, the framers of the Constitution — most of them reluctantly — accepted slavery as a price of union, although they adroitly avoided using the word in the document itself. Adoption of the Thirteenth Amendment in 1865 ended slavery as a legal institution, although more than a century later Americans, white as well as black, are still suffering from the wounds inflicted by the "peculiar institution."

The Thirteenth Amendment is itself peculiar in that it is the only provision of the Constitution that operates against private citizens as well as against governmental officials. In practice, however, relatively few controversies have arisen under this amendment and those that have come up have centered on alleged instances of "involuntary servitude" rather than actual slavery. In 1867, Congress passed an act making it a federal crime to hold persons in peonage — "a status or condition of compulsory service, based upon the indebtedness of the peon to the master." Thus, attempts to force anyone to work off a debt are illegal. "The undoubted aim of the Thirteenth Amendment as implemented by the Antipeonage Act," the Supreme Court said, "was not merely to end slavery but to maintain a system of completely free and voluntary labor throughout the United States."[7]

Compulsory military service has, many young people have thought, a real element of involuntary servitude; but in 1917 a unanimous Supreme Court gave this proposition short shrift, disposing of it in one long jumbled sentence: "contributing to the defense of the rights and honor of the nation" is a citizen's "supreme and noble duty."[8] While this decision is still ruling law, the Supreme Court in 1968 scalded as "a blatantly lawless" act, a local draft board's revocation of an exemption because the man had turned in his registration card as a protest against the war in Vietnam.[9]

Citizenship

Closely related to the right to freedom is the right to citizenship. In a world of nation-states, citizenship is "the right to have rights."[10] To be deprived of citizenship can mean being condemned to a status of a perpetually impoverished nomad. Because they are no longer citizens of their native lands, so-called "stateless persons" can be easily deported. Because they have no passports, they often find themselves unable to travel — legally — to other countries. If they do manage to emigrate, they usually are not entitled to work or even remain in the host country for more than a few months.

The Fourteenth Amendment — aimed at the infamous *Dred Scott*[11] ruling that a black could not be an American citizen — opens with a straightforward declaratory sentence: "All persons born or naturalized in the United States, and subject to the jurisdiction thereof, are citizens of the United States and of the State wherein they reside." Left unanswered, however, was whether Congress could revoke a person's citizenship as punishment for a crime. After some backing and filling, a majority of the Supreme Court held that Congress may not remove a person's citizenship for any reason. An individual may voluntarily renounce it, but only by a definite, specific repudiation. Neither desertion from the armed forces in wartime, draft evasion, nor voting in a foreign election constitutes a clear repudiation.[12]

Right to Travel

American citizenship, the Supreme Court has said, carries with it a right to travel within the United States free from legal restrictions and a similar right to travel abroad, subject only to very carefully drawn reg-

Over one hundred thousand American citizens of Japanese descent were denied their rights by the federal government during the Second World War. Aliens and citizens were indiscriminately evacuated from their homes, as with this group shown leaving San Francisco, and placed in detention camps in remote areas.

ulations that involve the federal government's authority to regulate foreign commerce, control immigration, and conduct foreign relations.[13] Although not mentioned in the Constitution, the right to travel has its origin in the First Amendment and economic necessity. If a citizen could not cross state lines or leave the country, his or her ability to speak to and associate with others who share political ideas would greatly diminish. Such restrictions, in a modern economy, could also drastically curtail a person's capacity to earn a livelihood.

The right to move freely within the United States means not only that a state may neither forbid nor regulate immigration from other states, but also that a state may not impose unreasonable disabilities on new arrivals. The Supreme Court has held unconstitutional state requirements for long periods of residence before a new member of the community can vote, receive welfare benefits, or have free hospital care.[14]

Equal Justice

The Fourteenth Amendment forbids only states, not the federal government, to deny any person "the equal protection of the laws." Indeed, the Constitution contains no general requirement that the federal government treat people equally. But the right to equal treatment seems so basic that the Supreme Court has ruled that it is included in the concept of "due process" embodied in the Fifth Amendment and so limits federal power no less than state.[15]

An employee of the Dallas Transit Company removes a sign requiring racially segregated seating from a bus following a 1956 ruling of the U.S. Supreme Court banning racial segregation on public transportation vehicles operating within a state. This decision (*Gayle* v. *Browder,* 352 U.S. 903) was one of a number of court rulings which applied the basic doctrine of the School Segregation Cases of 1954 to other aspects of life.

Racial Equality. Blacks have been the most obvious victims of unequal governmental treatment, although they have by no means been the only victims, as white immigrants, Hispanics, Orientals, Indians, and women of all races can testify. In 1896, the Supreme Court in *Plessy* v. *Ferguson* agreed that "separate but equal" accommodations for the races satisfied the Fourteenth Amendment.[16] While facilities in the South were almost always separate, they were seldom equal. Still, many decades elapsed before judges—and a longer time before other governmental officials—began to take the second half of the formula seriously. By the late 1930s, however, the Supreme Court had started its slow undermining of the basic doctrine of "separate but equal"; and when the great blow came in the School Segregation Cases of 1954, the Justices could point to sixteen years of rulings that had chipped away the legal foundations of racial segregation.[17]

Whatever criticism can be made about the slowness of the Justices' pace, it was faster than that of Presidents, senators, representatives, and most state officials. In any event, formal constitutional law has moved much closer to the ideal that Justice John Marshall Harlan I eloquently but vainly proclaimed in his dissent in *Plessy:* "Our Constitution is color-blind and neither knows nor tolerates classes among citizens."

Despite judicial rulings, a bevy of important civil rights laws enacted since the School Segregation Cases, and both publicly and privately sponsored programs of "affirmative action," much racial discrimination still exists in the affairs of private citizens, labor unions, small businesses, and large corporations. Moreover, some discrimination also remains in governmental policies, most obviously in continued racial segregation in public schools, especially those of northern cities.

For all its defense of equality, the Supreme Court has in recent years contributed to educational discrimination in two ways. First, a majority of the Justices has held that state officials need to approach problems of desegregating schools only on the basis of the offending districts and cannot be required to tackle the problem on a metropolitan or regional basis unless all school districts in that broader area have discriminated. On these grounds the Court invalidated a district judge's order directing Michigan to carry out desegregation not merely by reassigning pupils within the city of Detroit but also in surrounding suburbs.[18] Because Detroit itself is heavily black, the Supreme Court's restriction of remedies to the city has meant that full school integration there is impossible. The center city remains substantially black, the suburbs mostly white.

Second, in *San Antonio* v. *Rodriguez,* a majority of the Court held that states can lawfully allow local communities to supplement state funds for education with money raised by local property taxes.[19] This decision means that children in poorer areas run a substantial risk of receiving education inferior to that available to children in richer areas. Although the correlation is far from perfect, a larger proportion of blacks and Hispanics than whites are likely to live in poorer districts. In effect, the dissenters argued, this decision changes the constitutional guarantee of "equal protection" to "minimal protection."

Wealth. Other kinds of inequalities abound in the legal system, and some have racial ramifications. The most blatant are those based on wealth, as *Rodriguez* demonstrates. Judges take oaths to do equal justice between rich and poor, and most are loyal to that vow. The fault lies less in individual failings than in the fact that the American legal system is slow, cumbersome, and expensive. People with more skillful—and usually more expensive—attorneys have a decided advantage. The Supreme Court has tried to compensate by ruling that government must waive for the poor certain fees usually charged for use of the judicial system[20] and has held that in all serious criminal cases government must provide, free of charge, a lawyer if the defendant is too poor to afford his own.[21] But these attorneys, usually from legal aid bureaus, are often young and inexperienced or are already overburdened with work. Moreover, although help from legal aid organizations is sometimes available to the poor, neither the states nor the federal government has a constitutional obligation to provide free counsel in civil cases.

Statutory Classifications. The issue of equality is complicated by the fact that one sure way to treat people unequally is to apply exactly the same rule to everyone in all situations. A century ago, Anatole France ridiculed "the majestic equality" of French law that forbade both rich and poor to sleep under park benches. Today few people question the fairness of welfare laws that exclude multimillionaires from benefits or tax laws that would actually impose higher rates on the wealthy than on the poor.

Realizing that statutory classifications are often necessary, judges have tried to formulate rules to sort out permissible from impermissible distinctions. In the late 1960s, a majority of the Supreme Court constructed a two-tiered test. Where fundamental rights such as voting, speech, or religion are involved, judges should exercise "strict scrutiny" of any classifications. The government must show: that a "compelling" public interest is served by regulating the basic right; that other, less drastic, regulations, could not have protected that public interest; and that no "inherently suspect" classifications, such as race and to a lesser extent sex, were applied.[22] Where less fundamental rights have been involved—welfare payments, for example[23]—the Court has held that distinctions must only be "reasonably related" to achieving a valid public purpose. Judges need not strictly scrutinize classifications, although such tainted criteria as race could make any classification unreasonable.

Sex. The Supreme Court's sensitivity to discrimination based on sex is relatively recent, a product of agitation for women's liberation. In 1961, for instance, even the ultraliberal Warren Court could find no constitutional flaw in a Florida statute that required women, but not men, to file an application with a state official before serving on a jury.[24] It was not until 1975 that the Justices repented their male chauvinism about jury service.[25]

The Court is still divided over the extent to which sex is an "inherently suspect" classification, but at least the Justices have given "somewhat" stricter scrutiny to such statutory distinctions. They have sometimes allowed classifications by sex that have benefited women without hurting men, but have also struck down several regulations that favored one sex over the other.[26]

Freedom of Religion

When Madison proposed a bill of rights in 1789, he wanted the constitutional protection of freedom of religion to be broad in scope, specifically encompassing "liberty of conscience." In final form, however, what became the First Amendment read: "Congress shall make no law respecting an establishment of religion, or prohibiting the free exercise thereof. . . ."

There are two separate provisions here, one relating to "establishment of religion," the other to "free exercise." In many disputes the two are closely linked and sometimes demand opposite policies. For example, a young man drafted into the armed forces may need a chaplain in order freely to practice his religion. On the other hand, the government's paying the salary and expenses of chaplains and subjecting them to military discipline certainly entangles the government with religion. Similarly, either or both clauses may conflict with other constitutional guarantees. A statute that provides free bus transportation for all schoolchildren except those attending religious schools may deny those children "equal protection."

Antiestablishment. For a time, the Supreme Court's practice was to speak dogmatically about "a wall of separation between church and state," but to act pragmatically. More recently, the Justices have conceded that the Constitution does "not call for total separation between church and state; total separation is not possible in an absolute sense. Some relationship between government and religious organizations is inevitable."[27] The Court has come to favor a flexible, three-pronged test to determine the constitutionality of governmental aid to religion: (1) the purpose of the aid must be secular not religious; (2) the primary effect of the aid must not be to advance one religion or all religions; and (3) that aid must not constitute "excessive entanglement" of the state in religious affairs. Over the years the Court has allowed states to supply free bus transportation[28] and textbooks[29] to parochial school children and has found no flaw in the federal government's making funds available to church-affiliated colleges and universities or in a state's giving general grants to all private institutions of higher learning, including those run by religious groups.[30] On the other hand, the Justices have found "excessive entanglement" in an arrangement whereby a state would pay a portion of the salaries of parochial school teachers to teach such subjects as mathematics and science.[31]

Efforts to integrate religious training into curricula of public schools have also had a mixed judicial reception. In 1948, the Court invalidated a "released time" program for religious instruction.[32] Under this system, unpaid volunteers from local churches gave instructions on school property once a week to children whose parents wanted them to have such training. A majority of the Court thought that using public property and compulsory attendance laws constituted establishment. Four years later, however, the Court held constitutional a plan similar in almost all respects except that instructions were given off school property.[33]

The widespread practice of prayers and Bible reading in public schools has also generated a series of cases. For years the Justices avoided ruling on such rituals, but in 1962 they squarely faced the issue of the constitutionality of a prayer composed by the New York State Board of Regents: "Almighty God, we acknowledge our dependence upon Thee, and we beg Thy blessings upon us, our parents, our teachers, and our country." Students whose parents requested would be excused from this recitation; nevertheless, the Court ruled that the arrangement violated the First Amendment. Government, Justice Black said for the majority, "should stay out of the business of writing or sanctioning official prayers and leave that purely religious function to the people themselves and to those the people choose to look to for religious guidance."[34]

The following year, the Justices extended this ruling to strike down Pennsylvania's requirement of daily reading in public schools of verses of the Bible and recitation of the Lord's Prayer.[35]

Free Exercise. One of the earliest cases in which the Supreme Court considered free exercise of religion involved a challenge to an act of Congress outlawing polygamy in the territories. The statute was clearly directed against the Mormons, but in 1879 the Court sustained its validity, distinguishing between the right to *believe,* which was absolute, and the right to *act,* which was subject to normal criminal law.[36] Sixty-seven years later, the Court held that an antiprostitution statute could legitimately be applied to Mormons practicing polygamy.[37] A bare majority of the Justices said that polygamy was "a notorious example of promiscuity" that Congress could punish. The Court recognized the religious motivation behind the practice, but found that immaterial.

Sunday closing laws have also raised questions both of establishment—sanctioning the Christian day of rest—and of free exercise in that they force Jewish merchants to recognize the Christian sabbath and put them at a competitive disadvantage if they try to observe their own as well. A majority of the Supreme Court rejected both arguments,[38] but a few years later held that a state could not deny unemployment compensation to a Seventh Day Adventist who refused to accept a job that required him to work on Saturdays.[39]

Small religious sects have frequently suffered from government regulations impinging on their rituals and tabus. The Jehovah's Witnesses have been especially active in bringing offending public officials into court, and their litigation in the 1940s helped develop much of the law of the First Amendment. Interestingly, the Justices preferred to rest their decisions on the somewhat broader grounds of freedom of communication rather than on religious discrimination. The most notable victory of the Witnesses was over compulsory flag salutes. Since the Witnesses take the First Commandment literally—not to worship "graven images"—they refused to allow their children to participate in saluting the flag. In 1943 the Supreme Court reversed an earlier ruling and held that such laws[40] were unconstitutional interferences with religious freedom.

Almost twenty years later, the Court sustained the right of the "Old Order Amish" to take their children out of all schools after the eighth grade.[41] The Justices felt that the interest of the state in keeping children in school until they were sixteen years old was not sufficient to override the religious importance to the Amish of having their children immersed in the life of their own community, freed from the "worldly" influences of modern society.

Jehovah's Witnesses have been less successful in persuading courts to allow them to refuse emergency medical care. They interpret the scriptural injunction against "drinking blood" to forbid blood transfusions. But lower court judges, at the request of hospitals or physicians, have sometimes required Witnesses to submit themselves or their children to such treatment when their lives have been in danger and chances of recovery with a transfusion have been good.[42]

Test Oaths. In *Torcaso* v. *Watkins*, a unanimous Court invalidated a provision in the Maryland state constitution that required all persons holding office of profit or trust in the state to declare a belief in the existence of God. Torcaso had been denied a commission as a notary public because of a refusal to make such a declaration. "This Maryland religious test for public office," the Court said, "unconstitutionally invades the appellant's freedom of belief and religion and therefore cannot be enforced against him."[43] The Justices were doing little more here than recognizing that freedom to believe in God is not true freedom unless it includes the right not to believe.

Privacy

Justice Louis D. Brandeis once spoke of "the right to be let alone" as "the most comprehensive of rights and the right most valued by civilized men."[44] But Brandeis spoke in dissent. Despite the Fourth Amendment's protection against "unreasonable searches and seizures," the Supreme Court did not recognize a general right to privacy until 1965. Then, in *Griswold* v. *Connecticut,* speaking through William O. Douglas, a majority held that specific provisions of the Constitution had "penumbras"—shadowy regions next to specific things, here constitutional clauses. The general right to privacy, Douglas said, grew not only out of the Fourth Amendment but also from the First Amendment's protection of freedom of religion and association, the Third Amendment's prohibition against quartering troops in civilian homes in time of peace, the Fifth Amendment's ban against self-incrimination, and the Ninth Amendment's sweeping maxim that the rights listed in the first eight amendments were not exhaustive of basic civil liberties. Then, repeating the ancient language of natural rights, Douglas said for the Court: "We deal with a right of privacy far older than the Bill of Rights—older than our political parties, older than our school system."[45]

The specific issue in *Griswold* was whether a state that had a statute banning use of contraceptives could punish as an accessory a physician who advised married couples on contraception. The Court's answer was, of course, no. Douglas' opinion had stressed the sanctity of marriage against interference by government, but a few years later the Court struck down a Massachusetts statute that forbade distribution of contraceptives to unmarried people.[46] "If the right of privacy means anything," Justice William J. Brennan wrote for the majority, "it is the right of the *individual,* married or single, to be free from unwarranted governmental intrusion into matters so fundamentally affecting a person as the decision whether to bear or beget a child."

The Court has also invoked the right of privacy to invalidate state laws that forbid abortions unless the health of the mother is seriously endangered.[47] "The right of privacy," Justice Harry Blackmun said for the Court, "is broad enough to encompass a woman's decision whether or not to terminate her pregnancy," at least during the first three months of that pregnancy. After that time, the majority conceded, as the fetus becomes more and more capable of sustaining life on its own, the mother's right to privacy recedes and the state's interest in protecting life increases. "We therefore conclude," Blackmun wrote, "that the right of personal privacy includes the abortion decision, but that this right is not unqualified and must be considered against important state interests in regulation."

Curiously, a majority of the Justices in 1976 could see no merit in a constitutional claim made by two male homosexuals that enforcement of antisodomy laws against consenting adults for acts done in private violated their right to privacy. Without even hearing argument, the Court affirmed a decision by a lower federal court that such statutes were constitutional.[48]

Bodily Integrity

Some cases, like those ordering compulsory blood transfusions, touch on a subdivision of privacy, a right to bodily integrity. The Justices have indicated that such a right exists, but however fundamental it is hardly absolute. The Court has sustained compulsory vaccinations even against a challenge by a man who had a history of allergic reactions to such measures,[49] upheld a state authority to sterilize a feeble-minded young woman,[50] and validated obligatory blood tests for people accused of drunken driving.[51] On the other hand, the Court has struck down a law imposing sterilization as a punishment for crime[52] and invalidated use by police of a stomach pump to obtain evidence from an accused.[53] There may be an intelligent way of reconciling these decisions, but no Justice has yet had the imagination to explain it.

Basic Rights: Communication and Association

Because freedom of speech, press, assembly, association, and petition are vital to democratic political processes as well as being desirable means of self-expression, some Justices have said that these rights deserve a "preferred position" in the Constitution's hierarchy of values. But no formula can automatically solve all the problems that freedom of communication presents in a modern society. Even if one grants that rights to voice political opinions and join with others who share those opinions are absolutely necessary in a democracy, one still must confront questions about the limits on such rights. Do those rights include a right to: urge violent destruction of the political system of constitutional guarantees? publish documents that contain military secrets? call a neighbor dirty names or print false stories about his sexual conduct? film and show movies or stage live shows involving open performance of sexual intercourse?

All these questions basically ask at what point government may regulate rights of communication so as to protect other values that are important to society. As would be expected from the diversity of American life, we have not one answer but many. In the early cases that came to the Court after World War I, Justice Oliver Wendell Holmes proposed that the Justices sustain a regulation of communication only if what was spoken or written posed a "clear and present danger" to some important interest that government could protect.[54] In the test's first three applications, the Court used it to justify sending people to jail for arguing that the draft was unconstitutional and that the United States should not intervene in the Russian civil war. Later, Holmes and Justice Louis D. Brandeis tried to tighten the meaning of "clear and present danger" so that it would protect rather than threaten free speech. As Brandeis explained in 1927:

Those who won our independence by revolution were not cowards. They did not fear political change. They did not exalt order at the cost of liberty. . . . [N]o danger flowing from speech can be deemed clear and present, unless the incidence of the evil apprehended is so imminent that it may befall before there is opportunity for full discussion. If there be time to expose through discussion the falsehood and fallacies . . . the remedy to be applied is more speech, not enforced silence. Only an emergency can justify repression. . . .

Moreover, even imminent danger cannot justify resort to prohibition of these functions essential to effective democracy, unless the evil apprehended is relatively serious. . . . The fact that speech is likely to result in some violence or in destruction of property is not enough to justify its suppression. There must be the probability of serious injury to the State.[55]

In the 1930s and 1940s, the Court did occasionally use the test as Holmes and Brandeis wished, but the basic notion of "clear and present danger" remained vague. In the early 1950s both those who were terrified by the spectre of domestic communists and those who dismissed communist agitators as "miserable merchants of unwanted ideas" agreed that "clear and present danger" was not a useful rule to interpret the First Amendment. The former thought it was too restrictive of governmental power, the latter found it too restrictive of freedom of speech.

Since then five general approaches have been debated among judges and scholars. We shall briefly summarize each.

One approach, first suggested by Chief Justice Harlan Fiske Stone in the late 1930s,[56] holds that, because such rights as freedom of expression are vital to the democratic process they deserve special judicial protection—hence the term *preferred position*. Where such rights are involved, Stone said, courts should relax the usual presumption of constitutionality accorded statutes and place a heavier burden on government to justify any restrictions. (The similarity to the rule of "strict scrutiny" discussed under Equal Justice should be obvious, for "strict scrutiny" is a later and more specific application of "preferred position.")

Two very different kinds of objections have been lodged against this approach. One group of critics claims that the Constitution does not authorize judges to make distinctions in the importance of its various clauses. What rights a judge sees as "vital" or "fundamental" may be no more than a personal value judgment, which he has no authority to force on society. A second, much more libertarian, criticism holds that the notion of a preferred position for First Amendment rights does not go far enough. The First Amendment, these people point out, does not say that Congress shall have a greater burden of proving the constitutionality of laws regulating freedom of speech or press; rather it says simply "Congress shall make *no* law."

Balancing

As its name implies, *balancing* calls for judges to weigh against one another the interests that compete in a case and determine which prevails, or perhaps how much of each can co-exist. There are two immediate problems with this sort of rule. First, as its popularizer, the late Roscoe Pound, Dean of the Harvard Law School, warned, a judge must be careful not to pit interests of private individuals against interests of the public at large; otherwise the individual would always lose.[57] Rather one must translate an interest of an individual into a public interest. For example, in a free speech case, judges should not weigh the public's interest in preserving its constitutional processes against an individual's interest in liberty to advocate violent overthrow of the government. Instead, the second interest on the scale should be the public's concern in preserving a self-governing society in which people may freely debate opposing political views. The temptation to pit individual against public interests is often, however, overwhelming.

Second, no matter what interests are opposed, no judge or scholar has yet explained and justified the weights that should be put on various interests. Nor has anyone explained how a judge's scale of values should be calibrated. In the absence of such explanations—and perhaps more important, justifications—balancing may mean no more than a convenient cloak to hide a judge's reading his values into the Constitution.

Reasonableness

Another approach, often associated with Justice Felix Frankfurter, who served on the Supreme Court from 1939 until 1962, totally rejects the notion of a preferred position for any rights. Where a right conflicts with governmental authority or the rights of other individuals, Frankfurter agreed that a balance must be struck. But in a democracy, he argued, it must be the legislature that strikes that balance, not the judiciary.

Courts are not representative bodies. They are not designed to be a good reflex of a democratic society. Their judgment is best informed, and therefore most dependable, within narrow limits. Their essential quality is detachment, founded on independence. . . . Primary responsibility for adjusting the interests that compete in the situation before us of necessity belong to the Congress.[58]

The function of judges, Frankfurter maintained, was only to see if the "balance" that the legislature set was reasonable, not whether, in the judgment of the Supreme Court, it was "correct" or the "best" of possible alternatives.

Critics have retorted that Frankfurter's theory turns the courts into lunacy commissions, for he would allow judges to intervene only where they thought a legislature had acted irrationally. Others have pointed out that Frankfurter's approach would change the First Amendment to read:

Neither Congress nor the states shall make any law abridging the freedom of speech or press unless a majority of the appropriate legislature and the Supreme Court think such abridgment is reasonable.

But, whatever its shortcomings, Frankfurter's response, like that of balancing, emphasizes that freedom of communication can clash with other important constitutional values, like privacy, the right to a decent reputation, or the right of the people to have government restrain those who would use violent means to destroy the Constitution.

Literalness

The simplest solution has been that of Hugo L. Black, who was an Associate Justice of the Supreme Court from 1937 to 1971. After years of listening to arguments about the First Amendment, he came to the conclusion that it means exactly what it says.

My view is, without deviation, without exception, without any ifs, buts, or whereases, that freedom of speech means that government shall not do anything to people, or, in the words of Magna Carta, move against people, either for the views they have or the views they express or the words they speak or write. . . . I simply believe that "Congress shall make no law" means that Congress shall make no law.[59]

Thus Black voted against governmental power to punish those who spoke in favor of violent overthrow of the constitutional order or who screened movies that many people thought obscene. He also voted against the right of individuals, private citizens as well as public officials, to sue anyone who wrote falsehoods, deliberate or inadvertent, about their character. "Our First Amendment," he summed up, "was a bold effort . . . to establish a country with no legal restrictions of any kind upon the subjects people could investigate, discuss and deny."[60]

But, critics are quick to point out, Black excluded action as well as "symbolic speech" from the First Amendment's protection. He thought that such "symbolic" acts of communication as picketing,[61] wearing armbands,[62] or burning a draft card[63] or an American flag[64] were not protected by the First Amendment. The distinction that he drew in these cases between words and deeds is very thin. Not only is the usual purpose of words to cause deeds — "Words are the triggers of action," Judge Learned Hand once wrote — but verbal persuasion is typically interlaced with symbols. "We live by symbols," Oliver Wendell Holmes said, and nowhere is this more true than in politics. The flag, motherhood, the log cabin, the full dinner pail, Watergate, the donkey, the elephant, parades, and demonstrations are integral parts of American political debates, shorthand representations of politically laden values.

Justice Black also voted to convict demonstrators for parading in an orderly fashion outside a courtroom.[65] Judges and jurors, Black felt, should be insulated from popular influence. "Justice cannot be rightly administered," he explained, "nor are the lives and safety of prisoners secure, when throngs of people clamor against the processes of justice outside the courthouse or jailhouse door." These distinctions may be reasonable, indeed they may be both intelligent and necessary. But in effect they imply that communication of ideas is not an absolute that should always take precedence over other rights and other values.

Public versus Private Issues

Another approach, put forth by Professor Alexander Meiklejohn, combines literalness and reasonableness.[66] Insofar as *public issues* are involved, Meiklejohn asserted, officials must follow the literal words of the First Amendment and "make *no* law" abridging freedom of communication. It does not matter whether that public issue concerns advocacy of communism, intervention in the Middle East, or opposition to an incumbent President. "No law" means no restriction, none at all. Only in a situation in which political debate is unlimited can the people see all the alternatives and intelligently choose among them. Insofar as freedom of communication is related to self-government, it cannot legitimately be limited by governmental action.

On the other hand, Meiklejohn argued that where there were no issues of public policy involved but only issues of, say, obscenity or pornography, then the true test of constitutionality is, as Frankfurter stated it, one of reasonableness: Are the means reasonably related to a valid governmental purpose?

The obvious difficulty with this kind of approach is drawing a line between public and private issues. What kinds of books people may read or movies they can see, one can reason, are inherently public issues, just as is the kind of thing that one citizen may say or write about another. Moreover, such matters as sexual rules may be closely related both to a nation's general political culture and more specifically to how authoritarian or permissive it will be. The slogan, popular among students during the Vietnamese War, "make love not war," linked sexual customs dominant among the older generation with pent-up aggressiveness that expressed itself in international violence. Whether one accepts or rejects such a relationship, the point is, critics argue, that to allow restrictions on such ideas about sex is to limit debate over issues that are politically relevant and thus to reduce the area of self-government.

Judicial Practice

Over the decades since 1919, when freedom of communications first became an important issue for constitutional law, the Supreme Court has never followed a consistent doctrinal path and most cases have provoked bitter dissents. At times the Justices have seemed to be close to adopting one or the other approach, but, as with the cases involving religion, they have always acted more pragmatically than they have spoken. Outlines of different patterns have dimly emerged in various subissues.

National Security. When national security has been involved, the Justices have tended to balance — although still without telling us anything about the scale or the weights assigned to competing interests — government's authority to protect the political processes from violence against individuals' rights to speak out.[67] Predictably, by stating the problem in this way, the Court has tended to decide in favor of restricting freedom. At least during the period of the Warren Court (1953 – 1969), however, the Justices were sometimes able to arrive at a libertarian result by playing on legal technicalities.

Reputation and Free Press. When the right to freedom of the press (and less often freedom of speech) has conflicted with another person's right to privacy or a decent reputation, the Justices have also been pragmatic rather than doctrinaire. If the injured party has been a public official or a "public figure" — such as a labor-management negotiator or a noted football coach—the Court has required that he or she can sue for damages only on a showing that not only was the information false but the writer knew it was false or wrote it with reckless disregard for its truth or falsity. Political debate in a democracy, the Justices have reasoned, must be "robust," and that debate would become tame and tepid with a constant threat of a lawsuit hanging over participants' heads.[68]

On the other hand, when the injured party has been a private citizen, the Court has said that the normal rules for slander (for damaging oral attacks) or libel (written slurs) should apply, providing that the writer or speaker can be shown to have been at fault.[69] Certainly these decisions are based on a distinction that Meiklejohn and his followers could accept. And, although the Court has not specifically used such language, one can see in its opinions a genuine effort to balance freedom of the press against a right to privacy and fair reputation. There is, however, a wide and critical gap in the protection that judges will afford the latter right. Neither state nor federal officers can be sued in federal courts for statements they make in their official capacities, even if they make false charges against innocent private citizens.[70]

Obscenity and Pornography. Cases involving sex always make fascinating reading; but they also make hard law. On the one hand, most judges accept the notion that sexual norms have an important, albeit an unknown, effect on general political culture and that to try to freeze sexual morality is to try to exempt politically important matters from public discussion and choice. On the other hand, judges also know that many advocates of sexual license are hypocritically mouthing slogans about the new sexual freedom to justify profits earned by pandering to very old-fashioned lust. Thus judges have searched for "redeeming social value" in literature and movies that have been attacked as obscene or pornographic.

To say that the Justices have been less than consistent in this area and have disagreed sharply among themselves about proper rules is to engage in gross understatement. There are, however, some traces of a pattern. *Roth v. United States* (1957) forms a landmark because there the Justices faced up to problems of definitions and tests.[71] They did not reject the old rule that obscenity is not constitutionally protected but emphasized that "sex and obscenity are not synonymous." The Justices defined the latter term as "material which deals with sex in a manner appealing to prurient interest." Expressly rejecting a Victorian standard that a book might be judged obscene because of isolated passages, the Court established a new test: "whether to the average person, applying contemporary community standards, the dominant theme of the material taken as a whole appeals to prurient interest."

For effort and courage *Roth* rates high marks, but not for clarity. *Prurient* as it is defined in contemporary dictionaries means "a restless craving" or "itching," and is hardly more clear than the word *obscenity* itself. The Warren Court wrestled with the problem of definition on several other occasions, but without greater success. The Justices did say, however, that the way in which material was commercially advertised could be weighed in determining whether its basic appeal was to prurient interest.[72]

Although the Warren Court recognized a special problem where children were concerned and sustained a New York statute forbidding sales of girlie magazines to minors,[73] the general approach of the Justices was to allow as little restriction as possible. In contrast, the Court under Chief Justice Burger has been less fearful of censorship and more concerned about stopping the spread of "immoral" ideas. *California* v. *LaRue*[74] upheld state regulations banning "bottomless dancers" or acts of sexual intercourse in floor shows of establishments that sold liquor. Speaking for the majority, Justice William H. Rehnquist admitted that the regulations in question did outlaw "some forms of visual presentation which would not be found obscene under *Roth* and subsequent decisions of the Court." Nevertheless, Rehnquist found the state's interest in controlling use of alcoholic beverages—and the state's authority under the Twenty-first Amendment—sufficient to legitimize standards that could not be constitutionally applied in other situations.

What *LaRue* treated as an exceptional circumstance, *Miller* v. *California* turned into a general rule to allow governmental officials to forbid commercial exploitation of sex or nudity or "patently offensive representations or descriptions of ultimate sexual acts, normal or perverted, actual or simulated."[75] Speaking for six Justices, Warren Burger reiterated that obscenity was not protected by the First Amendment and that whether a given work was obscene was a question of fact. He continued:

The basic guidelines for the trier of fact must be: (a) whether "the average person, applying contemporary community standards" would find that the work, taken as a whole, appeals to the prurient interest . . . (b) whether the work depicts or describes, in a patently offensive way, sexual conduct specifically defined by the applicable state law, and (c) whether the work, taken as a whole, lacks serious literary, artistic, political, or scientific value. . . .

"Contemporary community standards," Burger added, are local not national and would probably vary from area to area.

Censorship. On one point, at least, there has historically been wide agreement among judges both here and in other common law countries. Freedom of speech and press protect against prior restraint, that is, against censorship. In some circumstances, most judges have said, a person may be held responsible for the effects of his or her words or writings, but no one should ever have to submit the content of his or her communication to a censor for clearance in advance. Yet, enough cases—frequently decided by divided votes—keep cropping up over the years to indicate that censorship is more prevalent in our society than fiercely libertarian pronouncements by judges would lead one to expect.

In 1931, *Near* v. *Minnesota* centered around a local district attorney's use of state law that branded as a public nuisance any periodical that regularly published obscene, lewd, or scandalous material. The district attorney had obtained an injunction against future publication of *The Saturday Press,* a weekly newspaper that mixed antisemitism with charges of corruption in Minneapolis politics. "This," a majority of the Supreme Court said about the injunction, "is the essence of censorship," but four of the Justices dissented.[76]

Eight years later, *Hague* v. *CIO* presented an even more crass kind of censorship, one that has probably occurred more often than it should in local politics. Boss Frank Hague of Jersey City, who once boasted "I am the law," used his full power to keep unions out of his private fiefdom. Not only did he deny labor organizers use of public halls in the city and threaten them with arrest if they tried to explain the provisions of federal law to workers, but when organizers did come into town he subjected them to humiliating searches, arrested them for distributing leaflets, and then forced them onto ferries leaving for Manhattan. A federal district judge granted an injunction against Hague, and the Supreme Court affirmed: "Wherever the title of streets and parks may rest, they have immemorially been held in trust for the use of the public and, time out of mind, have been used for the purposes of assembly, communicating thoughts between citizens, and discussing public questions."[77]

Frequently, problems of censorship have arisen where cities and towns require licenses for parades and public meetings. The Supreme Court has sustained the validity of such ordinances only where they are essentially nondiscretionary—that is, where the local official can impose only uniform regulations, such as limitations on the times and places for parades and meetings. If the official has discretion to allow a permit to one group and deny it to another, the Court has struck down the ordinance.[78]

The most famous of American disputes over censorhip occurred in 1971, when the *New York Times* and several other newspapers obtained and began to publish copies of a set of classified documents popularly known as *The Pentagon Papers.* Claiming that publication of information contained in those documents would endanger national security, the Department of Justice sought injunctions forbidding the newspapers to print them. The cases raced through the judicial process. Within eight days of the original filing in a federal district court, arguments had been heard and decisions handed down by courts at all three levels. Over protests from three Justices against that feverish haste, the Supreme Court held that there was a presumption that any previous restraint of expression was unconstitutional and that, in this instance, the government had not met the heavy burden of overcoming that presumption.[79]

Free Press and Fair Trial. The potential impact on jurors of newspaper stories or radio or television broadcasts poses a serious problem for American justice. Here a defendant's right under the Sixth Amendment to a fair trial by an "impartial jury" may conflict with newsmen's rights under the First Amendment to publish information. On occasion the Supreme Court has reversed convictions when the Justices have thought it probable that news media had so prejudiced a community that a panel of impartial jurors could not be chosen.[80] There are several remedies a trial judge may use when pretrial publicity about a case is widespread. These include delaying trial until passions have eased, allowing, if the defendant requests, the trial to be held in another community, or together with opposing counsel questioning potential jurors more closely than normal about possible prejudice. The basic, although hardly perfect, solution to excessive pretrial publicity lies in curbing police and prosecutors, who usually leak information to reporters. If the publicity continues during a trial at a pace that the judge fears might affect jurors already chosen, he may order them sequestered, that is, held under guard and isolated from the rest of the world, including their families, until the trial is completed and they have reached a verdict. Understandably, this remedy is not popular among jurors.

In cases that are likely to provoke great notoriety, some judges have taken the further step of barring newsmen from the hearings that precede actual trial as well as from the trial itself, at times even forbidding reporters to write about the evidence. In 1976 the Supreme Court finally addressed the constitutionality of such "gag" orders and struck them down as prior restraints. Pointing out the range of lesser means available to a trial judge to protect jurors against prejudicial information, the Court held that only truly extraordinary circumstances could justify such a form of censorship.[81]

Disclosure of Sources. An issue vital to a free press is the obligation of reporters to disclose at a trial or in investigations by grand juries their informants' names and offer full testimony about criminal activity of which they have knowledge. Many reporters have invoked the First Amendment as grounds for refusing to testify about such matters, claiming that if they testify future informants will be unwilling to provide the evidence from which convincing stories can be written and through which effective pressure can be brought to bear on government. The issue is a delicate one. Without a doubt, in some situations full disclosure can dry up sources of news, especially where, as in the Watergate scandals, some of the sources are public officials who prudently fear reprisal by more powerful public officials. On the other hand, reporters have the same obligation as other citizens to cooperate with law enforcement agencies; and newsmen are no less vulnerable to corruption than the rest of humanity. The Supreme Court, by a 5–4 vote, has come down on the side of requiring reporters to reveal their sources.[82]

"Chip! Chip! Chip!"

THE MILWAUKEE JOURNAL
Field Newspaper Syndicate, 1975

Reprinted courtesy of The Milwaukee Journal.

State court rulings such as the Nebraska "gag rule" decision criticized in the cartoon were severely limited by the U.S. Supreme Court in 1976.

The Darker Side of Civil Liberties

Americans have traditionally taken great pride in their freedom to vote, to criticize governmental officials, to form, join, and leave associations and political parties, to speak out or keep silent on issues of religion or politics or anything else that interested or bored them. Americans have also felt secure from the prying eyes of government's spies. They have believed that their government would let them alone unless they committed some act that was clearly defined by law as criminal. Most people, of course, are totally unfamiliar with the subtleties of Supreme Court rulings discussed in this chapter, but the general notion of constitutional liberty—"a government of laws and not of men"—has been a long standing American ideal.

In some measure, this traditional pride has been justified. Americans

In the shadow of the Capitol, federal officials guard microwave towers used in the interception of private communications.

enjoy a far greater range and depth of civil liberties than do citizens of communist countries or right-wing dictatorships. But some of that pride, the scandals of Watergate showed, was inflated. Even more ominously, evidence produced in 1975 and 1976 by a special Senate investigating committee headed by Senator Frank Church showed that some of Watergate's uglier violations of constitutional rights were common practices of some federal agencies and many were perhaps still corroding ideals of freedom.

At least since the 1930s, several federal agencies have been systematically spying on American citizens, shadowing them, opening their mail, reading their telegrams, tapping their telephones, "bugging" their homes, hotel rooms, and offices, and in several instances kidnapping and threatening them with bodily injury. The information so obtained has been carefully sorted and retained in computers' memory banks. During the mid-1970s the Federal Bureau of Investigation alone was keeping files on more than a half-million Americans.

The people subjected to these sorts of crimes have generally not been Russian spies, Palestinian terrorists, or even Mafia Dons, but law-abiding citizens whose political views and activities did not conform to what officials of the FBI, the Central Intelligence Agency, the National Security Agency, or the Internal Revenue Service thought "proper." As the Church committee reported:

The targets of intelligence activity have included political adherents of the right and the left, ranging from activists to casual supporters. Investigations have been directed against proponents of racial causes and women's rights, outspoken apostles of nonviolence and racial harmony; establishment politicians; religious groups; and advocates of new life styles.[83]

The principal objective of this massive gathering of information has not been to institute criminal proceedings—after all, it has never been a federal crime to advocate nonviolence, socialism, racial equality, or even women's rights. Rather the aim was to identify people with political views that seemed unorthodox and discover ways in which they might be harassed, blackmailed, or otherwise intimidated into abandoning their "wrong-headed" ideas.

In carrying out such policies, the FBI frequently resorted to burglary, or as the Bureau called it, "black bagging." Between 1960 and 1966, for instance, agents robbed offices of the Socialist Workers Party more than ninety times. And despite solemn assurances from the Director to Congress that his boys had ceased such naughty activities after 1971, they continued to do so for at least three or four more years. FBI operatives also infiltrated other organizations they deemed dangerous, such as the Women's Liberation Movement, dutifully noting the names of people who were so brazen as to attend meetings.

In another instance, FBI agents carried on a concerted campaign to destroy the reputation of Rev. Martin Luther King, Jr., the great black civil rights leader. Recognizing King's magnetic attraction to blacks and white liberals, J. Edgar Hoover, then Director of the FBI, reasoned that if King ever abandoned his advocacy of nonviolence and brotherly love he could unite all sorts of dissident elements. Therefore, Hoover concluded, the smart tactic would be to discredit King so that he could never pose a threat. "No holds were barred," the investigator in charge of the operation stated. FBI men followed King, tapped his telephone, and bugged his hotel rooms. At one juncture they even threatened to make public an allegedly damaging tape recording unless he committed suicide.[84]

The Internal Revenue Service readily joined in these widespread criminal activities. Ignoring the law that requires tax returns of citizens to be kept confidential, the IRS speedily made returns available to any and every federal official—and many state officers—who asked for them. IRS also conducted its own special tax audits of individuals of whose political views the Service disapproved—in addition, of course, to cooperating with the White House to harass the President's personal enemies and with the FBI to keep critics of the Bureau busy arguing with accountants.

One result of these actions was to blacken the reputations of the FBI and the IRS. (Because they have essentially been established to spy, it has been less shocking to find the CIA and NSA engaged in illegal snooping.) At one time, IRS was a model for a cynical world, demonstrating that tax collectors could be both honest and efficient. Now it is obvious that IRS has been riddled with officials who have only contempt for honesty and who measure efficiency in terms of punishment meted out to political foes. So, too, the FBI had been the premier American police force, bursting with integrity and respect for law but still able, through diligence and intelligence, to bring the shrewdest

"Yes, Mr. And Mrs. America —
This Is Your Life"

criminals to justice. That reputation now lies in a crumpled heap of felonies and deceptions. Sworn to uphold the law, large numbers of agents devoted their talents to destroying basic constitutional rights and did so with the approval, even urging of the Director, his assistants, and senior officials in the Department of Justice. For example, the Bureau commended the men responsible for stealing documents from the Socialist Workers party for their "sound judgment" and "great discretion" in committing felonies.

453

In part these people were overzealous. They rightly feared organizations, like the Weathermen and Black Panthers, that advocated and practiced violence. But as Justice Louis Brandeis warned a half century ago, "Men feared witches and burnt women."[85] A year later he added that "the greatest dangers to liberty lurk in insidious encroachment by men of zeal, well-meaning, but without understanding."[86] These particular men began by fearing spies and terrorists and ended by violating the rights of those who dared to stray from the middle road of politics. The progression of fear was easy for these people of flashing zeal and dull understanding: Terrorists are dangerous; and, as everyone knows, radicals sympathize with terrorists, therefore radicals are also dangerous; and everyone also knows that liberals tend to sympathize with radicals, therefore liberals are dangerous too. Finally, anyone who did not think like the Director of the FBI or the CIA and their minions was potentially a subversive and should be watched and perhaps even harassed.

In part, some of the officials involved were not so much zealous as corrupt. They saw and leaped at an opportunity to advance their careers by obtaining information that would please their superiors (whether office head, division chief, Director, or President). That they violated the law and their oaths to uphold that law faded before the chance for personal advancement. Testifying before the Church committee, William Sullivan, Assistant Director of the FBI, conceded that the Bureau's effort to "get" Martin Luther King "is not an isolated phenomenon . . . this was a practice of the Bureau down through the years. I might say it often became a real character assassination." Responding to questions whether he himself or any other FBI official ever objected to using criminal or immoral tactics, Sullivan said:

. . . never once did I hear anybody, including myself, raise the question, is this course of action which we have agreed upon lawful, is it legal, is it ethical or moral? We never gave any thought to this realm of reasoning, because we were just naturally pragmatists. The one thing we were concerned about [was] will this course of action work, will it get us what we want, will we reach the objective that we desire to reach?

As far as legality is concerned, moral or ethics, was never raised by myself or anybody else. . . . I think that this suggests really in government we are amoral.[87]

A more important result of this riot of governmentally sponsored crime will undoubtedly be further cynicism about honesty in politics and, far worse, perhaps even disdain for honesty and decency themselves. As Justice Brandeis also noted:

Our Government is the potent, the omnipresent teacher. For good or for ill, it teaches the whole people by its example. Crime is contagious. If the Government becomes a lawbreaker, it breeds contempt for law; it invites every man to become a law unto himself; it invites anarchy.[88]

Most important of all, these criminal activities could impose a "chilling effect" on political freedom—a fear, amply justified by past governmental policies, that to join unpopular organizations or to voice unorthodox ideas will bring serious risk of harassment by tax investigators, invasions of privacy by FBI agents, and perhaps even blackmail. To the extent that people do not exercise their constitutional rights because of fear of governmental repression, both the First Amendment and the cherished ideals of the American political tradition will shrink. Then it will become easier to accept the fundamental premise behind the activities uncovered by the Church committee: Governmental agencies like the FBI and IRS have a monopoly of political truth; they are our big brothers; we must love them and obey them and surrender this foolish notion espoused by communists like Thomas Jefferson, James Madison, and Abraham Lincoln, that we should think for ourselves.

Summary

This chapter has presented a double, even schizophrenic view of American civil liberties. The United States has a venerable tradition of individual freedom. Where formal constitutional clauses, statutes, executive orders, and judicial decisions have been involved, the record is generally in favor of liberty. That record has had its glaring faults, like slavery and racial discrimination, but, over the long haul, it has improved. It is also true that reasonable people can reasonably differ about whether existing statutes are too broad or judicial decisions too narrow; but, over the years, the arguments have more and more tended to converge within a context of respect for human dignity and liberty under law.

There is also a darker side, one that endangers the rights of all citizens. The evidence unearthed by the Church committee presents a modern instance in painful detail. Such spurts of repression have occurred before in American history. The Alien and Sedition Acts of 1798 made a mockery of the First and Fifth Amendments. Many of the prosecutions for sedition during World War I, the "Great Red Scare" of the 1920s, the imprisonment during World War II of more than a hundred thousand citizens of Japanese ancestry, the Cold War fright of the late 1940s and early 1950s, the FBI and the IRS during the late 1960s and early 1970s—all show the same pattern of hysterical officials violating their oaths of office in fierce determination to protect the American people from some imaginary seducer.

That the system has failed in the past and yet recovered does not mean that it will continue to survive crises. Governmental bureaucracies now have much more dangerous instruments than they did even a few decades ago. Sophisticated electronic devices can listen to conversations whether in the bedroom or telephone booth. Computers can store hundreds of millions of bits of information and, within a split second, regurgitate them in any pattern the operator desires. After recording a few innocent sentences of a telephone conversation, a skilled technician with modern equipment can reconstruct a tape that has the speaker confessing to rape and murder or planning to bomb the White House. Most ominously, the Watergate scandals and the findings of the Church committee indicate that there are hundreds, perhaps thousands, of officials in critically important—and powerful—executive agencies like the FBI, CIA, and IRS who have little real commitment to, or at least no understanding of, the Constitution or the broader American system of government.

Selected Bibliography

BECKER, CARL, *Freedom and Responsibility in the American Way of Life* (New York: Alfred A. Knopf, Inc., 1945). A beautifully written analysis of the compatibility of political authority and individual liberty.

BERNS, WALTER, *Freedom, Virtue and the First Amendment* (Baton Rouge, La.: Louisiana State University Press, 1957). A vigorous attack on the American tradition of freedom of expression.

CHAFEE, ZECHARIAH, *Free Speech in the United States* (Cambridge, Mass.: Harvard University Press, 1941). A classic in civil rights literature, by a noted legal scholar and defender of human liberty.

CLOR, HARRY M., *Obscenity and Public Morality: Censorship in a Liberal Society* (Chicago, Ill.: University of Chicago Press, 1969). A sophisticated attempt to develop a justification for censorship against obscenity in a free society.

DIONISOPOULOS, P. ALLAN, and CRAIG R. DUCAT, eds., *The Right to Privacy* (St. Paul, Minn.: West Publishing Co., 1976). A useful collection of cases and materials dealing with the developing law of privacy.

EMERSON, THOMAS I., *Toward a General Theory of the First Amendment* (New York: Random House, 1963). An effort to construct a formal legal doctrine to guide judges in deciding First Amendment cases.

FRIENDLY, FRED W., *The Good Guys, the Bad Guys and the First Amendment: Free Speech vs. Fairness in Broadcasting* (New York: Random House, 1975). A provocative discussion of problems of open debate and governmental regulation of television and radio.

LASSWELL, HAROLD D., *National Security and Individual Freedom* (New York: McGraw-Hill Book Company, 1950). An analysis of the dangers of a garrison state, even a supposedly democratic garrison state.

LEVY, LEONARD W., *Legacy of Suppression: Freedom of Speech and Press in Early American History* (Cambridge, Mass.: Harvard University Press, 1960). A myth-puncturing account of the rather low legal protection accorded freedom of expression in the good old days.

MEIKLEJOHN, ALEXANDER, *Free Speech and Its Relation to Self-Government* (New York: Harper & Row, 1948). A provocative and influential thesis that freedom of political expression ought to be an absolute right.

MILL, JOHN STUART, *On Liberty* (New York: Appleton-Century-Crofts,

1947). Originally published in 1851, a famous attempt to define the proper limits of freedom and authority.

PRITCHETT, C. HERMAN, *The American Constitution,* 3d ed. (New York: McGraw-Hill Book Company, 1976), chaps. 20–28. A lucid presentation of the law of the First Amendment.

Report of the Commission on Obscenity and Pornography (Washington, D.C.: Government Printing Office, 1970). A thoughtful, heavily documented, and much discussed report of a presidential commission.

SCHLISSEL, LILLIAN, ed., *Conscience in America: A Documentary History of Conscientious Objection in America, 1757–1967* (New York: E.P. Dutton & Co., Inc., 1968). The subtitle accurately describes this useful collection of documents.

SHAPIRO, MARTIN, *Freedom of Speech: The Supreme Court and Judicial Review* (Englewood Cliffs, N.J.: Prentice-Hall, Inc., 1966). An introductory analysis of Supreme Court treatment of free speech problems.

SORAUF, FRANK J., *The Wall of Separation: The Constitutional Politics of Church and State* (Princeton, N.J.: Princeton University Press, 1976). A scholarly analysis of a set of problems ranging from prayers in public schools to public aid to parochial schools.

TWENTIETH CENTURY FUND, *Rights in Conflict: Report of the Twentieth Century Fund Task Force on Justice, Publicity, and the First Amendment* (New York: McGraw-Hill Book Co., 1976). A penetrating analysis of the potential conflict between freedom of the press and an individual's right to a fair trial.

THOREAU, HENRY D., *On the Duty of Civil Disobedience* (New Haven, Conn.: Yale University Press, 1928). Originally published in 1849; an impassioned disquisition on the moral obligation of the individual to resist unjust governmental authority.

WESTIN, ALAN F., *Privacy and Freedom* (New York: Atheneum Publishers, 1967). A thorough study of the right to privacy and threats to its enjoyment—many of which have become even more real in the decade since publication of this book.

Chapter 17

Criminal Justice in a Free Society

How a nation handles problems caused by those people who break its rules forms a central aspect of political life. That process involves not only serious questions of civil liberties like those just discussed in Chapter 16. It also involves the quality of life that a society can enjoy free from restraint by criminals as well as from restraint by public officials. This chapter looks at the seriousness of crime in the United States, examines the formal, legal steps designed to protect the liberties of those who become enmeshed in the system of criminal justice, and analyzes some of the actual practices that allow police, prosecutors, judges, and, on occasion, defendants to evade those protections. We then discuss some of the implications that prisons pose for the future of a society that wishes to be free in fact as well as in name.

The Scope of Crime

Crime has become a cancer in American society. "Organized crime," whether run by Mafiosi families or more transient groups, is a major industry that sometimes stands at the throat of big cities, controlling some judges, prosecutors, police, and legitimate businesses as effectively as it engages in loan sharking, operates gambling establishments, directs prostitution, imports and distributes narcotics, and stands ready to kill or maim the uncooperative. Lesser organizations such as street gangs devote a greater percentage of their time to crimes of violence and can terrorize an entire neighborhood. Disorganized crime, in the form of the mugger who assaults and robs, threatens to turn urban streets into jungles. In that sort of environment, no honest person can enjoy real civil rights.

One can only guess at the incidence of crime because many, possibly most, crimes are not reported to the police, and police departments often find it politically expedient to inflate or deflate the figures that they have. The Federal Bureau of Investigation estimated that during 1975 10.2 million crimes against property and a million more against persons were committed in the United States.[1] A Gallup Poll conducted in December 1972 showed that one out of every three residents of metropolitan center cities had been mugged, robbed, assaulted, or burglarized in the preceding twelve months.

Costs

Most crimes of violence effect an ugly kind of discrimination because they have as their victims a disproportionately high share of poor and very poor people. A study of crime in thirteen large American cities during 1974 showed that residents with annual incomes under $3,000 were almost twice as likely as those with incomes over $25,000 to be the victim of any crime involving violence, more than three times as likely to be robbed and injured, and four times more likely to be

Figure 17.1
Crimes of Violence, 1970–1975
(percent change over 1970)

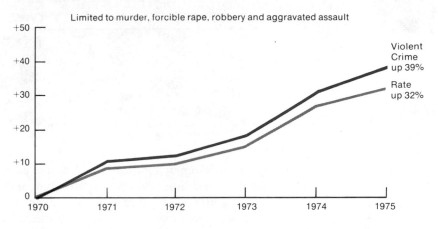

Source: Federal Bureau of Investigation, *Uniform Crime Reports in the United States – 1975* (Washington, D.C.: Government Printing Office, 1976), p. 13.

raped[2] — ratios that were similar to those obtained during the late 1960s by the President's Commission on Law Enforcement.

Furthermore, crime's relative injury to the poor is likely to be far more painful than to the well-to-do. A theft of $50 from a business executive creates no more than an inconvenience. But to an unskilled worker or a retired person that loss might mean eviction and would certainly cause a family to go hungry for days. When the target of a robbery is a store in a ghetto area, the cost, even the added cost of insurance, is passed on to the neighborhood in the form of higher prices. If robberies are frequent, the store will probably close, throwing additional people out of work and, for those who cannot afford an automobile, increasing the difficulties of shopping.

To prevent robberies, private industry spent about $6.5 billion in 1975 for guards, private police, and special equipment. These costs, of course, are passed on to consumers. The public bill for law enforcement — directly paid for by taxpayers and indirectly by those who need other governmental services — is staggering. Maintaining prisons, courts, police stations, specially equipped vehicles, radios, and arsenals of weapons is extraordinarily expensive, as are feeding and clothing 250,000 people in penitentiaries and thousands more in smaller jails and paying the salaries of more than a million prosecutors, police officers, prison guards, and probation officials. In 1974, spending for law enforcement at the state, local, and national level exceeded $16 billion.

The high rate of violent crime has imposed additional costs by lowering the quality of life for potential as well as actual victims. It keeps

people from enjoying theatres, libraries, parks, and other facilities for leisure, education, and cultural enrichment that urban centers provide as compensation for dirt, pollution, overcrowding, and other inconveniences. For a man—much less a woman—to go out at night on the streets of many neighborhoods in most urban centers is risky; and only a thief, a police decoy, or a fool is apt to walk alone after dark in lonely places like public parks. It comes as a shock to American tourists to see people strolling around Dublin, Madrid, Paris, or Rome at two in the morning. In the United States most city residents doublelock themselves securely in at nightfall, and more than a third of them have guns in their homes to protect against burglars.

Perhaps the most significant cost of crime is that it is eroding the bases of community at a time when a sense of national cohesion is badly needed. Knowledge among whites that blacks commit a very high percentage of crimes of violence increases fear of housing and school integration and intensifies racial prejudice. For their part, blacks, as the most frequent victims of violent crime, blame the police in particular for their problems and whites in general for not caring about their plight. Cutting across racial lines is an apparently growing distrust of all strangers. Such distrust may fragment American society in a way that will undermine the social cohesion essential to a stable constitutional democracy.

Risk Taking and Profit Making

The profits from crime are both enormous and tax free. The costs of goods stolen, embezzled, or destroyed by criminals came to $65 billion in 1975 and probably have risen in successive years. The risks tend to be low. Only a small minority of crimes result in an arrest—perhaps as few as one in every five—only a small percentage of those arrested are convicted, and hardly more than a bare majority of those who are convicted actually serve time in prison, as Table 17-1 indicates.

Table 17-1

Arrests, convictions, and sentences of all persons arrested on felony charges, 1975

City	Convicted	Sent to jail or prison
Washington, D.C.	33%	18%
Chicago	26%	15%
Baltimore	44%	28%
Detroit	58%	20%
Los Angeles County	46%	28%
San Diego County	34%	14%

Source: "Why Criminals Go Free,"*U.S. News & World Report,* May 10, 1976, p. 37.

Protecting Society

Law and Order

All these figures point to a critical set of problems whose immensity moves some people to advocate radical solutions, such as that illustrated by the Dick Tracy comic strip. The real issue, however, is far too complex to be solved by giving policemen licenses to kill at will or, more sensibly, giving them a freer hand, or even improving their efficiency and honesty, although the latter change is certainly needed.

At root, what is involved here is, again, the basic dilemma that faced the framers of the Constitution: how to make government (the police in this instance) strong enough to protect society without allowing government to be so strong as to oppress society. Unhappily for those who like simple solutions to difficult problems, "law and order" are two concepts, not a single idea. The notion of law is frequently in tension with order, for one of the essential functions of law is to restrain the officials who keep order.

If order were the only or even the primary value in a society, then freedom would be of little importance and the only standard for police conduct would be ability to prevent crime and catch criminals. But even then one could not be sure of achieving order; once freed from outside restraints, police might opt to further their own aims at the expense of society. It is hardly disrespectful to dedicated officials to suggest that as human beings they are vulnerable to the same sorts of temptations that beset the rest of mankind. The "police riot" in Chicago during the 1968 Democratic Convention indicates that policemen, if pushed, can become as unruly as any mob of civilians; and J. Edgar Hoover's vendetta against Rev. Martin Luther King, Jr., discussed in the preceding chapter, shows that even a distinguished peace officer can pervert law to serve personal malice.

The real question becomes how to preserve order *with* law and liberty, and there are no easy answers. Nowhere are the objectives of American criminal law authoritatively spelled out. And those aims that can be deduced from the Constitution, other legal norms, or actual practice are not necessarily consistent with each other. Historically, the criminal law was a public substitute for private revenge and without a doubt still retains much of that character. In part, the purpose of criminal law has also been to serve as a secular equivalent of Purgatory, a means of cleansing the criminal of his moral guilt, of forcing him "to pay his debt to society" for his sins. Another purpose has been to protect society either by deterring actual or potential lawbreakers or by isolating criminals from the rest of the population. Criminal law may also operate as a means of rehabilitating and reforming the offender.

Constitutional Provisions

The very differences among these aims and the inability of American political leadership to determine their order of importance contribute mightily to the problems of administering justice. Less confused, but by no means clear, are the substantive rights that the constitutional system tries to protect from abuse, deliberate or inadvertent, by those charged with applying criminal sanctions. By *substantive rights* we mean the essence of what is protected, in contrast to *procedural rights,* the obligations of public officials to follow certain specified steps before imposing punishment. The Constitution originally mentioned explicitly no substantive rights, although we can deduce from the various procedural guarantees there and in the Bill of Rights that the basic rights in the field of criminal justice are those to dignity and privacy, to physical freedom, to a fair trial if accused of crime, and to protection, if convicted, against certain kinds of punishment.

As written in 1787, the Constitution directly referred to only three of these. The framers safeguarded the right to a fair trial by forbidding both state and national governments to pass bills of attainder or ex post facto legislation.* Article III also carefully defines treason and limits the punishment that can be imposed for such a crime:

Treason against the United States shall consist only in levying war against them, or in adhering to their enemies, giving them aid and comfort. No person shall be convicted of treason unless on the testimony of two witnesses to the same overt act, or on confession in open court.

The Congress shall have power to declare the punishment of treason, but no attainder of treason shall work corruption of blood or forfeiture except during the life of the person attainted.

"Corruption of blood and forfeiture" refer to English practices of punishing the family of a convicted traitor either by death, imprisonment,

*These terms are defined in Chapter 4.

fines, or exile, or by forbidding succeeding generations to hold certain kinds of office or property.

More generally, the framers of the Constitution protected the basic right to freedom itself by providing in Article I that: "The privilege of the writ of habeas corpus shall not be suspended, unless when in cases of rebellion or invasion the public safety may require it." Sometimes called "the great writ of liberty," habeas corpus was especially designed to prevent arbitrary arrest or unlawful imprisonment. Where this right is available, any prisoner—or the lawyer or friend of the prisoner—who is being held by state or federal officers may ask the nearest court for a writ, ordering the officers to bring the prisoner into court and show legal cause for holding him. If such cause is not shown or if a charge is not brought, the court will order the prisoner released.

"Formal" Stages of Criminal Justice

To understand the way in which the system of criminal justice operates, one should have a clear view of the steps that the Constitution and statutes prescribe to protect the rights of an accused person during the process that takes place between the time when the police believe that they have solved a case and he or she actually begins to serve a sentence. At the same time, one should recognize that to some extent actual practice may differ from these formally prescribed rules. In this section we describe the stages formally outlined by law, and in the next section we turn to common practices.

Arrest

To arrest a suspect for an offense, a police officer is supposed to have "probable cause" to believe that the person has committed or is about to commit a crime. The difference between mere suspicion and probable cause is hardly precise. Some years ago, the Supreme Court defined *probable cause* as "reasonable ground of suspicion supported by circumstances sufficiently strong in themselves to warrant a cautious man in the belief that the party is guilty of the offense with which he is charged."[4] Generally speaking, a policeman should have some tangible evidence implicating a suspect—perhaps the officer sees a man actually commit a crime or a witness identifies the suspect as the guilty party.

Wherever possible, an arresting officer should have a *warrant*—an order from a judicial official, to whom the officer's evidence of probable cause has been submitted—to take a person into custody. (We use the term *judicial official* here because in federal district courts a magistrate, who is an assistant to a judge, rather than the judge himself, normally issues arrest and search warrants, hears charges against an ac-

Law Enforcement Code of Ethics

As a Law Enforcement Officer, *my fundamental duty is to serve mankind; to safeguard lives and property; to protect the innocent against deception, the weak against oppression or intimidation, and the peaceful against violence or disorder; and to respect the Constitutional rights of all men to liberty, equality and justice.*

I will *keep my private life unsullied as an example to all; maintain courageous calm in the face of danger, scorn, or ridicule; develop self-restraint; and be constantly mindful of the welfare of others. Honest in thought and deed in both my personal and official life, I will be exemplary in obeying the laws of the land and the regulations of my department. Whatever I see or hear of a confidential nature or that is confided to me in my official capacity will be kept ever secret unless revelation is necessary in the performance of my duty.*

I will *never act officiously or permit personal feelings, prejudices, animosities or friendships to influence my decisions. With no compromise for crime and with relentless prosecution of criminals, I will enforce the law courteously and appropriately without fear or favor, malice or ill will, never employing unnecessary force or violence and never accepting gratuities.*

I recognize *the badge of my office as a symbol of public faith, and I accept it as a public trust to be held so long as I am true to the ethics of the police service. I will constantly strive to achieve these objectives and ideals, dedicating myself before God to my chosen profession . . . law enforcement.*

cused, informs him of his constitutional rights, and sets bail. In state systems, the title magistrate is usually given to a minor judge who performs similar rather routine duties.) Obviously, there are many situations in which a policeman does not have time to go to court, and a warrant is not an absolute requirement for a valid arrest.

Search

Once an officer has made an arrest, he may search the prisoner, but judges in this country have been divided over just how extensive that search can be unless the policeman has obtained a warrant that follows the Fourth Amendment's requirements specifying the thing sought and the person or area to be examined. Indeed, the Supreme Court has crossed its own trail so often that the Justices have become wary of laying down general principles, claiming that this is the sort of problem that "can only be decided in the concrete factual context of the individual case."[5]

In general, the Supreme Court has restricted the area to be searched without a warrant to the person of the suspect and the immediate area under his control. The only lawful purposes of such a search are protecting the safety of the arresting officer and preventing the destruction of evidence.[6] But these are elastic terms that police are often able to stretch.

If the police wish to look into a suspect's home or office for evidence connecting him with a crime, they must, under normal circumstances, obtain a *search warrant*. To secure such a writ, police must go to a judicial officer and show that they have probable cause to believe that incriminating evidence is located at a particular address. The crucial word here is "normal." As in arrest, there may be many circumstances, such as the hot pursuit of a criminal into his home, in which courts allow police to proceed without a warrant.

Interrogation

The Fifth Amendment provides that no person "shall be compelled in a criminal case to be a witness against himself." The Supreme Court, in its controversial decision in *Miranda* v. *Arizona,* has required police to warn a suspect of his right to say nothing (and to have a lawyer at government's expense if the suspect cannot afford to hire one) as soon as they take him into custody.[7]

Although today American police probably seldom use violence to obtain a confession, only an exceptional person under arrest in a police station and surrounded by detectives would not experience considerable apprehension. From the point of view of solving crimes, this fear is quite functional. To ensure fair treatment, however, federal law requires U. S. officials to bring a prisoner "without unnecessary delay" before a judicial officer, who examines the charge and the evidence to make sure the suspect is being lawfully detained and again informs him of the charges against him and of his constitutional rights to silence and to free counsel. The judicial officer also sets the bail that the prisoner must post to be released, if the offense with which he is charged allows bail. In some jurisdictions, the magistrate can release the accused on his assurance that he will return for trial proceedings.

There is no clear line distinguishing necessary from unnecessary delay. The Supreme Court has said that federal police may wait to bring a prisoner before a magistrate until they have completed routine arrest procedures, checked out his alibi, and talked to the principal witnesses immediately available.[8] What federal officers are not supposed to do is begin a really probing interrogation of the suspect before he has been brought before a magistrate. The obvious purpose is not to promote police efficiency, but to make certain that the defendant knows his rights.

Formal state procedures vary but not nearly so much as informal police practices. The Supreme Court has not imposed on state officials quite the same requirement of rapid appearance before a magistrate, but *Miranda* v. *Arizona* held that due process of law obliges *all* enforcement officers to inform an accused of his constitutional rights. Furthermore, his lawyer may be present at all times the prisoner is under interrogation. If at any stage the prisoner changes his mind after first waiving his right to counsel, the interrogation is supposed to stop until his attorney can be present. The burden of proof that a defendant has freely and intelligently waived these rights is on the prosecution, if it attempts to introduce at a trial any statement or evidence obtained from questioning the accused.

Formal Charge

The Fifth Amendment requires that, for all serious federal crimes, the formal accusations be made by an *indictment* lodged by a *grand jury*. That jury, which historically functioned as an investigative body, is convened by the prosecutor in the jurisdiction. It hears evidence presented by the prosecutor and occasionally gathers evidence on its own. If a majority of the jurymen feel there is sufficient reason to bring a person to trial, they present a *true bill* and indict — that is, accuse — him.

The grand jury is a cumbersome instrument, and its use is one of the few provisions of the Bill of Rights that even the Warren Court did not make obligatory on the states. Although some states still use this process to initiate judicial proceedings, most allow prosecutors to accuse a defendant formally by filing with a court what is called an *information*.

Once a prisoner has been charged, the magistrate may review his earlier decision regarding bail. The Eighth Amendment provides only that "excessive bail shall not be required,"* a stipulation that does not prevent complete denial of bail in a very serious case. The judicial officer, if he decides to allow bail, sets a sum of money which the defendant will have to deposit (post) with the court. The amount is that which in the judicial officer's judgment is sufficient to insure the defendant's appearance at the trial. Because most defendants are not prosperous, bail bondsmen do a heavy business. For a fee, usually about 10 percent of the bail, they will post a bond guaranteeing bail and the defendant's presence at the trial. In most jurisdictions, these bondsmen can arrest and return the defendant if he tries to flee.

Bail practice raises several serious problems. First, when bail is denied or set so high that a prisoner cannot raise the money, he may have to stay in prison for many months. Not only will his earning power be at least temporarily destroyed and his dignity suffer, but his ability to gather evidence and prepare a defense will be curtailed. Ironically, although he may be kept in prison without being found guilty, if he is convicted he may be promptly freed, because suspended sentences are quite common, especially for first offenders.

Second, by establishing money as the basic criterion of whether a person stays in jail, bail practice discriminates against poorer defendants. Congress has done something about this problem. After several pilot studies showed that people released without bail showed up for trial about as often as those who had to put up money, Congress passed

*As of November 1976 the Supreme Court had never specifically held that states are bound by this clause, but that states are so bound appears to be a logical deduction from many decisions.

the Bail Reform Act of 1966. This statute, affecting only federal criminal procedure, requires that a judicial officer release on their own recognizance those accused of noncapital offenses who are unable to raise bail, unless the judicial official has strong reason to believe that the accused will not appear for trial. The statute also authorizes, but does not require, judicial officials to apply the same procedure to persons accused of capital offenses. In addition, Congress provided for swift appellate court review of decisions refusing release of an accused and ordered the Attorney General to give credit toward any prison sentence for the time a defendant spent in custody awaiting trial.

The problem of bail also involves society's interests in the protection of its other members. Some criminals released on bail commit fresh crimes within hours after regaining freedom; others intimidate potential witnesses or jurors. On the other hand, the law's presumption of innocence—and, of course, the Fifth and Fourteenth Amendments—bar imprisonment without trial. Traditionally, however, bail practices have resulted in a degree of deliberate *preventive detention*. Where judges believe that an accused is dangerous to society—and this belief may be grounded on very personal reasons—they often set very high bail or deny bail altogether. In the District of Columbia Crime Control Act of 1970, Congress took an additional step and formally authorized preventive detention for up to sixty days for a suspect accused of: (1) threatening a prospective witness or juror; (2) serious crimes and the judge believes him to be dangerous to the community; or (3) a crime of violence and has been convicted of such an offense within the previous ten years or committed a crime of violence while on probation, parole, or bail, or is a drug addict. These provisions raise very ticklish constitutional questions, and officials in the District of Columbia have been using the statute with great caution.

Trial

The Sixth Amendment says that an accused person has a right to a "speedy" trial, but delays between arrest and trial often run from three to six months and sometimes as long as a year. In 1974 Congress authorized criminal defendants not brought to trial in federal cases within a hundred days of arrest to petition a district judge to dismiss the charges against them. The statute, the Speedy Trial Act, excludes from the hundred days certain periods, such as those during which a defendant was not available for trial or was undergoing tests to determine his fitness to stand trial. But if the judge finds none of the specifically listed circumstances present, he must dismiss the charges. The Speedy Trial Act does not, of course, affect state courts, but several state legislatures and supreme courts are applying similar rules.

Federal and state trials for all serious crimes must be by jury, unless the defendant and, in some jurisdictions, the prosecution waive that right. At least in state courts, the vote to convict need not be unanimous,[9] and, for lesser offenses (still undefined), the jury may consist of fewer than twelve persons.[10] Neither the trial jury nor the grand jury has to be representative of the community at large in the sense of constituting a statistically neat cross-section, but the government may not systematically exclude people from jury service because of race, ethnic origin, or sex.[11]

The Sixth Amendment—which the Supreme Court has read as being included in, or *incorporated* in, the Fourteenth—sets procedural minimums for all trials: "the accused shall enjoy the right . . . to be informed of the nature and cause of the accusations; to be confronted with witnesses against him; to have compulsory process for obtaining witnesses in his favor, and to have assistance of counsel for his defense." As at the interrogation stage, the government must provide a lawyer for the accused if he cannot afford to hire one, and the attorney must have ample time to prepare his case.

Under the Fifth and Fourteenth Amendments, the defendant cannot be made to take the witness stand, nor can the prosecutor or judge comment to the jury about the defendant's not testifying, although nothing can prevent the jurymen from drawing their own conclusions. "The constitutional foundation underlying the privilege [against self-incrimination]," the Supreme Court has said, "is the respect a government—state or federal—must accord to the dignity and integrity of its citizens."[12]

In addition to considering these specific constitutional guarantees, an appellate court looks at the trial as a whole to ensure that it was fair in substance as well as procedure: to make certain, for example, that the basic statute under which the accused was charged was constitutional, that the trial was not conducted in an atmosphere of mob rule, that the presiding judge was unbiased, that the jury was not prejudiced by newspaper or other publicity, that the prosecutor did not introduce perjured testimony, and that a reasonable group of people could have concluded from the evidence actually presented that the accused was guilty.

The Fourth Amendment may come into play again at the trial, as may the Fifth, when the question of admissibility of evidence is involved. Since 1914 the Supreme Court has not allowed federal courts to hear evidence that was illegally obtained,[13] and in 1961 *Mapp* v. *Ohio* applied a similar exclusionary rule to state trials as well.[14] This policy has a double purpose. First, it is a means—just about the only practical means, though certainly not a completely effective one—of making police and prosecutors respect defendants' rights to privacy and to silence. Second, and equally fundamental, this policy protects the integrity of the judicial process. As Chief Justice Earl Warren said in one of his final opinions:

Courts which sit under our Constitution cannot and will not be made party to lawless invasions of the constitutional rights of citizens by permitting unhindered governmental use of the fruits of such invasions.[15]

Since Warren Burger succeeded Warren as Chief Justice (1969) and three other men chosen by Richard Nixon have come to the Supreme Court, a majority of the Justices have taken a less libertarian view of this rule, looking on it as a crude instrument to police the police. Burger has publicly said on several occasions that he is ready to scrap the policy as soon as someone can suggest a more expedient solution for controlling police.[16] As one would expect, the Court in its recent decisions has been creating exceptions to the exclusionary rule.

Electronic surveillance generally and wiretapping in particular have added another dimension to an already complex set of problems. In its first wiretapping case, *Olmstead* v. *United States* (1928), the Supreme Court ruled 5–4 that intercepting telephone conversations was not a search and seizure forbidden by the Fourth Amendment.[17] A decade later, however, the Justices found that the Federal Communications Act of 1934 had forbidden unauthorized interception of radio, telegraph, or telephone communications; and, under the exclusionary rule, evidence so obtained was inadmissible in federal courts.[18] *Mapp*'s extension of the exclusionary rule to state proceedings did not automatically make wiretap evidence inadmissible there because the Supreme Court distinguished between evidence obtained in violation of the Constitution—which state courts could not use—and evidence obtained in violation of a statute—which state courts could use.

Gradually, however, a majority of the Court came around to the view that *Olmstead* was wrong and that wiretapping and similar forms of bugging were searches and seizures that came within the scope of the Fourth Amendment.[19] Evidence so obtained by state officers would be admissible in the state courts only if the requirements of the Fourth Amendment were met.

This doctrine did nothing to change admissibility of evidence in federal courts, because the Court applied a stricter exclusionary rule there. But Congress in the Omnibus Crime Control Act of 1968 amended the Federal Communications Act. It is now illegal under most circumstances for private citizens or government officials to intercept messages without a warrant. State and federal officials must petition a court for permission and go through much the same procedure and show the same probable cause as in applying for a search warrant. An order can run for a maximum of thirty days, although it can be renewed following an application procedure very similar to the initial request. In emergency situations involving national security or organized crime, the Attorney General may himself authorize bugging for as long as forty-eight hours, if he uses that time to apply for a court order.

In general, the terms of the 1968 statute parallel the standards laid down in several recent Supreme Court decisions and bar from use in *any* judicial proceeding evidence obtained through *unlawful* eavesdropping. Some troublesome legal problems remain, however. First, an order for thirty days of wiretapping is far more inclusive than the usual search warrant, which allows a search at one time only. Second, the privacy of people other than the person named in the judicial authorization may be invaded since the suspect may talk with—and about—a large number of people. Third, notice of the authorization will normally be given the suspect only after the surveillance is completed, not as with a search warrant when the order is executed.

A fourth problem, that of the President's authority to order wiretapping under his own constitutional duty "to take care that the laws be faithfully executed," also remains, although in 1972 the Supreme Court cleared up some doubt. In a case with the delightful title of *United States* v. *U. S. District Court,* the Justices held that, even in investigations of "domestic security," wiretaps without judicial authorization violated the Fourth Amendment.[20] Evidence obtained either directly or indirectly from such unconstitutional activity could not be used in court. The Department of Justice had based its case on the inherent power of the Chief Executive as well as on that provision of the Omnibus Crime Control Act which stated that nothing in the statute shall "be deemed to limit the constitutional power of the President to take such measures as he deems necessary to protect the United States against the overthrow of the Government by force or other unlawful means, or against any other clear and present danger to the structure or existence of the Government."

For the Court, Justice Lewis F. Powell found that this language conferred no new power on the President. "It merely provides that the Act shall not be interpreted to limit or disturb such power as the President may have under the Constitution. In short, Congress simply left presidential powers where it found them." Stressing that a different situation might exist if the executive were tracking foreign agents, Powell held that where only domestic organizations were concerned, the President and his subordinates could conduct a "reasonable" search of telephone conversations only by submitting the case to a magistrate and obtaining a warrant. "Security surveillances," Powell lectured Richard Nixon, the President who had selected him for the Court, "are especially sensitive because of the inherent vagueness of the domestic security concept, the necessarily broad and continuing nature of intelligence gathering, and the temptation to utilize such surveillances to oversee political dissent. We recognize, as we have before, the constitutional basis of the President's domestic security role, but we think it must be exercised in a manner compatible with the Fourth Amendment."

Appeal

The Bill of Rights does not specifically mention a right to appeal a conviction, but the federal government and all the states allow at least one such appeal as a matter of statutory right. State procedures are usually more restrictive than federal; but state prisoners who can show that their trials were unfair and that the state judicial system does not allow a full review can ask a federal district judge for a writ of habeas corpus.[21] Whatever appellate procedure a state provides cannot discriminate on the basis of ability to pay. A state must, for example, furnish impoverished convicts with free transcripts of the trial and free legal counsel for at least one appeal.

Punishment

The Eighth Amendment—like most other constitutional provisions discussed in this chapter, incorporated into the Fourteenth—forbids imposition of "cruel and unusual punishments." That prohibition is hardly precise, and some Justices have candidly conceded that they interpret its meaning in light of the "evolving standards of decency that mark the progress of a maturing society."[22] The Court has been understandably reluctant to use such a vague criterion to strike down legislation, but it has occasionally done so. In 1910 the Justices held invalid a statute that authorized twelve years at hard labor in chains for embezzlement,[23] and in 1962 invalidated a California law that made drug addiction—the Justices said it was a disease—a crime.[24]

The death penalty poses the most awesome constitutional problem. In 1972 *Furman* v. *Georgia* held by a 5–4 vote that, as applied in the United States, death was a cruel and unusual punishment.[25] Each Justice wrote his own opinion; two of the majority thought that it was basically offensive to human dignity, and three others believed that it was being imposed capriciously.

Four years later, after Congress and thirty-five states had enacted new statutes to meet some of the objections of *Furman,* the Justices held (7–2) that death was not of and by itself a constitutionally forbidden punishment.[26] At the same time the Court placed severe procedural restrictions on sentences of death, striking down in the process statutes that made death an automatic punishment for certain crimes. The Justices were again badly divided in their reasoning and wrote six opinions, none of which was able to command more than three votes.

From this morass of words it appears that lawfully to kill a convicted human being government must divide the trial into two sections. In the first, the court determines the guilt or innocence of the accused. In the second part, assuming a verdict of guilty, the defendant must be allowed to present evidence showing mitigating circumstances and the prosecutor evidence of aggravating circumstances. The latter include such factors as the defendant's having been earlier convicted of another murder or having committed this murder while committing another felony. The court—judge or jury—must then weigh these circumstances and can impose a death sentence only on a finding that the aggravating circumstances outweigh any mitigating circumstances. A further check that seems required is *automatic* and full review of all death sentences by the state's highest court, with specific statutory instruc-

Isadore Hodges, one of thirteen inmates of "death row" at the Tennessee State Prison, was spared execution in the electric chair by the U.S. Supreme Court's ruling in 1972 that the death penalty as then applied was unconstitutional.

tions to go beyond the usual kinds of appellate review and insure that the penalty is not out of line with that imposed in similar cases within the state.

Double Jeopardy

If a defendant is acquitted, he can never be retried for that particular offense again. That is the clear message of the Fifth Amendment: "nor shall any person be subject for the same offense to be twice put in jeopardy of life or limb. . . ."Although this clause applies to state as well as federal cases, it is subject to certain exceptions. A particular crime could violate *both* state and federal law, and the guarantee does not protect a person from being prosecuted by both governments for such an offense. Even where a person has violated only a federal or a state law, that single deed may be criminal under several statutes. In such circumstances the accused may be tried and convicted for each separate offense. Again, freedom from double jeopardy does not prevent the prosecution from bringing a person to trial a second time when a higher court has set aside the original finding of guilt because of procedural errors.

Actual Practices of Criminal Justice

It is easy to understand why a law enforcement officer would prefer wider freedom than the Constitution, statutes, and judges give him. It is also easy to understand — although not to justify — why a policeman would sometimes break the law to catch a criminal. To a dedicated policeman, crime is not simply a mass of unpleasant statistics. He works every day amid the human suffering it causes and sees the blood, gore, wasted lives, and crippled minds of adults and, worse, of youngsters who will never have a chance at a decent living. He is likely to come to despise lawbreakers and to be deeply motivated to protect society from their activities. He is also likely to be frustrated and angry at the requirements that the legal system often imposes on him. For instance, when a policeman makes an arrest, he does not presume the accused innocent. If an honest officer were not convinced of the suspect's guilt he would not make the arrest. He has conducted an investigation, examined the evidence, and drawn what to him are logical conclusions.

At the same time, one must remember that a policeman's desire to curb crime is functional for his career ambitions. His promotion within the police force depends in large part on his success in solving cases and making arrests that lead to convictions. As a trained expert, he probably also takes professional pride in his work. Criticism by reporters, elected officials, or superiors on the force that he or his colleagues are not behaving efficiently can be stinging. Moreover, these people may be reprimanding him for operating *within* the law — inefficiently, that is, in terms of catching criminals. Those kinds of criticism — and sanctions imposed by being passed over for promotion — can push police to operate outside the law. As we saw in the preceding chapter, many agents of the Federal Bureau of Investigation and the Internal Revenue Service committed a variety of felonies to please their bosses. There is no reason to believe that state and local officers are morally stronger.

Especially when working on a "big case," a serious felony like premeditated murder or large-scale sale of narcotics, police almost always scrupulously follow the letter of the law. They know that the case is likely to end up in a lengthy trial during which a trial judge and perhaps appellate judges will protect the civil rights of the accused by carefully examining not only the nature of the evidence but also the way in which it was obtained. Police are apt to be equally scrupulous in dealing with affluent citizens or successful criminals, because both types of people probably know their legal rights, have their own lawyers, and perhaps also have easy access to reporters or public officials outside the force. In many cases, when the police think that the crime does not cause a disturbance (such as propositioning a prostitute) and the offender is basically a decent citizen, they give him far more lenient treatment that the law specifies.

In the usual case, however, the law enforcement officer is tougher in his actions, knowing that seldom will there be an examination in open court of the way in which evidence was obtained.[27] As a practical matter, the police are usually familiar with the habits of small-time thieves, pickpockets, prostitutes, pimps, runners for numbers rackets, operators of small gambling games, and drug addicts. They can pick up most of these people and search them for incriminating evidence without probable cause. Both the suspect and the officer may know that the law forbids such action, but both also know that if the petty criminal, or even the innocent poor man or woman, complicates the policeman's work by insisting on constitutional rights, the policeman can make life miserable. For the same reasons, after being taken into custody the accused often does not insist on his right to silence — although he may lie outrageously — or to an attorney, at least at the interrogation stage.

Studies of the impact of the *Miranda* decision on the behavior of suspects have shown that a large percentage of prisoners who are advised of their rights — and not all are informed — quickly waive them.[28] In part they do so because they wish to appear cooperative, in part because they really do not understand what is being told them — criminals are typically well below average in intelligence — and in part because they do not trust lawyers to take their side against the police. *Miranda,* of course, makes little difference to the successful professional criminal, who knows precisely what his rights are and is not likely to say anything to the police unless he gets a promise of leniency or immunity in return.

A standard police technique is to allow a petty crook to go free, letting him know that he can be leaned on any time, and then to use both gratitude and fear to persuade him to act as an informer. In payment for occasional tips, a policeman may give him a few dollars — often out of the officer's own pocket — and not go out of his way to check into how he earns his living otherwise. The efficiency of a police force in arresting big-time criminals is a function of its intelligence system, which in turn is based largely on underworld informants. Police agents can infiltrate a gang only at grave risk and great difficulty and can do so only once before blowing their cover. But the society of criminals has its own networks of communications, and tapping these can provide steady payoffs that police calculate are worth the cost of letting a few small fish go free.

The Trial Substitute

Even where a more serious offense is involved, the police may, through deliberate choice, ignorance, or overzealousness, exceed legal bounds. They may have arrested the suspect on a flimsy suspicion, searched his property more extensively than the Fourth Amendment permits, failed to provide proper warnings, questioned him longer than the law allows before charging him before a magistrate, or even threatened physical violence. But none of these flaws is necessarily fatal to a conviction, for one of the most important facts about American criminal justice is that most cases never go to trial. An overwhelming majority and, in some jurisdictions, perhaps as many as nine out of ten nontraffic convictions are obtained through guilty pleas. In 1971, for instance, 98,000 out of 101,000 convictions obtained in New York City's misdemeanor courts were by guilty pleas. In the first ten months of the same year, 95 percent of convictions for felonies in the Bronx were the result of pleas of guilty.

Thus, the normal culmination of the legal process is not a trial where a judge can examine police procedures, but *plea bargaining,* a negotiating process over the charge lodged against the defendant. The prisoner may tacitly begin his bargaining by cooperating with the police and by not insisting on his rights. Even if the police do not let him go free, they may be willing to book him on a less serious offense. It is with the prosecutor, however, that the main bargaining occurs. In some state—but never federal—jurisdictions, the trial judge may participate in the negotiations; in a few states, both the prosecuting and defense attorneys must stipulate that no bargaining has occurred, although everyone, including the judge, knows that it has.

In essence, the defendant offers to plead guilty if the prosecutor will ask the judge for leniency or will reduce the charge—for example, from assault with a deadly weapon to simple assault, or from selling drugs to illegal possession of narcotics. If there have been police irregularities at the arrest or investigatory stages, the defense attorney can use this fact in his negotiations, stressing that part of the prosecution's evidence would be thrown out of court.

Both sides are pushed toward this kind of bargaining. The defendant often has been convicted at least once before and he knows that the evidence against him is weighty, possibly damning; while his own protestations of innocence—which may be all that he can offer in his defense—are not likely to be convincing. Even when he is innocent and can put up a good defense, if he is poor and cannot raise bail, he may have to stay in jail longer awaiting trial than he would if convicted and sentenced. Moreover, it is a statistical fact that judges tend to impose stiffer punishment on persons convicted after a full trial than they do for the same offense if the accused pleads guilty.[29] And, of course, the defendant can usually plead guilty to a lesser crime than he would be tried for.

For his part, the prosecutor usually has a small, overworked staff facing a huge backlog of cases. There is always a big trial demanding attention. If he can get rid of less important business without riling the police or making a mockery of the law, a busy prosecutor is generally happy to do so. To maximize his bargaining position, the prosecutor often charges the defendant with a more serious crime than the one on which he thinks he can get a conviction if the case actually goes to trial.

The judge usually knows what is going on, even where plea bargaining is illegal. He also realizes that he presides over a court *originally* designed to serve a small, uncomplicated rural society, a tribunal that could not possibly function in an urban environment if it had to accord a full and fair trial to even a small percentage of defendants. His docket is stacked with cases. A typical judge on an urban court that handles lesser criminal cases may have to dispose of more than a thousand non-traffic cases every month, and perhaps as many traffic offenses. His colleagues on courts of higher jurisdiction have fewer but more complicated cases, and they too are usually far behind in their dockets.

Justices of the Supreme Court are quite aware of what happens in the criminal courts and have sustained the use of plea bargaining, provided that the trial judge makes sure that the negotiations have been "intelligent and voluntary." Indeed, Chief Justice Burger wrote for the Court in 1971 that plea bargaining "is an essential component of the administration of justice. Properly administered, it is to be encouraged."[30] On the other hand, the National Advisory Commission on Criminal Justice Standards and Goals, a group of distinguished policemen, lawyers, judges, professors, and penologists, reviewed the evidence for and against the practice and came to a conclusion that "totally condemns plea bargaining as an institution. . . . The only concession that the Commission is willing to make is that total elimination of the practice will take appreciable time."[31]

Prisons, Rehabilitation, and Social Reform

A Society of Captives

Confusion over the purposes of criminal law is depressingly reflected in what happens to that relatively small percentage of criminals who are convicted and imprisoned. Most prisons are at best custodial insti-

Efforts to provide prison inmates with opportunities to learn something besides the criminal trades vary greatly from prison to prison. At the Federal Correctional Institution at Fort Worth, Texas, some prisoners are trained in the construction trades in preparation for admission into union apprenticeship programs upon release.

tutions that do little, if anything, to rehabilitate offenders. At worst — and the worst seems normal — prisons are merely schools that have very strict rules about attendance, maim the minds and bodies of amateurs, and train them to become hardened professional criminals.

If a prisoner goes to a newer minimum-security institution, the process is likely to be painful and boring, but the odds are that it will not be oppressive. Confinement in an older style penitentiary or maximum-security prison, however, entails severe, even savage punishment. First, the facilities are usually dilapidated and badly overcrowded. After all, the comfort of convicted felons has a low priority for taxpayers' dollars. In Florida, for example, as many as ten inmates are packed into a single cell measuring twelve by fifteen feet. In 1976, federal district judges ruled that penitentiaries in Alabama, Florida, Louisiana, and Mississippi were so heavily overcrowded as to impose cruel and unusual punishment on prisoners.

Worse, however, than the physical conditions is the psychological atmosphere of terror that pervades a penitentiary. Sociologists have coined the word *prisonalization* to describe the social and psychological processes by which an inmate is assimilated into the life of a prison. In essence, the prisoner joins a society of criminals who live inside the walls a life of more sordid violence than they knew outside. The new man—or woman—quickly learns that, while the warden and guards keep prisoners from freedom, the real determinants of how a prisoner lives inside—or whether he or she lives at all—are fellow inmates. When the doors shut, the prisoners' own rules operate, and penitentiaries abound in extortion, assaults that often result in serious injuries, sometimes in blindings or cripplings, and occasionally in death, as well as homosexual activities that include prostitution, brutal gang rapes, and active cooperation forced by threats of mayhem. A prisoner learns to conform to these practices not by choice but by necessity. It is little wonder that life under these conditions does nothing to enable a man or woman to live a useful, productive life in a free society.[32]

The larger society takes little interest in what happens to the human being who will be incarcerated in this environment. "It must be ironic to a prisoner," Chief Justice Burger has remarked, "to recall that society spared no expense to provide him with three, four, or five trials and appeals, at enormous costs, but then proceeds to forget his plight" once he has been imprisoned.

In 1971 the bloody revolt of prisoners at Attica, New York, took forty-three lives and revealed how oppressive conditions inside really were. In 1976, prison officials admitted that the situation at Attica was still as bad as it had been five years earlier. Moreover, in some respects, the situation in most maximum-security penal institutions is likely to get worse even if more and more money is spent to improve physical facilities. Legislators, judges, prosecutors, and prison officials try to keep young offenders and first offenders out of penitentiaries by giving suspended sentences, providing alternative facilities where some contact with normal life can be maintained, and allowing early parole when there seems a chance for rehabilitation. These may all be needed reforms; but each of them, insofar as it is effective, screens out for the big prisons the really hardened criminals, the professionals as well as the sociopaths and psychopaths. These people inside prison are not apt to react more favorably to attempts to control or rehabilitate them than they did outside. One result is likely to be more and more unrest and even open revolt in the larger penitentiaries.

Reform

Police who are both efficient and law abiding, judicial procedures that are scrupulously fair, and prisons that reform rather than brutalize are all important elements in coping with the myriad problems of crime. But however honest, dedicated, and efficient, neither police, prosecutors, judges, nor prison officials get at the roots of crime. Controlling crime is tightly linked to broader societal reform. No program can be

Figure 17.2
Percent Repeaters
by Type of Crime in 1972

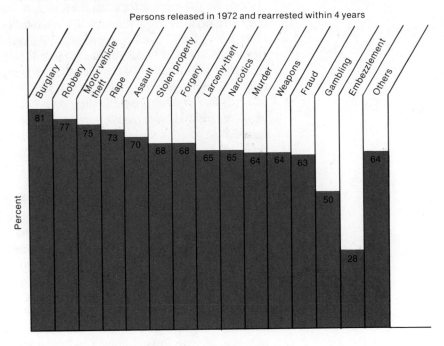

Persons released in 1972 and rearrested within 4 years

Percent

Burglary 81
Robbery 77
Motor vehicle theft 75
Rape 73
Assault 70
Stolen property 68
Forgery 68
Larceny-theft 65
Narcotics 65
Murder 64
Weapons 64
Fraud 63
Gambling 50
Embezzlement 28
Others 64

Source: Federal Bureau of Investigation, *Uniform Crime Reports in the United States – 1975* (Washington, D.C.: Government Printing Office, 1976), p. 45.

successful over the long run unless drug addiction is dramatically lessened and the economic and social conditions that encourage crime are drastically improved. The frustrations of life in overcrowded urban slums, of discrimination, and of broken homes and the humiliations and deprivations of unemployment and of living off welfare in a land of plenty may not cause crime, but they do make crime appear a more attractive alternative—a dangerous though possibly effective means of escape from the nightmare of the ghetto.

Moreover, as much as it pains most liberal intellectuals to admit it, a considerable number of people are not capable of living and working peacefully in a community. Whether because of sin, genetic defects, physical disabilities, mental disease, scars from earlier abuses by parents or society, these warped humans will again and again commit crimes of violence. Prison terms can interrupt but hardly end their careers. A large number of other "habitual criminals" have made breaking the law a life's work and, having become skilled at their trade, can see little point in joining the "straight" world.

How to cope with either group has so far exceeded the combined capacities of clergy, penologists, psychiatrists, and parole officers and certainly remains far beyond the reach of prison guards. These "repeaters" form the core of the quarter of a million men and women who populate prisons. Few inmates are residents of maximum-security prisons unless they have been previously *convicted* of one or two felonies. In gross statistical terms, because the odds of arrest and conviction are so low, it is probable that most of these people committed many felonies before being imprisoned. According to the FBI's data, 67 percent of prisoners who serve their time or receive pardons are within three years rearrested on serious charges. The corresponding figure for those paroled—and thus supposedly helped and supervised by law enforcement officers—is 64 percent, not a comforting difference. Indeed, in 1976, U. S. Attorney General Edward H. Levi advocated abolition of the federal parole system. It had become, he argued, not only ineffective but counterproductive in that a prisoner becomes eligible for parole and is often released after serving only one third of his sentence.

Other less radical proposals for reform have urged definite sentences for shorter terms than prisoners now typically receive (but longer than what they typically serve). Still others have advocated stiff and automatic sentences for habitual criminals. These suggestions presume that society can deter criminals by the threat of punishment. But, as we have already seen, some people are incapable of lives that our society considers normal and lawful. They are largely immune to a rational calculus of pain versus gain. One can change these people's conduct only by remedying the underlying physical, psychological, or social causes of their conditions. For the skilled professional criminal who can rationally weigh the risks of being imprisoned against the profits from crime, the odds seem all in his favor. There are simply too many opportunities for crime for any police force to block most of them, as the statistics cited earlier in this chapter illustrate.

What we have talked about here—efficient and law abiding police, a fair judicial system, prisons that help rehabilitate rather than destroy personality, individual moral regeneration, curing physical and psychological defects—provides an insuperable challenge for any society that operates in the real world. That perfect justice and goodness are utopian dreams, however, is a poor excuse for a society as rich as that of America not to strive to come nearer to those goals.

Summary

This chapter underlined the serious and gnawing problem of crime in America and stressed the difficulties of controlling such "deviant conduct" while maintaining a government under law, a wide measure of individual freedom, and respect for human dignity. A truly free society needs protection from both criminals and police. Without a doubt, there are many badly needed reforms in police practices and judicial procedures. But the failings there are not so overwhelming as is the political system's inability to provide what so many people see as a viable alternative to a life of crime. Whether the fault is due to individual shortcomings or to flaws in the system, the streak of violence that Chapter 2 described as running through American history still leaves a bright and ugly red stain on the nation's life.

Selected Bibliography

BANTON, MICHAEL, *The Policeman in the Community* (New York: Basic Books, Inc., 1964). A basic study of the relationship between the police and the public.

BLUMBERG, ABRAHAM S., *Criminal Justice* (Chicago, Ill.: Quadrangle Books, 1967). A searing analysis of plea bargaining and its implications for due process of law.

CAMPBELL, JAMES S., J. R. SAHNID, and D. P. STANG, *Law and Order Reconsidered: A Staff Report to the National Commission on the Causes and Prevention of Violence* (Washington, D. C.: Government Printing Office, 1969). A very useful study that re-evaluates the earlier work of the President's Commission on Law Enforcement and Administration of Justice, cited below.

CASPAR, JONATHAN D., *American Criminal Justice: The Defendant's Perspective* (Englewood Cliffs, N. J.: Prentice-Hall, Inc., 1972). A description of the way the police, prosecutors, and courts operate, based on interviews with people charged with criminal activity.

CHEVIGNY, PAUL, *Police Power: Police Abuses in New York City* (New York: Pantheon Books, 1969). A sharply critical account of the behavior of a relatively good police force; argues that abuses are the results of social pressures on the police.

COLE, GEORGE F., ed., *Criminal Justice: Law and Politics* (Belmont, Cal.: Duxbury Press, 1972). A carefully selected collection of some of the best recent literature on the police, the courts, and law enforcement generally.

GOLDFARB, RONALD L., *Jails: The Ultimate Ghetto of the Criminal Justice System* (Garden City, N. Y.: Anchor Press/Doubleday, 1975). A study of jails as pretrial detention centers.

GOLDFARB, RONALD L., and LINDA R. SINGER, *After Conviction* (New York: Simon and Schuster, Inc., 1973). A scholarly, detailed history and analysis of the ineffectual operations of the penal system.

LEVY, LEONARD W., *Against the Law: The Nixon Court and Criminal Justice* (New York: Harper & Row, 1974). An impassioned argument that Nixon's nominees on the Supreme Court are destroying historic safeguards of individual rights.

MITFORD, JESSICA, *Kind and Usual Punishment: The Prison Business* (New York: Vintage Books, 1974). A popular but useful (and readable) account of life in prison.

NATIONAL ADVISORY COMMISSION ON CRIMINAL JUSTICE STANDARDS AND GOALS, *National Conference on Criminal Justice* (Washington, D. C.: Government Printing Office, 1973). An effort by a distinguished group of public officials and private citizens to formulate a program to reform the entire system of criminal justice.

PACKER, HERBERT L., *The Limits of the Criminal Sanction* (Stanford, Calif.: Stanford University Press, 1968). An exciting inquiry into the relations between society and criminal law, and a challenge to the social utility of much of that law.

PRESIDENT'S COMMISSION ON LAW ENFORCEMENT AND ADMINISTRATION OF JUSTICE, *The Challenge of Crime in a Free Society* (Washington, D. C.: Government Printing Office, 1967). A monumental study surveying the entire field of criminal justice and making more than 200 specific recommendations for reform.

RADZINOWICZ, LEON, and MARVIN E. WOLFGANG, eds., *Crime and Justice* (New York: Basic Books, Inc., 1971). 3 vols. A massive collection, available in an inexpensive paperback edition, of leading articles by lawyers, philosophers, and social scientists.

ROSETT, ARTHUR, and DONALD R. CRESSEY, *Justice by Consent: Plea Bargains in the American Courthouse* (Philadelphia: J. P. Lippincott Company, 1976). A nontechnical analysis of plea bargaining by a lawyer and a sociologist, both of whom had earlier worked for the President's Commission on Law Enforcement and the Administration of Justice.

SKOLNICK, JEROME H., *Justice without Trial: Law Enforcement in Democratic Society* (New York: John Wiley and Sons, Inc., 1966). A skillfully done work combining the rich detail of an original case study with broad generalizations from existing knowledge.

SYKES, GRESHAM M., *The Society of Captives: A Study of a Maximum Security Prison* (Princeton, N. J.: Princeton University Press, 1958). A short but fascinating account of life in a state prison.

VAN DEN HAAG, ERNEST, *Punishing Criminals* (New York: Basic Books, Inc., 1975). A controversial argument by a psychiatrist that society has not only the right but the duty to make punishment fit the crime rather than the criminal, as much of modern criminology holds.

UNGAR, SANFORD J., *FBI* (Boston: Little, Brown and Company, 1975). A journalist's detailed and critical study of the FBI: although completed before the scandals that racked the FBI in 1976 produced much new valuable information about the Bureau's operations, this volume is still the best account.

WHITTEMORE, L. H., *Cop: A Closeup of Violence and Tragedy* (New York: Holt, Rinehart & Winston, Inc., 1969). Three vignettes of the working lives of policemen; provides a series of informative insights into the human problems of law enforcement.

WILSON, JAMES Q., *Varieties of Police Behavior* (Cambridge, Mass.: Harvard University Press, 1968). An interesting analysis of how police operate and how they could become more effective managers of social conflict.

Part Eight

Conclusion

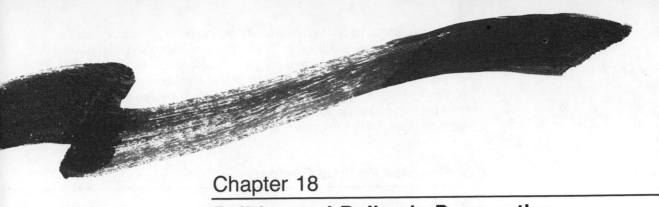

Chapter 18
Politics and Policy in Perspective

A Complex Political System
The Illustrative Case of the SST
Prospects

WE HAVE TRIED to further understanding of the American system of government by first placing it in its historical, cultural, and institutional setting and then describing how its formal and informal processes operate—the choice of leaders, the practical and legal restrictions on their power, and the character of citizens' rights. We have also described the way the system produces and carries out policy decisions and some of the ways these policy choices shape American life.

A Complex Political System

To this point our analyses have of necessity been organized around the various separate components of the American system, not the process as a whole. In reality, of course, Congress, the courts, the President and federal executives, political parties, the Constitution, federalism, and other elements of American politics constantly interact with each other. Rarely does one component operate in isolation. Instead, many elements of the political process are involved in developing and implementing almost all public policies.

An act of Congress, for example, may first take shape in an executive agency, or in a congressional subcommittee, or in an interest group. The problem addressed by this law may have been an issue in a presidential or congressional campaign. Or what happened in the campaign may have delayed consideration of a new policy. For example, despite widespread dissatisfaction with the welfare "mess," neither a Democratic Congress nor a Republican President was willing to give the other potential credit at the polls by cooperating to produce more rational and effective legislation before the election of 1972. In 1976, they offered a rerun of that scenario. No serious efforts at reform were undertaken by Congress or President Ford, at least in part because of the impending national election.

In some instances, widespread constituency pressures may greatly increase the importance to elected officials of such issues as abortion or gun control. Public attitudes, reflected in polls, election results, and letters to newspapers and elected officials, can play a significant role in framing legislative agendas and in determining the content of policies.

More generally, particular policy proposals inevitably are influenced by widespread public attitudes about government, its responsibilities, and its effectiveness. Shifts in public concerns, priorities, and confidence in government constantly sift through to elected officials and so affect the nature and content of public policy. So does the nation's pattern of economic and social development. Both domestic and foreign policy making are shaped at every stage by the social, economic, demographic, and technological realities of a highly urbanized and industrialized society.

As any important legislative proposal moves through the maze of government, its content is affected by a variety of officials—federal bureaucrats, the President and his aides, representatives and senators on the appropriate committees and subcommittees, other members of Congress, and congressional staff. If the proposal deals with domestic affairs, state and local governments will try to insure that their particular constituencies are treated fairly in the distribution of federal funds and responsibilities. The shape of the legislation is also influenced by past and anticipated rulings of federal courts, as well as by the general powers of and limitations on government set forth in the Constitution.

Once passed, a law continues to involve many elements of the political system. Enacting legislation is only one step in the policy process. Carrying out laws means action by federal administrative or regulatory agencies, the White House, and congressional committees and subcommittees. Rules and regulations must be developed within the executive branch or federal regulatory agencies. To implement the law, new administrative structures may have to be created, or old ones reorganized. Staffs usually have to be acquired, professional expertise developed, and equipment purchased.

All these activities depend heavily on the availability of funds to carry out the particular policy. To secure funds, administrative agencies submit budget requests to the Office of Management and Budget in accordance with general guidelines developed by the President and his most trusted advisers. OMB officials review these requests in light of overall resources and priorities. Their recommendations for particular programs and agencies become a key element in the development of the President's budget. Next comes detailed review in Congress, by the general budget and appropriations committees and subcommittees in each house.

After securing legal authority and appropriations, agencies move on to make thousands of determinations necessary to carry out almost any public policy. Is a particular businessman or individual eligible for assistance under the statutory provisions and administrative regulations? Does an exporter qualify for an exemption from a particular trade restriction? Do the laser guns ordered by the Department of Defense meet federal contract specifications? Are the matching arrangements proposed by a city consistent with the rules governing a federal sewer program? Which of 200 applicants should receive the fifteen federal grants available in the field of energy conservation?

For most domestic programs, implementation also depends heavily on the activity of state and local governments. Lack of matching funds or different local priorities may preclude participation in some federal programs. Differences in funding and administrative capabilities produce very different results among states and localities in "national" programs for welfare, health, job training, education, and law enforcement. Implementation may be slowed by political pressures, as in the case of major changes in federal transportation policy enacted by Congress in the early 1970s, which permitted use of highway taxes for mass transit. In many states, road builders, highway users, and other automotive interests strongly resisted diversion of "their" funds to public transportation. Another factor in implementation is lack of information among many local officials about new federal policies, a factor that reduced use of highway funds for public transportation.

At every step in the process of implementation, other elements of the political system become involved. Administrative agencies constantly compete for funds and responsibilities. Agencies lobby with budget officials, the White House, and congressional committees and subcommittees. So do interested groups of all kinds. Particular administrative decisions are closely watched by some members of Congress, as well as by corporations, unions, state and local governments, foreign nations, and other interests affected by the powers and actions of the agency in question. Judicial rulings may expand or restrict an agency's powers, discretion, or procedures. Public opinion can affect the carrying out of policy, as can disclosures of official cupidity or stupidity by enterprising journalists or disgruntled public employees. Implementation, as well as policy, is altered from time to time by election results. Newly elected leaders at the national, state, and local levels usually shift priorities, change policies, and replace some top officials.

Laws, of course, are only one type of policy. Other kinds of policy determinations also involve a variety of the components of the political system. Decisions by federal courts ordering desegregation of public schools have resulted largely from law suits filed by civil rights groups challenging policies of local school officials. In the wake of actions by federal judges, opponents of integration have rioted, local school boards have wrestled with complex plans designed to implement or evade court orders, and mayors and other elected officials have tried to satisfy the courts without losing their local base of support. In Washington, Presidents have unhappily resorted to military force to quell disturbances resulting from efforts to desegregate schools. Intense constituency pressures have led many members of Congress to attempt to eliminate busing from the remedies available to federal judges in dealing with school desegregation. And officials of the Departments of Justice and Health, Education, and Welfare have been consistently criticized, both for applying too much and too little pressure on local school districts that failed to desegregate.

Because of the complexity of the political process, issues rarely can be neatly compartmentalized. Even such broad categories as foreign policy and domestic policy are seldom water tight, because foreign policies almost always raise domestic issues. Defense spending and assistance to other nations reduce resources available for domestic needs. Development of new weapons is justified on the grounds of threats from abroad, but support for and opposition to particular military programs often depend on which sections of the country will obtain defense contracts and bases. Middle Eastern policy affects petroleum prices, and thus the cost of oil, and so the entire domestic economy.

Encouraging favorable trade relationships with friendly nations may threaten domestic industries that cannot meet the competition of cotton goods produced in Taiwan or shoes made in Brazil. The question of how far the United States extends its jurisdiction over coastal waters is hardly an abstract issue of international law for commercial fishermen in Maine and California who compete with the formidable fishing fleets of Japan and the Soviet Union.

The Illustrative Case of the SST

Development of public policy on commercial supersonic aircraft provides an excellent example of the interplay of foreign and domestic policy and the involvement of most political components of the American system in a single issue. Back in the late 1950s, advances in aviation technology stirred interest in supersonic airliners. Builders of aircraft and federal aviation officials saw great promise in supersonic airplanes, as, of course, did the commercial airlines. SSTs (supersonic transports) soaring over twice the speed of sound would drastically reduce travel time between major cities of the world. Development of the SST by American firms would permit the United States to retain its pre-eminent role in the production of commercial aircraft. But the estimated costs of designing and testing a supersonic airliner were beyond the resources of the aviation industry. As a result, the Federal Aviation Agency concluded that public funds would be required to assist development of the new airplane, and in 1961 Congress responded with an initial appropriation of $11 million.

The following year, the French and British governments announced a joint effort to develop their own SST, the Concorde, and similar work was also underway in the Soviet Union. The prospect of foreign competition created a sense of urgency in the United States. In 1963, President Kennedy decided to commit the federal government wholeheartedly to underwriting development of the SST by private industry. Under Kennedy's plan, which was announced one day after Pan American World Airways ordered six Concordes, 75 percent of the estimated development costs of the SST would be financed by taxpayers' dollars.

Over the next nine years, Congress appropriated $841 million for the SST. Supporters of the program, led by the two senators from Washington, the home of Boeing Aircraft, rested their case on national prestige and the necessity of insuring continued American superiority in civil aviation. Failure to develop the SST, they argued, would adversely affect the nation's balance of payments by as much as $16 billion by 1980, because dollars to purchase the new aircraft would flow out of rather than into the United States. Strong support for the SST came from business, labor, and political leaders, including Boeing's chairman, the president of the AFL-CIO, and the governor of Washington. Groups like the National Committee for SST and Industry and Labor for SST were formed to bolster congressional backers of the SST and the Federal Aviation Agency, which was the principal supporter of the project within the executive branch.

Opposition to federal subsidies for the SST grew steadily during the 1960s. The planes promised to be extremely noisy, generating sonic booms that could disturb millions of people, thus adding significantly to already severe noise problems around major airports. In addition, the new aircraft would pollute the upper atmosphere, perhaps adversely affecting the ozone layer that protects the earth from the sun's radiation. Because of the high cost of the aircraft itself and its prodigious consumption of fuel, travel on SSTs would be expensive. Why, asked critics, should the federal government subsidize an aircraft that would serve only a small proportion of the population, mostly affluent businessmen and wealthy "jet setters"? More generally, increasing numbers of Americans were no longer convinced that expensive technological developments like the SST automatically meant "progress." And environmental concerns were rising to the forefront of national political consciousness. Among the foes of the SST were such groups as the Friends of the Earth, Environmental Action, the Sierra Club, and Zero Population Growth.

By 1971, the opponents of the SST in Congress were sufficiently numerous to reverse the policy of three Presidents who had supported federal subsidies. Bolstering opposition were persistent doubts within the executive branch over the economic feasibility and scientific desirability of SSTs. After weeks of intense lobbying by both sides, the SST was killed on close votes in the House and Senate. With President Nixon strongly in favor of the SST, party lines were relatively important in the congressional voting, particularly in the House, where most Republicans backed it. A key factor in the House vote, as pointed out in Chapter 11, was the Legislative Reorganization Act of 1970, which provided for recording teller votes. With environmental concerns rising, many congressmen who had previously supported the SST on unrecorded votes were unwilling to antagonize environmentalists on a recorded vote.

With federal support ended, Boeing and General Electric, the prime contractors, abandoned the project. The issue of supersonic aircraft, however, was not yet resolved. During the same year that Congress was rejecting additional funds for the SST, both the Anglo-French Concorde and the Russian TU-144 were undergoing test flights. By 1975, Concorde was ready for regular passenger service. Now the question became whether the United States would permit SSTs to operate within its territorial limits. Requests from Air France and British Airways for permission to fly Concorde into New York and Washington were favorably received by the Federal Aviation Agency. In recommending that the Secretary of Transportation approve SST service,

"They're environmentalists watching for migratory birds and SST's!"

FAA concluded that the aircraft was neither excessively noisy nor a significant threat to the atmosphere.

Residents of areas surrounding jet airports vigorously protested. Noise levels, they argued, would be intolerable. To support their case, they pointed to FAA's own environmental impact statement on Concorde, which conceded that the SST would be four times noisier during take-off than the newest subsonic jets. Support for their objections came from the U.S. Environmental Protection Agency, which found Concorde's noise levels unacceptable for operations in densely settled areas such as those surrounding Kennedy International Airport in New York. Environmental groups also protested that the SST wasted fuel and that not enough was known about the hazards posed to health by Concorde's impact on the atmosphere. Responding to these concerns, members of Congress sought to amend federal airport legislation in order to ban Concorde.

Proponents of Concorde contended that local concerns should not be permitted to endanger relations with Britain and France. The Secretary of State urged fair treatment for two of the nation's oldest allies. British and French officials argued that agreements with the United States protected their airliners against discriminatory treatment. London and Paris also spoke ominously about retaliating against American airlines and commercial aircraft produced in the United States. To press their case, the two nations and their airlines dispatched top officials, hired lobbyists, and engaged politically influential Washington law firms.

Early in 1976, Secretary of Transportation William T. Coleman, Jr.

French and British lobbyists press the case for the Concorde SST with a legislator on the floor of the New Jersey Assembly in Trenton.

announced a national policy on Concorde. In reaching his decision, Coleman had convened a public hearing at which British and French officials, federal agencies, members of Congress, state and local political leaders, and a variety of other interests defended or attacked the aircraft. Coleman then decided to approve a limited number of daily flights into New York and Washington for a trial period of sixteen months. President Ford promptly supported Secretary Coleman's decision.

The American system of government, however, provides multiple means of access to power; and the way was not yet cleared for Concorde to fly to the two cities. Opponents continued to seek support in Congress for legislation to ban SSTs, arguing that the limited number of flights would grow once Concorde had its gigantic tires in the door. Anti-SST groups went to court as well in an effort to overturn the decision, the Environmental Defense Fund filing a motion for an injunction immediately after Secretary Coleman had announced his policy.

Although these efforts to block Concorde at the national level failed, supporters of Concorde had additional hurdles to overcome elsewhere in a decentralized political system. In New York, permission was required from the Port of New York Authority, the bistate agency that controls the metropolitan area's airports. Any action by the Port Authority, in turn, could be vetoed by the governor of New Jersey or the governor of New York. By the time Secretary Coleman had established federal policy, Governor Hugh Carey of New York was already on record against Concorde flights into Kennedy International Airport. Other local officials, as well as such groups as the Metro Suburban Aircraft Noise Association, the National Organization to Insure a

Sound-Controlled Environment (NOISE), and the Emergency Coalition to Stop the SST, immediately began to press the Port Authority to deny permission to Air France and British Airways.

Responding to these pressures, the New York legislature quickly passed a bill establishing noise standards that effectively barred supersonic aircraft from Port Authority airports. For the New York law to have any effect, however, New Jersey had to pass a similar statute. To prevent enactment, London and Paris dispatched officials to Trenton to lobby for the SST. Although New Jersey took no action, the Port Authority, in the face of Governor Carey's position, rejected the requests of Air France and British Airways for permission to inaugurate Concorde service at Kennedy International Airport. Only after evaluating at least six months of Concorde operations at other airports, especially the impact of the SST's noise levels, would the Port Authority reconsider its policy.

Still the matter was not ended. Britain and France refused to accept the Port Authority's prohibition and announced plans to go to federal court to test the constitutional authority of a state agency to interfere with interstate and foreign commerce. Federal officials indicated that new national policies were needed to prevent state and local governments from hindering the efficient operation of national and international aviation. Opponents of Concorde answered by claiming that the states had "a clear right, and indeed a pressing responsibility, to protect the health and welfare of their residents by taking any action necessary to effectively reduce excessive jet noise."[1]

By early 1977, sixteen years after the initial decision to subsidize SSTs, most of the major issues concerning public policy on supersonic aircraft were still unresolved. How much service, at what airports, and under what sort of restrictions remained unanswered questions. So did the larger question of federal support for development of an American SST, an issue that was revived once the Anglo-French Concorde entered commercial service.

What is boomingly clear from the SST's travails is the complexity of American political processes. Political conflict over the SST has involved basic constitutional questions, international relations, questions of national purpose and priorities, shifting public attitudes on technology and environmental protection, and different views of the costs and benefits of public actions. Experts have differed over scientific, economic, and technological questions raised by development and use of supersonic aircraft. International, national, and varying local perspectives have produced clashing views and interests. And almost every component of the political system has become involved over the years — Congress and its committees and voting methods, the President and a variety of executive officials and agencies, political parties, federal courts, state and local governments, and a host of interest groups ranging from foreign governments and their agents to neighborhood civic associations.

Prospects

In the course of examining the varied components of the American political system, what may have escaped notice—but should not have—is the fragility of constitutional democracy. Each of the tiles of ideals and trust that together form a democratic system is brittle. Collectively they can topple into a shattered heap of anarchy or be reglued into a pattern of dictatorship. Like most aspects of modern industrial societies, constitutional democracy depends on adherence to norms of peaceful behavior and free exchange of ideas. Acceptance of these norms rather than physical force makes a democracy possible. Public officials can be murdered; speakers can easily be shouted down; universities closed; constitutional rights trampled by police or by mobs of neighbors or strangers; and the electoral process corrupted by the apathy of voters or by the grandiose ambitions of candidates.

Despite this inherent fragility, essentially the same governmental structure has survived in the United States for almost 200 years—a monument to the wisdom of the framers of the Constitution and to the skill of succeeding generations of politicians. That this governmental structure has survived *and* produced a great measure of individual freedom and a general level of prosperity unequaled almost anywhere in the world is even more significant. Yet for contemporary Americans there are dismaying items on the debit side of the ledger. The United States continues to face serious crises in both foreign and domestic affairs.

The current international situation raises many issues of the debate over America's role as a world power that has gone on intermittently since 1898. One could almost say that the issues are similar to those George Washington discussed with his advisers after the outbreak of the French Revolution or those that Thomas Jefferson considered before sending the Navy and Marines to retaliate against the Barbary Pirates. There is one all important difference, however: the present problems occur against a backdrop of nuclear and biological weapons that can obliterate life on this planet.

The end of the war in Southeast Asia, which preoccupied American foreign policy and domestic politics for almost a decade, settled few questions. Relations with Vietnam, Thailand, China, Korea, Taiwan, and other Asian nations still pose a variety of problems and opportunities. Equally troublesome are questions of American policy toward Greece and Turkey, Israel, the Arab world, black Africa, and Latin America. Relations with adversaries of three decades in Eastern Europe and even with close allies are not straightforward and simple. Nor is it clear how the United States can help developing nations maintain their independence, attain some degree of internal freedom, and achieve a measure of prosperity or, in the case of some, feed their growing and hungry populations. If imperialism has become repugnant to most Americans, isolationism can only be a fatuous dream in a shrunken world. We can ask Cain's ancient question about being our brothers' keepers, but the answer will be unchanged.

The problem in foreign affairs is to find wisdom. In domestic politics, the problem is to find both wisdom and the power to carry out that wisdom. Previous chapters have stressed the ways in which the American system divides political power and makes it difficult to transform energy from a potential to a kinetic state. The results of that difficulty are plain.

More than a hundred years after Emancipation, racial injustice is still eroding ideals of human dignity as well as a constitutional command of equality; urban blight is spreading; private industries continue to scar the landscape, pollute the water, and foul the air at murderous rates. The welfare system can be most charitably described as inadequate, if indeed it is a system at all. In the midst of abundance, millions of children go hungry every day; and thousands are literally starving to death. Black and Puerto Rican ghettos are crowded with well-fed rats and ill-nourished people, people as rejected as the white poor of Appalachia or the Indian poor on the reservations. Well-off Americans apparently continue to hope that the patience of these people is as boundless as their poverty.

Crime threatens to turn cities into jungles, and epidemics of narcotics addiction menace entire generations. A President who waged two campaigns behind battle cries of law and order and promised to attack crime "without pity" gathered around him as his closest advisers a gang who, to maintain themselves in power, sold governmental favors in exchange for huge campaign contributions, and organized burglary and armed robbery against the opposition party and political dissidents. Moreover, that President invoked the name of national security to allow those same men to commit additional felonies of obstructing justice and suborning perjury in order to hide the first set of crimes.

But even before the stream of criminal prosecutions had been freshened by a rivulet of White House officials, the judicial system had been in dire trouble. That it is functioning at all is largely due to the fact that only a small percentage of crimes ever result in actual trials. Concomitantly, rehabilitation of convicted criminals is warmly endorsed in speeches but ignored in budgets. Only a handful of dedicated officials show deep concern.

It is difficult to explain how the richest nation in the world, one that can wage massive wars, rebuild the economy of Western Europe, design and deploy intercontinental ballistic missiles, and put men on the moon and rockets on Mars, cannot muster the physical resources and the will to conquer poverty, crime, and racial injustice at home. The cause may lie in what Duane Lockard has called "perverted priorities,"[2] putting second things first. Or it may result from what Theodore J. Lowi terms "interest group liberalism,"[3] a belief that government not only *does* work through a bargaining process among powerful interest groups but that that is the way government *ought* to function.

In either case, the Madisonian system of fragmented power must bear much of the blame. As we have seen, the legal structure of federalism itself poses no real obstacle to the exercise of national power. The difficulties lie in the fragmentation that permeates American government. The parties, the Congress, the bureaucracy, and even the national courts are to some extent infused with a kind of fractionalism that shatters and obscures authority and responsibility. To be adopted, a national policy must usually be cut and sewn into a bizarre, almost psychedelic patchwork so that almost every special constituency interest gets a piece of the action. To be carried out, a policy must be further tailored to fit the ideas and ambitions of federal, state, and local bureaucrats and the interests they represent. Rationality, in terms of programmatic efforts to attack a serious problem, rarely plays a central role in this bargaining process.

As long as the demands on government were small, as long as those making the demands could be satisfied with immediate symbolic gains and gradual material gains, the Madisonian system performed well. It still performs well for groups who have become politically entrenched and who want only to make minor adjustments in the status quo. But it is hard on newcomers. And there are now large groups of blacks, Indians, Hispanic Americans, and poor whites who are relatively new actors in politics and who do not seem likely soon to be absorbed into the mainstream of American life. Almost two decades ago, a distinguished political scientist warned that the system was so preoccupied with cleavages among those who were participating in politics that it had "become insensitive to the interests of the largest minority in the world."[4] Members of that minority are now demanding real, not merely symbolic, gains; they are demanding them quickly, not slowly; and they are demanding them on a national scale, not piecemeal.

For all the debits, there is also a credit side to the political ledger. The values protected by a system of fragmented power are numerous. Such arrangements safeguard the rights of many minorities by providing them with vantage points from which they can oppose and even block hostile governmental action. It promotes stability and peaceful change by encouraging negotiation, bargaining, and compromise. It produces public policy by a process approaching consensus, albeit consensus among a restricted clientele.

The system not only checks power against power and ambition against ambition — and so provides a strong incentive for legislators to counter efforts by the President to set himself above the Constitution. It also checks intelligence against intelligence and virtue against virtue. Built in is the assumption that no single individual or small group is all wise or all virtuous or is likely to have a monopoly of what wisdom and goodness humans may possess. The system, when it works, thus forces competition among ideas as well as among individuals, and so allows voters a choice.

These are not trivial accomplishments. Limited government and even popular government must inevitably rest on the legitimacy of opposition to those currently in power and in favor. And it was the wanton contempt of this basic right of citizens to propose, debate, and adopt alternative courses of action that made the events of the Watergate scandals so dangerous to free government.

It must also be kept in mind that the Madisonian system is providing a public institutional forum for many minority groups pressing for reform. Surveys of public opinion indicate that only a minority of American adults, and a smaller minority of white adults, see multitudinous problems of central cities as critical, or favor federal action to desegregate schools, enforce fair employment practices, or provide a minimum standard of living for all citizens.

The crux of the dilemma facing the United States is how to preserve the obvious benefits the Madisonian system bestows while lowering the costs of operating that system to the point where government, especially the federal government, can cope effectively and democratically with the unholy trinity of crime, poverty, and racial injustice. By "effectively" we imply no utopian vision of governmental officials wiping out social problems like a platoon of janitors cleaning blackboards; we mean only that government must formulate and administer programs that will bring remedies substantial enough to provide real help in the present and realistic hope for the future. By "democratically" we mean securing the approval of a majority of the people in the country, not for the details of any plan but for the general ends and means of a coherent program.

To win approval for what must be done requires leadership that is skilled both in persuasion and, in the best sense of the word, in manipulation. In the past, the United States has sometimes found that kind of leadership, usually in war, but occasionally in peace. Most recently, Lyndon B. Johnson was able to build on the legacy of John F. Kennedy to begin a war against poverty and a campaign for civil rights that went beyond tokenism. His tragedy was in dissipating his financial resources and his moral as well as political capital in Vietnam just when his management of Congress was creating and exploiting opportunities for far-reaching social reform.

If an open political system is to survive in the United States, it will do so because of positive political leadership that faces up to existing problems and convinces both private citizens and public officials that these problems are serious and interrelated; that they must be attacked, attacked immediately, and attacked together by coordinated and expensive programs.

In spite of Watergate, effective American government remains presidential government. Because of the moral or political ineptitude of a particular President, Congress may frustrate or even dominate the White House. In fact, if they are doing their work properly, congressmen should be able to restrain presidential power and even, on occasion, to neutralize that power, for the President is neither infallible nor impeccable. But over the long run, as we have said so many times in this book, if there is to be positive, effective leadership in American politics, it can come only from the White House. Even then, the Madisonian system may stalemate. But without presidential leadership, there can be no hope that the system can move with any speed or in a controlled direction.

The great challenge to a President is to bring together not just a majority of worried whites sufficiently numerous to keep his party in control of the White House for another four years, but to bring a whole people together. Confronting problems of foreign or domestic politics, his first legitimate task is to persuade by evidence and reason—not by violence, repression, or deception—other public officials and a large majority of private citizens to face up to existing problems, for they cannot be wished away or hidden behind glib phrases coined by hucksters from Madison Avenue. His second and more difficult task is to motivate those people to act, at a minimum, like prudent conservatives and opt for change while the option is still theirs. His function is not to repress but to liberate, not to deceive but to convince, not to calm but to excite, not to stagnate but to lead.

Literal Print

The Constitution of the United States of America

[Preamble]   We the People of the United States, in Order to form a more perfect Union, establish Justice, insure domestic Tranquility, provide for the common defence, promote the general Welfare, and secure the Blessings of Liberty to ourselves and our Posterity, do ordain and establish this Constitution for the United States of America.

Article I

Section 1
[Legislative Powers]

All legislative Powers herein granted shall be vested in a Congress of the United States, which shall consist of a Senate and House of Representatives.

Section 2
[House of Representatives, How Constituted, Power of Impeachment]

The House of Representatives shall be composed of Members chosen every second Year by the People of the several States, and the Electors in each State shall have the Qualifications requisite for Electors of the most numerous Branch of the State Legislature.

No Person shall be a Representative who shall not have attained to the Age of twenty-five Years, and been seven Years a Citizen of the United States, and who shall not, when elected, be an inhabitant of that State in which he shall be chosen.

Representatives and *direct Taxes*[1] shall be apportioned among the several States which may be included within this Union, according to their respective Numbers, *which shall be determined by adding to the whole Number of free Persons, including those bound to Service for a Term of Years,* and excluding Indians not taxed, *three fifths of all other Persons.*[2] The actual Enumeration shall be made within three Years after the first Meeting of the Congress of the United States, and within every subsequent Term of ten Years, in such Manner as they shall by Law direct. The Number of Representatives shall not exceed one for every thirty Thousand, but each State shall have at Least one Representative; *and until such enumeration shall be made, the State of New Hampshire shall be entitled to chuse three, Massachusetts*

[1]Modified by Sixteenth Amendment.
[2]Modified by Fourteenth Amendment.

eight, Rhode-Island and Providence Plantations one, Connecticut five, New-York six, New Jersey four, Pennsylvania eight, Delaware one, Maryland six. Virginia ten, North Carolina five, South Carolina five, and Georgia three.[3]

When vacancies happen in the Representation from any State, the Executive Authority thereof shall issue Writs of Election to fill such Vacancies.

The House of Representatives shall chuse their Speaker and other Officers; and shall have the sole Power of Impeachment.

Section 3
[The Senate, How Constituted, Impeachment Trials]

The Senate of the United States shall be composed of two Senators from each State, *chosen by the Legislature thereof,*[4] for six Years; and each Senator shall have one Vote.

Immediately after they shall be assembled in Consequence of the first Election, they shall be divided as equally as may be into three Classes. The Seats of the Senators of the first Class shall be vacated at the Expiration of the second Year, of the second Class at the Expiration of the fourth Year, and of the third Class at the Expiration of the sixth Year, so that one third may be chosen every second Year: *and if vacancies happen by Resignation, or otherwise, during the Recess of the Legislature of any State, the Executive thereof may make temporary Appointments until the next Meeting of the Legislature, which shall then fill such Vacancies.*[5]

No person shall be a Senator who shall not have attained to the Age of thirty Years, and been nine Years a Citizen of the United States, and who shall not, when elected, be an Inhabitant of that State for which he shall be chosen.

The Vice President of the United States shall be President of the Senate, but shall have no Vote, unless they be equally divided.

The Senate shall chuse their other Officers, and also a President pro tempore, in the Absence of the Vice President, or when he shall exercise the Office of President of the United States.

The Senate shall have the sole Power to try all Impeachments. When sitting for that Purpose, they shall be on Oath or Affirmation. When the President of the United States is tried, the Chief Justice shall preside: And no Person shall be convicted without the Concurrence of two thirds of the Members present.

Judgment in Cases of Impeachment shall not extend further than to removal from Office, and disqualification to hold and enjoy any Office of honor, Trust or Profit under the United States: but the Party convicted shall nevertheless be liable and subject to Indictment, Trial, Judgment and Punishment, according to Law.

---

[3]Temporary provision.
[4]Modified by Seventeenth Amentment.
[5]*Ibid.*

Section 4
[Election of Senators and Representatives]

The Times, Places and Manner of holding Elections for Senators and Representatives, shall be prescribed in each State by the Legislature thereof; but the Congress may at any time by Law make or alter such Regulations, except as to the Places of chusing Senators.

The Congress shall assemble at least once in every Year, and such Meeting shall be on the first Monday in December, unless they shall by Law appoint a different Day.[6]

Section 5
[Quorum, Journals, Meetings, Adjournments]

Each House shall be the Judge of the Elections, Returns and Qualifications of its own Members, and a Majority of each shall constitute a Quorum to do Business; but a smaller Number may adjourn from day to day, and may be authorized to compel the Attendance of absent Members, in such Manner, and under the Penalties as each House may provide.

Each House may determine the Rules of its Proceedings, punish its Members for disorderly Behavior, and, with the Concurrence of two thirds, expel a Member.

Each House shall keep a Journal of its Proceedings, and from time to time publish the same, excepting such Parts as may in their Judgment require Secrecy; and the Yeas and Nays of the Members of either House on any question shall, at the Desire of one fifth of the present, be entered on the Journal.

Neither House, during the Session of Congress, shall, without the Consent of the other, adjourn for more than three days, nor to any other Place than that in which the two Houses shall be sitting.

Section 6
[Compensation, Privilieges, Disabilities]

The Senators and Representatives shall receive a Compensation for their Services, to be ascertained by Law, and paid out of the Treasury of the United States. They shall in Cases, except Treason, Felony and Breach of the Peace, be privileged from Arrest during their Attendance at the Session of their respective Houses, and in going to and returning from the same; and for any Speech or Debate in either House, they shall not be questioned in any other Place.

No Senator or Representative shall, during the time for which he was elected, be appointed to any civil Office under the authority of the United States, which shall have been created, or the Emoluments whereof shall have been encreased during such time; and no Person holding any Office under the United States, shall be a Member of either House during his Continuance in Office.

Section 7
[Procedure in Passing Bills of Resolutions]

All Bills for raising Revenue shall originate in the House of Representatives; but the Senate may propose or concur with Amendments as on other Bills.

Every Bill which shall have passed the House of Representatives and the Senate, shall, before it becomes a Law, be presented to the

---

[6]Modified by Twentieth Amendment.

President of the United States; if he approve he shall sign it, but if not he shall return it, with his Objections to that House in which it shall have originated, who shall enter the Objections at large on their Journal, and proceed to reconsider it. If after such Reconsideration two thirds of that House shall agree to pass the Bill, it shall be sent, together with the Objections, to the other House, by which it shall likewise be reconsidered, and if approved by two thirds of that House, it shall become a Law. But in all such Cases the Votes of both Houses shall be determined by Yeas and Nays, and the Names of the Persons voting for and against the Bill shall be entered on the Journal of each House respectively. If any Bill shall not be returned by the President within ten Days (Sundays excepted) after it shall have been presented to him, the Same shall be a Law, in like Manner as if he had signed it, unless the Congress by their Adjournment prevent its Return, in which Case it shall not be a Law.

Every Order, Resolution, or Vote to which the Concurrence of the Senate and House of Representatives may be necessary (except on a question of Adjournment) shall be presented to the President of the United States; and before the Same shall take Effect, shall be approved by him, or being disapproved by him, shall be repassed by two thirds of the Senate and House of Representatives, according to the Rules and Limitations prescribed in the Case of a Bill.

Section 8
[Power of Congress]

The Congress shall have Power

To lay and collect Taxes, Duties, Imposts and Excises, to pay the Debts and provide for the common Defence and general Welfare of the United States; but all Duties, Imposts and excises shall be uniform throughout the United States;

To borrow Money on the Credit of the United States;

To regulate Commerce with foreign Nations, and among the several States, and with the Indian Tribes;

To establish an uniform Rule of Naturalization, and uniform Laws on the subject of Bankruptcies throughout the United States;

To coin Money, regulate the Value thereof, and of foreign Coin, and fix the Standard of Weights and Measures;

To provide for the Punishment of counterfeiting the Securities and current Coin of the United States;

To establish Post Offices and post Roads;

To promote the Progress of Science and useful Arts, by securing for limited Times to Authors and Inventors the exclusive Rights to their respective Writings and Discoveries;

To constitute Tribunals inferior to the supreme Court;

To define and Punish Piracies and Felonies committed on the high Seas, and Offences against the Law of Nations;

To declare War, grant Letters of Marque and Reprisal, and make Rules concerning Captures on Land and Water;

To raise and support Armies, but no Appropriation of Money to that

Use shall be for a longer Term than two Years;

To provide and maintain a Navy;

To make Rules for the Government and Regulation of the land and naval forces;

To provide for calling for the Militia to execute the Laws of the Union, suppress Insurrections and repel Invasions;

To provide for organizing, arming, and disciplining, the Militia, and for governing such Part of them as may be employed in the Service of the United States, reserving to the States respectively, the Appointment of the Officers, and the Authority of training the Militia according to the discipline prescribed by Congress;

To exercise exclusive Legislation in all Cases whatsoever, over such District (not exceeding ten Miles square) as may, by Cession of particular States, and the Acceptance of Congress, become the Seat of the Government of the United States, and to exercise like Authority over all Places purchased by the Consent of the Legislature of the State in which the Same shall be, for the Erection of Forts, Magazines, Arsenals, dock-Yards, and other needful Buildings;—And

To make all Laws which shall be necessary and proper for carrying into Execution the foregoing Powers, and all other Powers vested by this Constitution in the Government of the United States, or in any Department or Officer thereof.

Section 9   *The Migration or Importation of such Persons as any of the States now existing shall think proper to admit, shall not be prohibited by the Congress prior to the Year one thousand eight hundred and eight, but a Tax or Duty may be imposed on such Importation, not exceeding ten dollars for each Person.*[7]

The privilege of the Writ of Habeas Corpus shall not be suspended, unless when in Cases of Rebellion or Invasion the public Safety may require it.

No Bill of Attainder or ex post facto Law shall be passed.

No Capitation, or other direct, Tax shall be laid, unless in Proportion to the Census or Enumeration herein before directed to be taken.[8]

No Tax or Duty shall be laid on Articles exported from any State.

No Preference shall be given by any Regulation of Commerce or Revenue to the Ports of one State over those of another; nor shall vessels bound to, or from, one State, be obliged to enter, clear, or pay Duties in another.

No Money shall be drawn from the Treasury, but in Consequence of Appropriations made by Law; and a regular Statement and Account of the Receipts and Expenditures of all public Money shall be published from time to time.

The Constitution of the United States of America

[7]Temporary provision.
[8]Modified by Sixteenth Amendment.

No Title of Nobility shall be granted by the United States: And no Person holding any Office of Profit or Trust under them, shall, without the Consent of the Congress, accept of any present, Emolument, Office, or Title, of any kind whatever, from any King, Prince, or foreign State.

Section 10
[Restrictions
Upon Powers of States]

No State shall enter into any Treaty, Alliance, or Confederation; grant Letters of Marque and Reprisal; coin Money; emit Bills of Credit; make any Thing but gold and silver Coin a Tender in Payment of Debts; pass any Bill of Attainder, ex post facto Law, or Law impairing the Obligation of Contracts, or grant any Title of Nobility.

No State shall, without the Consent of the Congress, lay any Imposts or Duties on Imports or Exports, except what may be absolutely necessary for executing its inspection Laws: and the net Produce of all Duties and Imposts, laid by any State on Imports or Exports, shall be for the use of the Treasury of the United States; and all such Laws shall be subject to the Revision and Control of the Congress.

No State shall, without the Consent of Congress, lay any Duty of Tonnage, keep Troops, or Ships of War in time of Peace, enter into any Agreement or Compact with another State, or with a foreign Power, or engage in War, unless actually invaded, or in such imminent Danger as will not admit of Delay.

Article II

Section 1
[Executive Power,
Election, Qualifications
of the President]

The executive Power shall be vested in a President of the United States of America. *He shall hold his Office during the Term of four years and, together with the Vice President, chosen for the same Term, be elected as follows.*[9]

Each State shall appoint, in such Manner as the Legislature thereof may direct, a Number of Electors, equal to the whole Number of Senators and Representatives to which the State may be entitled in the Congress: but no Senator or Representative, or Person holding an Office of Trust or Profit under the United States, shall be appointed an Elector.

The electors shall meet in their respective States, and vote by ballot for two Persons, of whom one at least shall not be an Inhabitant of the same State with themselves. And they shall make a List of all the Persons voted for, and of the Number of Votes for each; which List they shall sign and certify, and transmit sealed to the Seat of the Government of the United States, directed to the President of the Senate. The President of the Senate shall, in the Presence of the Senate and House of Representatives, open all the Certificates, and the Votes shall then be counted. The Person having the greatest Number of Votes shall be

*The Constitution of the
United States of America*

---

[9]Number of terms limited to two by Twenty-second Amendment.

the President, if such Number be a Majority of the whole Number of Electors appointed; and if there be more than one who have such Majority and have an equal Number of Votes, then the House of Representatives shall immediately chuse by Ballot one of them for President; and if no person have a Majority, then from the five highest on the list the said House shall in like Manner chuse the President. But in chusing the President, the Votes shall be taken by States, the Representation from each State having one Vote; A quorum for this Purpose shall consist of a Member or Members from two-thirds of the States, and a Majority of all the States shall be necessary to a Choice. In every Case, after the Choice of the President, the person having the greatest Number of Votes of the Electors shall be the Vice President. But if there should remain two or more who have equal vote, the Senate shall chuse from them by Ballot the Vice President.[10]

The Congress may determine the Time of chusing the Electors, and the Day on which they shall give their Votes; which Day shall be the same throughout the United States.

No Person except a natural born Citizen, or a Citizen of the United States, at the time of the Adoption of this Constitution, shall be eligible to the Office of President; neither shall any Person be eligible to that Office who shall not have attained to the Age of thirty-five Years, and been fourteen Years a Resident within the United States.

In Case of the Removal of the President from Office, or his Death, Resignation, or Inability to discharge the Powers and Duties of the said Office, the same shall devolve on the Vice President, and the Congress may by Law provide for the Case of Removal, Death, Resignation, or Inability, both of the President and Vice President, declaring what Officer shall then act as President, and such Officer shall act accordingly, until the Disability be removed, or a President shall be elected.

The President shall, at stated Times, receive for his Services, a Compensation, which shall neither be encreased nor diminished during the Period of which he shall have been elected, and he shall not receive within that Period any other Emolument from the United States, or any of them.

Before he enter on the Execution of his Office, he shall take the following oath or Affirmation: — "I do solemnly swear (or affirm) that I will faithfully execute the Office of President of the United States, and and will to the best of my Ability, preserve, protect and defend the Constitution of the United States."

Section 2
[Powers of the President]

The President shall be Commander in Chief of the Army and Navy of the United States, and of the Militia of the several States, when called into the actual Service of the United States; he may require the Opinion, in writing, of the principal Officer in each of the executive Depart-

The Constitution of the United States of America

[10]Modified by Twelfth and Twentieth Amendments.

ments, upon any Subject relating to the Duties of their respective Offices, and he shall have Power to grant Reprieves and Pardons for Offences against the United States, except in Cases of Impeachment.

He shall have Power, by and with the Advice and Consent of the Senate to make Treaties, provided two thirds of the Senators present concur; and he shall nominate, and by and with the Advice and Consent of the Senate, shall appoint Ambassadors, other public Ministers and Consuls, Judges of the Supreme Court, and all other Officers of the United States, whose Appointments are not herein otherwise provided for, and which shall be established by Law: but the Congress may by Law vest the Appointment of such inferior Officers, as they think proper, in the President alone, in the Courts of Law, or in the Heads of Departments.

The President shall have Power to fill up all Vacancies that may happen during the Recess of the Senate, by granting Commissions which shall expire at the End of their next Session.

Section 3
[Powers and Duties of the President]

He shall from time to time give to the Congress Information of the State of the Union, and recommend to their Consideration such Measures as he shall judge necessary and expedient; he may, on extraordinary Occasions, convene both Houses, or either of them, and in Case of Disagreement between them, with Respect to the Time of Adjournment, he may adjourn them to such Time as he shall think proper; he shall receive Ambassadors and other public Ministers; he shall take Care that the Laws be faithfully executed, and shall Commission all the Officers of the United States.

Section 4
[Impeachment]

The President, Vice President and all civil Officers of the United States shall be removed from Office on Impeachment for, and Conviction of, Treason, Bribery, or other high Crimes and Misdemeanors.

Article III

Section 1
[Judicial Power, Tenure of Office]

The judicial Power of the United States, shall be vested in one supreme Court, and in such inferior Courts as the Congress may from time to time ordain and establish. The Judges, both of the supreme and inferior Courts, shall hold their Offices during good Behavior, and shall, at stated Times, receive for their Services, a Compensation, which shall not be diminished during their Continuance in Office.

Section 2
[Juristiction]

The judicial Power shall extend to all Cases, in Law and Equity, arising under this Constitution, the Laws of the United States, and Treaties made, of which shall be made, under their Authority; — to all Cases affecting Ambassadors, other public Ministers and Consuls; — to all Cases of admiralty and maritime Jurisdiction; — to Controversies to which the United States shall be a party; — to Controversies between two or more States;—*between a State and Citizens of another State*;—between Citizens of different States;—between Citizens of the same State claiming Lands under Grants of different States, *and between a State,* or the Citizens thereof, *and foreign States, Citizens or Subjects.*[11]

In all Cases affecting Ambassadors, other public Ministers and Consuls, and those in which a State shall be Party, the supreme Court shall have original Jurisdiction. In all the other Cases before mentioned, the supreme Court shall have appelate Jurisdiction, both as to Law and Fact, with such Exceptions, and under such Regulations as Congress shall make.

The Trial of all Crimes, except in Cases of Impeachment, shall be by Jury; and such Trial shall be held in the State where the said Crimes shall have been committed; but when not committed within any State, the Trial shall be at such Place or Places as the Congress may by Law have directed.

Section 1
[Treason, Proof and Punishment]

Treason against the United States, shall consist only in levying War against them, or in adhering to their Enemies, giving them Aid and Comfort. No Person shall be convicted of Treason unless on the Testimoney of two Witnesses to the same overt Act, or on Confession in open Court.

The Congress shall have Power to declare the Punishment of Treason, but no Attainder of Treason shall work Corruption of Blood, or Forfeiture except during the Life of the Person attained.

Article IV

Section 2
[Faith and Credit Among States]

Full Faith and Credit shall be given in each State to the public Acts, Records, and judicial Proceedings of every other State. And the Congress may by general Laws prescribe the Manner in which such Acts, Records and Proceedings shall be proved, and the Effect thereof.

Section 3
[Privileges and Immunities, Fugitives]

The Citizens of each State shall be entitled to all Privileges and Immunities of Citizens in the several States.

A person charged in any State with Treason, Felony or other Crime, who shall flee from Justice, and be found in another State, shall on Demand of the executive Authority of the State from which he fled, be delivered up to be removed to the State having Jurisdiction of the Crime.

No person held to Service or Labour in one State, under the Laws thereof, escaping into another, shall, in Consequence of any Law or

[11]Modified by Eleventh Amendment.

Regulation therein, be discharged from such Service or Labour, but shall be delivered up on Claim of the Party to whom such Service or Labour may be due.[12]

Section 3
[Admission of New States]

New States may be admitted by the Congress into this Union; but no new State shall be formed or erected within the Jurisdiction of any other State; nor any State be formed by the Junction of two or more States, or Parts of States, without the Consent of the Legislatures of the States concerned as well of the Congress.

The Congress shall have Power to dispose of and make all needful Rules and Regulations respecting the Territory or other Property belonging to the United States; and nothing in this Constitution shall be so construed as to Prejudice any Claims of the United States, or of any particular State.

Section 4
[Guarantee of
Republican Government]

The United States shall guarantee to every State in this Union a Republican Form of Government, and shall protect each of them against Invasion; and on Application of Legislature, or of the Executive (when the Legislature cannot be convened) against domestic Violence.

Article V

[Ammendment
of the Constitition]

The Congress, whenever two thirds of both Houses shall deem it necessary, shall propose Amendments to this Constitution, or, on the Application of the Legislatures of two thirds of the several States, shall call a Convention for proposing Amendments, which, in either Case, shall be valid to all Intents and Purposes, as Part of this Constitution, when ratified by the Legislatures of three fourths of the several States, or by Conventions in three fourths thereof, as the one or the other Mode of Ratification may be proposed by the Congress; *Provided that no Amendment which may be made prior to the Year One thousand eight hundred and eight shall in any Manner affect the first and fourth Clauses in the Ninth Section of the first Article,*[13] and that no State, without its Consent, shall be deprived of its equal Suffrage in the Senate.

Article VI

[Debts, Supremacy, Oath]

All Debts contracted and Engagements entered into, before the Adoption of this Constitution, shall be as valid against the United States under this Constitution, as under the Confederation.

This Constitution, and the Laws of the United States which shall be

[12]Repealed by the Thirteenth Amendment.
[13]Temporary provision.

made in Pursuance thereof; and all Treaties made, or which shall be made, under the Authority of the United States, shall be the supreme Law of the Land; and the Judges in every State shall be bound thereby, any Thing in the Constitution or Laws of any State to the Contrary notwithstanding.

The Senators and Representatives before mentioned, and the Members of the several State Legislatures, and all executive and judicial Officers, both of the United States and of the several States, shall be bound by Oath or Affirmation, to support this Constitution; but no religious Test shall be required as a Qualification to any Office or public Trust under the United States.

Article VII

[Ratification & Establishment]   The Ratification of the Conventions of nine States, shall be sufficient for the Establishment of this Constitution between the States so ratifying the Same.[14]

done in Convention by the Unanimous Consent of the States present the Seventeenth Day of September in the Year of our Lord one thousand seven hundred and Eighty seven and of the Independence of the United States of America the Twelfth. *In Witness* whereof We have hereunto subscribed our Names,

G:⁰WASHINGTON—
Presidt, and Deputy from Virginia

New Hampshire	{ John Langdon Nicholas Gilman
Massachusets	{ Nathaniel Gorham Rufus King
Connecticut	{ Wm Saml Johnson Roger Sherman
New York	Alexander Hamilton
New Jersey	{ Wil: Livingston David Brearley Wm Paterson Jona: Dayton

[14]The Constitution was submitted on September 17, 1787, by the Constitutional Conventions, was ratified by the conventions of several states at various dates up to May 29, 1790, and became effective on March 4, 1789.

Pennsylvania	B Franklin Thomas Mifflin Robt Morris Geo. Clymer Thos. FitzSimons Jared Ingersoll James Wilson Gouv Morris
Delaware	Geo Read Gunning Bedfor Jun John Dickinson Richard Bassett Jaco: Broom
Maryland	James McHenry Dan of St Thos. Jenifer Danl Carroll
Virginia	John Blair— James Madison Jr.
North Carolina	Wm Blount Richd Dobbs Spaight Hu Williamson
South Carolina	J. Rutledge Charles Cotesworth Pinckney Charles Pinckney Pierce Butler
Georgia	William Few Abr Baldwin

Amendments to the Constitution

The first ten amendments were proposed by Congress on September 25, 1789; ratified and adoption certified on December 15, 1791.

Amendment I

[Freedom of Religion, of Speech, and of the Press]

Congress shall make no law respecting an establishment of religion, or prohibiting the free exercise thereof; or abridging the freedom of speech, or of the press; or the right of the people peaceably to assemble, and to petition the Government for a redress of grievances.

Amendment II

[Right to Keep and Bear Arms]

A well regulated Militia, being necessary to the security of a free State, the right of the people to keep and bear Arms, shall not be infringed.

Amendment III

[Quartering of Soldiers]

No Soldier shall, in time of peace be quartered in any house, without the consent of the Owner, nor in time of war, but in a manner to be prescribed by law.

Amendment IV

[Security from Unwarrantable Search and Seizure]

Amendments to the Constitution

The right of the people to be secure in their persons, houses, papers, and effects, against unreasonable searches and seizures, shall not be violated, and no Warrants shall issue, but upon probable cause, supported by Oath or affirmation, and particularly describing the place to be searched, and the persons or things to be seized.

Amendment V

[Rights of Accused Persons in Criminal Proceedings]

No person shall be held to answer for a capital, or otherwise infamous crime, unless on a presentment or indictment of a Grand Jury, except in cases arising in the land or naval forces, or in the Militia, when in actual service in time of War or in public danger; nor shall any person be subject for the same offence to be twice put in jeopardy of life or limb; nor shall be deprived of life, liberty, or property, without due process of law; nor shall private property be taken for public use, without just compensation.

Amendment VI

[Right to Speedy Trial, Witnesses, Etc.]

In all criminal prosecutions, the accused shall enjoy the right to a speedy and public trial, by an impartial jury of the State and district wherein the crime shall have been committed, which district shall have been previously ascertained by law, and to be informed of the nature and cause of the accusation; to be confronted with the witnesses against him; to have compulsory process for obtaining Witnesses in his favor, and to have the Assistance of Counsel for his defence.

Amendment VII

[Trial by Jury in Civil Cases]

In suits at common law, where the value in controversy shall exceed twenty dollars, the right of trial by jury shall be preserved, and no fact tried by a jury shall be otherwise re-examined in any Court of the United States, than according to the rules of the common law.

Amendment VIII

[Bails, Fines, Punishments]

Excessive bail shall not be required, nor excessive fines imposed, nor cruel and unusual punishments inflicted.

Amendment IX

[Reservation of Rights of People]

The enumeration in the Constitution, of certain rights, shall not be construed to deny or disparage others retained by the people.

Amendment X

[Powers Reserved to States or People]

The powers not delegated to the United States by the Constitution, nor prohibited by it to the States, are reserved to the States respectively, or to the people.

Amendment XI

[Proposed by Congress on March 4, 1794; declared ratified on January 8, 1798.]

[Restriction of Judicial Power]

The Judicial power of the United States shall not be construed to extend to any suit in law or equity, commenced or prosecuted against one of the United States by Citizens of another State, or by Citizens or Subjects of any Foreign State.

Amendment XII

[Proposed by Congress on December 9, 1803; declared ratified on September 25, 1804.]

[Election of President and Vice President]

The Electors shall meet in their respective state, and vote by ballot for President and Vice-President, one of whom, at least, shall not be an inhabitant of the same state with themselves; they shall name in their ballots the person voted for as President, and in distinct ballots the person voted for as Vice-President, and they shall make distinct lists of all persons voted for as President, and all persons voted for as Vice-President, and of the number of votes for each, which lists they shall sign and certify, and transmit sealed to the seat of the government of the United States, directed to the President of the Senate;—The President of the Senate shall, in presence of the Senate and House of Representatives, open all the certificates and the votes shall then be counted;—The person having the greatest number of votes for President, shall be the President, if such number be a majority of the whole number of Electors appointed; and if no person have such majority, then from the persons having the highest numbers not exceeding three on the list of those voted for as President, the House of Representatives shall choose immediately, by ballot, the President. But in choosing the President, the votes shall be taken by states, the representation from each state having one vote; a quorum for this purpose shall consist of a member or members from two-thirds of the states, and a majority of all states shall be necessary to a choice. And if the House of Representatives shall not choose a President whenever the right of choice shall devolve upon them, before the fourth day of March next following, then the Vice-President, shall act as President, as in the case of the death or other constitutional disability of the President. The person having the greatest number of votes as Vice-President, shall be the Vice-President, if such a number be a majority of the whole numbers of Electors appointed, and if no person have a majority, then from the two highest numbers on the list, the Senate shall choose the Vice-President; a quorum for the purpose shall consist of two-thirds of the whole number of Senators, and a majority of the whole number shall be necessary to a choice. But no person constitutionally ineligible to the office of President shall be eligible to that of Vice-President of the United States.

Amendment XIII

[Proposed by Congress on January 31, 1865; declared ratified on December 18, 1865.]

Section 1
[Abolition of Slavery]

Neither slavery nor involuntary servitude, except as a punishment for crime whereof the party shall have been duly convicted, shall exist within the United States, or any place subject to their jurisdiction.

Section 2
[Power to Enforce this Article]

Congress shall have power to enforce this article by appropriate legislation.

Amendment XIV

[Proposed by Congress on June 13, 1866; declared ratified on July 28, 1868.]

Section 1
[Citizenship Rights not to be Abridged by States]

All persons born or naturalized in the United States, and subject to the jurisdiction thereof, are citizens of the United States and of the State wherein they reside. No State shall make or enforce any law which shall abridge the privileges or immunities of citizens of the United States; nor shall any State deprive any person of life, liberty, or property, without due process of law; nor deny to any person within its jurisdiction the equal protection of the laws.

Section 2
[Apportionment of Representatives in Congress]

Representatives shall be apportioned among the several States according to their respective numbers, counting the whole number of persons in each State, excluding Indians not taxed. But when the right to vote at any election for the choice of electors for President and Vice-President of the United States, Representatives in Congress, the Executive and Judicial officers of a State, or the members of the Legislature thereof, is denied to any of the male inhabitants of such State, being twenty-one years of age, and citizens of the United States, or in any way abridged, except for participation in rebellion, or other crime, the basis of representation therein shall be reduced in the proportion which the number of such male citizens shall bear to the whole number of male citizens twenty-one years of age in such State.

Section 3
[Persons Disqualified from Holding Office]

No person shall be a Senator or Representative in Congress, or elector of President and Vice-President, or hold any office, civil or military, under the United States, or under any State, who, having previously taken an oath, as a member of Congress, or as an officer of the United States, or as a member of any State legislature, or as an executive or judicial officer of any State, to support the Constitution of the United States, shall have engaged in insurrection or rebellion against the same, or given aid or comfort to the enemies thereof. But Congress may by a vote of two-thirds of each House, remove such disability.

Section 4
[What Public Debts are Valid]

The validity of the public debt of the United States, authorized by law, including debts incurred for payment of pensions and bounties for services in suppressing insurrection or rebellion, shall not be questioned. But neither the United States nor any State shall assume or pay any debt or obligation incurred in aid of insurrection or rebellion against the United States, or any claim for the loss of emancipation of any slave; but all such debts, obligations and claims shall be held illegal and void.

Section 5
[Power to Enforce this Article]

The Congress shall have power to enforce, by appropriate legislation, the provisions of this article.

Amendment XV

[*Proposed by Congress on February 26, 1869; declared ratified on March 30, 1870.*]

Section 1
[Negro Suffrage]

The right of citizens of the United States to vote shall not be denied or abridged by the United States or by any State on account of race, color, or previous condition of servitude.

Section 2
[Power to Enforce this Article]

The Congress shall have power to enforce this article by appropriate legislation.

Amendment XVI

[*Proposed by Congress on July 12, 1909; declared ratified on February 25, 1913.*]

[Authorizing Income Taxes]

The Congress shall have power to lay and collect taxes on incomes, from whatever source derived, without apportionment among the several States, and without regard to any census or enumeration.

Amendment XVII

[*Proposed by Congress on May 13, 1912; declared ratified on May 31, 1913.*]

[Popular Election of Senators]

The Senate of the United States shall be composed of two Senators from each State, elected by the people thereof, for six years; and each

Senator shall have one vote. The electors in each State shall have the qualifications requisite for electors of the most numerous branch of the State Legislature.

When vacancies happen in the representation of any State in the Senate, the executive authority of such State shall issue writs of election to fill such vacancies: Provided, That the Legislature of any State may empower the executive thereof to make temporary appointment until the people fill the vacancies by election as the Legislature may direct.

This amendment shall not be so construed as to affect the election or term of any Senator chosen before it becomes valid as part of the Constitution.

Amendment XVIII

[Proposed by Congress December 18, 1917; declared ratified on January 29, 1919.]

Section 1
[National Liquor Prohibition]

After one year from ratification of this article the manufacture, sale, or transportation of intoxicating liquors within, the importation thereof into, or the exportation thereof from the United States and all territory subject to the jurisdiction thereof for beverage purposes is hereby prohibited.

Section 2
[Power to Enforce this Article]

The Congress and the several states shall have concurrent power to enforce this article by appropriate legislation.

Section 3
[Ratification within Seven Years]

This article shall be inoperative unless it shall have been ratified as an amendment to the Constitution by the legislatures of the several states, as provided in the Constitution, within seven years from the date of the submission hereof to the states by the Congress.

Amendment XIX

[Proposed by Congress on June 4, 1919; declared ratified on August 26, 1920.]

[Women Suffrage]

The right of the citizens of the United States to vote shall not be denied or abridged by the United States or by any state on account of sex.

Congress shall have power, by appropriate legislation, to enforce the provision of this article.

Ammendment XX

[*Proposed by Congress on March 2, 1932; declared ratified on February 6, 1933.*]

Section 1
[Terms of Office]

The terms of the President and Vice-President shall end at noon on the 20th day of January, and the terms of the Senators and Representatives at noon on the 3rd day of January, of the years in which such terms would have ended if this article had not been ratified; and the terms of their successors shall then begin.

Section 2
[Time of Convening Congress]

The Congress shall assemble at least once in every year, and such meeting shall begin at noon on the 3rd day of January, unless they shall by law appoint a different day.

Section 3
[Death of President-Elect]

If, at the time fixed for the beginning of the term of the President, the President elect shall have died, the Vice-President elect shall become President. If a President shall not have been chosen before the time fixed for the beginning of his term, or if the President elect shall have failed to qualify, then the Vice-President elect shall act as President until a President shall have qualified; and the Congress may by law provide for the case wherein neither a President elect nor a Vice-President elect shall have qualified, declaring who shall then act as President, or the manner in which one who is to act shall be selected, and such person shall act accordingly until a President or Vice-President shall have qualified.

Section 4
[Election of the President]

The Congress may by law provide for the case of the death of any of the persons from whom the House of Representatives may choose a President whenever the right of choice shall have devolved upon them, and for the case of the death of any of the persons from whom the Senate may choose a Vice-President whenever the right of choice shall have devolved upon them.

Section 5

Sections 1 and 2 shall take effect on the 15th day of October following ratification of this article.

Section 6

This article shall be inoperative unless it shall have been ratified as an amendment to the Constitution by the legislatures of three-fourths of the several States within seven years from the date of its submission.

Amendment XXI

[*Proposed by Congress on February 20, 1933; declared ratified on December 5, 1933.*]

The eighteenth article of amendment to the Constitution of the United States is hereby repealed.

The transportation or importation into any State, Territory, or Possession of the United States for delivery or use therein of intoxicating liquors, in violation of the laws thereof, is hereby prohibited.

Section 3

This article shall be inoperative unless it shall have been ratified as an amendment to the Constitution by conventions in the several States, as provided in the Constitution, within seven years from the date of the submission hereof to the States by the Congress.

Amendment XXII

[Proposed by Congress on March 21, 1947; declared ratified on February 26, 1951.]

Section 1
[Tenure of
President Limited]

No person shall be elected to the office of President more than twice, and no person who has held the office of President, or acted as President, for more than two years of a term to which some other person was elected President shall be elected to the Office of the President more than once. But this Article shall not apply to any person holding the Office of President when this Article was proposed by the Congress, and shall not prevent any person who may be holding the office of President, during the term within which this Article becomes operative from holding the office of President or acting as President during the remainder of such term.

Section 2

This Article shall be inoperative unless it shall have been ratified as an amendment to the Constitution by the legislatures of three-fourths of the several states within seven years from the date of its submission to the States by the Congress.

Amendment XXIII

[Proposed by Congress on June 21, 1960; declared ratified on March 29, 1961.]

Section 1
[Electoral College
Votes for the
District of Columbia]

*Amendments to the
Constitution*

The District constituting the seat of Government of the United States shall appoint in such manner as the Congress may direct:

A number of electors of President and Vice President equal to the whole number of Senators and Representatives in Congress to which the District would be entitled if it were a State, but in no event more than the least populous State; they shall be in addition to those appointed by the States, but they shall be considered, for the purposes of the election of President and Vice President, to be electors appointed by a State; and they shall meet in the District and perform such duties as provided by the twelfth article of amendment.

Section 2 The Congress shall have power to enforce this article by appropriate legislation.

Amendment XXIV

[*Proposed by Congress on August 27, 1963; declared ratified on January 23, 1964.*]

Section 1
[Anti-Poll Tax]

The right of citizens of the United States to vote in any primary or other election for President or Vice President, for electors for President or Vice President, or for Senator or Representative of Congress, shall not be denied or abridged by the United States or any State by reasons of failure to pay any poll tax or other tax.

Section 2 The Congress shall have power to enforce this article by appropriate legislation.

Amendment XXV

[*Proposed by Congress on July 7, 1965; declared ratified on February 10, 1967.*]

Section 1
[Vice President to Become President]

In case of the removal of the President from office or his death or resignation, the Vice President shall become President.

Section 2
[Choice of a New Vice President]

Whenever there is a vacancy in the office of the Vice President, the President shall nominate a Vice President who shall take the office upon confirmation by a majority vote of both houses of Congress.

Section 3
[President may Declare own Disability]

Whenever the President transmits to the President pro tempore of the Senate and the Speaker of the House of Representatives has written declaration that he is unable to discharge the powers and duties of his office, and until he transmits to them a written declaration to the contrary, such powers and duties shall be discharged by the Vice President as Acting President.

Section 4
[Alternative Procedures to Declare and to End Presidential Disability]

Whenever the Vice President and a majority of either the principal officers of the executive departments, or of such other body as Congress may by law provide, transmit to the President pro tempore of the Senate and the Speaker of the House of Representatives their written declaration that the President is unable to discharge the powers and duties of his office, the Vice President shall immediately assume the powers and duties of the office as Acting President.

Thereafter, when the President transmits to the President pro tempore of the Senate and the Speaker of the House of Representatives his written declaration that no inability exists, he shall resume the powers and duties of his office unless the Vice President and a majority of either the principal officers of the executive department, or of such other body as Congress may by law provide, transmit within four days to the President pro tempore of the Senate and the Speaker of the House of Representatives their written declaration that the President is unable to discharge the powers and duties of his office. Thereupon Congress shall decide the issue, assembling within 48 hours for that purpose if not in session. If the Congress, within 21 days after receipt of the latter written declaration, or, if Congress is not in session, within 21 days after Congress is required to assemble, determines by two-thirds vote of both houses that the President is unable to discharge the powers and duties of his office, the Vice President shall continue to discharge the same as Acting President; otherwise, the President shall resume the powers and duties of his office.

Amendment XXVI

[*Proposed by Congress on March 23, 1971; declared ratified on June 30, 1971.*]

Section 1 The right of citizens of the United States, who are eighteen years of age or older, to vote shall not be denied or abridged by the United States or by any State on account of age.

Section 2 The Congress shall have the power to enforce this article by appropriate legislation.

Proposed Amendment XXVII

[*Proposed by Congress on March 22, 1972.*]

Section 1 Equality of rights under the law shall not be denied or abridged by the United States or by any State on account of sex.

Section 2 The Congress shall have power to enforce, by appropriate legislation, the provisions of this article.

Section 3 This amendment shall take effect two years after date of ratification.
[*To become effective this amendment must be ratified by 38 state legislatures prior to March 22, 1979.*]

Notes

Notes to Chapter 2

[1]David M. Potter, *People of Plenty: Economic Abundance and the American Character* (Chicago, Ill.: University of Chicago Press, 1954), especially chap. 4.

[2]Richard Hofstadter, *Anti-Intellectualism in American Life* (New York: Alfred A. Knopf, Inc., 1963).

[3]Morris Janowitz, *The Professional Soldier: A Social and Political Portrait* (New York: The Free Press of Glencoe, 1960).

[4]Giovanni Sartori, *Democratic Theory* (New York: Frederick A. Praeger, 1965), p. 97.

[5]Gabriel A. Almond and Sidney Verba, *The Civic Culture* (Princeton, N.J.: Princeton University Press, 1963), chap. 12. For a useful overview—and an annotated bibliography—of the role of personality and politics, see Fred I. Greenstein, *Personality and Politics: Problems of Evidence, Inference, and Conceptualization* (Chicago, Ill.: Markham Publishing Company, 1969).

[6]*Olmstead v. United States,* 277 U.S. 438, dissenting opinion (1928).

[7]*Brown v. Board of Education,* 347 U.S. 483 (1954).

[8]*The Federalist,* No. 51 (New York: Random House, 1937), Modern Library Edition, p. 337.

[9]James W. Prothro and Charles M. Grigg, "Fundamental Principles of Democracy: Bases of Agreement and Disagreement," *Journal of Politics,* XXII (1960), p. 276.

[10]Almond and Verba, *The Civic Culture,* Parts II and III.

[11]For a discussion of the scarcity of politically knowledgeable and sophisticated citizens, see Philip E. Converse, "The Nature of Belief Systems in Mass Publics," in David E. Apter, ed. *Ideology and Discontent* (New York: The Free Press of Glencoe, 1964), p. 206

[12]Jefferson to James Madison, December 20, 1787; quoted in Alpheus T. Mason, ed., *Free Government in the Making,* 3rd ed. (New York: Oxford University Press, 1965), p. 320.

[13]The best discussion of the concept of the "rules of the game" can be found in David B. Truman, *The Governmental Process* (New York: Alfred A. Knopf, 1955), chaps. 12, 14, and 16.

[14]Charles Frankel, *High on Foggy Bottom: An Outsider's Inside View of Government* (New York: Harper & Row, 1968), p. 108.

[15]Committee for Economic Development, *Improving the Public Welfare System* (New York: April 1970), pp. 9–10.

[16]*The Other America: Poverty in the United States* Baltimore, Md.: Penquin Books, 1962), p. 22.

[17]Harrington, *The Other America,* pp. 23–24.

[18]*Report of the National Advisory Commission on Civil Disorders* (Washington, D.C.: Government Printing Office, 1968), p. 1.

[19]W. E. B. Du Bois, *The Souls of Black Folk* (Chicago, Ill.: A. C. McClung & Co., 1903), p. 3.

[20]See William W. Ellis, *White Ethics and Black Power: The Emergence of the West Side Organization* (Chicago, Ill.: Aldine Publishing Co., 1969).

[21]See the data collected in Angus Campbell and Howard Schuman, "Racial Attitudes in Fifteen American Cities," in *Supplemental Studies for the National Advisory Commission on Civil Disorders* (Washington, D.C.: Government Printing Office, 1968), especially in chap. 4.

[22]See David H. Bayley and Harold Mendelsohn, *Minorities and the Police* (New York: The Free Press of Glencoe, 1969), especially chap. 6.

[23]Campbell and Schuman, "Racial Attitudes in Fifteen American Cities," p. 6.

[24]Nathan Glazer and Daniel P. Moynihan, *Beyond the Melting Pot: The Negroes, Puerto Ricans, Jews, Italians, and Irish of New York City* (Cambridge, Mass.: The Massachusetts Institute of Technology Press, 1963), p. 290.

[25]Charles Tilly, "Collective Violence in European Perspective," in Hugh Davis Graham and Ted Robert Gurr, eds., *Violence in America: Historical and Comparative Perspectives*, A Staff Report to the National Commission on the Causes and Prevention of Violence (Washington, D.C.: Government Printing Office, 1969), I, 5.

[26]Henry Fairlie, "The Distemper of America," *Interplay*, IV (1969), p. 6.

[27]See the articles collected in Charles S. Bullock, III, and Harrell R. Rodgers, Jr., eds., *Black Political Attitudes: Implications for Political Support* (Chicago: Markham Publishing Company, 1972), Part I.

[28]See the Becoming a Citizen Series prepared by the Immigration and Naturalization Service. Book 1: *Our American Way of Life;* Book 2: *Our United States;* Book 3: *Our Government*, rev. ed. (Washington, D.C.: Government Printing Office, 1969).

[29]Norton Long, "The Local Community as an Ecology of Games," *American Journal of Sociology*, XLIV (1958), p. 151; reprinted in Long, *The Polity* (Chicago: Rand McNally, 1962), p. 153.

Notes to Chapter 3

[1]The Commission on Population Growth and the American Future, *Population and the American Future* (Washington, D.C.: Government Printing Office, 1972), p. 25.

[2]See Jerome R. Pickard, "U.S. Metropolitan Growth and Expansion, 1970–2000, with Population Projections," in The Commission on Population Growth and the American Future, *Demographic and Social Aspects of Population Growth* (Washington, D.C.: Government Printing Office, 1972).

[3]York Willbern, *The Withering Away of the City* (University, Ala.: University of Alabama Press, 1964), pp. 9–10.

[4]Charles E. Silberman, "The City and the 'Negro,'" *Fortune*, March 1962, pp. 88–89.

[5]The National Commission on Civil Disorders, *Report* (Washington, D.C., Government Printing Office, 1968), p. 91.

[6]Mayor Henry W. Maier, Milwaukee, Wis., quoted in William E. Farrell, "Milwaukee Problems Still Seem Solvable," *New York Times*, Sept. 29, 1975.

[7]See Walter S. Mosberg, "A Blue Collar Town Fears Urban Renewal Perils Its Way of Life," *Wall Street Journal*, November 2, 1970.

[8]Robert C. Wood, *Suburbia* (Boston: Houghton Mifflin, 1959), p. 83.

[9]See *Milliken v. Bradley*, 418 U.S. 717 (1974).

[10]*San Antonio Independent School District v. Rodriguez*, 411 U.S. 1 (1973).

[11]*Milliken v. Bradley*, 418 U.S. 717 (1974).

[12]*Warth v. Seldin*, 422 U.S. 490 (1975).

Notes to Chapter 4

[1]*McCulloch v. Maryland*, 4 Wheaton 316, 415 (1819).

[2]*The Anatomy of Liberty* (New York: Trident Press, 1963), p. 7.

[3]Charles C. Tansill, ed., *Documents Illustrative of the Formation of the Union of the*

American States (Washington: Government Printing Office, 1927), p. 315. (Unless otherwise indicated references to Tansill refer to his reprinting of James Madison's notes on debates during the Convention.)

[4]Clinton Rossiter, *1787:The Great Convention* (New York: The Macmillan Company, Inc., 1966), p. 52.

[5]James Madison, *Vices of the Political System in the United States* (1787); reprinted in Alpheus T. Mason, ed., *Free Government in the Making,* 3d ed. (New York: Oxford University Press, 1965), p. 172.

[6]Tansill, p. 618.

[7]See John P. Roche, "The Founding Fathers: A Reform Caucus in Action," *American Political Science Review,* LV (1961), pp. 799–816.

[8]"Notes on Virginia," reprinted in Mason, *Free Government in the Making,* p. 165.

[9]Tansill, p. 126.

[10]*Ibid.,* p. 165.

[11]*Ibid.,* pp. 834–835.

[12]*Ibid.,* p. 358.

[13]*Ibid.,* p. 771. (Here the reference is to the notes taken by Robert Yates at the Convention rather than by Madison.)

[14]*Ibid.,* p. 588.

[15]*The Federalist,* No. 14.

[16]*Ibid.,* No. 51.

[17]*Ibid.*

[18]Richard Neustadt makes this point most emphatically; see his "Presidential Government," *International Encyclopedia of the Social Sciences,* XII, 451, 453.

[19]*Marbury v. Madison,* 1 Cranch 137, 177 (1803).

[20]*The Nature of the Judicial Process* (New Haven, Conn.: Yale University Press, 1921), p. 113.

[21]Tansill, p. 162.

[22]*Ibid.,* p. 163.

[23]*Ibid.,* p. 461.

[24]G. Hunt, ed., *The Writings of James Madison* (New York: G. P. Putnam's Sons, 1904), V, 272.

[25]Reprinted in Mason, *Free Government in the Making,* p. 325.

[26]Reprinted in Hunt, *The Writings of James Madison,* V, 385.

[27]See their book, *All the President's Men* (New York: Simon and Schuster, Inc., 1974), later made into a movie.

[28]*United States v. Nixon,* 418 U.S. 683 (1974).

[29]*Schneider v. Smith,* 390 U.S. 17, 25 (1968).

Notes to Chapter 5

[1]See especially *Pennsylvania v. Nelson,* 350 U.S. 497 (1956).

[2]4 Wheaton 316, 421 (1819).

[3]See, for example, *Luther v. Borden,* 7 Howard 1 (1849); and *Pacific Telephone Co. v. Oregon,* 223 U.S. 118 (1912).

[4]See the decision of the Supreme Court in *In re Debs,* 158 U.S. 564 (1895), a case that grew out of this same episode.

[5]*Texas v. White,* 7 Wallace 700 (1869).

[6]See *Baker v. Carr,* 369 U.S. 186 (1962) and *Reynolds v. Sims,* 377 U.S. 533 (1964). These cases are discussed in Chapter 8.

[7]William H. Riker, *Federalism: Origin, Operation, Significance* (Boston, Mass.: Little, Brown & Company, 1964), p. 152.

Notes to Chapter 6

[1]These two aspects of political power are emphasized in Peter Bachrach and Morton Baratz, "Two Faces of Power," *American Political Science Review,* LVIII (1962), pp. 947–952.

²See E. E. Schattschneider, *The Semi-Sovereign People* (New York: Holt, Rinehart and Winston, 1966), p. 71.

³David Ricci, *Community Power and Democratic Theory* (New York: Random House, 1971), pp. 168–169.

⁴See *The Power Elite* (New York: Oxford University Press, 1956).

⁵The classic studies of community power were undertaken by Helen and Robert Lynd in Muncie, Indiana; see *Middletown* (New York: Harcourt Brace Jovanovich, 1929) and *Middletown in Transition* (New York: Harcourt Brace Jovanovich, 1939). Also significant is Floyd Hunter's analysis of influence in Atlanta, Georgia, in *Community Power Structure* (Chapel Hill, N.C.: University of North Carolina Press, 1953).

⁶G. William Domhoff, *The Higher Circles* (New York: Random House, 1970), p. 109.

⁷Robert A. Dahl, "Business and Politics: A Critical Appraisal of Political Science," in Mason Haire and Paul F. Lazarsfield, eds., *Social Science Research on Business* (New York: Columbia University Press, 1959), p. 36.

⁸See *Who Governs?* (New Haven, Conn.: Yale University Press, 1961).

⁹Robert A. Dahl, *Pluralist Democracy in the United States* (Chicago: Rand McNally, 1967), p. 386.

¹⁰Sidney Verba and Norman H. Nie, *Political Participation in America: Political Democracy and Social Equality* (New York: Harper & Row, 1972), p. 208.

¹¹For an excellent analysis of the early stages of this campaign, see Stanley Kelley, Jr. *Professional Public Relations and Political Power* (Baltimore, Md.: The Johns Hopkins Press, 1956), chap. 3.

¹²Stuart R. Schram, *The Political Thought of Mao Tse-tung* (New York: Frederick A. Praeger, 1963), p. 209.

¹³Wallace S. Sayre and Herbert Kaufman, *Governing New York City* (New York: Russell Sage Foundation, 1960), p. 710.

¹⁴Dahl, *Who Governs?* p. 279.

¹⁵Eldridge Cleaver, "Three Notes from Exile," *Ramparts*, VIII (1969), p. 35.

¹⁶See Verba and Nie, *Political Participation in America*, chap. 10.

¹⁷Sayre and Kaufman, *Governing New York City*, pp. 716, 719.

Notes to Chapter 7

¹James Bryce, *The American Commonwealth*, rev. ed. (New York: Crowell-Collier and Macmillan Company, Inc., 1914), II, 3.

²V. O. Key, Jr., *Politics, Parties, and Pressure Groups*, 5th ed. (New York: Thomas Y. Crowell Company, 1964), p. 207.

³See the interesting article by Maurice Klain, "A New Look at the Constituencies: The Need for a Recount and a Reappraisal," *American Political Science Review*, XLIX (1955), pp. 1105–1119, in which it is shown that multimember state districts are far more common in the United States than has generally been recognized.

⁴Austin Ranney and Willmoore Kendall, *Democracy and the American Party System* (New York: Harcourt Brace Jovanovich, 1956), pp. 161–164.

⁵This southern strategy, usually credited to Attorney General William Mitchell, is outlined by one of Mitchell's former assistants, Kevin P. Phillips, in *The Emerging Republican Majority* (New Rochelle, N.Y.: Arlington House, 1969). In his dedication, Phillips gives Richard M. Nixon equal credit as the "architect" of this plan.

⁶Austin Ranney and Willmoore Kendall, *Democracy and the American Party System* (New York: Harcourt Brace Jovanovich, 1956), pp. 161–164.

⁷Austin Ranney, "Parties in State Politics," in Herbert Jacob and Kenneth N. Vines, eds., *Politics in the American States: A Comparative Analysis*, 2d ed. (Boston: Little, Brown and Company), p. 87. See also Duane Lockard, *The Politics of State and Local Government*, 2d ed. (New York: Crowell-Collier, Macmillan, Inc., 1969), pp. 176–177.

⁸Herbert McClosky, Paul Hoffman, and Rosemary O'Hara, "Issue Conflict and Consensus among Party Leaders and Followers," *American Political Science Review*, 54 (1960), pp. 406–427.

⁹Key, *Politics, Parties, and Pressure Groups*, p. 327

¹⁰Adlai Stevenson, *What I Think* (New York: Harper & Row, 1956), pp. ix–x.

¹¹Paul T. David, Ralph Goldman, and Richard Bain, *The Politics of National Party Conventions* (Washington, D.C.: The Brookings Institution, 1960), p. 84.

[12]Duane Lockard, *The Politics of State and Local Government,* 2d ed. (New York: The Macmillan Co., 1969), p. 211.

[13]James M. Burns, *The Deadlock of Democracy,* rev. ed. (Englewood Cliffs, N.J.: Prentice-Hall, Inc., 1963), p. 1.

[14]Pendleton Herring, *The Politics of Democracy* (New York: Holt, Rinehart and Winston, Inc., 1940), p. 132.

[15]Key, *Politics, Parties, and Pressure Groups,* p. 206.

Notes to Chapter 8

[1]Kenneth Prewitt, *The Recruitment of Political Leaders: A Study of Citizen-Politicians* (Indianapolis, Ind.: The Bobbs-Merrill Company, Inc., 1970).

[2]For a discussion, see C. Vann Woodward, *The Strange Career of Jim Crow,* 2d rev. ed. (New York: Oxford University Press, 1966).

[3]*Brown v. Board of Education,* 347 U.S. 483 (1954).

[4]*Dunn v. Blumstein,* 405 U.S. 330 (1972).

[5]369 U.S. 186 (1962).

[6]*Wesberry v. Sanders,* 376 U.S. 1 (1964).

[7]377 U.S. 533 (1964).

[8]*Mahan v. Howell,* 410 U.S. 315 (1973).

[9]Edward R. Tufte, "The Relationship between Seats and Votes in Two Party Systems," *American Political Science Review,* LXVII (1973), p. 551.

[10]*Gomillion v. Lightfoot,* 364 U.S. 339 (1961).

[11]"Determinants of the Outcomes of Midterm Congressional Elections," *American Political Science Review,* LXIX (1975), p. 812.

[12]*Politics, Parties, and Pressure Groups,* 3rd ed. (New York: Thomas Y. Crowell Company, 1955), pp. 462–463.

[13]P. Lazarsfeld, B. Berelson, and H. Gaudet, *The People's Choice: How the Voter Makes Up His Mind in a Presidential Campaign* (New York: Duell, Sloan and Pearce, Inc., 1944); B. Berelson, P. Lazarsfeld, and W. McPhee, *Voting* (Chicago: University of Chicago Press, 1954); Angus Campbell, Phillip E. Converse, Warren E. Miller, and Donald E. Stokes, *The American Voter* (New York: John Wiley and Sons, Inc., 1960), especially chap 4; and data released by the University of Michigan's Survey Research Center after the 1960, 1964, 1968, and 1972 elections.

[14]Stanley Kelley, Jr., "The Presidential Campaign," in Paul T. David, ed., *The Presidential Election and Transition 1960–1961* (Washington, D.C.: The Brookings Institution, 1961), p. 57.

[15]See Stanley Kelley, Jr., *Professional Public Relations and Political Power* (Baltimore, Md.: The Johns Hopkins Press, 1956); and Joe McGinniss, *The Selling of the President 1968* (New York: Trident Press, 1969).

[16]This section depends heavily on the works of Herbert E. Alexander cited in the selected bibliography, personal conversations with him, and his paper prepared for delivery at the meetings of the International Political Science Association (August 1976), "Developments in United States Election Law, 1971–1976."

[17]*Buckley v. Valeo,* 424 U.S. 1 (1976).

Notes to Chapter 9

[1]*Report of the United States Commission on Civil Rights 1959* (Washington, D.C.: Government Printing Office, 1959), Book I, p. 191.

[2]Much information about recent causes of nonvoting is contained in U.S. Bureau of the Census, "Voter Participation in November 1974," *Current Population Reports,* Series P-20, No. 275 (January 1975).

[3]See Stanley Kelley, Jr., Richard E. Ayres, and William G. Bowen, "Registration and Voting," *American Political Science Review,* LXI (1967), p. 359.

[4]Gabriel A. Almond and Sidney Verba, *The Civic Culture* (Princeton, N.J.: Princeton University Press, 1963), pp. 145–146.

⁵For a discussion of the findings, see Jae-On Kim, J. R. Petrocik, and S. N. Enockson, "Voter Turnout among the Various States: Systemic and Individual Components," *American Political Science Review*, LXIX (1975), p. 107.

⁶*Participation in America: Political Democracy and Social Equality* (New York: Harper & Row, Publishers, 1972). We draw especially heavily on chaps. 3–6.

⁷See generally Robert E. Lane, *Political Life: Why People Get Involved in Politics* (New York: The Free Press, 1959).

⁸p. 335.

⁹This classification was developed by V. O. Key, Jr., "A Theory of Critical Elections," *Journal of Politics,* XVII (1955), p. 3; and elaborated by Angus Campbell, Philip E. Converse, Warren E. Miller, and Donald E. Stokes, *Elections and the Political Order* (New York: John Wiley and Sons, Inc., 1966), chaps. 2 and 3.

¹⁰*The Responsible Electorate* (Cambridge, Mass.: Harvard University Press, 1966), p. 30.

¹¹Philip E. Converse, "The Nature of Belief Systems in Mass Publics," in David E. Apter, ed., *Ideology and Discontent* (New York: The Free Press, 1964).

¹²Paul F. Lazarsfeld, Bernard B. Berelson, and Hazel Gaudet, *The People's Choice: How the Voter Makes Up His Mind in a Presidential Campaign* (New York: Duell, Sloan & Pearce-Meredith Press, 1944).

¹³Paul R. Abramson, "General Change in American Electoral Behavior," *American Political Science Review,* LXVIII (1974), p. 93.

¹⁴"Interpreting the Election Results," in Paul T. David, ed., *The Presidential Election and Transition 1960–1961* (Washington, D.C.: The Brookings Institution, 1961), p. 175.

¹⁵Philip E. Converse, Warren E. Miller, Jerrold G. Rusk, and Arthur G. Wolfe, "Continuity and Change in American Politics: Parties and Issues in the 1968 Election," *American Political Science Review,* LXIII (1969), pp. 1104–1105.

¹⁶Robert A. Dahl, *Who Governs?* (New Haven, Conn.: Yale University Press, 1961), p. 305.

¹⁷For examples, see Robert E. Lane's two books: *Political Ideology: Why the American Common Man Believes What He Does* (New York: The Free Press, 1962), and *Political Thinking and Consciousness: The Private Life of the Political Mind* (Chicago, Ill.: Markham Publishing Company, 1969).

¹⁸"The Simple Act of Voting," *American Political Science Review,* LXVIII (1974), p. 574.

¹⁹William Schneider, "Issues, Voting, and Cleavages," *American Behavioral Scientist,* XVIII (1974), p. 111.

²⁰"Determinants of the Outcomes of Midterm Congressional Elections," *American Political Science Review,* XLIX (1975), p. 812.

²¹See Philip E. Converse, "Change in the American Electorate," in Angus Campbell and Philip E. Converse, eds., *The Human Meaning of Social Change* (New York: Russell Sage Foundation, 1972).

²²Norman H. Nie, Sidney Verba, and John R. Petrocik, *The Changing American Voter* (Cambridge, Mass.: Harvard University Press, 1976), chap. 10.

Notes to Chapter 10

¹Richard E. Neustadt, "Politicians and Bureaucrats," in David B. Truman, ed. *The Congress and America's Future,* The American Assembly, (Englewood Cliffs, N.J.: Prentice-Hall, 1965), p. 111.

²Quoted in Theodore C. Sorensen, *Kennedy* (New York: Harper & Row, 1965), p. 426.

³See Ronald C. Moe and Steven C. Tell, "Congress as Policy-Maker," *Political Science Quarterly,* 85 (1970), pp. 443–470.

⁴*The Federalist* (New York: Random House, 1937), No. 58, p. 380.

⁵Stephen K. Bailey, *Congress in the Seventies* (New York: St. Martin's Press, 1970), p. 89.

⁶Walter Kravitz, staff director, Budget Committee, U.S. House of Representatives, quoted in "Congress May Step Up Oversight of Programs," *Congressional Quarterly Weekly Report* (March 22, 1975), p. 597.

[7]U.S. Congress, House of Representatives, Select Committee on Government Research, *Federal Research and Development Programs: First Progress Report* (Washington, D.C.: Government Printing Office, 1964), p. 8.

[8]*Watkins v. United States,* 354 U.S. 178, 187–188 (1957).

[9]See *United States v. Rumely,* 345 U.S. 41 (1953); *Watkins v. United States,* cited above, note 8; *Quinn v. United States,* 349 U.S. 155 (1955); and *Emspak v. United States,* 349 U.S. 190 (1955).

[10]Michael J. Kirwan, *How to Succeed in Politics* (New York: Macfadden Books, 1964), p. 20. Kirwan served for a number of years as chairman of the Democratic Congressional Campaign Committee.

[11]See H. Douglas Price, "The Congressional Career Then and Now," in Nelson Polsby, ed., *Congressional Behavior* (New York: Random House, 1971), pp. 14–27.

[12]Nelson W. Polsby, "Strengthening Congress in National Policymaking," *The Yale Review* (Summer 1970), p. 485.

[13]Representative Edward G. Biester, quoted in James Goodman, "The House, It Is Slow A-Changing, They Say," *Evening Times* (Trenton, N.J.), July 14, 1971.

[14]Quoted in Richard D. Lyons, "Patman Joins Growing List of Retiring Congressmen," *New York Times,* Jan. 15, 1976.

[15]Elmer B. Staats, Controller General of the United States, quoted in Jon Margolis, "The G.A.O. Is Congress's Unpopular Watchdog," *New York Times,* May 18, 1975.

Notes to Chapter 11

[1]*Congressional Government* (Boston, Mass.: Houghton Mifflin Company, 1885), p. 58.

[2]Lewis A. Froman, Jr., and Randall B. Ripley, "Conditions for Party Leadership," *American Political Science Review,* LIX (1965), p. 52.

[3]Donald E. Stokes and Warren E. Miller, "Party Government and the Salience of Congress," *Public Opinion Quarterly,* XXVI (1962), p. 545.

[4]Randall B. Ripley, *Party Leaders in the House of Representatives* (Washington, D.C.: The Brookings Institution, 1967), p. 159.

[5]H. Douglas Price, "The Electoral Arena," in David B. Truman, ed., *The Congress and America's Future,* The American Assembly, (Englewood Cliffs, N.J.: Prentice-Hall, 1965), p. 32.

[6]"Halt of Sentinel Is Traced to a 10-Month-Old Memo," *New York Times,* February 9, 1969.

[7]Warren E. Miller and Donald E. Stokes, "Constituency Influence in Congress," *American Political Science Review,* LVII (1963), pp. 54–55.

[8]Miller and Stokes, "Constituency Influence in Congress," p. 52.

[9]See Julius Turner, *Party and Constituency: Pressure on Congress.* Revised ed. by Edward V. Schneier, Jr. (Baltimore, Md.: The Johns Hopkins Press, 1970), p. 111.

[10]376 U.S. 1 (1964).

[11]Representative Timothy E. Wirth (D., Colo.), quoted in Marjorie Hunter and David E. Rosenbaum, "Defeats Split Bitter House Democrats," *New York Times,* July 2, 1975. Wirth, thirty-five years old at the time of his election, had been employed by the Department of Health, Education and Welfare in Washington before running for Congress.

[12]Max Farrand, *The Framing of the Constitution* (New Haven, Conn.: Yale University Press, 1926), p. 74.

[13]Representative Thomas P. O'Neill, Jr. (D., Mass.), Majority Leader, House of Representatives, quoted in Hunter and Rosenbaum, "Defeats Split Bitter House Democrats."

[14]Richard E. Fenno, Jr., "The Internal Distribution of Influence: The House," in The American Assembly, David B. Truman, ed., *The Congress and America's Future,* The American Assembly, (Englewood Cliffs, N.J.: Prentice-Hall, 1965), p. 63.

[15]*My First Fifty Years in Politics* (New York: McGraw-Hill, 1960), pp. 182–183.

[16]See Randall B. Ripley, "The Party Whip Organizations in the United States House of Representatives," *American Political Science Review,* LVIII (1964), pp. 561–576.

Notes

[17]Quoted in Charles L. Clapp, *The Congressman: His Work As He Sees It* (Washington, D.C.: The Brookings Institution, 1963), p. 24.

[18]See Richard F. Fenno, "The House Appropriations Committee as a Political System," *American Political Science Review*, LVI (1962), pp. 310–324.

[19]Representative Edward Mezvinsky (D., Iowa), quoted in James M. Naughton, "Congress Getting Younger; Reform Period Is Foreseen," *New York Times*, Oct. 3, 1974. Mezvinsky, first elected in 1972, was chairman of the caucus of freshmen Democrats in the House in the Ninety-third Congress.

[20]Representative Jonathan B. Bingham (D., N.Y.), quoted in James M. Naughton, "Upheaval in the House," *New York Times*, Jan. 17, 1975.

[21]See Douglas Cater, *Power in Washington* (New York: Random House, 1964).

[22]Turner, *Party and Constituency*, p. 88.

[23]See Lewis A. Froman, Jr., *The Congressional Process* (Boston, Mass.: Little Brown and Company, 1967), p. 18.

[24]Representative David R. Obey (D., Wisc.), quoted in "Democrats to Study Changes in Recorded Teller Voting," *Congressional Quarterly Weekly Report*, xxx (Jan. 22, 1972), p. 153.

Notes to Chapter 12

[1]Louis M. Koenig, *The Chief Executive* (New York: Harcourt Brace Jovanovich, 1964), p. 13.

[2]*Our Chief Magistrate and His Powers* (New York: Columbia University Press, 1916), p. 139.

[3]*Theodore Roosevelt: An Autobiography* (New York: Crowell-Collier and Macmillan, Inc., 1913), p. 389.

[4]Richard E. Neustadt, *Presidential Power* (New York: John Wiley and Sons, Inc., 1960), pp. 158–159.

[5]*Ibid.*, pp. 164–167.

[6]Lyndon Baines Johnson, *The Vantage Point: Perspectives of the Presidency, 1963–1969* (New York: Holt, Rinehart & Winston, Inc., 1971), p. 566.

[7]For interesting analyses of Nixon's personality, see: Bruce Mazlish, *In Search of Nixon: A Psychohistorical Inquiry* (New York: Basic Books, Inc., 1972); and James David Barber, *The Presidential Character: Predicting Performance in the White House* (Englewood Cliffs, N.J.: Prentice-Hall, Inc., 1972), especially Part V.

[8]Quoted in Neustadt, *Presidential Power*, pp. 9–10.

[9]*Ibid.*, p. viii.

[10]Johnson, *The Vantage Point*, p. 450.

[11]*United States v. Curtiss-Wright Export Corp.*, 299 U.S. 304 (1936), and *Missouri v. Holland*, 252 U.S. 416 (1920).

[12]*The President: Office and Powers*, 4th ed. (New York: New York University Press, 1957), p. 172. (Italics omitted.)

[13]*United States v. Curtiss-Wright Export Corp.*

[14]The earliest example is *Little v. Barreme*, 2 Cranch 170 (1804).

[15]Emmet John Hughes, *The Living Presidency* (Baltimore, Md.: Penguin Books, 1974), p. 205.

[16]Quoted in Rowland Evans, Jr., and Robert D. Novak, *Lyndon B. Johnson: The Exercise of Power* (New York: The New American Library, Inc., 1966), p. 490.

[17]Robert A. Dahl and Charles E. Lindblom, *Politics, Economics, and Welfare* (New York: Harper & Row, 1953), p. 342.

[18]For a detailed historical summary, see: *Presidential Vetoes: Records of Bills Vetoed and Action Taken Thereon by the Senate and House of Representatives, First Congress through the Ninetieth Congress, 1789–1968*, compiled by the Senate Library under the direction of Francis R. Valeo (Washington, D.C.: Government Printing Office, 1969).

[19]*Train v. City of New York*, 420 U.S. 35 (1975); see also *Train v. Campaign Clean Water*, 420 U.S. 136 (1975).

[20]Analysis in this section depends heavily on Louis Fisher, *Presidential Spending Power* (Princeton, N.J.: Princeton University Press, 1975).

[21]*United States v. Nixon*, 418 U.S. 683 (1974).

[22]Johnson, *The Vantage Point,* p. 30.

[23]The remark was by Kermit Gordon; quoted in *ibid.,* p. 440.

[24]*Ex parte Merryman,* 17 Federal Cases 144 (No. 9487) (1861).

[25]*The Nature of the Judicial Process* (New Haven, Conn.: Yale University Press, 1921), p. 168.

[26]Barber, *The Presidential Character,* pp. 17–18.

Notes to Chapter 13

[1]This section depends heavily on Richard F. Fenno, *The President's Cabinet* (Cambridge, Mass.: Harvard University Press, 1959), and Emmet John Hughes, *The Living Presidency* (Baltimore, Md.: Penguin Books, 1974), chap. 5.

[2]Richard E. Neustadt, "Approaches to Staffing the Presidency," *American Political Science Review,* LVII (1963), p. 857.

[3]Kermit Gordon, "Reflections on Spending," in J. D. Montgomery and A. Smithies, eds., *Public Policy* (Cambridge, Mass.: Harvard University Press, 1966), XV, 12–13.

[4]For assessments of the National Security Council, see the articles collected in Keith C. Clark and Laurence J. Legere, eds., *The President and the Management of National Security* (New York: Frederick A. Praeger, 1969), as well as the introduction by the editors. See also Morton H. Halperin with Priscilla Clapp and Arnold Kanter, *Bureaucratic Politics and Foreign Policy* (Washington, D.C.: The Brookings Institution, 1974).

[5]*New Dimensions of Political Economy* (Cambridge, Mass.: Harvard University Press, 1966), p. 17.

[6]*Ibid.,* p. 54.

[7]See Norman C. Thomas, "Presidential Advice and Information: Policy and Program Formulation," *Law and Contemporary Problems,* XXXV (1970), p. 540.

[8]For a close analysis of Wilson and House, see Alexander L. George and Juliette L. George, *Woodrow Wilson and Colonel House: A Personality Study* (New York: The John Day Company, 1956). For a general account of such "inside advisers," see Louis W. Koenig, *The Invisible Presidency* (New York: Holt, Rinehart & Winston, Inc., 1960).

[9]Arthur Link, *Woodrow Wilson and the Progressive Era 1900–1917* (New York: Harper & Row, Publishers, 1954), p. 28.

[10]For a brilliant account of the relationship between FDR and Harry Hopkins, see Robert E. Sherwood, *Roosevelt and Hopkins* (New York: Bantam Books, Inc., 1950).

[11]Quoted in *ibid.,* I, 3.

[12]*Humphrey's Executor v. United States,* 295 U.S. 602 (1935).

[13]Gordon, "Reflections on Spending," cited above in note 3, pp. 13–14.

[14]*Go East, Young Man: The Early Years* (New York: Random House, 1974), p. 305.

[15]Quoted in Richard E. Neustadt, *Presidential Power* (New York: John Wiley & Sons, Inc., 1961), p. 39.

[16]Quoted in Hughes, *The Living Presidency,* p. 141.

[17]See Arthur M. Schlesinger, Jr., *The Age of Roosevelt,* vol. II, *The Coming of the New Deal* (Boston: Houghton Mifflin Company, 1959), chap. 32.

Notes to Chapter 14

[1]*Youngstown Sheet and Tube Co. v. Sawyer,* 343 U.S. 579 (1952).

[2]*NAACP v. Button,* 371 U.S. 415 (1963).

[3]*Congressional Record,* XXI, 2460.

[4]See especially the two books by C. Herman Pritchett, *The Roosevelt Court* (New York: Crowell-Collier and Macmillan, 1948) and *Civil Liberties and the Vinson Court* (Chicago, Ill.: University of Chicago Press, 1954); and Glendon A. Schubert, *The Judicial Mind* (Evanston, Ill.: Northwestern University Press, 1965).

[5]Benjamin N. Cardozo, *The Nature of the Judicial Process* (New Haven, Conn.: Yale University Press, 1921), pp. 112–113.

[6]See *United States v. Lanza,* 260 U.S. 377 (1922); *Abbate v. United States,* 359 U.S. 187 (1959); and *Bartkus v. Illinois,* 359 U.S. 121 (1959).

⁷See, for example, *Pierce v. Society of Sisters,* 268 U.S. 510 (1925); and *Barrows v. Jackson,* 346 U.S. 249 (1953).

⁸*Brown v. Board of Education,* 349 U.S. 294 (1955); there were four cases here, one each from Delaware, Kansas, South Carolina and Virginia.

⁹*Baker v. Carr,* 369 U.S. 186 (1962); *Wesberry v. Sanders,* 376 U.S. 1 (1964); and *Reynolds v. Sims,* 377 U.S. 533 (1964).

¹⁰But Harry Kalven and Hans Zeisel, *The American Jury* (Boston, Mass.: Little, Brown and Company, 1966), have shown that judges typically come to the same conclusions as jurors.

¹¹*New York Times v. Sullivan,* 376 U.S. 254, 285 (1964).

¹²*Ex parte McCardle,* 7 Wallace 506 (1869).

¹³See Richard A. Watson and Rondal G. Downing, *The Politics of Bench and Bar: Judicial Selection under the Missouri Nonpartisan Court Plan* (New York: John Wiley and Sons, Inc., 1969).

¹⁴Quoted in David M. Silver, *Lincoln's Supreme Court* (Urbana, Ill.: University of Illinois Press, 1956), p. 208.

¹⁵U.S. Senate, Committee on the Judiciary, *Hearings on the Nomination of Abe Fortas to be Chief Justice of the United States,* 90th Cong., 2d Sess., p. 191 Washington D.C. Government Printing Office, (1968).

¹⁶Quoted in Harold W. Chase, "Federal Judges: The Appointing Process," *Minnesota Law Review,* LI (1966), p. 204.

¹⁷*The Supreme Court of the United States* (New York: Columbia University Press, 1928), p. 75.

¹⁸*Chandler v. Judicial Council,* 398 U.S. 74 (1970).

Notes to Chapter 15

¹Quoted in Alpheus T. Mason, *The Supreme Court: Palladium of Freedom* (Ann Arbor, Mich.: University of Michigan Press, 1962), p. 72.

²These early cases are discussed in Charles Warren, *The Supreme Court in United States History* (Boston: Little, Brown and Company, 1922), chap. 1. The more important decisions were: *United States v. Yale Todd,* decided in 1794 but not officially reported until 1852, 13 Howard 52; *Hylton v. United States,* 3 Dallas 171 (1796); and *Calder v. Bull,* 3 Dallas 386 (1798).

³1 Cranch 137 (1803).

⁴*Annals of Congress,* 7th Cong., 1st Sess., p. 179.

⁵*Little v. Barreme,* 2 Cranch 170 (1804).

⁶James D. Richardson, ed., *A Compilation of the Messages and Papers of the Presidents* (Washington, D.C.: Bureau of National Literature and Art, 1908), II, 582.

⁷4 Wheaton 316 (1819).

⁸Richardson, *A Compilation of the Messages and Papers of the Presidents,* VI, 9.

⁹U.S. Senate, Subcommittee on Separation of Powers, *Hearings: The Supreme Court,* 90th Cong., 2d Sess. (1968), p. 130.

¹⁰Walter F. Murphy and Joseph Tanenhaus, "Public Opinion and the United States Supreme Court," in Joel Grossman and Joseph Tanenhaus, eds., *Frontiers of Judicial Research* (New York: John Wiley and Sons, Inc., 1969), p. 273; Murphy, Tanenhaus, and Daniel L. Kastner, *Public Evaluations of Constitutional Courts* (Beverly Hills, Cal.: Sage Publications, 1973).

¹¹Robert A. Dahl, "Decision-Making in a Democracy; The Supreme Court as a National Policy-Maker," *Journal of Public Law,* VI (1957), p. 279; and Charles L. Black, Jr., *The People and the Court* (New York: Crowell-Collier and Macmillan, 1960), chap. 3.

¹²*Pennsylvania v. Nelson,* 350 U.S. 497 (1956). See also *Brotherhood of Railroad Trainmen v. Howard,* 343 U.S. 768 (1952), and *Sullivan v. Little Hunting Park,* 396 U.S. 229 (1969).

¹³For a discussion of the group phase of decision making on the Supreme Court, see Walter F. Murphy, *Elements of Judicial Strategy* (Chicago, Ill.: University of Chicago Press, 1964), chaps. 3 and 7.

[14]Robert A. Dahl and Charles E. Lindblom, *Politics, Economics, and Welfare* (New York: Harper & Row, 1953), p. 342.

[15]The statement was by Thomas Corcoran, quoted in Louis Koenig, *The Invisible Presidency* (New York: Holt, Rinehart and Winston, 1960), p. 286.

[16]*Smith v. Allwright,* 321 U.S. 649 (1944); and *Terry v. Adams,* 345 U.S. 461 (1953).

[17]See Chapter 8 for a listing and discussion of these cases.

[18]Quoted in J. Woodford Howard, *Mr. Justice Murphy: A Political Biography* (Princeton, N.J.: Princeton University Press, 1968), p. 228.

[19]*Dred Scott v. Sandford,* 19 Howard 393 (1857).

[20]*Brown v. Board of Education,* 347 U.S. 483 (1954).

[21]*West Virginia v. Barnette,* 319 U.S. 624, 640 (1943).

Notes to Chapter 16

[1]See the discussion in Carl L. Becker, *The Declaration of Independence* (New York: Random House, 1958), chap. 2.

[2]*Abrams v. United States,* 250 U.S. 616 dissenting opinion (1919).

[3]Letter of October 17, 1788, in Gaillard Hunt, ed., *The Writings of James Madison* (New York: G.P. Putnam's Sons, 1904), V, 274.

[4]7 Peters 243 (1833).

[5]*Gitlow v. New York,* 268 U.S. 652 (1925).

[6]*Palko v. Connecticut,* 302 U.S. 319 (1937).

[7]*Pollock v. Williams,* 322 U.S. 4 (1944).

[8]*Selective Draft Act Cases,* 245 U.S. 366 (1917).

[9]*Oestereich v. Board No. 11,* 393 U.S. 233 (1968).

[10]Chief Justice Earl Warren in *Trop v. Dulles,* 356 U.S. 86 (1958).

[11]*Dred Scott v. Sandford,* 19 Howard 393 (1857).

[12]See especially *Afroyim v. Rusk,* 387 U.S. 253 (1967).

[13]For foreign travel, see: *Kent v. Dulles,* 357 U.S. 116 (1958), and *Aptheker v. Rusk,* 378 U.S. 500 (1964); for domestic travel, see: *Shapiro v. Thompson,* 394 U.S. 618 (1969); *Dunn v. Blumstein,* 405 U.S. 330 (1972); and *Memorial Hospital v. Maricopa County,* 415 U.S. 250 (1974).

[14]For welfare benefits, see *Shapiro,* cited in note 13; for voting, see *Dunn,* cited in note 13; and for free hospital care, see *Memorial Hospital,* also cited in note 13.

[15]*Bolling v. Sharpe,* 347 U.S. 497 (1954).

[16]163 U.S. 537 (1896).

[17]347 U.S. 483 (1954).

[18]*Milliken v. Bradley,* 418 U.S. 717 (1974).

[19]411 U.S. 1 (1973).

[20]For example, waiver of fee charged to prepare a transcript of trial so that loser may appeal, *Griffin v. Illinois,* 351 U.S. 12 (1956); waiver of fee charged to began a suit for divorce, *Boddie v. Connecticut,* 401 U.S. 371 (1971); but, curiously, the court refused to require a waiver of a fee for a pauper to file for bankruptcy, *United States v. Kras,* 409 U.S. 434 (1973).

[21]*Gideon v. Wainwright,* 372 U.S. 335 (1963); *Argersinger v. Hamlin,* 407 U.S. 25 (1972).

[22]See *Shapiro v. Thompson,* cited above note 13, and *Harper v. Virginia,* 383 U.S. 663 (1966). For a discussion whether sex is an inherently suspect criterion, see the debate between Justices Brennan and Stewart in *Schlesinger v. Ballard,* 419 U.S. 498 (1975).

[23]*Dandridge v. Williams,* 397 U.S. 471 (1970).

[24]*Hoyt v. Florida,* 368 U.S. 57 (1961).

[25]*Taylor v. Louisiana,* 419 U.S. 522 (1975).

[26]See, for example, *Schlesinger,* cited above note 22; *Reed v. Reed,* 404 U.S. 71 (1971); *Frontiero v. Richardson,* 411 U.S. 677 (1973); *Pittsburgh Press v. Pittsburgh,* 413 U.S. 376 (1973); and *Weinberger v. Wiesenfeld,* 420 U.S. 636 (1975).

[27]*Lemon v. Kurtzman,* 403 U.S. 602 (1971).

[28]*Everson v. Ewing Township,* 330 U.S. 1 (1947).

[29]*Cochran v. Louisiana,* 281 U.S. 370 (1930); *Board of Regents v. Allen,* 392 U.S. 236 (1968).

[30]*Tilton v. Richardson,* 403 U.S. 672 (1971); and *Roemer v. Maryland,* 49 L. Ed. 2d, 179 (1976).

[31]*Lemon v. Kurtzman,* 403 U.S. 602 (1971).

[32]*McCollum v. Board,* 333 U.S. 203 (1948).

[33]*Zorach v. Clauson,* 343 U.S. 606 (1952).

[34]*Engel v. Vitale,* 370 U.S. 421, 435 (1962).

[35]*Abington School District v. Schempp,* 374 U.S. 203, 226, (1963); see also *Chamberlin v. Dade County,* 377 U.S. 402 (1964).

[36]*Reynolds v. United States,* 98 U.S. 145 (1879); *Davis v. Beason,* 133 U.S. 333 (1890).

[37]*Cleveland v. United States,* 329 U.S. 14 (1946).

[38]*McGowan v. Maryland,* 366 U.S. 420 (1961); *Gallagher v. Crown Kosher Super Market,* 366 U.S. 617 (1961); *Two Guys From Harrison v. McGinley,* 366 U.S. 582 (1961); *Braunfield v. Brown,* 366 U.S. 599 (1961).

[39]*Sherbert v. Verner,* 374 U.S. 398 (1963).

[40]*West Virginia v. Barnette,* 319 U.S. 624 (1943).

[41]*Wisconsin v. Yoder,* 406 U.S. 205 (1972).

[42]*Application of Georgetown College,* 331 F. 2d 1000 (1964); *United States v. George,* 239 F. Supp. 752 (1965); *John F. Kennedy Memorial Hospital v. Heston,* 58 N.J. 576 (1971); *Powell v. Columbia Presbyterian Medical Center,* 267 N.Y.S. 2d 450 (1965). On the other hand, see, *In re Osborne,* 294 A. 2d 372 (1972); *In re Estate of Brooks,* 205 N.E. 2d 435 (1965); and *Erickson v. Dilgard,* 252 N.Y. S. 2d 705 (1962).

[43]367 U.S. 488 (1961).

[44]*Olmstead v. United States,* 277 U.S. 438 (1928).

[45]381 U.S. 479 (1965).

[46]*Eisenstadt v. Baird,* 405 U.S. 438 (1972).

[47]*Roe v. Wade,* 410 U.S. 113 (1973).

[48]*Doe v. Commonwealth's Attorney,* 425 U.S. 901 (1976).

[49]*Jacobson v. Massachusetts,* 197 U.S. 11 (1905).

[50]*Buck v. Bell,* 274 U.S. 200 (1927).

[51]*Breithaupt v. Abram,* 352 U.S. 432 (1957).

[52]*Skinner v. Oklahoma,* 316 U.S. 535 (1942).

[53]*Rochin v. California,* 342 U.S. 165 (1952).

[54]*Schenck v. United States,* 249 U.S. 47 (1919).

[55]*Whitney v. California,* 274 U.S. 357, concurring opinion (1927).

[56]*United States v. Carolene Products,* 304 U.S. 144 (1938).

[57]"A Survey of Social Interests," *Harvard Law Review,* LVII (1943), p. 1.

[58]*Dennis v. United States,* 341 U.S. 494, concurring opinion (1951).

[59]*A Constitutional Faith* (New York: Alfred A. Knopf, 1969), p. 45.

[60]"The Bill of Rights," *New York University Law Review,* XXXV (1960), p. 865.

[61]*Milk Wagon Drivers Union v. Meadowmoor Dairies,* 312 U.S. 287, dissenting opinion (1941); *Giboney v. Empire Storage,* 336 U.S. 490 (1949).

[62]*Tinker v. Des Moines,* 393 U.S. 503, dissenting opinion (1969).

[63]*United States v. O'Brien,* 391 U.S. 367 (1968).

[64]*Street v. New York,* 394 U.S. 576, dissenting opinion (1969).

[65]*Cox v. Louisiana,* 379 U.S. 559, dissenting opinion (1965).

[66]*Free Speech and Its Relation to Self-Government* (New York: Harper & Brothers, 1948), and *Political Freedom: The Constitutional Powers of the People* (New York: Oxford University Press, 1965).

[67]*Dennis v. United States,* cited above in note 58; *Yates v. United States,* 354 U.S. 298 (1957); *Barenblatt v. United States,* 360 U.S. 109 (1959).

[68]The basic case here is *New York Times v. Sullivan,* 376 U.S. 254 (1964).

[69]The basic case here is *Gertz v. Welsh,* 418 U.S. 323 (1974).

[70]For federal officials, *Barr v. Mateo,* 360 U.S. 564 (1959); for state officials, *Paul v. Davis,* 424 U.S. 693 (1976).

[71]354 U.S. 476 (1957).

[72]*Ginzburg v. United States,* 383 U.S. 463 (1966).

[73]*Ginsberg v. New York,* 390 U.S. 629 (1968).

[74]409 U.S. 109 (1972).

[75]413 U.S. 15 (1973).

[76]283 U.S. 697 (1931).

[77]307 U.S. 496 (1939).

[78]For instance: *Lovell v. Griffin,* 303 U.S. 444 (1938); *Cox v. New Hampshire,* 312 U.S. 569 (1941); *Niemotko v. Maryland,* 340 U.S. 268 (1951).

[79]*New York Times v. United States,* 403 U.S. 713 (1971).

[80]See, for instance, *Sheppard v. Maxwell,* 384 U.S. 333 (1966).

[81]*Nebraska Press Association v. Stuart,* 49 L. Ed. 2d, 683 (1976).

[82]*Branzburg v. Hayes,* 408 U.S. 665 (1972).

[83]U.S. Senate, Select Committee to Study Governmental Operations with Respect to Intelligence Activities, *Final Report,* Book II, p. 7, 94th Congress, 2d Session.

[84]Book III of the Church committee's *Final Report* has a 106-page summary of the FBI's efforts to discredit Rev. King.

[85]*Whitney v. California,* cited above note 55.

[86]*Olmstead v. United States,* cited above note 44.

[87]Quoted in *Final Report,* Book III, p. 135.

[88]*Olmstead,* cited above note 44.

Notes to Chapter 17

[1]Federal Bureau of Investigation, *Uniform Crime Reports for the United States— 1974* (Washington, D.C.: Government Printing Office, 1976).

[2]Law Enforcement Assistance Administration, *Criminal Victimization Surveys in 13 American Cities* (Washington, D.C.: Government Printing Office, 1975).

[3]Law Enforcement Assistantance Administration, National Criminal Justice Information and Statistics Service, SD-EE No. 7, and Bureau of the Census, *State and Local Government Special Studies, No. 77: Expenditure and Employment Data for the Criminal Justice System 1974* (Washington, D.C.: Government Printing Office, 1976).

[4]*Stacey v. Emory,* 97 U.S. 642 (1877).

[5]*Sibron v. New York,* 392 U.S. 59 (1968).

[6]*Chimel v. California,* 395 U.S. 752 (1969).

[7]384 U.S. 436 (1966).

[8]*Mallory v. United States,* 354 U.S. 449 (1957).

[9]*Johnson v. Louisiana,* 406 U.S. 356 (1972); *Apodoca v. Oregon,* 406 U.S. 404 (1972).

[10]*Johnson,* cited above note 9.

[11]Race: *Norris v. Alabama,* 294 U.S. 587 (1935); ethnic group: *Hernandez v. Texas,* 347 U.S. 475 (1954); sex: *Taylor v. Louisiana,* 419 U.S. 522 (1975).

[12]*Miranda,* cited above note 7.

[13]*Weeks v. United States,* 232 U.S. 383 (1914).

[14]367 U.S. 643 (1961).

[15]*Terry v. Ohio,* 392 U.S. 1 (1968).

[16]For example, *Bivens v. Six Unknown Federal Narcotics Agents,* 403 U.S. 388, dissenting opinion (1971).

[17]277 U.S. 438 (1928).

[18]*Nardone v. United States,* 302 U.S. 379 (1937).

[19]*Berger v. New York,* 388 U.S. 31 (1967); *Katz v. United States,* 389 U.S. 347 (1967).

[20]407 U.S. 297 (1972).

[21]*Francis v. Henderson,* 48 L. Ed. 2d, 149 (1976); and *Stone v. Powell,* 49 L. Ed. 1067 (1976). These decisions actually restricted use of habeas corpus by state prisoners. The earlier rule had been that a state prisoner could seek habeas corpus as a means of challenging the constitutionality of state action against him unless it could be shown that he was deliberately avoiding state procedures that were open to him.

[22]Chief Justice Earl Warren in *Trop v. Dulles,* 356 U.S. 86 (1958).

[23]*Weems v. United States,* 217 U.S. 349 (1910).

[24]*Robinson v. California,* 370 U.S. 660 (1962). In *Powell v. Texas,* 392 U.S. 514 (1968), however, the Court ruled that the factual record was not adequate to determine if drunkenness was a disease and so sustained the constitutionality of a statute punishing public intoxication.

[25]408 U.S. 238 (1972).

[26]The leading cases are *Gregg v. Georgia,* 49 L. Ed. 2d, 859 (1976); *Roberts v. Louisiana,* 49 L. Ed. 2d, 974 (1976); *Woodson v. North Carolina,* 49 L. Ed. 2d, 944 (1976); and *Green v. Oklahoma,* 49 L. Ed. 2d, 1214 (1976).

[27]Jerome H. Skolnick, *Justice Without Trial: Law Enforcement in Democratic Society* (New York: John Wiley and Sons, Inc., 1966), and Arthur Rosett and Donald R. Cressey, *Justice by Consent: Plea Bargains in the American Courthouse* (Philadelphia: J.P. Lippincott Company, 1976), provide two useful, well written accounts of how the system actually works.

[28]Many of these studies are discussed in U.S. Senate, Committee on the Judiciary, *Hearings: Controlling Crime through More Effective Law Enforcement,* 90th Cong., 1st Sess. (1967). See also, Note, "Interrogations in New Haven: The Impact of *Miranda,*" *Yale Law Journal,* LXXVI (1967), p. 1519; and Richard H. Seeburger and R. Stanton Wettick, Jr., "Miranda in Pittsburgh—A Statistical Study," *University of Pittsburgh Law Review,* XXIX (1967), p. 1.

[29]Note, "The Influence of the Defendant's Plea on Judicial Determination of Sentence," *Yale Law Journal,* LXVI (1956), p. 204; Herbert Jacob and James Eisenstein, "Sentences and Other Sanctions in the Criminal Courts," *Political Science Quarterly,* XL (1976), p. 617.

[30]*Santobello v. New York,* 404 U.S. 257 (1971).

[31]National Advisory Commission on Criminal Justice Standards and Goals, *National Conference on Criminal Justice* (Washington, D.C.: Government Printing Office, 1973).

[32]See the literature excerpted in Leon Radzinowicz and Marvin Wolfgang, eds., *Crime and Justice,* vol. 3, *The Criminal in Confinement* (New York: Basic Books, Inc., 1971), Part I.

Notes to Chapter 18

[1]New York State Senator John D. Caemmerer, quoted in Alfonso A. Narvaez, "Briton Sees Court Ruling as Last Word on SST's," *New York Times,* March 16, 1976.

[2]Duane Lockard, *The Perverted Priorities of American Politics* (New York: Crowell-Collier, Macmillan, Inc., 1970).

[3]Theodore J. Lowi, *The End of Liberalism: Ideology, Policy, and the Crisis of Public Authority* (New York: W. W. Norton and Company, Inc. 1969).

[4]E. E. Schattschneider, *The Semi-Sovereign People* (New York: Holt, Rinehart and Winston, 1960), p. 108.

Credits

Chapter 1 Photo, page 3, courtesy of UPI. Figure 1.1, page 5, © 1976 by The New York Times Company. Reprinted by permission. Photo, page 9, courtesy of the U.S. Environmental Protection Agency. Figure 1.2, page 10, © 1976 by The New York Times Company. Reprinted by permission. Photo, page 12, by Richard Stromberg. Photo, page 17, courtesy of the U.S. National Aeronautics and Space Administration.

Chapter 2 Photo, page 25, from the collection of the Library of Congress. Table 2–1, page 32, reprinted by permission. Table 2–2, page 38, reprinted by permission.

Chapter 3 Figure 3.3, page 59, © 1975 by The New York Times Company. Reprinted by permission. Box, page 65, from National Advisory Commission on Civil Disorders, *Report* (Washington, D.C.: Government Printing Office, 1968), pp. 1–2. Photo, page 69, courtesy of the U.S. Environmental Protection Agency. Table 3–1, page 74, copyright 1974 Congressional Quarterly Inc. Reprinted by permission.

Chapter 4 Photo, page 85, courtesy of Wide World Photos. Print, page 88, courtesy of The Bettmann Archive. Poster, page 92, reproduced from the collection of the Library of Congress. Photo, page 101, courtesy of UPI.

Chapter 5 Table 5–1, page 115, data from U.S. Bureau of the Census. Figure 5.1, page 118, reprinted by permission from TIME, The Weekly Newsmagazine; Copyright Time Inc. 1974. Figure 5.2, page 120, reprinted from *Newsweek,* December 15, 1975. Newsweek-Ib Ohlsson. Reprinted by permission. Figure 5.3, page 122, from *New York Times,* February 4, 1975. © 1975 by The New York Times Company. Reprinted by permission. Figure 5.4, page 130, Newsweek-Fenga & Freyer. Reprinted by permission.

Chapter 6 Photo, page 144, courtesy of UPI. Photo, page 148, courtesy of UPI. Photo, page 149, courtesy of UPI. Photo, page 154, courtesy of the U.S. Environmental Protection Agency.

Chapter 7 Photos, page 171, courtesy of Wide World Photos. Figure 7.1, page 173, copyright © 1976 by Little, Brown and Company. Reprinted by permission. Unnumbered table, page 175, reprinted by permission of Center for Political Studies, University of Michigan. Table 7–1, page 177, copyright 1964, 1968, 1970, 1972, 1975, 1976 Congressional Quarterly Inc. Reprinted by permission. Print, page 185, courtesy of Jo-Anne Naples.

Chapter 8 Photo, page 197, courtesy of UPI. Table 8–1, page 200, reprinted by permission. Figure 8.1, page 203, data copyright 1970, 1974 Congressional Quarterly Inc.

Reprinted by permission. Figure itself © 1966 by The New York Times Company. Reprinted by permission. Photo, page 209, by Arthur Grace. Photo, page 210, courtesy of Wide World Photos. Table 8–3, page 211, reprinted by permission. Table 8–4, page 213, reprinted by permission of The Gallup Poll (The American Institute of Public Opinion). Table 8–5, page 217, reprinted by permission of the publisher from *Financing the 1972 Election* by Herbert E. Alexander (Lexington, Mass.: Lexington Books, D. C. Heath and Company, 1976). Table 8–6, page 218, reprinted by permission of the publisher from *Financing the 1972 Election* by Herbert E. Alexander (Lexington, Mass.: Lexington Books, D. C. Heath and Company, 1976). Photo, page 222, courtesy of UPI.

Chapter 9 Table 9–1, page 229, adaptation of Table 2–1, page 31, from *Participation in America* by Sidney Verba and Norman Nie. Copyright © 1972 by Sidney Verba and Norman Nie. Reprinted by permission of Harper & Row, Publishers, Inc. Table 9–2, page 238, reprinted by permission of The Gallup Poll (The American Institute of Public Opinion). Figure 9.1, page 241, based on data from *Gallup Opinion Index,* Report No. 112 (October 1974), p. 27; Report No. 128 (March 1976), p. 15; and Gallup Poll press release, May 27, 1976. Reprinted by permission of The Gallup Poll (The American Institute of Public Opinion). Table 9–3, page 246, reprinted by permission.

Chapter 10 Figure 10.1, page 259, from U.S. Congress, Senate, Committee on Government Operations, *Congressional Budget Reform* (Washington, D.C.: Government Printing Office, 1974), pp. 15–16. Photo, page 266, courtesy of UPI. Figure 10.2, page 267, from *Congressional Quarterly,* June 21, 1975, p. 1291. Original source is Common Cause. Copyright 1975 Congressional Quarterly Inc. Reprinted by permission of Common Cause and Congressional Quarterly Inc. Figure 10.3, page 269, reprinted by permission. Copyright © 1971 by Random House.

Chapter 11 Photo, page 279, courtesy of UPI. Newsletter, page 283, courtesy of Congressman Charles E. Bennett. Figure 11.1, page 287, © 1976 by The New York Times Company. Reprinted by permission. Photo, page 291, courtesy of UPI. Table 11–1, page 295, most data from *Congressional Directory 1975* (Washington, D.C.: Government Printing Office, 1976). Figure 11.2, page 299, reprinted by permission. Photo, page 302, courtesy of UPI. Photo, page 308, by James K. W. Atherton, The Washington Post. Reprinted by permission.

Chapter 12 Photo, page 323, courtesy of UPI. Photo, page 327, courtesy of Wide World Photos. Photo, page 329, courtesy of UPI. Photo, page 331, courtesy of UPI. Photo, page 341, courtesy of UPI. Photo, page 345, courtesy of UPI.

Chapter 13 Photo, page 354, courtesy of The White House/David Hume Kennerly. Photo, page 355, courtesy of UPI. Photo, page 361, courtesy of Wide World Photos. Photo, page 363, courtesy of The White House/David Hume Kennerly.

Chapter 14 Print, page 379, courtesy of The Bettmann Archive. Photo, page 391, courtesy of UPI. Photo, page 397, courtesy of the Supreme Court Historical Society.

Chapter 15 Figure 15.1, page 403, copyright 1972 Congressional Quarterly Inc. Reprinted by permission. Photo, page 413, courtesy of UPI.

Chapter 16 Photo, page 433, courtesy of UPI. Photo, page 434, courtesy of UPI. Photo, page 451, courtesy of American Telephone & Telegraph Co.

Chapter 17 Figure 17.1, page 461, from FBI, *Uniform Crime Reports in the United States, 1975* (Washington, D.C.: Government Printing Office, 1976), p. 13. Table 17–1, page 463, reprinted from "U.S. News & World Report." Copyright 1976 U.S. News & World Report, Inc. Box, page 466, from FBI, *Uniform Crime Reports in the United States,* 1975 (Washington, D.C.: Government Printing Office, 1976), p. 8. Photo, page 474, courtesy of UPI. Photo, page 479, by Leo M. Dehnel, U.S. Bureau of Prisons. Figure 17.2, page 481, from FBI, *Uniform Crime Reports in the United States,* 1975 (Washington, D.C.: Government Printing Office, 1976), p. 45.

Credits

Chapter 18 Photo, page 496, courtesy of Wide World Photos.

Index

G

Gallup polls, 124, 175, 203, 219, 233, 239, 460
Garfield, James A., 148
Garvey, Marcus, 41
General Accounting Office (GAO), 273–274, 342
Getty, John Paul, 140
George III, 380
German-Americans, 43
Gerrymander, 198
Ghetto, 38, 41, 64, 481; see also Blacks; Cities
Gorham, Nathaniel, 89
Goldwater, Barry, 188, 213, 234
Government, 2, 9;
  confidence in, 180;
  constitutional, 6, 82;
  dangerous, 89–91;
  democratic, 29, 31, 89, 118;
  difficulties in action, 105–106;
  federal, see National government;
  "free," 4, 104, 501
  growth of, 8, 9, 11, 14–15, 54;
  intervention by, 7;
  limited, 4, 6, 83–100, 105, 110, 368–370, 427, 500–501;
  local, see Local government;
  republican, 4;
  representative, 4;
  role of, 237;
  socialization, 49;
  state, see State Government
Governors, 124, 126, 131, 141, 183, 212, 330, 340, 493
Grand Jury, 430, 468
"Grandfather Clauses," 196
Grant-in-aid, 120, 123
Grant, U., 320
Great Depression, 25, 116, 175, 235
"Great Red Scare," 455
Great Society, see Johnson, Lyndon B.
Greek Americans, 43
Griswold v. Connecticut, 439
Greenback Party, 172
Gross National Product, (GNP), 11
Grier, Robert, 398
Guaranteed Annual Income, 43, 74
Gulf of Tonkin Resolution, 255, 335
Gun Control, 232, 490

H

Habit, 2
Habeas Corpus, 428, 465

Hague, Frank, 148, 448
Hague v. CIO, 448
Hamilton, Alexander, 88–89, 166, 193
Hancock, John, 88
Hand, Learned, 444
Harding, Warren G., 178, 320–321, 332
Harlan, John Marshall, 434
Harrington, Michael, 36
Harris, Louis, 33
Haynsworth, Clement, 394
Health, Education, and Welfare, U.S. Department of, 7, 261, 492
Heller, Walter, 358
Hemingway, Ernest, 45
Henry, Patrick, 88
Herring, Pendleton, 187
Hickel, Walter J., 261
Highway programs, 8, 175, 254, 491–492
Hobbes, Thomas, 90
Holmes, Oliver Wendell, 398, 403, 405, 427, 441, 444
Homosexuality, 440, 480
"Honeymoon," 332
Hoover, Herbert, 178, 325, 358, 366
Hoover, J. Edgar, 452, see also Federal Bureau of Investigation
Hopkins, Harry, 359, 361
House, Edward M., 359
House of Representatives, U.S., 92;
  appropriations, 296;
  caucuses, 297–298;
  Committee of the Whole, 309, 311;
  Committees and subcommittees, 298–301;
  Education and Labor, 296;
  election of, 98, 104, 168, 199–204;
  Government Operations, 296;
  impeachment, 96, 103, 288, 334;
  Internal Security, 295;
  Judiciary, 296;
  policy committees;
  political parties, 178;
  presidential elections, 168, 204, 215–216;
  presiding officers, 216, 290–293;
  redistricting, 199–201;
  revenue bills, 288;
  Rules, 287, 292, 296, 307;
  SST, 494;
  Watergate, 102–103;
  Ways and Means, 296;
Housing, 8, 63–65, 72–73, 152, 254
Housing and Urban Development,

U.S. Department of, 7, 123, 261
Hughes, Charles Evans, 215, 396, 398, 403
Hughes, Emmet John, 336
Humphrey, Hubert, 206, 216, 234
Hungate, William L., 270

I

Immigrants and immigration, 24–26, 41–43, 48, 62, 64, 105, 174, 307, 433
Impeachment, 95, 103, 261, 288, 333–334, 398, 407, 415; see also Nixon, Richard M.; Watergate.
Impeachment: The Constitutional Problems, 333
Impoundment, 94, 102, 340–343
Imprisonment, 265
Income Tax, 219, 397
Incumbency, 34, 200, 205, 240–241, 286
Independent candidates, 221
Independent voters, 211
Independent Regulatory Commissions, 362
Indians, American, 36, 45, 93, 105, 153–154, 499
Indictment, 430, 468
Individualism, 14, 83
Industrialization, 11, 25–26, 490
Inflation, 7, 11
Injunction, 2, 380
Information, 8, 30, 96, 102, 322, 352–362, 367
Innocence, presumption of, 469
Intellectuals, 213, 481
Intelligence, military, 352
Interdependence, 11, 43, 54, 70, 115
Interests and Interest Groups, 6, 8–9, 11, 15–16, 71, 87, 94, 98, 116, 118, 124, 139, 142–145, 150–152, 155, 159, 164–165, 167, 170, 183, 187, 353, 360, 364, 381
"Interest-Group Liberalism," 499
Intergovernmental cooperation, 128–130
Interior, U.S. Department of, 123, 129, 261
Internal Revenue Service, 14, 101–102, 117, 129, 451–452, 455–456, 475
Interrogation, 467–468
Interview, 244–247
Interstate Commerce Commission